D1459880

INTERNATIONAL TRADE IN GOODS
AND FACTOR MOBILITY

INTERNATIONAL TRADE IN GOODS AND FACTOR MOBILITY

Kar-yiu Wong

The MIT Press
Cambridge, Massachusetts
London, England

This book was set in Times Roman by Windfall Software using ZzTEX and was printed and bound in the United States of America.

Library of Congress Cataloging-in-Publication Data

Wong, Kar-yiu, 1950–
    International trade in goods and factor mobility / Kar-yiu Wong.
        p.   cm.
    Includes bibliographical references and index.
    ISBN 0–262–23179–4
1. International trade—Mathematical models.   2. Commercial
policy—Mathematical models.   3. Economies of scale—Mathematical
models.   4. Equilibrium (Economics)—Mathematical models.
5. Comparative advantage (International trade)—Mathematical models.
I. Title.
HF1379.W637   1995
382′.01′5118—dc20   95–1493
                                                                    CIP

To Kin and Yau

Contents

Preface

I have long felt that the theory of international trade has paid too much attention to trade in goods and far too little to factor mobility. If one picks up a book on international trade, he or she would probably find that the bulk of the volume is about international trade in goods, with the underlying assumption that factors are internationally immobile. Discussion of international factor movements receives only a small fraction of the total coverage.

Empirically, the international movement of factors has become increasingly significant. Theoretically, the theories of international trade developed in the past decade or two are still limited by the assumption of no international factor movement. As this book demonstrates, relaxing this assumption can give rise to many important results and makes these theories more interesting.

This book comes out of my research on international trade. Some of the results reported here have appeared in previous papers, but many of them are new and have never been published. The writing of this volume has led me to systematically review nearly the whole field of international trade. Not only have I had the chance to think about many of the questions and issues that I have raised in various publications, but I have also had the pleasure of fully appreciating other people's work. I survey many issues and theories, and I present my own answers and solution to some of the unanswered or controversial questions. Regardless of whether my answers and analyses are right or wrong, I sincerely hope that this book can serve as a catalyst for further thinking, and I would be very grateful if readers would send me constructive comments.

My interest in the theory of international factor movements and their interactions with international trade in goods began with a challenging question posed by Professor Jagdish Bhagwati when I was a graduate student and his research assistant at Columbia University in 1981. He was commenting on the debate in Great Britain over the enactment of the immigration legislation of 1905. One of the controversial issues in that debate was whether restrictions on the inflow of foreign, labor-intensive products could be replaced by the inflow of cheap foreign labor. He asked me to analyze the impacts of international goods trade, international capital movement, and international labor movement systematically in one unified framework, and to compare the policies of allowing the movement of different combinations of goods and factors.

This question got me hooked on the issues, and in a few months I had come up with a new theoretical framework and a ranking of different trade and factor mobility policies. The framework and the results were reported in a paper that appeared in the *Journal of International Economics* in 1983. I would like to take this opportunity to thank him for posing this question, for being a superb supervisor, for giving me guidance and support through the years, and for introducing me to the German *Gastarbeiter* system through a joint project with him and Dr. Klaus-Werner Schatz of the Kiel Institute of World Economy.

Many other teachers at Columbia University have also helped shape my views on international trade: Ronald Findlay, Robert Feenstra, and Kelvin Lancaster on the trade side, and Robert Mundell, Maurice Obstfeld, and Guillermo Calvo on the finance side. I have also benefited a lot from Richard Brecher of Carleton University and Tatsuo Hatta of Osaka University, who were visiting Columbia when I was writing my dissertation. All deserve my sincere thanks.

Many friends have helped me professionally over the years, and I have benefited greatly from their advice, suggestions, and comments. Also valuable is the experience I have gained from working with some of my friends on different projects. Both the work experience and the results of these projects were extremely helpful to me in writing this book, as the references make clear.

The start of this book project can be traced to a lunch in Seattle in the summer of 1990 with Lise Solomon, an acquisition assistant at The MIT Press, who encouraged me to write a book on international trade. Then I had an unexpected visit to my office by Terry Vaughn, the Press's acquisitions editor for economics, during the summer workshops of the Econometric Society in Seattle, June 1992. This book project would never have gotten off the ground, however, without the encouragement and advice of my colleague and friend, Neil Bruce.

In writing this book, I received direct help from many people. Murray C. Kemp applied his well-known critical mind and patience to the reading of the entire draft of this book and has given me many constructive comments. Neil Bruce, who has lent me support from the very beginning of this project, is always available to assist. The many conversations with him were very stimulating. Hong Hwang of the Taiwan National University, who visited my department in the academic year of 1992–1993, helped me sort out some of the confusing ideas and contradictory results in the literature of imperfect competition. There were many other people who have read part of the manuscript and provided comments and suggestions for improvement. I am very grateful for their help. The drafts of most of the chapters have been used in my trade courses at the University of Washington. I would like to thank both current and former students for their comments. Special thanks should go to Grace Hsiu-Yi Chan, who carefully read the entire manuscript and made numerous suggestions. Needless to say, none of these people are responsible for any remaining errors and shortcomings.

I would also like to thank the University of Washington for providing me with a year of sabbatical leave in 1992–93 so that I could concentrate on writing.

Last but not least, I am very grateful to my family, who has given me a lot of encouragement and support. Their understanding and caring have made me feel less guilty for spending numerous nights and weekends in my office.

I INTRODUCTION

1 Introduction

1.1 Introduction

This book covers the theory of international trade in goods and factor mobility. It analyzes issues related to international trade in goods, international factor mobility, and the interactions between the two. The topics are examined both extensively and intensively; these topics include the pure theory of international trade, welfare economics, policy analysis, and some special issues such as multinational corporations and international labor migration. In presenting the analysis in the following chapters, both sophisticated techniques and simple economic intuitions and diagrams are used. The readers should find these analytical tools useful in understanding some very complicated issues and in applying them to the examination of other trade problems.

One of the most important features of this book is its emphasis on the importance of international factor mobility in the theory of international trade. This feature can be compared with what one finds in most books on international trade, where international trade is considered nearly synonymous to international trade in goods. International factor mobility is either neglected or discussed only marginally.

There are many reasons why international factor mobility receives so little attention in the literature, but two can be mentioned here. The first is that historically economic relationships between countries have been determined mainly through the movement of goods. Except for some sporadic periods, international factor movements were insignificant because movements of factors were generally carried out under strict government regulations, or were very costly. There were occasional periods during which the gaps between factor prices in different countries became so large and irresistible that some significant movement of factors did occur, but these periods did not happen too often.

The second reason that international factor movement has not received enough attention in the literature is that under certain conditions, the theory of international trade in goods can be extended to cover international factor mobility. For example, in the Arrow–Debreu-type general equilibrium framework, factor inputs can be regarded as negative outputs. In such a framework, production outputs and factor inputs can be analyzed simultaneously and symmetrically. This approach has been applied to the theory of international trade. It is widely believed that the theory of international trade in goods established in this type of general equilibrium framework can be extended to cover international factor mobility. For example, the law of comparative advantage was initially developed to explain countries' patterns of trade in goods, but it can be applied to explain countries' patterns of factor movement. The theory of optimal tariff on an imported good may also be used to explain optimal taxation on factors that move across country borders. Another application of the theory of international trade in goods in the area of international factor mobility is the gains from trade theorem. It has been proved that when a country moves from autarky to free trade, its welfare—measured either in terms of a social utility function or in terms of individuals' utility when compensation is allowed—increases. Under certain conditions, this theorem applies equally well to trade in goods and/or factor movements. (See Chapters 8 and 14 for the applications and limitations of this and other related theorems.)

The relationship between international trade in goods and factor mobility is best summarized by the important work of Mundell (1957). By applying the factor price equalization theorem (Samuelson, 1948, 1949; Lerner, 1952), Mundell shows that international trade in goods and factor mobility are substitutes in two senses: Either of them reaches the same world equilibrium, and an increase in the volume of one will discourage the volume of the other. Therefore, in terms of reaching the world equilibrium it does not matter whether only international trade in goods or international factor mobility is allowed, or both are allowed at the same time.

These views are limited, however, and more systematic and thorough analysis of international factor mobility is needed. The world has changed so much that movements of factors between countries are no longer insignificant. Some evidence about the significance of international factor movement will be presented in the last section of this chapter. For the time being, it can be noted that movements of factors between countries are significant and can have sizable impacts on countries' trade in goods and on their economic welfare.

It has also become increasingly apparent that there are many issues about international factor mobility that require further study. Some newer issues have arisen from the development of new theories of international trade, notably those based on increasing returns and imperfect competition. Most of these theories address international trade in goods, however, with no movement of factors internationally. Can these theories simply be applied to international factor mobility, in the sense that factor mobility and trade in goods are treated symmetrically? I will show that they cannot.

As this book demonstrates, there are many cases in which the Mundell substitutability between trade in goods and factor mobility does not hold. In many frameworks, the world equilibrium depends on whether only international trade in goods or international factor mobility is allowed, or both are allowed. It is incorrect in these frameworks to apply the theory of international in goods to international factor mobility, and the latter should be analyzed carefully.

1.2   Factor Content of Trade

In this and the following six sections, I briefly explain the theoretical significance of international factor mobility. Looking at the factor content of trade is
an alternative way of interpreting international trade in goods. Instead of determining the physical quantities of goods traded between countries, one can
focus on the amount of factors embodied in the goods. Therefore international
trade in goods can be regarded as indirect movements of factors.

The factor content of trade became a topic of interest when it was needed
to test the Heckscher-Ohlin theorem in a multicommodity framework, or to
extend the theorem to a multicommodity framework. It was discovered that it
is difficult to predict a country's trade patterns when there are more than two
tradable goods. By focusing on the amount of factors embodied in the moving
goods, one can develop an alternative approach to making predictions about
foreign trade.

Strictly speaking, the theory of factor content of trade is not a theory of international factor mobility, because it is still assumed that factors are immobile
internationally. However, because the factor content of trade is the indirect
movement of factors, there is a relationship between it and the direct movement of factors.

1.3   Interactions between Trade in Goods and Factor Mobility

Many trade theorems are established under the assumption that only goods
move between countries. Because the international movement of factors is getting more significant, it is important to examine whether these theorems still
hold when factors move at the same time. Moreover, there are significant interactions between trade in goods and factor mobility, and these interactions
should be studied carefully. Neglecting these interactions in the study of international trade in goods may lead to misleading results.

For example, in the neoclassical framework with two tradable goods, the
patterns of trade of countries depend on comparative, not absolute, advantages.
This property is summarized by the law of comparative advantage. When international capital mobility is permitted, the law can be generalized to cover
the movements of goods and capital, but this generalization is weak because it
gives only an "on average" implication. It is of little use in predicting the direction of movement of a particular commodity, or the direction of movement
of capital.

In the traditional framework with two tradable goods and moving capital, a common and fruitful approach is to examine how international capital
movement may affect the comparative advantages (in terms of the goods) of

6 Chapter 1

the countries. In two extreme cases that depend on the sluggishness of capital movement, separate theories of comparative advantage can be established. In these cases, not just the comparative, but also the absolute, advantages of the countries are important in determining the patterns of trade. This is quite different from the traditional results derived with the assumption of no international factor mobility.

1.4 International Factor Mobility with External Economies of Scale

One common way to relax the assumption of constant returns is to assume external economies of scale. Economies of scale are said to be external to firms if firms ignore these effects in choosing their production point. External economies of scale can be national or international, depending on whether the production functions of firms are affected by just the outputs in the economy or by world outputs. Both types of external economies have important implications for international trade in goods and factor mobility.

Under national external economies, free trade generally does not lead to factor price equalization, even if the usual assumptions such as identical technologies and diversification are made. Thus substitutability between international trade in goods and factor mobility, which is a core result in the neoclassical framework, breaks down. This has two important implications. First, free trade is not efficient in terms of world welfare. Second, when international factor mobility is also allowed under free trade, factors move internationally. Very little has been done to analyze this phenomenon.

As the latter part of this book shows, there are many interesting interactions between international trade in goods and international factor mobility in the presence of external effects. For example, it will be shown that under free trade with national external economies, capital tends to move from a smaller country to a larger country. If only international capital movement but not trade in goods is allowed, however, capital tends to move from a bigger country to a smaller country. In fact, it will be shown that international trade in goods only, international capital movement only, and international trade in goods plus capital movement generally lead to different world equilibria.

If international external economies are assumed, the results are closer to those found in the neoclassical framework. For example, under certain conditions free trade in goods leads to factor price equalization. This is contrary to the corresponding results noted under national external economies of scale. The implication is that international capital movement will not occur when free trade in goods prevails, or that international trade in goods only and in goods plus capital movement have the same world equilibrium. But if only international capital movement is allowed, will the world achieve the same equilibrium as that under free trade in goods? The answer depends on certain conditions.

1.5   International Factor Mobility with Monopolistic Competition

Monopolistic competition and differentiated products is one way of explaining intraindustry trade, an important phenomenon that has received much attention in the literature. Differentiation between products produced by different firms means that each firm has certain monopoly power. This represents an important departure from the neoclassical framework, and the assumption of perfect competition is appropriately dropped. It is usually assumed that with production differentiation firms have internal economies of scale. The implication of this assumption is that in equilibrium, no two firms will produce the same product (variety).

Because of product differentiation, it is important to specify consumers' preferences. Two approaches can be found in the literature: the love of variety approach and the ideal variety approach. These two approaches can be regarded as special cases of a more general approach (see Chapter 6).

Product differentiation has important implications on international factor movement. To illustrate some of these implications, let us consider a case in which capital can move freely internationally while no trade in goods is allowed. Owners of capital that work in another country repatriate the earnings back to their home.

How do capital owners decide whether to move their capital abroad? In the neoclassical framework with homogeneous products and no uncertainty, one can assume that the movement of factors depends on the gaps between the real factor prices in two countries. When products are differentiated, the decision to go abroad depends not only on the real factor price gaps, but also on the number of varieties produced in the two countries.

Two implications about international capital movement in the presence of product differentiation can be noted. First, international capital mobility can be analyzed under the love of variety approach or the ideal variety approach. Both approaches may lead to different equilibria. Second, under either approach, free international capital movement may not lead to equalization of the price of the moving factor. This is different from the corresponding result in the neoclassical framework.

A full analysis of international capital mobility with product differentiation is complicated, however, because although its movement depends on the numbers of varieties in the countries, it affects the number of varieties in the countries. This effect must be fully taken into account in deriving the equilibrium.

International factor mobility in the presence of product differentiation can have other implications. For example, in the neoclassical framework, an inflow of a factor (such as capital) tends to have a negative price effect on the owners of competing factors (such as native capitalists), because it tends to drive down the domestic price of the factor. An inflow of a factor may increase the domestic number of varieties, however, and this could represent a positive indirect effect on the residents in the host country. If the positive indirect effect of an inflow of foreign capital outweighs its negative price effect, the movement of capital may benefit all factors in the host country.

1.6   International Factor Mobility with Oligopoly

Oligoplistic industries are common in the world. This phenomenon has received much attention in the theory of international trade, and trade with oligopoly is one of the important topics in the theory. Many interesting yet not-so-intuitive results have been derived. Because many of these oligopolistic industries are also sources of foreign direct investment, neglecting international factor movement in the theory of trade with oligopoly could yield misleading results.

On the other hand, the presence of oligopolistic firms can have significant implications on international trade in goods and international factor movement. First, as explained in detail in Chapter 7, a free-trade-in-goods equilibrium depends on many factors including the interaction between the oligopolistic firms. Because these firms are not price takers, even with identical and constant-returns technologies, identical and homothetic preferences, and diversification, free trade in general may not lead to factor price equalization when oligopolistic firms are present.

The second thing one can note regarding international factor mobility is that in terms of world equilibrium, it can never substitute international trade in goods. When trade in goods is allowed so that the markets in the countries are integrated, whether international movements of goods actually take place, oligopolistic firms in different countries are competing with each other. Such competition between firms in different countries disappears when trade in goods is replaced by international movement of factors. This means that international trade in goods can achieve something (e.g., the change in market structure) that international factor mobility cannot. Thus international trade in goods and factor mobility must lead the world to different equilibrium points.

If factor price equalization is not achieved under free trade in goods, which is likely, then an equilibrium is no longer efficient in terms of world welfare.

Moreover, factors have incentives to move internationally under free trade when they are allowed. As a result, international trade in goods alone, international factor mobility alone, and international trade in goods plus factor mobility all give different world equilibria.

1.7   Multinational Corporations and Foreign Direct Investment

Foreign direct investment, a phenomenon with growing significance that receives more and more attention in the literature, is something more than international capital movement. Certain issues related to foreign direct investment cannot be explained by the traditional theory within the neoclassical framework. For example, it is observed that firms that invest overseas also borrow overseas. It seems that to capture higher returns is not the only motives of investing abroad. It is also observed that foreign direct investment is usually done by nonfinancial firms. Thus firms play an important role in foreign investment. In particular, very often the firm that invests abroad is also a firm that exports to the host country. This means that the relationship between exports and investment must be carefully examined in developing a successful theory of foreign direct investment.

The role of a multinational corporation in foreign direct investment has long been recognized in the literature. A firm with some competitive advantages in a foreign country has three options: to export, to invest, and to license its technology. Many papers treat these three options as exclusive options, which implies that if a firm chooses to go multinational, exporting and licensing must be inferior options. It is assumed that, in general, two (or three) options will not be chosen at the same time. This approach is not consistent with what actually occurs.

In this book, I have a chapter devoted to analyzing different issues concerning multinational corporations and foreign direct investment. The approach I take in that chapter is relatively new. Although I fully recognize the public-good nature of some of the advantages of a firm, I believe that foreign direct investment is more than just setting up a subsidiary plant in another country. It also involves the transfer of a bundle of assets owned by the firm that can be used in the source country if foreign investment does not take place. If the supply of these assets is limited at least in the short run, then foreign direct investment must be at the expense of production of the parent firm.

Using a unified model, the chapter on multinational corporations also analyzes other related issues such as licensing decisions and technological transfer and diffusion. The chapter also analyzes the phenomenon of quid pro quo and tariff-jumping foreign investment.

1.8   International Labor Migration

International labor migration is a very special type of factor movement because it involves not just the movement of the factor but also the movement of the factor owners. Workers must move before they can render their services abroad. There are several new issues related to international migration that one does not find when analyzing international trade in goods and capital movement.

Migration can be permanent or temporary depending on the duration of stay of the affected workers. In the former case, migrants become permanent residents in the host country and have no plan to move back to the source country. In the second case, migrants are aware of the probability of going back in the forseeable future, whether the return is voluntary or under constraints such as government regulations. A successful theory of international labor migration must distinguish between permanent migration and temporary migration because they have different impacts on the host and source countries.

Chapter 14 focuses on international labor migration. In it I discuss the different features of permanent and temporary migration, and their impacts on the source and host countries. Three issues concerning these two types of migration are especially important. First, how does migration affect welfare of the source and host countries? Second, what policies may the governments of these two countries consider in improving national welfare? Third, external effects of employment may be present. A rigorous model to analyze the role of external effects of employment in international labor migration is presented. The model shows the difficulty of extending the theory of international trade in goods to international labor migration.

The analysis of international labor migration becomes more fruitful when homogeneity of labor is not assumed. Three issues related to the analysis of labor homogeneity can be identified. The first deals with the type of labor that moves abroad. In some countries, there are concerns when skilled workers migrate out, causing a "brain drain." The second issue is that migration of labor may have important income distributional effects, affecting various types of workers in different ways. This is why restrictions on immigration are greeted with varying degrees of resistence by different groups in the host country. The third issue concerning heterogeneity of labor arises when the skill levels of workers are allowed to be determined endogenously, and when endogeneity is linked to international labor migration. Two important channels through which the skill of workers can be improved are identified: learning by doing and education. In the former case, a worker has to work in order to gain skill, while in the latter case, a worker has to use up some of the time that might be spent on working and earning in order to get education. In either case, a worker may be able to choose where he or she gets work experience or education, and where he or she works. The decision depends on a list of factors in the source and host countries. When the decision is to get education in the source country but work in a host country, brain drain occurs.

The literature usually analyzes permanent migration, temporary migration, and brain drain separately. In Chapter 14, I show that these three types of migration can be determined endogenously. The type of migration (including no migration) depends on the market conditions in the source and host countries. A simple overlapping generations model is presented to explain the decision of a potential migrant.

Another feature of international labor migration that distinguishes it from other types of international factor movement is that migrants may be illegal. Immigration is restricted by most countries, but sometimes the incentives to move are so large that some people decide to move illegally at the risk of being caught and deported.

1.9   Other Features of This Book

Despite its emphasis on the importance and significance of international factor mobility and the interactions between trade in goods and factor mobility, this book also has an extensive coverage of different issues in the theory of international trade. In analyzing many of these issues, new techniques and new approaches have been suggested, and new results are obtained. These attempts are briefly described:

1. *Interactions between International Trade in Goods and Capital Movement*   In analyzing the interactions between international trade in goods and international capital movement, new techniques have been developed. The techniques allow me to derive the world equilibrium and to analyze policy impacts in a simple way. A new way of analyzing "cross-hauling" of international capital movement in the presence of trade in goods is provided.

2. *External Economies of Scale*   A convenient way of analyzing a general equilibrium framework with external economies of scale is suggested. It is used to predict the patterns of trade in some cases. The first-best policy for such an economy to achieve Pareto optimality is explained. Sufficient conditions for gains from trade for an economy in the absence of the first-best policy are derived.

3. *Monopolistic Competition and Differentiated Products*   A general approach to analyzing the preferences of consumers in the presence of differentiated products is given. A simple way to analyze the general equilibrium nature of such an economy is presented. The first-best policy to achieve the Pareto optimality is explained, and gains from trade conditions are derived.

4. *Oligopoly*   In addition to analyzing different models of oligopolistic industries, the roles of transport costs and arbitrage in intraindustry trade are explained. A simple way of analyzing a general equilibrium model with an oligopolistic industry is suggested. The first-best policies are given. Strategic trade policies, trade wars, and alternatives to trade wars are explained with a unified framework.

5. *Welfare Economics of International Trade*   In this book I analyze different approaches to comparing the welfare levels of two situations. I then summarize the fundamental results using six core theorems, including two corollaries, which are valid whether or not a social utility function exists (with an additional assumption of no inferior goods for one of the theorems under the social utility approach), and whether compensation using lump-sum transfers or consumption taxes is used. I also analyze gains from trade for economies with incomplete markets or overlapping generations.

Another feature of this book is that it provides extensive surveys of many different theories of international trade in goods and factor mobility. The theories are presented using some unified models and notation. I have made attempts to extend, generalize, and synthesize these theories. These surveys are helpful to those readers who want to understand recent development in the literature and some basic analytical techniques.

1.10   Structure of This Book

This book is divided into six parts. The first part is the introduction. Part II, which consists of chapters 2 to 4, discusses the pure theory of international trade in the neoclassical framework. The framework is characterized by constant returns to scale and perfect competition. Chapter 2 presents the major techniques of analyzing the neoclassical general equilibrium framework. Chapter 3 analyzes two major topics: comparative advantage and factor content of trade. The basic laws of comparative advantage are presented, and factor content of trade explained. Factor content of trade can in some cases be a fruitful approach to analyzing patterns of trade by focusing on the factors embodied in the moving goods. This chapter also examines the relationship between factor accumulation and dynamic comparative advantage.

In Chapter 4 international capital mobility is examined. Several issues concerning the relationship between international trade in goods and international capital movement are presented. These issues include the validity of core trade theorems, the possibility of diversification under trade, and the stability of equilibrium. Using two simple graphical techniques that are explained in the chapter, these issues can be examined with relative ease. The chapter also analyzes comparative and absolute advantage in the presence of capital mobility and cross-hauling of capital movements.

Part III of this book covers models without constant returns to scale or perfect competition. Three types of models are investigated in successive chapters. The models are external economies of scale, monopolistic competition and product differentiation, and oligoply. As explained earlier, external economies of scale are external effects that firms ignore in their production decisions. Chapter 5 describes external economies of scale in detail and examines the relationship between international trade in goods and international factor movement.

Chapter 6 focuses on a model of monopolistic competition and product differentiation. In considering product differentiation, two important features must be noted. The first is the type of preferences under consideration. Two extreme types have been assumed: the love of variety approach and the ideal variety approach. The second feature, which makes product differentiation models interesting, is that variety is endogenous in the model. The chapter presents a simple model to analyze certain issues related to international trade in goods and international factor mobility. In particular, the possibility of intraindustry trade is discussed.

The focus of Chapter 7 is oligopoly. This type of model has captured the interest of trade theorists for two reasons. First, there are only a limited number of firms in the model. Thus the interactions between the firms and the firms' strategies are important elements of the model. They have to be fully considered in the analysis. Second, under certain conditions, there exists intraindustry trade in identical products between countries. Chapter 7 examines the possibility of intraindustry trade in different cases. Much of the literature on trade with oligopoly assumes partial equilibrium frameworks. Although these frameworks are simple to use and to bring out the intuition behind intra-industry trade, they are not suitable for analyzing international factor mobility because factor prices and factor endowment constraints are not explicitly considered. The chapter presents frameworks for partial equilibrium and general equilibrium that can be used to analyze several issues related to intraindustry trade and international factor mobility.

Part IV deals with the welfare economics of international trade. Chapter 8 has two major parts. The first discusses different ways of measuring welfare of a multihousehold economies. Unless the households are identical with identical factor endowments and preferences, finding an index to represent the welfare of the economy is not easy and not without controversy. Several approaches are surveyed. Two of them are more common in the trade literature: the social utility approach and the compensation approach, and compensation can be made using either lump-sum transfers or commodity taxation. The second part of the chapter proves six core theorems of neoclassical welfare

economics in international trade. These theorems have important policy implications and are valid under either the social utility approach (except that one of
the theorems requires no inferior goods) or the compensation approach using
lump-sum transfers or commodity taxes.

Chapter 9 looks at the gains from trade in five types of economies with
imperfections. These economies are external economies of scale, monopolistic competition, oligopoly, incomplete markets, and overlapping generations.
Chapter 9 shows that for these models, trade is not necessarily gainful. For the
first three models, the chapter determines some sufficient conditions for gainful trade. For the other two types of models, it shows that the government can
use policies such as compensation to make sure that autarkic equilibrium is not
preferred to free trade.

Part V, which consists of chapters 10 through 12, covers policy analysis for
different models. Chapter 10 presents the theory of distortions and the principle of optimal policy intervention. It points out that all of the models analyzed
in chapters 5 through 7 are distorted, and argues that a competitive equilibrium in any of these models is not Pareto optimal. The chapter also explains
what policy the government can have to maximize a social utility function for
the models with external economies of scale or monopolistic competition and
product differentiation.

Chapter 11 examines different policies for the government in the presence
of international trade in goods and factor mobility. In addition to examining
the effects of trade taxes and income taxes on moving factors, the chapter derives the optimal policies for the government. Two other issues are covered
in the chapter. The first is related to the impacts of international factor mobility when international trade in goods is present. Two separate cases are
discussed, depending on whether the optimal policy on the trading goods is
being imposed. The second issue is about comparing the impacts of international capital mobility and international labor mobility, and about the choice
between these two factor mobility policies.

Chapter 12 is about strategic trade policies. The word "strategic" refers to
two cases. First, there is an oligopolistic industry in which there are a limited
number of firms in each of the countries. The firms have certain monopoly
power, and there are strategic reasons for imposing trade taxes or subsidies
that one would not find in the neoclassical framework. This chapter has an
emphasis on the effects of government policies on the strategic interactions
between the oligopolistic firms at home and those firms in another country.
This chapter also derives the optimal policy intervention in this type of model,
and points out some problems of implementing these policies.

The second case covered in Chapter 12 involves two active governments,
whether or not the industries are oligopolistic. Trade war and retaliation between the governments are analyzed. This chapter also points out that there

are several alternatives to trade war that could make both countries better off. The last part of this chapter covers strategic policies toward international factor mobility.

The last part, Part VI, covers two special topics, multinational corporations (Chapter 13) and international labor migration (Chapter 14).

1.11   Rising Significance of International Trade in Goods and Factor Movements

There is evidence that international trade in goods and factor mobility are growing significantly over time in the world. To facilitate our investigation, I have divided the world into two groups: industrial countries (ICs) and developing countries (DCs).

First consider the growth of income in the world and in these regions. Figure 1.1 presents the real GDPs of these regions from 1963 to 1990. These GDPs, given in the form of indices, are taken from the *International Financial Statistical Yearbook*, 1992, published by the International Monetary Fund. The base year was converted to 1963 for the ease of comparison.

The three curves in Figure 1.1 show the continuing growth of the world and the two subgroups of countries. What is interesting to note is that the group of DCs as a whole was growing faster than the group of ICs. More specifically, in the given period of twenty-seven years, the real GDP of the world increased

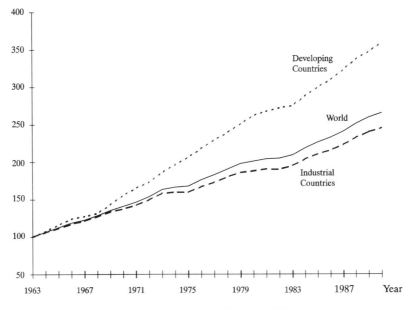

Figure 1.1   Growth of real GDP indices (1963=100), 1963–1990

Table 1.1
Annual growth rates of real GDP, merchandise exports, and outward direct investment

Year	World	Industrial countries	Developing countries
A. Real GDP (percent)			
1963–70	5.0	4.7	6.5
1971–80	3.2	2.8	4.7
1981–90	2.7	2.6	3.0
1963–90	3.7	3.4	4.8
B. Real merchandise exports (percent)			
1963–70	10.2	8.1	12.4
1971–80	3.6	7.3	−1.5
1981–90	4.4	4.0	5.0
1963–90	5.6	6.4	4.5
C. Real outward direct investment (percent)			
1971–80	3.6	3.7	1.2
1981–90	13.4	13.0	26.4
1970–90	8.2	8.1	9.3

Sources: International Monetary Fund, *Direction of Trade Statistics,* various issues; *International Financial Statistics Yearbook,* various issues; *Balance of Payments Statistics Yearbook,* various issues.

by 1.7 times from 100 to 266, while the expansion of ICs as a whole was 1.5 times and that of the group of DCs was 2.6 times.

The details about the growth rates of these country groups are given in Table 1.1. As shown in part (A) of the table, the annual growth rates of real GDPs of the world, the ICs, and the DCs in the period from 1963 to 1990 are 3.7 percent, 3.4 percent, and 4.8 percent, respectively. Economic growth was not even during those years, however. Faster growth was recorded in the years from 1963 to 1970. Growth slowed down considerably in the 1970s due to the first oil crisis. The second oil crisis in 1979 did about the same damage to many countries in terms of growth in the early 1980s, although the world managed to post an average annual growth rate of 2.7 percent in that decade.

In Figure 1.2, I compare the growth of the volumes of merchandise export of the world, the ICs, and the DCs from 1963 to 1990. The export volumes of the ICs and DCs are deflated by their respective export unit value with 1985 = 100, and they are then summed up to give the real export of the world. The volumes of export are interpreted as measures of the excess supplies and international competitiveness in trade in goods of these countries.

In the decade from 1963 to 1973, ICs and DCs expanded their exports each year. In the first six years of that decade, the ICs were more important suppliers of goods to other countries. In each of the next three years, however,

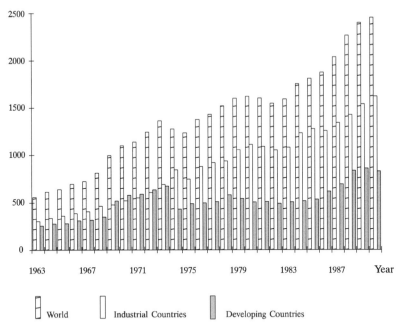

Figure 1.2 Growth of merchandise export at constant prices of 1985, billions of
U.S. dollars, 1963–1990

the growth rates of the DCs were so phenomenal that they actually exported more goods than the ICs did.

In 1973 came the devastating oil crisis. The volume of trade plummeted in most countries and the exports of the DCs were especially hit hard. In 1974, the total volume of exports of the DCs dropped to US$432 Bn from US$673 Bn in the previous year, with a shrinkage rate of 36 percent. Just when the DCs were about to recover from the rising price of oil, in 1979 the second oil crisis occurred. It was not until the second half of the 1980s that the DCs started to pick up steam in exporting more goods to other countries.

It is interesting to note that the ICs seemed to have been hurt less than the DCs by the two oil crises. Although their exports did show some shrinkage after the shocks, they quickly regained ground, and their growth appeared to be nonstoppable. Nothing is better at indicating the power of the ICs in trade than the share of export of these countries in the world. In 1963, the ICs' volume of export was only 54 percent, which means that ICs and DCs exported approximately the same volumes. In 1990, however, the ICs' export share was 66 percent, which is nearly twice of the share of the DCs.

Despite the disruption caused by the two oil crises, both the ICs and the DCs had high growth rates of export in the period from 1963 to 1990. For example, as shown in part (B) of Table 1.1, the ICs experienced an annual growth rate of

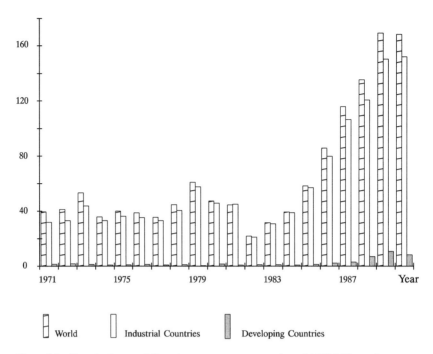

Figure 1.3 Growth of outward direct investment at constant prices of 1985, billions of
U.S. dollars, 1971–1990

its export of 6.4 percent while that of the DCs was 4.5 percent. That the DCs
had a lower annual growth rate in this period is due to its drop in real export in
the 1970s. It is clear from the table that in fact the DCs expanded their exports
to other countries more successfully than the ICs did both in the 1960s and in
the 1980s.

Another interesting phenomenon is that, except in the 1970s for the DCs,
the growth rates of export volume for the countries were much faster than their
economies. This suggests that as countries grow, they get more interdependent
through trade in goods.

Now consider the world, the ICs, and the DCs as sources of direct investment in the period from 1971 to 1990. Figure 1.3 shows the amounts of direct
investments (outward direct investments) from all countries, from the ICs, and
from the DCs for those years. The investment figures from the ICs and DCs
had been deflated by the export unit values (1985 = 100), and they were then
summed up to give the world's total. The first thing that can be noted in Figure 1.3 is that the ICs contributed nearly all of the direct investment in the
world. In each and every year in this period, the share of direct investment
from the ICs was more than 93 percent. In fact, in 1979, 99.5 percent of the
direct investment in the world originated from industrial countries.

The two oil crises also had negative impacts on direct investment across countries. The direct investment for the world as a whole dropped right after the oil shocks and, as in the case of foreign export, the DCs appeared to be hit more severely.

The economic growth and stability in the 1980s, on the other hand, have greatly encouraged the movement of capital across countries. This can be confirmed by Figure 1.3 or by part (C) of Table 1.1. For example, from 1981 to 1990, direct investment from the ICs grew by an annual rate of 13 percent while that the annual growth rate of the DCs was 26.4 percent, or more than double of that for the ICs. Again, the growth of direct investment for any region in those periods was higher than that of foreign export, which in turn was higher than that of GDP.[1]

---

1. For more evidence about the surge of foreign direct investment in the United States in the 1980s, see Graham and Krugman (1993), and Wong and Yamamura (1995).

II   PURE THEORY: THE NEOCLASSICAL MODELS

General Equilibrium with Constant Returns and Perfect Competition

Many trade issues are related to resource allocation and interactions between different sectors in an economy. Satisfactory analysis of these issues requires specific knowledge about the characteristics of the economies in question and techniques used to examine the interactions between different sectors and between consumption and production. To analyze these issues, trade theorists rely on general equilibrium frameworks to arrive at quantitative relationships between different parts of one or more economies. Many general equilibrium frameworks have been constructed to tackle different problems.

This chapter presents some of the more common general equilibrium frameworks used in the literature, which are important tools for analyzing problems that have challenged trade economists for a long time. These frameworks differ in terms of their dimensions and other properties, but they share some common assumptions: Two of these assumptions are constant-returns technologies and perfect competition.

This chapter derives some useful analytical techniques and important results that are used frequently. It begins with the two-factor, two-sector (2×2) framework, which is regarded as the fundamental general equilibrium framework. Despite its low dimension, it is a simple way of examining possible interactions between sectors. After it has been used to derive some important results, this framework is extended to other frameworks with different dimensions. The dual general equilibrium approach, which has been proved to be extremely useful in high-dimensional frameworks, is developed later.

2.1 The Two-Factor, Two-Sector Framework

This framework has the following properties:

1. One economy is endowed with fixed amounts of two homogeneous factors, labor (L) and capital (K). Denote the endowments of labor and capital by $\overline{L}$ and $\overline{K}$, respectively.

2. Two sectors produce two homogeneous goods, labeled goods 1 and 2. The production function of sector i, $i = 1, 2$, is

$$Q_i = F_i(K_i, L_i), \tag{2.1}$$

where Q_i is the output, and K_i and L_i are respectively the amounts of capital and labor employed in the sector.[1] Each production function is increasing,

---

1. One justification for the existence of a sectoral production function for sector i is that all the firms in sector i, $i = 1, 2$, have identical and constant-returns technologies. Denote the (common) production function of the jth firm in sector i by $Q_i^j = F_i(K_i^j, L_i^j)$ where K_i^j and L_i^j are capital and labor inputs, respectively. Suppose that there are n_i identical firms in that sector. If these

concave, linearly homogeneous, and differentiable up to the necessary order in inputs. Both factors are indispensible in the production in the sense that $F_i(0, L_i) = F_i(K_i, 0) = 0$.

3. Markets are perfectly competitive.

4. Factors are perfectly mobile between sectors.

5. Prices are perfectly flexible.

Because the production function given in assumption 2 is linearly homogeneous, the output-labor ratio of sector i can be given by the function $f_i(k_i) \equiv F_i(k_i, 1)$, where $k_i \equiv K_i/L_i$ is the capital-labor ratio. Thus

$$Q_i = L_i f_i(k_i) \equiv L_i F_i(K_i/L_i, 1). \tag{2.2}$$

Sector 1 relative to sector 2 is said to be capital (respectively labor) intensive if, when given the same factor prices in both sectors, $k_1 > k_2$ (respectively $k_1 < k_2$). The marginal products of capital and labor are respectively equal to

$$F_{iK}(K_i, L_i) \equiv \frac{\partial F_i(K_i, L_i)}{\partial K_i} = \frac{df_i}{dk_i} \equiv f_i'(k_i) \tag{2.3a}$$

$$F_{iL}(K_i, L_i) \equiv \frac{\partial F_i(K_i, L_i)}{\partial L_i} = f_i(k_i) - k_i f_i'(k_i). \tag{2.3b}$$

By condition (2.3), the marginal products of factors depend on the capital-labor ratios only. We assume that for $k_i > 0$, $f_i'(k_i) > 0$, and $f_i''(k_i) < 0$. Sometimes it is convenient to impose the Inada conditions: $\lim_{k_i \to 0} f_i(k_i) = 0$, $\lim_{k_i \to \infty} f_i(k_i) = \infty$, $\lim_{k_i \to 0} f_i'(k_i) = \infty$, and $\lim_{k_i \to \infty} f_i'(k_i) = 0$.

Perfect competition and cost minimization means that factors are paid their values of marginal products. Denote the wage rate by w, the rental rate of capital by r, and the price of good i by p_i. Perfect mobility of factors across sectors and *diversification in production*, that is, positive outputs of both goods, lead to equalization of factor prices in both sectors:

$$r = p_1 f_1' = p_2 f_2' \tag{2.4a}$$

$$w = p_1(f_1 - k_1 f_1') = p_2(f_2 - k_2 f_2'). \tag{2.4b}$$

---

firms face the same prices, then in equilibrium they must employ the same amounts of labor and capital, producing the same output level. This gives the sectoral output and the sectoral production function:

$$Q_i = \sum_j Q_i^j = n_i Q_i^j = n_i F_i(K_i^j, L_i^j)$$

$$= F_i(n_i K_i^j, n_i L_i^j) = F_i(K_i, L_i),$$

where linear homogeneity of the function has been used.

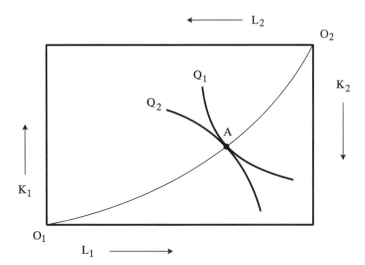

Figure 2.1

Conditions (2.4) imply that in equilibrium the two sectors have the same marginal rate of technical substitution.

This result can be illustrated by the Edgeworth box diagram in Figure 2.1. The size of the box is the given labor endowment (measured horizontally) and capital endowment (measured vertically) in the economy. Any point inside the box represents an allocation of the factors between the sectors (measured from O_1 for sector 1 and from O_2 for sector 2). The diagram shows a representative isoquant for sector 1 (labeled Q_1) and one for sector 2 (labeled Q_2). These two isoquants are tangent to each other at point A. The locus of points of tangency between the two isoquant maps for the sectors is called the *efficiency locus*. By (2.4), the sectors must have the same wage-rental ratio, and, because of cost minimization, also the same marginal rate of technical substitution. In other words, the production point must be on the efficiency locus, and if the commodity prices are known, the exact location of the production point can be determined.

The slope of ray O_1A (respectively O_2A) gives the sector's capital-labor ratio k_1 (k_2). If sector 1 is labor intensive, as in the case shown in the diagram, the efficiency locus must be below the diagonal except at O_1 and O_2. Alternatively, if sector 1 is capital intensive, the efficiency locus is above the diagonal. Different points on the efficiency locus give different factor intensties of the sectors. Note that with homothetic production functions and fixed factor endowments, factor intensity ranking of the sectors cannot be reversed. In other words, the efficiency locus cannot be partly above the diagonal and partly below it. To see why, suppose that the factor intensity ranking is reversed so that due to continuity of the production functions the efficiency locus cuts the diagonal at a point other than the origins. At this point, an isoquant for sector 1 is tangent to an isoquant for sector 2. Because the production functions are homothetic, other isoquants of the sectors must have the same slope at different points on the diagonal. This means that the efficiency locus coincides with the diagonal. This is the case when both sectors have the same capital-labor ratio. If the sectors have different capital-labor ratios, the efficiency locus must be entirely above or below the diagonal (except at the two origins). Of course, if factor endowments are not fixed, then for some technologies, factor intensity reversal is possible (Samuelson, 1948, 1949; Minhas, 1962). Alternatively, factor intensity reversal is possible when there are more than two factors, even if factor endowments are fixed (Wong, 1990).

Given diversification in production (positive outputs in all sectors), conditions (2.4) form a subsystem of the economy, with four equations and six unknowns: w, r, k_1, k_2, p_1, and p_2. If the two commodity prices p_1 and p_2 are given or taken as parameters, then these equations can be solved for the factor prices and capital-labor ratios. This gives a very important implication: With diversification, factor prices depend only on commodity prices, not on factor endowments. For an application of this result, consider a small open economy with diversification and facing given world prices. A change in the quantities of factors working in the economy, either through factor accumulation or international factor movements, will not affect factor prices. As a result, when given commodity prices and diversification, the technologies appear to be of the fixed-coefficient type because the capital-labor ratios of the sectors are fixed.

Denote the wage-rental ratio by ω, which under cost minimization is equal to the marginal rate of technical substitution in each sector, or

$$\omega = \frac{w}{r} = \frac{f_i}{f_i'} - k_i, \qquad i = 1, 2, \tag{2.5}$$

which gives the implicit dependence of the capital-labor ratio on the wage-rental ratio in each sector. Differentiate both sides of (2.5) and rearrange terms to give

$$\frac{dk_i}{d\omega} = -\frac{(f_i')^2}{f_i f_i''} > 0. \tag{2.6}$$

The economic intuition behind equation (2.6) is that as a factor becomes relatively more expensive, cost-minimizing firms tend to substitute it with another factor that is relatively cheaper.

The positive relationship between k_i and ω can also be proved by Figure 2.2. Consider sector i, $i = 1, 2$. The iso-cost line AB, which has a (negative)

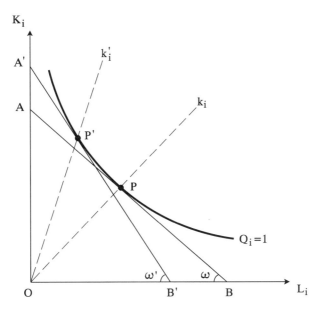

Figure 2.2

slope equal to the initial wage-rental ratio ω, is tangent at point P to the unit isoquant labeled $Q_i = 1$. Ray OP, called the expansion path, from the origin is the locus of cost-minimizing input mix under the given factor prices. Thus the slope of line OP equals the corresponding capital-labor ratio, k_i. An increase in the wage-rental ratio to ω' shifts the iso-cost line to A'B', which is tangent to the unit isoquant at P'. The diagram shows an increase in the capital-labor ratio, $k_i' > k_i$, as the firms are using less of the more expensive factor (labor) in production.

2.2   Unit Cost Function and Input-Ouput Coefficients

Using the production function of sector i given previously, I can define the unit cost function as

$$c_i(w, r) = \min_{a_{Ki}, a_{Li}} \{wa_{Li} + ra_{Ki} : F_i(a_{Ki}, a_{Li}) \geq 1\}. \tag{2.7}$$

The values of a_{Ki} and a_{Li} that solve the problem are the cost-minimizing capital-output and labor-output ratios, respectively. The unit cost function has the following properties:

1. It is increasing, differentiable, concave, and linearly homogeneous in factor prices.

2. By the envelope theorem, its derivatives are the optimal input-output coefficients that solve the problem in (2.7):

$$\frac{\partial c_i}{\partial w} = a_{Li}(w, r) \tag{2.8a}$$

$$\frac{\partial c_i}{\partial r} = a_{Ki}(w, r) \tag{2.8b}$$

Conditions (2.8) are called Shephard's lemma (Shephard, 1953).

3. The input-output coefficients, when expressed as functions of factor prices, are homogeneous of degree zero in factor prices.

4. Because the unit cost function is concave, its Hessian (second-order derivatives) matrix is negative semi-definite and has nonpositive diagonal elements; thus

$$\frac{\partial a_{Ki}}{\partial r}, \quad \frac{\partial a_{Li}}{\partial w} \leq 0. \tag{2.9a}$$

Because input-output coefficients are homogeneous of degree zero, (2.9a) implies that

$$\frac{\partial a_{Ki}}{\partial w}, \quad \frac{\partial a_{Li}}{\partial r} \geq 0. \tag{2.9b}$$

Conditions (2.9a) and (2.9b) mean that a cost-minimizing firm tends to use more of the less expensive factor and less of the more expensive factor, which is similar to a result I derived earlier.

Under perfect competition, firms producing positive outputs earn zero profit, which means that unit costs are equal to output prices, that is,

$$c_1(w, r) = w a_{L1} + r a_{K1} = p_1 \tag{2.10a}$$

$$c_2(w, r) = w a_{L2} + r a_{K2} = p_2. \tag{2.10b}$$

The input-output coefficients can also be used to state the full-employment conditions. With constant-returns technologies, $a_{ji} Q_i$ is the cost-minimizing derived demand for factor j to produce Q_i units of good i. Perfect price flexibility and inter-sectoral factor mobility imply full employment of factors:

$$a_{L1} Q_1 + a_{L2} Q_2 = \overline{L} \tag{2.11a}$$

$$a_{K1} Q_1 + a_{K2} Q_2 = \overline{K}. \tag{2.11b}$$

Let $\widehat{y} \equiv dy/y$ represent the rate of growth of any variable y. Differentiate equations (2.10) and (2.11), and rearrange terms to give

$$\theta_{L1}\widehat{w} + \theta_{K1}\widehat{r} = \widehat{p}_1 - [\theta_{L1}\widehat{a}_{L1} + \theta_{K1}\widehat{a}_{K1}] \tag{2.12a}$$

$$\theta_{L2}\widehat{w} + \theta_{K2}\widehat{r} = \widehat{p}_2 - [\theta_{L2}\widehat{a}_{L2} + \theta_{K2}\widehat{a}_{K2}] \tag{2.12b}$$

$$\lambda_{L1}\widehat{Q}_1 + \lambda_{L2}\widehat{Q}_2 = \widehat{L} - [\lambda_{L1}\widehat{a}_{L1} + \lambda_{L2}\widehat{a}_{L2}] \tag{2.12c}$$

$$\lambda_{K1}\widehat{Q}_1 + \lambda_{K2}\widehat{Q}_2 = \widehat{K} - [\lambda_{K1}\widehat{a}_{K1} + \lambda_{K2}\widehat{a}_{K2}], \tag{2.12d}$$

where θ_{ji} is factor j's share in sector i, and λ_{ji} is the fraction of factor j working in sector i; for example, $\theta_{L1} = wa_{L1}/p_1$ and $\lambda_{L1} = L_1/L$. With zero profit and full employment, I have

$$\theta_{Li} + \theta_{Ki} = 1 \qquad i = 1, 2 \tag{2.13a}$$

$$\lambda_{j1} + \lambda_{j2} = 1 \qquad j = K, L. \tag{2.13b}$$

Note that condition (2.11b) can be written as

$$\frac{L_1}{L}\frac{K_1}{L_1} + \frac{L_2}{L}\frac{K_2}{L_2} = \frac{\overline{K}}{\overline{L}}, \tag{2.14}$$

which reduces to

$$\lambda_{L1}k_1 + \lambda_{L2}k_2 = \overline{k}, \tag{2.14'}$$

where $\overline{k} = \overline{K}/\overline{L}$. Condition (2.14′) shows that when both goods are produced, the overall capital-labor ratio is a weighted average of the two sectors' capital-labor ratios.

Define θ and λ as

$$\theta = \begin{pmatrix} \theta_{L1} & \theta_{K1} \\ \theta_{L2} & \theta_{K2} \end{pmatrix} \qquad \text{and} \qquad \lambda = \begin{pmatrix} \lambda_{L1} & \lambda_{L2} \\ \lambda_{K1} & \lambda_{K2} \end{pmatrix}.$$

Using the conditions in (2.13), the determinants of θ and λ are equal to

$$|\theta| = \theta_{L1} - \theta_{L2} = \theta_{K2} - \theta_{K1} \tag{2.15a}$$

$$|\lambda| = \lambda_{L1} - \lambda_{K1} = \lambda_{K2} - \lambda_{L2}. \tag{2.15b}$$

Using the definitions of θ_{ji} and λ_{ji}, and the zero-profit conditions, the determinants of θ and λ are also equal to

$$|\theta| = \frac{wL_1}{wL_1 + rK_1} - \frac{wL_2}{wL_2 + rK_2} = \frac{\omega(k_2 - k_1)}{(\omega + k_1)(\omega + k_2)} \tag{2.15a'}$$

$$|\lambda| = \frac{L_1}{\overline{L}} - \frac{K_1}{\overline{K}} = \frac{L_1 L_2(k_2 - k_1)}{\overline{L}\,\overline{K}}. \tag{2.15b'}$$

Thus both $|\theta|$ and $|\lambda|$ are positive if and only if sector 1 is labor intensive.

Turning back to equations (2.12a) and (2.12b), I note that the first-order condition for the cost-minimizing problem given in (2.7) is that $dc_i = w\, da_{Li} + r\, da_{Ki} = 0$, which implies that

$$\theta_{Li}\widehat{a}_{Li} + \theta_{Ki}\widehat{a}_{Ki} = 0 \qquad i = 1, 2. \tag{2.16}$$

Substitute (2.16) into equations (2.12a) and (2.12b) to give

$$\theta_{L1}\widehat{w} + \theta_{K1}\widehat{r} = \widehat{p}_1 \quad . \tag{2.17a}$$

$$\theta_{L2}\widehat{w} + \theta_{K2}\widehat{r} = \widehat{p}_2. \tag{2.17b}$$

On the other hand, equations (2.12c) and (2.12d) can be written in an alternative form by defining σ_i as the elasticity of substitution of sector i, that is,

$$\sigma_i = \frac{\widehat{a}_{Ki} - \widehat{a}_{Li}}{\widehat{w} - \widehat{r}} \qquad i = 1, 2. \tag{2.18}$$

Equations (2.16) and (2.18) can be solved to give

$$\widehat{a}_{Li} = -\theta_{Ki}\sigma_i(\widehat{w} - \widehat{r}) \tag{2.19a}$$

$$\widehat{a}_{Ki} = \theta_{Li}\sigma_i(\widehat{w} - \widehat{r}), \qquad i = 1, 2. \tag{2.19b}$$

The values of $\widehat{a}_{Li}$ and $\widehat{a}_{Ki}$ in (2.19) are substituted into (2.12c) and (2.12d) to give

$$\lambda_{L1}\widehat{Q}_1 + \lambda_{L2}\widehat{Q}_2 = \widehat{L} + \delta_L(\widehat{w} - \widehat{r}) \tag{2.17c}$$

$$\lambda_{K1}\widehat{Q}_1 + \lambda_{K2}\widehat{Q}_2 = \widehat{K} - \delta_K(\widehat{w} - \widehat{r}), \tag{2.17d}$$

where $\delta_L = \lambda_{L1}\theta_{K1}\sigma_1 + \lambda_{L2}\theta_{K2}\sigma_2$ and $\delta_K = \lambda_{K1}\theta_{L1}\sigma_1 + \lambda_{K2}\theta_{L2}\sigma_2$. The four equations in (2.17) are called the *equations of change*.

2.3   The Stolper-Samuelson and the Rybczynski Theorems

I now make use of the equations of change to derive two important properties of the present framework. Without loss of generality, I assume that sector 1 is labor intensive unless stated otherwise. This implies that $|\theta|$ and $|\lambda|$ are both positive. First solve equations (2.17a) and (2.17b) for the changes in factor prices:

$$\widehat{w} = \frac{\theta_{K2}\widehat{p}_1 - \theta_{K1}\widehat{p}_2}{|\theta|} \tag{2.20a}$$

$$\widehat{r} = \frac{\theta_{L1}\widehat{p}_2 - \theta_{L2}\widehat{p}_1}{|\theta|}. \tag{2.20b}$$

Suppose that $\widehat{p}_1 > \widehat{p}_2$, and let $\widehat{p}_1 = \widehat{p}_2 + \psi$ where $\psi > 0$. Conditions (2.20) reduce to

$$\widehat{w} = \widehat{p}_1 + \frac{\theta_{K1}}{|\theta|}\psi \qquad (2.21\text{a})$$

$$\widehat{r} = \widehat{p}_2 - \frac{\theta_{L2}}{|\theta|}\psi \qquad (2.21\text{b})$$

Because $|\theta| > 0$ due to the factor intensity ranking, I have

$$\widehat{w} > \widehat{p}_1 > \widehat{p}_2 > \widehat{r}. \qquad (2.22\text{a})$$

Similarly, if $\widehat{p}_2 > \widehat{p}_1$, I have

$$\widehat{r} > \widehat{p}_2 > \widehat{p}_1 > \widehat{w}. \qquad (2.22\text{b})$$

Conditions (2.22) are called the *magnification effects* (Jones, 1965). Of course when $\widehat{p}_1 = \widehat{p}_2$, then $\widehat{w} = \widehat{p}_1 = \widehat{p}_2 = \widehat{r}$. The special case in which there is an increase in only one commodity price is summarized by the Stolper-Samuelson theorem (Stolper and Samuelson, 1941):[2]

The Stolper-Samuelson Theorem   A rise in the price of a commodity will increase the real reward of the factor used intensively in the sector and decrease the real reward of the other factor.

The Stolper-Samuelson theorem can be explained using simple economic reasoning. Suppose that good 2 becomes more expensive while the price of good 1 is fixed. This encourages the production of good 2. Expansion of sector 2 draws labor and capital from sector 1. By assumption sector 1 is labor intensive. The simultaneous expansion of sector 2 and contraction of sector 1 will create an excess demand for capital and an excess supply of labor, thus pushing up the rental rate but pushing down the wage rate. Furthermore, with firms in sector 2 earning zero profit, an increase in p_2 plus a decrease in the wage rate means that r must have grown faster than p_2.

Note that equations (2.20) and (2.19) confirm one result I obtained earlier. By (2.20), if $\widehat{p}_1 = \widehat{p}_2 = 0$, the factor prices are fixed. This shows the one-to-one correspondence between commodity prices and factor prices. Furthermore, by (2.19), the input-output coefficients are also fixed. Once commodity prices are given and diversification is assumed, factor prices and

---

2. Note that the theorem is stated in terms of the real rewards of the factors, where real rewards are factor prices deflated by any linear combination of the commodity prices. By the magnification effect, if the price of the labor-intensive good rises, the wage rate will increase more than both commodity prices do, implying that the real wage rate is higher. The real rental rate decreases because the nominal rental rate does, while one commodity price increases and the other does not change.

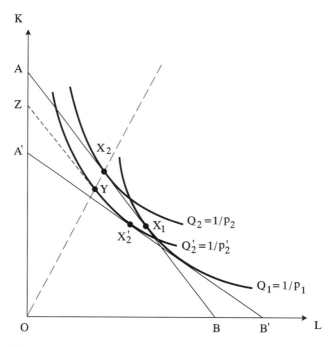

Figure 2.3

input-output coefficients are not affected by factor endowments or international factor movements.

The relationship between commodity prices and factor prices can be illustrated by the well-known *Lerner diagram* (Lerner, 1952) in Figure 2.3. Denote the initial commodity prices by p_i, $i = 1, 2$. The diagram shows two isoquants of the sectors, $Q_i = 1/p_i$, $i = 1, 2$, sector 2 being capital intensive. The isoquants are tangent at points X_1 and X_2 to a common iso-cost line AB represented by the following equation:

$$wL + rK = 1. \tag{2.23}$$

With respect to the output level $Q_i = 1/p_i$, point X_i is the cost-minimizing production point. At point X_i, both the revenue and cost for the sector equal unity, implying zero profit.[3]

By equation (2.23), the slope of AB is equal to $-\omega$, with a horizontal intercept of $1/w$ and a vertical intercept of $1/r$. Thus I have a compact diagram showing the relationship between commodity prices and factor prices.

---

3. The actual production point of sector i will be a point on ray OX_i, and its exact location depends on the output of the sector.

Figure 2.3 provides a simple, graphical way of proving the Stolper-Samuelson theorem. Suppose that p_2 increases to p_2' while p_1 remains unchanged. Corresponding to this higher price, I draw a new isoquant for sector 2, $Q_2' = 1/p_2'$, as shown. This isoquant and the unchanged isoquant Q_1 are tangent to a new iso-cost line A'B'. The new wage rate w' (respectively new rental rate r') is given by the reciprocal of the horizontal (respectively vertical) intercept of line A'B'. It is immediately clear, by comparing the original and new intercepts on the horizontal and vertical axes, that the wage rate falls (OB < OB') and the rental rate increases (OA > OA'). What is left to show is that r increases by a greater proportion than p_2.

Draw a ray from the origin that passes through X_2, cutting the new isoquant Q_2' at point Y. Construct line YZ parallel to AB where Z is on the vertical axis. Then

$$\frac{\Delta r}{r} = \frac{r' - r}{r} = \frac{1/\text{OA}' - 1/\text{OA}}{1/\text{OA}} = \frac{\text{AA}'}{\text{OA}'}$$

and

$$\frac{\Delta p_2}{p_2} = \frac{p_2' - p_2}{p_2} = \frac{1/\text{OY} - 1/\text{OX}_2}{1/\text{OX}_2} = \frac{\text{YX}_2}{\text{OY}} = \frac{\text{ZA}}{\text{OZ}},$$

where the last equality is due to the fact that YZ is parallel to AX$_2$. It is clear from the diagram that OA' < OZ and AA' > ZA. Thus $\Delta r/r > \Delta p_2/p_2$. Combining the results gives the Stolper-Samuelson theorem.

The relationship between commodity prices, factor prices, and capital-labor ratios is frequently described by a well-known diagram in Figure 2.4 (Samuelson, 1949; Johnson, 1957).[4] The positive relationship between ω and k_i comes from (2.6). The diagram shows the case in which sector 2 is capital intensive at all revelant factor prices. Because of this factor intensity ranking, ω increases with p_1/p_2; thus the schedule on the left is positively sloped, and by the Stolper-Samuelson theorem, at any point it is steeper than a ray from the origin to that point.

I now turn to the relationship between factor endowments and outputs when commodity prices, and thus factor prices, are kept constant. Solve equations (2.17c) and (2.17d) for the changes in outputs to give:

$$\widehat{Q}_1 = \frac{\lambda_{K2}\widehat{L} - \lambda_{L2}\widehat{K}}{|\lambda|} \tag{2.24a}$$

$$\widehat{Q}_2 = \frac{\lambda_{L1}\widehat{K} - \lambda_{K1}\widehat{L}}{|\lambda|}. \tag{2.24b}$$

---

4. A detailed treatment of this technique is given in Kemp (1969) and Bhagwati and Srinivasan (1983a).

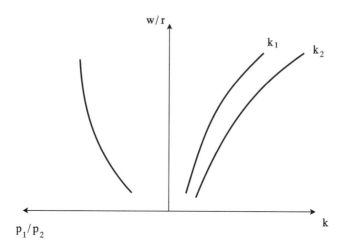

Figure 2.4

Using the value of $|\lambda|$ given in (2.15b), I can show that if $\widehat{\widehat{L}} > \widehat{\widehat{K}}$ then

$$\widehat{Q}_1 > \widehat{\widehat{L}} > \widehat{\widehat{K}} > \widehat{Q}_2. \tag{2.25a}$$

Similarly, if $\widehat{\widehat{K}} > \widehat{\widehat{L}}$ then

$$\widehat{Q}_2 > \widehat{\widehat{K}} > \widehat{\widehat{L}} > \widehat{Q}_1. \tag{2.25b}$$

Equations (2.25a) and (2.25b) are also called the magnification effects (Jones, 1965). Of course when $\widehat{\widehat{K}} = \widehat{\widehat{L}}$, then $\widehat{Q}_1 = \widehat{\widehat{L}} = \widehat{\widehat{K}} = \widehat{Q}_2$. The special case in which there is an increase in the endowment of only one factor is summarized by the Rybczynski theorem (Rybczynski, 1955).

The Rybczynski Theorem   Given no factor intensity reversal, diversification in production, and constant commodity (and thus factor) prices, an increase in the endowment of a factor will increase by a greater proportion the output of the sector which uses the factor intensively, and decrease the output of the other sector.

A simple economic intuition can be used to explain the Rybczynski theorem. Suppose that the labor endowment increases while the capital endowment is fixed. Given constant commodity prices, factor prices and the input-output coefficients of both sectors are fixed. Thus the labor-intensive sector must expand in order to absorb the additional labor. Furthermore, it must expand at the expense of the capital-intensive sector because the additional capital it needs for its expansion must come from the latter. When the capital-intensive sector contracts, it releases not just capital but also labor, meaning that the rate

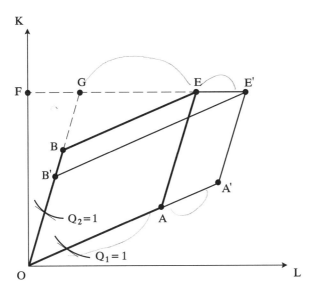

Figure 2.5

of increase in labor employment and thus the rate of increase in output in the labor-intensive sector is greater than that in the labor endowment.

The relationship between outputs and factor endowments can be illustrated diagrammatically. Figure 2.5 shows the unit isoquants of the sectors that are tangent to different iso-cost lines. The iso-cost lines have a slope of the (negative) exogenously given wage-rental ratio, ω. If $p_1 \neq p_2$, the two iso-cost lines do not coincide, as in the case shown. This is the major difference between this diagram and the Lerner diagram. Point E represents the initial factor endowments, $\overline{K}$ and $\overline{L}$. Construct parallelgram OAEB, where the adjacent sides OA and OB pass through the points of tangency between the iso-cost lines and the unit isoquants. Slopes of OA and OB are, respectively, the capital-labor ratios in the sectors, k_1 and k_2, at the given factor prices. Parallelgram OAEB thus gives the equilibrium resource allocation in the economy: Lines OA and OB represent the output levels of the sectors when measured along OA and OB, and they represent the employment of labor (respectively capital) in the sectors when measured horizontally (respectively vertically). It can be seen from the diagram that for full employment of all factors and diversification in production, ray OE has to lie between ray OA and ray OB. This reflects condition (2.14′) that the aggregate capital-labor ratio is a weighted average of the capital-labor ratios of the sectors. For this reason, the space bounded by rays OA and OB is called the *cone of diversification* under the given factor prices.

Figure 2.5 provides a simple graphical way of proving the Rybczynski theorem. Suppose now that there is an increase in the labor endowment, which in the diagram is represented by a rightward shift of the endowment point E to point E' so that length EE' equals the increase in labor endowment. Because commodity prices are given, factor prices and input-output coefficients are unchanged. Using this result, construct a new parallelgram, OA'E'B' where the slopes of OA' and OB' represent the initial (unchanged) capital-labor ratios of sectors 1 and 2, respectively. Lines OA' and OB' thus represent the new output levels of the sectors. Comparing these levels with the old ones, it is clear from the diagram that production of good 1 rises while that of good 2 falls. What is left to show is that the rate of increase in good 1 output is greater than that in labor endowment. To do that, construct horizontal line EF and extend OB to cut EF at G. Note that $\Delta \overline{L}/\overline{L} = $ EE'/EF and that $\Delta Q_1/Q_1 = $ AA'/OA = EE'/EG, where the last equality comes from the properties of similar triangles. Because EG < EF, we have $\Delta Q_1/Q_1 > \Delta \overline{L}/\overline{L}$. Combining the results gives the Rybczynski theorem.

Note that the Rybczynski theorem is proved in the diversified two-by-two framework with constant prices and the assumption of no factor intensity reversal (FIR). The assumption of diversification in production for the validity of the theorem is well known, but the requirement of no FIR is not. I have proved that FIR cannot occur for an economy with fixed factor endowments, but in the case in which the theorem is considered, factor endowments change and FIR is a real possibility. As a result, it is interesting to determine whether the Rybczynski theorem is still valid when FIR cannot be ruled out.

Figure 2.6 shows the case in which the technology exhibits two FIRs, so that the initial price ratio p^o corresponds to three wage-rental ratios, ω^o, ω', and ω'', with sector 2 capital intensive at ω^o and ω'' but labor intensive at ω'. I assume that the economy's initial capital-labor ratio is $\overline{k}^o$, with ω^o being the initial wage-rental ratio so that the corresponding capital-labor ratios in sectors 1 and 2 are k_1^o and k_2^o, respectively, with $k_2^o > k_1^o$.

The line segments AB and BC in the diagram are good measures of the distribution of labor between the sectors. Using the diagram and condition (2.14'), I have

$$\frac{\text{AB}}{\text{BC}} = \frac{k_2^o - \overline{k}^o}{\overline{k}^o - k_1^o} = \frac{\lambda_{L1}}{\lambda_{L2}}. \tag{2.26}$$

Because at constant factor prices the input-output coefficients are constant, the ratio of line segment AB to line segment BC is directly proportional to the ratio of the output levels of the two sectors.

Suppose now that the labor endowment is increased so that the capital-labor ratio falls and moves to another cone of diversification. Let me keep the commodity price ratio fixed at p^o. This means that the wage-rental ratio can no longer be constant.

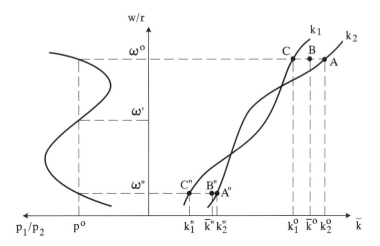

Figure 2.6

Suppose first that there is one (or an odd number of) FIR. A possible wage-rental ratio is given by ω' in Figure 2.6. Because the factor intensity ranking is reversed, whether the Rybczynski theorem is valid or not is no longer a meaningful question because the theorem assumes a constant capital-labor ranking. Suppose instead that the labor endowment increases to an extent that there are two (or an even number of) FIRs. A possible wage rate is ω'', as shown in Figure 2.6. I assume that the economy remains diversified so that at the wage-rental ratio ω'', $k_2'' > \bar{k}'' > k_1''$, as shown in the diagram. I want to argue that the Rybczynski theorem is not valid. Note that corresponding to ω'' the ratio $A''B''$ to $B''C''$ is again a measure of the distribution of labor between the sectors:

$$\frac{A''B''}{B''C''} = \frac{\lambda_{L1}''}{\lambda_{L2}''}. \tag{2.26'}$$

Because $\bar{k}''$ can be anywhere between k_1'' and k_2'', the outputs of the sectors are not predictable and the theorem is not valid.

When the Rybczynski theorem is valid in the absence of FIR, it has many applications, especially in predicting changes in outputs under fixed prices due to factor accumulation or international factor movements. For example, suppose that the domestic labor force grows. In Figure 2.7, price line AB, which has a slope of the exogenously given (negative) relative price of good 1, p, is tangent to the production possibility frontier (PPF) TT at point Q, which also represents the initial output levels. (I will have more discussion about the production point later.) Suppose that there is an increase in the labor endowment due to population growth or labor inflow. The PPF will shift out to T'T', assuming that sector 2 is capital intensive. If commodity prices do not change,

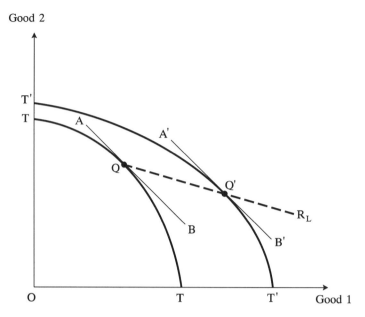

Figure 2.7

the point of tangency Q′ between the new price line A′B′, which is parallel to AB, and T′T′ represents the new production point. By the Rybczynski theorem, the new production point Q′ represents a higher output level of good 1 and a lower output level of good 2. The locus of the production point as labor grows is called the Rybczynski line for labor R_L. Using equations (2.24) and noting that $\widehat{K} = 0$, the slope of the Rybczynski line is equal to

$$\frac{\mathrm{d}Q_2}{\mathrm{d}Q_1}\bigg|_{R_L} = -\frac{Q_2}{Q_1}\frac{\lambda_{K1}}{\lambda_{K2}} = -\frac{f_2 k_1}{f_1 k_2}.$$

This means that the Rybczynski line is negatively sloped. Moreover, the slope is constant because under constant commodity prices, k_i and f_i are constant. (So the Rybczynski line is indeed a straight line.)

Similarly, an increase in the capital stock will shift the production point along the Rybczynski line for capital R_K, which has a slope of

$$\frac{\mathrm{d}Q_2}{\mathrm{d}Q_1}\bigg|_{R_K} = -\frac{Q_2}{Q_1}\frac{\lambda_{L1}}{\lambda_{L2}} = -\frac{f_2}{f_1}.$$

It is easy to show that the Rybczynski line R_K is steeper than the price line, which in turn is steeper than the Rybczynski line R_L.[5]

---

5. By (2.4a), the slope of the price line is $-p_1/p_2 = -f_2'/f_1'$. Because the two sectors have the same wage-rental ratio, as given by (2.4), I have

Another important property of the present framework can be obtained from equations (2.20) and (2.24). For example, using the definitions of θ_{ji}, equation (2.20a) gives the effect of p_1 on w:

$$\frac{\partial w}{\partial p_1} = \frac{w}{p_1} \frac{\theta_{K2}}{|\theta|} = \frac{k_2 f_1}{k_2 - k_1},$$

where (2.15a) and the zero-profit conditions (2.10) have been used. Using the definitions of λ_{ji}, equation (2.24a) gives the effect of L on Q_1:

$$\frac{\partial Q_1}{\partial L} = \frac{Q_1}{L} \frac{\lambda_{K2}}{|\lambda|} = \frac{k_2 f_1}{k_2 - k_1} = \frac{\partial w}{\partial p_1}.$$

The same technique can be used to derive other effects. Thus I have

$$\frac{\partial w}{\partial p_i} = \frac{\partial Q_i}{\partial L} \tag{2.27a}$$

$$\frac{\partial r}{\partial p_i} = \frac{\partial Q_i}{\partial K}, \quad i = 1, 2. \tag{2.27b}$$

Equations (2.27) are called the reciprocity relation, which shows the symmetry between the output effects of factor endowments and the input effects of commodity prices in this framework. The reciprocity relation in a higher dimensional framework will be derived later.

$$\frac{f_1}{f_1'} - k_1 = \frac{f_2}{f_2'} - k_2.$$

Because $k_2 > k_1$ by assumption, this condition implies

$$\frac{f_2}{f_1} > \frac{f_2'}{f_1'},$$

that is, the Rybczynski line R_K is steeper than the price line. This condition can be rewritten as

$$k_1 \left(\frac{f_1}{f_1' k_1} - 1 \right) = k_2 \left(\frac{f_2}{f_2' k_2} - 1 \right).$$

Because $k_2 > k_1$, I have

$$\frac{f_1}{f_1' k_1} - 1 > \frac{f_2}{f_2' k_2} - 1,$$

or, after rearranging terms

$$\frac{f_2'}{f_1'} > \frac{f_2 k_1}{f_1 k_2},$$

that is, the price line is steeper than the Rybczynski line R_L.

2.4   The Gross Domestic Product (GDP) Function

The gross domestic product (GDP) function, which is also called the gross national production (GNP) function or revenue function, is a powerful tool for analyzing resource allocation and production in an economy. The GDP function is an important component of the dual approach. Being analogous to the restricted profit function for a firm in microeconomics, the GDP function has two major advantages as compared with the traditional, primal approach, which emphasizes production functions of the sectors. First, it can easily be extended to a higher dimensional framework. Second, the aggregate supplies of goods and the market factor prices can be obtained by differentiating the GDP function, assuming differentiability, whereas in the traditional approach, to obtain the equilibrium values of these variables requires solving a system of equations.[6] Furthermore, the derivatives of the GDP function are useful in deriving more properties of the structure of the economy.

Let me first introduce some new notation. There are $m \geq 1$ factors and $n \geq 2$ goods in the economy. The following variables are defined:

$\mathbf{v} \equiv m$-dimensional vector of factor endowments;

$\mathbf{v}_i \equiv m$-dimensional vector of factors employed in sector i, $\sum_i \mathbf{v}_i = \mathbf{v}$;

$\mathbf{w} \equiv m$-dimensional vector of factor prices;

$\mathbf{Q} \equiv n$-dimensional vector of outputs;

$\mathbf{p} \equiv n$-dimensional vector of goods prices; and

$\mathbf{a}_i \equiv Q_i^{-1}\mathbf{v}_i \equiv m$-dimensional vector of factors to produce one unit of good i.

For the time being, I assume no international factor movement, implying that the given factor endowments are the maximum amounts of factors available to firms. Denote the production possibility set (PPS) of the economy by $\Gamma(\mathbf{Q}, \mathbf{v}) \leq 0$ which is assumed to be closed, bounded from above, and convex. Given factor endowments, $\Gamma(\mathbf{Q}, \mathbf{v}) = 0$ is the equation of the production possibility frontier (PPF) of the economy. Free disposal is allowed. The GDP function $g(\mathbf{p}, \mathbf{v})$ is defined as

$$g(\mathbf{p}, \mathbf{v}) = \max_{\mathbf{Q}} \{\mathbf{p} \cdot \mathbf{Q} : \Gamma(\mathbf{Q}, \mathbf{v}) \leq 0\}, \tag{2.28}$$

---

6. For more discussion about the applications of the dual approach, see Diewert (1974), Chipman (1979), Dixit and Norman (1980), Woodland (1982), and Kohli (1991). Kohli (1991) also explains how the GDP function of an economy is estimated.

where "·" represents an inner product of two vectors. Condition (2.28) states that the GDP function of an economy with given factor endowments and facing given commodity prices is the maximum value of outputs by choosing the optimal, feasible resource allocation.

Three points about this function can be noted. First, in the absence of international factor movement, gross *national* product (GNP) is equivalent to gross *domestic* product (GDP). In such a case, I will call the function defined in (2.28) GDP function and GNP function interchangeably. Second, the function in (2.28) is called *gross* domestic product function, not *net* domestic product function because the outputs in (2.28) include allowances for capital depreciation. Third, in the GDP function, commodity prices are arguments. If the economy is a small open economy under free trade, the commodity prices are the exogenously given world prices. If the economy is a large one or a closed one, then commodity prices are treated as parameters in the GDP function (but have to be determined endogenously).

The definition of the GDP function given in (2.28) is quite general. For example, it is applicable whether the economy is closed or open, whether nontradable goods are present, and whether joint production exists.

The solution of the problem given by (2.28) can be denoted by $\mathbf{Q}(\mathbf{p}, \mathbf{v})$. If the solution is unique, $\mathbf{Q}(\mathbf{p}, \mathbf{v})$ represents the competitive outputs in the economy with the given commodity prices and factor endowments. Two explanations for this important result can be provided. First, it is clear that the present framework is an Arrow-Debreu type general equilibrium framework, and it is well known that in such a framework the first theorem of welfare economics holds, meaning that a competitive equilibrium is Pareto efficient. Thus the competitive outputs maximize the GDP of the economy.

Second, consider the special case in which no joint production exists while sectoral production functions are given by $Q_i = F_i(\mathbf{v}_i)$, $i = 1, \ldots, n$. The GDP function can be written in an alternative form:

$$g(\mathbf{p}, \mathbf{v}) = \max_{\mathbf{Q}, \{\mathbf{v}_i\}} \left\{ \mathbf{p} \cdot \mathbf{Q} : Q_i \leq F_i(\mathbf{v}_i), \text{ and } \sum_i \mathbf{v}_i \leq \mathbf{v}, \ i = 1, \ldots, n \right\}.$$

Define the Lagrangean function

$$\mathcal{L} = \mathbf{p} \cdot \mathbf{Q} + \sum_{i=1}^{n} \phi_i [F_i(\mathbf{v}_i) - Q_i] + \mathbf{w} \cdot \left[\mathbf{v} - \sum_{i=1}^{n} \mathbf{v}_i \right],$$

where $\{\phi_i\}$ and $\mathbf{w}$ are Lagrangean multipliers. Using the Lagrangean function, the GDP function can be given by

$$g(\mathbf{p}, \mathbf{v}) = \max_{\mathbf{Q}, \{\mathbf{v}_i\}} \min_{\mathbf{w}, \{\phi_i\}} \mathcal{L}. \tag{2.28'}$$

The first-order conditions are

$$\frac{\partial \mathcal{L}}{\partial Q_i} = p_i - \phi_i \leq 0 \tag{2.29a}$$

$$\frac{\partial \mathcal{L}}{\partial v_{ji}} = \phi_i F_{ij}(\mathbf{v}_i) - w_j \leq 0 \tag{2.29b}$$

$$\frac{\partial \mathcal{L}}{\partial \phi_i} = F_i(\mathbf{v}_i) - Q_i \geq 0 \tag{2.29c}$$

$$\frac{\partial \mathcal{L}}{\partial w_j} = v_j - \sum_i v_{ji} \geq 0 \tag{2.29d}$$

$$i = 1, \ldots, n; \quad j = 1, \ldots, m,$$

where $F_{ij}(\mathbf{v}_i) \equiv \partial F_i / \partial v_{ji}$ is the marginal product of factor j in sector i. If the economy produces a positive output of good i, then by (2.29a), $p_i = \phi_i$. If sector i employs a positive amount of factor j, then $v_{ji} > 0$ and by (2.29b), $w_j = \phi_i F_{ij}$. These results are combined to give

$$w_j = p_i F_{ij}(\mathbf{v}_i). \tag{2.30}$$

By interpreting w_j as the market price of factor j, condition (2.30) is identical to conditions (2.4). This means that with the allocation of resources determined by profit-maximizing firms, the first-order conditions of the GDP function are satisfied. (Convexity of technologies implies the second-order conditions.) In other words, the firms choose production individually as if they are jointly maximizing the gross domestic product of the economy.

Graphically, the optimality of a competitive equilibrium means that the production point occurs at the point of tangency Q between price line AB and the PPF in Figure 2.7.

In the case with no joint production, the GDP function can be defined in an alternative way:

$$g(\mathbf{p}, \mathbf{v}) = \min_{\mathbf{w}} \{\mathbf{w} \cdot \mathbf{v} : p_i \leq c_i(\mathbf{w}), \quad i = 1, \ldots, n\}. \tag{2.28''}$$

The constraint $p_i \leq c_i$ in (2.28'') comes from the zero-profit condition of a firm under perfect competition. The condition $p_i > c_i$ cannot occur in an equilibrium because if it does, then firms in sector i earn positive profit and they will expand their production. If in equilibrium $p_i < c_i$, the output of good i is zero because the profit with a positive output is negative. Thus $p_i = c_i$ if sector i has a positive output.

To see the equivalence between (2.28) and (2.28''), let us recall the Lagrangean function in (2.28'). The order of minimization and maximization does not matter, and by rearranging terms the GDP function can be written in the following different forms:

$$g(\mathbf{p}, \mathbf{v}) = \max_{\mathbf{Q}, \{\mathbf{v}_i\}} \min_{\mathbf{w}, \{\phi_i\}} \left\{ \mathbf{p} \cdot \mathbf{Q} + \sum_i \phi_i [F_i(\mathbf{v}_i) - Q_i] + \mathbf{w} \cdot \left[\mathbf{v} - \sum_i \mathbf{v}_i \right] \right\}$$

$$= \max_{\mathbf{Q}} \min_{\mathbf{w}} \left\{ \mathbf{w} \cdot \mathbf{v} + \right.$$

$$\left. \sum_i Q_i \left\{ p_i - \min_{\mathbf{a}_i} \max_{\phi_i} \left[\mathbf{w} \cdot \mathbf{a}_i + \phi_i \big(1 - F_i(\mathbf{a}_i)\big) \right] \right\} \right\}$$

$$= \max_{\mathbf{Q}} \min_{\mathbf{w}} \left\{ \mathbf{w} \cdot \mathbf{v} + \sum_i Q_i \{ p_i - c_i \} \right\}, \tag{2.31}$$

where, by (2.7), the unit cost function is given by

$$c_i(\mathbf{w}) = \min_{\mathbf{a}_i} \max_{\phi_i} \left[\mathbf{w} \cdot \mathbf{a}_i + \phi_i \big(1 - F_i(\mathbf{a}_i)\big) \right].$$

The expression in (2.31) is the definition of the GDP function in terms of (2.28″), with $\mathbf{Q}$ interpreted as Lagrangean multipliers. This result means that the GDP function can be regarded as the maximum total value of feasible outputs or the minimum total payment to factors.

The factor-payment approach to the GDP function in a two-factor, two-sector framework can be illustrated by Figure 2.8. The unit cost function of each sector can be represented by a map of unit-cost schedules that is convex

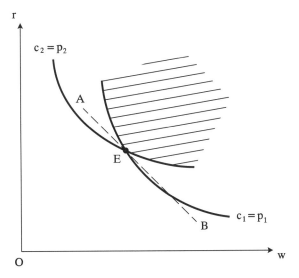

Figure 2.8

to the origin. The diagram shows one unit-cost schedule for each sector corresponding to its exogenously given commodity price. By Shephard's lemma, or by equations (2.8), the slope of schedule $c_i(w, r)$ is equal to

$$\left.\frac{dr}{dw}\right|_{c_i} = -\frac{\partial c_i/\partial w}{\partial c_i/\partial r} = -\frac{a_{Li}}{a_{Ki}} = -\frac{1}{k_i}.$$

For sector i, any unit-cost schedules above schedule c_i shown in Figure 2.8 have values greater than p_i. This means that the shaded area represents all combinations of factor prices that satisfy the constraints $p_i \leq c_i$, $i = 1$, $\ldots, n$.

In Figure 2.8, line AB represents the budget line of the economy with a slope of $-\overline{L}/\overline{K}$. By (2.28''), the equilibrium factor prices that minimize total factor payment are represented by point E. Note that in the case shown in the diagram, line AB is between the tangents to the two unit-cost schedules at point E, which confirms the previous result that the aggregate capital-labor ratio is a weighted average of the capital-labor ratios of the sectors.[7]

More properties of the GDP function are given next.

2.4.1   The Output Side

Keeping the factor endowments fixed, the GDP function has the following properties.

1. It is increasing, linearly homogeneous, and convex in prices $\mathbf{p}$. (Convexity is proved in the appendix.) I assume that it is twice differentiable in $\mathbf{p}$.[8] Differentiability is not required for most of the results shown here, but it greatly simplifies the analysis.

2. By the envelope theorem, the partial derivatives of the GDP function with respect to $\mathbf{p}$ are

$$\frac{\partial g}{\partial p_i} = Q_i(\mathbf{p}, \mathbf{v}), \qquad i = 1, \ldots, n. \tag{2.32}$$

3. By (2.32), $Q_i(\mathbf{p}, \mathbf{v})$ is homogeneous of degree zero in $\mathbf{p}$ and linearly homogeneous in $\mathbf{v}$.

---

7. Depending on commodity prices and factor endowments, the economy may be completely specialized in production. Suppose that in Figure 2.8 line AB is much steeper (with more labor and/or less capital) so that it is tangent to schedule c_1 at a point above point E. Then the economy produces good 1 only, because at that point of tangency, $c_2 > p_2$.

8. Differentiability of the GDP function is violated if the number of goods is greater than the number of factors, because at given $\mathbf{p}$, the production of the sectors is indeterminate. A well-known example is the Ricardian model (explained later). In these cases, I assume that the derivatives of the GDP function are sets. For the properties of the function when it is not differentiable, see Dixit and Norman (1980).

4. By Euler's theorem and the results in (3), I have

$$0 = \sum_{\ell=1}^{n} p_\ell \frac{\partial Q_i}{\partial p_\ell} \tag{2.33a}$$

$$Q_i = \sum_{j=1}^{m} v_j \frac{\partial Q_i}{\partial v_j}. \tag{2.33b}$$

By Young's theorem and using (2.32), I have

$$\frac{\partial Q_i}{\partial p_\ell} = \frac{\partial^2 g}{\partial p_\ell \partial p_i} = \frac{\partial^2 g}{\partial p_i \partial p_\ell} = \frac{\partial Q_\ell}{\partial p_i}.$$

Substitute this result into (2.33a) to give

$$0 = \sum_{\ell=1}^{n} p_\ell \frac{\partial Q_\ell}{\partial p_i}. \tag{2.34}$$

Note that by using the envelope theorem, condition (2.34) is the first-order condition for the maximization problem in (2.28). It implies that the price hyperplane is tangent to the production possibility frontier at the production point. In the case with two sectors, in Figure 2.7, price line AB is tangent to the PPF at the production point.

5. Let $g_{\mathbf{pp}}$ be the $n \times n$ matrix of the second-order derivatives of $g(\mathbf{p}, \mathbf{v})$ with respect to prices. Because $g(\mathbf{p}, \mathbf{v})$ is convex in $\mathbf{p}$, $g_{\mathbf{pp}}$ is positive semi-definite. This implies that the diagonal elements of $g_{\mathbf{pp}}$ are non-negative, that is,

$$\frac{\partial^2 g}{\partial p_i{}^2} = \frac{\partial Q_i}{\partial p_i} \geq 0, \qquad i = 1, \ldots, n,$$

which means that the supply schedule of any sector is not downward sloping.

2.4.2   The Input Side

When given commodity prices, the GDP function has the following properties.

1. It is increasing, linearly homogeneous, and concave in $\mathbf{v}$. (Concavity is proved in the appendix.) It is assumed to be twice differentiable.

2. By the envelope theorem and the minimization problem in (2.28″), the partial derivatives of $g(\mathbf{p}, \mathbf{v})$ with respect to factor endowments are

$$\frac{\partial g}{\partial v_j} = w_j(\mathbf{p}, \mathbf{v}), \qquad j = 1, \ldots, m. \tag{2.35}$$

3. By (2.35), the factor price $w_j(\mathbf{p}, \mathbf{v})$ is linearly homogeneous in $\mathbf{p}$ and homogeneous of degree zero in $\mathbf{v}$.

4. By Euler's theorem and the results in (3), I have

$$w_j = \sum_{i=1}^{n} p_i \frac{\partial w_j}{\partial p_i} \tag{2.36a}$$

$$0 = \sum_{\ell=1}^{m} v_\ell \frac{\partial w_j}{\partial v_\ell}. \tag{2.36b}$$

Using (2.35) and Young's theorem, (2.36b) reduces to

$$0 = \sum_{\ell=1}^{m} v_\ell \frac{\partial w_\ell}{\partial v_j}. \tag{2.37}$$

Condition (2.37), which is analogous to (2.34), also comes from the first-order condition of the minimization problem in (2.28'').

5. Let $g_{\mathbf{vv}}$ be the $m \times m$ matrix of the second-order derivatives of $g(\mathbf{p}, \mathbf{v})$ with respect to factor endowments. Because $g(\mathbf{p}, \mathbf{v})$ is concave in $\mathbf{v}$, $g_{\mathbf{vv}}$ is negative semi-definite. This means that the diagonal element $g_{\mathbf{vv}}$ is nonpositive, that is,

$$\frac{\partial^2 g}{\partial v_j{}^2} = \frac{\partial w_j}{\partial v_j} \leq 0, \qquad j = 1, \ldots, m,$$

which states that the demand schedule of any factor is not positively sloped. Note that in the special case with diversification and equal numbers of factors and sector, as in the previous two-by-two framework, factor prices are independent of factor endowments under constant commodity prices, that is,

$$\frac{\partial w_k}{\partial v_j} = 0, \qquad j, k = 1, \ldots, m.$$

2.4.3 Cross Effects

We now look at the effects of commodity prices on factor prices and the effects of factor endowments on outputs.

1. Applying Young's theorem, we have the famous *reciprocity relation*:

$$\frac{\partial w_j}{\partial p_i} = \frac{\partial^2 g}{\partial p_i \partial v_j} = \frac{\partial^2 g}{\partial v_j \partial p_i} = \frac{\partial Q_i}{\partial v_j}. \tag{2.38}$$

The reciprocity relation for the previous two-by-two framework is given in equations (2.27a) and (2.27b). Note that equation (2.38) does not represent the Rybczynski theorem or the Stolper-Samuelson theorem, because the signs of the partial derivatives are not known in the equation.

2. Using the reciprocity relation in (2.38), equations (2.33b) and (2.36a) reduce to

$$Q_i = \sum_{j=1}^{m} v_j \frac{\partial w_j}{\partial p_i} \tag{2.39a}$$

$$w_j = \sum_{i=1}^{n} p_i \frac{\partial Q_i}{\partial v_j}. \tag{2.39b}$$

Equation (2.39b) is especially useful. The term on the left-hand side is the price of factor j, while the right-hand side gives the marginal value product of the factor, that is, the rate of increase in the national product with respect to the endowment of factor j. For example, in the 2×2 framework, the rental rate of capital can be given by

$$r = p_1 \frac{\partial Q_1}{\partial K} + p_2 \frac{\partial Q_2}{\partial K}.$$

The intuition behind equation (2.39a) and (2.39b) is simple. Recall that one can use the output-value approach or the factor-payment approach to defining the GDP function; so we have $\mathbf{p} \cdot \mathbf{Q}(\mathbf{p}, \mathbf{v}) = \mathbf{w}(\mathbf{p}, \mathbf{v}) \cdot \mathbf{v}$. Differentiation of the latter equation with respect to p_i, using the envelope theorem, gives equation (2.39a); differentiation of it with respect to v_j gives equation (2.39b). Thus, in the present framework, Q_i is the shadow value of p_i while w_j is the shadow price of factor j.

The above framework and the GDP function can now be extended to allow international factor movements. Suppose that the first m^t factors can move across countries and the remaining $m^n = m - m^t$ are immobile. Partition the factor endowment vector so that $\mathbf{v} = (\mathbf{v}^t, \mathbf{v}^n)$ where $\mathbf{v}^t$ corresponds to the mobile factors and $\mathbf{v}^n$ corresponds to the immobile factors. Similarly, partition the factor price vector so that $\mathbf{w} = (\mathbf{w}^t, \mathbf{w}^n)$.

When factors can move across countries, there are two approaches to analyzing the production side of the economy. The first approach is to treat the amounts of factor movements as parameters. Let the m^t-dimensional vector $\mathbf{k}$ represent the amounts of foreign factors flowing into and working in the economy (negative elements for factors flowing out). The total factors available to domestic firms are $(\mathbf{v}^t + \mathbf{k}, \mathbf{v}^n)$. Thus the gross domestic product of the economy is given by the GDP function $g(\mathbf{p}, \mathbf{v}^t + \mathbf{k}, \mathbf{v}^n)$.

In the second approach to analyzing international factor movement, the prices instead of the quantities of the mobile factors are treated as parameters. In this approach, mobile factors are regarded as negative outputs. Let $\mathbf{r}$ be the m^t-dimensional vector of exogenously given prices of the mobile factors.[9] I now define the following function:

9. Two recent examples that use the second approach to analyze the production of an economy are Kohli (1991) and Kemp and Wong (1995a). Kohli (1991) treats imports as an input, or a negative output, while Kemp and Wong (1995a) consider international capital movement.

$$\widetilde{g}(\mathbf{p}, \mathbf{r}, \mathbf{v}) = \max_{\mathbf{Q}, \mathbf{k}} \left\{ \mathbf{p} \cdot \mathbf{Q} - \mathbf{r} \cdot \mathbf{k} : \Gamma(\mathbf{Q}, \mathbf{v}^t + \mathbf{k}, \mathbf{v}^n) \leq 0 \right\}. \tag{2.40}$$

Denote the solution by $(\widetilde{\mathbf{Q}}, \widetilde{\mathbf{k}})$. The interpretation of the function in (2.40) is that the economy, treating $\mathbf{r}$ as the cost of the mobile factors, chooses the optimal movement of these factors and the optimal production to maximize the revenue less the payment to foreign factors.

I want to compare the two maximization problems in (2.28) and (2.40). To facilitate my comparison, imagine that there are two identical economies (identical technologies and factor endowments) named α and β, which are facing the same exogenously given commodity prices $\mathbf{p}$. I use the first approach for economy α and the second approach for economy β.

Let me first suppose that economy β is facing the prices of the mobile factors $\mathbf{r}$. Under the second approach, the function given by (2.40) determines the optimal output equal to $\widetilde{\mathbf{Q}} = \widetilde{\mathbf{Q}}(\mathbf{p}, \mathbf{r}, \mathbf{v})$ and optimal factor inflow equal to $\widetilde{\mathbf{k}} = \widetilde{\mathbf{k}}(\mathbf{p}, \mathbf{r}, \mathbf{v})$. I now consider economy α and suppose that it is given exogenous amounts of the mobile factors equal to $\widetilde{\mathbf{k}}$. Using the first approach as described by (2.28), its optimal output is equal to $\mathbf{Q} = \mathbf{Q}(\mathbf{p}, \mathbf{v}^t + \widetilde{\mathbf{k}}, \mathbf{v}^n)$.

These two functions give the same output levels, that is, $\widetilde{\mathbf{Q}}(\mathbf{p}, \mathbf{r}, \mathbf{v}) = \mathbf{Q}(\mathbf{p}, \mathbf{v}^t + \widetilde{\mathbf{k}}, \mathbf{v}^n)$, as long as the equilibrium production point is unique for each economy. To understand why, note that because both economies have the same factors and the same technologies, economy β is able to produce output $\mathbf{Q}$ but it chooses to produce $\widetilde{\mathbf{Q}}$. From the definition of function $\widetilde{g}(\mathbf{p}, \mathbf{r}, \mathbf{v})$ given by (2.40),

$$\mathbf{p} \cdot \widetilde{\mathbf{Q}} - \mathbf{r} \cdot \widetilde{\mathbf{k}} \geq \mathbf{p} \cdot \mathbf{Q} - \mathbf{r} \cdot \widetilde{\mathbf{k}},$$

or

$$\mathbf{p} \cdot \widetilde{\mathbf{Q}} \geq \mathbf{p} \cdot \mathbf{Q}. \tag{2.41a}$$

On the other hand, economy α can produce $\widetilde{\mathbf{Q}}$ (economy β's output) but it chooses to produce $\mathbf{Q}$. So from the definition of function $g(\mathbf{p}, \mathbf{v}^t + \widetilde{\mathbf{k}}, \mathbf{v}^n)$ given in (2.28), I have

$$\mathbf{p} \cdot \mathbf{Q} \geq \mathbf{p} \cdot \widetilde{\mathbf{Q}}. \tag{2.41b}$$

Comparing (2.41a) and (2.41b) gives

$$\mathbf{p} \cdot \mathbf{Q} = \mathbf{p} \cdot \widetilde{\mathbf{Q}}. \tag{2.42}$$

Assuming a unique production point, the two functions give the same optimal output vector. Furthermore, condition (2.42) and the definition of function $\widetilde{g}$ given by (2.40) imply the following relationship between the two GDP functions:

$$\widetilde{g}(\mathbf{p}, \mathbf{r}, \mathbf{v}) = g(\mathbf{p}, \mathbf{v}^t + \widetilde{\mathbf{k}}, \mathbf{v}^n) - \mathbf{r} \cdot \widetilde{\mathbf{k}}. \tag{2.43}$$

I can now show the equivalence of the input sides of the functions. Denote the market factor prices in economy α by $\mathbf{w} = (\mathbf{w}^t, \mathbf{w}^n)$, which are obtained by partially differentiating function $g(\mathbf{p}, \mathbf{v}^t + \widetilde{\mathbf{k}}, \mathbf{v}^n)$ with respect to factor endowments. Similarly, denote the prices of the immobile factors in economy β by $\widetilde{\mathbf{w}}^n$, which are equal to the derivatives of $\widetilde{g}(\mathbf{p}, \mathbf{r}, \mathbf{v})$ with respect to the immobile factors. Using the input approach to the GDP functions, functions g and $\widetilde{g}$ can be given alternatively by

$$g(\mathbf{p}, \mathbf{v}^t + \widetilde{\mathbf{k}}, \mathbf{v}^n) = \mathbf{w}^t \cdot (\mathbf{v}^t + \widetilde{\mathbf{k}}) + \mathbf{w}^n \cdot \mathbf{v}^n \tag{2.44a}$$

$$\widetilde{g}(\mathbf{p}, \mathbf{r}, \mathbf{v}) = \mathbf{r} \cdot \mathbf{v}^t + \widetilde{\mathbf{w}}^n \cdot \mathbf{v}^n. \tag{2.44b}$$

Making use of (2.43), conditions (2.44) can be combined together to give

$$\mathbf{w}^t \cdot (\mathbf{v}^t + \widetilde{\mathbf{k}}) + \mathbf{w}^n \cdot \mathbf{v}^n = \mathbf{r} \cdot (\mathbf{v}^t + \widetilde{\mathbf{k}}) + \widetilde{\mathbf{w}}^n \cdot \mathbf{v}^n.$$

Thus if functions g and $\widetilde{g}$ give a unique vector of factor prices, then $(\mathbf{w}^t, \mathbf{w}^n) = (\mathbf{r}, \widetilde{\mathbf{w}}^n)$.

The equivalence between these two approaches in terms of outputs and factor prices is not surprising because in the Arrow-Debreu type general equilibrium frameworks inputs can be regarded as negative outputs. Thus, with respect to function g, the economy chooses the optimal outputs when total (national and foreign) factors are given. In terms of function $\widetilde{g}$, the economy chooses instead the optimal outputs and optimal amounts of the mobile factors, taking the prices of the mobile factors and the endowments of the immobile factor as fixed. What I have shown is that these two approaches imply the same optimal outputs and factor prices.

It should be noted, however, that functions g and $\widetilde{g}$ are not equivalent. Function g gives the gross domestic product of the economy, but the interpretation of function $\widetilde{g}$ is slightly complicated. Consider the special case in which all moving factors $\mathbf{k}$ earn factor prices in the domestic economy. In other words, foreign factors working in the domestic economy receive market prices and repatriate without taxes, and national factors working abroad are taxed to the full extent by the foreign government so that they remit back the same income as what they would get should they be working in the domestic economy. In this special case, function $\widetilde{g}$ represents the gross national product of the economy.

This analysis can be used to develop a graphical method of deriving the gross national product of a 2×2 economy when foreign factors are working inside it. Refer to Figure 2.9: TT is the production possibility frontier (PPF) before any factor movement. Suppose now that a certain amount of foreign capital flows in, shifting the PPF out to T'T'. Let the new price line be A'B',

Good 2

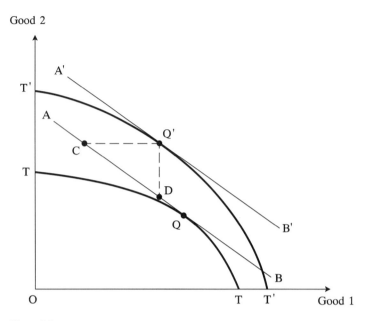

Figure 2.9

which is tangent to T'T' at the new production point Q'. Line A'B' represents the gross domestic product of the economy, and Q' can be called the GDP point. Suppose that the foreign capital owners in the economy receive the domestic rental rate in the absence of any income taxes and that they repatriate their income out of the economy. The previous analysis shows that the GNP of the economy in the presence of foreign capital inflow is the same as its GNP (which is the same as GDP) before the foreign capital inflow if the commodity prices are fixed. Let me construct another price line AB, which is parallel to A'B' and is tangent to the pre-factor-flow PPF denoted by TT. Line AB then represents the GNP of the economy. Furthermore, the factor income repatriation can also be shown graphically. For example, if the foreign factor owners repatriate good 1 (respectively 2) only, the amounts of goods left behind are represented by point C (respectively D), which is to the left of (respectively vertically below) point Q. If a combination of the goods is repatriated, the basket of goods available to the economy after repatriation is represented by a point between C and D. Note that line AB is just a hypothetical line, and it does not have to be the actual pre-factor-flow price line (although it is if the economy is a small open one that allows free trade in goods before and after the capital movement). This means that the technique is applicable whether the economy has monopoly power in goods trade or is a small open economy.

2.5   The Ricardian Model

The GDP approach to analyzing the production side of an economy is general because it is not limited by the dimension of the economy, but, its generality is also its limitation. I now consider two special frameworks with low dimensions: the Ricardian framework and the specific-factors model.

As Jones and Scheinkman (1977) argue, the 2×2 framework is special because its dimensionality is low and because the number of factors is equal to the number of sectors. The Ricardian and the specific-factors models are two ways of extending this 2×2 framework: In the Ricardian model, the number of sectors is greater than the number of factors, and in the specific-factors model, the number of factors is greater than the number of sectors.[10] These models can thus be used to examine the implications of having more factors than sectors, or more sectors than factors. I wish to show whether the results I obtained from the 2×2 framework survive if the numbers of factors and sectors are different. In particular, I investigate the following four relationships: that between factor endowments and output levels, that between factor endowments and factor prices, that between commodity prices and output levels, and that between commodity prices and factor prices.

It should be pointed out, however, that all these three models can be described by the GDP function explained previously and thus have some common properties such as convexity of the production possibility set, nonnegative supplies of goods, and so on.

In the Ricardian model, there are two sectors ($n = 2$) and one homogeneous factor, labor ($m = 1$).[11] Linear homogeneity of the production functions requires that the labor-output coefficients of sector i, a_i, $i = 1, 2$, are constants. This means that the production functions can be written as

$$Q_i = L_i/a_i, \qquad i = 1, 2. \tag{2.45}$$

The production functions given by (2.45) have an important implication: The average product and marginal product of labor in sector i are constant, being equal to $1/a_i$. Using these production functions, I now derive the properties of this model.

---

10. Ethier (1984) provides an excellent survey of the analysis of higher dimensional issues in trade theory.

11. The Ricardian model introduced here is of the simplest, but the most common, form. For extension, see Findlay (1974) when a second factor, capital, is present, and Dornbusch et al. (1977) for a Ricardian model with a continuum of goods.

If firms in sector i have positive outputs, cost minimization implies the following inverse demand for labor:

$$w_i = p_i/a_i \qquad i = 1, 2. \tag{2.46}$$

With perfect labor mobility between the sectors, the wage rates in the sectors are equalized, that is, $w_1 = w_2 = w$. Because under autarky both goods are produced (if consumers consume both goods), condition (2.46) then gives an important result about the autarkic prices

$$\frac{p_1^a}{p_2^a} = \frac{a_1}{a_2}, \tag{2.47}$$

where the superscript "a" denotes the value of a variable under autarky. Condition (2.47) is interesting because it shows that the autarkic price ratio depends only on the labor-output coefficients but not on the preferences of the residents (as long as both goods are produced under autarky). This result, which is the most crucial property of the Classical model of a closed economy, was later observed by Samuelson (1951) to be true in more general models and is summarized by the following theorem (a proof is given in the appendix).

The Nonsubstitution Theorem   Suppose that there is one primary factor indispensible to production, there is no joint production, technologies exhibit constant returns to scale, and markets are perfectly competitive. The equilibrium commodity prices relative to the wage rate are unique.

The importance of the theorem is that even if substitution between inputs are technically possible, the optimal input-output coefficients of firms are unique and independent of the demand conditions and the endowment of the primary factor.

I now turn back to the production functions given in (2.45). The full-employment condition in (2.11) can be rewritten for the present model:

$$a_1 Q_1 + a_2 Q_2 = \overline{L}. \tag{2.48}$$

Equation (2.48) gives all possible combinations of the outputs of the sectors when given labor endowment, and thus can be regarded as the equation of the PPF. The equation can be illustrated by line TT in Figure 2.10. The horizontal (respectively vertical) intercept of TT, that is, $\overline{L}/a_1$ (respectively $\overline{L}/a_2$), are the maximum output of good 1 (respectively 2) when all labor is employed in that sector. The slope of the PPF (negative of the marginal rate of transformation) is equal to $-a_1/a_2$, which, according to (2.47), is equal to the slope of the autarkic price line.

Figure 2.10 shows several very important properties about the price-output relationship in the Ricardian model. Suppose that the price line coincides with

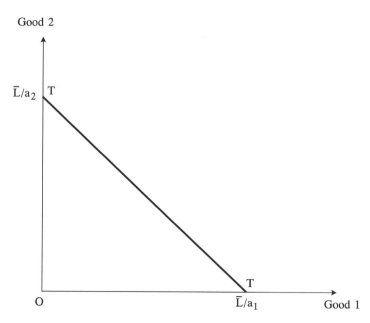

Figure 2.10

the PPF, as under an interior autarkic equilibrium, so that firms in both sectors are producing positive outputs. The production point is somewhere on the PPF. However, any point on the PPF satisfies the cost-minimizing condition given by (2.46). This implies that if the price line coincides with the PPF, the production point is indeterminate. (Of course, I can pin down the location of the production point if consumption demands are known.) In fact, for all models with more sectors than factors, the production point is in general indeterminate, meaning that the GDP function is not differentiable with respect to commodity prices.[12]

Suppose that initially both sectors have positive outputs, and that there is a small increase in the relative price of good 1. The price line becomes steeper than the PPF and the economy is completely specialized in the production of good 1. Any further increase in the relative price of good 1 will have no effect on production. Furthermore, as long as the output of any one good is positive before and after the change in a price, the wage rate will change by the same proportion as the change in the price of the good. If the production pattern is completely reversed by an increase in the relative price of good 1 (producing

12. For example, Samuelson (1953) and Melvin (1968) show that with two factors and three sectors, the production possibility surface is ruled, that is, composed of straight lines. When a price hyperplane touches a flat portion of the production possibility surface, it gives multiple production points.

only good 2 initially but only good 1 finally), the rate of change of the wage rate can be greater or smaller than that of the price of good 1.

I next turn to the output effect of factor endowment. Suppose that the labor endowment is increased under constant commodity prices. This shifts the PPF outward in a parallel fashion. If initially both outputs are positive, the production point remains indeterminate. If initially only one good, such as good 1, is produced, its output is increased by the same proportion as the change in the labor endowment.

2.6   The Specific-Factors Model

In this model, a factor such as capital in each sector is assumed to be specific to the sector so that no capital movement between the sectors exists (hence the name specific-factors). Labor, on the other hand, can move freely between the sectors. As a result, there is one rental rate for the capital stock in each sector, and in general the two rental rates are different.[13]

The specific-factors model can be analyzed by extending the 2×2 model described earlier. First, sector specificity of capital means that condition (2.4a) should be replaced by two separate conditions:

$$r_1 = p_1 f_1'(k_1) \tag{2.49a}$$

$$r_2 = p_2 f_2'(k_2), \tag{2.49b}$$

where r_i is the rental rate of capital in sector i, $i = 1, 2$. Conditions (2.4b) (2 equations), (2.49a), and (2.49b) now have four equations, but there are seven unknowns: p_1, p_2, w, r_1, r_2, k_1, and k_2. This means that even if the commodity prices are given, the equations cannot be solved for the remaining unknowns. The whole system of equations has to be solved simultaneously and the endogenous variables generally depend on all exogenous variables including factor endowments. Thus even if commodity prices are given, factor prices in general depend also on factor endowments.

The model can be solved in a simple way. Recall that $F_{iL}(\overline{K}_i, L_i)$ is the marginal product of labor in sector i, where $\overline{K}_i$ is the given capital stock in that sector. By using the labor endowment constraint, condition (2.4b) can be rewritten as

$$p_1 F_{1L}(\overline{K}_1, L_1) = p_2 F_{2L}(\overline{K}_2, \overline{L} - L_1). \tag{2.50}$$

---

13. This model is also called Ricardo-Viner, or Jones-Neary, model. See Ricardo (1817, Chapter 7), Viner (1931, 1950), Jones (1971a), and Neary (1978a, 1978b). It should be pointed out that important contributions to the theory have also been made by many other people.

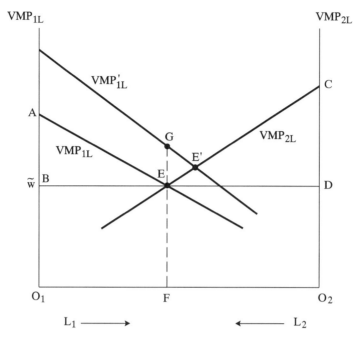

Figure 2.11

Because the capital stocks in the sectors are given, if commodity prices are given, then condition (2.50) can be solved for the unknown: L_1. Once L_1 is known, other variables can be determined (in terms of the commodity prices and factor endowments).

The solution can be illustrated nicely by a simple diagram. In Figure 2.11, the horizontal axis represents the economy's given labor endowment. A point in the diagram shows the labor employments in sector 1 (L_1, measured from O_1 to the right) and sector 2 (L_2, measured from O_2 to the left). When given the commodity prices and capital stocks in the sectors, schedules labeled VMP_{iL}, which are negatively slope because F_{iL} is falling, show the value of marginal product of labor in sector i, $VMP_{iL} = p_i F_{iL}$. (Ignore schedule VMP'_{1L} for the time being.) The intersecting point between the schedules, point E, satisfies condition (2.50). Thus this is the equilibrium point, with O_1F of the labor working in sector 1 and O_2F working in sector 2. The equilibrium wage rate is $\tilde{w}$. The area below each VMP curve is the value of the output of the sector. The area bounded by each sector's VMP schedule and the horizontal line representing the wage rate is the income earned by the capital owners in that sector. So area ABE is equal to $r_1\overline{K}_1$ and area CDE is $r_2\overline{K}_2$.

The diagram shows that corresponding to each relative price, there is in general a unique production point (with strictly concave production functions). So the indeterminacy of production point mentioned in the Ricardian model does not exist here. I showed earlier that the production possibility set is convex. Thus in the present model the PPF does not have a flat portion (when given strictly convex technologies) and the PPF is strictly concave to the origin.

The effects of a change in the commodity prices can be determined as follows. Suppose that p_1 rises while p_2 remains fixed. Because $VMP_{iL} = p_i F_{iL}$, schedule VMP_{1L} shifts up equiproportionately to VMP'_{1L} while schedule VMP_{2L} does not change. This gives a new equilibrium point E'. It is easy to conclude from the diagram that the price change leads to an increase in L_1 and thus Q_1 (because $\overline{K}_1$ is fixed), a decrease in L_2 and Q_2, an increase in w and r_1, and a decrease in r_2. Thus the supply of good 1 is positively related to its relative price.

How can we compare the rises in p_1 and r_1? To answer this question, assume (hypothetically) that the equilibrium point is at G, which is on schedule VMP'_{1L} and directly above point E. At point G, the wage rate rises by the same proportion as p_1, and so does r_1. The actual equilibrium point is point E', meaning that the wage rate in fact has not risen by that much, and thus that r_1 has actually risen more than in the hypothetical case, that is, the rate of increase in r_1 is greater than that of p_1. Because the relationship between p_1 and r_1 does not depend on the capital-labor ratios in the sectors, however, it is difficult to conclude whether the Stolper-Samuelson theorem is valid.

Let me turn to the effects of an increase in a factor endowment. First consider an increase in $\overline{L}$. In Figure 2.12, origin O_2 shifts to O'_2 by a distance of $\Delta\overline{L}$, the increase in labor endowment. At the same time, the whole schedule VMP_{2L} shifts to the right by the same amount in a parallel fashion. The new schedule, VMP'_{2L}, cuts schedule VMP_{1L} at a new equilibrium point, point E'. Comparing the initial and the new equilibrium points, I get an increase in L_1 and thus Q_1, a decrease in the wage rate and thus a rise in both rental rates. I also see from the diagram that the horizontal gap (EF) between the two VMP schedules for sector 2 is greater than the increase in labor employment in sector 1, meaning that L_2 and thus Q_2 also increase. Obviously the Rybczynski theorem is not valid in its original form because an increase in the labor endowment increases the production of both sectors. This result is shown by the positively sloped Rybczynski schedule for labor R_L in Figure 2.13, which is the locus of the production point under given commodity prices as labor endowment changes. The slope of this schedule is

$$\frac{dQ_2}{dQ_1}\bigg|_{R_L} = \frac{F_{2L}dL_2}{F_{1L}dL_1} = \frac{p_1 F_{2L} F_{1LL}}{p_2 F_{1L} F_{2LL}} > 0,$$

where the last equality is obtained by differentiating (2.50). Note that in general this schedule is not a straight line.

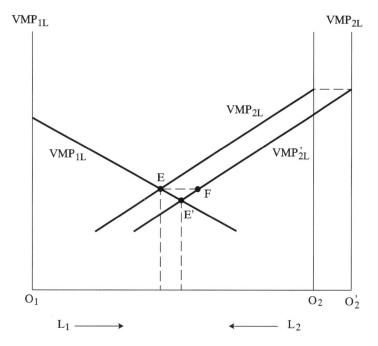

Figure 2.12

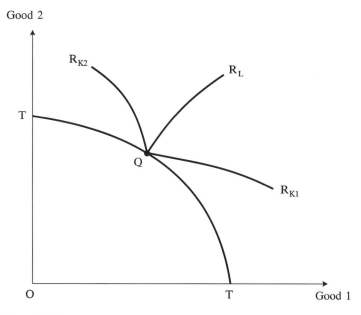

Figure 2.13

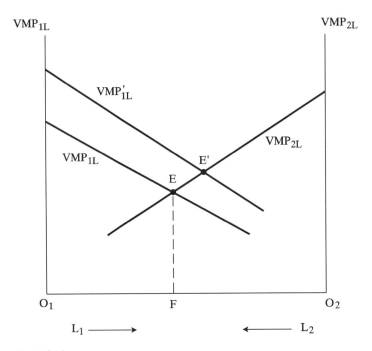

Figure 2.14

I next consider an increase in the sector-1 capital stock. Because the production function is linearly homogeneous in the two factors, labor and capital in each sector must be complements in the sense that an increase in capital increases the sector's marginal product of labor. As a result, in Figure 2.14 schedule VMP_{1L} shifts up to VMP'_{1L}. The diagram shows an increase in w, L_1 and Q_1, and a decrease in r_2, L_2 and Q_2. Furthermore, because the commodity price of good 1 has not changed, zero profit means that an increase in w must imply a decrease in r_1. This point can also be proved by the downward sloping unit-cost schedule in Figure 2.8. An increase in w is reflected by a downward movement along the unit-cost schedule for sector 1, and a drop in r_1. The changes in the sectors' outputs is illustrated by the downward sloping Rybczynski for sector-1 capital, R_{K1} in Figure 2.13. The same analysis can also be used to derive the Rybczynski schedule for sector-2 capital, R_{K2}, which is negatively sloped as shown.

The specific-factors model has been extended in two directions. First, Mussa (1974), Mayer (1974a), Neary (1978a, 1978b), and Grossman (1983) regard sector specificity of capital as a short-run phenomenon. In the long run, capital can move between sectors to equalize the rental rates, and this model reduces to the 2×2 model.

Under this approach, we have two PPFs: the long-run PPF characterized by rental rate equalization, and the short-run PPF that corresponds to the given allocation of capital. Both PPFs are concave to the origin, but the short-run PPF is below the long-run PPF except that they are tangent to each other at the point corresponding to the initial production with rental rate equalization. In fact, for each allocation of capital between the sectors there is a short-run PPF, which is below but tangent at one point to the long-run PPF.

The second way of extending the specific-factors model is to treat the capital stocks in the two sectors as two different types of factors, and in a more general model both sectors (possibly) employ all three factors. This implies a three-factor, two-sector model. (See Batra and Casas, 1976; Ruffin, 1981; Thompson, 1986; Wong, 1990.)

2.7   Consumption Demand

So far I have concentrated on the production side of the economy. I now turn to its consumption side. There have been many ways suggested in the literature to aggregate the consumer preferences in the economy. In this section (and throughout this book), I concentrate on two major approaches. The first is to allow differences between the preferences of households. The second is to use some simplifications to aggregate the consumption demands of different households.[14]

2.7.1   Many Households with Different Preferences

Suppose that there are H households in the economy. Denote the consumption of the hth household by the n-dimensional vector $\mathbf{C}^h$ and assume that its preferences can be represented by the utility function $u^h(\mathbf{C}^h)$, which is increasing, quasi-concave, and differentiable. Using this utility function, I can define the corresponding expenditure function $e^h(\mathbf{p}, u^h)$, which is increasing, differentiable, linearly homogeneous, and concave in $\mathbf{p}$ and increasing in the utility level u^h. I assume that all households face the same set of prices, although this assumption can be relaxed.

The compensated demand for goods is given by the partial derivatives of the expenditure function with respect to prices, $e_{\mathbf{p}}^h(\mathbf{p}, u^h)$. Utility maximization by any two households implies equalization of marginal rate of substitution between any pair of commodities the households consume. Their consumption can be graphically represented by a point on the contract curve in the Edgeworth box diagram. This gives efficiency in consumption.

14. There is one interesting approach due to Gorman (1953), which has been used in the literature. See Chipman and Moore (1973) and Woodland (1982) for an extension of the Gorman approach.

The aggregate compensated consumption demand is the summation of households' consumption bundles

$$\tilde{\mathbf{C}}(\mathbf{p}, u^1, \ldots, u^H) = \sum_h e_{\mathbf{p}}^h(\mathbf{p}, u^h). \tag{2.51}$$

The expression in (2.51) is quite general, because the preferences of households can differ in many ways. Such a generality has its limitations. First, the aggregate consumption of a good depends not only on commodity prices, but also on the utility levels of households. This means that in general it also depends on income distribution. Second, because this approach considers the utility levels of all households, it is complicated for analyzing national welfare.

2.7.2   A Social Utility Function

Because of the difficulty of the general approach mentioned previously, different ways have been suggested to represent national welfare by an aggregate utility function or a social utility function and to derive aggregate consumption from that function. The simplest way is to assume that there is only one household in the economy or that the consumption of the economy is determined by a dictator. The welfare of the economy is the same as the welfare of the single household or it is measured by the welfare of the dictator, but the assumption of one household or a dictator is too strong. Here I discuss three other approaches: (1) identical preferences and endowments among households, (2) identical and homothetic preferences among households, and (3) the existence of a social utility function. I assume that all households face the same commodity prices.

Identical Preferences and Endowments

If all households have identical preferences and endowments, they must make the same consumption choice, and in equilibrium they have the same utility level. This means that the utility level of each household is good enough to represent the welfare level of the economy. Thus, in this case, I can use the utility function of any household to represent the welfare of the economy.

Identical and Homothetic Preferences

Suppose that the preferences of households are identical and homothetic. They thus have the same expenditure function. Denote the expenditure function of the hth household by $e(\mathbf{p}, u^h)$. Homotheticity means that the expenditure function is separable: $e(\mathbf{p}, u^h) = \tilde{e}(\mathbf{p})\phi(u^h)$, where $\phi(.)$ is an increasing function. The aggregate expenditure equals $\sum_h e(\mathbf{p}, u^h) = \sum_h \tilde{e}(\mathbf{p})\phi(u^h) =$

$\widetilde{e}(\mathbf{p})\sum_h \phi(u^h)$. Denote the national income by I. In equilibrium and assuming no satiation, I have

$$I = \widetilde{e}(\mathbf{p})\sum_h \phi(u^h),$$

which gives

$$\sum_h \phi(u^h) = \frac{I}{\widetilde{e}(\mathbf{p})}. \qquad (2.52)$$

The aggregate demand given in (2.51) reduces to

$$\widetilde{\mathbf{C}} = \widetilde{e}_\mathbf{p}(\mathbf{p})\sum_h \phi(u^h) = \widetilde{e}_\mathbf{p}(\mathbf{p})\frac{I}{\widetilde{e}(\mathbf{p})}, \qquad (2.51')$$

where (2.52) has been used. Two important results follow. First, by (2.51'), the aggregate consumption demand depends on the commodity prices and national income, but not on income distribution. Second, assuming nonsatiation, define an utility level u so that $I = e(\mathbf{p}, u)$. Because the expenditure function is strictly increasing when satiation is absent, $e(\mathbf{p}, u)$ can be interpreted as the social expenditure function, with u interpreted as the social utility level.

A Social Utility Function

Another approach to measuring aggregate consumption and national welfare is to make use of a social utility function. Under this approach, a social utility function is used to rank-order all possible aggregate consumption bundles. Assuming that the social utility function is a "well-behaved" utility function, many of the results in the neoclassical theory of consumption can be extended to an economy. (More discussion about the merits and drawbacks of this approach is given in chapter 8.)

One sufficient condition for the existence of a social utility function is the existence of a social welfare function and an optimal income distribution to maximize social welfare (Samuelson, 1956). To see his argument, let me assume a Bergson-Samuelson social welfare function given by $W(u^1, \ldots, u^H)$, where $u^h = u^h(\mathbf{C}^h)$. Suppose that the consumption bundles of the households are chosen to maximize the social welfare level subject to the constraint that the value of the aggregate consumption is not greater than the national income, I, that is,

$$\max_{\mathbf{C}^1,\ldots,\mathbf{C}^H} \left\{ W\left[u^1(\mathbf{C}^1), \ldots, u^H(\mathbf{C}^H)\right] : \mathbf{p}\cdot\sum_{h=1}^{H}\mathbf{C}^h \leq I \right\}. \qquad (2.53)$$

Define $\mathbf{C} = \sum_h \mathbf{C}^h$. The maximization problem in (2.53) can be written as

$$\max_{\mathbf{C}} \left\{ \max_{\mathbf{C}^2,\ldots,\mathbf{C}^H} \left\{ W\left[u^1(\mathbf{C} - \sum_{h=2}^{H} \mathbf{C}^h), \ldots, u^H(\mathbf{C}^H) \right] \right\} : \mathbf{p} \cdot \mathbf{C} \leq I \right\}. \quad (2.53')$$

The maximum welfare obtained in (2.53'), which depends on prices $\mathbf{p}$ and national income I, can be represented by a new function $\widetilde{V}(\mathbf{p}, I)$. Denote the function inside the large parentheses in (2.53') by $u(\mathbf{C})$, that is, $u(\mathbf{C})$ is defined as

$$u(\mathbf{C}) = \max_{\mathbf{C}^2,\ldots,\mathbf{C}^H} W\left[u^1(\mathbf{C} - \sum_{h=2}^{H} \mathbf{C}^h), \ldots, u^H(\mathbf{C}^H) \right].$$

When given the aggregate consumption bundle $\mathbf{C}$, function $u(\mathbf{C})$ can be interpreted as the maximum social welfare level by allocating the bundle optimally among the households. Assuming differentiability of the social welfare function and the utility functions of the households, the first-order conditions of the above problem imply that the households must have the same marginal rate of substitution between any two goods they consume. This result has the important implication that in a decentralized economy, the government does not have to decide the quantity of each good each household should consume to solve the above problem. By appropriately allocating income among the households, the consumption bundles the households choose to maximize their utility levels also jointly maximize the social welfare function.

Function $\widetilde{V}(\mathbf{p}, I)$ can be defined as the maximum social welfare level by choosing the aggregate consumption bundle subject to the budget constraint:

$$\widetilde{V}(\mathbf{p}, I) = \max_{\mathbf{C}} \left\{ u(\mathbf{C}) : \mathbf{p} \cdot \mathbf{C} \leq I \right\}.$$

These results imply that maximizing the social welfare function can be broken up into two steps. First, the aggregate consumption bundle is chosen to maximize $u(\mathbf{C})$ subject to the budget constraint, and second, the aggregate consumption bundle is allocated optimally among the households. This means that $u(\mathbf{C})$ is the maximum social welfare function when the economy is given the aggregate consumption $\mathbf{C}$, and it is called the *social utility function*. Furthermore, $\widetilde{V}(\mathbf{p}, I)$ is interpreted as the dual to $u(\mathbf{C})$ and is called the *social indirect utility function*.

Some important properties of $u(\mathbf{C})$ are given as follows. First, if all households' utility functions are increasing (respectively continuous, differentiable) in consumption goods and the social welfare function is increasing (respectively continuous, differentiable) in utility levels, then so is $u(\mathbf{C})$ in $\mathbf{C}$.[15] Second, if the households' utility functions are increasing and concave and the social welfare function is increasing and quasi-concave, $u(\mathbf{C})$ is quasi-concave. (Quasi concavity is proved in the appendix.)

Given the properties of $u(\mathbf{C})$, the indirect utility function $\widetilde{V}(\mathbf{p}, I)$ has the following properties: It is continuous (or even differentiable), quasi-convex in $\mathbf{p}$, increasing in I, and homogeneous of degree zero in $(\mathbf{p}, I)$.

If a social utility function $u(\mathbf{C})$ exists, I can define the social expenditure function $e(\mathbf{p}, u)$ which is increasing, differentiable, concave, and linearly homogeneous in $\mathbf{p}$ and increasing and differentiable in u. The aggregate compensated demand for goods is

$$\widetilde{\mathbf{C}}(\mathbf{p}, u) = e_{\mathbf{p}}(\mathbf{p}, u). \tag{2.54}$$

2.8   Direct and Indirect Trade Utility Functions

In the rest of this chapter, I assume for simplicity the existence of a social utility function $u(\mathbf{C})$, which is increasing, differentiable, and quasi-concave. Further assume that in the absence of any distortions in consumption, the households, taking prices as given, jointly choose the aggregate consumption bundle, which maximizes the social utility function. Using the social utility function, I can define the economy's *direct trade utility* (DTU) function, *indirect trade utility* (ITU) function, and *input utility* function—three compact and convenient ways of summarizing the preferences and technologies of the economy.

Denote $\mathbf{E}$ (respectively $\mathbf{M} \equiv -\mathbf{E}$) as the n-dimensional vector of exported (respectively imported) goods. Negative elements of $\mathbf{E}$ represented goods imported. For the time being, I assume no international factor movement. The direct trade utility function (Meade, 1952) is defined as

$$U(\mathbf{E}, \mathbf{v}) = \max_{\mathbf{C}, \mathbf{Q}} \{u(\mathbf{C}) : \mathbf{C} = \mathbf{Q} - \mathbf{E}, \text{ and } \Gamma(\mathbf{Q}, \mathbf{v}) \leq 0\}. \tag{2.55}$$

In other words, the DTU function is the maximum utility level of the economy by choosing the optimal consumption and production bundles when the export levels $\mathbf{E}$ are chosen exogenously. Note that no commodity prices or budget constraints appear in the definition of the DTU function.

---

15. To prove that $u(\mathbf{C})$ is increasing in $\mathbf{C}$, suppose that there exists another bundle $\mathbf{C}' \geq \mathbf{C}$. It can be imagined that the increase in the goods is given to one of the households such as the first household. The social welfare level increases. In fact the maximum social welfare level with $\mathbf{C}'$ may be even higher.

The DTU function is continuous and quasi-concave in $\mathbf{E}$ and $\mathbf{v}$, increasing in $\mathbf{v}$ and decreasing in $\mathbf{E}$. Continuity and monotonicity are obvious, and quasi concavity is proved in the appendix. Even though the definition of the DTU function is not subject to any budget constraint, there is some relationship between the optimal consumption bundle and the optimal production bundle in (2.55). To incorporate the constraints, define the Lagrangean function $\mathcal{L}' \equiv \{u(\mathbf{C}) + \mathbf{h} \cdot (\mathbf{Q} - \mathbf{C} - \mathbf{E}) - \alpha\,\Gamma(\mathbf{Q}, \mathbf{v})\}$ where α is a Lagrangean multiplier and $\mathbf{h}$ is an n-dimensional vector of Lagrangean multipliers. The DTU function can be written in the following alternative form:

$$U(\mathbf{E}, \mathbf{v}) = \max_{\mathbf{C},\mathbf{Q}} \min_{\mathbf{h},\alpha} \mathcal{L}'$$

$$\equiv \max_{\mathbf{C},\mathbf{Q}} \min_{\mathbf{h},\alpha} \left\{ u(\mathbf{C}) + \mathbf{h} \cdot (\mathbf{Q} - \mathbf{C} - \mathbf{E}) - \alpha\,\Gamma(\mathbf{Q}, \mathbf{v}) \right\}. \tag{2.55'}$$

Differentiate the Lagrangean function by C_i and Q_i respectively, $i = 1, \ldots, n$, to give some of the first-order conditions:

$$\frac{\partial \mathcal{L}'}{\partial C_i} = u_i - h_i \leq 0 \tag{2.56a}$$

$$\frac{\partial \mathcal{L}'}{\partial Q_i} = h_i - \alpha\,\Gamma_i \leq 0, \tag{2.56b}$$

where u_i is the marginal utility of good i and $\Gamma_i \equiv \partial \Gamma / \partial Q_i$. Note that if $\Gamma(\mathbf{Q}, \mathbf{v})$ is not differentiable, Γ_i is interpreted as a set. Consider any goods i and ℓ that are produced and consumed. With the inequalities being replaced by equalities, equations (2.56a) and (2.56b) are combined together to give

$$\frac{u_i}{u_\ell} = \frac{\Gamma_i}{\Gamma_\ell}. \tag{2.57}$$

Note that Γ_i / Γ_ℓ is the marginal rate of transformation between goods i and ℓ. Thus (2.57) states that in solving the DTU problem in (2.55), the marginal rate of substitution is set to be the same as the marginal rate of transformation for any pair of goods that are consumed and produced domestically. This condition is illustrated in Figure 2.15 for the 2×2 framework. For an export vector of $(E_1, -M_2)$, the optimal consumption point is at C and the optimal production point is at Q, where $PQ = E_1$ and $PC = M_2$. The tangent to the indifference curve at C is parallel to the tangent to the PPF at Q.

By the envelope theorem, the partial derivatives of the DTU function are

$$\frac{\partial U}{\partial E_i} = -h_i, \qquad i = 1, \ldots, n \tag{2.58a}$$

$$\frac{\partial U}{\partial v_j} = -\alpha\,\Gamma_j \qquad j = 1, \ldots, m, \tag{2.58b}$$

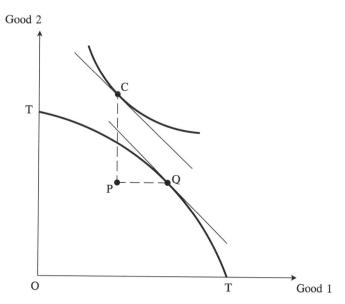

Good 2

Figure 2.15

where $\Gamma_j \equiv \partial\Gamma/\partial v_j$. Note again that if $\Gamma(\mathbf{Q}, \mathbf{v})$ is not differentiable with respect to v_j, then $\partial U/\partial v_j$ is interpreted as a set. Condition (2.58a) has an important implication. Consider any two goods i and ℓ, which are consumed and produced domestically. Condition (2.58a) gives

$$\frac{\partial U/\partial E_i}{\partial U/\partial E_\ell} = \frac{h_i}{h_\ell}. \tag{2.59}$$

Comparing conditions (2.56), (2.57) and (2.59), I get

$$\frac{\partial U/\partial E_i}{\partial U/\partial E_\ell} = \frac{u_i}{u_\ell} = \frac{\Gamma_i}{\Gamma_\ell}. \tag{2.59'}$$

To see the significance of (2.59'), consider again the two-by-two framework introduced above. The DTU function in this framework can be represented by the trade indifference curves in Figure 2.16. Three indifference curves labeled u^2, u^a, and u^1 are shown. Because the DTU function is decreasing in $\mathbf{E}$, the utility level is increasing in the direction toward the northwest. So $u^2 > u^a > u^1$. Because the origin represents autarky, u^a is the autarkic utility level. The slope of a trade indifference curve is equal to

$$\frac{\mathrm{d}M_2}{\mathrm{d}E_1} = -\frac{\mathrm{d}E_2}{\mathrm{d}E_1} = \frac{\partial U/\partial E_1}{\partial U/\partial E_2} = \frac{u_1}{u_2}.$$

Thus condition (2.59') shows that the slope of a trade indifference curve is numerically equal to that of the social indifference curve and that of the PPF

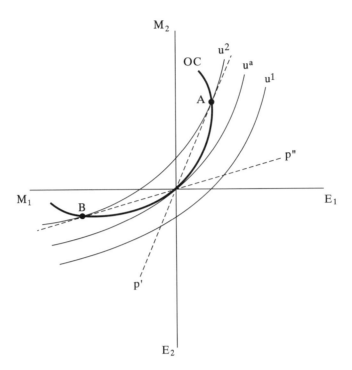

Figure 2.16

at the corresponding points. The slope of the indifference curve labeled u^a at the origin is equal to the autarkic price ratio.

I now turn to another function called the indirect trade utility (ITU) function (Woodland, 1980).[16] Assuming no international factor mobility for the time being, the ITU function is defined by

$$V(\mathbf{p}, \mathbf{v}, b) = \max_{\mathbf{C}} \{u(\mathbf{C}) : \mathbf{p} \cdot \mathbf{C} \leq g(\mathbf{p}, \mathbf{v}) + b\}, \tag{2.60}$$

where b is the amount of transfer the economy received from other countries. Intuitively, the ITU function gives the maximum utility level of the economy when it faces commodity prices $\mathbf{p}$ and receives a transfer of b. The solution $\mathbf{C}(\mathbf{p}, \mathbf{v}, b)$ gives the optimal consumption bundle of the economy. Because I assume that the households choose consumption bundles that jointly maximize the social utility function, $\mathbf{C}(\mathbf{p}, \mathbf{v}, b)$ is indeed the aggregate consumption demand. Both the DTU and ITU functions give the social utility level. Because the DTU function does not specify the budget constraint, in many cases the ITU function is a more useful analytical technique.

---

16. Even though his main focus is the direct trade utility function, Chipman (1979) discusses many issues related to the indirect trade utility function.

One simple feature of the ITU function is that it can be derived from the social indirect utility function $\widetilde{V}(\mathbf{p}, I)$ introduced earlier by replacing national income with $g(\mathbf{p}, \mathbf{v}) + b$, that is, $V(\mathbf{p}, \mathbf{v}, b) \equiv \widetilde{V}(\mathbf{p}, g(\mathbf{p}, \mathbf{v}) + b)$.

The ITU function is quasi-convex in $\mathbf{p}$, increasing and quasi-concave in $\mathbf{v}$, and increasing in b, and homogeneous of degree zero in $(\mathbf{p}, b)$. Quasi convexity is proved in the appendix. I assume that it is differentiable in $(\mathbf{p}, \mathbf{v})$.[17]

There are some more useful properties of the ITU function. Define the following Lagrangean function $\mathcal{L} \equiv u(\mathbf{C}) + \lambda[g(\mathbf{p}, \mathbf{v}) + b - \mathbf{p} \cdot \mathbf{C}]$. Assuming differentiability, the partial derivatives of the ITU function can be obtained by using the envelope theorem:

$$\frac{\partial V}{\partial p_i} = \lambda[Q_i(\mathbf{p}, \mathbf{v}) - C_i] = \lambda E_i(\mathbf{p}, \mathbf{v}, b) \qquad i = 1, \ldots, n \qquad (2.61\text{a})$$

$$\frac{\partial V}{\partial v_j} = \lambda w_j(\mathbf{p}, \mathbf{v}, b) \qquad j = 1, \ldots, m \qquad (2.61\text{b})$$

$$\frac{\partial V}{\partial b} = \lambda, \qquad (2.61\text{c})$$

where $\lambda = \lambda(\mathbf{p}, \mathbf{v}, b)$, the Lagrangean multiplier, is interpreted as the marginal utility of income. A useful result is that combining (2.61a) and (2.61c) gives the export supply function of good i

$$E_i(\mathbf{p}, \mathbf{v}, b) = \frac{\partial V / \partial p_i}{\partial V / \partial b}.$$

I now examine the autarky equilibrium of an economy before I introduce an important application of the ITU function. Commodity prices $\mathbf{p}^a \geq \mathbf{0}(n)$, where $\mathbf{0}(n)$ is a n-dimensional vector of zeroes, are said to be autarkic prices if and only if the resulting excess demands of all markets are nonpositive. In terms of the GDP and expenditure functions introduced earlier, the autarkic equilibrium conditions can be stated as

$$e_\mathbf{p}(\mathbf{p}, u) = g_\mathbf{p}(\mathbf{p}, \mathbf{v}) \qquad (2.62\text{a})$$

$$e(\mathbf{p}, u) = g(\mathbf{p}, \mathbf{v}) \qquad (2.62\text{b})$$

On the left-hand side of (2.62a) is the compensated demand for goods; the right-hand side gives the aggregate supply of goods. Condition (2.62b) is the budget constraint of the economy. Note that for simplicity I present only the equations for those sectors in which excess demand is zero. There are $n + 1$ equations (n equations in 2.62a and 1 in 2.62b) and $n + 1$ variables (n autarkic prices $\mathbf{p}$ and utility u^a). Because both the expenditure function and the GDP

---

17. The ITU function is differentiable if the GDP function is. If it is not differentiable, $\partial V / \partial p_i$ and $\partial V / \partial v_j, i = 1, \ldots, n, j = 1, \ldots, m$, are sets.

function are linearly homogeneous in $\mathbf{p}$, if I multiply both sides of (2.62a) by $\mathbf{p}$, I get (2.62b). This means that one of the $n + 1$ equations is redundant. This result, which is not surprising, is called Walras's law. Thus I can only solve for at most the $n - 1$ relative prices and the utility level.

The ITU function can be used to provide an alternative way of deriving the autarkic equilibrium.

Theorem of Autarkic Commodity Prices (Woodland, 1980)   The commodity prices $\mathbf{p}^a \geq \mathbf{0}(n)$ are autarkic prices if and only if

$$V(\mathbf{p}^a, \mathbf{v}, 0) \leq V(\mathbf{p}, \mathbf{v}, 0) \qquad \text{for all} \qquad \mathbf{p} \geq \mathbf{0}(n).$$

Three points about the theorem can be noted. First, it may appear that by using the theorem one can find the nominal autarkic prices. This is not true, because $V(\mathbf{p}, \mathbf{v}, 0)$ is homogeneous of degree zero in $\mathbf{p}$. Thus if $\mathbf{p}^a$ minimizes $V(\mathbf{p}, \mathbf{v}, 0)$, so does $\alpha \mathbf{p}^a$ for any constant $\alpha > 0$. Second, in the previous proof, differentiability of the ITU function is not required. If the function is differentiable, then the necessary part of the theorem of autarkic commodity prices can be proved easily. If $\mathbf{p}^a$ are autarkic prices, then $E_i(\mathbf{p}^a, \mathbf{v}, 0) \geq$ for all $i = 1, \ldots, n$. This implies, by (2.61a), that $\partial V / \partial p_i \geq 0$, meaning that $V(\mathbf{p}^a, \mathbf{v}, 0)$ is a turning point. Quasi convexity of V with respect to $\mathbf{p}$ guarantees that the turning point is a minimum.

The third point about the theorem is that it seems to be contradictory to the notion that the economy as a whole is maximizing social utility. There is actually no contradiction between these two concepts because when an economy maximizes its social utility function, it is *taking commodity prices as given* (or the consumers are taking prices as given). The commodity prices, when treated as parameters or given exogenously to a small open economy, affect the maximum utility level that the economy can achieve. The ITU function expresses the dependence of the maximum utility level on the commodity prices. The theorem of autarkic commodity prices states that the maximum utility level reaches the minimum when the economy is facing the autarkic prices. This is the basic idea of the theory of gains from trade, which I will talk more about in later chapters.

The DTU and ITU functions defined in (2.55) and (2.60), respectively, can easily be extended to allow international factor movement. Suppose that the first m^t factors are mobile and $\mathbf{k}$ represents the amounts of foreign mobile factors working in the home country. As explained before, there are two approaches to analyzing the production side of the economy. Here I take the first one and redefine the DTU and the ITU function, as

$$U(\mathbf{E}, \mathbf{v}^t + \mathbf{k}, \mathbf{v}^n) = \max_{\mathbf{C}, \mathbf{Q}} \{u(\mathbf{C}) : \mathbf{C} = \mathbf{Q} - \mathbf{E},$$

$$\text{and } \Gamma(\mathbf{Q}, \mathbf{v}^t + \mathbf{k}, \mathbf{v}^n) \leq 0\} \qquad (2.63a)$$

$$V(\mathbf{p}, \mathbf{v}^t + \mathbf{k}, \mathbf{v}^n, b) = \max_{\mathbf{C}} \{u(\mathbf{C}) : \mathbf{p} \cdot \mathbf{C} \le g(\mathbf{p}, \mathbf{v}^t + \mathbf{k}, \mathbf{v}^n) + b\}. \qquad (2.63b)$$

With free trade and no government transfer, b is equal to the repatriation by national factors working abroad less the repatriation by foreign factors working in the economy. To see how the ITU function is used to evaluate the welfare of an economy, I can make use of its derivatives in (2.61) to measure changes in welfare:

$$dV = V_{\mathbf{p}} \cdot d\mathbf{p} + V_{\mathbf{v}}^t \cdot (d\mathbf{v}^t + d\mathbf{k}) + V_{\mathbf{v}}^n \cdot d\mathbf{v}^n + V_b \, db$$

$$= \lambda \big[\mathbf{E} \cdot d\mathbf{p} + \mathbf{r} \cdot d\mathbf{k} + \mathbf{w} \cdot d\mathbf{v} + db \big], \qquad (2.64)$$

where $V_{\mathbf{p}}$ is the n-dimensional Jacobian vector of V with respect to $\mathbf{p}$, $V_{\mathbf{v}}^t$ is the m^t-dimensional Jacobian vector of V with respect to the mobile factors and $V_{\mathbf{v}}^n$ is the m^n-dimensional Jacobian vector of V with respect to $\mathbf{v}^n$. I can illustrate how condition (2.64) is applied to measure changes in national welfare in the following case. Consider a small trading economy with fixed factor endowments under free trade in goods and in the mobile factors. In this case, the transfer is equal to $b = -\mathbf{r} \cdot \mathbf{k}$. Thus $db = -\mathbf{r} \cdot d\mathbf{k} - \mathbf{k} \cdot d\mathbf{r}$. Substituting this expression into (2.64) to give

$$dV = \lambda \big[\mathbf{E} \cdot d\mathbf{p} - \mathbf{k} \cdot d\mathbf{r} \big]. \qquad (2.64')$$

Suppose that there is an improvement in its term of trade in the sense that

$$\mathbf{E} \cdot d\mathbf{p} - \mathbf{k} \cdot d\mathbf{r} > 0.$$

This result and condition (2.64') imply that $dV > 0$, that is, an improvement in the terms of trade for a small open economy is beneficial (Kemp, 1962; Krueger and Sonnenschein, 1967; Wong, 1991a). Using the terminology in Wong (1991a), $\mathbf{E} \cdot d\mathbf{p}$ is called the *commodity terms of trade* and $-\mathbf{k} \cdot d\mathbf{r}$ the *factor terms of trade*. It is important to note that in the presence of international factor movements, an improvement in the commodity terms of trade alone is not sufficient for a welfare improvement.

I now turn to another function called the *input utility function*, which is defined as

$$V^I(\mathbf{w}, \mathbf{v}, b) = \max_{\mathbf{C}} \Big\{ u(\mathbf{C}) : \mathbf{c}(\mathbf{w}) \cdot \mathbf{C} \le \mathbf{w} \cdot \mathbf{v} + b \Big\}, \qquad (2.65)$$

where $\mathbf{c}(\mathbf{w})$ is the n-dimensional vector of unit cost functions. On the right-hand side of (2.65), $\mathbf{w} \cdot \mathbf{v}$ is the national product of the economy, and thus $\mathbf{w} \cdot \mathbf{v} + b$ is the economy's national income. Because $\mathbf{c}(\mathbf{w})$ is the unit cost vector, $\mathbf{c}(\mathbf{w}) \cdot \mathbf{C}$ is thus the total cost of producing the consumption bundle $\mathbf{C}$.

There are two interpretations of the input utility function. First, if the economy is a small open economy receiving a transfer of b, and if free movement of all factors is allowed under the exogenously given factor prices $\mathbf{w}$, then the function gives the maximum utility level the economy can achieve. If the economy is not a small open economy, then $\mathbf{w}$ will be treated as parameters. Second, suppose that the economy trades in goods with the rest of the world under prices $\mathbf{p}$ and that the economy is diversified in production in the sense that it produces positive outputs of all the goods it consumes. Because firms earn zero profit, the unit costs equal commodity prices, $\mathbf{c}(\mathbf{w}) = \mathbf{p}$. This means that given a transfer of b and the factor prices that give zero profit, the input utility function is the maximum utility of the economy.

Properties of the input utility function can be derived using the techniques developed here. The proofs are omitted here, but interested readers are referred to Wong (1983, 1986a). The input utility function is convex and homogeneous of degree zero in $\mathbf{w}$, concave, linearly homogeneous and increasing in $\mathbf{v}$, and increasing in b. Define the Lagrangean function: $\mathcal{L} = u(\mathbf{C}) + \lambda[\mathbf{w} \cdot \mathbf{v} - \mathbf{c}(\mathbf{w}) \cdot \mathbf{C}]$. By the envelope theorem, the partial derivatives of the functions are

$$\frac{\partial V^I}{\partial w_i} = \lambda[v_i - v_i^c]$$

$$\frac{\partial V^I}{\partial v_j} = \lambda w_j$$

$$\frac{\partial V^I}{\partial b} = \lambda$$

$$i, j = 1, \ldots, m,$$

where λ is the marginal utility of income, and $v_i^c \equiv \sum_\ell a_{i\ell} C_\ell$ is the consumption demand for factor i. The consumption demand for factor i is the quantity of factor i firms demand to produce the consumption bundle. Moreover, the function provides a neat way of determining the autarkic factor prices in the economy:

Theorem of Autarkic Factor Prices (Wong, 1983)   The factor prices $\mathbf{w}^a \geq \mathbf{0}(m)$ are autarkic prices if and only if

$$V^I(\mathbf{w}^a, \mathbf{v}, 0) \leq V^I(\mathbf{w}, \mathbf{v}, 0) \qquad \text{for all} \qquad \mathbf{w} \geq \mathbf{0}(m).$$

Some applications of this theorem and the input utility function will be provided in the next chapter.

2.9   Stability of Equilibrium

Stability of equilibrium is one of the most important topics in theoretical analyses of economic models. Very often it yields a lot of information about the properties of a model.

2.9.1 Some Basic Concepts

An equilibrium of a system is said to be stable if the system has an adjustment mechanism so that starting from a given point it moves automatically to the equilibrium as time approaches infinity. The equilibrium is said to be *globally stable* if the starting point can be anywhere in the system, or *locally stable* if the starting point has to be in the neighborhood of the equilibrium point.

Depending on what variables take the major responsibility in adjusting, stability commonly can be divided into two types: The price adjustment or the *Walrasian stability*, and the quantity adjustment or the *Marshallian stability*. The former is based on the *tâtonnement* process.[18]

Several reasons can be offered to explain why stability of equilibrium is important, and why they deserve careful study.

1. In theoretical work, an equilibrium usually is obtained by solving a system of equations. This is not what is done in the real world to search for an equilibrium, because no one knows (or cares about) these equations. Therefore if an equilibrium derived in a theoretical work is to represent what is observed in the real world, one has to explain how the real world would reach this equilibrium. Furthermore, being able to show that the equilibrium of a theoretical system is stable increases one's confidence in the internal consistency of the model.

2. Because it is important to focus on stable equilibria, if a theoretical model yields multiple equilibria, in many cases one can rule out unstable equilibria in the analysis.

3. In many cases, whether an equilibrium in a theoretical work is stable depends on the values of parameters. To get a stable equilibrium, one can set bounds on some of the parameters.

4. In theoretical work, it is usually important to determine the effects of changes in exogenous variables—an exercise called comparative statics. Samuelson (1947, Chapters 9 and 10) points out that there is a dual relationship between comparative statics and the stability of equilibrium, which he calls the *correspondence principle*.

The correspondence principle has three important implications. First, an analysis of the stability conditions can reveal important information about comparative statics, and vice versa. Second, a stable equilibrium often yields "normal" comparative statics effects, and in many cases "perverse" comparative statics effects can be ruled out if unstable equilibria are not considered. It is argued that unstable equilibria can be ruled out because in the real world

---

18. For a description of the *tâtonnement* and the *non-tâtonnement* processes, see Takayama (1985, 339–345).

unstable equilibria nearly never exist (Samuelson, 1947). Third, even if unstable equilibria are not ruled out theoretically, the adjustment mechanism often guarantees that perverse comparative statics effects do not exist (Samuelson, 1971). This result is called the *global correspondence principle.*

In the literature of international trade, an example in which the second and third implications of the correspondence principle can be applied is the transfer problem. Suppose that a country gives a transfer to another country. It is commonly believed that the donor country is hurt and the receiving country gains, except in some "perverse" cases. It has been shown that in the type of frameworks considered, these perverse cases occur when the equilibrium is not Walrasian stable (Samuelson, 1952; Chipman, 1974).[19]

To illustrate the second and third implications of the correspondence principle, let me consider a market in which the price of the good adjusts according to the *tâtonnement* process. In Figure 2.17, schedule S is the supply schedule that bends backward, and schedule D is the demand schedule.[20] In the case shown, there are three equilibria at points A, B, and C. By the *tâtonnement* process, the price adjusts upward if there is excess demand or downward if there is excess supply. It is easy to see that equilibria A and C are Walrasian stable, but equilibrium B is unstable.

Suppose that there is an increase in demand so that the demand schedule shifts out to schedule D', as shown in the diagram. Schedule D' cuts the supply schedule at points A', B', and C'. If the economy starts from a stable equilibrium, A or C, it will shift to a new stable equilibrium such as A' or C'. A movement from A to A', or from C to C', represents a "normal" price effect, because the increase in demand has created a rise in the price. However, if the economy shifts from point B to point B', there is a fall in the price, implying a "perverse" response. Thus in this case a perverse price-demand response requires a Walrasian unstable equilibrium.

Samuelson (1947) points out that the perverse case is rare because an unstable equilibrium is almost never observed. In 1971, he notes (Samuelson, 1971) that even if the initial equilibrium is at point B in the diagram, under a *tâtonnement* process a perverse case will not be observed. The reason is that at the initial price level (that corresponds to point B in Figure 2.17), there is an excess demand. Under the *tâtonnement* process, the price will rise, not fall,

---

19. Immiserizing transfers can occur even with a stable equilibrium if it is a bilateral transfer in a multicountry framework (Bhagwati, Brecher, and Hatta, 1983), or if there are domestic distortions (Bhagwati and Brecher, 1982; Bhagwati, Brecher, and Hatta, 1985; Beladi, 1990), or if part of the transfer is absorbed by administrative procedures, by transportation, by costly rent-seeking, or in downright waste (Kemp and Wong, 1993).

20. The example is adopted from the one in Samuelson (1971). The market he examines is the foreign exchange market of the donor country. An increase in the demand for foreign exchange is due to a transfer it gives to another country.

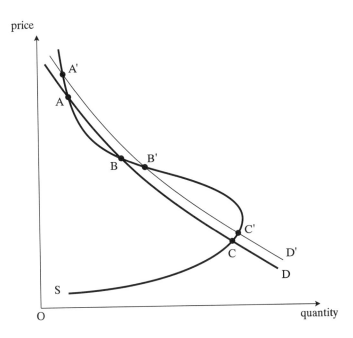

Figure 2.17

until point A′ is reached. This means that the shock will move the market not to a new unstable equilibrium but to a new equilibrium point such as A′. In the present case the new price is higher than the initial one and there is no perverse price-output response. This illustrates the global correspondence principle.

2.9.2   Stability of an Autarkic Equilibrium

I now show that in the present framework with a quasi-concave social utility function, convex technologies, and perfect competition, an autarkic equilibrium is unique and globally stable. I first state and prove the following results.

Result 2.1   Given a quasi-concave social utility function, the Weak Axiom of Revealed Preference (WARP) holds for the economy, that is, given any two non-negative price vectors $\mathbf{p}$, $\mathbf{p}' \geq \mathbf{0}(n)$, and the corresponding consumption bundles $\mathbf{C}$ and $\mathbf{C}'$, respectively,

$$\text{if } \mathbf{p} \cdot \mathbf{C}' \leq \mathbf{p} \cdot \mathbf{C}, \text{ then } \mathbf{p}' \cdot \mathbf{C}' < \mathbf{p}' \cdot \mathbf{C}. \tag{2.66}$$

The idea behind the WARP is that if under the price vector $\mathbf{p}$, the economy can afford $\mathbf{C}'$ but instead chooses $\mathbf{C}$, then the former bundle cannot yield a higher utility than the latter one does. When the economy decides to choose $\mathbf{C}'$ when the prices are $\mathbf{p}'$, it must be because at these prices $\mathbf{C}$ is not affordable.

That this axiom holds for the economy is due to the existence of a well-behaved social utility function.

I now explain how the WARP is applied. Denote the excess (import) demand functions (correspondences) for goods by $\mathbf{M}(\mathbf{p}) \equiv \mathbf{C}(\mathbf{p}, g(\mathbf{p}, \mathbf{v})) - \mathbf{Q}(\mathbf{p}, \mathbf{v})$, where fixed factor endowments are for simplicity dropped from the excess demand functions (correspondences). Let $\mathbf{p}^a$ be an autarkic price vector.

Result 2.2   Given the budget constraint (Walras's law), the WARP, convex technologies, and perfect competition, for all $\mathbf{p} \geq \mathbf{0}(n)$ and $\mathbf{p} \neq \phi \mathbf{p}^a$ for any constant $\phi > 0$, I have

$$\mathbf{p}^a \cdot \mathbf{M}(\mathbf{p}) > 0. \tag{2.67}$$

Result 2.2 states that under all non-autarkic prices, the aggregate value of excess demands evaluated using autarkic prices must be positive. To prove this result, suppose that there exist two price vectors $\mathbf{p}$ and $\mathbf{p}' \geq \mathbf{0}(n)$ so that

$$\mathbf{p} \cdot \mathbf{M}' \leq \mathbf{p} \cdot \mathbf{M}, \tag{2.68}$$

where $\mathbf{M}$ and $\mathbf{M}'$ are the corresponding excess demand functions. Since $\mathbf{Q}$ and $\mathbf{Q}'$ are the corresponding outputs, convex technologies and profit maximization of firms imply that

$$\mathbf{p} \cdot \mathbf{Q}' \leq \mathbf{p} \cdot \mathbf{Q}. \tag{2.69}$$

Adding up conditions (2.68) and (2.69), I have

$$\mathbf{p} \cdot \mathbf{C}' \leq \mathbf{p} \cdot \mathbf{C}. \tag{2.68'}$$

Using the WARP (condition (2.66)), condition (2.68') implies that

$$\mathbf{p}' \cdot \mathbf{C}' < \mathbf{p}' \cdot \mathbf{C}. \tag{2.70}$$

Reversing the roles of $\mathbf{p}$ and $\mathbf{p}'$, condition (2.69) can be written as

$$\mathbf{p}' \cdot \mathbf{Q}' \geq \mathbf{p}' \cdot \mathbf{Q}. \tag{2.69'}$$

Subtract condition (2.69') from (2.70) to give

$$\mathbf{p}' \cdot \mathbf{M}' < \mathbf{p}' \cdot \mathbf{M}. \tag{2.71}$$

Thus condition (2.68) and the WARP imply condition (2.71). Now let $\mathbf{p}'$ be an autarkic equilibrium price vector and denote it by $\mathbf{p}^a$. This means that the corresponding excess demands are nonpositive, $\mathbf{M}^a \leq \mathbf{0}(n)$. Since $\mathbf{p} \geq \mathbf{0}(n)$, I have $\mathbf{p} \cdot \mathbf{M}^a \leq 0$. Because of the budget constraint (Walras's law), $\mathbf{p} \cdot \mathbf{M} = 0$ for all $\mathbf{p} \geq \mathbf{0}(n)$. This means that if $\mathbf{p}'$ is an autarkic price vector, condition

(2.68) always holds. Using the above result, I conclude that (2.71) always holds. Again because of Walras's law, I have $\mathbf{p}^a \cdot \mathbf{M}^a = 0$. Condition (2.71) then implies Result 2.2.

Note that Varian (1992, pp. 399–400) proves a similar result for a pure exchange economy.

Result 2.3   (Arrow, Block, and Hurwicz, 1959; Hotaka, 1971) Given Walras's law, homogeneity of the excess demand functions, and gross substitutability of goods, for all $\mathbf{p} \geq \mathbf{0}(n)$ and $\mathbf{p} \neq \phi \mathbf{p}^a$ for any constant $\phi > 0$, I have

$$\mathbf{p}^a \cdot \mathbf{M}(\mathbf{p}) > 0.$$

In Result 2.3, goods are said to be gross substitutes if an increase in any price while all other prices are fixed will increase the demands for all goods other than that of the initial good. I now prove that under the conditions stated in Results 2.2 and 2.3, an autarkic equilibrium is both unique and globally stable.

Result 2.4   If $\mathbf{p}^a \cdot \mathbf{M}(\mathbf{p}) > 0$ for all $\mathbf{p} \geq \mathbf{0}(n)$ and $\mathbf{p} \neq \phi \mathbf{p}^a$ for any constant $\phi > 0$, where $\mathbf{p}^a$ is an autarkic price vector, then the equilibrium price vector is unique.

To prove this result, suppose that $\mathbf{p}^a$ and $\widetilde{\mathbf{p}}$ are two autarkic price vectors and $\mathbf{p}^a \neq \phi \widetilde{\mathbf{p}}$ for any constant $\phi > 0$. At the latter equilibrium, $\mathbf{M}(\widetilde{\mathbf{p}}) \leq \mathbf{0}(n)$. Multiply $\mathbf{M}(\widetilde{\mathbf{p}})$ by $\mathbf{p}^a$, and I have

$$\mathbf{p}^a \cdot \mathbf{M}(\widetilde{\mathbf{p}}) \leq \mathbf{0}(n). \tag{2.72}$$

However, condition (2.72) contradicts condition (2.67). Thus I must have a unique autarkic price vector.

Result 2.5   Suppose that the price of good i, $i = 1, \ldots, n$, adjusts according to $\dot{p}_i = \theta_i M_i(\mathbf{p})$ where θ_i is a positive constant. If Walras's law holds, and if $\mathbf{p}^a \cdot \mathbf{M}(\mathbf{p}) > 0$ for all $\mathbf{p} \geq \mathbf{0}(n)$ and $\mathbf{p} \neq \phi \mathbf{p}^a$ for any constant $\phi > 0$, where $\mathbf{p}^a$ is the autarkic price vector, then the autarkic equilibrium is globally stable.

A sketch of this result is provided as follows. Define a function $L = \sum_i \left[(p_i - p_i^a)/\theta_i \right]^2$. I wish to show that L is a Liaponov function.[21] First, note that $L \geq 0$. At the equilibrium point, $L = 0$, and at other points, $L > 0$. The rate of change of L with respect to time is

---

21. For the properties of a Liaponov function, see Takayama (1985, pp. 347–356) or Varian (1992, pp. 484–485).

$$\dot{L} = 2 \sum_i \left(\frac{p_i - p_i^a}{\theta_i} \right) \dot{p}_i$$

$$= 2 \sum_i \left(p_i - p_i^a \right) M_i(\mathbf{p})$$

$$= -2 \sum_i p_i^a M_i(\mathbf{p}) \qquad\qquad \text{[Walras's law]}$$

$$< 0. \qquad\qquad\qquad\qquad\qquad \text{[condition (2.67)]}$$

This means that function L is declining over time, and I conclude that (assuming boundedness of the prices) it is a Liaponov function and that the equilibrium is globally stable.

Results 2.4 and 2.5 are related, because if an equilibrium is globally stable, it must be unique.

Result 2.6   Suppose that Walras's law holds. Given a quasi-concave social utility function, convex technologies, and perfect competition, or given gross substitutability of all goods and homogeneity of excess demands, an autarkic equilibrium is unique and Walrasian stable.

2.10   The Offer Curve

The ITU function is closely related to the DTU function. To show the relationship between these two functions, note that the ITU function can be defined in an alternative way:

$$V(\mathbf{p}, \mathbf{v}, b) = \max_{\mathbf{E}} \{ U(\mathbf{E}, \mathbf{v}) : \mathbf{p} \cdot \mathbf{E} + b \geq 0 \}. \tag{2.60$'$}$$

In (2.60$'$), $\mathbf{p} \cdot \mathbf{E} + b \geq 0$ is the budget constraint, or the trade account balance, of the economy. To see that (2.60$'$) is equivalent to (2.60), note that using the definitions of the DTU and GDP functions, (2.60$'$) can be written as

$$V(\mathbf{p}, \mathbf{v}, b) = \max_{\mathbf{C}, \mathbf{Q}, \mathbf{E}} \left\{ u(\mathbf{C}) : \mathbf{C} = \mathbf{Q} - \mathbf{E}, \ \Gamma(\mathbf{Q}, \mathbf{v}) \leq 0, \ \mathbf{p} \cdot \mathbf{E} \geq -b \right\}$$

$$= \max_{\mathbf{C}, \mathbf{Q}} \left\{ u(\mathbf{C}) : \mathbf{p} \cdot \mathbf{C} \leq \mathbf{p} \cdot \mathbf{Q} + b, \ \Gamma(\mathbf{Q}, \mathbf{v}) \leq 0 \right\}$$

$$= \max_{\mathbf{C}} \left\{ u(\mathbf{C}) : \mathbf{p} \cdot \mathbf{C} \leq g(\mathbf{p}, \mathbf{v}) + b \right\}.$$

The definition of the ITU function in (2.60$'$) is useful. For example, its first-order condition gives

$$\frac{\partial U/\partial E_i}{\partial U/\partial E_\ell} = \frac{p_i}{p_\ell}, \tag{2.73}$$

for any two traded goods i and ℓ. Equation (2.73) states that the optimal trade point occurs at a point of tangency between a trade indifference curve and a price line.

The locus of $\mathbf{E}$, where $\mathbf{E} = \mathbf{E}(\mathbf{p}, \mathbf{v}, b)$ for some $\mathbf{p} \geq \mathbf{0}(n)$ and b, is called the *offer surface* of the economy (or *offer curve* when there are two traded goods). Points on the offer surface must satisfy the budget constraint in (2.60'): $\mathbf{p} \cdot \mathbf{E} + b = 0.$[22] For example, with $b = 0$, Figure 2.16 shows two price lines p' and p'' passing through the origin. The locus of the points of tangency such as A and B is the offer curve of the economy.

The offer curve has the following properties:

1. If $b = 0$, it exists only in the first and third quadrants in Figure 2.16 because of the budget constraint of the economy.

2. It sooner or later bends backward and toward the axes representing the imported goods. This occurs when the income effect of a price change outweighs the substitution effect.

3. If $b = 0$, it touches a trade indifference curve at the origin and has a slope of the autarky price ratio. To see why, totally differentiate the budget constraint (trade balance) to give $\mathbf{p} \cdot d\mathbf{E} + \mathbf{E} \cdot d\mathbf{p} = 0$. At the autarkic point, $\mathbf{E} = \mathbf{0}(n)$. This implies that $\mathbf{p} \cdot d\mathbf{E} = 0$, which means that the price vector is perpendicular to the offer surface, or that the price line is tangent to the offer curve for the two-good case shown in Figure 2.16.

4. For $b = 0$, it is on or above the autarkic price line p^a through the origin. It is because with quasi-convex preferences and convex technologies, the trade indifference curve u^a is on or above the autarkic price line, and u^a is the minimum utility level with respect to commodity prices for the economy.

2.11   International Trade Equilibrium

I now introduce a second country. Let me label the two countries the "home" country and the "foreign" country. Both countries have economies characterized by the above framework, but they may have different endowments, technologies, and preferences. I denote the variables of the foreign country by asterisks. (Home country variables do not have asterisks.)

---

22. I use equality rather than inequality in the budget constraint because of the assumption of nonsatiation.

Suppose that all goods are tradable while the first m^t factors but not the rest can move across countries.[23] As I explained before, the GDP function can be written as $g(\mathbf{p}, \mathbf{v}^t + \mathbf{k}, \mathbf{v}^n)$, where $\mathbf{k}$ represents the inflow of foreign factors (negative elements for outflow of domestic factors). The ITU function is then stated as $V(\mathbf{p}, \mathbf{v}^t + \mathbf{k}, \mathbf{v}^n, b)$. For convenience drop factor endowments from relevant functions. For example, the ITU function can be written as $V(\mathbf{p}, \mathbf{k}, b)$. Assuming differentiability of the ITU function, the export supply function of sector i, $i = 1, \ldots, n$, is defined as

$$E_i(\mathbf{p}, \mathbf{k}, b) = \frac{\partial V/\partial p_i}{\partial V/\partial b} = \frac{1}{\lambda}\frac{\partial V}{\partial p_i}.$$

Making use of the export functions, the free-trade equilibrium conditions are

$$\mathbf{E}(\mathbf{p}, \mathbf{k}, b) + \mathbf{E}^*(\mathbf{p}^*, \mathbf{k}^*, b^*) = 0 \tag{2.74a}$$

$$\mathbf{k} + \mathbf{k}^* = 0 \tag{2.74b}$$

$$\mathbf{p} = \mathbf{p}^* \tag{2.74c}$$

$$\mathbf{r}(\mathbf{p}, \mathbf{k}) = \mathbf{r}^*(\mathbf{p}^*, \mathbf{k}^*) \tag{2.74d}$$

$$b = -b^* = -\mathbf{r}(\mathbf{p}, \mathbf{k}) \cdot \mathbf{k}. \tag{2.74e}$$

Conditions (2.74a) and (2.74b) give the equilibrium conditions for the goods and capital markets, while conditions (2.74c) and (2.74d) are due to equalization of the prices of the trading goods and moving factors. The prices of the mobile factors, $\mathbf{r}(\mathbf{p}, \mathbf{k})$ and $\mathbf{r}^*(\mathbf{p}^*, \mathbf{k}^*)$, are equal to the differentiation of the GDP functions with respect to the mobile factors. In condition (2.74e), the transfer is due to the repatriation of income earned by the moving factors.

In conditions (2.74), there are $2n + 2m^t + 2$ equations to solve for $2n + 2m^t + 2$ unknowns: $\mathbf{p}, \mathbf{p}^*, \mathbf{k}, \mathbf{k}^*, b$, and b^*. Because of the budget constraints of the countries (Walras's law), two of the equations are redundant so that I can choose one of the goods or factors as the numeraire and set its price to be unity (assuming that it is positive). If I choose a home tradable good as a numeraire so that its price is unity, then by (2.74c) the equilibrium foreign price of the good is also unity. Denote the solution by $(\mathbf{k}_0, \mathbf{k}_0^*, \mathbf{p}_0, \mathbf{p}_0^*, b_0, b_0^*)$.

Recall the offer curve of a two-good economy explained in the previous section. For the home country, the foreign offer curve shows all trade opportuni-

23. The assumption that all goods are tradable is made to simplify my notation but can easily be relaxed. If nontradable goods are present, equilibrium condition (2.74a) can be broken up into three conditions, with the first condition representing zero excess demand in the world markets of the tradable goods, and the second and third conditions representing zero excess demand of the nontradable goods in the home and foreign countries, respectively. Alternatively, the equilibrium prices of the nontradable goods in the countries can be derived by using the theorem of autarkic commodity prices.

ties it faces; similarly, the home offer curve represents the trade opportunities for the foreign country. This result provides a graphical method of depicting the free trade equilibrium in this simple framework. In Figure 2.16, if I super-impose a diagram showing the foreign offer curve in such a way that the E_1 axis coincides with the M_1^* axis, and the M_2 axis with the E_2^* axis, then the intersecting point of the two offer curves represents the free-trade equilibrium.

I now examine the stability conditions of the trading model in (2.74). For two reasons, Results 2.1 to 2.4 may not be applied to analyze the stability of an international equilibrium. Even if I assume the existence of a social utility function for each country, the Weak Axiom of Revealed Preference (WARP) may not hold for the countries as a whole. Without the WARP, condition (2.67) may not be true, and an international equilibrium may not be unique and globally stable.

Secondly, in Results 2.3 and 2.4, a *tâtonnement* process is assumed. Such an adjustment process can be extended to international trade in goods. However, for international factor movements, the assumption of a *tâtonnement* process is much stronger. It is more reasonable to assume that a disequilibruim in an international factor market exists in the form of a gap between factor prices in the two countries, and the factor flows between countries in response to the factor price gap. In other words, for international factor movement, it is more appealing to allow quantity (factor flows) adjustment instead of price adjustment.

Let me define two functions: n-dimensional $\Theta(\mathbf{p}, \mathbf{k}) \equiv -\big[\mathbf{E}(\mathbf{p}, \mathbf{k}, b) + \mathbf{E}^*(\mathbf{p}, -\mathbf{k}, -b)\big]$ and m-dimensional $\Phi(\mathbf{p}, \mathbf{k}) \equiv \big[\mathbf{r}(\mathbf{p}, \mathbf{k}) - \mathbf{r}^*(\mathbf{p}, -\mathbf{k})\big]$ where b is given by (2.74e). Function $\Theta(\mathbf{p}, \mathbf{k})$ represents the excess demands for the goods and $\Phi(\mathbf{p}, \mathbf{k})$ is the domestic prices of the mobile factors over those of the foreign prices. It is clear that at the equilibrium point, $\Theta(\mathbf{p}_0, \mathbf{k}_0) = \mathbf{0}(n)$ and $\Phi(\mathbf{p}_0, \mathbf{k}_0) = \mathbf{0}(m')$.

I here assume the following adjustment equations:

$$\dot{\mathbf{p}} = \Theta(\mathbf{p}, \mathbf{k}) \tag{2.75a}$$

$$\dot{\mathbf{k}} = \Phi(\mathbf{p}, \mathbf{k}). \tag{2.75b}$$

There is an asymmetry in the adjustment rules in (2.75). Condition (2.75a) is based on a *tâtonnement* (Walrasian) process while condition (2.75b) assumes quantity (Marshallian) adjustments.

Conditions (2.75) allow me to analyze the dynamic adjustment of the variables. Here I consider for simplicity a linear approximation system and local stability. Expanding the Taylor series of Θ and Φ around the equilibrium point, I have

$$\begin{bmatrix} \dot{\mathbf{p}} \\ \dot{\mathbf{k}} \end{bmatrix} = \begin{bmatrix} \Theta_{\mathbf{p}} & \Theta_{\mathbf{k}} \\ \Phi_{\mathbf{p}} & \Phi_{\mathbf{k}} \end{bmatrix} \begin{bmatrix} \mathbf{p} - \mathbf{p}_0 \\ \mathbf{k} - \mathbf{k}_0 \end{bmatrix}, \tag{2.76}$$

where the derivatives of functions Θ and Φ are evaluated at the equilibrium point. Denote the $(n + m') \times (n + m')$ matrix in (2.76) by Ω. To have (local) stability, the real part of any eigenvalue of Ω must be negative. A sufficient condition for this condition is that Ω is negative semidefinite. Alternatively, the Routh-Hurwitz condition gives the necessary and sufficient condition for negative real parts of eigenvalues. A necessary condition for the Routh-Hurwitz condition is that the trace of Ω is negative.[24] Note that by Walras's law, if all but one of the markets are stable, so is the last one.

In the 2×2 system, if only the goods are tradable and if no international factor movements are allowed, the stability condition for each market is that the aggregate export supply is increasing in its own price. By Walras's law, if one market is stable, so is the other one. Thus the stability analysis can concentrate on just the good-1 market, for example. Define p as the relative price of good 1 and denote the export function for good 1 of the home country by $E_1(p, 0, 0)$ (negative for an import). As before, foreign variables are distinguished by asterisks. The stability condition that the trace of Ω is negative reduces to

$$\frac{\partial E_1}{\partial p} + \frac{\partial E_1^*}{\partial p^*} > 0. \tag{2.77}$$

Without loss of generality, assume that the home country exports good 1 and imports good 2. Thus its export is $E_1 > 0$ and import is $M_2 > 0$. Similarly, let $M_1^* = -E_1^* > 0$. Define the following elasticities:

$$\varepsilon^e \equiv \frac{p}{E_1} \frac{\partial E_1}{\partial p}, \quad \text{home elasticity of export;}$$

$$\varepsilon \equiv -\frac{1/p}{M_2} \frac{\partial M_2}{\partial 1/p} = \frac{p}{M_2} \frac{\partial M_2}{\partial p}, \quad \text{home elasticity of import;}$$

$$\varepsilon^* \equiv -\frac{p^*}{M_1^*} \frac{\partial M_1^*}{\partial p^*} = -\frac{p^*}{E_1^*} \frac{\partial E_1^*}{\partial p^*}, \quad \text{foreign elasticity of import;}$$

Making use these elasticities and the fact that $\varepsilon^e + 1 = \varepsilon$[25] condition (2.77) reduces to

$$\varepsilon + \varepsilon^* > 1, \tag{2.77'}$$

which is the Marshall-Lerner condition.[26]

---

24. For a discussion about stability of equilibrium see, for example, Takayama (1985, pp. 302–319).

25. The condition that $\varepsilon^e + 1 = \varepsilon$ can be obtained by differentiating the trade balance equation $pE_1 = M_2$.

26. It is interesting to note that although condition (2.77') is due to Marshall (and Lerner), it is based on the Walrasian adjustment process.

Appendix

This appendix proves some of the results stated in this chapter.

1. I first prove that the GDP function is convex in $\mathbf{p}$. Consider any two price vectors, $\mathbf{p} \geq \mathbf{0}(n)$ and $\mathbf{p}' \geq \mathbf{0}(n)$. Define $\mathbf{p}'' = \phi\mathbf{p} + (1 - \phi)\mathbf{p}'$ where $0 \leq \phi \leq 1$, and let the corresponding optimal output be $\mathbf{Q}''$. Because $\mathbf{Q}''$ is feasible, the definition of the GDP function implies

$$g(\mathbf{p}, \mathbf{v}) \geq \mathbf{p} \cdot \mathbf{Q}'' \tag{A.1a}$$

$$g(\mathbf{p}', \mathbf{v}) \geq \mathbf{p}' \cdot \mathbf{Q}''. \tag{A.1b}$$

Multiply (A.1a) by ϕ and (A.1b) by $(1 - \phi)$, and add up these two equations to give

$$\phi g(\mathbf{p}, \mathbf{v}) + (1 - \phi)g(\mathbf{p}', \mathbf{v}) \geq \mathbf{p}'' \cdot \mathbf{Q}'' = g(\mathbf{p}'', \mathbf{v}),$$

which is the condition for convexity.   ■

2. I next prove that the GDP function is concave in $\mathbf{v}$. Consider two factor endowments, $\mathbf{v}$ and $\mathbf{v}'$, and define $\mathbf{v}'' = \phi\mathbf{v} + (1 - \phi)\mathbf{v}'$ where $0 \leq \phi \leq 1$. Denote the optimal factor prices that solves the problem in (2.28″) when factor endowments are $\mathbf{v}''$ by $\mathbf{w}''$. Thus $g(\mathbf{p}, \mathbf{v}'') = \mathbf{w}'' \cdot \mathbf{v}''$. Because $\mathbf{w}''$ is feasible, that is, $c_i(\mathbf{w}'') \geq \mathbf{p}_i$ for all i, the definition of the GDP function gives

$$g(\mathbf{p}, \mathbf{v}) \leq \mathbf{w}'' \cdot \mathbf{v} \tag{A.2a}$$

$$g(\mathbf{p}, \mathbf{v}') \leq \mathbf{w}'' \cdot \mathbf{v}' \tag{A.2b}$$

Multiply (A.2a) by ϕ and (A.2b) by $(1 - \phi)$ and add up the two equations to give

$$\phi g(\mathbf{p}, \mathbf{v}) + (1 - \phi)g(\mathbf{p}, \mathbf{v}') \leq \mathbf{w}'' \cdot \mathbf{v}'' = g(\mathbf{p}, \mathbf{v}''),$$

which implies concavity.   ■

3. I now prove that if the households' utility functions are concave and if the social welfare function is quasi-concave, then the social utility function is quasi-concave. Consider two aggregate consumption bundles $\mathbf{C}$ and $\mathbf{C}'$. Let the corresponding optimal consumption bundles of the hth household be $\mathbf{C}^h$ and $\mathbf{C}^{h'}$, $\mathbf{C} = \sum_h \mathbf{C}^h$ and $\mathbf{C}' = \sum_h \mathbf{C}^{h'}$. Denote the social welfare function by the following compact form $W[u^h(\mathbf{C}^h)]$. Thus $u(\mathbf{C}) = W[u^h(\mathbf{C}^h)]$ and $u(\mathbf{C}') = W[u^h(\mathbf{C}^{h'})]$. Choose ϕ where $0 \leq \phi \leq 1$, and define $\mathbf{C}^{h''} = \phi\mathbf{C}^h + (1 - \phi)\mathbf{C}^{h'}$ and $\mathbf{C}'' = \phi\mathbf{C} + (1 - \phi)\mathbf{C}' = \sum_h \mathbf{C}^{h''}$. Note that $\{\mathbf{C}^{h''}\}$ may not be the optimal distribution of the aggregate consumption bundle. Because the utility function $u^h(.)$ is concave, I have

$$u^h(\mathbf{C}^{h''}) \geq \phi u^h(\mathbf{C}^h) + (1 - \phi)u^h(\mathbf{C}^{h'}). \tag{A.3}$$

Quasi concavity of $u(\mathbf{C})$ comes from the following relations:

$$u(\mathbf{C}'') \geq W[u^h(\mathbf{C}^{h''})]$$

$$\geq W[\phi u^h(\mathbf{C}^h) + (1 - \phi)u^h(\mathbf{C}^{h'})]$$

$$\geq \min \left\{ W[u^h(\mathbf{C}^h)],\, W[u^h(\mathbf{C}^{h'})] \right\}$$

$$= \min \left\{ u(\mathbf{C}),\, u(\mathbf{C}') \right\}.$$

The first inequality is due to the definition of $u(\mathbf{C})$ and the fact that the consumption bundle $\mathbf{C}^{h''}$ given to the hth household may not maximize the social welfare function. The second inequality comes from (A.3) and the fact that $W[\,.\,]$ is increasing. The third one is due to quasi concavity of the social welfare function. ∎

4. I now prove that the DTU function is quasi-concave. Consider two export and factor endowment vectors $(\mathbf{E}, \mathbf{v})$ and $(\mathbf{E}', \mathbf{v}')$. Let the corresponding optimal consumption and production choices be $(\mathbf{C}, \mathbf{Q})$ and $(\mathbf{C}', \mathbf{Q}')$, where $\mathbf{C} = \mathbf{Q} - \mathbf{E}$ and $\mathbf{C}' = \mathbf{Q}' - \mathbf{E}'$. By definition, $U(\mathbf{E}, \mathbf{v}) = u(\mathbf{C})$ and $U(\mathbf{E}', \mathbf{v}') = u(\mathbf{C}')$. Choose ϕ so that $0 \leq \phi \leq 1$ and define $\mathbf{C}'' = \phi \mathbf{C} + (1 - \phi)\mathbf{C}'$ and $\mathbf{Q}'' = \phi \mathbf{Q} + (1 - \phi)\mathbf{Q}'$. Let $\mathbf{E}'' = \mathbf{Q}'' - \mathbf{C}''$. Using the definitions of $\mathbf{C}''$ and $\mathbf{Q}''$, I have $\mathbf{E}'' = \phi \mathbf{E} + (1 - \phi)\mathbf{E}'$. By quasi concavity of the social utility function, $u(\mathbf{C}'') \geq \min[u(\mathbf{C}), u(\mathbf{C}')]$, and by convexity of the PPS, $\Gamma(\mathbf{Q}'', \mathbf{v}'') \leq 0$, that is, $\mathbf{Q}''$ is feasible. This implies that by the definition of the DTU function, $U(\mathbf{E}'', \mathbf{v}'') \geq u(\mathbf{C}'')$. Combining these results gives

$$U(\mathbf{E}'', \mathbf{v}'') \geq \min[U(\mathbf{E}, \mathbf{v}), U(\mathbf{E}', \mathbf{v}')],$$

which implies quasi concavity. ∎

5. To prove quasi convexity of the ITU function in $\mathbf{p}$, consider two price vectors $\mathbf{p} \geq \mathbf{0}(n)$ and $\mathbf{p}' \geq \mathbf{0}(n)$. Choose ϕ where $0 \leq \phi \leq 1$, and define $\mathbf{p}'' = \phi \mathbf{p} + (1 - \phi)\mathbf{p}'$. Let the corresponding optimal consumption bundle be $\mathbf{C}''$. I need to show that

$$\mathbf{p} \cdot \mathbf{C}'' \leq g(\mathbf{p}, \mathbf{v}) + b \qquad \text{or} \qquad \mathbf{p}' \cdot \mathbf{C}'' \leq g(\mathbf{p}', \mathbf{v}) + b. \tag{A.4}$$

Suppose not, that is,

$$\mathbf{p} \cdot \mathbf{C}'' > g(\mathbf{p}, \mathbf{v}) + b \tag{A.5a}$$

$$\mathbf{p}' \cdot \mathbf{C}'' > g(\mathbf{p}', \mathbf{v}) + b. \tag{A.5b}$$

Multiply (A.5a) by ϕ and (A.5b) by $(1 - \phi)$, and add up the two equations to give

$$\mathbf{p}'' \cdot \mathbf{C}'' > \phi g(\mathbf{p}, \mathbf{v}) + (1 - \phi) g(\mathbf{p}', \mathbf{v}) + b \geq g(\mathbf{p}'', \mathbf{v}) + b. \tag{A.6}$$

The last inequality in (A.6) is due to convexity of $g(\mathbf{p}, \mathbf{v})$ in $\mathbf{p}$. However, (A.6) is contradictory to the budget constraint and the fact that $\mathbf{C}''$ is the optimal consumption bundle at $\mathbf{p}''$. Thus (A.4) holds, which in turn implies

$$V(\mathbf{p}'', \mathbf{v}, b) \leq \max \left[V(\mathbf{p}, \mathbf{v}, b), V(\mathbf{p}', \mathbf{v}, b) \right],$$

which is the condition for quasi convexity. To prove quasi concavity of the ITU function in $\mathbf{v}$, consider two possible factor endowment vectors $\mathbf{v} \geq \mathbf{0}(m)$ and $\mathbf{v}' \geq \mathbf{0}(m)$. For $0 \leq \phi \leq 1$, define $\mathbf{v}'' = \phi \mathbf{v} + (1 - \phi) \mathbf{v}'$. I want to show that the following condition must hold

$$\mathbf{p} \cdot \mathbf{C} \leq g(\mathbf{p}, \mathbf{v}'') + b \qquad \text{or} \qquad \mathbf{p} \cdot \mathbf{C}' \leq g(\mathbf{p}, \mathbf{v}'') + b. \tag{A.7}$$

Suppose not, that is,

$$\mathbf{p} \cdot \mathbf{C} > g(\mathbf{p}, \mathbf{v}'') + b \tag{A.8a}$$

$$\mathbf{p} \cdot \mathbf{C}' > g(\mathbf{p}, \mathbf{v}'') + b. \tag{A.8b}$$

Multiply (A.8a) by ϕ and (A.8b) by $(1 - \phi)$, and add up the equations to give

$$\mathbf{p} \cdot \left[\phi \mathbf{C} + (1 - \phi) \mathbf{C}' \right] > g(\mathbf{p}, \mathbf{v}'') + b \geq \phi g(\mathbf{p}, \mathbf{v}) + (1 - \phi) g(\mathbf{p}, \mathbf{v}') + b. \tag{A.9}$$

The last inequality in (A.9) is due to concavity of $g(\mathbf{p}, \mathbf{v})$ in $\mathbf{v}$. On the other hand, multiply the budget constraint at $\mathbf{v}$ by ϕ and that at $\mathbf{v}'$ by $(1 - \phi)$ and add up the equations to give

$$\mathbf{p} \cdot \left[\phi \mathbf{C} + (1 - \phi) \mathbf{C}' \right] \leq \phi g(\mathbf{p}, \mathbf{v}) + (1 - \phi) g(\mathbf{p}, \mathbf{v}') + b. \tag{A.10}$$

Equations (A.9) and (A.10) are contradictory to each other. This means that (A.7) is true, and it implies

$$V(\mathbf{p}, \mathbf{v}'', b) \geq \min \left[V(\mathbf{p}, \mathbf{v}, b), V(\mathbf{p}, \mathbf{v}', b) \right],$$

which is the condition for quasi concavity. ∎

6. To prove the theorem of autarkic commodity prices, denote the optimal consumption and production bundles corresponding to $\mathbf{p}^a$ by $\mathbf{C}^a$ and $\mathbf{Q}^a$, respectively. Suppose that $\mathbf{p}^a \geq \mathbf{0}(n)$ are autarkic prices, meaning that $\mathbf{C}^a \leq \mathbf{Q}^a$. Multiply both sides of the latter expression by any $\mathbf{p} \geq \mathbf{0}(n)$, giving $\mathbf{p} \cdot \mathbf{C}^a \leq \mathbf{p} \cdot \mathbf{Q}^a$. By the definition of the GDP function, $\mathbf{p} \cdot \mathbf{Q}^a \leq g(\mathbf{p}, \mathbf{v})$. Combining these results gives $\mathbf{p} \cdot \mathbf{C}^a \leq g(\mathbf{p}, \mathbf{v})$, which means that $\mathbf{C}^a$ is feasible at prices $\mathbf{p}$. Thus $V(\mathbf{p}^a, \mathbf{v}, 0) \leq V(\mathbf{p}, \mathbf{v}, 0)$.

Next suppose that $V(\mathbf{p}^a, \mathbf{v}, 0) \leq V(\mathbf{p}, \mathbf{v}, 0)$ for all $\mathbf{p} \geq \mathbf{0}(n)$. Take any $\widetilde{\mathbf{p}} \geq \mathbf{0}(n)$ and denote the corresponding consumption and production by $\widetilde{\mathbf{C}}$ and $\widetilde{\mathbf{Q}}$.

That $\widetilde{\mathbf{C}}$ was not chosen when the prices are $\mathbf{p}^a$ means that $\mathbf{p}^a \cdot \widetilde{\mathbf{C}} \geq g(\mathbf{p}^a, \mathbf{v})$. By the definition of the GDP function, $g(\mathbf{p}^a, \mathbf{v}) \geq \mathbf{p}^a \cdot \widetilde{\mathbf{Q}}$. These two results give

$$\mathbf{p}^a \cdot \widetilde{\mathbf{C}} \geq \mathbf{p}^a \cdot \widetilde{\mathbf{Q}}.$$

This expression is combined with the budget constraint when the prices are $\widetilde{\mathbf{p}}$ to give

$$(\widetilde{\mathbf{p}} - \mathbf{p}^a) \cdot (\widetilde{\mathbf{Q}} - \widetilde{\mathbf{C}}) \geq 0. \tag{A.11}$$

Choose $\widetilde{\mathbf{p}}$ so that it is equal to $\mathbf{p}^a$ except the ith good. Thus (A.11) reduces to

$$(\widetilde{p}_i - p_i^a)(\widetilde{Q}_i - \widetilde{C}_i) \geq 0. \tag{A.11$'$}$$

Thus $(\widetilde{Q}_i - \widetilde{C}_i) \geq 0$ if $\widetilde{p}_i > p_i^a$ and $(\widetilde{Q}_i - \widetilde{C}_i) \leq 0$ if $\widetilde{p}_i < p_i^a$. Denote the right-hand (respectively left-hand) limits of $\widetilde{C}_i$ and $\widetilde{Q}_i$ as $\widetilde{p}_i$ is greater than and approaches p_i^a by $\widetilde{C}_i^+$ and $\widetilde{Q}_i^+$ (respectively $\widetilde{C}_i^-$ and $\widetilde{Q}_i^-$). (A.11$'$) implies that $\widetilde{Q}_i^+ - \widetilde{C}_i^+ \geq 0$ and $\widetilde{Q}_i^- - \widetilde{C}_i^- \leq 0$. In particular, if $p_i^a > 0$ and the production and consumption functions are continuous at p_i^a, then $\widetilde{Q}_i = \widetilde{C}_i$. If $p_i^a = 0$ then $\widetilde{Q}_i \geq \widetilde{C}_i$. Similar analysis can be extended to other markets. So $\mathbf{p}^a$ is an autarkic price vector. ∎

7. I now prove the nonsubstitution theorem for an economy with $n \geq 2$ sectors. Because sector i, $i = 1, \ldots, n$, may use labor and other goods (including itself) in its production, its unit cost function can be written as $c_i(\mathbf{p}, w)$. Using the facts that the function is linearly homogeneous, and that firms earn zero profit in equilibrium, I have

$$\sum_{j=1}^{n} p_j \frac{\partial c_i}{\partial p_j} + w \frac{\partial c_i}{\partial w} = c_i(\mathbf{p}, w). \tag{A.12}$$

Define $\widetilde{p}_j \equiv p_j / w$. Because $c_i(\mathbf{p}, w)$ is linearly homogeneous, its derivatives are homogeneous of degree zero. Both sides of condition (A.12) can be divided by w to give

$$\sum_{j=1}^{n} \widetilde{p}_j \frac{\partial c_i}{\partial p_j} + \frac{\partial c_i}{\partial w} = c_i(\widetilde{\mathbf{p}}, 1), \qquad i = 1, \ldots, n. \tag{A.13}$$

There are n equations in (A.13), which are used to solve for the n commodity prices relative to the wage rate. Assuming a unique solution, I get the theorem. ∎

3   Comparative Advantage and Factor Content of Trade

Adam Smith's *Wealth of Nations* and his theory of absolute advantage initiated the interest in explaining and predicting countries' patterns of trade. Since that time, trade theorists have developed many different theories to analyze and predict trade patterns. In this chapter, I investigate some of those theories and present some recent theoretical developments.

I begin with a fundamental concept called natural trade and a basic result that has many applications. This basic result comes originally from Ricardo's theory of comparative advantage, which can be disaggregated into two components. The first comes directly from the properties of the classical model while the other component, which was later called the law of comparative advantage, is not specific to the classical model but instead can be applied to many other models. This law, and its generalization to higher dimensional frameworks, are explained.

I then discuss a new approach to comparative advantage: factor content of trade. Under this approach, instead of measuring the quantity of goods that flow internationally and the directions of their movements, one measures the quantities of factors embodied in the flowing goods. The usefulness of this approach is that extension to higher dimensional frameworks is relatively painless and more results can be obtained. There are also relationships between factor content of trade and international factor movements.

The original theorems of comparative advantage are derived in static models. Because factors are assumed to be perfectly mobile within an economy (and possibly between economies), an equilibrium is treated as long-run. These static models are characterized by exogenously given factor endowments. There has been interest in examining the patterns of trade in a dynamic context. Some of these dynamic models and their results are discussed later.

3.1   Natural Trade

Natural trade in goods and factor services exists under certain conditions. Consider the m-factor, n-sector framework of two countries (home and foreign countries) introduced in the previous chapter. Suppose that all goods are tradable and that the first m^t factors are internationally mobile. Denote the inflow of foreign factors by the m^t-dimensional vector $\mathbf{k}$ (negative elements for outflow of domestic factors).[1] Use a superscript "w" to denote world levels of domestic prices ($\mathbf{p}$) and prices of the mobile factors ($\mathbf{r}$). Domestic price levels do not have superscript "w". Trade is said to be natural if the following condition holds:

---

1. For simplicity I assume no nontradable goods. If some goods are not tradable, the equilibrium can be analyzed using the techniques suggested in the previous chapter.

$$(\mathbf{p} - \mathbf{p}^w) \cdot \mathbf{M} + (\mathbf{r} - \mathbf{r}^w) \cdot \mathbf{k} \geq 0. \tag{3.1}$$

In (3.1), $(\mathbf{p} - \mathbf{p}^w)$ and $(\mathbf{r} - \mathbf{r}^w)$ are the gaps between domestic and world prices. The left-hand side of (3.1) represents the tax revenue less subsidy expenditure on trading goods and factors. In other words, trade is natural if the government does not have a positive net subsidy expenditure on trading goods and factors.[2]

Five points about natural trade can be noted. First, transport costs have not been ruled out. Second, free trade is a special case of natural trade with $\mathbf{p} = \mathbf{p}^w$ and $\mathbf{r} = \mathbf{r}^w$. Third, no export or import subsidy on any good is only a sufficient but not a necessary condition for a natural trade. Fourth, if trade is balanced so that $\mathbf{p}^w \cdot \mathbf{M} + \mathbf{r}^w \mathbf{k} = 0$, condition (3.1) reduces to

$$\mathbf{p} \cdot \mathbf{M} + \mathbf{r} \cdot \mathbf{k} \geq 0. \tag{3.1$'$}$$

Fifth, natural trade is an assumption stronger than what is needed for some of the results (such as gains from trade) that are explained later.

There are more applications of condition (3.1) later in this chapter, but for the time being let me illustrate the concept of natural trade in the two-factor, two-sector model. With no international factor movement but balanced trade, condition (3.1$'$) reduces to

$$p_1 M_1 + p_2 M_2 \geq 0. \tag{3.2}$$

Making use of the trade balance equation $p_1^w M_1 + p_2^w M_2 = 0$ and depending on the pattern of trade, either

$$\frac{p_1}{p_2} \geq \frac{E_2}{M_1} = \frac{p_1^w}{p_2^w} \quad \text{if} \quad M_1 > 0 \tag{3.3a}$$

or

$$\frac{p_1}{p_2} \leq \frac{M_2}{E_1} = \frac{p_1^w}{p_2^w} \quad \text{if} \quad M_1 < 0, \tag{3.3b}$$

where $E_i = -M_i$ is the level of export of good i. Condition (3.3) states that under natural trade the domestic relative price of the exportable is not greater than its world relative price, no matter what the country's pattern of trade is.

Natural trade and condition (3.3) can be illustrated in Figure 3.1. Without loss of generality, I assume that the economy exports good 1. Line P and P$'$ are two domestic price lines, with a slope equal to $-p_1/p_2$. Line P^w is the world price line with a slope of $-p_1^w/p_2^w$. By condition (3.3), the world price line is

---

2. The term "natural trade" is due to Deardorff (1980). Because of condition (3.1), which requires non-negative tariff revenue, it is also called "trade under self-financing tariffs" by Ohyama (1972).

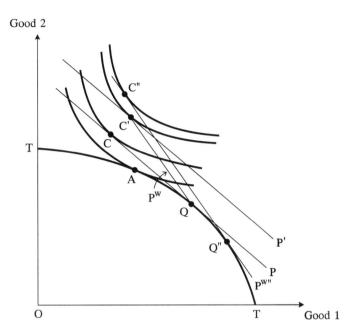

Good 2

Figure 3.1

steeper than the domestic price line. Assuming that any tax revenue the government receives is distributed to the households in a lump-sum fashion, the gap between domestic price lines P and P′ is equal to the tariff revenue given by the terms on the lefthand side of (3.1). Thus line P, which is tangent to the production possibility frontier (PPF) at the production point Q, represents the national product of the economy while line P′ represents the national income of the economy.[3] By the definition of natural trade, line P′ must be above line P. The consumption is at point C′ at which a social indifference curve is tangent to line P′. The diagram also shows the autarkic point A at which a social indifference curve is tangent to the PPF. The tangent (not shown in the diagram) to the PPF at point A represents the autarkic price line. Comparing the autarkic price line, the domestic price line under trade P, and the world trade price line P^w in the diagram, I can establish the following condition

$$\frac{p_1^a}{p_2^a} < \frac{p_1}{p_2} < \frac{p_1^w}{p_2^w}, \tag{3.4}$$

---

3. If, however, the economy does not receive the revenue, as in the case of voluntary export restraints imposed by the other country, the consumption point of the economy will be at the point of tangency C between a social indifference curve and the price line P in Figure 3.1. In this case, national product of the economy is the same as its national income.

for the country that exports good 1. If free trade exists, the second inequality is replaced by equality, and if the world price ratio is the same as the autarkic price ratio, the first inequality is also replaced by an equality. Therefore a more general expression is

$$\frac{p_1^a}{p_2^a} \le \frac{p_1}{p_2} \le \frac{p_1^w}{p_2^w}. \tag{3.4$'$}$$

If the country exports good 2, the inequality ranking in (3.4$'$) is reversed.

To illustrate the implications of natural trade, I also show the free trade equilibrium for a small open economy in Figure 3.1. A second world price line, P$^{w''}$, is tangent to the PPF at the free-trade production point Q$''$ and a higher indifference curve at the consumption point C$''$. Points Q$''$ and C$''$ are the two extreme points of the hypotenuse of the free-trade trade triangle, while points Q and C$'$ are those for the trade triangle under natural trade. A comparison of the sizes of these two triangles shows that the volume of trade is smaller under natural trade than under free trade.

The detrimental effect of natural trade on the volume of trade is also illustrated in Figure 3.2. Under free trade, the offer curve of the home country is depicted by curve OC. Trade restrictions under natural trade due to a fixed tar-

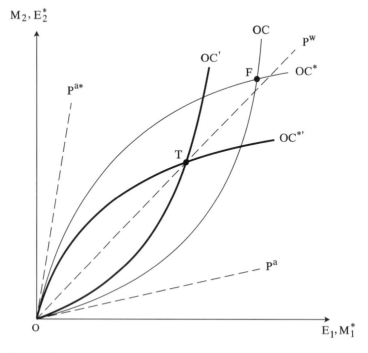

Figure 3.2

iff rate, for example, shift the offer curve inward to OC', meaning that at any given world price ratio, the trade triangle is smaller.

3.2   The Law of Comparative Advantage

For the time being, consider a two-country, two-good framework. Without loss of generality, I assume that the home country exports good 1. Because the two countries face the same world prices under trade, (3.4') can be applied to both countries to give

$$\frac{p_1^a}{p_2^a} \leq \frac{p_1}{p_2} \leq \frac{p_1^w}{p_2^w} \leq \frac{p_1^*}{p_2^*} \leq \frac{p_1^{a*}}{p_2^{a*}}, \tag{3.5}$$

where as before the variables of the foreign countries were distinguished by an asterisk. Condition (3.5) states that if the home country exports good 1, it must have a lower autarkic relative price of good 1 and the world relative price of good 1 under trade must be in between the autarkic relative prices of good 1 in the two countries. The more interesting case is of course the one in which the autarkic prices of countries are known and they are used to predict patterns of trade. Suppose that I have

$$\frac{p_1^a}{p_2^a} < \frac{p_1^{a*}}{p_2^{a*}}. \tag{3.6}$$

Given condition (3.6), condition (3.5) excludes the possibility that the home country exports good 2.[4] By condition (3.6), the home (respectively foreign) country is said to have a comparative advantage in good 1 (respectively 2). Thus if trade exists, the home country must export good 1. These results are summarized by the following law:

The Law of Comparative Advantage   Assume that natural trade exists between the countries: (1) Each country exports the good in which it has a comparative advantage; and (2) the world price ratio under trade is in between the autarkic price ratios in the countries.

In a two-sector framework, the law of comparative advantage can be illustrated by Figure 3.2. OC and OC* are the offer curve under free trade of the home and foreign countries. For example, natural trade due to fixed tariffs imposed by government shifts these offer curves to OC' and OC*'. Because of the definition of natural trade, the offer curve of each country must shift toward to the axis that represents its importable good. Point T is the equilibrium

---

4. If the home country exports good 2, then condition (3.5) with the reversed order holds, but it violates condition (3.6).

point under natural trade. The diagram shows the case in which condition (3.6) holds, meaning that the home country has a comparative advantage in good 1. The diagram confirms parts (1) and (2) of the law.

In the previous chapter, I showed that the autarkic price of each good in the Ricardian model is proportional to its labor-output coefficient, that is,

$$\frac{p_1^a}{p_2^a} = \frac{a_1}{a_2}.$$

Thus if the home country versus the foreign country is more efficient in producing good 1 in the sense that its ratio of sector-1 labor-output coefficient to sector-2 labor-output coefficient is lower, that is,

$$\frac{a_1}{a_2} < \frac{a_1^*}{a_2^*}, \tag{3.7}$$

then the relative price of good 1 is lower in the home country under autarky and condition (3.6) holds. By the law of comparative advantage, the home country exports good 1. This result is summarized as follows.

The Ricardo Theorem of Comparative Advantage   Each country exports the good in which it has a comparative labor-productivity advantage (Ricardo, 1817. Chapter 7).

Conceptually, the Ricardo theorem of comparative advantage can be broken up into two components: (1) Each country exports the good in which it has a comparative advantage; (2) The comparative advantage of a country is the good which, vis-à-vis the other country, has a lower labor-output ratio relative to that of the other good. It is noted that part (1) of this theorem is part (1) of the law of comparative advantage.

The significance of the Ricardo theorem of comparative advantage is that autarkic price ratios, and thus patterns of trade, of two trading countries are explained entirely by the countries' technologies, and their preferences do not play any role (as long as both goods are produced under autarky).

The law of comparative advantage also applies to international factor movements. Consider a two-factor, two-sector model and suppose that capital is mobile with capital owners repatriating good 1. (The result does not depend on which goods they repatriate.) Only repatriation of goods, but not trade in goods, is allowed. If the price of capital relative to good 1 is cheaper in the foreign country under autarky, meaning that the foreign autarkic rental rate in terms of good 1 is lower than that in the home country, then foreign capital owners will have an incentive to move their capital to the home country. This gives part (1) of the law. Furthermore, following the Rybczynski theorem and for the host country, the capital inflow will encourage the output of the capital-intensive good (say, good 1) while discouraging that of the labor-intensive good (good 2) in the home country. Assuming no inferior goods, the domestic equilibrium relative price of good 1 will drop. By the Stolper-Samuelson theorem, the real rental rate falls. Just the opposite exists in the foreign country. Thus the world equilibrium rental rate in terms of good 1 is between the autarkic rental rates. This gives part (2) of the law.

3.3   The Factor Endowment Theory of Comparative Advantage

The Heckschler-Ohlin theorem of comparative advantage, which is based on the factor endowments of the trading countries, is the most important theory of trade patterns in the neoclassical models. This section examines its content, interpretation, and applications. For the time being, let me consider the theorem in the framework described in the previous chapter and the previous section in the present chapter: two factors, two sectors, and two countries which have identical and linearly homogeneous production functions, and identical and homothetic preferences.

The Heckscher-Ohlin theorem is stated as follows:

The Heckscher-Ohlin Theorem   Suppose that there are two trading goods and that trade is natural. Each country exports the good which uses its abundant factor intensively (Heckscher, 1919; Ohlin, 1933).

There are two ways of defining factor abundance. The home country vis-à-vis the foreign country is said to be labor abundant and capital scarce according to the price definition if the home country has a lower wage-rental ratio under autarky. It is labor abundant according to the physical or quantity definition if

$$\frac{\overline{K}}{\overline{L}} < \frac{\overline{K}^*}{\overline{L}^*}. \tag{3.8}$$

I first prove the Heckscher-Ohlin theorem using the price definition of factor abundance. Without loss of generality, let good 1 be labor intensive. The one-to-one correspondence between factor prices and commodity prices developed in Chapter 2 shows that if the home country vis-à-vis the foreign country has a lower autarkic wage-rental ratio, then identical technologies imply that it must have a lower relative price of labor-intensive good 1. By the law of comparative advantage, it can be concluded that the home country exports good 1 under natural trade.

I now prove the theorem using the quantity definition of factor abundance. The proof can be divided into the following steps.

1. I start with a hypothetical situation in which the foreign factor endowments are constant multiples of the home factor endowments. Because by assumption the two countries have identical, convex, and constant-returns technologies, and identical, quasi-convex, and homothetic preferences, the two countries have the same autarkic commodity price ratio, which is assumed to be unique. Thus in this hypothetical situation trade does not exist even if it is allowed.

2. Suppose that the home country receives a fixed additional amount of labor. Condition (3.8) is satisfied, meaning that the home country is labor abundant while the foreign country is capital abundant.

3. By the Rybczynski theorem, the increase in labor endowment in the home country leads to an expansion of its output of labor-intensive good 1 and a contraction of its output of good 2 at the original price ratio. Given homothetic preferences, the output changes lead to an excess supply of good 1 and an excess demand for good 2 in the country. A new autarkic equilibrium in the home country is reached, with a lower price ratio of good 1 than that in the foreign country.

4. By the law of comparative advantage, the home country exports good 1 and imports good 2. This gives the Heckscher-Ohlin theorem.

The Rybczynski theorem plays a very important role in step 3 of this proof. I show in the previous chapter that the validity of the Rybczynski theorem requires certain conditions: no factor intensity reversal (FIR), diversification in production, and constant prices. This raises the question: If complete specialization or FIR cannot be ruled out so that the Rybczynski theorem is no longer valid, how would the validity of the Heckscher-Ohlin theorem be affected?[5]

To answer this question, first relax the assumption of diversification in production. Suppose that in step (3) of the proof, the increase in labor endowment in the home country is so significant that at the original price ratio the home country specializes in producing the labor-intensive good, good 1. This creates an excess supply of good 1 and an excess demand for good 2 if prices do not change. So the autarkic relative price of good 1 must drop. One can then take step (4) of the proof to give the Heckscher-Ohlin theorem. This means that in applying the Rybczynski theorem, one does not need the assumption of diversification at the initial autarkic prices.

I now turn to the validity of the Heckscher-Ohlin theorem in the presence of FIR. It is usually believed that when FIR cannot be ruled out, the theorem

---

5. Validity of the Rybczynski theorem also requires constant commodity prices. In proving the Heckscher-Ohlin theorem, constant commodity prices are assumed in the hypothetical situation in order to compare the excess demands in the countries.

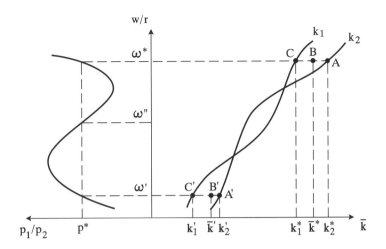

Figure 3.3

is not valid;[6] however, I argue that even if FIR is present the theorem *remains valid if factor intensities of sectors are ranked using the actual capital-labor ratios.*

I now explain in detail the possible validity of the Heckscher-Ohlin theorem in the presence of FIR. Figure 3.3 is similar to a diagram given in the previous chapter. With a capital-labor ratio of $\overline{k}^*$, the foreign autarkic relative price of good 1 and wage-rental ratio are p^* and ω^*, respectively. Following step (1) of the preceding proof, the home country's capital-labor ratio is initially equal to $\overline{k}^*$. An increase in labor endowment (step 2) lowers the home country's capital-labor ratio to a new level denoted by $\overline{k}'$. If $\overline{k}^*$ and $\overline{k}'$ are separated by odd number of FIRs, the countries have different factor intensity rankings, and thus it is usually claimed that the Heckscher-Ohlin theorem must be violated for at least one country. It is also claimed that the theorem is still not valid even if $\overline{k}^*$ and $\overline{k}'$ are separated by even numbers of FIRs so that the countries have the same factor intensity ranking. This argument is shown in Figure 3.3, in which there are two FIRs between $\overline{k}^*$ and $\overline{k}'$. Following step (3) of the preceding proof, I hypothetically keep the commodity price ratio in the country at p^*. The wage-rental ratio changes because of the FIRs. Denote the corresponding capital-labor ratios in sector i by k_i', $i = 1, 2$. As analyzed in the previous chapter, if the new home capital-labor ratio is such that $\overline{k}'$ is slightly less that k_1' (respectively slightly greater than k_2'), the home country is specialized in producing good 1 (respectively good 2). Because the pattern of production of the home country is no longer predictable, the good exported

6. See, for example, Jones (1956–1957) and Ethier (1988, p. 135).

by the home country is not known unless the exact value of $\bar{k}'$ is given. This means that being labor abundant is not sufficient to predict the patterns of trade of the countries. Thus, as is usually stated, the Heckscher-Ohlin theorem is not valid when FIR is present.

I now argue that the preceding pessimistic view is misplaced and that the theorem is still valid if the actual capital-labor ratios of trading goods are used to rank the factor intensities of the sectors. Without loss of generality, suppose that the home country exports good 2 while the foreign country exports good 1 under free trade. Let me again refer to Figure 3.3, except that p^* is now interpreted as the free-trade price ratio faced by both countries. Based on this pattern of trade, I compare the capital-labor ratio of sector 2 in the home country, which is equal to k'_2 as given by the diagram, with that of sector 1 in the foreign country, k^*_1. Figure 3.3 gives $k'_2 < k^*_1$. From this, I can say that good 2 is labor intensive and good 1 is capital intensive. Because the home country is labor abundant and it exports the labor-intensive good 2, I thus conclude that the Heckscher-Ohlin theorem is valid, whether or not FIR is present. This conclusion stands even if the home country exports good 1. In this case, I need to compare k'_1 with k^*_2. Because $k'_1 < k^*_2$, good 1 is now labor intensive and exported by the labor-abundant country, the home country. This is just what the theorem states.

Some remarks about the present interpretation of the theorem are needed.

1. It is possible that under p^* both countries have the same ratio of output of good 1 to output of good 2. Because of identical and homothetic preferences, the countries have no incentive to trade. To allow for this possibility and still have the Heckscher-Ohlin theorem, I slightly modify the theorem to say that *if trade exists*, each country exports the good that uses its abundant factor intensively where factor intensities are defined using the actual capital-labor ratios of the trading goods to rank the factor intensities of the sectors.

2. Knowledge of not only the technology but also the trade equilibrium is needed to determine the factor intensity ranking.

3. The validity of the theorem does not depend on the number of FIRs, or whether there is FIR.

4. So far, I have used the physical definition of factor abundance. If two countries are in different cones of diversification, the physical and price definitions of factor abundance are equivalent. Thus the theorem is valid no matter which definition of factor abundance is used.

5. If FIR is present, the theorem, though valid, is not useful in predicting patterns of trade. This is because if FIR is present, factor endowments of the countries alone are no longer sufficient to predict their patterns of trade.

Ranking factor intensities of sectors by using actual capital-labor ratios is not new in the literature, although it is new to use this method to show that the Heckscher-Ohlin theorem is still valid when FIR exists. As I show later, this method is related to the concept of factor content of trade.

3.4 Goods Trade and Factor Prices

International trade affects not just resource allocation within an economy but also the prices of the immobile factors. This section examines how international trade in goods could influence factor prices in two trading partners. It first derives the conditions under which factor prices are equalized, and then examines the implications when factor prices are not equalized.

3.4.1 Equalized Factor Prices

The factor price equalization theorem is one of the most important theorems in the present framework.

Factor Price Equalization Theorem   The trading countries have the same factor prices (Samuelson, 1948, 1949; Lerner, 1952).

This theorem, which has important empirical and theoretical implications, is based on a list of strong conditions. The following are six of these conditions, but, as will be seen later, they are still not sufficient for the theorem.

1. The countries have identical, linearly homogeneous technologies.

2. There are no trade impediments and no transport costs.

3. There are equal numbers of goods and factors.

4. All goods are tradable but all factors are not mobile internationally.

5. Both countries are producing all the goods under trade.

6. All markets are competitive and in the long run all firms are making zero profit.

Some of these conditions are similar to what are needed for the Heckscher-Ohlin theorem: identical and linearly homogeneous technologies and competitive markets. Others are much stronger than what I showed before. For example, condition (2) implies free trade with no transport costs, which is more restrictive than natural trade. Condition (5) requires diversification in production, but no such condition is needed for the Heckscher-Ohlin theorem. It should be pointed out, however, that the validity of the factor price equalization theorem is independent of the demand side of the countries.

The theorem can be illustrated and proved by using the GDP function introduced in Chapter 2. When the free-trade commodity prices have been determined and denoted by $\mathbf{p}$, the factor prices can be determined from the GDP function. As a result, the factor prices must satisfy the following conditions:

$$\mathbf{c}(\mathbf{w}) = \mathbf{p}, \tag{3.9}$$

where $\mathbf{c}$ is the n-dimensional vector of unit cost functions. The equality instead of inequality in condition (3.9) is due to the assumptions that all goods are produced and that firms earn zero profits. Identical technologies across countries imply that condition (3.9) applies to both countries which are facing the same set of commodity prices due to assumption (2). In condition (3.9), there are n equations and m unknowns (the factor prices). Assumptions (3) to (5) imply that $m = n$.

Because (3.9) applies to both countries, whether they have the same factor prices reduces to the following question: When given a set of commodity prices, can condition (3.9) be solved for a unique set of factor prices? In other words, the question is whether the unit cost functions are globally univalent or invertible.[7] Define the Jacobian matrix of $\mathbf{c}(\mathbf{w})$ as $\mathbf{A}(\mathbf{w})$ where, by Shephard's lemma, a representative element of $\mathbf{A}(\mathbf{w})$ is the input-output coefficient, a_{ji}. Then the Gale-Nikaido condition (Gale and Nikaido, 1965) states that $\mathbf{c}(\mathbf{w})$ is globally invertiable if all the principle minors of $\mathbf{A}(\mathbf{w})$ are positive. For practical purposes, I consider only positive factor prices. In the two-factor, two-sector framework, the Gale-Nikaido condition is satisfied if the sectors have different capital-labor ratio and a unique factor intensity ranking, that is, no FIR.[8]

3.4.2   Unequal Factor Prices

Despite the attention the factor price equalization theorem receives in the literature, the equalization of factor prices in different countries is not observed in the real world. It is easy to offer explanation of such divergence between the theoretical results and reality because as I showed earlier, the validity of the theorem requires a set of restrictive conditions. If any single condition is violated, factor price equalization is not likely. For example, in the proof of the theorem, if firms do not earn zero profit or the output of a particular sector

---

7. The inverse function theorem (or the implicit function theorem) can be used to check local invertibility of $\mathbf{c}(\mathbf{w})$. For the factor price equalization theorem, however, global invertibility of $\mathbf{c}(\mathbf{w})$ is needed because the factor endowments of two trading partners can differ in all possible ways. See Takayama (1972, Chapter 18), Woodland (1982, Chapter 4), or Ethier (1984) for further discussion.

8. In a two-factor, two-sector framework, the Gale-Nikaido condition reduces to (1) $a_{11}, a_{22} > 0$ and (2) $a_{11}a_{22} - a_{12}a_{21} > 0$. Condition (1) is satisfied because both factors are indispensable. If the sectors have different capital-labor ratios, factors and sectors can be labeled in such a way that (2) is satisfied, but factor intensity ranking cannot be reversed.

is zero, then the unit cost function is not equal to the market price. Alternatively, in the presence of trade impediments or transport costs, commodity price equalization does not exist, let alone factor price equalization. Furthermore, the existence of FIR can ruin any possibility of equalization of factor prices.[9]

Although it is recognized that factor price equalization may not be possible if some of the conditions stated are violated, there is a presumption that factor prices tend to move closer under trade than under autarky. Although this presumption is appealing and true in some cases, in general it is not true.[10]

Consider the 2×2 framework and suppose that FIR exists. By the law of comparative advantage, the commodity price ratios of the countries move in opposite directions toward each other under natural trade. If trade is free and no transport costs are present, the price ratios will eventually be the same. The directions of changes in factor prices in each country depend on factor intensity ranking of the sectors and on whether FIRs exist. If the factor endowments of the countries are separated by an odd number of FIRs, then the countries have different factor intensity rankings. Thus the changes in commodity prices will shift the wage-rental ratios in the countries in the same direction, but the wage-rental ratios may become closer or farther apart. If the factor endowments are separated by even numbers of FIRs, the movements in commodity prices will shift the wage-rental ratios in opposite directions. This means that the wage-rental ratios will move toward or away from each other (Johnson, 1957).[11]

I now examine the free-trade factor prices of the two countries when they may not be equalized due to complete specialization in production (the number of factors being greater than the number of goods being produced), or due to the existence of FIRs. The conditions that will be derived are quite general because they cover the cases in which the factor prices are equalized.

Consider a framework with $m \geq 2$ factors, $n \geq 2$ sectors, and two countries. Countries still have identical technologies, but the number of goods may not be the same as that of factors. The notation introduced in the previous chapter is used.

Free trade and no transport costs imply equalization of commodity prices, $\mathbf{p} = \mathbf{p}^*$. By identical technologies and cost minimization, the foreign factor prices must satisfy $c_i(\mathbf{w}^*) \geq p_i$, for all $i = 1, \ldots, n$. Because the domestic

---

9. It is sometimes said that factor prices can be equalized in the presence of FIR if the factor endowments in the countries are not too different. This statement is not true because even if their factor endowments are very close, they may still be separated by an FIR.

10. An example in which factor prices move closer together is when trade impediments or transport costs are present in the 2×2 framework without FIR.

11. For a more recent example in which the wage-rental ratios of two trading countries diverge in the presence of two FIRs, see Deardorff (1986). Thompson (1986) examines the possibility of factor price polarization in a three-factor, two-sector model.

factor prices minimize the GDP function of the home country subject to the constraint that unit costs are not less than prices,

$$g(\mathbf{p}, \mathbf{v}) = \mathbf{w} \cdot \mathbf{v} \leq \mathbf{w}^* \cdot \mathbf{v}. \tag{3.10}$$

Condition (3.10) implies

$$(\mathbf{w} - \mathbf{w}^*) \cdot \mathbf{v} \leq 0$$

and by symmetry, for the foreign country,

$$(\mathbf{w}^* - \mathbf{w}) \cdot \mathbf{v}^* \leq 0,$$

which are combined together to give (Helpman, 1984a)

$$(\mathbf{w} - \mathbf{w}^*) \cdot (\mathbf{v} - \mathbf{v}^*) \leq 0. \tag{3.11}$$

Condition (3.11) states that under free trade, the prices of factors are *on average* lower (or not higher) in the country in which they are abundant. If factor prices are equalized, the weak inequality in (3.11) can be replaced by an equality.

Condition (3.11), however, is not good enough to be used to predict the movement of the prices of a particular factor in the countries. The condition allows the possibility that under trade the price of a particular factor is higher in the country where it is abundant.

A stronger result can be obtained if there are only two factors in the economy. Without loss of generality, assume that the home country is labor abundant, that is,

$$\frac{\overline{L}}{\overline{K}} > \frac{\overline{L}^*}{\overline{K}^*}. \tag{3.12}$$

With two factors, condition (3.10) reduces to

$$w\overline{L} + r\overline{K} \leq w^*\overline{L} + r^*\overline{K},$$

which, after rearranging terms, implies

$$(w - w^*)\frac{\overline{L}}{\overline{K}} \leq r^* - r. \tag{3.13a}$$

Similarly, for the foreign country,

$$(w - w^*)\frac{\overline{L}^*}{\overline{K}^*} \geq r^* - r. \tag{3.13b}$$

I now want to prove that $w \leq w^*$. Suppose that the opposite is true, that is $w > w^*$ or $(w - w^*) > 0$. Multiply both sides of (3.12) by $(w - w^*)$ to give

$$(w - w^*)\frac{\overline{L}}{\overline{K}} > (w - w^*)\frac{\overline{L}^*}{\overline{K}^*}. \tag{3.13c}$$

Combining (3.13a), (3.13b) and (3.13c),

$$r^* - r > r^* - r,$$

which is a contradiction. Thus $w \leq w^*$ must apply. Following the same line of argument, $r \geq r^*$. This gives the following theorem:

Factor Price Differential Theorem Assume identical technologies, free trade, and no transport costs. On average, factor prices must not be higher in the country in which the factors are abundant. If there are two factors in the countries, the price of each factor must not be higher in the country in which it is abundant.

3.5   Are Goods Trade and Factor Mobility Substitutes?

In this section I examine the relationship between goods trade and factor movements. In particular, I want to ask a question that often appears in the literature: Are they substitutes or complements?

Before answering the question, I first define the meaning of substitutability and complementarity between goods trade and factor movements. Here I focus on the following two meanings.[12]

1. Quantitative-Relationship Sense. Goods trade and factor movements are said to be substitutes (or complements) in the quantitative-relationship sense if an increase in the volume of trade will diminish (or augment) the level of factor movements and/or if an increase in the level of factor movements will diminish (or augment) the volume of trade.

2. Price-Equalization Sense. Goods trade and factor movements are substitutes if free trade in goods implies factor price equalization and/or free trade in factors implies commodity price equalization.

The above definitions of substitutability and complementarity represent their weak version. For a strong version, the term "and/or" in the preceding definitions is replaced by "and." Obviously, the strong version implies the weak version. In the literature, the quantitative-relationship meaning of substitutability is more common than the price-equalization meaning.[13]

---

12. For two more meanings of substitutability and complementarity, see Wong (1986b).

13. See, for example, Ohlin (1933), Markusen (1983), Svensson (1984), Markusen and Svensson (1985), and Jones and Neary (1984).

In this section, I assume that the countries have identical technologies. Substitutability between goods trade and factor movement with different technologies across countries is examined in Chapter 4. Here, I consider separately the case in which factor price equalization holds and the case in which factor price equalization does not hold.

3.5.1 When Factor Prices Are Equalized

When factor price equalization holds, "[t]he absence of trade impediments implies commodity-price equalization and, even when factors are immobile, a tendency toward factor-price equalization. It is equally true that perfect factor mobility results in factor-price equalization and, even when commodity movements cannot take place, in a tendency toward commodity-price equalization" (Mundell, 1957, p. 321). Therefore, as Mundell concluded, "commodity movements and factor movements are substitutes" in the strong and weak price-equalization senses.

In the neoclassical framework with factor price equalization, goods trade and factor movements are also substitutes in the strong and weak quantitative-relationship senses. Suppose that the home country relative to the foreign country is well endowed with labor but poorly endowed with capital. The home country is a small, open economy, exporting the labor-intensive good 1 and importing the capital-intensive good 2. (The following result does not depend on the sizes of the countries, patterns of trade, and factor intensity ranking.) Initially free trade prevails and factor movements do not exist even if they are allowed.

Suppose now that the home country imposes a small tariff on the imported good 2. This raises the domestic relative price of good 2, and by the Stolper-Samuelson theorem, the domestic real rental rate of capital goes up and domestic real wage rate drops. If factor movements are now permitted, foreign capital tends to flow into the home country or domestic labor tends to flow out.

For concreteness, suppose that only capital movement is allowed but there are no taxes on income repatriation. In Figure 3.4, point Q is the production point after the imposition of the tariff but before the inflow of foreign capital. The domestic price line P, the slope of which is the negative of the relative domestic price of good 1, is tangent to the production possibility frontier (PPF) of the economy at point Q. By the Rybczynski theorem, as foreign capital flows in, the production point moves along the Rybczynski line R_K in the diagram. Without loss of generality, we assume that foreign capital owners repatriate their income in terms of good 2. Suppose that after the inflow of a small amount of foreign capital the PPF shifts to T'T', and the new production point, which is called the gross domestic product (GDP) point, occurs at the

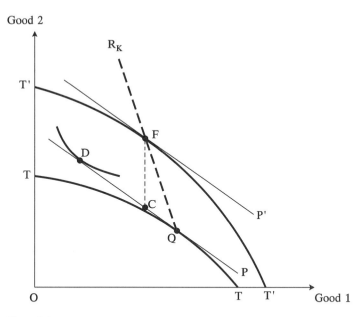

Figure 3.4

point of tangency between a new domestic price line P′ and the new PPF. As shown in the previous chapter, the gross national product (GNP) point is at point C, which is directly below point F and on the initial price line P.

Because domestic prices and rental rate are not affected by the amount of capital in the economy, more and more foreign capital flows in, shifting the GDP point (point F) up along the Rybcznski line R_K. This means that the GNP point (point C) also shifts up along domestic price line P. Sooner or later, point C reaches point D at which a social indifference curve is tangent to the price line P. At this point, the economy becomes autarkic in consumption because after paying for the foreign capital services, the home country gets exactly what it wants to consume at the domestic prices. Thus trade in goods ceases to exist. The initial tariff, no matter how small, is ultimately prohibitive.

Autarky in consumption is not the final equilibrium, however, because the domestic relative price of good 2 and the domestic real rental rate are still higher than those of the world. More foreign capital thus flows in, pushing up the production of good 2. In the absence of inferior goods, the relative price of good 2 drops, lowering the rental rate. This process continues until the rental rates in terms of good 2 in both countries are equalized. Because of identical technologies, the wage rates in terms of good 2 are also equalized and both countries must have the same unit cost in sector 1. In other words, free movement of capital has equalized not just the rental rates in terms of good 2 but also the wage rates and commodity prices.

The analysis shows that a trade impediment discourages goods trade, but encourages factor movements. A factor movement in response to factor price differential suppresses goods trade until the latter disappears.

Similar analysis can be used to show the opposite effect. This means that starting from a free factor movement equilibrium, an impediment on factor movement would encourage goods trade until commodity prices are equalized. Commodity price equalization implies factor price equalization and no factor movements. Thus, I have shown that factor movements diminish goods trade, and that goods trade also diminishes factor movements. They are substitutes.

In this analysis, the home country is assumed to be small. Does the size of the country matter? The answer is no. A tariff imposed by the home country on the imported good 2 makes the domestic relative price of good 2 higher than that in the foreign country, thus discouraging import. Again by the Stolper-Samuelson theorem, the domestic rental rate is greater than the foreign one, attracting foreign capital. By the Rybczynski theorem without the presence of inferior goods, the inflow of capital increases the domestic production of good 2 (capital intensive) but lowers that in the foreign country, further diminishing the volume of trade. Capital movement stops when factor prices, and thus commodity prices, are equalized.

Mundell's result has a strong implication about protection. If a country tries to discourage the inflow of a good, then the factor that is used intensively in the production of that good tends to flow in. Under the factor price equalization condition, the final equilibrium with factor movements is identical to that under free trade. Protection is entirely ineffective (at least in the long run).

3.5.2   When Factor Prices Are Not Equalized

If factor price equalization under free trade does not hold, then by definition goods trade and factor mobility are not substitutes in the strong price-equalization sense. They are, however, still substitutes in the weak price-equalization sense. Suppose that goods trade is not permitted but free capital movement is. In equilibrium, the rental rates in terms of good 2 (assuming that capital owners repatriate good 2) are equalized Due to identical technologies, factor prices and commodity prices are also equalized.

I now examine whether they are substitutes in the quantitative-relationship sense. Consider an initial free-trade equilibrium with no factor movements. If factor prices are not equalized then by the factor price differential theorem, the labor-abundant home country must have a higher rental rate and a lower wage rate than those in the foreign country. To simplify the analysis, I again assume that the home country is a small, open economy.

Suppose now that not just free trade but also free capital movement are permitted. Because of the differences in factor prices, foreign capital flows in, shifting out the domestic PPF and encouraging the production of good 2 but discouraging that of good 1. Without factor price equalization, no tariff is needed to induce factor movements. At constant commodity prices, the domestic production point will shift upward along the Rybczynski line R_K as in the previous case illustrated in Figure 3.4. (The diagram is still applicable in the present case, except that the domestic price line P also represents the world price line because of free trade.) As foreign capital flows in, the home country's level of import falls. Capital movement stops when factor and commodity prices are equalized.

Goods trade also diminishes factor movement as described previously. Thus I can conclude that they are substitutes in strong and weak quantitative-relationship senses.

3.6   The General Law of Comparative Advantage

I showed how the law of comparative advantage is used to prove the Heckscher-Ohlin theorem and to explain the patterns of trade of countries. Unfortunately, the law and the latter theorem are stated and proved in a framework with a low dimension: only two trading goods or factors.

Attempts have been made to apply the law of comparative advantage when the number of trading goods and factors is greater than two, but difficulties arise. Samuelson (1953) and Melvin (1968) argue that in a framework in which there are more goods than factors, the production is in general not determinate. (See also the Ricardian framework explained in the previous chapter.) With more goods than factors, the economy can in general export (or import) any goods.

A more direct challenge to the law of comparative advantage comes from Drabicki and Takayama (1979). Using a model of three goods, they show that a country may import the good that is cheaper under autarky (or export the good that is more expensive under autarky). Furthermore, they prove that the world commodity price ratios need not fall between the corresponding price ranges under autarky. A similar example is also provided in Dixit and Norman (1980, pp. 95–96).

As Drabicki and Takayama note, these results are not paradoxes but evidence that theorems derived in a two-sector framework may not be true in a multicommodity framework. The question is, can a theorem in a multicommodity framework that predicts the movements of goods and factors be developed?

Dixit and Norman (1980), Deardorff (1980), and Dixit and Woodland (1982) suggest a weaker version of the law of comparative advantage that does not depend on the numbers of goods and factors. To show their result, consider a framework with $m \geq 2$ factors and $n \geq 2$ goods. As before, I denote the autarkic and world equilibrium (net of any transport costs) values of a variable by superscripts "a" and "w" while the domestic values of variables under trade do not have any superscripts. An asterisk represents a foreign variable. All goods are tradable and the first m^t factors are mobile internationally.

Assuming natural trade as defined in (3.1), I need to show that in terms of a well-behaved social utility function a country is not worse off under a natural trade than under autarky. With the inflow of foreign factors denoted by $\mathbf{k}$ and the commodity prices denoted by $\mathbf{p}$, the GDP of the economy is given by $g(\mathbf{p}, \mathbf{v}^t + \mathbf{k}, \mathbf{v}^n)$. The transfer the country receives from the rest of the world due to goods trade and factor movement is equal to

$$b' = (\mathbf{p} - \mathbf{p}^w) \cdot \mathbf{M} - \mathbf{r}^w \cdot \mathbf{k}, \tag{3.14}$$

where $(\mathbf{p} - \mathbf{p}^w) \cdot \mathbf{M}$ is the net tariff revenue and $\mathbf{r}^w \cdot \mathbf{k}$ is the payment to the foreign factor owners. The national income (GNP) of the economy is

$$I = g(\mathbf{p}, \mathbf{v}^t + \mathbf{k}, \mathbf{v}^n) + b'$$
$$= \mathbf{w} \cdot \mathbf{v} + \mathbf{r} \cdot \mathbf{k} + (\mathbf{p} - \mathbf{p}^w) \cdot \mathbf{M} - \mathbf{r}^w \cdot \mathbf{k}$$
$$= \mathbf{w} \cdot \mathbf{v} + b$$
$$= g(\mathbf{p}, \mathbf{v}) + b, \tag{3.15}$$

where (3.14) has been used and $b = (\mathbf{p} - \mathbf{p}^w) \cdot \mathbf{M} + (\mathbf{r} - \mathbf{r}^w) \cdot \mathbf{k}$, which is the net transfer the country receives from the rest of the world. By the definition of natural trade, $b \geq 0$. By condition (3.15), the maximum utility the economy achieves under the natural trade is given by the indirect trade utility (ITU) function $V(\mathbf{p}, \mathbf{v}, b)$. Making use of the properties of the ITU function, I have the following rankings

$$V(\mathbf{p}, \mathbf{v}, b) \geq V(\mathbf{p}, \mathbf{v}, 0) \geq V(\mathbf{p}^a, \mathbf{v}, 0), \tag{3.16}$$

where the first inequality is due to the fact that the ITU function is increasing in b; and the second inequality is due to the theorem of autarkic prices proved in the previous chapter. The result in (3.16) can be summarized by the following theorem:[14]

The Theorem of Gain from Natural Trade   Natural trade is better than no trade.

Three remarks about this important theorem can be noted. First, because free trade is a special case of natural trade, the theorem implies that free

14. In the literature it is sometimes said that "some (restricted) trade is better than no trade." This may not be correct if the natural trade condition is not satisfied. See Bhagwati (1968a) for three counterexamples.

trade is better than no trade. Second, natural trade is only a sufficient but not necessary condition for gain from trade. Third, the theorem is proved under the condition that a social utility function exists. It is interesting to see whether the same conclusion can be drawn without relying on a social utility function. This is done in Chapter 8.

I now make use of the theorem of gain from natural trade to examine countries' comparative advantages. I begin with the home country. By the theorem, the consumption bundle under the natural trade $\mathbf{C}$ yields a utility level not lower than that yielded by the autarkic consumption bundle $\mathbf{C}^a$. This implies that under autarky, the natural trade consumption bundle cannot be less expensive than the autarkic consumption bundle, or the economy would have chosen $\mathbf{C}$ instead of $\mathbf{C}^a$. This means that

$$\mathbf{p}^a \cdot \mathbf{C}^a \leq \mathbf{p}^a \cdot \mathbf{C}. \tag{3.17}$$

From the definition of the GDP function, I have

$$\mathbf{p}^a \cdot \mathbf{Q}^a \geq \mathbf{p}^a \cdot \mathbf{Q} - \mathbf{r}^a \cdot \mathbf{k}, \tag{3.18}$$

as both $(\mathbf{Q}^a, \mathbf{0}(m^t))$ and $(\mathbf{Q}, -\mathbf{k})$ are feasible but $(\mathbf{Q}^a, \mathbf{0}(m^t))$ is chosen under autarky (with no international factor movements), where $\mathbf{0}(j)$ is a j-dimensional vector of zeroes. With nonsatiation, the budget constraint of the economy under autarky is

$$\mathbf{p}^a \cdot \mathbf{Q}^a = \mathbf{p}^a \cdot \mathbf{C}^a, \tag{3.19}$$

Combining conditions (3.17), (3.18), and (3.19) gives

$$\mathbf{p}^a \cdot \mathbf{M} + \mathbf{r}^a \cdot \mathbf{k} = \mathbf{p}^a \cdot (\mathbf{C} - \mathbf{Q}) + \mathbf{r}^a \cdot \mathbf{k} \geq 0. \tag{3.20}$$

Condition (3.20) states that the sum of the values of imports of goods and factors, evaluated at autarky prices, is non-negative.

Following the same line of argument, I have a similar condition for the foreign country:

$$\mathbf{p}^{a*} \cdot \mathbf{M}^* + \mathbf{r}^{a*} \cdot \mathbf{k}^* \geq 0. \tag{3.21}$$

Because the trade equilibrium conditions are

$$\mathbf{M} + \mathbf{M}^* = \mathbf{0}(n)$$

$$\mathbf{k} + \mathbf{k}^* = \mathbf{0}(m^t),$$

conditions (3.20) and (3.21) can be combined to give

$$(\mathbf{p}^a - \mathbf{p}^{a*}) \cdot \mathbf{M} + (\mathbf{r}^a - \mathbf{r}^{a*}) \cdot \mathbf{k} \geq 0. \tag{3.22}$$

Condition (3.22) gives the following theorem:

The General Law of Comparative Advantage   On average a country imports those goods and factors that are more expensive and exports those goods
and factors that are less expensive under autarky.

The general law of comparative advantage is much weaker than the law
of comparative advantage proved in a framework with two tradable goods or
factors. It is so weak that it is unable to predict the direction of movement
of a particular good or factor even if the autarkic prices in both countries are
known, and it is also unable to compare the domestic prices of goods and
factors under natural trade with those under autarky.

3.7   Chain Version of Comparative Advantage

This section explains a stronger way than the general law of comparative
advantage to predict the patterns of trade in a multigood world when there are
only two factors. Assuming identical technologies and no FIR for any pair of
goods, rank and label all the goods so that good 1 is the most capital-intensive,
and the last good (the nth good) is the most labor-intensive, that is,

$$k_1 > k_2 > \ldots > k_n. \tag{3.23}$$

Without loss of generality, assume that the home country is capital abundant.
Consider first the case in which *factor prices are not equalized under free
trade* due to complete specialization. I showed before that the rental rate must
be lower and the wage rate higher in the home country than in the foreign
country. The home factor prices (w, r) and the foreign factor prices (w^*, r^*)
under free trade are depicted by points H and F, respectively, in Figure 3.5.

I first prove the following result: If the home unit cost of sector i, $i =
1, \ldots, (n - 1)$, is at least as high as the foreign unit cost, then the unit costs
of all more labor-intensive sectors must be higher in the home country at the
prevailing factor prices. Without loss of generality, suppose that $c_i(w, r) \geq
c_i(w^*, r^*)$, that is, given the factor prices it is at least as expensive to produce
good i in the home country as in the foreign country. Figure 3.5 shows the
unit-cost schedules of sectors i and $i + 1$, which are labeled c_i and c_{i+1},
respectively. Both schedules intersect at point F, which corresponds to the
foreign factor prices. These two schedules thus give the foreign unit costs of
producing the goods under trade. Because by construction sector $i + 1$ is more
labor intensive than sector i, schedule c_{i+1} must be steeper than schedule c_i at
point F.

Because it is more costly to produce good i in the home country, the home
factor-price point, H, must be above schedule c_i. This relation is shown in the

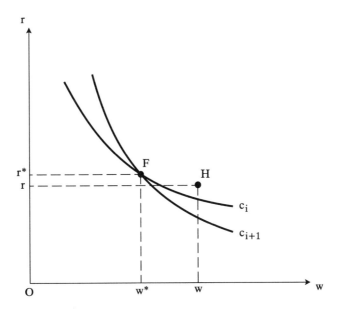

Figure 3.5

diagram. It is clear from the diagram that point H must also be above schedule c_{i+1}, meaning that the unit cost of producing good $i + 1$ is higher in the home country than in the foreign country. Thus I have shown that if it is at least as expensive to produce a good in the home country as in the foreign country, it is more expensive to produce all more labor-intensive goods in the home country.

I reverse the preceding analysis to argue that if it is at least as costly to produce a good in the foreign country as in the home country, then it is more costly to produce all more capital-intensive goods in the foreign country.

This result is illustrated in the Lerner diagram in Figure 3.6 for the case $n = 4$. Given the trade commodity prices, I construct the unit-dollar isoquants for the sectors, $Q_i = 1/p_i$, $i = 1, \ldots, 4$. Because the home country has a higher wage-rental ratio, the home unit-dollar iso-cost line HH' is steeper than the foreign one FF', with the former being tangent to isoquants Q_1 and Q_2, and the latter being tangent to Q_2, Q_3, and Q_4. Note that if an isoquant corresponding to the prevailing price is above the unit-dollar iso-cost, then the unit cost is greater than the price and the good will not be produced.[15] In the case shown in the diagram, the home country produces good 1 (and possibly good 2) while the foreign country produces goods 3 and 4 (and possibly good 2).

---

15. To see why, consider good 3. Construct another isoquant of the sector, which is tangent to HH'. This isoquant, which is closer to the origin than the isoquant labeled $Q_3^* = 1/p_3$, corresponds to a price of good 3 higher than p_3, meaning that a price higher than p_3 is needed to break even for firms in the home sector. So under trade the home firms produce zero output of the good.

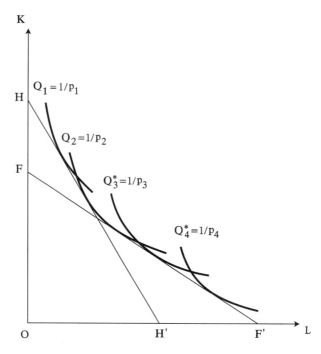

Figure 3.6

The preceding result has two implications. First, the capital-abundant (home) country must produce good 1 to good i and the labor-abundant (foreign) country must produce good j to good n, $1 < i \leq j < n$. Note that it is possible that $i = j$, meaning that good i, called the marginal good, is produced in both countries. In Figure 3.6, good 2 is the marginal good so its unit-dollar isoquant is tangent to HH' and FF'. Second, when both countries have different factor endowments, at least one of them is completely specialized, that is, it does not produce all goods.[16]

Now consider a more special case in which the countries have identical and homothetic preferences. In this case, the countries must consume all goods, meaning that each country must import those goods it is not producing. This means that the home country must export goods 1 to i and import goods j to n. It may export or import the marginal good. Thus I have

The Chain Version of the Heckscher-Ohlin Theorem   Suppose that free trade exists between the two countries. With no FIR, rank and label all goods

---

16. Note that a balanced trade means that every country must produce and export some goods, and thus that a country's unit-dollar iso-cost line cannot be entirely below that of the other country, because this implies that this country gets negative profit no matter what goods it produces.

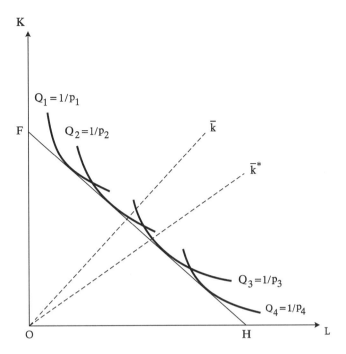

Figure 3.7

according to condition (3.23). If factor prices are not equalized, the capital-abundant country exports goods 1 to i and imports goods j to n, $1 < i \leq j < n$. The marginal good (at most one) in between i and j may be exported by either countries.

The chain version of the Heckscher-Ohlin theorem was first proposed by Jones (1956–1957), but Bhagwati (1972a) show that it is not true if factor prices are equalized. Deardorff (1979) provides a formal proof of the theorem in the absence of factor price equalization under free trade. Deardorff (1979) also shows that the theorem remains valid if tariffs or intermediate goods, but not both, are present.

To see why the theorem is not valid when factor prices are equalized, consider Figure 3.7. The two countries have the same unit-dollar iso-cost line FH. The home capital-labor ratio is shown by the ray labeled $\bar{k}$ and the foreign ratio shown by ray $\bar{k}^*$. Because the home country is capital abundant, ray $\bar{k}$ must be steeper than ray $\bar{k}^*$. The diagram can now be used to show that information about the factor endowments is no longer sufficient to predict patterns of production, let alone patterns of trade in various countries. For example, it is possible that the home country produces and exports goods 1 and 3 while the foreign country produces and exports goods 2 and 4, or the home country produces and exports goods 2 and 4 while the foreign country produces and exports goods 1 and 3. In general, countries' preferences have to be known in order to determine their production and trade.

3.8   Different Concepts of Factor Content of Trade

Factor content of trade is not a new approach to analyzing international trade. It was developed by researchers who considered the simple 2×2 framework to be too far away from the multifactor, multisector real world. It was first employed by Leontief (1953) in his famous test of the Heckscher-Ohlin theorem, and later formalized theoretically by Travis (1964), Vanek (1968), Melvin (1968), and many others. Under this approach, instead of examining the observed quantities and types of goods that move across borders of countries, one measures the quantities of factors embodied in the trading goods. Thus international trade in goods is interpreted as indirect flows of factor services. This approach is used to extend the Heckscher-Ohlin theorem and to provide some convenient way to compare the factor prices in two or more trading partners.

To introduce the idea of factor content of trade, the present analysis is limited to the two-country framework with the home country and the foreign country trading with each other. Disaggregate the trading commodities into two components: the goods the home country imports and the goods it exports. Define $\mathbf{G}^M$ as the n-dimensional vector of commodities the home country imports and $\mathbf{G}^E$ as that of commodities it exports. Vectors $\mathbf{G}^M$ and $\mathbf{G}^E$ contain non-negative elements. The home country's import vector can be written in the following form:

$$\mathbf{M} \equiv \mathbf{G}^M - \mathbf{G}^E. \tag{3.24}$$

The foreign country's variables are again distinguished by asterisks.

Corresponding to the vectors of commodities $\mathbf{G}^M$ (the home country's import), $\mathbf{G}^E$ (its export) and $\mathbf{C}$ (its consumption) define $\mathbf{v}^{GM}$ as the actual quantities of factors embodied in $\mathbf{G}^M$, $\mathbf{v}^{GE}$ as the actual quantities of factors embodied $\mathbf{G}^E$, and $\mathbf{v}^C$ as the actual quantities of factors embodied in $\mathbf{C}$.

Recall that $\mathbf{A}(\mathbf{w})$ is the $m \times n$ matrix of input-output coefficients. The factors embodied in $\mathbf{G}^E$ are equal to

$$\mathbf{v}^{GE} = \mathbf{A}(\mathbf{w})\mathbf{G}^E.$$

On the other hand, the goods the home country imports are produced in the foreign country, meaning that the factors embodied in these goods are equal to

$$\mathbf{v}^{GM} = \mathbf{A}^*(\mathbf{w}^*)\mathbf{G}^M.$$

If the countries have identical technologies, we have $\mathbf{A}^*(\mathbf{w}) = \mathbf{A}(\mathbf{w})$ for all $\mathbf{w} \geq \mathbf{0}$.

According to Deardorff (1982), three different concepts of factor content of trade can be defined as follows:[17]

1. *Actual factor content of trade,* $\mathbf{v}^M$ The actual factor content of trade of the home country is defined as the actual quantities of factor services embodied in the goods it imports less those embodied in the goods it exports, that is,

$$\mathbf{v}^M \equiv \mathbf{v}^{GM} - \mathbf{v}^{GE} = \mathbf{A}^*(\mathbf{w}^*)\mathbf{G}^M - \mathbf{A}(\mathbf{w})\mathbf{G}^E. \tag{3.25}$$

The export of factor services can be defined as $\mathbf{v}^E = -\mathbf{v}^M$.

2. *Factor content based on domestic coefficients,* $\mathbf{v}^{MD}$ This refers to the quantities of factors embodied in the trading good computed using domestic input-output coefficients. Using the preceding notation, it is equal to

$$\mathbf{v}^{MD} = \mathbf{A}(\mathbf{w})\mathbf{G}^M - \mathbf{A}(\mathbf{w})\mathbf{G}^E = \mathbf{A}(\mathbf{w})\mathbf{M}. \tag{3.25'}$$

3. *Factor content based on actual content of consumption,* $\mathbf{v}^{MC}$ This refers to the actual quantities of factors embodied in the consumption bundle of the home country less the factor endowments in the economy. In other words,

$$\mathbf{v}^{MC} = \mathbf{v}^C - \mathbf{v}.$$

If the countries have identical technologies and equalized factor prices, then by (3.25) and (3.25'), we have $\mathbf{v}^M = \mathbf{v}^{MD}$. If it is further given that full employment exists, then $\mathbf{v}^M = \mathbf{A}\mathbf{M} = \mathbf{A}\mathbf{C} - \mathbf{A}\mathbf{Q} = \mathbf{v}^C - \mathbf{v} = \mathbf{v}^{MC}$. Under these conditions, the three concepts of factor content of trade are identical.

3.9   Factor Content of Trade for a Single Economy

In this section, I focus on a single economy and examine its factor content of trade. The economy trades with other countries, but for the time being I ignore its trading partners. The economy under consideration does not have to be a small one facing exogenously given commodity prices. What is required is that the equilibrium commodity prices have been determined. Of course, because the rest of the world has not been considered explicitly, this section can at best analyze the economy's factor content based on domestic coefficients, $\mathbf{v}^{MD}$.

There are several advantages for using factor content based on domestic technologies:

---

17. For convenience, factor content of trade is here defined as the net import of factor services whereas Deardorff (1982) defines it as the net export of factor services.

1. Because I focus on a single economy, there is no need to make assumptions such as identical technologies and preferences across countries, free trade, no transport costs, or factor price equalization.

2. Domestic technologies and factor content based on domestic technologies are easier to estimate. Estimating factor content of trade using the technologies of a country's trading partner can be very difficult, especially if the country is trading with a large number of countries.[18] This means that it is easier to test any hypotheses derived using domestic technologies.

3. I noted earlier that when there are identical technologies across countries and factor price equalization, factor content based on domestic technologies is equivalent to actual factor content, and if full employment is always given, all three concepts of factor content are equivalent.

4. Using the input utility function explained in the previous chapter, it is very easy to synthesize the related results in Wong (1983, 1986a), Neary and Schweinberger (1986), and Deardorff and Staiger (1988). This point together with (3) are important when I later examine factor content of trade with factor price equalization. The results in this section are also applicable later.[19]

Before the analysis is given, it should be noted that factor content based on domestic technologies is not the same as actual factor content of trade, and that the latter concept is more applicable when analyzing goods trade.

Recall that the input utility function of the home country is defined as

$$V^I(\mathbf{w}, \mathbf{v}, b) = \max_{\mathbf{C}} \left\{ \mathbf{c}(\mathbf{w}) \cdot \mathbf{C} \leq \mathbf{w} \cdot \mathbf{v} + b \right\},$$

where $\mathbf{c}(\mathbf{w})$ is the vector of unit cost functions and b is the transfer received from abroad. I showed that the derivatives of the input utility function with respect to factor prices are equal to the demand for factor services:

$$V_{\mathbf{w}}^I = \lambda \left[\mathbf{v} - \mathbf{A}(\mathbf{w})\mathbf{C} \right], \tag{3.26}$$

where λ is the marginal utility of income (assumed to be positive with no satiation).

As the home country is trading with other countries, interpret $\mathbf{p}$ as the equilibrium trade commodity prices and $\mathbf{w}$ as the corresponding factor prices. Assume incomplete specialization so that $\mathbf{p} = \mathbf{c}(\mathbf{w})$, that is, the firms are producing positive outputs of all the consumption goods and are earning zero profit.

---

18. This is the reason why Leontief (1953) uses the U.S. input-output table to estimate the labor and capital requirements for producing import competing commodities.

19. This section depends on the techniques and analysis in Wong (1983, 1986a) and the analyses in Neary and Schweinberger (1986) and Deardorff and Staiger (1988).

Denote the optimal output vector under trade by $\mathbf{Q}$. With full employment, $\mathbf{v} = \mathbf{A}(\mathbf{w})\mathbf{Q}$. The vector of import equals $\mathbf{M} = \mathbf{C} - \mathbf{Q}$. Thus the term inside the brackets in (3.26) is the negative of factor content of trade using domestic technologies, because

$$\mathbf{v}^{MD} = \mathbf{A}(\mathbf{w})\big[\mathbf{C} - \mathbf{Q}\big] = \big[\mathbf{A}(\mathbf{w})\mathbf{C} - \mathbf{v}\big]. \tag{3.27}$$

The first result is that subject to the budget constraint the current account given in terms of the value of factor content is balanced, because

$$\mathbf{w} \cdot \mathbf{v}^{MD} + b = \mathbf{w} \cdot \big[\mathbf{A}(\mathbf{w})\mathbf{C} - \mathbf{v}\big] + b = \mathbf{c}(\mathbf{w}) \cdot \mathbf{C} - \mathbf{w} \cdot \mathbf{v} + b = 0, \tag{3.28}$$

where $\mathbf{w} \cdot \mathbf{A}(\mathbf{w}) = \mathbf{c}(\mathbf{w})$ and where the last equality comes from the budget constraint.

Next, imagine that the economy, instead of trading with other countries, receives a gift of factor endowments equal to the factor content of trade. Its total factor endowments are $\mathbf{v} + \mathbf{v}^{MD}$. I argue that with $b = 0$, the initial factor price vector under trade, $\mathbf{w}$, is the same as the new autarkic factor price vector with the addition of $\mathbf{v}^{MD}$. To see why, first note that using condition (3.26), the national expenditure when given the factor price vector $\mathbf{w}$ is

$$\mathbf{w} \cdot [\mathbf{v} + \mathbf{v}^{MD}] = \mathbf{w} \cdot \mathbf{A}(\mathbf{w})\mathbf{C} = \mathbf{c}(\mathbf{w}) \cdot \mathbf{C}.$$

This means that the consumption vector under trade is still feasible. Note that the optimal consumption vector under trade is $\mathbf{C}$. Now the economy, with the gift of factors but under autarky and factor price vector $\mathbf{w}$, has the same national expenditure. So $\mathbf{C}$ remains the optimal consumption vector. The output vector, from condition (3.27), is $\mathbf{C}$. So all markets clear. In fact, $\mathbf{C}$ is the optimal output with the gift of factors because when given the factor endowments, $\mathbf{w} \cdot [\mathbf{v} + \mathbf{v}^{MD}]$ is the maximum national income that is the national expenditure. Thus consumers are jointly maximizing the social utility function, firms are jointly maximizing national income, and all markets clear, implying that $\mathbf{w}$ is the autarkic factor price vector.

Before deriving the third result, factor prices must be normalized. As explained in Chapter 2, $e(\mathbf{p}, u)$ is the social expenditure function, where u is the social utility level. Replacing $\mathbf{p}$ by $\mathbf{c}(\mathbf{w})$ creates $e(\mathbf{c}(\mathbf{w}), u)$.[20] Because the social utility function is assumed to be homothetic, the expenditure function can be written as $e(\mathbf{c}(\mathbf{w}), u) = u\,\bar{e}(\mathbf{w})$, where $\bar{e}(\mathbf{w})$ is defined in the following way:[21]

---

20. I can define a new function $\tilde{e}(\mathbf{w}, u) \equiv e(\mathbf{c}(\mathbf{w}), u)$, which Wong (1983) calls input expenditure function.

21. Actually, if the social utility function is homothetic, $e(\mathbf{c}(\mathbf{w}), u) = \phi(u)\bar{e}(\mathbf{w})$ where $\phi(u)$ is an increasing function. Because utility function is an ordinal measure, the social utility function can be redefined so that $e(\mathbf{c}(\mathbf{w}), u) = u\,\bar{e}(\mathbf{w})$.

$$\bar{e}(\mathbf{w}) \equiv \min_{\mathbf{C}} \left\{ \mathbf{c}(\mathbf{w}) \cdot \mathbf{C} : u(\mathbf{C}) \geq 1 \right\}.$$

Function $\bar{e}(\mathbf{w})$ is what Wong (1983) calls unit expenditure function, which is shown to be increasing and concave in $\mathbf{w}$. It is an exact measure of the cost of living. Now normalize factor prices so that $\bar{e}(\mathbf{w}) = 1$. Thus $e(\mathbf{c}(\mathbf{w}), u) = u$. For an economy with factor prices $\mathbf{w}$, the national income is $\mathbf{w} \cdot \mathbf{v} + b$, which implies that $e(\mathbf{c}(\mathbf{w}), u) = \mathbf{w} \cdot \mathbf{v} + b$. Combining these results gives $u = \mathbf{w} \cdot \mathbf{v} + b$.

The last result is very useful. Denote the autarkic factor prices of the economy without the gift of factors by $\mathbf{w}^a$. Recall that it is proved in the previous chapter that autarkic factor prices minimize the input utility function (with $b = 0$), that is,

$$\mathbf{w}^a \cdot \mathbf{v} \leq \mathbf{w} \cdot \mathbf{v} \quad \text{for all } \mathbf{w} \geq \mathbf{0} \text{ and } \bar{e}(\mathbf{w}) = 1. \tag{3.29}$$

I showed earlier that when a trading economy is given a gift of factors equal to the factor content of trade, the initial factor prices under trade are the autarkic factor prices of the economy with the gift. Consider two trade situations the economy may face, with factor prices $\mathbf{w}$ and $\mathbf{w}'$ and with no international transfer. Denote the corresponding factor content by $\mathbf{v}^{MD}$ and $\mathbf{v}^{MD'}$, respectively. Because $\mathbf{w}$ and $\mathbf{w}'$ are the autarkic factor prices of the economy with the gifts of $\mathbf{v}^{MD}$ and $\mathbf{v}^{MD'}$, condition (3.29) gives

$$\mathbf{w} \cdot (\mathbf{v} + \mathbf{v}^{MD}) \leq \mathbf{w}' \cdot (\mathbf{v} + \mathbf{v}^{MD}) \tag{3.30a}$$

$$\mathbf{w}' \cdot (\mathbf{v} + \mathbf{v}^{MD'}) \leq \mathbf{w} \cdot (\mathbf{v} + \mathbf{v}^{MD'}). \tag{3.30b}$$

Combining conditions (3.30a) and (3.30b) and arranging terms will give (Deardorff and Staiger, 1988),

$$(\mathbf{w} - \mathbf{w}') \cdot (\mathbf{v}^{MD} - \mathbf{v}^{MD'}) \leq 0. \tag{3.31}$$

Condition (3.31) states that an increase in the indirect import of some factor services, imputed using domestic technologies, will on average lower their prices. This result is a weak one in the sense that it cannot predict the movement of a particular factor price, but it is a useful one for two reasons. First, it is a testable hypothesis, and the information needed is not enormous. It only requires the knowledge of domestic technologies (such as an input-output table), trade data, and (normalized) factor prices under trade.

Second, it can be applied to any trade situation. In particular, suppose that the primed situation is autarky. This means that $\mathbf{v}^{MD'} = 0$ and $\mathbf{w}' = \mathbf{w}^a$. By using condition (3.31), Deardorff and Staiger (1988) show that

$$(\mathbf{w}^a - \mathbf{w}) \cdot \mathbf{v}^{MD} \geq 0. \tag{3.31'}$$

Condition (3.31′), which is true for any trade situation, is similar to the general law of comparative advantage derived earlier. It states that an economy indirectly imports those factor services that are more expensive under autarky. Again, this result cannot be used to predict the exact movement of a particular factor service.

I showed earlier that the indirect trade in factor services is balanced, $\mathbf{w} \cdot \mathbf{v}^{MD} = 0$. Thus (3.31′) can be written alternatively as

$$\mathbf{w}^a \cdot \mathbf{v}^{MD} \geq 0. \tag{3.31″}$$

3.10   Factor Content of Trade with Possibly Unequal Factor Prices

I now bring in the foreign country. Assume that the countries have identical technologies. For some results, I state explicitly that they are further assumed to have identical and homothetic preferences. The results in this section do not depend on factor price equalization, although they still hold when factor prices are indeed equalized.

3.10.1   Patterns of Indirect Trade in Factors

Recall that under trade the home country imports goods $\mathbf{M}$ given by (3.24), which has an actual factor content of $\mathbf{v}^M$ given by (3.25). Suppose now that the home country cannot import $\mathbf{M}$ but instead is given a gift of factor endowments of $\mathbf{v}^M$. Because the two countries have identical technologies, the home country is able to produce $\mathbf{Q}^a + \mathbf{M}$ using $\mathbf{v} + \mathbf{v}^M$ where $\mathbf{Q}^a$ is the original autarkic output vector. Suppose that the home country is facing autarkic commodity prices, $\mathbf{p}^a$. The definition of the GDP function gives

$$g(\mathbf{p}^a, \mathbf{v} + \mathbf{v}^M) \geq \mathbf{p}^a \cdot (\mathbf{Q}^a + \mathbf{M}). \tag{3.32a}$$

Denote the resulting vector of factor prices by $\mathbf{w}'$. Because $\mathbf{w}'$ and the original autarkic factor price vector are feasible and satisfy the nonpositive-profit condition, so again by the definition of the GDP function

$$\mathbf{w}' \cdot (\mathbf{v} + \mathbf{v}^M) \leq \mathbf{w}^a \cdot (\mathbf{v} + \mathbf{v}^M). \tag{3.32b}$$

Because $g(\mathbf{p}^a, \mathbf{v} + \mathbf{v}^M) = \mathbf{w}' \cdot (\mathbf{v} + \mathbf{v}^M)$ and $\mathbf{w}^a \cdot \mathbf{v} = \mathbf{p}^a \cdot \mathbf{Q}^a$, (3.32a) and (3.32b) can be combined together to give

$$\mathbf{w}^a \cdot \mathbf{v}^M \geq \mathbf{p}^a \cdot \mathbf{M}. \tag{3.33}$$

By the general law of comparative advantage or condition (3.20), and because of no international factor movement, $\mathbf{p}^a \cdot \mathbf{M} \geq 0$. Thus condition (3.33) gives

$$\mathbf{w}^a \cdot \mathbf{v}^M \geq 0. \tag{3.34a}$$

Condition (3.34a) is analogous to (3.31′), which was derived in the previous section. There is, however, a big difference between these two conditions. Condition (3.34a) is given in terms of the actual factor content of trade while in condition (3.31′) the factor content is imputed from domestic technologies. Of course, if factor price equalization exists, the two conditions are equivalent. An expression for the foreign country similar to that in (3.34a) can be obtained:

$$\mathbf{w}^{a*} \cdot \mathbf{v}^{M*} \geq 0. \tag{3.34b}$$

Because by (3.25) $\mathbf{v}^M = -\mathbf{v}^{M*}$, (3.34a) and (3.34 b) can be combined to give

$$(\mathbf{w}^a - \mathbf{w}^{a*}) \cdot \mathbf{v}^M \geq 0. \tag{3.35}$$

Condition (3.35) can be summarized by the following theorem:

Factor-Content Version of the General Law of Comparative Advantage   With identical technologies across countries, a country *on average* indirectly exports the factors which are cheaper under autarky (Deardorff, 1982; Ethier, 1984; Helpman, 1984a).

This theorem gives a relationship between the autarkic factor prices in the countries and the indirect trade in factor services computed using the country's technologies. It should, however, be noted that it requires identical technologies, that it is true only on average, and that factor price equalization is not needed. Furthermore, if there are more than two factors, then it cannot be used to predict the indirect movement of a particular factor even if all autarkic factor prices in the countries are given. If there are only two factors, capital and labor, and if the countries have identical and homothetic preferences, then a stronger result can be obtained. Let K^E and L^E be the indirect export of capital and labor, respectively. Then $-\mathbf{v}^M = (L^E, K^E)$ and $\mathbf{w} = (w, r)$. Conditions (3.34a) and (3.35) reduce to

$$w^a L^E + r^a K^E \leq 0 \tag{3.36a}$$

$$(w^a - w^{a*})L^E + (r^a - r^{a*})K^E \leq 0. \tag{3.36b}$$

Without loss of generality, assume that $w^a < w^{a*}$, that is, that labor service is cheaper in the home country under autarky. Because factor prices in both countries are normalized using the same true price index, we must have $r^a > r^{a*}$. Condition (3.36a) implies that at least one of L^E and K^E is nonpositive. I argue that L^E cannot be negative, or K^E is nonnegative and (3.36b) cannot be satisfied. This means that the home country cannot import (indirectly) the service of its cheaper factor, labor. Using the same argument, I say that the foreign country cannot import (indirectly) capital service. Combining these results, I conclude that if trade exists, each country exports the service of its cheaper factor.

The factor-content version of the general law of comparative advantage does not explain why a particular factor is relatively cheaper under autarky in one country. I now introduce a theory that is analogous to the Heckscher-Ohlin theorem. Suppose that the two countries have identical technologies and preferences. Recall condition (3.29) that under the present normalization, the autarkic home factor prices $\mathbf{w}^a$ minimizes national welfare, which is measured by $\mathbf{w} \cdot \mathbf{v}$, that is, $\mathbf{w}^a \cdot \mathbf{v} \leq \mathbf{w} \cdot \mathbf{v}$ for all $\mathbf{w} \geq \mathbf{0}$. Because $\mathbf{w}^{a*}$ is a feasible factor price vector for the home country, I have $\mathbf{w}^a \cdot \mathbf{v} \leq \mathbf{w}^{a*} \cdot \mathbf{v}$, or

$$(\mathbf{w}^a - \mathbf{w}^{a*}) \cdot \mathbf{v} \leq 0. \tag{3.37a}$$

The same result can be obtained for the foreign country, that is,

$$(\mathbf{w}^{a*} - \mathbf{w}^a) \cdot \mathbf{v}^* \leq 0. \tag{3.37b}$$

Combine conditions (3.37a) and (3.37b) together to give (Dixit and Norman, 1980)

$$(\mathbf{w}^a - \mathbf{w}^{a*}) \cdot (\mathbf{v} - \mathbf{v}^*) \leq 0. \tag{3.38}$$

The interpretation of condition (3.38) is that the factors that are abundant in a country are on average cheaper under autarky. Condition (3.38) and the factor-content of the general law of comparative advantage can be combined to say (very loosely) that each country exports its abundant factors. This result is very weak, however, because the inference is indirect and because in general it is useless to predict the movement of the service of a particular factor.

If there are only two factors, then a much stronger result can be obtained. Assume that the home country is abundant in labor. Because under the homotheticity assumption only scales of the countries matter, assume without loss of generality that $\overline{L} > \overline{L}^*$ and $\overline{K} < \overline{K}^*$. The condition then reduces to

$$(w^a - w^{a*})(\overline{L} - \overline{L}^*) + (r^a - r^{a*})(\overline{K} - \overline{K}^*) \leq 0. \tag{3.38'}$$

With the same normalization of factor prices in both countries, $(w^a - w^{a*})$ and $(r^a - r^{a*})$ must have different signs. By condition (3.38') and the assumption about factor abundance, it must be that $w^a < w^{a*}$ and $r^a > r^{a*}$. In other words, when there are only two factors, each factor must be cheaper under autarky in the country where it is abundant. This result and the factor-content version of the general law of comparative advantage can then be combined to give:

Factor-Content Version of the Heckscher-Ohlin Theorem   With two factors, a country exports the service of its abundant factor (Brecher and Choudhri, 1982a; Helpman, 1984a).

Note that this theorem is true whether or not factor price equalization holds, but it does require identical and constant-returns technologies and identical and homothetic preferences across countries.

A graphical proof of this theorem when factor prices are not equalized and when there are only two factors was provided by Brecher and Choudhri (1982a). Recall the case shown in Figure 3.6. The home country is capital abundant, good 1 is the most capital-intensive, and good 4 is the least. As explained earlier, the home country exports good 1 and possibly good 2, while the foreign country exports goods 3 and 4, and possibly 2. With balanced trade, the home country exports more capital service than it imports, and imports more labor service than it exports.

3.10.2   Two Testable Results in Terms of Factor Prices under Trade

Because autarkic factor prices are not observable, it is difficult to test conditions (3.35) and (3.38). I now introduce two related results, which depend on trade in factor services and factor prices under trade that may be observable. Using the previous notation, $\mathbf{G}^M$ is the gross import of goods by the home country, and $\mathbf{v}^{GM} \equiv \mathbf{A}(\mathbf{w}^*)\mathbf{G}^M$ are the amounts of factors embodied in $\mathbf{G}^M$. Suppose that the home country cannot import $\mathbf{G}^M$, but instead is given a gift of factors $\mathbf{v}^{GM}$. Under the free-trade commodity prices and because of identical technologies, the home country is able to use $\mathbf{v} + \mathbf{v}^{GM}$ to produce at least $\mathbf{Q} + \mathbf{G}^M$, that is, $\mathbf{p} \cdot \mathbf{G}^M \leq g(\mathbf{p}, \mathbf{v}^{GM})$. This implies

$$\mathbf{p} \cdot (\mathbf{Q} + \mathbf{G}^M) \leq g(\mathbf{p}, \mathbf{v} + \mathbf{v}^{GM})$$

$$\leq \mathbf{w} \cdot (\mathbf{v} + \mathbf{v}^{GM})$$

$$= \mathbf{p} \cdot \mathbf{Q} + \mathbf{w} \cdot \mathbf{v}^{GM}.$$

The two inequalities are due to the definition of the GDP function. The expression implies that

$$\mathbf{p} \cdot \mathbf{G}^M \leq \mathbf{w} \cdot \mathbf{v}^{GM}. \tag{3.39a}$$

Zero profit in the foreign country implies that

$$\mathbf{p} \cdot \mathbf{G}^M = \mathbf{w}^* \cdot \mathbf{v}^{GM}. \tag{3.39b}$$

Conditions (3.39a) and (3.39b) together give

$$(\mathbf{w} - \mathbf{w}^*) \cdot \mathbf{v}^{GM} \geq 0. \tag{3.40a}$$

Similarly, for the foreign country, I have

$$(\mathbf{w}^* - \mathbf{w}) \cdot \mathbf{v}^{GM*} \geq 0. \tag{3.40b}$$

Note that $\mathbf{v}^{GM*}$ are the factors embodied in the home country's exported goods. Thus the factor content of trade of the home country is $\mathbf{v}^M = \mathbf{v}^{GM} - \mathbf{v}^{GM*}$. Conditions (3.40a) and (3.40b) can be combined to give (Helpman, 1984a)

$$(\mathbf{w} - \mathbf{w}^*) \cdot \mathbf{v}^M \geq 0. \tag{3.41}$$

Condition (3.41) states that a country on average exports the services of the factors that are cheaper under free trade. Note that condition (3.41) necessarily is satisfied if factor price equalization holds. Condition (3.41) is testable if one can observe the factor prices under trade and estimate the factor content of trade using the appropriate technologies.

Another testable result is the one that was derived earlier and given in (3.11). It is repeated here:

$$(\mathbf{w} - \mathbf{w}^*) \cdot (\mathbf{v} - \mathbf{v}^*) \leq 0. \tag{3.11}$$

To test (3.11) knowledge about the factor endowments in the two countries is needed. Note that condition (3.11) is derived under the assumption of no intermediate inputs. Staiger (1986) shows that in the presence of intermediate inputs under free trade the condition is still true using direct, but not gross, factor content.

Again very loosely speaking, conditions (3.41) and (3.11) can be combined to say that a country on average exports the services of the abundant factors. Note further that the present result, using conditions (3.41) and (3.11), is similar to that based on conditions (3.35) and (3.38). Both of them use indirect inference, and both are very weak. They do have an important difference: The former uses trade factor prices while the latter uses autarkic prices.

3.10.3   Another Result

There is yet another way of analyzing factor content of trade without factor price equalization due to Bertrand (1972). The distinct feature of this approach is that factor content of trade is measured in terms of the values of factor services embodied in traded goods, evaluated at free-trade prices.

Assume that both countries consume a given ratio of the values of all domestic and foreign commodities. This means that each country will consume a given ratio of the values of the factor services used in producing the goods in the world. Therefore the value of the consumption demand for factor j's service under free trade can be written as

$$w_j v_j^C = \beta w_j v_j + \gamma w_j^* v_j^*, \qquad j = 1, \ldots, m, \tag{3.42}$$

where β and γ are variables whose values are determined under free trade. They are the same for all goods.

Rank (and relabel if necessary) the factors so that

$$\frac{w_1 v_1}{w_1^* v_1^*} \geq \frac{w_2 v_2}{w_2^* v_2^*} \geq \cdots \geq \frac{w_m v_m}{w_m^* v_m^*}. \tag{3.43}$$

The value of the export of the service of factor j is

$$w_j v_j^E = w_j v_j - w_j v_j^C = (1 - \beta) w_j v_j - \gamma w_j^* v_j^*, \tag{3.44}$$

where (3.42) has been used. The values of free-trade factor prices satisfy the following equilibrium, zero-trade-balance, condition

$$\sum_{j=1}^{m} w_j v_j^E = 0.$$

Condition (3.44) immediately gives the following theorem.

Factor Content of Trade with Possibly Unequal Factor Prices   Given condition (3.42), the home country exports the service of factor j if $(w_j v_j / w_j^* v_j^*)$ $> \theta$ and imports the service of factor k if $(w_k v_k / w_k^* v_k^*) < \theta$, where $\theta \equiv \gamma / (1 - \beta)$ (Bertrand, 1972).

3.11   Actual Factor Content of Trade with Equal Factor Prices

I now turn to the case in which factor prices are equalized. As explained before, with identical technologies and equal factor prices, the actual factor content of trade $\mathbf{v}^M$ is equal to the factor content based on domestic coefficients. As a result, the results in the previous two sections remain valid in this section. Because factor prices are equalized, however, I can derive more and stronger results.

With identical technologies and factor price equalization, $\mathbf{A}^*(\mathbf{w}^*) = \mathbf{A}(\mathbf{w})$, the actual factor content of trade defined in (3.25) reduces to

$$\mathbf{v}^M = \mathbf{A}(\mathbf{w})\big[\mathbf{G}^M - \mathbf{G}^E\big] = \mathbf{A}(\mathbf{w})\mathbf{M}. \tag{3.25''}$$

Because $\mathbf{M} = -\mathbf{M}^*$, the foreign country's import vector, and because of factor price equalization, $\mathbf{v}^M = -\mathbf{v}^{M*}$.

3.11.1   Some Basic Results

The results obtained earlier in respect to factor content for a single economy can be applied directly to the present cases in terms of actual factor content. Thus the following results are easily obtained:

1. *Balanced current account*

$$\mathbf{w} \cdot \mathbf{v}^M = \mathbf{w} \cdot \mathbf{A}(\mathbf{w})\mathbf{M} = \mathbf{p} \cdot (\mathbf{C} - \mathbf{Q}) = b. \tag{3.28$'$}$$

Thus zero balance in goods trade ($b = 0$) implies zero balance in trade in factor services.

2. *Comparison of two trade situations*   By applying condition (3.31),

$$(\mathbf{w} - \mathbf{w}') \cdot (\mathbf{v}^M - \mathbf{v}^{M'}) \le 0.$$

3. *Factor content and autarkic factor prices*   Condition (3.31$'$) implies that

$$(\mathbf{w} - \mathbf{w}^a) \cdot \mathbf{v}^M \le 0, \tag{3.45}$$

where $\mathbf{w}$ is the factor price vector under trade.

Condition (3.45) applies also to the foreign country, that is,

$$(\mathbf{w} - \mathbf{w}^{a*}) \cdot \mathbf{v}^{M*} \le 0, \tag{3.45$'$}$$

where $\mathbf{w}^{a*}$ is the autarkic factor price vector in the foreign country. Because $\mathbf{v}^M = -\mathbf{v}^{M*}$, (3.45) and (3.45$'$) can be combined together to give

$$(\mathbf{w}^a - \mathbf{w}^{a*}) \cdot \mathbf{v}^M \ge 0. \tag{3.45$''$}$$

Condition (3.45$''$), which is analogous to the general law of comparative advantage, states that each country on average imports indirectly through goods trade those factor services that are more expensive under autarky. This result can be called the general law of comparative advantage in factor content of trade. Recall condition (3.11), which states that factor prices are on average lower in the country in which they are abundant. This condition and the general law of comparative advantage in factor content of trade can be combined to establish the very loose concept that a country on average exports indirectly through trade the services of its abundant factors. These results are too weak to predict the movement of any factor except in the special case in which there are only two factors. Stronger results are obtained next.

3.11.2   Pattern of Trade in Factor Services with Many Factors

Label the factors according to their relative abundance in the home country versus the foreign country so that

$$\frac{v_1}{v_1^*} \ge \frac{v_2}{v_2^*} \ge \ldots \ge \frac{v_m}{v_m^*}. \tag{3.46}$$

In other words, the home country vis-à-vis the foreign country is most abundant in factor 1, next most abundant in factor 2, and so on. I now add the assumption that the countries have identical and homothetic preferences. This assumption and equalization of commodity prices under free trade imply that the countries spend the same share of their income on each commodity. In particular,

$$C_i = \alpha C_i^*, \qquad i = 1, \ldots, n, \tag{3.47}$$

where α is the ratio of home country's consumption of good i to foreign country's consumption of the good under free trade. The value of α depends on free-trade prices.

The home country's consumption demand for factor j under free trade is equal to $v_j^C = \sum_i a_{ji} C_i$, where a_{ji} is the input-output coefficient evaluated at free-trade factor prices and is the same in both countries because of identical technologies and factor price equalization. Using (3.47) and noting that the two countries have identical input-output coefficients, the consumption demand for factor j reduces to

$$v_j^C = \sum_i a_{ji} C_i = \alpha \sum_i a_{ji} C_i^* = \alpha v_j^{C*}. \tag{3.48}$$

Define $v_j^w \equiv v_j + v_j^*$ as the world endowment of factor j. Full employment of factor j implies that

$$v_j^C + v_j^{C*} = v_j + v_j^* \equiv v_j^w,$$

which, using (3.48), gives

$$v_j^C = \frac{\alpha v_j^w}{1 + \alpha} \tag{3.49a}$$

and

$$v_j^{C*} = \frac{v_j^w}{1 + \alpha}. \tag{3.49b}$$

Using (3.49a), the net export of service of factor j by the home country is

$$v_j^E \equiv v_j - v_j^C$$

$$= v_j - \frac{\alpha v_j^w}{1 + \alpha}$$

$$= \frac{v_j - \alpha v_j^*}{1 + \alpha}. \tag{3.50}$$

Condition (3.50) then gives the following result

$$v_j^E \begin{Bmatrix} > \\ = \\ < \end{Bmatrix} 0 \quad \text{if and only if} \quad \frac{v_j}{v_j^*} \begin{Bmatrix} > \\ = \\ < \end{Bmatrix} \alpha.$$

This important result is summarized in the following theorem:

Factor Content of Trade with Factor Price Equalization   Given factor price equalization, the home country exports the service of factor j if $v_j/v_j^* > \alpha$, and imports the service of factor ℓ if $v_\ell/v_\ell^* < \alpha$ (Vanek, 1968).

This is a very strong result. Imagine that two lines are drawn to divide the ranking of factor abundance given in (3.46) into three groups of factors. Factors on the left- (respectively right-) hand side are those that have $v_j/v_j^* >$ (respectively $<$) α, and those in between are given by $v_j/v_j^* = \alpha$. (It is possible that the middle group has no element. Then the two lines coincide with each other.) The home country exports the factors in the left-hand group and imports the factors in the right-hand group. It is true that the value of α depends on the technology and preferences of the countries, and it may be difficult to estimate. The theorem implies the following results: First, each country must export the service of the factor in which it is most abundant; and second, if a country exports a factor, it must also export all factors that are more abundant in the country.

3.11.3   Pattern of Trade in Factor Services with Two Factors

Stronger results can be obtained if there are only two factors, capital and labor, whether or not there are more than two goods. Let factor 1 represent capital and factor 2 represent labor. According to condition (3.46), the home country is abundant in capital. Using the preceding notation, K^C and L^C represent the consumption demands for capital and labor, and $K^E \equiv K - K^C$ and $L^E \equiv L - L^C$ are the export of capital service and export of labor service by the home country, respectively. The theorem of factor content of trade with factor price equalization implies that under free trade, the home country exports capital service and imports labor service, that is,

$$K^E > 0 > L^E. \tag{3.51}$$

Furthermore, as shown previously, the balance of trade is zero, that is, $rK^E + wL^E = 0$. Condition (3.51), which is the factor-content version of the Heckscher-Ohlin theorem established in the previous section, states that in a two-factor world, each country exports the service of its abundant factor.

The factor content of trade can be illustrated by the Edgeworth box in Figure 3.8. The size of the box represents the amounts of labor and capital in the world, and the endowment point E shows the distribution of the factors between the countries, with O as the home country's origin and O* as the foreign country's origin. Point E is above the diagonal, reflecting the assumption that

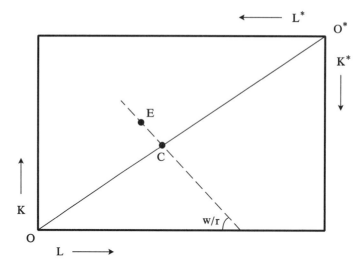

Figure 3.8

the home country is capital abundant. Because the countries have identical and homothetic preferences and are facing the same commodity and factor prices, they spend the same proportions of their income on capital and labor services. This means that the (indirect) consumption (of factors) of the home and foreign countries must be represented by a point on the diagonal of the box.

Suppose that free-trade factor prices are known. Then construct a line through E so that its slope equals the (negative) wage-rental ratio, and let this line cut the diagonal at point C. Because the trade in factor services is balanced, point C represents the consumption of factor services of the countries. The diagram clearly shows that the home country has an export of capital service and an import of labor service, confirming condition (3.51) and the factor-content version of the Heckscher-Ohlin theorem.

The factor content of trade can be expressed alternatively in terms of the capital-labor ratios of the exported and imported goods. Define $\mathcal{E}$ as the set of goods the home country exports, with G_i^E as the level of export of good i, $i \in \mathcal{E}$, and define $\mathcal{M}$ as the set of goods the country imports, with G_j^M as the level of import of good j, $j \in \mathcal{M}$. Denote the capital-output and labor-output ratios of sector i by a_{ki} and $a_{\ell i}$, respectively. Then by condition (3.51),

$$K^E = \sum_{i \in \mathcal{E}} a_{ki} G_i^E - \sum_{j \in \mathcal{M}} a_{kj} G_j^M > 0,$$

which implies

$$\sum_{i \in \mathcal{E}} a_{ki} G_i^E > \sum_{j \in \mathcal{M}} a_{kj} G_j^M. \tag{3.52a}$$

Similarly, using the second part of condition (3.51),

$$\sum_{i \in \mathcal{E}} a_{\ell i} G_i^E < \sum_{j \in \mathcal{M}} a_{\ell j} G_j^M. \tag{3.52b}$$

Noting that the terms in (3.52a) and (3.52b) are positive,

$$\frac{\sum_{i \in \mathcal{E}} a_{ki} G_i^E}{\sum_{i \in \mathcal{E}} a_{\ell i} G_i^E} > \frac{\sum_{j \in \mathcal{M}} a_{kj} G_j^M}{\sum_{j \in \mathcal{M}} a_{\ell j} G_j^M}. \tag{3.53}$$

Define $\theta_i^e \equiv a_{\ell i} G_i^E / \sum_{i \in \mathcal{E}} a_{\ell i} G_i^E$ and $\theta_j^m \equiv a_{\ell j} G_j^M / \sum_{j \in \mathcal{M}} a_{\ell j} G_j^M$. The variable θ_i^e (respectively θ_i^m) is the share of labor working in sector i in the total amount of labor employed in all exportable (respectively importable) sectors. Recall that k_i is the capital-labor ratio of sector i. Condition (3.53) thus implies that[22]

$$\sum_{i \in \mathcal{E}} \theta_i^e k_i > \sum_{j \in \mathcal{M}} \theta_j^m k_j. \tag{3.53'}$$

Condition (3.53') gives an alternative statement of the Heckscher-Ohlin theorem in this multigood, two-factor framework: The weighted average of the capital-labor ratios of the goods exported by the capital-abundant country is greater than the weighted average of the capital-labor ratios of the goods it imports, the weights being the share of labor employed in that sector in the total amount of labor employed in all exportable (or importable) sectors.

3.11.4   More Results (Leamer, 1980)

Sometimes there is interest in comparing the relative abundance of two factors in a multifactor framework. Take, for example, two factors i and j. Then the home country versus the foreign country is abundant in factor i relative to factor j if and only if

$$\frac{v_i}{v_i^*} > \frac{v_j}{v_j^*}. \tag{3.54}$$

Alternatively, the factor abundance condition (3.54) can be stated in terms of the world endowments of these two factors:

$$\frac{v_i}{v_j} > \frac{v_i^w}{v_j^w}. \tag{3.54'}$$

---

22. The result given by (3.53') is implicit in Leontief's calculation to be explained later, but apparently Chacholiades (1978) is first one to provide a rigorous proof of this expression.

Condition (3.50) can be rearranged to give

$$v_j^w = \frac{(1+\alpha)(v_j - v_j^E)}{\alpha}.$$

(3.55)

Substitute (3.55) into (3.54′) to give

$$\frac{v_i}{v_j} > \frac{v_i - v_i^E}{v_j - v_j^E}.$$

(3.56)

There are three alternative ways of writing condition (3.56):

1. Noting that the consumption demand for factor i is $v_i^C \equiv v_i - v_i^E > 0$,

$$\frac{v_i}{v_j} > \frac{v_i^C}{v_j^C}.$$

(3.57a)

2. Terms in (3.56) can be simplified to give

$$-v_i v_j^E > -v_j v_i^E.$$

(3.57b)

3. Condition (3.57b) can be rewritten as $-(v_i^C + v_i^E)v_j^E > -(v_j^C + v_j^E)v_i^E$, or

$$-v_i^C v_j^E > -v_j^C v_i^E.$$

(3.57c)

Conditions (3.57a) to (3.57c) will be used later to examine the Leontief paradox.

3.12   The Leontief Paradox and Factor Content of Trade

In testing the Heckscher-Ohlin theorem, Leontief (1953) makes use of the 1949 U.S. input-output table to estimate the total capital and labor requirements for one million dollars' worth of exports and those for one million dollars' worth of import replacements in 1947. His results, in terms of our notation, are

export of capital service, $K^{GE} = \$2,550,780$ (1947 prices);

export of labor service, $L^{GE} = 182.313$ man-year;

import of capital service, $K^{GM} = \$3,091,339$ (1947 prices); and

import of labor service, $L^{GM} = 170.004$ man-year;

He then calculates the ratios of capital to labor embodied in the exports and imports. To his surprise, the capital-labor ratio of the exports is lower than that of the imports, $K^{GE}/L^{GE} < K^{GM}/L^{GM}$. His results seem to suggest that the United States, which is believed to be capital-abundant relative to the world as a whole, exported labor-intensive goods and imported capital-intensive goods. This result is contradictory to the Heckscher-Ohlin theorem; hence it is called the Leontief paradox.

Many papers have been written to explain or resolve the paradox by criticizing his methodology or data, refuting the Heckscher-Ohlin theorem and its assumptions, or extending the theorem.[23] Here I discuss the relationship between the paradox and factor content of trade.

Leontief's framework of the U.S. economy is in fact multicommodity and two-factor. In his input-output table, there are thirty-eight tradable sectors and twelve nontradable sectors, which are consolidated from 200 industries, but there are only two factors (labor and capital). This is not the two-good, two-factor framework used to state and prove the Heckscher-Ohlin theorem. Thus the theorem cannot be tested directly. Leontief calculates the factor services embodied in the exports and imports using the U.S. technologies. By doing so, he uses the concept of factor content of trade fifteen years before it is formalized and developed separately by Vanek and Melvin in 1968.

Because of the nonexistence of an input-output table for the rest of the world, Leontief uses the U.S. input-output coefficients to compute the amounts of capital and labor required to replace the goods imported. If technologies are identical across countries and if factor price equalization holds, then both countries have the same input-output coefficients. If factor price equalization does not hold between the United States and the rest of the world, then Leontief's methodology to compute factor content of trade may not be appropriate.

To see the importance of using the appropriate input-output coefficients, refer back to Figure 3.3, which shows two reversals of factor intensity ranking. Suppose that the home country is labor abundant by the physical and price definitions of factor abundance. With factor intensity reversal, there is no direct relationship between autarkic goods prices and factor endowments. Suppose that $p^a < p^{a*}$. By the law of comparative advantage, the home country exports good 1 under free trade. Because the factor endowments of the two countries are in two different cones of diversification, factor price equalization is not possible.

The free-trade capital-labor ratios of the sectors in the same country show that good 1 is labor intensive ($k_2' > k_1'$ and $k_2^* > k_1^*$) in both countries. Thus the capital-abundant (foreign) country exports the labor-intensive good, contrary to the Heckscher-Ohlin theorem. This is the Leontief paradox.

---

23. See Chacholiades (1978, Chapter 11), Deardorff (1984), and Leamer (1984, Chapter 2) for surveys of the papers related to the Leontief Paradox. Leamer 1984 also provides a cross-country study of the sources of comparative advantage.

As discussed earlier, however, the theorem remains valid if the sectors are ranked according to the capital-labor ratios of the sectors that actually produce the traded goods. In other words, k_1' should be compared with k_2^*. Because $k_1' < k_2^*$, good 1 is said to be labor intensive and good 2 capital intensive. Thus the Heckscher-Ohlin theorem may be stated as follows: The capital-abundant (foreign) country exports the capital-intensive good. This means that one possible reason for the Leontief paradox is that in the presence of FIR, he computes and uses the wrong capital-labor ratio.

An alternative way of evaluating Leontief's methodology is suggested by Leamer (1980). He argues that the Leontief paradox rests on a simple conceptual misunderstanding. He shows that with more than two goods and factors, $K^{GE}/L^{GE} < K^{GM}/L^{GM}$ is compatible with either order of factor abundance. This means that Leontief's finding cannot be used to conclude whether the United States is capital abundant or labor abundant.

To determine whether trade data reveal that the United States versus the rest of the world is abundant in capital relative to labor, Leamer proposes three conditions as given by (3.57a) to (3.57c), depending on whether the United States is exporting or importing capital and labor. Thus each of the following conditions would suggest that the United States is revealed by trade to be capital abundant:

1. $K^{GE} - K^{GM} > 0$ and $L^{GE} - L^{GM} < 0$.

2. $K^{GE} - K^{GM} > 0$, $L^{GE} - L^{GM} > 0$, and $(K^{GE} - K^{GM})/(L^{GE} - L^{GM}) > K^C/L^C$.

3. $K^{GE} - K^{GM} < 0$, $L^{GE} - L^{GM} < 0$, and $(K^{GE} - K^{GM})/(L^{GE} - L^{GM}) < K^C/L^C$.

Leamer observes that in 1949, the United States exported capital and labor services. (The United States had a trade surplus in that year.) Thus he suggests that the correct way of determining whether the United States is revealed to be capital abundant is to use condition (2). In fact, he makes use of the production data of the United States in that year and shows that $(K^{GE} - K^{GM})/(L^{GE} - L^{GM}) > K^C/L^C$. So the United States is revealed to be capital abundant.

Despite Leamer's work, however, doubts still remain about whether that the paradox has really been resolved. Brecher and Choudhri (1982b) point out that the United States' exportation of labor services is by itself a paradox.[24] Using (3.50), the export of labor services of the home country (the United States) is

---

24. Baldwin (1971), using 1958 U.S. input-output data, also finds that the United States exported labor services, but Stern and Maskus (1981) seem to find that the paradox may have evaporated by 1972. See a discussion of the findings in Maskus (1985).

$$L^E = L - \frac{\alpha L^w}{1 + \alpha} = \frac{L - \alpha L^*}{1 + \alpha} \tag{3.58}$$

where $\alpha \equiv C/C^*$ is the ratio of the value of home country's (the United States) consumption to the foreign country's. Thus the United States exports labor services, $L^E > 0$, if and only if $L > \alpha L^*$, or

$$\frac{C_i}{L} < \frac{C_i^*}{L^*}. \tag{3.59}$$

Condition (3.59) implies that the United States has a lower per capita consumption than the rest of the world, a result that is hardly supported by statistical data.

Furthermore, there are some other features of the Leontief's results that Leamer did not explain well. First, in the counterexample in Leamer (1980), there are three goods and three factors. (The Leamer model has equal numbers of goods and factors.) In contrast, Leontief assumed only two factors, labor and capital. When there are only two factors, as Leamer showed, comparing K^{GE}/L^{GE} with K^{GM}/L^{GM}, which Leontief did, is the appropriate way of testing whether a country is revealed to be capital abundant.

Second, the United States had a significant trade surplus in 1947. The surplus clearly accounted for the U.S. net exports of capital and labor services Leamer found. The theoretical implications of a trade surplus in the Heckscher-Ohlin framework and theorem have not been well investigated in the literature. The fact that a trade imbalance is observed means that there are some features in the world that the framework has not captured but should have been included in empirical tests of the theorem.[25] It is not clear whether some of these features that contributed to the U.S. surplus may indicate the departures of some of the assumptions on which the Heckscher-Ohlin theorem is based.

Third, using the amounts of capital and labor services embodied in exports and imports, which Leontief found by assuming that the trade surplus was zero, it can be shown that the United States indeed had a net import of capital service and a net export of labor service, $K^E < 0$ and $L^E > 0$. In the Heckscher-Ohlin framework, this pattern of trade in factor services is not compatible with the presumption that the United States was a capital abundant country.

Fourth, more recent tests of the Heckscher-Ohlin-Vanek factor content theorem did not find evidence to support the theorem. For example, Maskus (1985)

---

25. Casas and Choi (1984, 1985) estimate the amounts of factors embodied in trading goods the United States would have under balanced trade conditions, and argue that the United States would have been a net importer of labor services under balanced trade.

performs the following three tests for the United States in a three-factor, thirty-four-country world using 1958 and 1972 data: (1) the United States exports a factor service if and only if its consumption of the factor relative to its endowment is lower than that for the world (see condition 3.58); (2) the revealed endowment rankings duplicate the actual endowment rankings; and (3) the export of a factor service by the United States implies a larger world expenditure per unit than that of the United States. He shows that (1) is violated for two of the factors (skilled labor and unskilled labor) for 1958 but is valid for the other factor (gross physical capital) for 1958 and for all three factors for 1972. Part (2) is in general violated, and so is (3) except for gross physical capital for 1958. His findings seem to contradict the results in Stern and Maskus (1981). In another test, Staiger (1988) finds that when the export of a factor service is expressed as a linear function of national and world endowments, there is evidence of misspecification. This suggests a correlation between countries' factor endowments and other characteristics of the countries that jointly determine patterns of trade.

Thus I come to an agreement with Brecher and Choudhri (1982b, p. 823) that "until it is demonstrated that one or more of these departures [from such assumptions as factor-price equalization, free trade, identical tastes, and homogeneous labor] can account for the net export of labor services by the United States, the Leontief paradox is still with us."

3.13   International Factor Movements and Factor Content of Trade

In the previous analysis, I compared international goods trade with factor movements in a simple two-good, two-factor framework. I showed that under certain conditions, they are substitutes. I also argued that goods trade can be interpreted as the exchange of factor services between two countries. Such interpretation was shown to be a very convenient way of analyzing goods trade in a multidimensional framework. Suppose now that international factor movements, instead of goods trade, is allowed between two countries. How would factor movements be different from goods trade? How differently would they affect the equilibria of both countries?

Free movements of all factors across countries lead to factor price equalization and, with identical technologies, commodity price equalization. Thus I can say that if factor price equalization holds under free goods trade and if equilibrium is unique, indirect flows of factor services are equivalent to direct factor movements. Either of them will result in the same world equilibrium. Furthermore, direct factor movements are identical to factor content of trade. This means that the theorem of factor content of trade with factor price equalization also applies to international factor movements. So if α is the ratio of home country's consumption of any good to foreign country's consumption of the same good under free trade or free factor movements, the home country will export directly factor j if $v_j/v_j^* > \alpha$ and import factor ℓ if $v_\ell/v_\ell^* < \alpha$.

Suppose that factor price equalization under free trade does not hold. Then how are the patterns of indirect trade in factors compared with the patterns of direct factor movements? This question can be answered by using the results obtained here.

By the general law of comparative advantage, the amounts of foreign factors flowing into the home country are related to the autarkic factor prices in the countries in the following way

$$(\mathbf{r}^a - \mathbf{r}^{a*}) \cdot \mathbf{k} \geq 0.$$

On the other hand, if free trade is allowed, condition (3.35) gives the relationship between the factor content of trade and autarkic factor prices: $(\mathbf{w}^a - \mathbf{w}^{a*}) \cdot \mathbf{v}^M \geq 0$. Combining these results, it can be said, loosely, that if a country indirectly exports a factor it will also tend to export the factor directly. These results are generally very weak. In the special case with two factors, the direction of indirect movement of a factor must be the same as that of direct movement of the factor.

3.14   Factor Accumulation and Dynamic Comparative Advantage

So far, the analysis is static as it is based on the assumption that factor endowments are fixed. Since the 1960s, there has been growing interest in examining the validity of some trade theorems in a dynamic context. A natural starting point is to make use of growth models that are constructed to analyze economic growth in the presence of factor accumulation. Because most of these models assume closed economies, extension of them has been made to allow international trade.[26] Many dynamic trade models assume one sector in an economy; for example, Negishi (1965), Hamada (1966), and Ruffin (1979), but these models are not suitable for analyzing the patterns of trade.

One serious attempt to investigate the effects of factor accumulation on comparative advantage is Findlay (1970). To the 2×2 framework, he introduces a third sector that produces capital. The two consumption goods are tradable. Labor and capital are not mobile internationally, a common assump-

---

26. See Findlay (1984) and Smith (1984) for two surveys of the work on trade theories in a dynamic context.

tion in this type of framework. The capital sector is also nontradable. With zero depreciation of capital, the amount of capital produced in the economy at any time is the increase in the capital stock in the economy. In equilibrium, investment is equal to saving. Findlay (1970) makes the assumption that the propensity to save is constant.

At any point in time, the factor endowments are given. Under the usual assumption that production adjusts and factors move across sectors instanta- neously and costlessly, the Findlay model behaves like the traditional 2×2 model in the short-run. Thus, if the world prices of the consumption goods at any time period are given under trade (assumed to be free), the pattern of trade of the country can be predicted using the method described. One appeal- ing result in Findlay (1970), which is compatible with what is observed for some countries, is the possibility of reversal of patterns of trade over time as countries are accumulating labor and capital.

At a steady state, a country has a constant capital-labor ratio. This means that when two trading countries are at their steady states, they have con- stant capital-labor ratios. Findlay (1970) shows that the Heckscher-Ohlin theorem holds for the countries at their steady states: The country that has a higher capital-labor ratio at steady state exports the capital-intensive good.

Although the Findlay model at a steady state looks similar to the static 2×2 model, there is a big difference between them: The steady-state capital- labor ratio of a country is not given exogenously, but instead is affected by other variables. Findlay (1970) identifies two exogenous variables: the rate of growth of labor, n, and the average propensity to save, s. By considering two countries that are marginally different from each other, Findlay shows that the country that has a higher rate growth of labor or that has a lower saving propensity has a comparative advantage in the labor-intensive good.[27] Some of the Findlay results are based on the assumption that both countries produce both consumption goods at steady states. Deardorff (1974) argues that this is a strong assumption.[28]

I now explain in more detail how the 2×2 framework can be modified to allow factor accumulation. Both goods are tradable in the world. One of them is a consumption good and the other is an investment. Such a model, which is an extension of the Uzawa two-sector growth model, is common in the

---

27. Findlay (1970) shows that if a country is not at a steady state, then it is possible that a country with a lower saving propensity has a comparative advantage in the capital-intensive good. This suggests the Leontief paradox. As Findlay argues, however, this possibility does not exist in the long run.

28. Deardorff (1974) also points out that Findlay's assumption that the capital-labor ratio of the nontradable capital sector is in between those of the other sectors in proving the dynamic stability of the model is not necessary.

trade literature, for example, Oniki and Uzawa (1965), Stiglitz (1970), Fischer and Frenkel (1972), and Smith (1977). Assume that the consumption sector is capital intensive.[29]

At any time, the factor endowments of a country are given. Its national income is represented by its GDP function $g = g(p, K, L)$, where p is the price of the consumption good, with the investment good chosen as the numeraire. Because K and L can vary over time, I drop the "bar" above them. For simplicity, I do not use any index to denote time.

The propensity to save is assumed to be constant, s. The economy as a whole saves a given proportion of its national income for investment. So investment is sg and, assuming zero depreciation for simplicity, this is the increase in capital stock:

$$\dot{K} = sg(p, K, L), \tag{3.60}$$

where the "dot" represents a derivative with respect to time. Because the GDP function is linearly homogeneous in factor endowments, condition (3.60) gives

$$\dot{K} = sL\widetilde{g}(p, k), \tag{3.60'}$$

where $\widetilde{g} = \widetilde{g}(p, k) \equiv g(p, k, 1)$, and $k \equiv K/L$ is the capital-labor ratio. Assume that labor grows at a constant rate of n. Using (3.60'), the rate of growth of the capital-labor ratio is

$$\dot{k} = \left(\frac{\dot{K}}{K} - \frac{\dot{L}}{L}\right)k = s\widetilde{g}(p, k) - nk. \tag{3.61}$$

A steady state of the economy requires that $\dot{k} = 0$, that is,

$$s\widetilde{g}(p, k) = nk. \tag{3.62}$$

Condition (3.62) is illustrated by schedule KK in Figure 3.9. To determine its slope, differentiate both sides of the condition and rearrange terms to give

$$\left.\frac{\mathrm{d}p}{\mathrm{d}k}\right|_{KK} = \frac{n - sr}{s(\partial\widetilde{g}/\partial p)}. \tag{3.63}$$

To find out the sign of the slope in (3.63), note that $\widetilde{g} = w + rk$. In a steady state, $s(w + rk) = nk$. Therefore at least in the neighborhood around a steady state, $n > sr$. I next show that given the factor intensity ranking, $\partial\widetilde{g}/\partial p \geq 0$. Refer to Figure 3.10. Schedules $c_C = p_C$ and $c_I = 1$ are the unit-cost schedules for the consumption and investment sectors, respectively, corresponding to the prevailing relative price p_C. Consider three possible cases, depending

---

29. Uzawa (1963) shows that in this type of model, a closed economy does not have a stable steady state if the investment good is capital intensive.

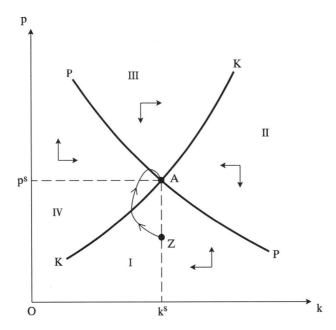

Figure 3.9

on the country's pattern of production. First, if the economy is diversified, the intersecting point of the schedules, E, represents the factor prices. Line AA' has a slope of $-1/k$ and passes through point E. Its horizontal intercept, A', gives the per capita national income, $\widetilde{g}$. If there is an increase in p_C to p'_C, then line AA' shifts to BB', implying an increase in $\widetilde{g}$. Second, if the economy is completely specialized in the consumption good, then line AA' must be tangent to schedule $c_C = p_C$ at point E. Again, when p_C increases, schedule c_C shifts out and the per capita national income goes up. Third, if the economy is completely specialized in the investment good, w and r (in terms of the investment good) are independent of p, so that the per capita national income is constant. In all these cases, $\partial \widetilde{g}/\partial p \geq 0$. Thus schedule KK in Figure 3.9 is positively sloped if the economy is diversified or completely specialized in the consumption good, but is a vertical line if the economy is completely specialized in the investment good.

Now turn to the adjustment of the price ratio. I assume that the preferences of the economy are homothetic. I first consider a closed economy. Assuming a *tâtonnement* process explained in Chapter 2, I postulate that the change in p is proportional to the excess demand for the consumption good:

$$\dot{p} = \alpha(C_C - Q_C) = \alpha L \Theta(p, k), \tag{3.64}$$

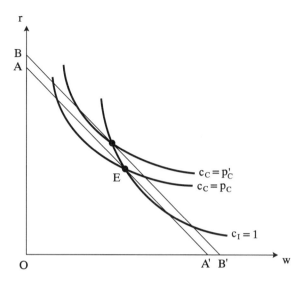

Figure 3.10

where α is a proportionality constant. Note that because of homotheticity of preferences and homogeneity of technologies, the excess demand can be written as $L\Theta(p, k)$. At a steady state, $\dot{p} = 0$, that is,

$$\Theta(p, k) = 0. \tag{3.65}$$

This steady state condition is illustrated by schedule PP in Figure 3.9.

To determine the slope of schedule PP, assume that when given factor endowments the system is stable in a Walrasian sense, meaning that $\Theta_p(p, k) < 0$, where the subscript denotes a partial derivative. If p is fixed, an increase in k when K grows faster than L will, by the Rybczynski theorem, increase the production of the consumption good by a greater proportion but decrease that of the investment. At the same time, the national income increases and the demand for each good will go up by the same proportion. As a result, an excess supply for the consumption good is created, leading to a downward pressure of p. This means that $\Theta_k < 0$. Thus the slope of schedule PP is equal to

$$\left.\frac{dp}{dk}\right|_{PP} = -\frac{\Theta_k}{\Theta_p} < 0.$$

Schedules PP and KK divide the space in the diagram into four regions. Making use of conditions (3.61) and (3.64), the directions of adjustment of the variables in these regions are represented by the arrows in the diagram. The intersecting point of the schedules, A, represents an autarkic steady state

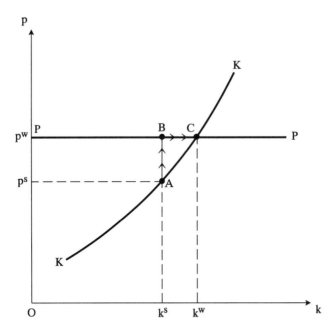

Figure 3.11

(k^s, p^s). If the economy is initially at point Z, not at the steady state point, a possible adjustment path is shown in the diagram.

I now turn to an open economy. For the time being, assume that the economy has no monopoly power so that in any time period the world price ratio is fixed at p^w, where $p^w > p^s$. Initially the economy is at the autarkic steady state point A in Figure 3.11. If free trade is now allowed, the schedule that describes zero adjustment of p becomes a horizontal line corresponding to p^w. At the same time, point A will shift to the new steady state point C. In the special case in which p adjusts instantaneously, point A jumps up to point B and then moves to the right to point C, as shown by the arrows. At point C, $s\widetilde{g}(p^w, k^w) = nk^w$ where the superscript "w" refers to the value at the new steady state. At this point, the production of the consumption good is greater than the autarkic production level because of an increase in its relative price and an increase in the capital-labor ratio. The economy may or may not be completely specialized in the production of the consumption good.[30]

In the period in which free trade is allowed, the economy has a static comparative advantage in the consumption good. (Factor endowments are fixed in

---

30. Note that in the model in Smith (1984), only the capitalists save. An implication of this assumption is that whenever the world price ratio is different from the autarkic one, no matter how small the difference is, the economy will be completely specialized.

the short-run.) Then the economy accumulates capital at a rate faster than the growth of labor as shown by the adjustment path in Figure 3.11. This enhances the comparative advantage of the economy in the consumption good so that it keeps on exporting this good. In other words, there is no reversal in the pattern of trade of the country. If, however, the country does not start from the autarkic steady state equilibrium, or if the price ratio does not adjust instantaneously so that capital-labor ratio decreases first (as in the case shown in Figure 3.9), reversal in comparative advantage is possible.

This analysis can be reversed to show the case in which $p^w < p^s$. In this case, the price ratio drops and the economy experiences a decumulation of capital. The economy has a short-run and a long-run comparative advantage in the investment good, but it may or may not be completely specialized in producing the good in the long-run.

Let me now drop the assumption that the home country is a small one. Label the economy discussed the home country and add another economy labeled the foreign country. Foreign variables are distinguished by asterisks. Both countries have identical technologies and preferences. Initially, the countries are not trading. The steady states of the countries are illustrated in Figure 3.12. Schedules PP and KK for the home country are the same as those in Figure 3.9. The foreign country has the same schedule PP because they have identical technologies and preferences. Using condition (3.62), it can easily be shown

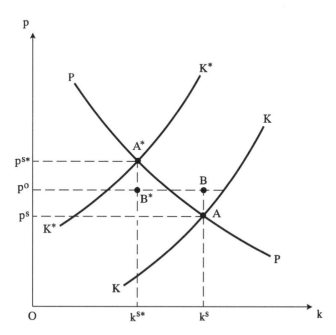

Figure 3.12

that if the foreign country has a lower saving propensity, $s^* < s$, and/or if the foreign country has a higher rate of labor growth, $n^* > n$, then schedule K*K* for the foreign country is above schedule KK for the home country, as shown in the diagram. The two autarkic steady states of the countries are depicted by points A and A*.

Suppose that initially both countries are at their steady states, represented by points A and A*. Then the home country has a lower relative price of the consumption good and a higher capital-labor ratio, meaning that it has an short-run comparative advantage in the consumption good. Suppose now that free trade between the countries is allowed, and that prices adjust instantaneously to clear markets. By the law of comparative advantage, the equilibrium price in that period is in between p^s and p^{s*}. Let it be p^o. This means that point A of the home country shifts up to point B while point A* of the foreign country shifts down to point B*. Furthermore, the home country exports the consumption good and accumulates capital, as explained before, while the foreign country exports the investment good and decumulates capital. Thus there is a generalization of the Heckscher-Ohlin theorem that in the long run, the country with a higher saving propensity or a lower labor growth rate exports the capital-intensive consumption good.

4 International Goods Trade and Capital Movement

The analysis in the previous chapter is based on two major and strong assumptions, that the countries have identical technologies and that there is no international capital movement. These two assumptions are relaxed in the present chapter. This chapter presents simple general equilibrium models and graphical apparatus to examine various issues related to international goods trade and capital movement.

The first issue investigated in this chapter is whether international capital movement may invalidate the four core trade theorems derived in Chapter 3. Indeed, it is shown that the presence of capital movement between countries invalidates some of these theorems. The rest of this chapter is devoted to analyzing the relationship between international goods trade and capital movement.

After examining the validity of these theorems, I relax the assumption of identical technologies between countries. This allows me to avoid the indeterminacy in factor mobility in the presence of free trade as described in Chapter 3. Obviously, without the assumption of identical technologies, the analysis can become quite complicated. Thus, one purpose of this chapter is to introduce two simple graphical apparatuses that are used to simplify the analysis. The first graphical apparatus focuses on the relationship between the commodity price ratio and the rental rate, and gives a good description of some of the properties of the production side of the countries. The second apparatus focuses on the relationship between a country's export level and capital inflow, and the equilibrium of the markets of one of the commodities and capital.

Using these two simple graphical apparatuses, this chapter examines several issues related to international goods trade and capital movement. For example, it examines existence and stability of equilibrium, and substitutability between trade in goods and capital movement. Also examined are the impacts of international capital movement on the patterns of trade of countries, and the relationship between comparative advantage and absolute advantage in the presence of capital movement. The last issue analyzed in this chapter is the phenomenon of "cross-hauling" of international direct investment. Using the specific-capital model, I provide a new look at this phenomenon.

4.1 The Fundamental Trade Theorems in the Presence of Capital Movement

This section examines the validity of the four fundamental trade theorems in the presence of international capital movement: the Rybczynski theorem, the Stolper-Samuelson theorem, the Heckscher-Ohlin theorem, and the factor price equalization theorem.[1] The neoclassical model described in

---

1. The earliest work on related issues are Leamer (1984) and Ethier and Svensson (1986). The present discussion is a synthesis and extension of their work.

Chapter 2 can be extended in two ways. First, free capital movement and free trade in goods are allowed, and second, I add one more factors so that there are again two immobile factors. Thus the following model has two goods (1 and 2) and three factors: capital (K), labor (L), and land (D).[2]

I begin the analysis with the home country, which is endowed with fixed endowments of capital $\overline{K}$, labor $\overline{L}$, and land $\overline{D}$. The production function of sector i is denoted by

$$Q_i = F_i(K_i, L_i, D_i),$$

which is continuously differentiable, increasing, linearly homogeneous and concave in inputs. Denote the rental rates of capital and land by r and s, and the wage rate by w.

Taking prices as given, firms in sector i jointly maximize the sectoral profit by choosing the appropriate inputs. Their problem can be described in the following way:

$$\max_{K_i, L_i, D_i} \left\{ p_i F_i(K_i, L_i, D_i) - r K_i - w L_i - s D_i \right\}. \tag{4.1}$$

By rearranging the terms, an alternative statement of their problem is

$$\max_{L_i, D_i} \left\{ \max_{K_i} \left[p_i F_i(K_i, L_i, D_i) - r K_i \right] - w L_i - s D_i \right\}. \tag{4.1'}$$

Let r_i ($\equiv r/p_i$) be the real rental rate in terms of good i, and let me define a new function for sector i:

$$H_i(L_i, D_i, r_i) \equiv \max_{K_i} \left[F_i(K_i, L_i, D_i) - r_i K_i \right]. \tag{4.2}$$

Denote the solution to the H_i problem by $K_i = G_i(L_i, D_i, r_i)$. From condition (4.1'), $G_i(L_i, D_i, r_i)$ can be interpreted as the derived demand for capital by sector i when given the real rental rate and labor and land inputs. Because the production function $F_i(K_i, L_i, D_i)$ is linearly homogeneous, condition (4.2) implies that $G_i(L_i, D_i, r_i)$ is linearly homogeneous in L_i and D_i when given r_i. This means that $H_i(L_i, D_i, r_i)$ is also linearly homogeneous in L_i and D_i when given r_i. Furthermore, by the envelope theorem, the derivatives of $H_i(L_i, D_i, r_i)$ with respect to L_i and/or D_i are equal to the corresponding derivatives of $F_i(K_i, L_i, D_i)$; for example,

$$H_{iL} \equiv \frac{\partial H_i}{\partial L_i} = \frac{\partial F_i}{\partial L_i}$$

---

2. For an analysis of these four theorems in another framework with higher dimensions, see Ethier and Svensson (1986). The dimensions of the present framework are kept as low as possible, because it is well known that increasing the dimensions of the framework can severely limit the validity of these theorems.

$$H_{iD} \equiv \frac{\partial H_i}{\partial D_i} = \frac{\partial F_i}{\partial D_i}.$$

I can further show that $H_i(L_i, D_i, r_i)$ is concave in L_i and D_i when given r_i. Thus $H_i(L_i, D_i, r_i)$ behaves like a production function. Substitute it into (4.1′) to give an alternative statement of the profit maximization problem:

$$\max_{L_i, D_i} \left\{ p_i H_i(L_i, D_i, r_i) - wL_i - sD_i \right\}. \tag{4.1″}$$

By treating $H_i(L_i, D_i, r_i)$ as a production function, condition (4.1″) can be used to define a framework that is similar to the two-factor, two-sector framework analyzed in the previous two chapters. The third factor, capital, which can move freely across countries, appears to play an indirect role through its effect on the real rental rates. This approach greatly simplifies the analysis.

4.1.1   The Rybczynski Theorem

Consider the home country and suppose that r, p_1 and p_2 are fixed. Without loss of generality, assume that sector 1 is land intensive, with a higher land-labor ratio than that in sector 2 at any given factor prices. As explained previously, $H_i(L_i, D_i, r_i)$ behaves like a production function with the usual properties. Thus in terms of functions $H_i(L_i, D_i, r_i)$, the model behaves like the 2×2 framework analyzed in Chapter 2, and the same analysis can be used to argue that given commodity and factor prices, an increase in the endowment of land (respectively labor) will increase H_1 (respectively H_2) and decrease H_2 (respectively H_1). Furthermore, the magnification effects hold: If $\widehat{D} > \widehat{L}$, then

$$\widehat{H}_1 > \widehat{D} > \widehat{L} > \widehat{H}_2, \tag{4.3}$$

where "$\widehat{}$" represents the rate of change of a variable.

Condition (4.3) is similar to the Rybczynski theorem, but it does not give output effects. To determine the latter, I have to find out the relationship between $\widehat{H}_i$ and $\widehat{Q}_i$, $i = 1, 2$. As shown in Chapter 2, when factor prices are given, the land-labor ratio in each sector is unchanged. Because the capital demand function $G_i(L_i, D_i, r_i)$ is linearly homogeneous in L_i and D_i, a fixed labor-land ratio implies fixed capital-labor and capital-land ratios. By homogeneity of $F_i(K_i, L_i, D_i)$ and $H_i(L_i, D_i, r_i)$, the ratio of any input to either Q_i or $H_i(L_i, D_i, r_i)$ is fixed. This means that $\widehat{Q}_i = \widehat{H}_i = \widehat{K}_i = \widehat{L}_i = \widehat{D}_i$. Making use of this result, I get the magnification effects and the Rybczynski theorem: If $\widehat{D} > \widehat{L}$, then

$$\widehat{Q}_1 > \widehat{D} > \widehat{L} > \widehat{Q}_2. \tag{4.3′}$$

The validity of the Rybczynski theorem is not surprising, because I have already shown that given commodity prices and capital rental rate, land-labor and capital-labor ratios are fixed. This implies a one-to-one correspondence between H_i and Q_i. Once we get (4.3), result (4.3′) immediately follows.

4.1.2   The Stolper-Samuelson Theorem

There are three prices that are treated as parameters when analyzing the production side of the economy: r, p_1 and p_2. I consider the effects of changes in these prices separately. First, I allow possible changes in commodity prices while r is fixed.

Define a_{ji} as the cost-minimizing amount of factor j to produce one unit of good i, $j = K, L, D$. The unit cost of sector i then equals $r\,a_{Ki} + w\,a_{Li} + s\,a_{Di}$. A positive output and zero profit imply

$$p_i = r\,a_{Ki} + w\,a_{Li} + s\,a_{Di}. \tag{4.4}$$

Differentiate both sides of (4.4), keeping r fixed and rearrange terms to give

$$\widehat{p}_i = \theta_{Li}\,\widehat{w} + \theta_{Di}\,\widehat{s} + \theta_{Ki}\,\widehat{a}_{Ki} + \theta_{Li}\,\widehat{a}_{Li} + \theta_{Di}\,\widehat{a}_{Di}, \tag{4.5}$$

where θ_{ji} is the share of factor j in the cost of producing good i. Cost minimization means that $\theta_{Ki}\widehat{a}_{Ki} + \theta_{Li}\widehat{a}_{Li} + \theta_{Di}\widehat{a}_{Di} = 0$. Equation (4.5) reduces to

$$\widehat{p}_i = \theta_{Li}\widehat{w} + \theta_{Di}\widehat{s}. \tag{4.5′}$$

Equations (4.5′) can be solved for $\widehat{w}$ and $\widehat{s}$

$$\widehat{w} = \frac{\theta_{D2}\widehat{p}_1 - \theta_{D1}\widehat{p}_2}{|\theta|} \tag{4.6a}$$

$$\widehat{s} = \frac{\theta_{L1}\widehat{p}_2 - \theta_{L2}\widehat{p}_1}{|\theta|} \tag{4.6b}$$

where

$$\theta = \begin{pmatrix} \theta_{L1} & \theta_{D1} \\ \theta_{L2} & \theta_{D2} \end{pmatrix}.$$

It is easy to show that if good 1 is land intensive with $D_1/L_1 > D_2/L_2$, then $|\theta| < 0$. Suppose that $\widehat{p}_1 > 0$, $\widehat{p}_2 = 0$, then $\widehat{s} > \widehat{p}_1 > 0 > \widehat{w}$. Similar results for the case in which good 1 is labor intensive can also be established. Thus I conclude that the Stolper-Samuelson theorem holds.

The magnification effects of changes in commodity prices on w and s are not valid in the sense that when $\widehat{p}_1 > \widehat{p}_2 > 0$, it is not necessarily true that $\widehat{s} > \widehat{p}_1 > \widehat{p}_2 > \widehat{w}$. To see why, consider the following example: Let $\theta_{L1} = 0.1$, $\theta_{D1} = 0.8$, $\theta_{L2} = 0.2$ and $\theta_{D2} = 0.1$. Thus $|\theta| = \theta_{L1}\theta_{D2} - \theta_{L2}\theta_{D1} = -0.15 < 0$. Further suppose that $\widehat{p}_1 = 0.15 > \widehat{p}_2 = 0.1$. Then by (4.6b) $\widehat{s} = 0.13$, which is less than $\widehat{p}_1$, violating the magnification effects.

The reason that the magnification effects no longer hold is because when sector i uses three factors, $\theta_{Li} + \theta_{Di}$ is less than unity and thus there is no longer any direct relationship between θ_{Li} and θ_{Di}, which is the case when only two factors are used.[3]

Now turn to the effects of an increase in r while commodity prices are fixed. Differentiate equation (4.4) and use the cost-minimizing condition to give

$$0 = \theta_{Ki}\widehat{r} + \theta_{Li}\widehat{w} + \theta_{Di}\widehat{s}, \quad i = 1, 2,$$

which can be solved for the changes in w and s:

$$\widehat{w} = \frac{\theta_{D1}\theta_{K2} - \theta_{D2}\theta_{K1}}{|\theta|}\widehat{r} \tag{4.7a}$$

$$\widehat{s} = \frac{\theta_{L2}\theta_{K1} - \theta_{L1}\theta_{K2}}{|\theta|}\widehat{r}. \tag{4.7b}$$

Several results can be obtained from (4.7). First, because commodity prices are fixed, zero profit implies that an increase in r must lead to a decrease in the price of at least one of the immobile factors. Second, by (4.7a), $\widehat{w}$ is positive as a result of an increase in r if

$$\frac{L_1}{L_2} > \frac{D_1}{D_2} > \frac{K_1}{K_2} \quad \text{or} \quad \frac{K_1}{K_2} > \frac{D_1}{D_2} > \frac{L_1}{L_2}.$$

Consider land as the middle factor if either of these relations is true. Similarly, by (4.7b), $\widehat{s} > 0$ as a result of an increase in r if labor is the middle factor. If alternatively capital is the middle factor, conditions (4.7) imply that an increase in r will lower both w and s. These results are summarized as follows: First, if capital is not the middle factor, then an increase in r hurts the middle factor and benefits the other immobile factor. Second, if capital is the middle factor, then an increase in r hurts both immobile factors.

4.1.3 The Factor Price Equalization Theorem

Suppose now that there are two countries with the usual assumptions: identical and linearly homogeneous production functions, no trade impediments and transport costs, no factor intensity reversal, and diversification in production.

With free capital mobility, rental rates are equalized. Because $H_i(L_i, D_i, r_i)$ behaves like a production function when r_i is treated as a parameter, I can use the traditional arguments to show that if commodity prices and the rental rate are equalized, the prices of labor and land must also be equalized.

---

3. Recall that with only two factors, the determinant of θ can be reduced to $\theta_{L1} - \theta_{L2}$.

4.1.4   The Heckscher-Ohlin Theorem

To examine the validity of this theorem, make the usual assumptions that the countries have identical technologies, and identical and homothetic preferences. Following the approach of Jones and Ruffin (1975), Ferguson (1978), and Leamer (1984), comparative advantages of the countries are analyzed under the assumption that world capital market always clears.

First look at the physical definition of factor abundance. I showed earlier that the Rybczynski theorem is valid in the presence of capital mobility. Thus at any given commodity prices and rental rate of capital, the home country, as compared with the foreign country, produces relatively more of the good that uses its abundant factor intensively. This means that with equalization of rental rates of capital, and if both countries have the same commodity prices and have identical and homothetic preferences, each country must have an excess supply of the good that uses its abundant factor intensively. This implies that if only free capital mobility is allowed, each country must have a lower relative price of the good that uses its abundant factor intensively, and thus a comparative advantage in that good. Thus the Heckscher-Ohlin theorem follows.

Then turn to the price definition of factor abundance. Without loss of generality, choose good 2 as the numeraire and assume that sector 1 is land intensive. I have shown that with international capital movement and when $\widehat{p}_1 > 0$ and $\widehat{p}_2 = 0$, then $\widehat{s} > \widehat{p}_1 > 0 > \widehat{w}$. Suppose that the home country is abundant in labor according to the price definition. So the home country has a higher s/w ratio in the absence of trade in goods (but after equalization of capital rental rates). Thus ruling out factor intensity reversal, the home country must have a higher relative price of good 1, that is, it has a comparative advantage in the labor-intensive good 2. Thus the Heckscher-Ohlin theorem follows.

4.2   Free Goods Trade and Capital Movement

In the previous section, I assume that the countries have identical technologies and show that perfect capital mobility preserves many results of the fundamental trade theorems. I now relax the assumption of identical technologies and preferences and consider a more general framework in which the countries can differ in any way in terms of technologies, preferences, and factor endowments. I do keep the assumptions of constant returns and perfect competition. The dimension of the present framework is kept low in order to get more insights.[4] Capital is mobile internationally, but labor is not.

---

4. Batra and Casas (1976) and Das and Lee (1979) consider a three-factor, two-sector model in which one of the factors, capital, is internationally mobile. The implication of having three factors in each country, whether the two immobile factors are sector-specific, is that the rental rate of

The techniques introduced in Chapter 2 are now used to derive the equilibrium under simultaneous goods trade and capital mobility. I first describe the economy of the home country. Choosing good 2 as the numeraire, define p as the relative price of good 1 and denote the given labor and capital endowments by $\overline{L}$ and $\overline{K}$, respectively. Suppose that an amount of foreign capital κ works in the home country (negative κ for an outflow of domestic capital). The home GDP function can be denoted by $g(p, \overline{K} + \kappa, \overline{L})$. To simplify the notation, I drop the fixed factor endowments from the GDP function, which is then written as $g(p, \kappa)$. The supply of good 1 is equal to $Q_1(p, \kappa) = \partial g / \partial p$, and the market rental rate of capital is given by $r(p, \kappa) = \partial g / \partial \kappa$. The foreign capital earns r per unit, which is repatriated out of the country.

Assuming the existence of a social utility function, I can define the indirect trade utility function (ITU) of the home country as $V(p, \kappa, b)$, where b is the transfer the country receives from the rest of the world, and where again for simplicity the fixed factor endowments are dropped from the function. With repatriation of the earnings of foreign capital and no other transfers, I have $b = -r\kappa$. As a result, the ITU function is simplified as $V(p, \kappa, -r\kappa)$. I define $I \equiv g(p, \kappa) - r\kappa$ as the national income level of the country.[5]

Denote the export of good 1 by $E_1 = E_1(p, \kappa, b)$ (negative E_1 for import of good 1). As explained in Chapter 2, E_1 is proportional to the derivative of the ITU function with respect to the relative price of good 1:

$$E_1(p, \kappa, b) = \frac{1}{\lambda} \frac{\partial V}{\partial p}, \tag{4.8}$$

where λ is the marginal utility of income. Without satiation, $\lambda > 0$. Alternatively, export of good 1 equals domestic production, $Q_1(p, \kappa)$, less domestic consumption, $C_1(p, I)$:

$$E_1(p, \kappa, b) = Q_1(p, \kappa) - C_1(p, I), \tag{4.9}$$

where $C_1(p, I)$ is the Marshallian demand for good 1. Define m_1 as the marginal propensity to consume good 1, that is, $m_1 \equiv p \partial C_1 / \partial I$. If no inferior goods are present, $0 < m_1 < 1$.

I can simplify condition (4.8) or (4.9) and define a reduced form export function:

$$\mathcal{E}_1(p, \kappa) \equiv E_1(p, \kappa, -r(p, \kappa)\kappa). \tag{4.10}$$

---

capital in each country is a function of the commodity price ratio and the quantity of capital that moves from one country to another.

5. Note that if domestic capital flows out (when κ is negative), it earns and repatriates back the foreign rental rate r^* in the absence of any foreign income taxes. So the national income is given by $g(p, \kappa) - r^*\kappa$. For simplicity and because at the equilibrium under free capital movement rental rates are equalized, I do not consider this case explicitly.

To economize the notation, use subscripts to denote partial derivatives of function $\mathcal{E}_1(p, \kappa)$: $\mathcal{E}_{1p} \equiv \partial \mathcal{E}_1(p, \kappa)/\partial p$ and $\mathcal{E}_{1\kappa} \equiv \partial \mathcal{E}_1(p, \kappa)/\partial \kappa$. It is well known that the sign of the price derivative $\mathcal{E}_{1p}$ is positive at the autarkic point but becomes negative when the offer curve bends backward (inelastic import demand). The effect of capital inflow on export can be obtained by differentiating condition (4.9) to give

$$\mathcal{E}_{1\kappa} = \frac{\partial Q_1}{\partial \kappa} - \frac{\partial C_1}{\partial \kappa} = \frac{\partial Q_1}{\partial \kappa} - \frac{m_1}{p}\frac{\partial I}{\partial \kappa}. \tag{4.11}$$

The capital effect depends on the pattern of production of the country. I analyze three possible cases separately.

Diversification in Production

If the economy is diversified, then by the Rybczynski theorem, $\partial Q_1/\partial \kappa$ is positive if and only if sector 1 is capital intensive. The effect of capital inflow on national income is

$$\frac{\partial I}{\partial \kappa} = \frac{\partial g}{\partial \kappa} - r - \kappa \frac{\partial r}{\partial \kappa}. \tag{4.12}$$

Because $\partial g/\partial \kappa = r$ and with diversification r depends only on p but not on κ, I have $\partial r/\partial k = 0$. Thus condition (4.12) reduces to

$$\frac{\partial I}{\partial \kappa} = 0. \tag{4.12'}$$

Because the national income remains constant when the relative commodity price is fixed, so does the consumption of goods. Thus (4.11) reduces to

$$\mathcal{E}_{1\kappa} = \frac{\partial Q_1}{\partial \kappa} = \frac{\partial r}{\partial p}, \tag{4.13a}$$

where the last equality is due to the reciprocity relation. Let us use r_p to denote $\partial r/\partial p$. By (4.13a), $\mathcal{E}_{1\kappa}$ is positive if and only if sector 1 is capital intensive.

Complete Specialization in Good 1

If the economy is completely specialized in good 1, the output of good 1 is given by its production function: $Q_1 = F_1(\overline{K} + \kappa, \overline{L})$, where all factors are allocated to sector 1. Denote the marginal product of capital by $F_{1K}(\kappa)$ and its derivative by $F_{1KK}(\kappa)$, where for convenience I drop the exogenously given capital and labor endowments from the functions. By assumption, $F_{1K} > 0$ and $F_{1KK} < 0$. The rental rate of capital is $r = pF_{1K}(\kappa)$, which depends on p and κ. Its derivatives are

$$\frac{\partial r}{\partial p} = F_{1K} > 0 \tag{4.14a}$$

$$\frac{\partial r}{\partial \kappa} = p F_{1KK} < 0. \tag{4.14b}$$

Using condition (4.14b), the capital effect on national income is

$$\frac{\partial I}{\partial \kappa} = \frac{\partial g}{\partial \kappa} - r - \kappa \frac{\partial r}{\partial \kappa} = -\kappa \frac{\partial r}{\partial \kappa} = -p\kappa F_{1KK} > 0.$$

The capital effect on consumption is then equal to

$$\frac{\partial C_1}{\partial \kappa} = \frac{m_1}{p} \frac{\partial I}{\partial \kappa} = -\frac{m_1 \kappa}{p} \frac{\partial r}{\partial \kappa}.$$

Substitute these results into (4.11) to give the effect of capital inflow on export:

$$\mathcal{E}_{1\kappa} = F_{1K} - \frac{m_1}{p} \frac{\partial I}{\partial k} = \frac{1}{p}\left(r + m_1 \kappa \frac{\partial r}{\partial \kappa}\right). \tag{4.13b}$$

To determine the sign of $\mathcal{E}_{1\kappa}$ note that $r + \kappa \partial r / \partial \kappa = \partial(r\kappa)/\partial \kappa$, which is the rate of change in the total payment to foreign capital with respect to capital inflow. Assume that this is positive.[6] Thus if no inferior goods exist so that $0 < m_1 < 1$, then $\mathcal{E}_{1\kappa} > 0$.

Complete Specialization in Good 2

If the economy produces good 2 only, the export function of good 1 reduces to $E_1 = -C_1$. The output of good 2 is given by its production function $Q_2 = F_2(\overline{K} + \kappa, \overline{L})$. Denote the marginal product of capital by $F_{2K}(\kappa)$ and its derivative by $F_{2KK}(\kappa)$, where $\overline{K}$ and $\overline{L}$ are dropped from the functions for simplicity. By assumption $F_{2K} > 0$ and $F_{2KK} < 0$. The rental rate of capital is the marginal product of capital in sector 2: $r = F_{2K}$. Thus the capital effect on national income is

$$\frac{\partial I}{\partial \kappa} = \frac{\partial g}{\partial \kappa} - r - \kappa \frac{\partial r}{\partial \kappa} = -\kappa \frac{\partial r}{\partial \kappa} = -\kappa F_{2KK} > 0.$$

This is used to give the capital effect on export:

$$\mathcal{E}_{1\kappa} = \frac{m_1 \kappa}{p} \frac{\partial r}{\partial \kappa} < 0. \tag{4.13c}$$

The foreign economy can be described in a similar way, except that foreign variables are distinguished by asterisks. For example, $E_1^* = \mathcal{E}_1^*(p^*, \kappa^*)$ is the foreign export function of good 1, p^* is the foreign relative price of good 1, and κ^* represents capital flowing into the foreign country (negative for capital flowing out).

---

6. There are many production functions, such as CES production functions, with which $r\kappa$ increases with κ. Alternatively, if the foreign country has monopoly power in capital supply, it will not send capital up to the point at which $r + \kappa \partial r / \partial \kappa$ is negative.

The equilibrium of the two countries with free goods trade and capital movement is described by the following conditions:

$$\mathcal{E}_1(p, \kappa) + \mathcal{E}_1^*(p^*, \kappa^*) = 0 \qquad (4.15a)$$

$$\kappa + \kappa^* = 0 \qquad (4.15b)$$

$$p = p^* \qquad (4.15c)$$

$$r(p, \kappa) = r^*(p^*, \kappa^*). \qquad (4.15d)$$

Condition (4.15a) is the clearing condition for the good-1 market while condition (4.15b) is due to the fact that in this two-country framework, capital flowing into the home country is the capital flowing out of the foreign country. The other two conditions give price equalization. Note that there is no equation describing the equilibrium of the good-2 market. It is because by Walras's law, equilibrium of the good-1 and capital markets implies equilibrium of the good-2 market. Recall that $r = r(p, \kappa)$ and $r^* = r^*(p^*, \kappa^*)$ are the derivatives with respect to capital endowment of the respective GDP functions of the countries. Depending on the pattern of production, the rental rate of each country may depend only on the relative price of good 1 or capital movement. The four conditions in (4.15) can be solved for the four unknowns: p, p^*, κ and κ^*.

The budget constraint of the economy defines the balance of current account of the home country (and thus that of the foreign country):

$$pE_1 + E_2 = r\kappa. \qquad (4.16)$$

4.3   Two Graphical Apparatuses

This section introduces two graphical apparatuses to depict the world equilibrium. These apparatuses, which in some sense are dual to each other, emphasize different variables in the framework. They are used later to derive many properties of the present model as well as the relationship between goods trade and capital movement.

4.3.1   The p–r Relation

First look at the home country. As noted, the rental rate (in terms of good 2) is given by the function, $r = r(p, \kappa)$. Treating κ as a parameter, this function is illustrated by schedule ABCD in Figure 4.1. The schedule consists of three parts. Curve BC represents the relation between p and r when the economy is diversified so that r does not depend on κ. By the Stolper-Samuelson theorem, BC is positively sloped if and only if good 1 is capital intensive. This is the case shown in the diagram. Because of the magnification effect, the slope of

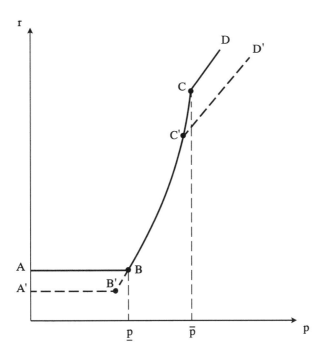

Figure 4.1

BC at any point is greater than that of a line from the origin to that point, meaning that the percentage increase in r is greater than that of p.

When given factor endowments and capital movement, define two price levels $\underline{p}$ and $\overline{p}$ so that when $p \leq \underline{p}$ the economy is completely specialized in good 2 and when $p \geq \overline{p}$ the economy is completely specialized in good 1. In the former case, the rental rate depends entirely on factor proportion, not on p, so that we have $r = F_{2K}(\kappa)$, which is the marginal product of capital in sector 2. Thus when given the value of κ, line segment AB in Figure 4.1 is a horizontal line. In the latter case with complete specialization in good 1, the rental rate is given by $r = p F_{1K}(\kappa)$. Given the value of κ, the p–r relation is line CD from the origin with a slope of $F_{1K}(\kappa)$.

An increase in κ will lower the marginal product of capital in a sector if only that good is produced, but it will not affect r at any given p as long as the economy is diversified. Thus in terms of Figure 4.1, when more foreign capital flows in, line AB shifts down and line CD gets less steep, while curve BC remains unchanged except that both points B and C shift down while both $\overline{p}$ and $\underline{p}$ drop. The new p–r curve is represented by A′B′C′D′.

Now bring in the foreign country. Figure 4.2 shows the r-schedule for the home country and the r^*-schedule for the foreign country before any international movement of capital. With different technologies across countries,

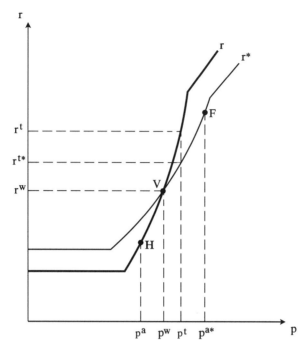

Figure 4.2

the two schedules do not coincide, but the diagram shows the case in which good 1 is capital intensive in both countries. Point H and point F show the autarkic relative price of good 1 and rental rate in the home and foreign countries, respectively. With $p^a < p^{a*}$, the home country is said to have a comparative advantage in good 1 in the absence of capital movement. If only goods trade is allowed, the home country exports good 1 and import good 2. Let the free-trade price ratio be equal to p^t. In the case shown in the diagram, the domestic free-trade rental rate is greater than the foreign rental rate under free trade. Thus when capital movement is now permitted, foreign capital will flow into the home country. As explained previously, capital movement will shift the line segments but not the curved parts of the schedules, but for simplicity, these shifts are not shown in the diagram.

Figure 4.2 shows the case in which the two schedules intersect at a point, V, on the curved parts of the schedules corresponding to diversification. It is clear that at point V conditions (4.15c) and (4.15d) are satisfied. It is tempting to conjecture that in such a case, an equilibrium exists with free goods trade and capital movement and with diversification in both countries, but this conjecture is wrong. I will explain why later.

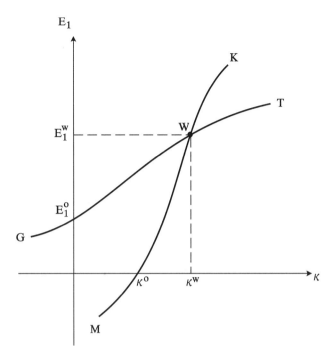

Figure 4.3

4.3.2 The E_1–κ Relation

I now turn to another graphical technique for analyzing international goods trade and capital movement. Under this approach, which was developed in Wong (1986a), the four equilibrium conditions in (4.15) are reduced to two schedules, labeled as GT and KM in Figure 4.3. *Schedule GT*, which comes from conditions (4.15a) to (4.15c), describes the equilibrium of the world good-1 market. Because condition (4.15d) may not be satisfied along schedule GT, however, the capital market does not necessarily clear. In contrast, *schedule KM* is based on conditions (4.15a), (4.15b), and (4.15d). It thus assumes the equilibrium of the capital market but not necessarily that of the good-1 market. A point of intersection between these two schedules, at which the four equilibrium conditions are satisfied, represents an equilibrium under free goods trade and capital movement. These schedules are described in more detail as follows.

Schedule GT

Substitute conditions (4.15b) and (4.15c) into (4.15a) to give

$$\mathcal{E}_1(p, \kappa) + \mathcal{E}_1^*(p, -\kappa) = 0. \tag{4.17}$$

Assuming that the partial derivative with respect to p of the sum of export functions does not vanish, equation (4.17) is inverted to give p as a function of κ, $p = \phi(\kappa)$. Function $\phi(\kappa)$ shows the equilibrium world free-trade relative price of good 1, as κ is given as a parameter. Function $\phi(\kappa)$ is substituted into the home export supply function to give

$$E_1 = \mathcal{E}_1(\phi(\kappa), \kappa) \equiv \Theta^G(\kappa). \tag{4.18}$$

Function $\Theta^G(\kappa)$, which is illustrated as schedule GT in Figure 4.3, shows the free-trade equilibrium export level of good 1 of the home country when κ is treated as a parameter. The vertical intercept of GT gives the level of export of good 1 by the home country in the absence of capital movement. This level of export of good 1, denoted by E_1^o in the diagram, can be positive or negative, depending on the comparative advantage of the home country before capital moves.

The slope of GT can be obtained as follows. Differentiate (4.17) and rearrange terms to give

$$\phi'(\kappa) = \frac{\mathcal{E}_{1\kappa*}^* - \mathcal{E}_{1\kappa}}{\mathcal{E}_{1p} + \mathcal{E}_{1p*}^*}, \tag{4.19}$$

which represents the effect of capital movement on the free-trade relative price of good 1. For Walrasian stability in the good-1 market at any given level of capital movement, I assume that $\mathcal{E}_{1p} + \mathcal{E}_{1p*}^* > 0$. Thus $\phi'(\kappa)$ has the same sign as $\mathcal{E}_{1\kappa*}^* - \mathcal{E}_{1\kappa}$. As explained previously, the values of $\mathcal{E}_{1\kappa}$ and $\mathcal{E}_{1\kappa*}^*$ depend on whether the countries are completely specialized. For example, if both countries are diversified, condition (4.13a) gives $\mathcal{E}_{1\kappa*}^* - \mathcal{E}_{1\kappa} = \partial r^*/\partial p^* - \partial r/\partial p$ which can be substituted into (4.19).

Differentiate the export supply function of the home country $E_1 = \mathcal{E}_1(p, \kappa)$ and use (4.19) to give the slope of schedule GT:

$$\left. \frac{dE_1}{d\kappa} \right|_{GT} = \frac{\mathcal{E}_{1p}\mathcal{E}_{1\kappa*}^* + \mathcal{E}_{1\kappa}\mathcal{E}_{1p*}^*}{\mathcal{E}_{1p} + \mathcal{E}_{1p*}^*}. \tag{4.20}$$

Recall that for Walrasian stability, $\mathcal{E}_{1p} + \mathcal{E}_{1p*}^*$ is assumed to be positive. Thus if both of them are positive, or if one of them is negative but of a sufficiently small magnitude, then GT is positively (respectively negatively) sloped if $\mathcal{E}_{1\kappa}$ and $\mathcal{E}_{1\kappa*}^*$ are both positive (respectively negative). As explained earlier, $\mathcal{E}_{1\kappa}$ is positive (respectively negative) if the home country is diversified and if good 1 is capital (respectively labor) intensive, or if the home country is specialized in good 1 (respectively 2). These conditions also apply to the foreign country.

Schedule KM

I now turn to another schedule, KM, which represents equilibria of the world capital market at different values of E_1 when commodity prices may not be equalized. Recall that for the home country $r = r(p, \kappa)$. Because the dependence of r on p and κ relies on the pattern of production of the country, I consider three different cases separately: (1) diversification, (2) specialization in good 1, and (3) specialization in good 2. The analysis applies also to the foreign country.

I analyze cases (1) and (2) first. In case (1), with diversification, the rental rate r depends on p but not on κ, and in case (2), with specialization in good 1, the rental rate is equal to $r = p F_{1K}(\kappa)$. In these two cases, I can express the domestic price ratio as $p = \rho(r, \kappa)$. The functional form of $\rho(r, \kappa)$ and its derivatives depend on the production pattern. For convenience, define $\rho_r \equiv \partial\rho/\partial r$ and $\rho_\kappa \equiv \partial\rho/\partial \kappa$. Under diversification, ρ_r is positive if and only if sector 1 is capital intensive, and ρ_κ is zero. If only good 1 is produced, totally differentiate $r = p F_{1K}(\kappa)$ and rearrange terms to give $\rho_r = 1/F_{1K} > 0$ and $\rho_\kappa = -p F_{1KK}/F_{1K} > 0$. For the foreign country, I also define $p^* = \rho^*(r^*, \kappa^*)$ when it is diversified or specialized in good 1.

Substitute these two price equations, and conditions (4.15b) and (4.15d) into condition (4.15a) to give

$$\mathcal{E}_1(\rho(r, \kappa), \kappa) + \mathcal{E}_1^*(\rho^*(r, -\kappa), -\kappa) = 0. \tag{4.21}$$

Assuming that $\mathcal{E}_{1p}\partial\rho/\partial r + \mathcal{E}_{1p^*}^* \partial\rho^*/\partial r^*$ does not vanish, condition (4.21) is inverted to give the equilibrium rental rate in terms of the capital movement, $r = \theta(\kappa)$. This function is substituted into the export supply function of the home country to give

$$E_1 = \mathcal{E}_1(\rho(\theta(\kappa), \kappa), \kappa) \equiv \Theta^K(\kappa). \tag{4.22}$$

Function $\Theta^K(\kappa)$ is represented by schedule KM in Figure 4.3. To interpret schedule KM, imagine that the home country gives a gift of E_1 of good 1 to the foreign country, and schedule KM represents the equilibrium value of κ under free capital movement. The horizontal intercept of the schedule gives the amount of free capital movement κ^o in the absence of goods trade. If the equilibrium of the world capital market is Walrasian stable, then the space in Figure 4.3 left (respectively right) of schedule KM represents a home rental rate higher (respectively lower) than the foreign rental rate.

The slope of schedule KM can be obtained as follows. Differentiate (4.21) and rearrange terms to give

$$\theta'(\kappa) = \frac{\mathcal{E}_{1\kappa^*}^* - \mathcal{E}_{1\kappa} + \mathcal{E}_{1p^*}^* \rho_{\kappa^*}^* - \mathcal{E}_{1p}\rho_\kappa}{\mathcal{E}_{1p}\rho_r + \mathcal{E}_{1p^*}^* \rho_{r^*}^*}. \tag{4.23}$$

Then differentiate (4.22) and use (4.23) to yield

$$\frac{dE_1}{d\kappa}\bigg|_{KM} = \frac{\mathcal{E}_{1p}\rho_r\mathcal{E}_{1\kappa^*}^* + \mathcal{E}_{1\kappa}\rho_{r^*}^*\mathcal{E}_{1p^*}^* + \mathcal{E}_{1p}\mathcal{E}_{1p^*}^*(\rho_r\rho_{\kappa^*}^* + \rho_{r^*}^*\rho_\kappa)}{\mathcal{E}_{1p}\rho_r + \mathcal{E}_{1p^*}^* \rho_{r^*}^*}, \tag{4.24}$$

which represents the slope of schedule KM. Note that when both economies are diversified, $\rho_\kappa = \rho_{\kappa*}^* = 0$, and $\mathcal{E}_{1\kappa}$ and ρ_r, and $\mathcal{E}_{1\kappa*}^*$ and ρ_{r*}^* always have the same sign. Thus under diversification, if both $\mathcal{E}_{1p}$ and $\mathcal{E}_{1p*}^*$ are positive, or if one of them is negative but is insiginificant in magnitude, a sufficient condition that schedule KM is positively (respectively negatively) sloped is that $\mathcal{E}_{1\kappa}$ and $\mathcal{E}_{1\kappa*}^*$ are both positive (respectively negative).

I now turn to case (3) in which one of the countries is specialized in good 2. Without loss of generality, assume that the home country produces only good 2 while the foreign country produces both goods or just good 1. For the home country producing only good 2, the rental rate is given by the marginal product of capital in that sector, $r = F_{2K}(\kappa)$. Substitute the equilibrium condition $r = r^*$ into the foreign function ρ^* defined previously to give $p^* = \rho^*(F_{2K}(\kappa), -\kappa)$ where $\kappa^* = -\kappa$ from (4.15b). As a result, in this case, p^* depends only on the amount of capital movement κ. Let us define $\psi^*(\kappa) \equiv \rho^*(F_{2K}(\kappa), -\kappa)$. The derivative of $\psi^*(\kappa)$ is equal to:

$$\psi^{*\prime}(\kappa) = \rho_{r*}^* F_{2KK} - \rho_{\kappa*}^*.$$

The sign of $\psi^{*\prime}(\kappa)$ depends on the foreign production pattern. If the foreign country is specialized in good 1, the above analysis shows that $\rho_{r*}^* > 0$ and $\rho_{\kappa*}^* < 0$, implying that the sign of $\psi^{*\prime}(\kappa)$ is ambiguous. If the foreign country is diversified, then $\rho_{\kappa*}^* = 0$, and $\psi^{*\prime}(\kappa) < 0$ if and only if good 1 is capital intensive. Using function $\psi^*(\kappa)$ and the equilibrium condition (4.15a), the export supply of the home country can be written as

$$E_1 = -\mathcal{E}_1^*(\psi^*(\kappa), -\kappa). \tag{4.22$'$}$$

Condition (4.22$'$) is illustrated by schedule KM in Figure 4.3 when the home country is specialized in good 2. The slope of schedule KM is obtained by differentiating condition (4.22$'$) and is equal to, after rearranging terms,

$$\left. \frac{dE_1}{d\kappa} \right|_{KM} = \mathcal{E}_{1\kappa*}^* - \mathcal{E}_{1p*}^* \psi^{*\prime}. \tag{4.24$'$}$$

As explained earlier, $\mathcal{E}_{1\kappa*}^* > 0$ and $\psi^{*\prime}(\kappa) < 0$ if and only if good 1 is capital intensive when the foreign economy is diversified. For Walrasian stability of equilibrium of the foreign good-1 market, $\mathcal{E}_{1p*}^*$ is assumed to be positive. Thus when the home country is specialized in good 2, schedule KM is positively sloped if the foreign country is specialized in good 1, or if good 1 is capital intensive when the foreign economy is diversified.

4.4   The Chipman Flat and Equilibrium with Diversification

Existence of an equilibrium described by conditions (4.15) can be proved by the usual method for an Arrow-Debreu type economy. An interesting question is whether there exists an *equilibrium* under which both countries are diversified in production. A related question is whether there exists an *efficient production point* with diversification in both countries. The latter question is weaker than the first one because it focuses on the production side of the economies without examining whether the efficient production point with diversification clear goods markets.

Whether there exists an equilibrium with diversification has long been an important question in the literature. Although Jones (1967) argues that countries tend to specialize in production under goods trade and capital movement, Kemp and Inada (1969), Chipman (1971), Uekawa (1972), and Brecher and Feenstra (1983) show that there are some fairly general conditions that are sufficient for the existence of an equilibrium with diversification.

Referring back to Figure 4.2, point V represents equalization of commodity prices and rental rates: Conditions (4.15c) and (4.15d) are satisfied. Because conditions (4.15a) and (4.15b) are not necessarily satisfied, however, it is wrong to conclude that the intersecting point V represents the world equilibrium. It is also incorrect to conclude that because the two p–r schedules of the countries have an intersection at a point on their curved parts, the two countries have an efficient production point with diversification. This is because if capital does move across countries, the linear segments of the two schedules shift. It is necessary to know whether the factor endowments of the countries can provide an intersecting point of the two p–r schedules with diversification.

To develop a formal analysis of an equilibrium with diversification, begin with the production levels of the goods in the world. Let $Q_i^w \equiv Q_i + Q_i^*$ be the total world output of good i. In Figure 4.4 schedule RSTU represents the production possibility frontier (PPF) of the world under goods trade and capital movement. Given convex technologies in both countries, the world PPF is concave to the origin. In the case in which the two p–r schedules in Figure 4.2 intersect at a point such as V on the diversification parts of the schedules the world PPF has a flat segment, shown as ST in Figure 4.4. This flat segment is also known as the *Chipman flat* based on a formula developed by Chipman (1971). It is possible that this flat segment degenerates into one single point.

Some properties of the Chipman flat are given as follows. When the commodity price ratio and the rental rate are maintained at the point of intersection between the diversification portions of the countries' p–r schedules in Figure 4.2, a continuous capital inflow at a constant rate into the home country

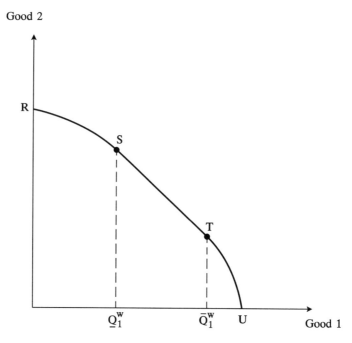

Figure 4.4

will cause an increase in the home output of the capital-intensive good and a decrease in that of the labor-intensive good at constant rates. This result is not surprising because the Rybczynski line is straight. At the same time, as foreign capital flows out, output levels in the foreign country are also changing at constant rates. These results together mean that the world outputs are also changing at constant rates. Under certain conditions (to be derived later), the constant rates of change of the world outputs are reflected as a linear segment of the world PPF.

Because the world commodity price ratio and rental rate that correspond to the Chipman flat are determined by the point of intersection between the diversification portions of the schedules in Figure 4.2, they are independent of preferences but, as explained later, they do depend on factor endowments. If the world equilibrium under free goods trade and capital movement is at a point on the Chipman flat, a small change in demand conditions in the countries is reflected by a shift of capital from one country to another rather than a change in prices. Furthermore, because under diversification commodity prices and hence factor prices remain unchanged, factor intensities are fixed, as in the case of fixed technical coefficients. This result is what Chipman (1971) called *the substitution theorem.*

I now explain how to determine the conditions for existence of a Chipman flat. Note that the slope of the world PPF is given by

$$\frac{dQ_2^w}{dQ_1^w} = \frac{\partial Q_2^w / \partial \kappa}{\partial Q_1^w / \partial \kappa} = \frac{\partial Q_2/\partial \kappa - \partial Q_2^*/\partial \kappa^*}{\partial Q_1/\partial \kappa - \partial Q_1^*/\partial \kappa^*}. \tag{4.25}$$

Condition (4.25) is quite general and it does not depend on whether the countries are diversified or specialized. The Chipman flat represents the case in which both countries are diversified. So for the time being I focus only on this case.

First look at the home country. Because it is diversified, there are two possibilities. If the sectors have different factor intensities, then, as proved in Chapter 2, I have

$$\frac{\partial Q_1}{\partial \kappa} = \frac{\partial r}{\partial p} = -\frac{f_1}{k_2 - k_1}. \tag{4.26}$$

If instead the two sectors have the same factor intensities, then the common capital-labor ratios of the sectors must be the same as the capital-labor ratio of the home economy under full employment. Because labor endowment is fixed, there is only one amount of capital working in the economy (and thus one unique level of capital movement across countries) that is consistent with full employment.

Assuming that each of the home and foreign countries has different capital-labor ratios between the sectors, I can apply (4.26) to give

$$\frac{\partial Q_1}{\partial \kappa} - \frac{\partial Q_1^*}{\partial \kappa} = \frac{\partial r}{\partial p} - \frac{\partial r^*}{\partial p^*} = \frac{f_1^*}{k_2^* - k_1^*} - \frac{f_1}{k_2 - k_1},$$

which is the difference between the slopes of the p–r schedules of the countries in Figure 4.2. In the case shown in Figure 4.2 in which the home p–r schedule is steeper than the foreign one, a transfer of capital from the foreign country to the home country implies a net increase in the output of good 1 in the world. In terms of Figure 4.4, this represents a downward and rightward movement along the world PPF. To get the slope of the Chipman flat, partially differentiate with respect to κ the gross domestic product equation of the home country, $g = p Q_1 + Q_2$, to give

$$p\frac{\partial Q_1}{\partial \kappa} + \frac{\partial Q_2}{\partial \kappa} = \frac{\partial g}{\partial \kappa} = r, \tag{4.27a}$$

where p remains constant along the flat. A similar result holds for the foreign country:

$$p^*\frac{\partial Q_1^*}{\partial \kappa^*} + \frac{\partial Q_2^*}{\partial \kappa^*} = \frac{\partial g^*}{\partial \kappa^*} = r^*. \tag{4.27b}$$

Using the fact that along the Chipman flat $p = p^* = p^w$ and $r = r^* = r^w$, subtract (4.27b) from (4.27a) to give

$$p^w \left(\frac{\partial Q_1}{\partial \kappa} - \frac{\partial Q_1^*}{\partial \kappa^*} \right) + \left(\frac{\partial Q_2}{\partial \kappa} - \frac{\partial Q_2^*}{\partial \kappa^*} \right) = 0.$$

By rearranging terms and using condition (4.25), I obtain the slope of the Chipman flat, the linear segment ST of the world PPF:

$$\left. \frac{dQ_2^w}{dQ_1^w} \right|_{ST} = -p^w.$$

Thus as long as both countries are diversified, the world PPF is flat.

Recall that $c_i(w, r)$ and $c_i^*(w^*, r^*)$ are the unit cost functions of sector i in the home and foreign countries, respectively. The following conditions jointly give the existence of a nondegenerating Chipman flat:

1. There exist $\widetilde{p} > 0$, $\widetilde{r} > 0$, $\widetilde{w} \geq 0$, $\widetilde{w}^* \geq 0$, which jointly satisfy

$$c_1(\widetilde{w}, \widetilde{r}) = c_1^*(\widetilde{w}^*, \widetilde{r}) = \widetilde{p}$$

$$c_2(\widetilde{w}, \widetilde{r}) = c_2^*(\widetilde{w}^*, \widetilde{r}) = 1.$$

2. Factor endowments in the world satisfy the following condition:

$$\min[\widetilde{k}_1, \widetilde{k}_2]\overline{L} + \min[\widetilde{k}_1^*, \widetilde{k}_2^*]\overline{L}^* < \overline{K} + \overline{K}^* < \max[\widetilde{k}_1, \widetilde{k}_2]\overline{L}$$
$$+ \max[\widetilde{k}_1^*, \widetilde{k}_2^*]\overline{L}^*.$$

3. If at the $(\widetilde{r}, \widetilde{p})$ point, $\widetilde{k}_2 \neq \widetilde{k}_1$ and $\widetilde{k}_2^* \neq \widetilde{k}_1^*$, then

$$\frac{\partial r}{\partial p} \neq \frac{\partial r^*}{\partial p^*}.$$

Condition (1) requires that in each sector in each country the unit cost is equal to the market price, ensuring that firms earn zero profit and are willing to produce positive outputs. This condition also means at least one intersection between the curved portions of the p–r schedules of the countries. Condition (2) ensures that given the amounts of labor endowments in the countries, the world has the amount of capital stock to be distributed between the countries so that they are diversified at the given $(\widetilde{w}, \widetilde{w}^*, \widetilde{r}, \widetilde{p})$. In other words, the world capital stock can be distributed between the countries so that the intersection point $(\widetilde{r}, \widetilde{p})$ is at the curved parts of the p–r schedules. Note that a necessary condition for condition (2) is:

2′. At $(\widetilde{r}, \widetilde{p})$, not both $\widetilde{k}_2 = \widetilde{k}_1$ and $\widetilde{k}_2^* = \widetilde{k}_1^*$ hold; or

2″. At $(\widetilde{r}, \widetilde{p})$, not both $\widetilde{p}\widetilde{f}_1 = \widetilde{f}_2$ and $\widetilde{p}\widetilde{f}_1^* = \widetilde{f}_2^*$ hold.

Condition $(2')$ is equivalent to condition $(2'')$ because under diversification $k_2 = k_1$ is equivalent to $pf_1 = f_2$.[7] If both equalities in condition $(2')$ are satisfied, condition (2) must be violated. If only one of the equalities in condition $(2')$ is satisfied, full employment of factors requires a fixed distribution of capital between the countries. For example, suppose that $\widetilde{k}_2 = \widetilde{k}_1$ and $\widetilde{k}_2^* \neq \widetilde{k}_1^*$. In equilibrium, the amount of capital fully employed in the home country equals $\widetilde{k}_1 \overline{L}$. The rest of the capital in the world is then allocated to the foreign country. Under given commodity prices, the outputs of goods 1 and 2 in the foreign country are fixed. The outputs of goods in the world are indeterminate, however, because capital and labor can be redistributed between the sectors within the home country, changing the outputs of the sectors. Such redistribution of capital and labor within the home country represents movements along the Chipman flat.

Condition (3) means that the two p–r schedules have different slopes at point $(\widetilde{p}, \widetilde{r})$. By equation (4.25), this condition implies that an international movement of capital will change the world output of good 1 (and thus that of good 2). In the case shown in Figure 4.2 in which $dr/dp > dr^*/dp^*$ at point V, a movement of capital from the foreign country to the home country will increase the output of good 1. A condition that is equivalent to (3) is:

$3'$. At $(\widetilde{r}, \widetilde{p})$, $(\widetilde{f}_1/\widetilde{f}_2) \neq (\widetilde{f}_1^*/\widetilde{f}_2^*)$.

To see the equivalence between (3) and $(3')$, note that $w = pf_1 - k_1 r = f_2 - k_2 r$. This condition is applied to both countries at the equilibrium point $(\widetilde{p}, \widetilde{r})$ to yield

$$\widetilde{r} = \frac{\widetilde{f}_2 - \widetilde{p}\widetilde{f}_1}{\widetilde{k}_2 - \widetilde{k}_1} = \frac{\widetilde{f}_2^* - \widetilde{p}\widetilde{f}_1^*}{\widetilde{k}_2^* - \widetilde{k}_1^*}. \tag{4.28}$$

Using (4.28), it can be shown that $\widetilde{f}_2/\widetilde{f}_1 = \widetilde{f}_2^*/\widetilde{f}_1^*$ is equivalent to $\widetilde{f}_1/(\widetilde{k}_2 - \widetilde{k}_1) = \widetilde{f}_1^*/(\widetilde{k}_2^* - \widetilde{k}_1^*)$. By using the expression of $\partial r/\partial p$ given in (4.26), I can thus conclude that conditions (3) and $(3')$ are equivalent.

If conditions (1) and (2) are satisfied, whether or not (3) is also satisfied, it is said that an efficient production with diversification under free goods trade and capital movement exists.[8] If, however, only conditions (1) and (2) but not condition (3) are satisfied, then a transfer of capital from one country to

---

7. The equivalency between $k_2 = k_1$ and $pf_1 = f_2$ under diversification can be proved by using the cost-minimization and perfect factor mobility conditions: $w = p(f_1 - k_1 f_1') = f_2 - k_2 f_2'$ and $r = pf_1' = f_2'$.

8. Uekawa (1972) derives more sufficient conditions for the existence of an efficient point with diversification.

another does not affect the world aggregate supply of each good. As a result, the Chipman flat degenerates to a point.[9]

I now use the preceding analysis to have a closer look at the world PPF. For illustration, let me focus only on the case in which good 1 is capital intensive in both countries, and $dr/dp > dr^*/dp^*$ at the efficient point $(\tilde{r}, \tilde{p})$. This is the case shown in Figure 4.2. Suppose first that both countries are diversified. Because by assumption $dr/dp > dr^*/dp^*$, a transfer of capital from the foreign country to the home country will increase the world's supply of good 1. In Figure 4.4, such a transfer of capital shifts a production point on the flat part ST down toward point T. This analysis can be applied to argue that in region RS in Figure 4.4, the home country is specialized in good 2 and/or the foreign country is specialized in good 1. Similarly, in region TU, the home country is specialized in good 1 and/or the foreign country is specialized in good 2.

Thus existence of a Chipman flat implies existence of an efficient point with diversification. It should be noted, however, that existence of a Chipman flat (or an efficient point with diversification) does *not* imply that at the world equilibrium as described by (4.15) both countries are diversified. In order to have an equilibrium with diversification, the equilibrium must be at a point on the Chipman flat.

A necessary and sufficient condition for existence of an equilibrium with diversification can be derived as follows. Denote the minimum and maximum world output of good 1 within the Chipman by $\underline{Q}_1^w$ and $\overline{Q}_1^w$, respectively, as shown in Figure 4.4. Furthermore, given world preferences and the world relative price of good 1, which is equal to the (negative) slope of the Chipman flat, I can compute the world demand for good 1 at this price. Denote this demand by $\tilde{C}_1^w$. Thus an equilibrium under diversification exists if and only if

$$\overline{Q}_1^w > \tilde{C}_1^w > \underline{Q}_1^w. \tag{4.29}$$

4.5   More Conditions for an Efficient Production with Diversification

In the previous section, I derived several sets of conditions for the existence of an efficient production with diversification. These conditions are quite general. In this section, I focus on a particular class of models in which more conditions

---

9. Thus if the countries have identical technologies and if factor price equalization exists, condition (3) is violated. Because conditions (1) and (2) can be satisfied, the Chipman flat degenerates to a point.

will be derived.[10] These models and conditions are used again in later sections to analyze other issues.

Suppose that the technologies of the home and foreign countries are different in such a way that their production functions have the following relation:

$$F_i(K_i, L_i) = F_i^*(b_{Ki}K_i, b_{Li}L_i), \quad \text{for all } K_i, L_i > 0, \tag{4.30}$$

where $b_{ji} > 0$. The technological parameters b_{ji} describe the differences between the countries' technologies. If $b_{ji} = 1$ for all $i = 1, 2$, $j = K, L$, then the countries have identical technologies. If $b_{K1} > 1$ (respectively $0 < b_{K1} < 1$) while $b_{L1} = 1$, for example, then the sector 1 of the home country relative to the same sector in the foreign country is more (less) productive in using capital. Specifically, I can say that sector i of home country is more productive than the same sector in the foreign country in the following senses:

1. Hicks-neutral: $b_{Li} = b_{Ki} = b_i > 1$.

2. Labor-augmenting: $b_{Li} > 1, b_{Ki} = 1$.

3. Capital-augmenting: $b_{Ki} > 1, b_{Li} = 1$.

The issue is the nature of the relationship between these technological parameters that should exist in order to yield an efficient production with diversification in both countries under free goods trade and capital movement.

To answer this question, let a_{ji} be the cost-minimizing input-output coefficient that depends on factor prices and technological change. This coefficient is observable. Define a new set of coefficients:

$$a'_{ji} = a_{ji}b_{ji}. \tag{4.31}$$

To interpret a'_{ji}, rearrange condition (4.31) to give

$$a_{ji} = a'_{ji}/b_{ji}$$

or, in terms of the "‸" operator:

$$\widehat{a}_{ji} = \widehat{a'}_{ji} - \widehat{b}_{ji}. \tag{4.32}$$

In (4.32), $\widehat{b}_{ji}$ is the contribution of technological change to the input-output coefficient. Thus $\widehat{a'}_{ji}$ can be interpreted as the change in input-output coefficient that is due to factor prices (when technologies remain fixed).[11] Note that

10. Variants of these models have been used in the literature, and are similar to the one suggested by Bhagwati (1964) as a generalized $2 \times 2 \times 2$ version of the Ricardian theory of comparative advantage.

11. The approach of disaggregating $\widehat{a}_{ji}$ comes from Jones (1965).

$\widehat{a}_{ji}$ is the rate of change of the observed input-output coefficient a_{ji}, and $\widehat{a}'_{ji}$ is the part of its rate of change that is due entirely to factor price changes.

The analysis begins with a set of technological parameters so that an efficient production point exists under diversification at $(\widetilde{p}, \widetilde{r})$.[12] I need to determine how the technological parameters may change so that the initial efficient point is still achieved. To answer this question, I hypothetically peg the commodity price ratio at the initial level $\widetilde{p}$, and then determine how the technological parameters may change so that the rental rate remain at $\widetilde{r}$.

I employ the techniques developed in Chapter 2. Denote the income share of factor j in sector i by θ_{ji}; for example, $\theta_{L1} \equiv w\, a_{L1}/p$ and $\theta_{L2} \equiv w\, a_{L2}$. Define

$$\phi_1 = \widehat{p} + \theta_{L1}\widehat{b}_{L1} + \theta_{K1}\widehat{b}_{K1} \tag{4.33a}$$

$$\phi_2 = \theta_{L2}\widehat{b}_{L2} + \theta_{K2}\widehat{b}_{K2}. \tag{4.33b}$$

For the home country, assuming diversification, the equations of change for factor prices derived in Chapter 2 are replaced by

$$\theta_{L1}\widehat{w} + \theta_{K1}\widehat{r} = \phi_1$$

$$\theta_{L2}\widehat{w} + \theta_{K2}\widehat{r} = \phi_2,$$

which can be solved for

$$\widehat{r} = \frac{\theta_{L1}\phi_2 - \theta_{L2}\phi_1}{|\theta|} \tag{4.34a}$$

$$\widehat{w} = \frac{\theta_{K2}\phi_1 - \theta_{K1}\phi_2}{|\theta|}, \tag{4.34b}$$

where $|\theta|$ is the determinant of θ. As shown in Chapter 2, $|\theta| = \theta_{L1} - \theta_{L2} = \theta_{K2} - \theta_{K1}$ and is positive if and only if sector 1 is labor intensive.

I now evaluate the home factor prices at the initial efficient point with diversification, fixing the price ratio so that $\widehat{p} = 0$. If the rental rate does not change either, then by (4.34a) the technological parameters must change in such a way that:

$$\theta_{L1}\phi_2 = \theta_{L2}\phi_1,$$

or, using the definitions of ϕ_1 and ϕ_2,

$$\theta_{L1}(\theta_{L2}\widehat{b}_{L2} + \theta_{K2}\widehat{b}_{K2}) = \theta_{L2}(\theta_{L1}\widehat{b}_{L1} + \theta_{K1}\widehat{b}_{K1}). \tag{4.35}$$

Condition (4.35) gives the relationship between the changes in the technological parameters in order to have efficient production with diversification.

---

12. This set is nonempty. For example, $b_{ji} = 1$ for all j and i is one element of the set.

I now consider several special cases. For convenience, I present only the cases in which *sector 1 in both countries is capital intensive*. Thus $|\theta| < 0$. (Other cases of factor intensity ranking can be analyzed in a similar way.)

4.5.1 Hicks-Neutral Technological Superiority

Suppose that $\widehat{b}_{Li} = \widehat{b}_{Ki} = \widehat{b}_i \neq 0$, $i = 1, 2$. Note that $\widehat{b}_i$ is not required to be positive so that the foreign country may in fact have technological superiority. Substitute $\widehat{b}_i$ into (4.35) to give

$$\theta_{L1}\widehat{b}_2 = \theta_{L2}\widehat{b}_1. \tag{4.36a}$$

Condition (4.36a) gives the relationship between b_1 and b_2, which is required for efficient production with diversification. Such relationship is shown diagrammatically by schedule HN in Figure 4.5. By rearranging the terms in (4.36a), the slope of schedule HN is derived:

$$\left.\frac{db_2}{db_1}\right|_{HN} = \frac{b_2\theta_{L2}}{b_1\theta_{L1}}.$$

Because sector 1 is capital intensive, $\theta_{L2} > \theta_{L1}$, implying $db_2/db_1 > b_2/b_1$, that is, schedule HN at any point is steeper than the ray from the origin to that point in Figure 4.5. Thus schedule HN cuts through the 45°-line at point $(1,1)$, and is entirely above it when $b_1 > 1$ and entirely below it when $b_1 < 1$.[13]

If b_1 and b_2 are represented by a point in the diagram not on schedule HN, they do not give an efficient production with diversification. For example, if $\widehat{b}_2 > 0$ and $\widehat{b}_1 = 0$, then (4.34a) gives $\widehat{r} < 0$. This means that starting from a point on schedule HN, an upward movement in Figure 4.5 (an increase in b_2) leads to a drop in the home rental rate at any given commodity price ratio. Thus if the countries are under free trade and are diversified, the domestic rental rate is always lower than the foreign rate. This leads to capital outflow from the home country to the foreign country, and in equilibrium at least one of the countries is completely specialized. Because of the assumed factor intensity ranking, the final equilibrium gives the following production pattern:

Production Patterns P1   The home country is specialized in good 2, and/or the foreign country is specialized in good 1.

Similarly, any point below schedule HN in Figure 4.5 represents a domestic rental rate higher than the corresponding foreign one under free trade as long as both countries are diversified. Foreign capital flows in until at least one of the countries is completely specialized with the following production pattern:

---

13. Schedule HN is not defined at the origin.

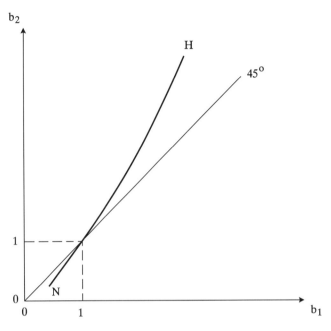

Figure 4.5

Production Patterns P2   The home country is specialized in good 1, and/or the foreign country is specialized in good 2.

4.5.2   Labor-Augmenting Technological Superiority

Now assume that $\widehat{b}_{Ki} = 0$ and $\widehat{b}_{Li} \neq 0$. It is necessary to find the relationship between $\widehat{b}_{L1}$ and $\widehat{b}_{L2}$ so that an efficient production under diversification exists. Substitute the values of these coefficients into (4.35) and simplify the terms to give

$$\widehat{b}_{L2} = \widehat{b}_{L1}. \tag{4.36b}$$

Condition (4.36b) thus gives the required relationship between the two technological parameters. Such relationship is illustrated by schedule LA in Figure 4.6. The slope of schedule LA can be obtained by rearranging the terms in (4.36b) to yield

$$\left. \frac{db_{L2}}{db_{L1}} \right|_{LA} = \frac{b_{L2}}{b_{L1}}.$$

This means that schedule LA coincides with the 45°-line from the origin (except at the origin where it is not defined). Again, points above schedule LA represent domestic rental rates lower than the foreign ones under free trade and diversification in both countries. Thus domestic capital is induced to move out

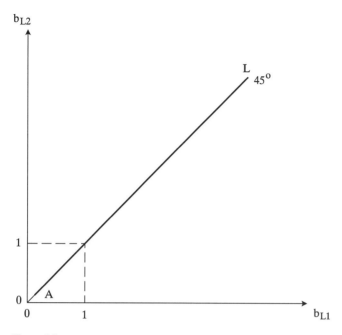

Figure 4.6

to the foreign country, leading to a final equilibrium characterized by production pattern P1. Similarly, points below schedule LA represent foreign capital flowing to the home country with production pattern P2 in equilibrium.

4.5.3 Capital-Augmenting Technological Superiority

I now assume $\widehat{b}_{Li} = 0$ and $\widehat{b}_{Ki} \neq 0$. Substitute these values into (4.35) to yield

$$\theta_{L1}\theta_{K2}\widehat{b}_{K2} = \theta_{L2}\theta_{K1}\widehat{b}_{K1},$$

or, after rearranging the terms,

$$k_2\widehat{b}_{K2} = k_1\widehat{b}_{K1}. \tag{4.36c}$$

Condition (4.36c) gives the relationship between b_{K1} and b_{K2} that is required for efficient production under diversification. Such relationship is illustrated by schedule KA in Figure 4.7. Rearranging the terms in (4.36c), I get

$$\left.\frac{db_{K2}}{db_{K1}}\right|_{KA} = \frac{k_1 b_{K2}}{k_2 b_{K1}},$$

which is the slope of schedule KA. Because $k_1 > k_2$ by assumption, the slope of schedule KA is greater than b_{K2}/b_{K1}. Thus schedule KA passes through the point at (1,1), and is entirely above (respectively below) the 45°-line from

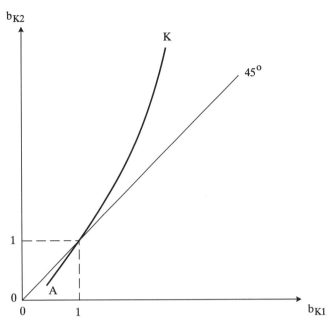

Figure 4.7

the origin when $b_{K1} >$ (respectively $<$) 1. Using the preceding analysis, it is easy to show that points in the region above (respectively below) schedule KA represents a lower (respectively higher) rental rate in the home country under free trade and diversification in both countries, and thus an outflow of domestic capital (respectively inflow of foreign capital) with production pattern P1 (respectively P2) in equilibrium.

4.6   Stability of Equilibrium

In Chapter 2 I derived conditions for Walrasian stability of equilibrium in a general framework. I now examine these conditions more closely in the present framework. I also derive the Marshallian conditions for stability.

With free trade in goods and capital services, there are five markets in the present framework: two commodity markets, the capital market, and one labor market in each country. For simplicity, as is usually done in the literature, labor markets are assumed to clear instantaneously always. So I concentrate on the three international markets. By Walras's law, if any two of these three markets are stable, so is the third. Thus the stability analysis can concentrate on the world good 1 and capital markets.

The Walrasian stability (price adjustment) is more common in the trade literature, and in a two-good framework it is summarized by the Marshall-Lerner condition. The Marshallian stability (quantity adjustment), however, is more relevant to our discussion in the present chapter. Only Marshallian stable equilibrium in the capital market is considered because, as will be seen later, this type of stability comes directly from the realistic assumption of capital owners' utility maximization.

4.6.1   Price Adjustment in the Goods Markets and Quantity Adjustment in the Capital Market

Assume that conditions (4.15b) and (4.15c) always hold, that is, $\kappa + \kappa^* = 0$ and $p = p^*$. Then postulate that p and κ adjust according to the following conditions:

$$\dot{p} = Z(p, \kappa) \equiv -\alpha^p \big[\mathcal{E}_1(p, \kappa) + \mathcal{E}_1^*(p, -\kappa) \big] \tag{4.37a}$$

$$\dot{\kappa} = R(p, \kappa) \equiv \alpha^k \big[r(p, \kappa) - r^*(p, -\kappa) \big], \tag{4.37b}$$

where $Z(p, \kappa)$ is proportional to the world's excess demand for good 1, and $R(p, \kappa)$ is proportional to the rental rate differential across countries. Two constants—$\alpha^p > 0$ and $\alpha^k > 0$—reflect the speeds of adjustment of the two variables. Condition (4.37a) states that the world relative price of good 1 increases if there is an excess demand for good 1 in the world, and condition (4.37b) represents the movement of capital by its owners from a country of lower rental rate to a country of higher rental rate. The adjustment condition of p can be justified by the *tâtonnement* process, and that of k is due to the pursuit of higher incomes by capital owners. Note that (4.37a) is the Walrasian stability adjusting condition for the good-1 market and (4.37b) is the Marshallian stability adjusting condition for the capital market.

Using subscripts to denote partial derivatives, I have

$$Z_p = -\alpha^p (\mathcal{E}_{1p} + \mathcal{E}_{1p*}^*)$$

$$Z_\kappa = -\alpha^p (\mathcal{E}_{1\kappa} - \mathcal{E}_{1\kappa*}^*)$$

$$R_p = \alpha^k (r_p - r_{p*}^*)$$

$$R_\kappa = \alpha^k (r_\kappa + r_{\kappa*}^*).$$

If both countries are diversified and if both countries have the same factor intensity ranking, $\text{sign}(Z_\kappa) = -\text{sign}(R_p)$. Note that $R_\kappa = 0$ if both countries are diversified or $R_\kappa < 0$ if at least one of the countries is completely specialized. Expand the Taylor series of the functions in (4.37) around the equilibrium point (p^w, κ^w) in (4.37), dropping the second and higher order terms, to give

$$\begin{pmatrix} \dot{p} \\ \dot{\kappa} \end{pmatrix} = \begin{pmatrix} Z_p & Z_\kappa \\ R_p & R_\kappa \end{pmatrix} \begin{pmatrix} p - p^w \\ \kappa - \kappa^w \end{pmatrix} = \mathbf{B} \begin{pmatrix} p - p^w \\ \kappa - \kappa^w \end{pmatrix},$$

where $\mathbf{B}$ is the matrix representing the partial derivatives of $Z(p,\kappa)$ and $R(p,\kappa)$. The system is (locally) stable if and only if the eigenvalues of $\mathbf{B}$ have negative real parts. This in turn requires that $\mathbf{B}$ has negative trace and positive determinant, that is,

$$Z_p + R_\kappa < 0 \tag{4.38a}$$

$$Z_p R_\kappa - R_p Z_\kappa > 0. \tag{4.38b}$$

In the special case in which both countries are diversified, $R_\kappa = 0$, and if it is further given that the countries have the same factor intensity ranking of the sectors, $R_p Z_\kappa < 0$. In this case, the stability conditions in (4.38) reduce to $Z_p < 0$, or $\mathcal{E}_{1p} + \mathcal{E}_{1p^*}^* > 0$.

4.6.2   Quantity Adjustment in the Goods and Capital Markets

I now drop the assumption that commodity price ratios are always equalized across countries. Instead, assume that $E_1 + E_1^* = 0$ (condition 4.15a), that is, one country's export is another country's import. I postulate that the transfer of good 1 adjusts according to the following equation:

$$\dot{E}_1 = -\beta^e (p - p^*), \tag{4.39a}$$

where $\beta^e > 0$ represents the speed of adjustment of E_1. This condition states that the home country is willing to export more of good 1 if its relative price is lower. For the capital market, assume an adjustment equation similar to the one given by (4.37b)

$$\dot{\kappa} = \beta^k (r - r^*), \tag{4.39b}$$

where $\beta^k > 0$. For simplicity β^e and β^k are assumed to be constants.

To apply conditions (4.39), let me invert $E_1 = \mathcal{E}_1(p,\kappa)$ to give $p = \mu(E_1, \kappa)$, which is interpreted as the price level (when given the capital movement κ) at which the home country is willing to export E_1. Define the partial derivatives as $\mu_E \equiv \partial\mu/\partial E_1$ and $\mu_\kappa \equiv \partial\mu/\partial\kappa$. By totally differentiating the home country's export function, it is easy to show that

$$\mu_E = \frac{1}{\mathcal{E}_{1p}}$$

$$\mu_\kappa = -\frac{\mathcal{E}_{1\kappa}}{\mathcal{E}_{1p}}.$$

The same price function for the foreign country can be defined as $p^* = \mu^*(E_1^*, \kappa^*) = \mu^*(-E_1, -\kappa)$, where $E_1 + E_1^* = 0$ and $\kappa + \kappa^* = 0$ have been used. Substitute these two price functions into conditions (4.39) to give

$$\dot{E}_1 = B(E_1, \kappa) \equiv -\beta^e\big[\mu(E_1, \kappa) - \mu^*(-E_1, -\kappa)\big] \tag{4.40a}$$

$$\dot{\kappa} = D(E_1, \kappa) \equiv \beta^k\big[r(\mu(E_1, \kappa), \kappa) - r^*(\mu^*(-E_1, -\kappa), -\kappa)\big], \tag{4.40b}$$

where $B(E_1, \kappa)$ and $D(E_1, \kappa)$ are two functions showing the price differential and the rental rate differential across countries. I use subscripts to denote partial derivatives; for example, $B_E \equiv \partial B/\partial E_1$, $B_\kappa \equiv \partial B/\partial \kappa$, and so on. Thus

$$B_E = -\beta^e(\mu_E + \mu^*_{E*}) = -\beta^e\left(\frac{1}{\mathcal{E}_{1p}} + \frac{1}{\mathcal{E}^*_{1p*}}\right)$$

$$B_\kappa = -\beta^e(\mu_\kappa + \mu^*_{\kappa*}) = \beta^e\left(\frac{\mathcal{E}_{1\kappa}}{\mathcal{E}_{1p}} + \frac{\mathcal{E}^*_{1\kappa*}}{\mathcal{E}^*_{1p*}}\right)$$

$$D_E = \beta^k(r_p\mu_E + r^*_{p*}\mu^*_{E*}) = \beta^k\left(\frac{r_p}{\mathcal{E}_{1p}} + \frac{r^*_{p*}}{\mathcal{E}^*_{1p*}}\right)$$

$$D_\kappa = \beta^k(r_p\mu_\kappa + r_\kappa + r^*_{p*}\mu^*_{\kappa*} + r^*_{\kappa*}) = \beta^k\left(r_\kappa + r^*_{\kappa*} - \frac{r_p\mathcal{E}_{1\kappa}}{\mathcal{E}_{1p}} - \frac{r^*_{p*}\mathcal{E}^*_{1\kappa*}}{\mathcal{E}^*_{1p*}}\right).$$

Based on the preceding analysis, (local) stability of an equilibrium requires that

$$B_E + D_\kappa < 0 \tag{4.41a}$$

$$B_E D_\kappa - B_\kappa D_E > 0. \tag{4.41b}$$

To interpret and apply the stability conditions in (4.41), I first derive two results. First, using the derivatives of $B(E_1, \kappa)$,

$$\frac{B_\kappa}{B_E} = -\frac{\mathcal{E}_{1\kappa}/\mathcal{E}_{1p} + \mathcal{E}^*_{1\kappa*}/\mathcal{E}^*_{1p*}}{1/\mathcal{E}_{1p} + 1/\mathcal{E}^*_{1p*}} = -\frac{\mathcal{E}_{1p}\mathcal{E}^*_{1\kappa*} + \mathcal{E}_{1\kappa}\mathcal{E}^*_{1p*}}{\mathcal{E}_{1p} + \mathcal{E}^*_{1p*}}. \tag{4.42}$$

Comparing (4.42) with equation (4.20), I see that $-B_\kappa/B_E$ is equal to the slope of schedule GT in Figure 4.3. Second, using the derivatives of $D(E_1, \kappa)$,

$$\frac{D_\kappa}{D_E} = -\frac{r_p\mathcal{E}_{1\kappa}/\mathcal{E}_{1p} + r^*_{p*}\mathcal{E}^*_{1\kappa*}/\mathcal{E}^*_{1p*} - r_\kappa - r^*_{\kappa*}}{r_p/\mathcal{E}_{1p} + r^*_{p*}/\mathcal{E}^*_{1p*}}$$

$$= -\frac{r_p\mathcal{E}_{1\kappa}\mathcal{E}^*_{1p*} + r^*_{p*}\mathcal{E}^*_{1\kappa*}\mathcal{E}_{1p} - \mathcal{E}_{1p}\mathcal{E}^*_{1p*}(r_\kappa + r^*_{\kappa*})}{\mathcal{E}_{1p}r^*_{p*} + \mathcal{E}^*_{1p*}r_p}. \tag{4.43}$$

If both countries are either diversified or specialized in the production of good 1, (4.43) can be compared with (4.24). Recall function $p = \rho(r, \kappa)$, which is obtained by inverting $r = r(p, \kappa)$ when neither country is specialized in good 2. I showed that $\rho_r = 1/r_p$ and $\rho_\kappa = -r_\kappa/r_p$. Using these relations for the two countries and rearranging the terms show that the righthand sides of (4.43) and (4.24) are identical in magnitude. Thus $-D_\kappa/D_E$ is equal to the slope of schedule KM in Figure 4.3. In fact, this result holds even if one of the countries is specialized in good 2. To see this point, assume that the home country produces good 2 only while the foreign country is diversified or specialized in producing good 1. Then the home country's rental rate is independent of p, meaning that $r_p = 0$. Using this result, (4.43) reduces to

$$\frac{D_\kappa}{D_E} = -\frac{r_{p*}^* \mathcal{E}_{1\kappa*}^* \mathcal{E}_{1p} - \mathcal{E}_{1p} \mathcal{E}_{1p*}^* (r_\kappa + r_{\kappa*}^*)}{\mathcal{E}_{1p} r_{p*}^*}$$

$$= -\mathcal{E}_{1\kappa*}^* + \frac{\mathcal{E}_{1p*}^* (r_\kappa + r_{\kappa*}^*)}{r_{p*}^*}. \tag{4.43'}$$

Recall that in (4.24'), function $p^* = \psi^*(k)$ is obtained by inverting the rental rate equalization condition $r(\kappa) = r^*(p^*, -\kappa)$. Thus by differentiation, $\psi^{*\prime}(\kappa) = (r_\kappa + r_{\kappa*}^*)/r_{p*}^*$. This result and a comparison of conditions (4.43') and (4.24') show that $-D_\kappa/D_E$ is equal to the slope of schedule KM even if the home country is specialized in good 2.

I now go back to the stability conditions (4.41). Rearranging the terms in (4.41b), I can conclude that if B_E and D_E have the same sign, then (4.41b) reduces to

$$-\frac{D_\kappa}{D_E} < -\frac{B_\kappa}{B_E}, \tag{4.44a}$$

that is, the slope of schedule KM is less than that of the schedule GT. Alternatively, if B_E and D_E have different signs, then (4.41b) reduces to

$$-\frac{D_\kappa}{D_E} > -\frac{B_\kappa}{B_E}, \tag{4.44b}$$

that is, the slope of schedule KM is greater than that of the schedule GT.

The stability results will help me in the analysis below put some constraints on the slopes of the two schedules.

4.7 Are Goods Trade and Factor Mobility Substitutes?

In the previous chapter, I examined substitutability between goods trade and factor mobility when the two countries have identical technologies (and some other properties). I now consider the cases in which technologies may not be identical across countries. This means that factor price equalization is generally not possible, and that goods trade and factor mobility are not substitutes in the price-equalization sense. As a result, in this section, I only consider substitutability and complementarity in the quantitative-relationship sense.

A former analysis of substitutability and complementarity can be given with the aid of Figure 4.3. First, I adopt the following system of labeling the countries and goods. Call the country the home country that receives capital from the other country under free capital movement but autarky in goods trade, and label the good "good 1" that the home country exports in the absence of any international capital movement.

In Figure 4.3, the vertical intercept of schedule GT, E_1^o, is the level of export of good 1 by the home country when capital is immobile internationally, and the horizontal intercept of schedule KM, k^o, is the amount of capital inflow when goods trade is not allowed. The present system of labeling the countries and goods guarantees that $E_1^o > 0$ and $k^o > 0$. (For simplicity, I ignore the cases in which one of them is zero.) Schedules GT and KM intersect at point W which gives E_1^w, the export level of good 1 by the home country, and k^w, the level of capital inflow, under free goods trade and capital mobility.

Using Figure 4.3, I give the following definitions:

Definition 1
1. Capital mobility diminishes (augments) goods trade if and only if the volume of trade under free goods trade and capital mobility is smaller (greater) than the volume of trade under free trade but no capital mobility, that is, if and only if $E_1^w < (>) E_1^o$.

2. Goods trade diminishes (augments) capital mobility if and only if the amount of capital transfer under free goods trade and capital mobility is smaller (greater) than the amount of capital transfer under free capital mobility but autarky in trade, that is, if and only if $k^w < (>) k^o$.

Definition 2
1. Goods trade and capital mobility are substitutes if and only if they diminish each other.

2. Goods trade and capital mobility are complements if and only if they augment each other.

In Definition 1, the effects of goods trade and capital mobility on each other are measured by comparing their levels under free goods trade or capital mobility with their levels at the final world equilibrium under free goods trade and capital mobility. This definition has the advantage of avoiding the ambiguity if schedules GT and KM are not monotonically increasing or decreasing. If I neglect the difference between discrete changes and marginal changes, Definition 1 is the same as the weak version of substitutability and complementarity defined in the previous chapter. Moreover, Definition 2 is the strong version of substitutability and complementarity defined previously. Note that both definitions allow the possibility that E_i^w and/or K_i^w is negative.

In general, to determine whether international trade in goods and capital movement are substitutes, information is needed about the equilibrium under free goods trade but no capital movement, the equilibrium under free capital mobility but autarkic in goods trade, and the equilibrium under free goods trade and capital mobility. In some cases, further conditions for substitutability or complementarity can be derived.[14]

Consider again the two-country framework described by conditions (4.30). Assume that the countries can differ in any ways except that they always have the same factor intensity ranking under diversification. Following the stability analysis in the previous section, assume that both $\mathcal{E}_{1p}$ and $\mathcal{E}_{1p*}^*$ are always positive or if one of them is negative, it is small in magnitude. This implies, as explained previously, that if both countries are diversified, schedules GT and KM in Figure 4.3 are positively (respectively negatively) sloped if sector 1 is capital (labor) intensive in both countries. Furthermore, B_E defined in the previous section is negative.

Next recall that $D_E = \beta^k(r_p/\mathcal{E}_{1p} + r_{p*}^*/\mathcal{E}_{1p*}^*)$. The assumed sign of $\mathcal{E}_{1p}$ and $\mathcal{E}_{1p*}^*$ implies that D_E is positive if sector 1 is capital intensive so that r_p and r_{p*}^* are positive. Using conditions (4.44) and recalling that $B_E < 0$, I can say that the sufficient conditions for a Marshallian stable world equilibrium under free goods trade and capital movement are (1) sector 1 is capital intensive in both countries (so that $D_E > 0$) and slope of schedule KM > slope of schedule GT > 0; or (2) sector 1 is labor intensive in both countries (so that $D_E < 0$) and slope of schedule KM < slope of schedule GT < 0.

Based on these conditions on stable equilibria, four interesting cases can be identified. These cases are illustrated in panels (a) to (d) in Figure 4.8. The effects of goods trade and capital movement on each other can also be identified. The results are:

Case 1. Both schedules are positively sloped and the home country receives capital under free goods trade. *Result:* GT augments KM and KM augments GT, implying that *goods trade and capital mobility are complements.*

Case 2. Both schedules are negatively sloped and the home country sends out capital under free goods trade. *Result:* GT diminishes KM and KM augments GT.

---

14. Wong (1988) suggests an alternative approach to measuring the effects of international factor movements on a country's volume of trade. Using his approach, which involves the estimation of the indirect trade utility function of an economy, it is found that for the United States a small labor inflow tends to augment the volume of trade but a small captial inflow has insignificant effects.

Case 3. Both schedules are negatively sloped and the home country receives capital under free trade. *Result:* GT augments KM and KM diminishes GT.

Case 4. Both schedules are negatively sloped and the home country receives capital under free trade. *Result:* GT diminishes KM and KM diminishes GT, implying that *goods trade and capital mobility are substitutes.*

I now explain case (1). (Other cases can be analyzed in the same way and are ignored here.) In this case, as illustrated in panel (a) of Figure 4.8, both schedules are positively sloped and sector 1 is capital intensive in both countries. As for the movement of capital, I showed earlier that if sector 1 is capital intensive in both countries and if the technological parameters are represented by points in the region below schedule HN in Figure 4.5, the home country will have a higher rental rate under free trade, leading to foreign capital inflow. Thus in panel (a) of Figure 4.8, goods trade and capital movement augment each other.

4.8   Patterns of Trade under International Capital Movement

It was shown in the previous chapter that the general law of comparative advantage can be used to explain the directions of movement of goods and capital under free goods trade and capital movement. The shortcoming of this law is that it is so general that it cannot be used to predict the direction of movement of a particular good or capital even if the autarkic prices of the tradable goods and mobile capital in both countries are known.

The patterns of trade of countries, however, remain a very important issue for trade theorists and government planners. At the same time, international capital movement has become a significant phenomenon in the world. Thus it is meaningful to investigate conditions under which patterns of trade and direction of international capital movement are predictable.

In this section, I take two different approaches to analyzing patterns of trade, depending on the speed of capital movement between countries: the perfect-capital-mobility (PCM) approach and the sluggish-capital-movement (SCM) approach.

4.8.1   The Perfect-Capital-Mobility (PCM) Approach

Under this approach, it is assumed that the international capital market adjusts quickly and costlessly so that it always clears (Jones and Ruffin, 1975; Ferguson, 1978). This implies that rental rates are always equalized across countries. A country is then said to have a comparative advantage in a good at a given international rental rate if the relative price of the good is lower than that in another country in the presence of capital mobility but autarky in goods trade.

(a)

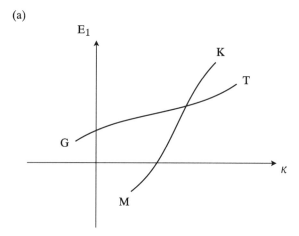

(b)

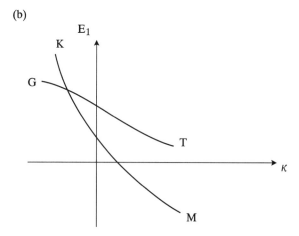

Figure 4.8

It is clear that a country's comparative advantage generally depends on the international rental rate chosen.

This approach can conveniently be illustrated using the p–r technique explained earlier. In panel (a) of Figure 4.9, schedule HH represents the p–r relation of the home country and schedule FF represents that of the foreign country. The diagram shows the case in which both schedules are positively sloped, that is, sector 1 in both countries is capital intensive. Furthermore, HH is always above FF when both countries are diversified, meaning that at any rental rate in both countries and with diversification, $p^* > p$. In other words, the home country has a *global comparative advantage in good 1*.

Panel (b) of Figure 4.9 shows another case in which schedules HH and FF cut each other once even though both countries remain diversified. Using the

(c)

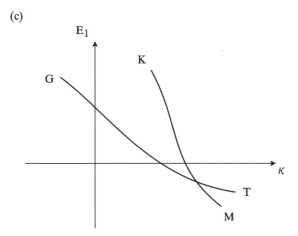

(d)

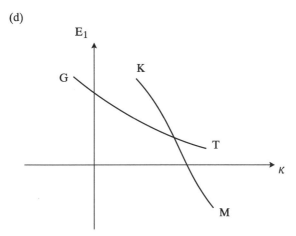

Figure 4.8

preceding definition, it can be said that the home country has a comparative advantage in good 1 if $r = r^* > r'$ and a comparative advantage in good 2 if $r = r^* < r'$. In this case, there is a *reversal of comparative advantage*.

Two features of this concept of comparative advantage can be noted. First, it is defined based on the technologies of the countries and independent of preferences and factor endowments. Second, it is closely related to the concept of existence of an efficient production with diversification analyzed earlier. Specifically, a country enjoys a global comparative advantage if and only if an efficient production with diversification does not exist. In this case, at least one country must be completely specialized under free goods trade and capital mobility. I can also say that if an efficient production with diversification exists, a reversal (or reversals) of comparative advantage exists.

(a)

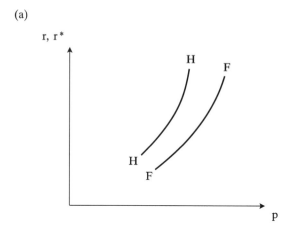

(b)

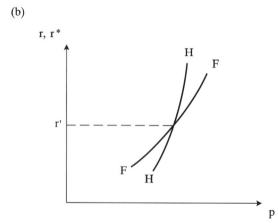

Figure 4.9

The preceding analysis can now be applied to predict patterns of trade in cases in which the technologies of the countries differ in the following ways: Hicks-neutral, labor-augmenting, or capital-augmenting. First derive conditions for global comparative advantage. For illustration purposes, continue to assume that sector 1 is capital intensive in both countries. When the countries have a Hicks-neutral, labor-augmenting, or capital-augmenting technological difference, the region below schedules HN, LA, or KA in Figure 4.5 to Figure 4.7, respectively, represents a higher rental rate in the home country than in the foreign country under free goods trade and diversification. This corresponds to the case shown in panel (a) in Figure 4.9. Thus the home country has a global comparative advantage in good 1. A similar analysis can be given to show that in the regions to the left of and above these schedules, the home country has a global comparative advantage in good 2. Obviously, comparative advantage reversal can occur only when the technological parameters are at points on these schedules.

4.8.2   The Sluggish-Capital-Mobility (SCM) Approach

In this approach, it is assumed that although goods markets clear instantaneously, capital moves very slowly between countries. In terms of Figure 4.3, this means that in the short run with the value of κ taken as given, the home export of good 1 adjusts quickly to clear the commodity markets, reaching a point on schedule GT. As capital moves slowly over time in response to the rental rate differential, the equilibrium of the good-1 market is represented by the movement of a point along schedule GT.

Under this approach, I can say that at any given value of κ, the home country has a comparative advantage in good 1 (respectively 2) if the corresponding value of E_1 as given by schedule GT is positive (respectively negative). It is then clear that the comparative advantage of a country depends on the level of capital movement, and it is possible that a country has a reversal of comparative advantage as capital moves.

In terms of Figure 4.3, existence of reversal of comparative advantage can be analyzed by comparing the signs of E_1^o and E_1^w. For illustration, suppose that $E_1^o > 0$. There is one reversal (or an odd number of reversals) in comparative advantage if $E_1^w < 0$ and there is no reversal (or an even number of reversals) in comparative advantage if $E_1^w > 0$.

This concept of comparative advantage can again be illustrated by the panels in Figure 4.8. In the cases shown in panels (a), (b), and (d), $E_1^w > 0$ and no reversal in comparative advantage exists. In panel (c), however, $E_1^w < 0$, and there is a reversal in comparative advantage.

Using the results in the previous section and Figure 4.8, two conclusions can be obtained immediately. Suppose that the two countries have the same factor intensity ranking.

1. If a reversal in comparative advantage occurs, the capital-receiving country tends to export the labor-intensive good under free trade but no capital movement. (Alternatively, if the capital-receiving country exports the capital-intensive good under free trade but no capital movement, then reversal in comparative advantage will not occur.)

2. If a reversal in comparative advantage occurs, capital mobility diminishes goods trade and goods trade augments capital mobility.

More results about the comparative advantages of the countries can be derived using the preceding framework in which the technologies of the countries differ in a Hicks-neutral, labor-augmenting, or capital-augmenting way.

Suppose that both countries have the same ratio of endowed capital to endowed labor, and that they have identical and homothetic preferences. For the countries' technologies, I begin with the assumption that they have identical technologies and imagine that the home country experiences a technological progress in one or both sectors. This allows the countries' technologies to differ from each other in certain ways. Note that for the time being I do not label the goods in such a way that the home country must export good 1 when free trade but no capital movement is allowed.

I first derive the effects of the technological progress on production. Recall ϕ_1 and ϕ_2 as defined in (4.33a) and (4.33b). During the technological progress, I hypothetically freeze the price ratio so that both countries still have the same price ratio. Thus $\widehat{p} = 0$. Combining (4.34a) and (4.34b), I have

$$\widehat{w} - \widehat{r} = \frac{\phi_1 - \phi_2}{|\theta|}. \tag{4.45}$$

This is the rate of change in the wage-rental ratio at given commodity prices when the technological parameters change.

Recall the equations of change for outputs derived in Chapter 2:

$$\lambda_{L1}\widehat{Q}_1 + \lambda_{L2}\widehat{Q}_2 = \widehat{L} - [\lambda_{L1}\widehat{a}_{L1} + \lambda_{L2}\widehat{a}_{L2}] \tag{4.46a}$$

$$\lambda_{K1}\widehat{Q}_1 + \lambda_{K2}\widehat{Q}_2 = \widehat{K} - [\lambda_{K1}\widehat{a}_{K1} + \lambda_{K2}\widehat{a}_{K2}]. \tag{4.46b}$$

As shown previously, $\widehat{a}_{ji} = \widehat{a}'_{ji} - \widehat{b}_{ji}$, where a'_{ji} is the input-output coefficient that depends solely on factor prices. Because factor endowments do not change, $\widehat{L} = \widehat{K} = 0$.

Denote the elasticity of substitution in sector i by σ_i so that

$$\widehat{a}'_{Ki} - \widehat{a}'_{Li} = \sigma_i(\widehat{w} - \widehat{r}). \tag{4.47}$$

Cost minimization of firms that take factor prices and technologies as given implies

$$w\mathrm{d}a'_{Li} + r\mathrm{d}a'_{Ki} = 0,$$

or, after rearranging terms,

$$\theta_{Li}\widehat{a}'_{Li} + \theta_{Ki}\widehat{a}'_{Ki} = 0. \tag{4.48}$$

Solving equations (4.47) and (4.48), I get

$$\widehat{a}'_{Li} = -\theta_{Ki}\sigma_i(\widehat{w} - \widehat{r}) \tag{4.49a}$$

$$\widehat{a}'_{Ki} = \theta_{Li}\sigma_i(\widehat{w} - \widehat{r}). \tag{4.49b}$$

Let me define $\delta_L \equiv \lambda_{L1}\theta_{K1}\sigma_1 + \lambda_{L2}\theta_{K2}\sigma_2 > 0$ and $\delta_K \equiv \lambda_{K1}\theta_{L1}\sigma_1 + \lambda_{K2}\theta_{L2}\sigma_2 > 0$. Using parameters $\widehat{a}'_{ji}$ as given by conditions (4.49) and using condition

(4.45), the equations of change (4.46) reduce to

$$\lambda_{L1}\widehat{Q}_1 + \lambda_{L2}\widehat{Q}_2 = \phi_L \tag{4.50a}$$

$$\lambda_{K1}\widehat{Q}_1 + \lambda_{K2}\widehat{Q}_2 = \phi_K, \tag{4.50b}$$

where $\phi_L = \lambda_{L1}\widehat{b}_{L1} + \lambda_{L2}\widehat{b}_{L2} + \delta_L(\phi_1 - \phi_2)/|\theta|$ and $\phi_K = \lambda_{K1}\widehat{b}_{K1} + \lambda_{K2}\widehat{b}_{K2} - \delta_K(\phi_1 - \phi_2)/|\theta|$. Using the definitions of ϕ_1 and ϕ_2 as given by (4.33), ϕ_L and ϕ_K reduce to

$$\phi_L = \frac{(X_{L1}\widehat{b}_{L1} + X_{L2}\widehat{b}_{L2} + X_{K1}\widehat{b}_{K1} + X_{K2}\widehat{b}_{K2})}{|\theta|} \tag{4.51a}$$

$$\phi_K = \frac{(Y_{L1}\widehat{b}_{L1} + Y_{L2}\widehat{b}_{L2} + Y_{K1}\widehat{b}_{K1} + Y_{K2}\widehat{b}_{K2})}{|\theta|}, \tag{4.51b}$$

where $X_{L1} = (\lambda_{L1}|\theta| + \theta_{L1}\delta_L)$, $X_{L2} = (\lambda_{L2}|\theta| - \theta_{L2}\delta_L)$, $X_{K1} = \delta_L\theta_{K1}$, $X_{K2} = -\delta_L\theta_{K2}$, $Y_{L1} = -\delta_K\theta_{L1}$, $Y_{L2} = \delta_K\theta_{L2}$, $Y_{K1} = (\lambda_{K1}|\theta| - \theta_{K1}\delta_K)$, and $Y_{K2} = (\lambda_{K2}|\theta| + \theta_{K2}\delta_K)$. Equations (4.50a) and (4.50b) can be solved for the rates of change of outputs:

$$\widehat{Q}_1 = \frac{\lambda_{K2}\phi_L - \lambda_{L2}\phi_K}{|\lambda|} \tag{4.52a}$$

$$\widehat{Q}_2 = \frac{\lambda_{L1}\phi_K - \lambda_{K1}\phi_L}{|\lambda|}. \tag{4.52b}$$

Because preferences are homothetic, both sectors have zero excess demand at given commodity prices if they grow by the same proportion, that is, $\widehat{Q}_1 = \widehat{Q}_2$. Alternatively, consider the following condition:

Condition C $\widehat{Q}_1 \geq \widehat{Q}_2$.

In condition C if a strict inequality holds, the home country has an excess supply of good 1 at the foreign autarkic commodity prices and zero capital movement, and the country has a comparative advantage in good 1 with no capital movement. If condition C holds with equality, both sectors have zero excess demand at the foreign autarkic prices. If, however, condition C does not hold, the home country has an excess supply of good 2 at these prices and thus a comparative advantage in good 2.

Because of conditions (4.52a) and (4.52b), condition C is equivalent to

$$\frac{\lambda_{K2}\phi_L - \lambda_{L2}\phi_K}{|\lambda|} \geq \frac{\lambda_{L1}\phi_K - \lambda_{K1}\phi_L}{|\lambda|}$$

or, after rearranging terms,

$$\frac{\phi_L}{|\lambda|} \geq \frac{\phi_K}{|\lambda|}. \tag{4.53}$$

Condition (4.53) can be simplified in the three special cases considered previously.

Hicks-Neutral Type Technological Difference

In this case, $\widehat{b}_{L1} = \widehat{b}_{K1} = \widehat{b}_1$ and $\widehat{b}_{L2} = \widehat{b}_{K2} = \widehat{b}_2$. Substituting the values of these parameters into (4.51), condition (4.53) reduces to

$$\frac{(|\lambda||\theta| + \delta_L + \delta_K)\widehat{b}_1}{|\lambda||\theta|} \geq \frac{(|\lambda||\theta| + \delta_L + \delta_K)\widehat{b}_2}{|\lambda||\theta|}. \tag{4.54}$$

Because $|\lambda|$ and $|\theta|$ always have the same sign, condition (4.54) reduces to

$$\widehat{b}_1 \geq \widehat{b}_2. \tag{4.54$'$}$$

When the difference between the countries' technologies is of the Hicks-neutral type, condition (4.54$'$) is equivalent to condition C. To see how this condition is applied, suppose that $\widehat{b}_1 > \widehat{b}_2$, that is, $\widehat{Q}_1 > \widehat{Q}_2$. Because the countries are initially identical, this means that the home country has an excess supply of good 1 at the initial price ratio. Thus the home country has a comparative advantage in good 1 (in the absence of international capital movement). Similarly, if $\widehat{b}_1 < \widehat{b}_2$, then the home country has a comparative advantage in good 2.

Graphically, condition (4.54$'$) with an equality is illustrated by schedule CM in panel (a) of Figure 4.10. Incidentally, schedule CM coincides with the 45°-line from the origin. In the region on the right- (respectively left-) hand side of schedule CM, $b_1 >$ (respectively $<$) b_2, meaning that the home country exports good 1 (respectively 2) when no capital movement is allowed. For simplicity, our analysis covers only the case corresponding to the space on the right-hand side of schedule CM. (The case corresponding to the space on the other side of the schedule can be analyzed in the same way.) The present case is the same as the previous one in which the goods are labeled so that the home country exports good 1 in the absence of capital movement.

I now allow capital movement and determine the conditions under which reversal in comparative advantage will occur. To do this, I add schedule HN derived earlier to Figure 4.10. This schedule represents all possible combinations of b_1 and b_2 that give equalized rental rates across countries under free goods trade. I have shown that under certain conditions comparative advantage reversal occurs only when sector 1 is labor intensive. This is the case shown in panel (a). Schedule HN is below (respectively above) schedule CM when $b_1 >$ (respectively $<$) 1. This schedule is derived using the preceding analysis and Figure 4.5, except that *I now assume that sector 1 is labor intensive*. In the region above schedule HN in panel (a) of Figure 4.10, the home country has a higher rental rate than the foreign country's under free goods trade (condition

(a)

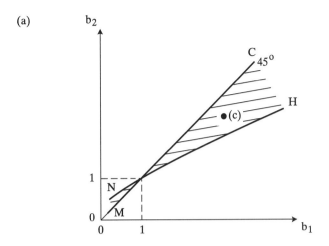

(b)

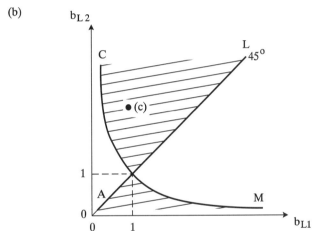

(c)

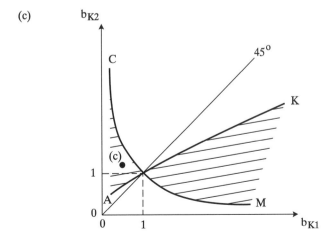

Figure 4.10

(4.34a) with $|\theta| > 0$) and so foreign capital tends to flow in when it is allowed. This leads to production pattern P1 explained previously, with the home country being specialized in captial-intensive good 2, or the foreign country being specialized in labor-intensive good 1, or both. In either case, the home country must sooner or later import good 1 as foreign capital gradually moves in.[15]

Thus in panel (a) of Figure 4.10 the shaded regions between schedules CM and HN give all possible combinations of b_1 and b_2 that cause comparative advantage reversal. For example, in the shaded region with $b_1 > 1$, the home country has a comparative advantage in good 1 with no capital movement, but at the final world equilibrium under free goods trade and capital mobility, the home country exports good 2. The point marked "(c)" in the diagram is a possible combination of b_1 and b_2 which gives rise to case (c) in Figure 4.8. In the regions above or below both schedules in the present diagram, the comparative advantage of the home country is not affected by the movement of capital.[16]

Labor-Augmenting Technological Difference

I now assume that $b_{K1} = b_{K2} = 1$ (so $\widehat{b}_{K1} = \widehat{b}_{K2} = 0$). Substitute these values into conditions (4.51) and (4.53) and rearrange terms to give

$$[\lambda_{L1}|\theta| + \theta_{L1}(\delta_L + \delta_K)]\widehat{b}_{L1} \geq [-\lambda_{L2}|\theta| + \theta_{L2}(\delta_L + \delta_K)]\widehat{b}_{L2}, \qquad (4.55)$$

where I have used the fact that $|\lambda|$ and $|\theta|$ have the same sign. Condition (4.55) is equivalent to condition C. This means that if the condition holds with a strict inequality, the home country has a comparative advantage in good 1 when no capital movement occurs.

Condition (4.55) with an equality is illustrated by schedule CM in panel (b) of Figure 4.10. Again the case in which sector 1 is labor intensive is examined. This means that $|\theta| > 0$. For simplicity I now consider only the case in which $\lambda_{L2}|\theta| > \theta_{L2}(\delta_L + \delta_K)$. (Other cases can be analyzed in a similar way.) This condition is satisfied if the elasticities of substitution of both sectors are sufficiently small. Given this condition, schedule CM is negatively sloped, passing through point $(1, 1)$. In the region to the right (respectively left) of schedule CM, condition (4.55) is satisfied with an inequality, and the home country has a comparative advantage in good 1 with no capital movement.

---

15. In the region below schedule HN in Figure 4.10 with sector 1 being labor intensive, or in Figure 4.5 with sector 1 being capital intensive, the countries have production patterns P2, with the home country specialized in good 1 and/or with the foreign country specialized in good 2.

16. Similarly, in the shaded region below point (1,1), the home country has a comparative advantage in good 2 with no capital movement, but at the final world equilibrium under free goods trade and capital mobility, the home country exports good 1.

To analyze comparative advantage reversal in the presence of capital movement, I add to the diagram schedule LA, which coincides with the 45°-line from the origin. This schedule is the locus of b_{L1} and b_{L2} for equalized rental rates across countries under free goods trade. In the region above (respectively below) the schedule, the home country has a higher (respectively lower) rental rate than the foreign country has under free goods trade but no capital movement. Condition (4.34a) (with $|\theta| > 0$) implies that if international capital movement is also allowed, then foreign (respectively home) capital is attracted to the other country.

The shaded regions in panel (b) of Figure 4.10 give possible values of (b_{L1}, b_{L2}) that can cause comparative advantage reversal. For example, in the shaded region when $b_{L2} > 1$, the home country has a comparative advantage in good 1 with no capital movement, but its higher rental rate under free goods trade attracts foreign capital inflow until it is specialized in good 2, the foreign country is specialized in good 1, or both. In either case, the home country exports good 2, meaning that its comparative advantage has been reversed. The point marked (c) in Figure 4.10 corresponds to case (c) in Figure 4.8.

Capital-Augmenting Technological Difference

I now assume that $b_{L1} = b_{L2} = 1$ ($\hat{b}_{L1} = \hat{b}_{L2} = 0$). Substitute these values into (4.53) and rearrange terms to give (with $|\lambda||\theta| > 0$):

$$\left[-\lambda_{K1}|\theta| + \theta_{K1}(\delta_L + \delta_K) \right]\hat{b}_{K1} \geq \left[\lambda_{K2}|\theta| + \theta_{K2}(\delta_L + \delta_K) \right]\hat{b}_{K2}. \qquad (4.56)$$

Condition (4.56) is equivalent to condition C with this type of technological difference between the countries. This condition with an equality is illustrated by schedule CM in panel (c) of Figure 4.10 when sector 1 is labor intensive. Concentrating only on the case in which $\lambda_{K1}|\theta| > \theta_{K1}(\delta_L + \delta_K)$, schedule CM is negatively sloped.[17] The region below (respectively above) the schedule represents combinations of b_{K1} and b_{K2} that give the home country a comparative advantage in good 1 (respectively 2). The diagram also shows schedule KA, which gives the locus of b_{K1} and b_{K2} so that the free-trade rental rates are equalized across countries. In the region above (respectively below) schedule KA, capital flows into (respectively out of) the home country so that under free trade and capital mobility, the countries sooner or later achieve production patterns P1 (respectively P2), with the home country exporting good 2 (respectively good 1).

Using these techniques, it can be shown that in the two shaded regions in panel (c) of Figure 4.10, the home country will experience a reversal of com-

---

17. The condition is satisfied if the elasticities of substitution in both sectors are small.

parative advantage as capital moves across countries. A possible combination of (b_{K1}, b_{K2}) that gives rise to the case shown in panel (c) of Figure 4.8 is marked with "(c)."

4.9   Comparative Advantage and Absolute Advantage

The theory of comparative advantage states that international trade is based on comparative advantages of countries. Even if a country has absolute disadvantages in all goods, it can still find some goods to export as long as the disadvantages in these goods are relatively less than those in other goods. Similarly, a country that has absolute advantages in all goods will not export everything; rather, it exports those goods in which it has relatively greater advantages.

In the previous section, I showed that in the presence of capital mobility, comparative advantage depends not only on technologies (and possibly on other factors such as preferences, factor endowments, taxes, and so on), but also on the level of capital movement. It is sometimes argued that when capital can move across countries, absolute advantage, not just comparative advantage, matters.

In this section, I examine the relationship between comparative advantage and absolute advantage (in goods) in the presence of capital mobility. I present two approaches to analyzing this relationship. The first is due to Jones (1980). Consider a "Ricardian" model in which two goods labeled 1 and 2 are produced by labor using fixed coefficients.[18] Labor is trapped within a country and cannot move internationally. The production of good 1 also requires another factor call "T." Unlike labor, factor T is footloose and can move between countries perfectly. Denote the given amount of labor used to produce one unit of good i by a_{Li}, $i = 1, 2$, and denote the amount of factor T used to produce one unit of good 1 by a_{T1}.

The home and the foreign countries trade with each other and with the rest of the world. Both of them are small so that external prices of goods and factor T are taken as given. Choosing good 2 as the numeraire, denote the world price of good 1 by p and the world price of factor T by s. Furthermore, denote the wage rates in the home and foreign countries by w and w^*.

First consider the home country. In equilibrium, all firms cannot have positive profit, meaning that

$$a_{L1}w + a_{T1}s \geq p \tag{4.57a}$$

$$a_{L2}w \geq 1. \tag{4.57b}$$

---

18. Jones (1980) also considers a "Heckscher-Ohlin" model in which there are two immobile factors in each country in addition to the footloose factor.

If a good is produced with positive output, the inequality in the corresponding equation in (4.57) is replaced by an equality, implying zero profit for the firms in the sector. The values of the prices and technological parameters then determine the pattern of production of the home country. Because the wage rate is flexible, it will adjust to make the country competitive so that it exports at least one good. Under certain conditions (to be shown later), the country can export both goods. This means that at least one of the equations in (4.57) must hold with an equality. To find out the production pattern of the country, combine conditions (4.57) together (using equalities) to give

$$\frac{a_{L1}}{a_{L2}} + a_{T1}s = p. \tag{4.58}$$

Condition (4.58) gives the relation between p and s under which the country with fixed technological parameters is willing to produce both goods. If the left-hand side of (4.58) is greater than the right-hand side, that is, when condition (4.57a) holds with an inequality, the country produces only good 2. If, however, the left-hand side of (4.58) is less than the right-hand side, the country is specialized in good 1.

The country's pattern of trade is illustrated in Figure 4.11. Condition (4.58) is shown by the line labeled "home." Its vertical intercept is a_{L1}/a_{L2} and its slope is equal to a_{T1}. Any point on the home line is compatible with diversification. Regions I and II (respectively III and IV), which are above (respectively below) the home line, represent complete specialization in good 1 (respectively 2).

The same analysis is applied to the foreign country. Thus in Figure 4.11, the line labeled "foreign" illustrates the dependence of its pattern of production on p and s. The diagram shows the case in which the following conditions hold

$$\frac{a_{L1}^*}{a_{L2}^*} > \frac{a_{L1}}{a_{L2}} \tag{4.59a}$$

$$a_{T1} > a_{T1}^*. \tag{4.59b}$$

By condition (4.59a), the home country is said to have a comparative advantage in terms of labor cost in good 1 vis-à-vis the foreign country, and condition (4.59b) implies that the foreign country vis-à-vis the home country has an absolute advantage in hiring factor T, which is essential in the production of good 1.

The production patterns depend on their comparative advantages and absolute advantages (or disadvantages) and on world prices. This point can be illustrated using Figure 4.11. The home and foreign lines divide the p–s space into four regions: I, II, III, and IV. For example, in region I (respectively III),

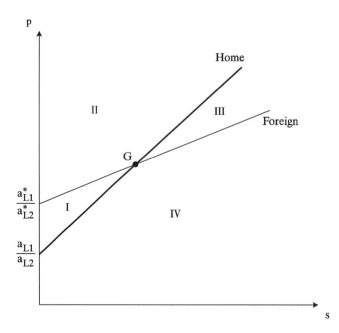

Figure 4.11

the home country is specialized in and exports good 1 (2) while the foreign
country is specialized in and exports good 2 (1).

Close examination of Figure 4.11 reveals that in the present model the countries may have some possible patterns of production and trade that are not
possible in the traditional Ricardian model. First, in region II (respectively IV),
both countries are specialized in producing and exporting good 1 (respectively
2). Second, at point G where the lines intersect, both countries are producing
goods 1 and 2. These strange production and trade patterns exist because the
countries are essentially trading not with each other but with the rest of the
world.

I now suggest another approach to analyzing the relationship between comparative advantage and absolute advantage. Recall the framework developed
in the previous sections. Suppose that the home country has a technological
superiority over the foreign country in producing both goods so that in the absence of capital movement it has no comparative advantage. The combination
of technological parameters that yield no comparative advantage depends on
the type of technological difference, the preferences, and factor endowments.
For concreteness, let me assume that the countries have identical and homothetic preferences, and that the factor endowments of the home country are
constant multiples of those of the foreign country. Suppose further that the
home country has a Hicks-neutral type technological difference over the for-

eign country (other types of technological differences are ignored here but can be analyzed using the same technique). The analysis in the previous section shows that if the following condition holds,

$$b_1 = b_2 > 1, \tag{4.60}$$

then with no capital mobility the home country vis-à-vis the foreign country has uniform absolute advantages in both goods but no comparative advantage. Condition (4.60) is independent of the factor intensity ranking of the sectors. Given this condition, there is no trade between the countries before any movement of capital. This result is consistent with the classical doctrine of comparative advantage.

If capital is permitted to flow across countries, however, the above no-trade point is no longer the world equilibrium. The consequence of capital movement depends on the factor intensity ranking of sectors. Consider first the case in which sector 1 is capital intensive in both countries. As the earlier analysis shows, condition (4.60) implies that at the autarky point, the rental rate in the home country is higher than that in the foreign country. Thus when at the no-trade point capital is allowed to move internationally, foreign capital will move to the home country. At the original price ratio, this movement of capital will create an excess supply of good 1 in the home country and an excess supply of good 2 in the foreign country. Thus the home country starts exporting good 1. The home country's export of good 1 and capital inflow can be described by schedules GT and KM in panel (a) in Figure 4.12. Three features of the diagram should be noted. First, because of the factor intensity rankings in the countries, schedules GT and KM are positively sloped under the condition that $\mathcal{E}_{1p}$, $\mathcal{E}_{1p*}^* > 0$. Second, schedule GT passes through the origin, meaning that no trade exists if capital movement is not allowed. Third, schedule KM is on the right-hand side of schedule GT at the zero trade level because at the no-trade point home rental rate is higher than the foreign one. The final equilibrium is at point W, with the home country exporting good 1. This means that despite the absence of comparative advantage before capital moves, its absolute advantages cause capital inflow and subsequent export of good 1.

The case in which sector 1 is labor intensive is very much different. It is illustrated in panel (b) of Figure 4.12. Both schedules GT and KM are negatively sloped. Schedule GT again passes through the origin because with no capital movement both countries have no comparative advantage and there is no trade. The absolute advantages of the home country always produce a higher rental rate in the country than in the foreign country at the no-trade point, irrespective of factor intensity ranking. Thus schedule KM is on the right-hand side of schedule GT at the zero trade level. Foreign capital tends to

(a)

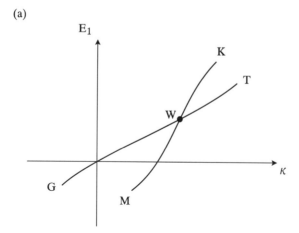

(b)

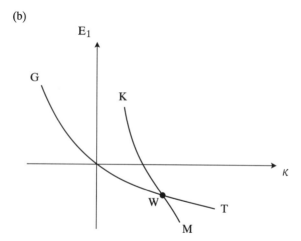

Figure 4.12

flow into the home country. Such capital inflow will cause an excess supply of
good 2 (the capital-intensive good) in the home country and an excess supply
of good 1 in the foreign country. Thus the home country starts exporting good
2. The final equilibrium is at point W, with the home country exporting good 2.
If I combine these results, I can say that in the presence of capital movement,
the country that has uniform absolute advantages in both goods will ultimately
export the capital-intensive good.

What the analyses in this section and the previous section show is that comparative advantage and absolute advantage, which are defined in terms of price
ratios in the countries, are no longer a fixed concept. In the presence of capital movement, they depend on the direction and level of capital movement. In
the previous section, I showed reversal of comparative advantage, and in this

section it is shown how absolute advantages can be turned into comparative advantages.

Because comparative advantages depend on actual capital movement, they can be affected by other factors that directly influence international capital movement, for example, taxes or subsidies on foreign capital earnings. To see this point, suppose that the home government imposes a tax on the earnings of (domestic and foreign) capital owners but there is no such tax in the foreign country so that the after-tax rental rate is lower in the home country than in the foreign country, despite the home country's technological superiority. At the no-trade point, therefore, domestic capital tends to flow out, leading to subsequent export of the labor-intensive good by the home country. Thus the income tax completely reverses the patterns of trade of the countries.

4.10   International Capital Movement with Sector-Specific Capital

So far I have been considering the neoclassical framework with perfect intersectoral factor mobility. It has, however, been pointed out that capital in the short-run is sector specific. Some economists even take one step further and assume that although capital is not mobile between sectors within an economy, it is mobile between the same sector in different economies (Caves, 1971, pp. 17–19). Although it may seem odd that capital is mobile not intersectorally but internationally, Batra and Ramachandran (1980) point out that international investment involves more than just transfer of capital. Technological knowledge, managerial know-how, superior marketing techniques, and so on are all embodied in international investment. These advantages usually are sector specific, but they can readily be used in the production of the same commodity in another country (see also Batra and Ramachandran 1980, p. 278, fn 4). Caves (1982) points out that international investment involves the transfer of a bundle of sector-specific assets from one country to another, and that assuming sector-specific capital may give theoretical results more reasonable than the neoclassical assumption of perfect intersectoral capital mobility. Caves' work was followed by a series of papers (Brecher and Findlay, 1983; Srinivasan, 1983; Neary and Ruane, 1988) on the welfare effects of international movement of capital that is specific to a sector but mobile internationally. A dynamic specific-factors model is given in Eaton (1987).

In this section, I analyze international capital movement in a specific-factors (SF) model. (There is a discussion about the issues related to foreign direct investment and multinational corporations in Chapter 13.) Important properties about this model are explained in Chapter 2. Here I explain how the equilibrium under international trade in goods and capital movement is determined and analyze the relationship between goods flow and capital movement.

To illustrate the role of sector specificity of capital in the presence of goods trade and capital movement, first consider the special case in which only one type of capital is mobile between two countries with identical technologies. Without loss of generality, suppose that only sector-1 capital is mobile internationally. This case is similar to the one analyzed in Section 4.1. Under the usual assumptions such as incomplete specialization, and free trade in goods and movement of sector-1 capital, factor prices equalize in the countries and there is no incentive for sector-2 capital to move internationally even if it is allowed to (Caves, 1971; Amano, 1977).[19] At such an equilibrium, there is an indeterminacy in terms of the distribution of sector-2 capital between the countries. This result is similar to the one in Mundell (1957) for international factor mobility under factor price equalization in the $2 \times 2 \times 2$ framework.

For more fruitful results, I turn to a more general framework in which the two countries allow movement of both types of capital and may have different technologies. Furthermore, the rental rates of capital may not be given exogenously and may be affected by capital movements. This framework, which is an extension of the one explained in Section 4.2, is used to analyze several issues including "cross-hauling" of foreign investment.

Let me first describe the home country. Denote the given endowment of sector-i capital by $\overline{K}_i$, $i = 1, 2$, and the inflow of sector-i foreign capital by κ_i (negative for outflow of home capital). The amount of sector-i capital working in the home country is thus equal to $K_i = \overline{K}_i + \kappa_i$. I can define the GDP function as $g(p, \kappa_1, \kappa_2)$, where for simplicity the fixed factor endowments are dropped from the function. The total payment given to the foreign capital is $r_1 \kappa_1 + r_2 \kappa_2$ where $r_i = r_i(p, \kappa_1, \kappa_2)$ is the rental rate of capital i. The payment is repatriated out of the country. Let me define $r_{ip} \equiv \partial r_i / \partial p$, $r_{ij} \equiv \partial r_i / \partial \kappa_j$, $i, j = 1, 2$. Based on the analysis given in Chapter 2, $r_{1p} > 0, r_{2p} < 0, r_{ij} < 0$.

With sector-specific capital, the home ITU function is written as $V(p, \kappa_1, \kappa_2, b)$, where $b = -r_1 \kappa_1 - r_2 \kappa_2$. As explained in Chapter 2, the derivatives of the ITU function give the export function of good 1, $E_1(p, \kappa_1, \kappa_2, b)$. Using condition (4.8), I can derive the reduced form of export function of good 1, which is written as $\mathcal{E}_1(p, \kappa_1, \kappa_2)$. To simplify the notation, I denote the partial derivatives of this function by $\mathcal{E}_{1p} \equiv \partial \mathcal{E}_1 / \partial p$, $\mathcal{E}_{1j} \equiv \partial \mathcal{E}_1 / \partial \kappa_j$, $j = 1, 2$.

The export and rental-rate functions depend on the pattern of production and can be analyzed using the technique described previously. For simplicity, I omit the details.

---

19. Free movement of sector-1 capital leads to sector-1 rental rate equalization. Because both countries have the same price of good 1 under free trade, and because firms in the sector must have zero profit, wage rates in the countries are also equalized. Furthermore, the same price of good 2 and wage rate in both countries must mean the same rental rate of sector-2 capital.

The same notation applies to the foreign country except that its variables are distinguished by asterisks. The equilibrium conditions are

$$\mathcal{E}_1(p, \kappa_1, \kappa_2) + \mathcal{E}_1^*(p^*, \kappa_1^*, \kappa_2^*) = 0 \tag{4.61a}$$

$$\kappa_i + \kappa_i^* = 0 \tag{4.61b}$$

$$p = p^* \tag{4.61c}$$

$$r_i(p, \kappa_1, \kappa_2) = r_i^*(p^*, \kappa_1^*, \kappa_2^*) \tag{4.61d}$$

$$i = 1, 2.$$

These six conditions, which are analogous to the equilibrium conditions in the presence of perfect intersectoral capital mobility, can be solved for the six unknowns: p, p^*, κ_j, and κ_j^*, $j = 1, 2$.

I now introduce a simple graphical method to solve these conditions. Substitute conditions (4.61b) and (4.61c) into (4.61a) to give

$$\mathcal{E}_1(p, \kappa_1, \kappa_2) + \mathcal{E}_1^*(p, -\kappa_1, -\kappa_2) = 0, \tag{4.62}$$

which is then solved for $p = \varrho(\kappa_1, \kappa_2)$. This is the world price of good 1 under free trade when the movements of both types of capital are given as parameters. Differentiate (4.62) and rearrange terms to give

$$\varrho_j \equiv \frac{\partial \varrho}{\partial \kappa_j} = \frac{\mathcal{E}_{1j}^* - \mathcal{E}_{1j}}{\mathcal{E}_{1p} + \mathcal{E}_{1p^*}^*} \tag{4.63}$$

for $j = 1, 2$. For Walrasian stability of the goods market at any level of capital movement, I again assume that $\mathcal{E}_{1p} + \mathcal{E}_{1p^*}^* > 0$. Thus the sign of ϱ_j depends on the sign of $\mathcal{E}_{1j}^* - \mathcal{E}_{1j}$, which is positive if a transfer of one unit of sector-j foreign capital to the home country at a given p decreases the excess supply of good 1 in the world market.

Substitute $p = \varrho(\kappa_1, \kappa_2)$ and condition (4.61b) into (4.61d) to give

$$r_i(\varrho(\kappa_1, \kappa_2), \kappa_1, \kappa_2) = r_i^*(\varrho(\kappa_1, \kappa_2), -\kappa_1, -\kappa_2). \tag{4.64}$$

The relationship between κ_1 and κ_2 for sector i as described by (4.64) is illustrated graphically by schedule R_i in Figure 4.13. This schedule represents the locus of κ_1 and κ_2 that clear the markets of good 1 and sector-i capital. To get the slope of this schedule, differentiate both sides of (4.64) and rearrange terms to give

$$\left.\frac{\partial \kappa_2}{\partial \kappa_1}\right|_{R_i} = -\frac{r_{i1} + r_{i1}^* + r_{ip}\varrho_1 - r_{ip^*}^*\varrho_1}{r_{i2} + r_{i2}^* + r_{ip}\varrho_2 - r_{ip^*}^*\varrho_2}. \tag{4.65}$$

Because the sign of ϱ_j is ambiguous, the sign of the slope of the schedule R_i as given by (4.65) is also ambiguous. In the special case in which both countries

(a)

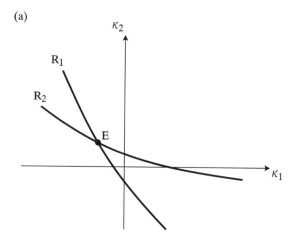

(b)

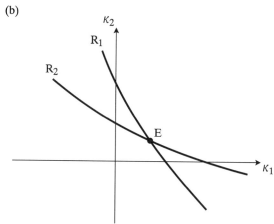

Figure 4.13

are facing given world price p, $\varrho_1 = \varrho_2 = 0$, and condition (4.65) reduces to

$$\left.\frac{\partial \kappa_2}{\partial \kappa_1}\right|_{R_i} = -\frac{r_{i1} + r_{i1}^*}{r_{i2} + r_{i2}^*} < 0. \tag{4.65'}$$

In Figure 4.13, I assume that both schedules are negatively sloped. The equilibrium is depicted by the intersecting point, E, of schedules R_1 and R_2. If capital flows from a place of low rental rate to a place of high rental rate, (local) stability of equilibrium requires that in the neighborhood around the equilibrium point schedule R_1 is steeper than schedule R_2.

One important phenomenon that has captured the attention of many trade economists is two-way flow, or "cross-hauling" of foreign investment (Hymer and Rowthorn, 1970; Caves, 1971; and Bhagwati, 1972). In the neoclassical framework with homogeneity of capital and certainty, it is not possible to have "cross-hauling" of capital. One way of explaining this phenomenon is to assume the presence of uncertainty (Razin and Wong, 1993). Alternatively, "cross-hauling" of capital can also arise in the presence of product differentiation (explained in Chapter 6) or intra-industry investment of oligopolistic firms in two countries (explained in Chapter 13). In the present chapter, this phenomenon can be explained by using the SF model.

Amano (1977) explains vigorously how the SF model can be applied to analyze international capital movement, but he concentrates on the case with identical technologies between countries, an assumption that severely limits the generality of his model and results. Batra and Ramachandran (1980) provide another rigorous SF model of international capital movement, but their attention in the paper is on the effects of income taxes on international investment. Probably the first SF model of "cross-hauling" of foreign investment without identical technologies is in Jones, et al. (1983). They consider a small open economy with a tradable sector and a nontradable sector. The price of the tradable good and the rental rates of the two types of sector-specific capital are exogenously given. They show that a change in the demand for the nontradable good or an international transfer will cause movement of the two types of capital to flow in opposite directions.

Two concepts of "cross-hauling" of foreign investment can be distinguished. The first concept can be illustrated by using Figure 4.13, where the origin is the no-capital-flow point, with or without trade in goods. Point E thus shows the movements of capital at the equilibrium under free trade in goods and capital movement. Panels (a) and (b) show two different possible cases. In panel (a), point E is in the second quadrant, showing that domestic sector-1 capital flows out while foreign sector-2 capital moves to the home country: The two types of capital move in opposite directions. This is the first concept of "cross-hauling" of foreign investment, that is, at a free trade plus capital movement equilibrium, foreign capital from one sector works in the same sector in the home country while home capital from another sector works in the same sector in the foreign country. In panel (b), the equilibrium point is in the first quadrant, meaning that both types of foreign capital flow to the home country, and there is no "cross-hauling" of foreign investment. The analysis thus shows that "cross-hauling" of foreign investment exists if and only if the world equilibrium point is in the second or fourth quadrant in Figure 4.13.

The second concept of "cross-hauling," which is considered in Jones, et al. (1983), is to use an initial equilibrium under free trade and capital mobility (not necessarily the autarky) as a reference point and then examine the movement of the two types of capital after a shock such as a change in tastes or a change in government policy. This concept can also be illustrated by using the present model and Figure 4.13. Because both sectors in the present model are tradable, I consider the effects of some shocks that are not analyzed in Jones, et al. (1983).

Suppose first that there is a technological progress or a decrease in the amount of capital in the home sector 1. At each value of κ_2, more foreign sector-1 capital will flow to the home country. This shifts schedule R_1 to the right. Schedule R_2 may also shift because the good-1 market is disturbed and function $p = \varrho(\kappa_1, \kappa_2)$ may change. If I assume that the effect of a change in $p = \varrho(\kappa_1, \kappa_2)$ is sufficiently small, and if schedule R_2 is negatively sloped, the new equilibrium point, as compared with the initial one, must represent sector-1 capital flowing from the foreign country to the home country and sector-2 capital flowing in an opposite direction, that is, "cross-hauling" of foreign investment.

A stronger result can be obtained in the special case in which the two countries are initially identical, with identical technologies, preferences, and factor endowments (same amounts of capital in each of the sectors). In this case, schedules R_1 and R_2 have some interesting properties. First, $\mathcal{E}_{1j} = \mathcal{E}_{1j}^*$ for $j = 1, 2$. By condition (4.63), $\varrho_j = 0$, implying that condition (4.65) for the slope of schedule R_j reduces to (4.65'), that is, the schedule is negatively sloped in the neighborhood close to the origin. Second, the schedules intersect at the origin because no trade or capital movement will occur. Suppose now that the foreign country has slightly more of sector-1 capital, or that the home country has a small technological progress in sector 1. The analysis in the previous paragraph shows that the home country gains sector-1 capital but loses some sector-2 capital. In this case, "cross-hauling" of foreign investment exists.

I now consider the next case in which the home country experiences an increase in labor endowment. With given levels of κ_1 and κ_2, the rental rate in each sector goes up, meaning that schedule R_1 shifts to the right and schedule R_2 shifts up (neglecting the effects that come from the commodity prices). Then even if both schedules are negatively sloped, it is still not clear whether "cross-hauling" of foreign investment has occured. The only conclusion possible is that the home country has more of at least one of the two types of capital.

III PURE THEORY: VARIABLE RETURNS AND IMPERFECT COMPETITION

External Economies of Scale

The analysis given so far is based on the assumption of perfect competition and constant returns to scale. In this and the following two chapters, I relax this assumption and examine commodity trade and factor mobility in frameworks that do not have perfect competition and constant returns at the same time. In this chapter I focus on external economies of scale.

A firm is said to be experiencing economies of scale if an increase in its production brings some technological advantages (or disadvantages) to the firm's production process. In some cases, an increase in a firm's production has a spillover effect in the sense that it also brings technological advantages (or disadvantages) to other firms' production process. A very common case is the one in which the technological advantages a firm gains come from the production levels of certain industries (including its own).

Economies of scale are said to be external to a firm if these advantages are ignored by firms because the economies-of-scale effects come from factors the firm has little or no control of. One example is that such effects come from the industry production level when there are a large number of firms.

In theoretical work, it is usually assumed that firms, while ignoring external economies of scale, behave like firms in competitive markets, perceiving that their production functions exhibit constant returns to scale. As will be shown later, firms under these conditions earn zero profit in the long run. In this sense, external economies of scale are said to be compatible with perfect competition.

Such treatment of external economies of scale originated with Marshall (1890) and was later refined by Edgeworth, Haberler, Graham, Knight, Tinbergen, Ohlin, Meade, and others.[1] Modern treatment of external economies of scale began with Minabe (1966), Jones (1968), Kemp (1964, 1969), Melvin (1969), and Chipman (1970). Much more work was done in the 1970s and 1980s. Today there is a good understanding of frameworks with external economies, but different issues are still of interest to trade theorists and there are still many open questions that call for more research.

This chapter presents and extends some of the results developed in the literature, and examines the relationship between international commodity trade and factor mobilty under external economies of scale. Surprisingly, very few papers, with a few exceptions such as Melvin (1969), Markusen (1983), and Panagariya (1986), have investigated international factor mobility under variable returns to scale. There is a big void in the literature. What I show is that in the presence of external economies of scale, international trade in goods and factor mobility have very different effects on the world. I show that the usual notion that theorems of international trade in goods can be applied to interna-

---

1. See Chipman (1965) for a survey.

tional factor mobility by simply assuming that factors are negative outputs is no longer valid when external economies of scale are present.

5.1   External Effects in Production

Consider an economy endowed with $m \geq 1$ exogenously given factors that can be employed to produce $n \geq 2$ homogeneous goods. Each of the n sectors consists of a large number of identical firms. A representative firm, or firm f, of sector i, $i = 1, \ldots, n$, has technology described by the following production function:

$$Q_i^f = F_i(\mathbf{v}_i^f, \mathbf{Z}), \tag{5.1}$$

where Q_i^f is its output and $\mathbf{v}_i^f \in R_+^m$ is the vector of its factor inputs. The term $\mathbf{Z}$ in the production function is a vector of all other variables that may also affect the output of the firm. $\mathbf{Z}$ is different from $\mathbf{v}_i^f$ in the sense that the firm treats $\mathbf{Z}$ as exogenously given. The exogeneity of $\mathbf{Z}$ is only the firm's perception. For the society, $\mathbf{Z}$ is affected by production of the economy. I will be more explicit about the elements of $\mathbf{Z}$ later, but for the time being, I keep this generality in order to develop some general results about externality.

The production function in (5.1), when $\mathbf{Z}$ is treated as constant, behaves like a neoclassical production function. More specifically, it is differentiable, linearly homogeneous, and concave in $\mathbf{v}_i^f$. The firm, acting competitively and taking $\mathbf{Z}$ as given, makes use of the production function to maximize its profit.

Summing up the outputs of the firms, I get the aggregate output of sector i, that is,

$$Q_i \equiv \sum_f Q_i^f = \sum_f F_i(\mathbf{v}_i^f, \mathbf{Z}) = F_i(\mathbf{v}_i, \mathbf{Z}), \tag{5.2}$$

where $\mathbf{v}_i = \sum_f \mathbf{v}_i^f$. The last equality in (5.2) is due to linear homogeneity of the production function in all factor inputs. Condition (5.2) represents the sectoral production function.

To determine factor demands of the firms, two concepts of marginal products of factor j should be distinguished. Using the terminology of Panagariya (1980), the *private marginal product* (PMP) of factor j for a firm in sector i, PMP_{ij}, is defined as the contribution of a marginal unit of the factor to the firm's output, holding variables $\mathbf{Z}$ constant, that is,[2]

---

2. Private marginal product is also called subjective marginal product, and social marginal product, which is introduced later, is also called objective marginal product (Chipman, 1965).

$$PMP_{ij} = \frac{\partial F_i}{\partial v_{ij}^f}. \tag{5.3}$$

Note that because of identical technology, all the firms in sector i employ the same amounts of factors in equilibrium and thus has the same PMP of factor j. In view of the sectoral production function given by condition (5.2), PMP_{ij} is also given by

$$PMP_{ij} = \frac{\partial F_i}{\partial v_{ij}}. \tag{5.3'}$$

The *social marginal product* (SMP) of factor j in sector i is defined as the total impact of a marginal unit of the factor on the whole sector's output, that is,

$$SMP_{ij} = \frac{\partial F_i}{\partial v_{ij}} + \sum_h \left[\frac{\partial F_i}{\partial Z_h} \frac{\partial Z_h}{\partial v_{ij}} \right]. \tag{5.4}$$

A comparison of (5.3') and (5.4) shows that the difference between the PMP and SMP of the factor comes from the terms within the square brackets in (5.4), which represent the external effects of a marginal increase in factor j in sector i.

Denote the price of factor j by w_j, $j = 1, \ldots, m$, and the price of good i by p_i, $i = 1, \ldots, n$. Define the corresponding price vectors: $\mathbf{w} = \{w_j\}$ and $\mathbf{p} = \{p_i\}$. Because firm f is a price taker and treats $\mathbf{Z}$ as fixed, the cost-minimizing factor demand is given by

$$w_j = p_i PMP_{ij} = p_i \frac{\partial F_i}{\partial v_{ij}}. \tag{5.5}$$

Condition (5.5) means that factor j is demanded up to the point at which its wage rate is equal to the value of its private marginal product. From the firm's point of view, it is maximizing its profit, but from the society's point of view, the employment of the factors is not optimal because the external effects are neglected.

The total payment of the firm to the factors is equal to

$$\sum_j w_j v_{ij}^f = p_i \sum_j v_{ij}^f \frac{\partial F_i}{\partial v_{ij}^f} = p_i Q_i^f, \tag{5.6}$$

where it is noted that F_i is linearly homogeneous in all factors. Condition (5.6) has an interesting implication: The factor payment is equal to the revenue of the firm so that it earns zero profit in the long-run. This result is compatible with perfect competition.

More properties of the production of the economy can be obtained by defining a GDP function similar to the one defined in Chapter 2:

$$\breve{g}(\mathbf{p}, \mathbf{v}, \mathbf{Z}) = \max_{\mathbf{Q}, \{\mathbf{v}_i\}} \mathbf{p} \cdot \mathbf{Q} \quad \text{s.t.} \quad F_i(\mathbf{v}_i, \mathbf{Z}) \geq Q_i, \quad \text{for all } i,$$

$$\sum_i \mathbf{v}_i \leq \mathbf{v}, \tag{5.7}$$

where $\mathbf{v}$ represents the factor endowments of the economy. Let v_j be an element of $\mathbf{v}$, and full employment implies that $v_j = \sum_i v_{ij}$. Define the following Lagrangian function:

$$\mathcal{L} = \mathbf{p} \cdot \mathbf{Q} + \sum_i \phi_i \left[F_i(\mathbf{v}_i, \mathbf{Z}) - Q_i \right] + \mathbf{w} \cdot (\mathbf{v} - \sum_i \mathbf{v}_i). \tag{5.8}$$

Denote the solution to the Lagrangian problem (5.8) by $\breve{\mathbf{Q}}(\mathbf{p}, \mathbf{v}, \mathbf{Z})$ and $\breve{\mathbf{w}}(\mathbf{p}, \mathbf{v}, \mathbf{Z})$.

The first-order conditions of this problem are given by

$$\frac{\partial \mathcal{L}}{\partial Q_i} = p_i - \phi_i \leq 0 \tag{5.9a}$$

$$\frac{\partial \mathcal{L}}{\partial v_{ij}} = \phi_i \frac{\partial F_i}{\partial v_{ij}} - w_j \leq 0. \tag{5.9b}$$

Condition (5.9a) states that if the equilibrium output of good i is positive, then ϕ_i is equal to the market price of good i. By (5.9b), if factor j is employed in sector i, which implies that the output of the sector is positive, then w_j is interpreted as the market price of factor j. Using these two results, one can see that condition (5.9b) is identical to condition (5.5). This means that if the values of $\mathbf{Z}$ in the GDP function are those the firms face but regard as constant, then $\breve{Q}(\mathbf{p}, \mathbf{v}, \mathbf{Z})$ represents the aggregate outputs jointly chosen by the firms, and the value of the GDP function is the GDP of the economy.

Using the Lagrangian function in (5.8) and the envelope theorem, the partial derivatives of $\breve{g}$ are given by

$$\frac{\partial \breve{g}}{\partial p_i} = \breve{Q}_i(\mathbf{p}, \mathbf{v}, \mathbf{Z}) \tag{5.10a}$$

$$\frac{\partial \breve{g}}{\partial v_j} = \breve{w}_j(\mathbf{p}, \mathbf{v}, \mathbf{Z}) \tag{5.10b}$$

$$\frac{\partial \breve{g}}{\partial Z_h} = \sum_i \phi_i \frac{\partial F_i}{\partial Z_h} = \sum_i p_i \frac{\partial F_i}{\partial Z_h}. \tag{5.10c}$$

In (5.10c), I use the fact that $\phi_i = p_i$ if the equilibrium output of good i is positive. If the equilibrium output of good i is zero, then let $\partial F_i / \partial Z_h$ be zero, meaning that a change in Z_h does not affect the output of the good. As I explained earlier, if $\mathbf{Z}$ is given at the equilibrium values, conditions (5.10a) and (5.10b) give the market outputs and factor prices.

5.2   Output-Generated External Effects

In the previous section, I considered a general framework and derived some properties of external effects. Without specifying what these external effects are, however, there is not too much I can say. In this section, I am more explicit about the external effects.

Following the terminology in Kemp (1969), the external effects are *output-generated* if $\mathbf{Z}$ contains the output levels of some sectors and that the external effects are *factor-generated* if $\mathbf{Z}$ contains factors employed in some sectors. I here consider only output-generated externality because they are more common in the literature, but factor-generated externality will be considered in Chapter 14.

5.2.1   The Model

For expositional purposes, I make the following assumptions:

1. In function $F_i(\mathbf{v}_i, \mathbf{Z})$, $\mathbf{Z}$ contains only its own output level. Thus, the sectoral production function is written as

$$Q_i = F_i(\mathbf{v}_i, Q_i). \tag{5.2'}$$

As mentioned, when taking Q_i as given, function $F_i(\mathbf{v}_i, Q_i)$ is assumed to be differentiable, linearly homogeneous, and concave in $\mathbf{v}_i$. Assuming that $F_i(\mathbf{v}_i, Q_i)$ is invertible in Q_i, an alternative form of the production function in (5.2') is

$$Q_i = H_i(\mathbf{v}_i). \tag{5.2''}$$

2. Function $H_i(\mathbf{v}_i)$ given by (5.2'') is homothetic in factor inputs so that the marginal rate of technical substitution is independent of its output level. This implies that the sectoral production function in (5.2') is separable and can be written as

$$Q_i = h_i(Q_i)\widetilde{F}_i(\mathbf{v}_i), \tag{5.11}$$

where $h_i(Q_i) > 0$ for $Q_i > 0$. With the production function given by (5.11), the marginal rate of technical substitution between factors j and k is equal to $(\partial \widetilde{F}_i/\partial v_{ij})/(\partial \widetilde{F}_i/\partial v_{ik})$, which does not depend on the output level.

In the literature, it is sometimes further assumed that $h_i(Q_i)$ is given by the function $Q_i^{\varepsilon_i}$ where ε_i is a constant. Condition (5.11) then reduces to

$$Q_i = \left[\widetilde{F}_i(\mathbf{v}_i)\right]^{1/(1-\varepsilon_i)}. \tag{5.11'}$$

The production function in (5.11') is homogenous of degree $1/(1 - \varepsilon_i)$. In the following analysis, unless stated explicitly, I keep the generality of function $h_i(Q_i)$ so that the production function is homothetic but may not be homogeneous.

Recall that each firm in the sector ignores external effects. This means that each firm regards $h_i(Q_i)$ as a constant. This is the case when the output of each firm depends on the industry output, but each firm is so small that it perceives that its production has little or negligible effect on the industry output. Thus in a first approximation, the industry output is considered constant by each firm.

The main reason for making assumptions (1) and (2), which are common in the literature, is that they greatly simplify the analysis and allow me to highlight the implications of external effects. The techniques to be developed later can be used to analyze other cases.

Using the production function given by (5.11), I say that $h_i'(Q_i)$ is positive (respectively negative) if and only if the external effect is positive (respectively negative). In the present special case in which the external effect comes from its own output, I can say that the production function $H_i(\mathbf{v}_i)$ exhibits increasing (respectively decreasing) returns to scale. If $h_i'(Q_i) = 0$, then the external effect is zero and $H_i(\mathbf{v}_i)$ exhibits constant returns to scale.

Define the *rate of variable returns to scale* (VRS) for sector i as the elasticity of function $h_i(Q_i)$, that is,

$$\varepsilon_i = \frac{Q_i}{h_i(Q_i)} \frac{\mathrm{d}h_i(Q_i)}{\mathrm{d}Q_i} = h_i'(Q_i)\widetilde{F}_i.$$

The sign of ε_i is the same as that of $h_i'(Q_i)$, meaning that it is positive if and only if the production function exhibits increasing returns to scale (IRS). For a reason to be explained later, it is assumed that $\varepsilon_i < 1$. As explained, if ε_i is constant, the production function reduces to the one given by (5.11').

Because $h_i(Q_i)$ is regarded as a constant by each firm, the inverse demand for factor j by the industry is

$$w_j = p_i h_i(Q_i) \frac{\partial \widetilde{F}_i}{\partial v_{ij}}. \tag{5.5'}$$

Condition (5.5') has a very important implication. With output-generated external effects and with homothetic production functions given by (5.11), whether or not intersectoral externality is included, factors are employed by firms so that the marginal rate of technical substitution between any two factors is equalized across firms and sectors. This implies that production must occur on the efficiency locus and on the production possibility frontier (PPF).

The social marginal product of factor j in sector i, however, is given by

$$SMP_{ij} = \frac{\partial Q_i}{\partial v_{ij}} = h_i(Q_i)\frac{\partial \widetilde{F}_i}{\partial v_{ij}} + h_i'(Q_i)\widetilde{F}_i\frac{\partial Q_i}{\partial v_{ij}} = \frac{h_i(Q_i)}{1 - \varepsilon_i}\frac{\partial \widetilde{F}_i}{\partial v_{ij}}. \tag{5.12}$$

In order to have a positive social marginal product, it is assumed that $\varepsilon_i < 1$. This is to avoid being in the land of Cockaigne. (Kemp, 1969.)

5.2.2 Production Possibilities

Define $\widetilde{Q}_i \equiv Q_i/h_i(Q_i)$ and $\widetilde{p}_i \equiv p_i h_i(Q_i)$. With output-generated external effects, it is more convenient to define a new GDP function, which is analogous to function $\breve{g}(\mathbf{p}, \mathbf{v}, \mathbf{Z})$ defined by (5.7):

$$g(\widetilde{\mathbf{p}}, \mathbf{v}) = \max_{\mathbf{Q},\{\mathbf{v}_i\}} \widetilde{\mathbf{p}} \cdot \widetilde{\mathbf{Q}} \quad \text{s.t.} \quad \widetilde{F}_i(\mathbf{v}_i) \geq \widetilde{Q}_i, \quad \text{for all } i,$$

$$\sum_i \mathbf{v}_i \leq \mathbf{v}. \tag{5.7'}$$

Note that the two GDP functions are equivalent if the variables in $\mathbf{Z}$ are appropriately defined.

Function $g(\widetilde{\mathbf{p}}, \mathbf{v})$ defined by condition (5.7') behaves, in terms of $\widetilde{\mathbf{p}}$ and $\mathbf{v}$, like the GDP function explained in Chapter 2. The derivative of the function with respect to $\widetilde{p}_i$ is equal to

$$\frac{\partial g}{\partial \widetilde{p}_i} = \widetilde{Q}_i(\widetilde{\mathbf{p}}, \mathbf{v}). \tag{5.13}$$

Using the definition of $\widetilde{Q}_i$,

$$Q_i = h_i(Q_i)\widetilde{Q}_i(\widetilde{\mathbf{p}}, \mathbf{v}) \quad \text{for all } i = 1, \ldots, n. \tag{5.13'}$$

Condition (5.13') represents a system of n equations. If the commodity prices and factor endowments are given, these equations can be solved for the n outputs of the sectors.

In view of the system of equations given by (5.13'), I distinguish between the *real system* represented by $(\{Q_i\}, \{p_i\})$, and the *virtual system* represented $(\{\widetilde{Q}_i\}, \{\widetilde{p}_i\})$. Because the virtual system behaves like the traditional framework, to derive the properties of the real system it is often more convenient to start with the properties of the virtual system.

One feature of an equilibrium represented by the system of equations in (5.13') is that the outputs may be determinate even though the number of goods is greater than the number of factors. Recall that for an economy under constant returns, if the number of goods is greater than the number of factors, the production possibility surface may be "ruled," that is, it may consist of straight lines. In the present economy, the locus of outputs that satisfy (5.13′) may not be a straight line, even if there are more sectors than factors.

Another feature of the system of equations in (5.13′) is that in some cases these equations preclude the possibility of zero outputs of certain sectors (when given $\mathbf{p}$ and $\mathbf{v}$). Suppose the production functions are homogeneous so that ε_i is constant for all i. I want to find out whether $Q_i = 0$ can occur in an equilibrium when given $\mathbf{p}$ and $\mathbf{v}$. Consider first the case when $\varepsilon_i > 0$, that is, the sector is subject to increasing returns to scale (IRS). In this case, when $Q_i \to 0$, $h_i(Q_i) \to 0$, which in turn implies that $\widetilde{p}_i \to 0$. Because the GDP function in terms of $\widetilde{\mathbf{p}}$ and $\widetilde{\mathbf{Q}}$ behaves regularly, $\widetilde{p}_i \to 0$ implies $\widetilde{Q}_i \to 0$. The values of these parameters are compatible with condition (5.13′), meaning that $Q_i = 0$ may exist in an equilibrium if ε_i is constant and positive, no matter what commodity prices are. Consider next the case in which ε_i is constant and negative, that is, the sector is subject to decreasing returns to scale (DRS). When $Q_i \to 0$, I have $h_i(Q_i) \to \infty$ and $\widetilde{p}_i \to \infty$, but when $\widetilde{p}_i \to \infty$, $\widetilde{Q}_i$ becomes very large, and this contradicts the initial assumption that $Q_i \to 0$. Summarizing these results, I have: In an equilibrium under given commodity prices and factor endowments and homogeneous production functions, the output of a sector subject to IRS or CRS may be zero but that of the sector subject to DRS cannot be zero. This result for a two-sector, one-factor economy was first given by Panagariya (1981). Note that this result and that in Panagariya (1981) are proved under the assumption that the rates of VRS are constant.

One further feature of the preceding system of equations is the possibility of multiple equilibria for a small open economy facing exogenously given world prices. To illustrate such a possibility, let me consider the following example:

Example 5.1   Suppose that there are two sectors but there is only one factor, labor. Let its endowed amount be 2. The production functions are $Q_1 = Q_1^{0.5}L_1$ and $Q_2 = L_2$. In other words, sector 1 is subject to IRS and sector 2 to CRS. Suppose that the relative price of good 1, p, is equal to 1. Then the following three points satisfy the equations in (5.13′): $(Q_1, Q_2) = (1, 1)$, $(0, 2)$ and $(4, 0)$. The first equilibrium, which is an interior solution, involves positive outputs of the goods, and in the other two the economy is completely specialized. In fact, it can be shown that $(0, 2)$ is always an equilibrium for all finite prices.

An interior production point under given commodity prices is usually more interesting. For the economy described in Example 5.1, an interior equilibrium, if it exists, must be unique. To see why, note that in order to have an interior solution, the virtual system, which is a Ricardian framework, must have an interior solution. This means that to have diversification, the virtual relative price, $\tilde{p}$, must be equal to 1. This implies that $p = 1/h_1(Q_1) = Q_1^{-0.5}$, or $Q_1 = p^{-2}$, meaning that given p, there is only one value of Q_1 that is compatible with diversification.

It does not mean that for every given price ratio, there always exists an interior solution. In the preceding example, p^{-2} cannot be greater than the maximum output of good 1 that the economy can produce when given the labor endowment. When the labor endowment is equal to 2, the maximum output of good 1 is 4. This means that in order to have diversification, the price ratio cannot be lower than $Q_1^{-0.5}$, or 0.5.

I now turn to a more general model in which ε_i may or may not be constant. I first apply the GDP function defined in (5.7') to derive the following reciprocity relations:

1. $(1 - \varepsilon_i)\dfrac{\partial Q_i}{\partial p_k} = (1 - \varepsilon_k)\dfrac{\partial Q_k}{\partial p_i};$

2. $\displaystyle\sum_k p_k \dfrac{\partial Q_i}{\partial p_k} = 0;$

3. $\displaystyle\sum_i (1 - \varepsilon_i) p_i \dfrac{\partial Q_i}{\partial p_k} = 0;$

4. $(1 - \varepsilon_i)\dfrac{\partial Q_i}{\partial v_j} = \dfrac{\partial w_j}{\partial p_i};$

5. $\displaystyle\sum_i (1 - \varepsilon_i) p_i \dfrac{\partial Q_i}{\partial v_j} = w_j;$

6. $\dfrac{\partial w_\ell}{\partial v_j} = \dfrac{\partial w_j}{\partial v_\ell};$

$$i, k = 1, \ldots, n; \qquad j, \ell = 1, \ldots, m.$$

These relations, which are analogous to those in the framework with constant returns derived in Chapter 2, are proved in the appendix. Relation (2) implies that Q_i is homogeneous of degree zero in commodity prices. Relations (1) and (3) to (6) are proved by Inoue (1981) under the assumption that the rates of VRS are independent of output levels. It is here shown that Inoue's assumption is not needed for these five and the other relations.

To derive more properties about the production possibilities of the economy, it is convenient to use output function $\tilde{Q}_i(\tilde{\mathbf{p}}, \mathbf{v})$.[3] Totally differentiate both sides of $Q_i = h_i \tilde{Q}_i$ to give

---

3. Note that $h_i(Q_i)\tilde{Q}_i(\tilde{\mathbf{p}}, \mathbf{v}) \equiv \check{Q}_i(\mathbf{p}, \mathbf{v}, \mathbf{Z})$.

$$dQ_i = \widetilde{Q}_i h_i' dQ_i + h_i d\widetilde{Q}_i = \frac{h_i}{(1 - \varepsilon_i)} d\widetilde{Q}_i. \tag{5.14}$$

I define $\psi_i = h_i/(1 - \varepsilon_i) > 0$. Condition (5.14) can be written alternatively as

$$dQ_i = \psi_i d\widetilde{Q}_i. \tag{5.14'}$$

Condition (5.14$'$) can be used to determine the marginal rate of transformation, MRT. To be more explicit, let me for the time being consider a two-sector economy, $n = 2$. Therefore the MRT is equal to

$$\frac{dQ_2}{dQ_1} = \frac{\psi_2}{\psi_1} \frac{d\widetilde{Q}_2}{d\widetilde{Q}_1} = \frac{h_2(1 - \varepsilon_1)}{h_1(1 - \varepsilon_2)} \frac{d\widetilde{Q}_2}{d\widetilde{Q}_1}. \tag{5.15}$$

I have explained that the GDP function defined in (5.7$'$) behaves, in terms of $\widetilde{\mathbf{p}}$ and $\widetilde{\mathbf{Q}}$, like the traditional GDP function with CRS technologies. This means that the set of possible $\widetilde{\mathbf{Q}}$ is convex and the frontier of this set is negatively (or nonpositively) sloped. Denote the virtual production possibility frontier (PPF) by $\widetilde{Q}_2 = T(\widetilde{Q}_1)$, and $T' \leq 0$ and $T'' \leq 0$. Therefore the MRT given by (5.15) reduces to

$$\frac{dQ_2}{dQ_1} = \frac{\psi_2}{\psi_1} T' \leq 0. \tag{5.15'}$$

Because ψ_1, and ψ_2 are both positive, condition (5.15$'$) implies that the real PPF (hereafter simply called PPF for convenience) of the present economy under variable returns to scale is non-positively sloped, or is negatively sloped if the virtual PPF is.[4]

The MRT is also related to the price ratio. Recall that the present GDP function behaves normally in terms of $\widetilde{\mathbf{Q}}$ and $\widetilde{\mathbf{p}}$. Thus

$$\frac{d\widetilde{Q}_2}{d\widetilde{Q}_1} = -\frac{\widetilde{p}_1}{\widetilde{p}_2}.$$

Because $\widetilde{p}_i = p_i h_i$, condition (5.15) thus gives

$$\frac{dQ_2}{dQ_1} = -\frac{h_2(1 - \varepsilon_1)}{h_1(1 - \varepsilon_2)} \frac{\widetilde{p}_1}{\widetilde{p}_2} = -\frac{1 - \varepsilon_1}{1 - \varepsilon_2} \frac{p_1}{p_2}. \tag{5.16}$$

Condition (5.16) shows that unless the two sectors have the same rates of VRS, the price line is not tangent to the PPF. In particular, if $\varepsilon_2 > (<) \varepsilon_1$ then the PPF is steeper (less steep) than the price line at the production point.

---

4. It should be noted that in deriving the slope of the PPF, no inter-sectoral externality is assumed. Herberg, et al. (1982) show that with intersectoral externality, the sign of the slope of the PPF is ambiguous. See also Herberg (1969) and Kemp (1969).

In general, the relationship between the MRT and the price line as given by (5.16) is not constant. If ε_1 and ε_2 are constant, then the wedge between the MRT and the price line is constant. Thus as one travels down the PPF, the price line will get steeper (respectively less steep) if and only if the MRT increases (respectively decreases). In other words, the price-output effect is perverse if and only if the PPF is (locally) convex to the origin.[5]

5.2.3   Curvature of the Production Possibility Frontier

I now analyze the curvature of the PPF. Totally differentiate both sides of (5.15′) to give

$$\frac{d^2 Q_2}{dQ_1^2} = T'' \frac{\psi_2}{\psi_1} \frac{d\widetilde{Q}_1}{dQ_1} + T' \frac{\psi_1 \psi_2' (dQ_2/dQ_1) - \psi_2 \psi_1'}{\psi_1^2}$$

$$= \frac{\psi_2}{\psi_1^2} \left[T'' + \psi_2' (T')^2 - \psi_1' T' \right]. \tag{5.17}$$

Equation (5.17), which appears in slightly different forms in many papers in the literature, can be traced back to Tinbergen (1945, p. 191). To determine the sign of $d^2 Q_2/dQ_1^2$, I have to evaluate ψ_i'. First note that

$$\varepsilon_i' = \frac{h_i(h_i' + Q_i h_i'') - Q_i (h_i')^2}{h_i^2} = \frac{h_i'(1 - \varepsilon_i) + Q_i h_i''}{h_i}.$$

Using this condition,

$$\psi_i' = \frac{(1 - \varepsilon_i)h_i' + h_i \varepsilon_i'}{(1 - \varepsilon_i)^2} = \frac{2h_i'(1 - \varepsilon_i) + Q_i h_i''}{(1 - \varepsilon_i)^2}. \tag{5.18}$$

The value of ψ_i' as given by (5.18) is substituted into (5.17) to determine the curvature of the PPF. In general, the sign of ψ_i' is ambiguous, implying that the curvature of the PPF is also ambiguous. The PPF under VRS may be concave downward or convex downward, or may even be partly concave and partly convex.

I now try to find some conditions under which the curvature of the PPF is known. First consider *the special cases in which the rates of VRS of the sectors are constant*, that is, the productions functions are homogeneous.

By differentiating $h_i(Q_i) = Q_i^{\varepsilon_i}$, keeping ε_i constant,

$$h_i' = \varepsilon_i Q_i^{\varepsilon_i - 1}$$

$$h_i'' = -\varepsilon_i(1 - \varepsilon_i) Q_i^{\varepsilon_i - 2}.$$

---

5. This result is due to Markusen and Melvin (1981). Herberg and Kemp (1969, Theorem 5) note that in general the normality of output responses is not related to the curvature of the PPF.

Using these two conditions, ψ_i' reduces to

$$\psi_i' = \frac{\varepsilon_i}{(1 - \varepsilon_i)Q_i^{1-\varepsilon_i}}. \tag{5.19}$$

Condition (5.19) shows that ψ_i' has the same sign as ε_i, that is, ψ_i' is negative if and only if sector i exhibits decreasing returns to scale. When ψ_i' is substituted into (5.17), I get:

Result 5.1 Given homogeneous production functions with constant ε_i, the PPF is concave to the origin if both sectors are subject to nonincreasing returns to scale. It is strictly concave if, in addition, the rates of VRS are finite in magnitude and if the virtual PPF is strictly concave or the PPF is negatively sloped and at least one sector is subject to DRS.

Three features of Result 5.1 can be noted. First, it is a global result. Second, homogeneity of both production functions is required, otherwise DRS is not sufficient for a concave PPF. (See conditions (5.17) and (5.18).) Third, it does not depend on whether factors are indispensable in the sectors, or on whether some of the factors are immobile between sectors.

I now turn to more general cases in which the production functions may or may not be homogeneous. The problems of these cases is that it is difficult to find general conditions for global concavity of the PPF. Thus I focus on local concavity. I first show the following result:

Result 5.2 The PPF is (locally) concave to the origin if both sectors are subject to non-increasing returns ($h_i' \leq 0$, $i = 1, 2$) and if either one of the following conditions holds:

1. $h_i'' \leq 0$;

2. $d\varepsilon_i'/dQ_i \leq 0$;

3. the elasticity of output with respect to scale is non-increasing;

4. $d^2(Q_i/L_i)/dQ_i^2 \leq 0$ when capital-labor ratio is fixed.

Conditions (1) and (2) follow immediately from (5.18). Conditions (3) and (4) are due to Mayer (1974a).[6] The elasticity of output with respect to scale is equal to $1/(1 - \varepsilon_i)$. Differentiation of it and using condition (2) immediately gives condition (3). Next note that $Q_i/L_i = h_i \tilde{f}_i(k_i)$ where k_i is the capital-labor ratio and $\tilde{f}_i(k_i) \equiv \tilde{F}_i(k_i, 1)$. Assuming that k_i is constant,

---

6. Mayer (1974b) states one more condition: the long-run average cost (LAC) curve is convex downward. This condition is based on the assumption that factor prices are fixed while the output of a sector changes.

$d^2(Q_i/L_i)/dQ_i^2 \leq 0$ is equivalent to $h_i'' \leq 0$. Using condition (1), I have condition (4).

I now focus on the curvature of the PPF when the output of a good is close to zero (in neighborhoods close to an axis). Let me consider the following conditions and definitions:

1. *Condition A* $-T'$ has positive lower and finite upper bounds, and $-T''$ has finite upper bound.

2. *Condition B*   As Q_i approaches zero, ψ_i' approaches ∞ (respectively $-\infty$) if $\varepsilon_i >$ (respectively $<$) 0, while ψ_j' is finite, $j \neq i$.

3. *The Herberg-Kemp curvature*   The PPF of an economy is said to have the *Herberg-Kemp curvature* if it is strictly concave (respectively convex) to the origin in the neighborhood of zero output of good i if sector i shows decreasing (respectively increasing) returns in that neighborhood, irrespective of the returns to scale in another sector.

4. *The Tinbergen curvature*   The PPF of an economy is said to have the *Tinbergen curvature* if it is strictly convex (respectively concave) to the origin in the neighborhood of zero output of good i if sector i shows decreasing (respectively increasing) returns in that neighborhood, irrespective of the returns to scale in another sector.

The Herberg-Kemp or Tinbergen curvature is one possible property of the production possibility frontier of an economy under variable returns to scale. Both are local properties because they describe the curvature of the PPF only in the regions when the output of a good is close to zero. Both are strong results, however, in the sense that the curvature of the PPF depends on the returns to scale of the sector whose output is close to zero but not on those of the other sector as long as the value of the latter sector's ψ_j' is finite.

Conditions A and B give the following famous result:

Result 5.3   Given Conditions A and B, the PPF has the Herberg-Kemp curvature (Herberg and Kemp, 1969).

Result 5.3 is due to the fact that Conditions A and B imply that as $Q_i \to 0$, ψ_i' becomes so significant in magnitude that it dominates ψ_j' of the other sector so that the sign of $d^2 Q_2 / dQ_1^2$ in condition (5.17) is the same as the sign of ψ_i', which, under Condition B, depends on the returns to scale. By condition (5.17) the PPF has the curvature indicated in Result 5.3.

I now find some cases in which conditions A and B are satisfied. Condition A is satisfied if there is only one factor so that the virtual system is a Ricardian one. In this case, the virtual PPF is a negatively sloped straight line, $T' < 0$ and

$T'' = 0$. Such a framework is common in the literature; for example, Chipman (1970), Panagariya (1980), Ethier (1979, 1982a, and 1982b), Helpman (1984b), and Krugman (1987a).

The following condition gives a sufficient condition for Condition B.

Result 5.4   If both sectors' production functions are homogeneous (with constant rates of VRS), then Condition B is satisfied.

Result 5.4 can be proved by applying condition (5.19). By using this result, Result 5.3 reduces to

Result 5.3′   Given Condition A and homogeneous production functions, the PPF has the Herberg-Kemp curvature (Herberg and Kemp, 1969).

Note that it is possible that as $Q_2 \to 0$, $\psi_2 \to 0$. In this case, I get

$$\lim_{Q_2 \to 0} \frac{\mathrm{d}^2 Q_2}{\mathrm{d} Q_1{}^2} = 0. \tag{5.20}$$

An example that gives condition (5.20) is provided by Mayer (1974b). However, Herberg and Kemp (1975) point out that condition (5.20) is not equivalent to the condition that $\mathrm{d}^2 Q_2 / \mathrm{d} Q_1{}^2$ is positive for Q_2 positive but sufficiently small. Thus even without the assumption of a homogeneous production function but when condition (5.20) exists, Result 5.3′ holds. Another point about Result 5.3′ is that it does not depend on whether some factors are immobile as long as there is at least one mobile factor (Herberg and Kemp, 1991; Wong, 1994a).[7]

I now turn to the Tinbergen curvature, which is opposite to the Herberg-Kemp curvature. Such possible form of the PPF apparently was first analyzed and shown in a diagram in Tinbergen (1945, p. 192; 1954, p. 181). Recently, the Tinbergen curvature has been regarded as wrong (Panagariya, 1980; Helpman, 1984b). However, this verdict is not correct, as the following example, which is taken from Wong (1994b), shows:

Example 5.2   Suppose that $h_i = a_i + b_i Q_i + c_i Q_i^2$, where all parameters are finite and $a_i > 0$. If b_i and/or c_i is negative, a_i is sufficiently large so that h_i is positive for all possible values of Q_i. It can be shown that

$$\varepsilon_i = \frac{Q_i(b_i + 2c_i Q_i)}{h_i} \tag{5.21a}$$

---

7. Markusen and Melvin (1984) suggest that Result 5.3 is not applicable if some factors are sector specific. Herberg and Kemp (1991) argue that the result is applicable if there are more than one mobile factors. Wong (1994a) shows that it is applicable even if there is only one mobile factor.

$$\psi_i' = \frac{2h_i(a_i b_i + 3a_i c_i Q_i - c_i^2 Q_i^3)}{(a_i - c_i Q_i^2)^2} \tag{5.21b}$$

There is only one factor, labor, and its endowment is unity. Let the parameters have the following values:

$a_1 = 0.8$ $a_2 = 1.2$

$b_1 = 0.2$ $b_2 = -0.1$

$c_1 = 0$ $c_2 = -0.1$.

Using these values, the maximum values of goods 1 and 2 (when the output of the other good is zero) are both equal to unity. Substituting these values into (5.21a) shows that sector 1 is subject to IRS and sector 2 subject to DRS. With only one factor, the virtual economy is a Ricardian one, and the virtual PPF in terms of $\widetilde{Q}_1$ and $\widetilde{Q}_2$ is a straight line with a slope of -1, that is, $T' = -1$ and $T'' = 0$. Because $\psi_2 > 0$, condition (5.17) implies that the sign of $d^2 Q_2 / d Q_1^2$ is the same as that of $(\psi_1' + \psi_2')$. When $Q_1 \to 0$ $(Q_2 \to 1)$, $\psi_1' + \psi_2' = -0.28 < 0$, meaning that the PPF is concave to the origin. When $Q_2 \to 0$ $(Q_1 \to 1)$, $\psi_1' + \psi_2' = 0.3 > 0$, implying that the PPF is convex to the origin. These results together show that the PPF of the present economy has the Tinbergen curvature.

Turning from the properties of the PPF to other properties, define the unit cost function of sector i under VRS:

$$c_i(\mathbf{w}, Q_i) = \min_{\mathbf{a}_i} \mathbf{w} \cdot \mathbf{a}_i \quad \text{s.t.} \quad F_i(\mathbf{a}_i, Q_i) \geq 1, \tag{5.22}$$

where $\mathbf{a}_i$ is the vector of per-unit inputs in sector i. Because the production function is homothetic, $F_i(\mathbf{a}_i, Q_i) = h_i(Q_i)\widetilde{F}_i(\mathbf{a}_i)$, I can define $\widehat{\mathbf{a}}_i = h_i(Q_i)\mathbf{a}_i$. Consider the following function

$$\widetilde{c}_i(\mathbf{w}) = \min_{\mathbf{a}_i} \mathbf{w} \cdot \widehat{\mathbf{a}}_i \quad \text{s.t.} \quad \widetilde{F}_i(\widehat{\mathbf{a}}_i) \geq 1. \tag{5.22'}$$

Because $h_i(Q_i)\widetilde{F}(\mathbf{a}_i) = \widetilde{F}(h_i(Q_i)\mathbf{a}_i)$, a comparison of the functions in (5.22) and (5.22') shows that

$$c_i(\mathbf{w}, Q_i) = \widetilde{c}_i(\mathbf{w})/h_i(Q_i). \tag{5.23}$$

Condition (5.23) is a useful one because function $\widetilde{c}_i(\mathbf{w})$, which is called the virtual unit cost function, behaves like the unit cost function in a framework with CRS. One immediate application of this condition is that the zero profit condition for sector i, $p_i \geq c_i(\mathbf{w}, Q_i)$, is equivalent to $\widetilde{p}_i \geq \widetilde{c}_i(\mathbf{w})$. Using this result, the GDP function given by (5.7') can be defined alternatively as

$$g(\widetilde{\mathbf{p}}, \mathbf{v}) = \min_{\mathbf{w}} \mathbf{w} \cdot \mathbf{v} \quad \text{s.t.} \quad \widetilde{p}_i \geq \widetilde{c}_i(\mathbf{w}) \quad \text{for all } i. \tag{5.7''}$$

More applications of function $\widetilde{c}_i(\mathbf{w})$ are provided later.

5.3   Prices, Output Levels, and Factor Endowments

I now investigate more properties of the present framework concerning the relationships between commodity and factor prices, output levels, and factor endowments. The main focus of this section is about the validity of the Rybczynski theorem and the Stolper-Samuelson theorem in this framework. Many researchers, including Minabe (1966), Jones (1968), Kemp (1969), Herberg and Kemp (1969), Mayer (1974c), Panagariya (1980), Inoue (1981), Chang (1981), Herberg et al. (1982), Ide and Takayama (1991, 1993), and Ishikawa (1994) have examined these questions and derived conditions under which these theorems may or may not hold. I now present some of their results and provide some extensions. For simplicity, I focus on the two-factor, two-sector framework (with diversification) analyzed previously.

My notation is the same as that in Chapter 2 and in the previous two sections. For example, w is the wage rate and r the rental rate of capital. I adopt the preceding approach and begin with the derivation of the equations of change. (See Wong, 1994a for an alternate approach using the virtual GDP function.)

Because firms are price takers and pay factors according to their private marginal products, the zero-profit condition (5.6) (for the industry) can be written as

$$wL_i + rK_i = p_i h_i \left(L_i \frac{\partial \widetilde{F}_i}{\partial L_i} + K_i \frac{\partial \widetilde{F}_i}{\partial K_i} \right) = p_i h_i \widetilde{F}_i = p_i Q_i. \tag{5.6'}$$

Total differentiation of this condition gives

$$\theta_{Li}\widehat{w} + \theta_{Ki}\widehat{r} = \widehat{Q}_i + \widehat{p}_i - (\theta_{Li}\widehat{L}_i + \theta_{Ki}\widehat{K}_i), \tag{5.24}$$

where "$\widehat{}$" denotes the rate of change of a variable, and

$$\theta = \begin{pmatrix} \theta_{L1} & \theta_{K1} \\ \theta_{L2} & \theta_{K2} \end{pmatrix} = \begin{pmatrix} \dfrac{wL_1}{p_1 Q_1} & \dfrac{rK_1}{p_1 Q_1} \\ \dfrac{wL_2}{p_2 Q_2} & \dfrac{rK_2}{p_2 Q_2} \end{pmatrix}.$$

Using the factor demand condition given by (5.5'), condition (5.12) can be restated as

$$(1 - \varepsilon_i)\mathrm{d}Q_i = h_i \frac{\partial \widetilde{F}_i}{\partial L_i} \mathrm{d}L_i + h_i \frac{\partial \widetilde{F}_i}{\partial K_i} \mathrm{d}K_i = \frac{w\mathrm{d}L_i + r\mathrm{d}K_i}{p_i},$$

which can be rearranged to give

$$(1 - \varepsilon_i)\widehat{Q}_i = \theta_{Li}\widehat{L}_i + \theta_{Ki}\widehat{K}_i. \tag{5.25}$$

Using (5.25), (5.24) can be expressed as

$$\theta_{L1}\widehat{w} + \theta_{K1}\widehat{r} = \widehat{p}_1 + \varepsilon_1\widehat{Q}_1 \tag{5.26a}$$

$$\theta_{L2}\widehat{w} + \theta_{K2}\widehat{r} = \widehat{p}_2 + \varepsilon_2\widehat{Q}_2. \tag{5.26b}$$

Full employment of the factors are described by the following equations

$$L_1 + L_2 = L \tag{5.27a}$$

$$K_1 + K_2 = K. \tag{5.27b}$$

Totally differentiate the equations in (5.27) to give

$$\lambda_{L1}\widehat{L}_1 + \lambda_{L2}\widehat{L}_2 = \widehat{L} \tag{5.28a}$$

$$\lambda_{K1}\widehat{K}_1 + \lambda_{K2}\widehat{K}_2 = \widehat{K}, \tag{5.28b}$$

where

$$\lambda = \begin{pmatrix} \lambda_{L1} & \lambda_{L2} \\ \lambda_{K1} & \lambda_{K2} \end{pmatrix} = \begin{pmatrix} \dfrac{L_1}{L} & \dfrac{L_2}{L} \\ \dfrac{K_1}{K} & \dfrac{K_2}{K} \end{pmatrix}.$$

Denote the elasticity of substitution by $\sigma_i = (\widehat{K}_i - \widehat{L}_i)/(\widehat{w} - \widehat{r})$. Equation (5.25) then gives

$$\widehat{L}_i = (1 - \varepsilon_i)\widehat{Q}_i - \sigma_i\theta_{Ki}(\widehat{w} - \widehat{r}), \tag{5.29a}$$

$$\widehat{K}_i = (1 - \varepsilon_i)\widehat{Q}_i + \sigma_i\theta_{Li}(\widehat{w} - \widehat{r}). \tag{5.29b}$$

Using (5.29), the full-employment conditions (5.28) can be written as

$$\lambda_{L1}(1 - \varepsilon_1)\widehat{Q}_1 + \lambda_{L2}(1 - \varepsilon_2)\widehat{Q}_2 = \widehat{L} + \delta_L(\widehat{w} - \widehat{r}) \tag{5.30a}$$

$$\lambda_{K1}(1 - \varepsilon_1)\widehat{Q}_1 + \lambda_{K2}(1 - \varepsilon_2)\widehat{Q}_2 = \widehat{K} - \delta_K(\widehat{w} - \widehat{r}), \tag{5.30b}$$

where $\delta_L = \lambda_{L1}\theta_{K1}\sigma_1 + \lambda_{L2}\theta_{K2}\sigma_2 > 0$, and $\delta_K = \lambda_{K1}\theta_{L1}\sigma_1 + \lambda_{K2}\theta_{L2}\sigma_2 > 0$. The framework is now described by the equations of change (5.26) to (5.30), which form the basis of our analysis.

Without loss of generality, assume that sector 1 is capital intensive. Then I have

$$|\lambda| = \lambda_{L1} - \lambda_{K1} = \lambda_{K2} - \lambda_{L2} < 0,$$

$$|\theta| = \theta_{L1} - \theta_{L2} = \theta_{K2} - \theta_{K1} < 0.$$

5.3.1   Validity of the Rybczynski Theorem under Constant Factor Prices

Because in the presence of VRS there does not exist a one-to-one correspondence between commodity prices and factor prices, I first examine the validity of the Rybczynski theorem under constant factor prices, that is, $\widehat{w} = \widehat{r} = 0$. Define

$$\lambda' = \begin{pmatrix} \lambda'_{L1} & \lambda'_{L2} \\ \lambda'_{K1} & \lambda'_{K2} \end{pmatrix} = \begin{pmatrix} \lambda_{L1}(1-\varepsilon_1) & \lambda_{L2}(1-\varepsilon_2) \\ \lambda_{K1}(1-\varepsilon_1) & \lambda_{K2}(1-\varepsilon_2) \end{pmatrix}$$

The term λ'_{ji}, which is positive, can be interpreted as the per unit demand for factor j in sector i.[8] The determinant of λ' can be shown to be

$$|\lambda'| = |\lambda|(1-\varepsilon_1)(1-\varepsilon_2) < 0.$$

Using the definition of λ', (5.30) can be solved for the output effects of changes in factor endowments:

$$\widehat{Q}_1 = \frac{\lambda'_{K2}\widehat{L} - \lambda'_{L2}\widehat{K}}{|\lambda'|} = \frac{\lambda_{K2}\widehat{L} - \lambda_{L2}\widehat{K}}{|\lambda|(1-\varepsilon_1)} \tag{5.31a}$$

$$\widehat{Q}_2 = \frac{\lambda'_{L1}\widehat{K} - \lambda'_{K1}\widehat{L}}{|\lambda'|} = \frac{\lambda_{L1}\widehat{K} - \lambda_{K1}\widehat{L}}{|\lambda|(1-\varepsilon_2)}. \tag{5.31b}$$

Using (5.31) gives

Result 5.5   The Rybczynski theorem under constant factor prices without magnification effects holds under VRS (Jones, 1968).

In proving Result 5.5, Jones (1968) does not assume homothetic production function but does make the assumption that $\lambda'_{ji} > 0$ for all factors and sectors.

I now turn to the possibility of magnification effect, which Jones (1968) does not consider. Rearrange the terms in (5.31) to give

$$(1-\varepsilon_1)\widehat{Q}_1 = \frac{\lambda_{K2}\widehat{L} - \lambda_{L2}\widehat{K}}{|\lambda|} \tag{5.32a}$$

$$(1-\varepsilon_2)\widehat{Q}_2 = \frac{\lambda_{L1}\widehat{K} - \lambda_{K1}\widehat{L}}{|\lambda|}. \tag{5.32b}$$

Conditions (5.32) are similar to the corresponding ones in a neoclassical framework. Thus I have

8. If the production function is not homothetic, λ'_{ji} may be negative. In Jones (1968), which does not use homothetic production functions, it is assumed to be positive. A similar assumption is made in Mayer (1974c), Chang (1981), and Ide and Takayama (1991, 1993).

Result 5.6   Suppose that factor prices are held constant. A weak version of the magnification effects of the Rybczynski theorem exists in the sense that if $\widehat{K} > \widehat{L} \geq 0$, then $(1 - \varepsilon_1)\widehat{Q}_1 > \widehat{K} > \widehat{L} > (1 - \varepsilon_2)\widehat{Q}_2$, or if $\widehat{L} > \widehat{K} \geq 0$, then $(1 - \varepsilon_2)\widehat{Q}_2 > \widehat{L} > \widehat{K} > (1 - \varepsilon_1)\widehat{Q}_1$.

Result 5.6 immediately implies that *under given factor prices, if both industries are subject to nondecreasing returns to scale, and if* $\widehat{K} > \widehat{L} \geq 0$, *then* $\widehat{Q}_1 > \widehat{K} > \widehat{L} > (1 - \varepsilon_2)\widehat{Q}_2$, *or if* $\widehat{L} > \widehat{K} \geq 0$, *then* $\widehat{Q}_2 > \widehat{L} > \widehat{K} > (1 - \varepsilon_1)\widehat{Q}_1$. In the special case in which if $\widehat{K} > \widehat{L} = 0$, then $\widehat{Q}_1 > \widehat{K} > \widehat{L} > \widehat{Q}_2$, or if $\widehat{L} > \widehat{K} = 0$, then $\widehat{Q}_2 > \widehat{L} > \widehat{K} > \widehat{Q}_1$ (Herberg, et al. 1982).

5.3.2   Validity of the Stolper-Samuelson Theorem

Assuming that $\widehat{L} = \widehat{K} = 0$, equations in (5.30) can be solved for the changes in outputs:

$$\widehat{Q}_1 = \frac{(\lambda_{K2}\delta_L + \lambda_{L2}\delta_K)}{|\lambda|(1 - \varepsilon_1)}(\widehat{w} - \widehat{r}) \tag{5.33a}$$

$$\widehat{Q}_2 = -\frac{(\lambda_{K1}\delta_L + \lambda_{L1}\delta_K)}{|\lambda|(1 - \varepsilon_2)}(\widehat{w} - \widehat{r}). \tag{5.33b}$$

Conditions (5.33a) and (5.33b) are substituted into (5.26). Rearranging the terms gives

$$\theta'_{L1}\widehat{w} + \theta'_{K1}\widehat{r} = \widehat{p}_1 \tag{5.34a}$$

$$\theta'_{L2}\widehat{w} + \theta'_{K2}\widehat{r} = \widehat{p}_2, \tag{5.34b}$$

where

$$\theta' = \begin{pmatrix} \theta'_{L1} & \theta'_{K1} \\ \theta'_{L2} & \theta'_{K2} \end{pmatrix} = \begin{pmatrix} \theta_{L1} - \dfrac{\mu_2\varepsilon_1}{|\lambda|(1 - \varepsilon_1)} & \theta_{K1} + \dfrac{\mu_2\varepsilon_1}{|\lambda|(1 - \varepsilon_1)} \\ \theta_{L2} + \dfrac{\mu_1\varepsilon_2}{|\lambda|(1 - \varepsilon_2)} & \theta_{K2} - \dfrac{\mu_1\varepsilon_2}{|\lambda|(1 - \varepsilon_2)} \end{pmatrix}$$

and where $\mu_1 = \lambda_{K1}\delta_L + \lambda_{L1}\delta_K > 0$, and $\mu_2 = \lambda_{K2}\delta_L + \lambda_{L2}\delta_K > 0$. It is easy to show that $\theta'_{L1} + \theta'_{K1} = \theta'_{L2} + \theta'_{K2} = 1$, which implies that

$$|\theta'| = \theta'_{K2} - \theta'_{K1} = \theta'_{L1} - \theta'_{L2} = |\theta| - \frac{\mu_1\varepsilon_2}{|\lambda|(1 - \varepsilon_2)} - \frac{\mu_2\varepsilon_1}{|\lambda|(1 - \varepsilon_1)}. \tag{5.35}$$

Making use of (5.34), the effects of changes in commodity prices on factor prices can be written as

$$\widehat{w} = \frac{\theta'_{K2}\widehat{p}_1 - \theta'_{K1}\widehat{p}_2}{|\theta'|} \tag{5.36a}$$

$$\widehat{r} = -\frac{\theta'_{L2}\widehat{p}_1 - \theta'_{L1}\widehat{p}_2}{|\theta'|}. \tag{5.36b}$$

The variable θ'_{ji} can be interpreted as a measure of the effect of an increase in a factor price on the average cost of production of a sector. In general, the sign of θ'_{ji} is ambiguous, even if the production function is homothetic. Jones (1968), Mayer (1974c), Chang (1981), and Ide and Takayama (1991, 1993) assume that θ'_{ji} is positive for all factors and sectors, meaning that with a fixed set of factor endowments, an increase in any factor price must increase the (average) cost of producing each commodity. This assumption is not as restrictive as it appears. I can note from the definition of θ'_{ji} that if both sectors are subject to nonincreasing returns, then $\theta'_{L1} \geq 0$ and $\theta'_{K2} \geq 0$. Thus from (5.36), I get

Result 5.7   Assuming that $\theta'_{ji} \geq 0$, the Stolper-Samuelson theorem is valid if and only if $|\theta'|$ is negative. If, however, $|\theta'| > 0$, then the opposite of the Stolper-Samuelson theorem is true so that an increase in a commodity price will increase the factor that is not used intensively in the sector (Jones, 1968).

Now drop the assumption that $\theta'_{ji} \geq 0$. Note that if both sectors are subject to nonincreasing returns, then $|\theta'| < 0$. Thus conditions (5.36) give

Result 5.8   Given fixed factor endowments, if both industries are subject to nonincreasing returns to scale, then

$$\widehat{w}/\widehat{p}_1 < 0 \quad \text{if } \widehat{p}_2 = 0$$

$$\widehat{r}/\widehat{p}_2 < 0 \quad \text{if } \widehat{p}_1 = 0.$$

Note that Result 5.8 is not the Stolper-Samuelson theorem; although an increase in p_1 implies a decrease in w, the result does not mention how r may change. (The effect of an increase in p_2 can be interpreted in the same way.) To derive a sufficient condition for the theorem, note that the output effects of prices are normal if an increase in a relative price leads to an increase in its output but a decrease in the other output. By solving the equations in (5.26), the changes in factor prices are given by

$$\widehat{w} = \frac{\theta_{K2}(\widehat{p}_1 + \varepsilon_1\widehat{Q}_1) - \theta_{K1}(\widehat{p}_2 + \varepsilon_2\widehat{Q}_2)}{|\theta|} \tag{5.37a}$$

$$\widehat{r} = -\frac{\theta_{L2}(\widehat{p}_1 + \varepsilon_1\widehat{Q}_1) - \theta_{L1}(\widehat{p}_2 + \varepsilon_2\widehat{Q}_2)}{|\theta|}. \tag{5.37b}$$

If both industries are subject to nondecreasing returns to scale, ε_1 and ε_2 are both nonnegative but less than unity. If output effects of prices are normal when $\widehat{p}_1 > \widehat{p}_2 \geq 0$, then $\widehat{Q}_1 > 0 > \widehat{Q}_2$, which implies $\widehat{p}_1 + \varepsilon_1\widehat{Q}_1 \geq \widehat{p}_1 > \widehat{p}_2 \geq \widehat{p}_2 + \varepsilon_2\widehat{Q}_2$. Equations (5.37) imply that $\widehat{r} > \widehat{p}_1 + \varepsilon_1\widehat{Q}_1 > \widehat{p}_2 + \varepsilon_2\widehat{Q}_2 > \widehat{w}$. Combining the results, I must have $\widehat{r} > \widehat{p}_1 > \widehat{p}_2 > \widehat{w}$. Similarly, if $\widehat{p}_2 > \widehat{p}_1 \geq 0$, then $\widehat{w} > \widehat{p}_2 > \widehat{p}_1 > \widehat{r}$. These results are summarized as follows:

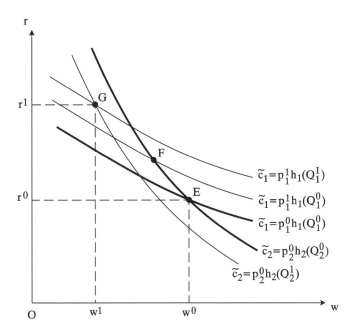

Figure 5.1

Result 5.9 Suppose that both industries are subject to nondecreasing returns to scale, and that output effects of price increases are normal. The Stolper-Samuelson theorem with magnification effects holds.

Result 5.9, which was first noted in Wong (1989c), is useful when it is needed to examine economies under nondecreasing returns (as commonly assumed in the literature) because most other results are related to economies with nonincreasing returns.

The intuition behind Result 5.9 can be illustrated graphically. In Figure 5.1, the initial commodity prices are p_i^0 and initial outputs are Q_i^0. Thus the schedules $\tilde{c}_i$ show the unit-cost schedules of the virtual system. As defined previously, initially $\tilde{c}_i = p_i^0 h_i(Q_i^0)$. The intersecting point of these two unit-cost schedules, E, gives the initial factor prices (w^0, r^0). Suppose that p_1 is increased to p_1^1. If the unit cost functions do not depend on output levels, as in the neoclassical framework with CRS, the final point is at F and the Stolper-Samuelson theorem is satisfied. In the present framework with nondecreasing returns in both sectors, if the outputs respond normally to an increase in p_1, the final outputs are $Q_1^1 > Q_1^0$ and $Q_2^1 < Q_2^0$ where the superscript "1" represents the new value. With IRS in both sectors, the $\tilde{c}_1$ schedule shifts further up and the $\tilde{c}_2$ schedule shifts down. (If sector i is subject to CRS, its unit cost schedule is independent of the output changes.) A comparison of the new intersecting point, G, and the initial intersecting point, E, reveals that the Stolper-Samuelson theorem with magnification effects holds.

5.3.3   Commodity Prices and Output Levels

Result 5.9 requires normal output effects of price changes. It is now the time to find conditions under which these effects are normal. Substitute (5.36a) and (5.36b) into (5.33) to give

$$\widehat{Q}_1 = \frac{\mu_2(1-\varepsilon_2)}{|\lambda'||\theta'|}(\widehat{p}_1 - \widehat{p}_2) \tag{5.38a}$$

$$\widehat{Q}_2 = -\frac{\mu_1(1-\varepsilon_1)}{|\lambda'||\theta'|}(\widehat{p}_1 - \widehat{p}_2), \tag{5.38b}$$

Conditions (5.38a) and (5.38b) can be used to give the following results:

Result 5.10   (1) The output of each good responds positively to its relative price if and only if $|\theta'|$ is negative. (2) The output of each good responds positively to its relative price if both sectors are subject to nonincreasing returns, $\varepsilon_1, \varepsilon_2 \leq 0$.

Result 5.11   In the neighborhood of zero output of good i, its output responds perversely to an increase in its relative price if and only if the sector is subject to increasing returns.

Results 5.10 and 5.11 are due to Herberg and Kemp (1969). To get Result 5.11 from the preceding analysis, note that when $Q_i \to 0$, we have $|\lambda| \to 0$ and $\mu_i \to 0$. Thus

$$\lim_{Q_i \to 0} \frac{\widehat{Q}_i}{\widehat{p}_1 - \widehat{p}_2} = (-1)^i \frac{1}{\varepsilon_i}.$$

5.3.4   Validity of the Rybczynski Theorem under Constant Commodity Prices

I now turn to the Rybczynski theorem under constant commodity prices. Assume that the commodity prices remain constant, that is, $\widehat{p}_1 = \widehat{p}_2 = 0$. Equations in (5.26) can be solved for the rates of change of the factor prices:

$$\widehat{w} = \frac{\theta_{K2}\varepsilon_1\widehat{Q}_1 - \theta_{K1}\varepsilon_2\widehat{Q}_2}{|\theta|} \tag{5.39a}$$

$$\widehat{r} = -\frac{\theta_{L2}\varepsilon_1\widehat{Q}_1 - \theta_{L1}\varepsilon_2\widehat{Q}_2}{|\theta|}. \tag{5.39b}$$

The values of $\widehat{w}$ and $\widehat{r}$ in (5.39) can be substituted into (5.30) to yield a relationship between factor endowments and output levels:

$$\lambda''_{L1}\widehat{Q}_1 + \lambda''_{L2}\widehat{Q}_2 = \widehat{L} \tag{5.40a}$$

$$\lambda''_{K1}\widehat{Q}_1 + \lambda''_{K2}\widehat{Q}_2 = \widehat{K}, \tag{5.40b}$$

where

$$\lambda'' = \begin{pmatrix} \lambda''_{L1} & \lambda''_{L2} \\ \lambda''_{K1} & \lambda''_{K2} \end{pmatrix} = \begin{pmatrix} \lambda'_{L1} - \dfrac{\varepsilon_1\delta_L}{|\theta|} & \lambda'_{L2} + \dfrac{\varepsilon_2\delta_L}{|\theta|} \\ \lambda'_{K1} + \dfrac{\varepsilon_1\delta_K}{|\theta|} & \lambda'_{K2} - \dfrac{\varepsilon_2\delta_K}{|\theta|} \end{pmatrix}.$$

It is easy to show that

$$|\lambda''| = |\lambda'| - \frac{\mu_2\varepsilon_1(1-\varepsilon_2) + \mu_1\varepsilon_2(1-\varepsilon_1)}{|\theta|}, \tag{5.41}$$

or, using (5.35),

$$|\lambda''||\theta| = |\lambda'||\theta'|. \tag{5.41'}$$

Equations in (5.40) can be solved for the effects of factor endowments on commodity outputs:

$$\widehat{Q}_1 = \frac{\lambda''_{K2}\widehat{L} - \lambda''_{L2}\widehat{K}}{|\lambda''|} \tag{5.42a}$$

$$\widehat{Q}_2 = -\frac{\lambda''_{K1}\widehat{L} - \lambda''_{L1}\widehat{K}}{|\lambda''|}. \tag{5.42b}$$

By (5.40), λ''_{ji} can be interpreted as the increase in the per unit demand for factor j by sector i under constant commodity prices. Jones (1968), Mayer (1974c), Chang (1981), and Ide and Takayama (1991, 1993) assume that it is positive for all factors and sectors. Using this assumption and condition (5.40), I have

Result 5.12   If $\lambda''_{ji} > 0$ for all sectors and factors, the Rybczynski theorem (without magnification effects) under constant commodity prices is valid if and only if $|\lambda''|$ is negative (Jones, 1968).

Result 5.12 implies that if $\lambda''_{ji} > 0$ for all sectors and factors and if $|\lambda''| > 0$, however, then the opposite of the Rybczynski theorem is true.

Result 5.13   If both industries are subject to nonincreasing returns to scale, then (Herberg at al., 1982)

$$\widehat{Q}_1/\widehat{L} < 0 \quad \text{if } \widehat{K} = 0$$

$$\widehat{Q}_2/\widehat{K} < 0 \quad \text{if } \widehat{L} = 0.$$

Result 5.14   Suppose that both industries are subject to nondecreasing returns to scale, and that price-output responses are always normal in the sense that an increase in the relative price of a good increases the output of the good but decreases the output of the other good. Then the weak version of the Rybczynski theorem (without magnification effects) holds.

Results 5.13 and 5.14 can be proved by using the reciprocity relations and the corresponding results for the Stolper-Samuelson theorem. Alternatively, Result 5.13 can be proved by using equations (5.42) and the fact that if both industries are subject to nonincreasing returns to scale, $|\lambda''|$ is negative while λ''_{L1} and λ''_{K2} are positive.

5.4   Stability of Production Equilibrium

The previous section shows that the relationships between output levels, prices, and factor endowments depend crucially on the signs of $|\theta'|$ and $|\lambda''|$. Condition (5.41') implies that $|\theta'|$ and $|\lambda''|$ have the same sign because $|\lambda'|$ and $|\theta|$ have the same sign. The definitions of θ' and λ'' can be used to determine their signs, and in fact one sufficient condition under which they are of the right sign (negative given that sector 1 is capital intensive) is when both sectors are subject to nonincreasing returns to scale. If at least one of the sectors is subject to IRS, then to get the signs of these two determinants would require more information about the technologies.

An alternative way to determine their signs, as first suggested by Mayer (1974c), is to check the conditions for stability of equilibrium. These conditions may be used to put some bounds on the signs of these two determinants. Mayer's work is extended by Chang (1981), and Ide and Takayama (1991) suggest a simpler and more intuitive adjustment rule. The adjustment rules in these papers, which are based on Marshall's quantity adjustment concept, draw the same conclusion: If an equilibrium is stable, then the price-output effects are normal and there are important implications on the validity of the Rybczynski theorem and the Stolper-Samuelson theorem. I now present their adjustment rules and their implications.[9] I will later compare their results with the stability of an autarkic or international equilibrium.

5.4.1   The Ide-Takayama Adjustment Rule

First define $z \equiv Q_1/Q_2$, and let p^s be the supply price of good 1 relative to good 2. The supply price is the price at which the firms are just breaking even.

---

9. Neary (1978a, 1978b) uses the same approach to show that in the presence of factor market distortions and sector specific factors, perverse price-output response can be ruled out at stable equilibria.

In other words, it is the price I examined in the previous section. Conditions (5.38a) and (5.38b) can be combined to give

$$\widehat{z} = \frac{\mu}{A}\widehat{p}^s, \tag{5.43}$$

where $A = |\lambda'||\theta'|$ and $\mu = \mu_1(1 - \varepsilon_1) + \mu_2(1 - \varepsilon_2) > 0$. Either conditions (5.38) or condition (5.43) show that the price-output effects are normal if and only if A is positive.

Suppose that the economy is a small open economy facing the world relative price of good 1, p^w. Ide and Takayama (1991) suggest the following output adjustment rule:

$$\dot{z} = a\left(\frac{p^w}{p^s} - 1\right) = \phi(z), \tag{5.44}$$

where a is a positive constant and the dot above a variable represents its derivative with respect to time. The rationale behind condition (5.44), which is based on the output adjustment process due to Marshall (1890), is that firms are willing to expand their outputs if their profits are positive, that is, p^w is greater than the unit cost. The equilibrium value of z, denoted by $\bar{z}$, solves $\phi(z) = 0$. Thus $\bar{z}$ is said to be (locally) dynamically stable in the Marshallian sense if and only if $\phi'(\bar{z}) < 0$. Using (5.43) and (5.44) gives

$$\phi'(z) = -\frac{ap^w}{(p^s)^2}\frac{\mathrm{d}p^s}{\mathrm{d}z} = -\frac{ap^w}{\mu p^s z}A. \tag{5.45}$$

Condition (5.45) states that the production equilibrium is Marshallian stable if and only if $A > 0$. Using condition (5.43), a production equilibrium is Marshallian stable if and only if output responses to prices are normal.

Conditions (5.44) and (5.45) can be illustrated in Figure 5.2. The schedule labeled p^s gives the possible relationship between the supply price and output ratio; p^w is the exogenously given world relative price of good 1 for the present small open economy. Three possible production equilibria labeled A, B, and C are shown. First examine point A. Suppose that there is a small shock so that there is a small increase in z, where point D corresponds to the new value of z. In the diagram, p' then represents the corresponding supply price of good 1, which is required to yield zero profit for the firms in sector 1. Because the prevailing price is p^w, firms in sector 1 are actually earning negative profit, and by condition (5.44) or (5.45), z falls until point A is again reached. This means that point A is Marshallian stable. The same analysis can be used to argue that point C is also stable but point B is not. Summarizing these results, a production equilibrium is Marshallian stable if and only if the supply price schedule is positively sloped.

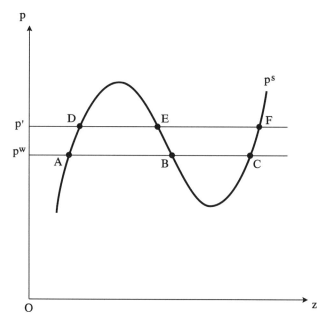

Figure 5.2

The intuition behind the relationship between Marshallian stability of a production equilibrium and output responses can be illustrated by Figure 5.3. In the diagram, TT is the PPF of an economy facing exogenously given world prices. Suppose that point B is the initial production point, and P^s is the supply price line in the sense that its (negative) slope is the initial world price ratio and the ratio of the unit costs of the sectors. There is an increase in the world relative price of good 1 and P_1^w and P_2^w are two new world price lines. If point B is Marshallian stable, output of good 1 increases and output of good 2 decreases. This gives a production point such as point D on the PPF lower than point B. At point D, the unit costs of the sectors are equal to their world prices.

Another application of Marshallian stability is that if I further assume (as Jones and others do) that the appropriate parameters, λ'_{ji}, θ'_{ji} and λ''_{ji}, are all positive, the Rybczynski theorem and the Stolper-Samuelson theorem hold.

5.4.2   The Mayer-Chang Adjustment Rules

Mayer (1974c) suggests the following adjustment rules:

$$\dot{Q}_1 = d_1(p_1^w - c_1(w, r, Q_1)) \tag{5.46a}$$

$$\dot{Q}_2 = d_2(p_2^w - c_2(w, r, Q_2)) \tag{5.46b}$$

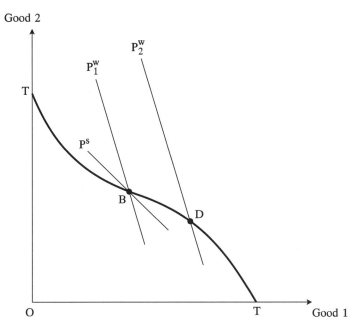

Figure 5.3

$$\dot{w} = d_3(L_1 + L_2 - \overline{L}) \tag{5.46c}$$

$$\dot{r} = d_4(K_1 + K_2 - \overline{K}), \tag{5.46d}$$

where d_i is a positive constant for all i. Note that the first two adjustment rules for the commodity markets are of the Marshallian type (quantity adjustment) while the last two are of the Walrasian type (price adjustment). Take a linear approximation of the preceding adjustment system around an equilibrium point by differentiating the expressions with respect to Q_1, Q_2, w and r. Let J denote the Jacobian matrix of this linear system. The equilibrium is said to be stable if and only if the Routh-Hurwitz conditions are satisfied. One of the conditions is that the determinant of J is positive. Mayer (1974c) and Chang (1981) show that the determinant of J is positive if and only if $A > 0$.

The I-T and the M-C adjustment rules produce the same necessary condition for stability of a production equilibrium. There are, however, some differences between their rules and results. Under the I-T rule, $A > 0$ is a necessary and sufficient condition for stability of an equilibrium but under the M-C rules, it is only a necessary condition. The I-T rule is simpler because it focuses on the adjustment of the output ratio while the M-C rules allow adjustment of the two factor markets and two output markets. Implicitly Ide and Takayama (1991) assume that the factor markets adjust instantaneously and are always in equilibrium.

5.4.3   Correspondence Principle

By the M-C and I-T adjustment rules, if a production equilibrium is Marshallian stable, then the price-output response is normal and the Rybczynski and Stolper-Samuelson theorems are valid. But what happens if at a production point the variable A defined earlier is negative? Obviously, the production equilibrium is not Marshallian stable and perverse comparative statics responses are possible, but is this a matter of concern?

According to the correspondence principle suggested by Samuelson (1947), there is no need to worry about perverse comparative statics results because unstable production equilibria are almost never observed in the real world. This idea was extended in Samuelson (1971) to argue that even if the initial production equilibrium is not stable, normal comparative statics results are obtained in a global context. This result, which is called the global correspondence principle, was later applied by Bhagwati et al. (1987) and Kemp et al. (1990) to the theory of international trade. In the present framework with external economies of scale, Ide and Takayama (1991) show that the perverse comparative statics results will never be observed, irrespective of whether the initial production equilibrium is Marshallian stable.

The argument of Ide and Takayama can be illustrated by Figure 5.2. The initial world price ratio is p^w, yielding three equilibria, A, B, and C. I showed earlier that points A and C are stable but point B is not. Suppose that point B is the initial production equilibrium. The world price ratio is now raised slightly to $p' > p^w$. If the equilibrium moves from point B to point E, then there is a perverse price-output response. According to the adjustment rule given by (5.44), however, point B will not move to point E. To see why, note that at point B the supply price is equal to p^w, the original world price ratio, and this price is less than the prevailing price, meaning that firms in sector 1 will expand their outputs and z increases. This process continues until point F is reached. In other words, the price-output response must be normal. Furthermore, the Rybczynski and Stolper-Samuelson theorems are both valid.

It should be noted, however, that how the correspondence principle is applied depends on the mechanism of adjustment of the economic system. In the previous analysis, I assume a Marshallian adjustment mechanism. There are economies-of-scale models analyzed in the literature that have Marshallian unstable production equilibrium, but Walrasian stable autarkic equilibrium. I will show some of these examples in the next section.

5.5   Autarkic Equilibrium

In order to derive the autarkic equilibrium, the preferences of the economy must be specified. Assume that its preferences can be represented by a social utility function given by $u = u(\mathbf{C})$, where $\mathbf{C} = (C_1, C_2, \ldots, C_n)$ and where C_i is the aggregate consumption of good i. The national income is equal to $g(\widetilde{\mathbf{p}}, \mathbf{v}) + b$, where b is the international transfer the economy receives. The problem of the economy is to choose the consumption bundle to maximize its utility subject to the budget constraint, taking prices as given. This allows me to define the indirect trade utility (ITU) function under VRS:

$$V(\mathbf{p}, \mathbf{v}, b) = \max_{\mathbf{C}} \left\{ u(\mathbf{C}) + \lambda[g(\widetilde{\mathbf{p}}, \mathbf{v}) + b - \mathbf{p} \cdot \mathbf{C})] \right\}, \qquad (5.47)$$

where λ is the Lagrange multiplier that is interpreted as the marginal utility of income. This function is analogous to the ITU function under CRS I explained in Chapter 2.

In an autarkic equilibrium, $Q_i \geq C_i$ for all i where C_i is chosen to maximize the social utility function. In the two-factor, two-sector framework, an autarkic equilibrium can be illustrated in an alternative way. Define the demand price of good 1 relative to good 2, which is denoted by p^d, as the marginal rate of substitution when the economy's ratio of consumption of good 1 to consumption of good 2 is equal to z. Thus an autarkic equilibrium can be defined as one at which the ratio of consumption of good 1 to consumption of good 2 is equal to the corresponding output ratio under the condition that $p^d = p^s$. Such an equilibrium is depicted by point E in Figure 5.4. Denote the autarkic value of z by z^a.

The three panels in Figure 5.4 show three possible cases. The demand price schedule in each panel, which is labeled p^d, shows the relationship between the demand price ratio and the consumption quantity ratio. In the case in which the preferences are convex and homothetic, the demand schedule is downward sloping. In panel (a), the supply price schedule is positively sloped whereas in panels (b) and (c) it is negatively sloped. An intersecting point between the two schedules represents an autarkic equilibrium. An autarkic equilibrium is said to be an interior one if at that point the outputs of both goods are positive.

Two properties of an interior autarkic equilibrium deserve close examination: uniqueness and stability. These two properties are related to stability of a production equilibrium. I first examine the uniqueness problem.

Consider again a two-factor, two-sector framework and assume homothetic preferences. Using the analysis in the previous section, if production equilibria under all possible prices are stable, the supply schedule in Figure 5.4 is positively sloped. (This is the case shown in panel a.) It is then easy to see that an interior autarkic equilibrium, if it exists, is unique.

The present technique can be used to argue that uniqueness of an interior production equilibrium when given commodity prices does not imply unique-

(a)

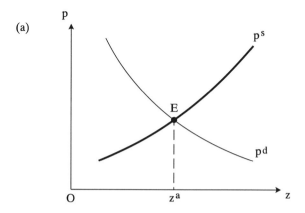

(b)

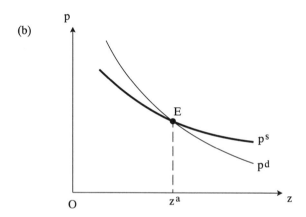

(c)

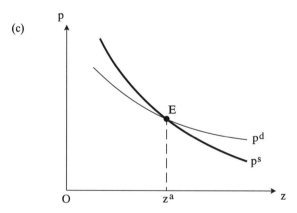

Figure 5.4

ness of autarkic equilibrium. An interior production equilibrium is said to
be unique if, when given any commodity prices, there exists only one set
of outputs that yield zero profits to firms. In terms of Figure 5.4, this means
that the slope of the supply price schedule is monotonic. On the other
hand, autarkic equilibrium is said to be unique if the demand price schedule cuts the supply price schedule only once. The diagram shows clearly
that if the supply price schedule is monotonically positively sloped,
an autarkic equilibrium is unique. If, however, the supply price schedule
is negatively sloped (when a production equilibrium is not Marshallian
stable), then there can be more than one intersection point between the two
schedules.

The following example, which was suggested by Chipman (1970), shows an
economy that has an unique autarkic equilibrium with a positive wage rate and
full employment.

Example 5.3 Consider the economy described in Example 5.1. The production functions are $Q_1 = Q_1^{\varepsilon_1} L_1$ and $Q_2 = L_2$. The labor endowment
is equal to 2. The social utility function is $u = C_1^{\alpha} C_2^{1-\alpha}$, $0 < \alpha < 1$. With
this function the economy will not choose to consume at a corner. It is easy
to show that the marginal rate of substitution between the two goods is
equal to

$$\frac{\partial u/\partial C_1}{\partial u/\partial C_2} = \frac{\alpha}{1-\alpha} \frac{C_2}{C_1},$$

which in equilibrium is equal to the price ratio, p. I have shown that in order to have positive outputs of both goods, the price ratio and the output of
good 1 is related by $p = 1/Q_1^{\varepsilon_1}$. (See Example 5.1 and the discussion following it.) These conditions and the equilibrium conditions $C_i = Q_i$ gives
the unique equilibrium: $Q_1 = C_1 = (2\alpha)^{1/(1-\varepsilon_1)}$, $Q_2 = C_2 = 2 - 2\alpha$ and $p = (2\alpha)^{-\varepsilon_1/(1-\varepsilon_1)}$.

Because in the preceding example the social utility function is of the Cobb-
Douglas type, one may conjecture that with a CES-type social utility function,
an autarkic equilibrium is also unique. Unfortunately, this conjecture is not
correct. See Helpman (1984b) for an example that shows two possible interior
autarkic equilibria for an economy with the technologies in Example 5.3 but a
CES-type social utility function.

Stability of an autarkic equilibrium in the Marshallian sense can be analyzed
by postulating the following output adjustment rule (Ide and Takayama, 1993):

$$\dot{z} = a\left(\frac{p^d}{p^s} - 1\right) = \phi(z). \tag{5.44'}$$

Condition (5.44′) is a generalization of condition (5.44).[10] I show that in panels (a) and (b) of Figure 5.4 the autarkic equilibria are stable. For example, if $z < z^a$, then $p^d > p^s$. By condition (5.44′), z increases. Alternatively, if $z > z^a$, then $p^d < p^s$ and z decreases.

Stability of an equilibrium can also be analyzed using the Walrasian approach, which emphasizes price adjustment. Figure 5.4 can be used to compare Walrasian stability and Marshallian stability of an autarkic equilibrium. Thus the autarkic equilibrium shown in panel (a) of Figure 5.4 is both Marshallian and Walrasian stable, but the autarkic equilibrium shown in panel (b) of Figure 5.4 is only Marshallian stable but not Walrasian stable.[11]

Note that the stability condition in (5.44′) describes an autarkic equilibrium, and it should not be confused with the stability condition of a production point given by (5.44) (due to Ide and Takayama) or (5.46) (due to Mayer and Chang). A production point is Marshallian stable if the supply price schedule is positively sloped (or if the price-output responses are normal), as is the one in panel (a) of Figure 5.4. In panel (b), the autarkic equilibrium is Marshallian stable but a production point is not because the supply schedule is negatively sloped. In panel (c), the autarkic equilibrium is Walrasian stable but the production point and the autarkic equilibrium are not Marshallian stable.

I now examine the effects of factor accumulation on an autarkic equilibrium. Without loss of generality, assume that sector 1 is capital intensive. Further assume that both sectors are subject to nondecreasing returns and that the output responses to prices are normal. In other words, consider a supply price schedule like the one in panel (a) of Figure 5.4. Given these conditions, Results 5.9 and 5.14 imply that both the Stolper-Samuelson theorem with magnification effects and the Rybczynski theorem without magnification effects are valid. These results are very useful in the present analysis.

Suppose that $\widehat{K} \geq \widehat{L} \geq 0$ with at least one inequality. Because outputs respond normally to changes in commodity prices, Result 5.14 implies that under constant commodity prices z increases. Because preferences are homothetic, the increase in z will lower the autarkic relative price of good 1. In terms of panel (a) of Figure 5.4, the supply price schedule shifts to the right, causing a drop in the relative price of good 1. Furthermore, with sufficiently mild scale-economies effect the Stolper-Samuelson theorem implies that the real reward of capital drops and that of labor rises.

---

10. Condition (5.44′) is similar to the adjustment rule in the one-factor model of Ethier (1982a). Panagariya (1986) also has an analysis of the stability of an autarkic equilibrium, and he postulates two different adjustment rules.

11. Note that the model in Ethier (1979, 1982a, 1982b) has an autarkic equilibrium described by schedules similar to those in panel (b) of Figure 5.4. He is aware of the fact that the autarkic equilibrium is not Walrasian stable.

Suppose instead that $\widehat{L} > \widehat{K} \geq 0$ so that the economy has more labor. The analysis can be reversed to show that given normal price-output responses, there must be a decrease in the output ratio, Q_1/Q_2, an increase in relative price of good 1, an increase in the real rental rate but a decrease in the real wage rate.

5.6 Foreign Trade under National Economies of Scale

I now extend the preceding analysis to a two-country model in order to analyze foreign trade. When trade is possible, a fundamental question is how the external effects should be defined. When two countries are linked to each other by trade, the economies of scale that are external to firms may come not only from the output of the industry within the domestic economy, but may also come from the output of the same industry in a trading partner. Then how should function $h_i(.)$ be defined? (I continue to ignore interindustry externality.)

In the trade literature, two extreme approaches have been taken. In the first approach, external economies are assumed to come only from the same sector in the country so that international external effects are not present. In the second approach, externality depends on the output of the sector in the world. I analyze these two approaches separately, first taking the case of national economies of scale.

5.6.1 Offer Curves and International Equilibrium

To determine an international equilibrium between two countries, I first derive the offer curve of a country. Figure 5.5 shows a country with three production and consumption points under exogenously given commodity prices. Q_AQ_D is the PPF of the economy. P_1, P_2, and P_3 are three parallel price lines with a slope equal to (negative) the price ratio, and Q_A, Q_B, and Q_D are three possible production points (see Example 5.1). Points Q_A and Q_D represent complete specialization. Three indifference curves tangent to these three price lines are drawn. The tangency points are the corresponding consumption points, C_A, C_B, and C_D. These three possible sets of consumption and production points lead to three trade triangles, which are represented by points A, B, and D in Figure 5.6. This diagram also shows the price line that passes through these three points and the origin.

If the same procedure is repeated with other price ratios, I can trace out the offer curve of the economy, HDKOBNAL in Figure 5.6.[12] Several properties of an offer curve can be presented as follows.

---

12. For more details about the derivation of an offer curve, see Kemp (1969, Chapter 8), Chacholiades (1978, Chapter 7), and Wong (1995a).

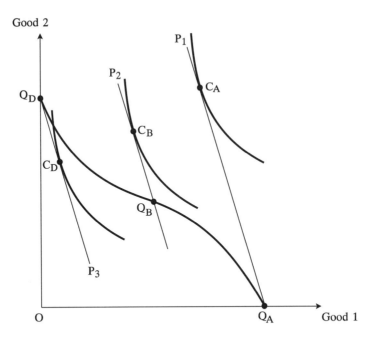

Figure 5.5

1. Because the PPF is not necessarily concave to the origin, the offer curve may not be concave to the axis that represents the imported good.

2. The part of the offer curve, HK, represents complete specialization in good 2, and the part LN represents complete specialization in good 1.

3. The slope of the offer curve at the origin is equal to the autarkic price ratio. To see this point, write the balance of trade equation as $pE_1 + E_2 = 0$. Differentiating this equation totally and evaluating it at $E_1 = E_2 = 0$ will give this result.

4. In the absence of international transfers, the offer curve exists in the first and third quadrants only. This is due to the economy's budget constraint.

5. The offer curve is convex downward at the origin if and only if the autarkic equilibrium is Walrasian stable.

Property (5) can be proved by making use of Figure 5.4. If the supply price schedule is on the right-hand side of the demand price schedule when the price ratio is slightly greater than the autarkic, then the equilibrium is Walrasian stable and there is an excess supply of good 1. As a result, the offer curve is convex downward at the origin. Alternatively, if the autarkic equilibrium is not Walrasian stable, the offer curve is concave downward at the origin, as Figure 5.5 shows.

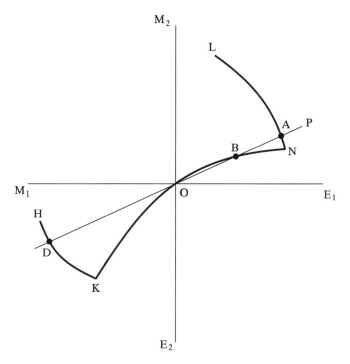

Figure 5.6

It should be pointed out that in the literature, it is common to draw the offer curve of an economy under increasing returns so that it is concave downward at the origin (for example, see Kemp 1969 and Chacholiades 1978). The models in Melvin (1969), Markusen and Melvin (1981), and Ethier (1979, 1982a, 1982b) also have such a property. Two things from the present analysis can be noted. First, the presence of IRS does not imply an offer curve that is concave downward at the origin. Second, if the offer curve is concave downward at the origin, its autarkic equilibrium is not Walrasian stable.

I now bring together the offer curves of two trading partners, which are labeled the home country and the foreign country. An international equilibrium is a point of intersection between the two offer curves. Figure 5.7 shows several possible cases, with OC representing the offer curve of the home country and OC* that of the foreign country. Panel (a) shows a unique international equilibrium, point A, at which the home country is completely specialized in good 1 and the foreign country completely specialized in good 2. In panel (b), there are three possible international equilibria, points A, B, and C. As explained before, at A the home is completely specialized in good 1 and the foreign country completely specialized in good 2. At point B, both countries are diversified, and at point C, the home country is completely specialized in

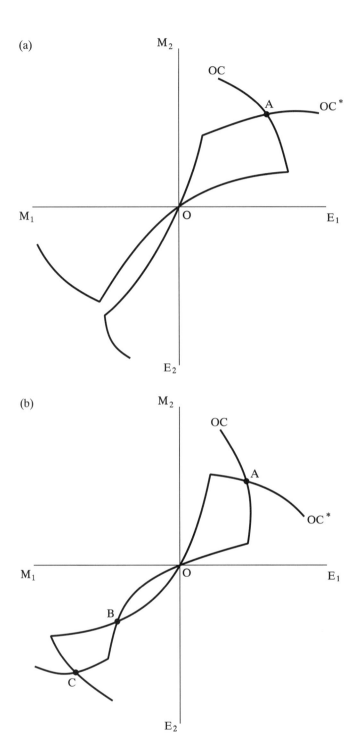

Figure 5.7

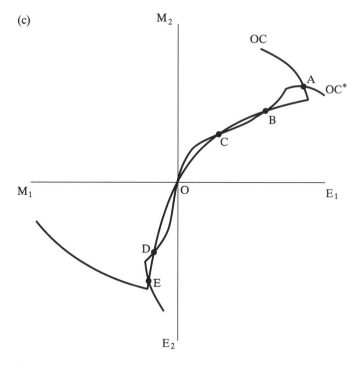

Figure 5.7

good 2 while the foreign country is completely specialized in good 1. Panel (c) represents the rare case in which there are five equilibria. At points B, C, and D, both countries are diversified while at points A and E, at least one of them is completely specialized.

5.6.2   Stability of International Equilibrium

With the possibility of multiple equilibria under free trade between the countries, one can use conditions of stability of equilibrium to avoid the consideration of some of them. To analyze stability of an international equilibrium, I continue to adopt the Marshallian adjustment rules (Marshall, 1879, Chapter 2). The Marshallian concept of stability, which is based on quantity adjustment, has the advantage that a trading point can be off the offer curve of either country or even off both offer curves. Such a concept has also been used by Kemp (1969, Chapter 8). I first introduce his adjustment rules in terms of export levels, and then explain how his concept can be formalized. The Marshallian concept of stability is based on the following assumptions. First, when an economy is not in equilibrium, its exportable sector adjusts its output while the consumption of goods and the production of the importable remain fairly constant. Second, the firms in a sector increase (respectively decrease) their

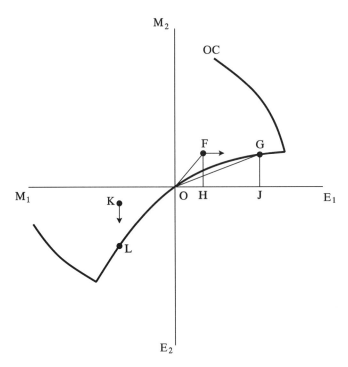

Figure 5.8

outputs when they have positive (respectively negative) profits, that is, when the demand price is greater than the supply price.

I now use the preceding assumptions to show how an economy adjusts when it is not in equilibrium. Consider the offer curve OC in Figure 5.8. Suppose that for some reason the trading point is at F, with the economy exporting OH of good 1 and importing FH of good 2. The external relative price of good 1 is given by the slope of OF. Point F is compared with a point on the offer curve, G. Both points have the same import of good 2, but point G represents a higher level of export (OJ > OH). At any point on the offer curve domestic firms earn zero profit, and the slope of OG thus represents the average cost of producing good 1 relative to the price of good 2. Thus if the trading point is at F, firms in sector 1 earn positive profits and they are willing to expand their outputs. The export of good 1 by the economy increases, moving the trading point to the right until point G is reached. Using the same argument, if the trading point is a point in the third quadrant above the offer curve such as point K, firms in sector 2 (which is now the exportable sector) expand their outputs, moving the trading point downward to point L.

I now apply the adjustment rules to determine the stability of the equilibria shown in Figure 5.7. For illustrative purpose, I reproduce panel (b) of Fig-

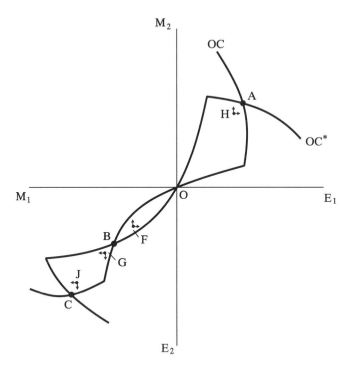

Figure 5.9

ure 5.7 in Figure 5.9. First analyze the equilibrium at point B. Suppose that there exists a small shock and the trading point shifts to point F. Using the adjustment rules explained previously, the home sector 1 and the foreign sector 2 will expand their outputs, shifting the trading point to the right and upward, as shown by the arrows. As a result, the trading point shifts *away* from the original equilibrium, implying that the equilibrium at B is not stable. The adjustments of other trading points such as points G, H, and J are summarized by the arrows. Thus I conclude that equilibrium point B is unstable while those at points A and C are stable.

The same argument can be applied to determine the stability of equilibria in the other two panels of Figure 5.7. In panel (a), the unique equilibrium is stable. In panel (c), equilibria A, C and E are stable but equilibria B and D are unstable. Panel (c) is especially interesting, because it shows two features about stability of equilibria: First, if there are more than one equilibria, then the equilibria are alternatively stable and unstable (Marshall, 1879, p. 24). Second, even in the presence of VRS, it is possible to have a stable equilibrium with diversification in both countries (equilibrium C in panel c).

I have shown that the Marshallian concept of stability of international equilibrium is simple and easy to use, even though Marshall did not provide any explanation about the adjustment rules. Because Marshall focused on the adjustment of the export level, rather than the adjustment of the production of the exportable good, his adjustment rules have been criticized for being logically inconsistent (Chipman, 1965). Amano (1968), however, argues that in the Marshallian framework, the domestic sector can be explicitly considered, and a set of adjustment rules that are based on consumers and firms' optimization behaviors can be stated. He assumes that at a temporary (short-run) equilibrium in which the outputs are fixed, prices adjust to clear the markets in a Walrasian way. These equilibrium prices are the demand prices and the resultant export vectors give the trading point mentioned previously. Firms in both sectors in both countries then expand or contract their outputs when their demand prices are greater or smaller than their supply prices. Stability conditions can then be derived. Because Amano (1968) assumes constant returns to scale, his stability conditions cannot be directly applied in the present framework, but his condition can easily be extended. For example, Panagariya (1986) considers a specific-factors model and assumes that commodity price ratio adjusts to clear the markets while labor within each economy moves between sectors in response to wage differential. Ethier (1982a), on the other hand, assumes that given any output levels, the demand price always adjusts instantaneously to clear the markets. This assumption allows him to consider exclusively the adjustment in terms of the commodity production.

5.7   Patterns of Trade

I now make use of the offer curve techniques developed in the previous chapter to investigate how IRS may affect the patterns of trade of two countries. In the following sections, I focus mainly on a two-sector, two-factor, two-country framework that has the following features:

1. The countries have identical technologies. Sector 1 is capital-intensive and subject to IRS while sector 2 is labor-intensive and subject to CRS.

2. The countries have identical and homothetic preferences.

3. Unless stated otherwise, the rate of VRS in sector 1 is not significant and relevant production equilibria are Marshallian stable as defined previously.[13]

---

13. Note that if there is only one factor in the model, and if at least one sector (maybe two) is subject to IRS, an interior production equilibrium is never Marshallian stable. To see why, recall that in Section 5.3 it is shown that the virtual price line is tangent to the virtual PPF. With only one factor, the virtual PPF is a straight line, that is, T' is a constant. Then $-T' = \widetilde{p} = h_1 p / h_2$ where $\widetilde{p}$ and p are the virtual price ratio and real price ratio, respectively. Differentiate both sides of the above equation and rearrange terms to give

This means that the supply price schedule is positively sloped like the one in panel (a) of Figure 5.4 and that the price-output responses are normal.

Condition (1) can easily be relaxed so that sector 2 is also subject to IRS. The cases of DRS in either sector can be analyzed in the same way but they are less interesting. Condition (2) is crucial because it removes any demand bias. Condition (3) is also crucial for some of the results obtained later. Unless stated otherwise, I do not make the assumption that the rate of IRS of sector 1 is constant.

The main purpose of this section is to determine the roles of IRS in determining the patterns of trade of two countries. I begin with some simple, special cases in order to draw some intuition before I turn to more general cases.

5.7.1 Identical Factor Endowments

In this case, the two countries are identical. If for each country an autarkic equilibrium with diversification is unique, then they must have the same autarkic equilibrium with diversification. If free trade is now allowed, will they trade?

Because the countries have the same autarkic equilibrium, obviously no trade is an equilibrium. In this case the offer curves of the countries are tangent to each other at the origin. In addition to this equilibrium, there may be other equilibria in which at least one of the countries is completely specialized. Under the Marshall-Kemp-Ethier adjustment rules, the no-trade equilibrium *may or may not be stable*: It is stable (respectively unstable) if the price-output responses are normal (respectively perverse) under autarky in each country so that its offer curve is convex (respectively concave) downward at the origin.

The case that is often analyzed in the literature is the one in which the no-trade equilibrium is unstable. (See, for example, Kemp, 1969; Melvin, 1969; Chacholiades, 1978; Ethier, 1979, 1982a, 1982b; Krugman, 1987a; and Rauch, 1989.) This case is shown in panel (a) of Figure 5.10. Suppose that at the no-trade equilibrium point, point O, there is a small shock so that the firms in the home sector 1 have a small increase in output while those in the foreign country have a small decrease in output. Because of IRS, these home firms are able to lower their average costs. This makes them more competitive relative to the foreign firm. The home firms will produce more, lowering

---

$$\frac{\mathrm{d}Q_1}{\mathrm{d}p} = \frac{h_1 h_2}{p(h_1 h_2' T' - h_2 h_1')} < 0,$$

because $T' < 0$. Thus the output response is perverse and the production equilibrium is not Marshallian stable. This result, which is a generalization of a result in Ethier (1982a), holds even if both sectors are subject to IRS and whether the rates of VRS are constant. When there are two factors, however, this result may not hold. By conditions (5.38) and (5.35), output responses are normal if the degrees of IRS of the sectors are not significant.

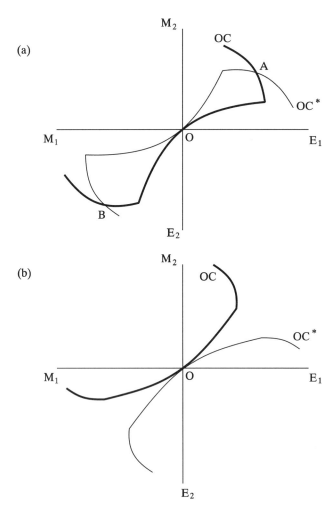

Figure 5.10

their average cost even further. The opposite happens to the foreign counter-part. This process continues until the stable equilibrium point A is reached, with the home country completely specialized in good 1, the foreign country completely specialized in good 2, or both. Alternatively, if the initial shock leads to a small increase in the output of good 1 in the foreign country, the process is reversed until point B is reached.

If, however, the price-output responses are normal, then the offer curves of the countries will have the curvature at the origin shown in panel (b) of Figure 5.10. In this case, the no-trade international equilibrium is stable in the Marshallian sense. This implies that trade does not exist between the countries even if it is allowed.

Figure 5.10 shows several important features of trade under external economies of scale. First, contrary to what is commonly believed in the literature, IRS alone is not sufficient for international trade (Wong, 1995a). In addition to IRS, a Marshallian unstable no-trade equilibrium or other adjustment rules is needed to lead the countries to trade. Second, if trade exists, the patterns of trade may be indeterminate because of existence of multiple equilibria. Third, the autarkic price ratios are not useful for predicting the patterns of trade because they are identical. Fourth, if trade exists, the world price ratio may not be in between the autarkic price ratios of the countries.[14] Thus this part of the law of comparative advantage does not hold.

5.7.2   Identical Capital-Labor Ratio but Different Sizes

I now turn to another case in which the home and foreign countries have the same capital-labor ratio but different sizes of economies. In particular, I assume that the home country is bigger.

I showed earlier given normal price-output responses that an increase in the size of an economy will lower its autarkic relative price of good 1. This means that the home (bigger) country's autarkic relative price of good 1 is lower than that of the foreign country and it has a comparative advantage in good 1.

In this case, as in the previous one, multiple equilibria can exist, and some of them are stable. If no additional information is available, it is not possible to predict which of them will be the outcome. Thus once again the patterns of trade may not be determinate, and it is possible to have an equilibrium in which a country imports the good in which it has a comparative advantage. For example, the home country imports good 1.

Two solutions have been suggested to solve the indeterminacy. Markusen and Melvin (1981) point out that there exists at least one stable equilibrium in which the home country exports good 1. This result can be explained by using panel (b) of Figure 5.7 or by using Figure 5.9. Because the home country has a lower autarkic relative price of good 1, its offer curve is less steep than the foreign offer curve at the origin. Because of the income effect, sooner or later a point will be reached beyond which the country is willing to export less as the relative export price is improved further. This means that the offer curve of each country will sooner or later get closer to the axis of its importable sector. In terms of the diagrams, the offer curves of the countries must intersect at

---

14. The law of comparative advantage states that in a two-good framework, the world price ratio lies between the autarkic price ratios of the two countries. In the present case, the countries have the same autarkic ratio. The law of comparative advantage would imply that the world price ratio is equal to the countries' autarkic price ratio. The analysis shows that in the present framework, the world price ratio may be different from the common autarkic price ratio, thus violating this part of the law of comparative advantage.

least once in the first quadrant. In fact, the outermost equilibrium point must be stable because at this point the home offer curve cuts the foreign offer curve from below.

The Markusen-Melvin result, however, is rather weak because it merely states that the home country may export good 1. Ethier (1982a) suggests a stronger result: If the productions of the sectors in the countries adjust according to the Marshall-Kemp-Ethier adjustment rules, each country will export the good in which it has a comparative advantage. For example, because the home country has a comparative advantage in good 1, the home firms in sector 1 will notice that when trade is allowed the foreign relative price of good 1 is higher than the domestic relative price. Thus they have an incentive to expand their production. As these firms produce more, their unit cost drops, inducing more production and export of good 1. The opposite occurs in the foreign country. This process continues until a stable trade equilibrium is reached. In the present model, the equilibrium must be the intersecting point in the first quadrant of Figure 5.9 closest to the origin, with the home country exporting good 1. As a result, this part of the law of comparative advantage is still valid (Wong, 1995a). At this equilibrium, however, it is possible that both countries are diversified under free trade.[15]

5.7.3   Other Cases

These analytical techniques can now be used to examine the patterns of trade in other cases. Suppose that the home country has more capital but the same amount of labor as the foreign country. I showed earlier that with normal price-output responses, the home country has a lower autarkic relative price for good 1. Thus using the Ethier approach and the arguments given previously, I can conclude that the home country exports good 1 when free trade is allowed.

On the other hand, if the home country has more labor but the same amount of capital as the foreign country, good 1 must be relatively more expensive in the home country before trade. Then the foreign country will export good 1.

I now try to generalize the results. Assume that the world has fixed amounts of labor and capital. I want to see how different ways of distributing the factors between the countries may affect the patterns of trade of the countries. Figure 5.11 illustrates the situation. Points O and O* are the origins of the home and foreign countries, respectively. Suppose that point M, the midpoint of the diagonal, is the endowment point, meaning that the two countries have the same factor endowments. I showed earlier that the patterns of trade are indeterminate. If the endowment point is at point A when the home country has more

---

15. In the framework in Ethier (1982a), at least one country is completely specialized under free trade because the autarkic equilibrium with diversification is unique.

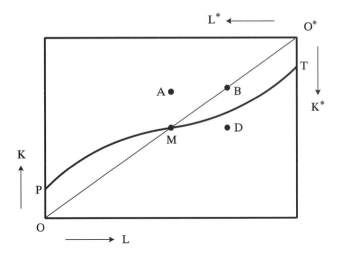

Figure 5.11

capital but the same amount of labor as the foreign country, or at point B when the home country is bigger with the same capital-labor ratio, the Marshallian adjustment rule implies that the home country exports good 1. If, however, the endowment point is at point D, with the home country having more labor but the same amount of capital as the foreign country, then the home country imports good 1. The combined results allow the construction of a pattern-of-trade schedule PMT in the diagram so that an endowment point above it implies that the home country exports good 1 while an endowment point below it implies that the home country imports good 1. This schedule is in general between the diagonal and a horizontal line through point M.

The diagram illustrates the factors that determine the patterns of trade in the presence of IRS: the *scale effect* and the *factor-proportion effect*. The scale effect states that if a country gets bigger while its capital-labor ratio remains constant, then it is more likely that it will export good 1. The factor-proportion effect states that if a country gets more capital or less labor while the endowment of the other factor is fixed, then it is more likely to export good 1. Versions of the Heckscher-Ohlin Theorem are given in Panagariya (1983) and Wong (1995a).

5.8   Factor Prices under Free Trade

I now examine the factor prices in the two countries under free trade. Because the goal is to analyze international factor movements, the analysis in this section focuses on absolute factor prices (in terms of the numeraire, good 2).[16] Keep the framework with the two countries described previously and for the time being assume that the countries have the same capital-labor ratio in order to neutralize the factor-proportion effect, that is, the endowment point is on the diagonal of the box in Figure 5.11. I want to determine the factor prices under free trade in the two countries.

Even though the countries have identical technologies, the fact that sector 1 is subject to IRS means that if the countries have different output levels of good 1, they usually do not have identical factor prices. Thus, in general, I do not expect factor price equalization, as the following analysis shows.[17]

Consider first the case in which the countries have identical factor endowments. These two countries may or may not trade with each other, depending on whether they have normal price-output effects under autarky. If they do have normal price-output responses, they do not trade but they still have the same commodity prices. In this case, they also have the same factor prices.

If they trade, then the patterns of trade are indeterminate. Suppose that the home country exports good 1. Because this case is similar to the case in which the home country is bigger with the same capital-labor ratio as the foreign country, I analyze these two cases simultaneously.

As I mentioned, if the home country, being bigger or not smaller, exports good 1 under free trade, the two countries may be diversified or may be completely specialized. The factor prices in the two countries under different patterns of specialization are determined in Figure 5.12. The schedule labeled $\tilde{c}_2$ is the common unit-cost schedule for sector 2 of the virtual system of each country when the countries are facing the same price of good 2. Because good 2 is the numeraire and because sector 2 is subject to CRS, this schedule has the following equation $\tilde{c}_2(w, r) = 1$, and its location is not affected by the production in the countries. The schedule labeled $\tilde{c}_1$ represents the unit cost for sector 1 of the home virtual system, and it is described by the equation $\tilde{c}_1(w, r) = p^f h_1(Q_1^f)$ where p^f is the free-trade price ratio and Q_1^f is the home country's output of good 1 under free trade. The schedule labeled $\tilde{c}_1^*$ is the corresponding unit-cost schedule for sector 1 in the foreign country, and its equation is $\tilde{c}_1^*(w, r) = p^f h_1(Q_1^{f*})$, where Q_1^{f*} is the foreign country's output of good 1 under free trade. In the diagram, I also construct two rays, OX and OY, so that OX (respectively OY) is the locus of all points at which the (negative) slope of a unit-cost schedule for sector 1 (respectively sector 2) is equal

16. For analysis on the relative factor prices in the countries under free trade, see Laing (1961), Kemp (1964, 1969), Melvin (1969), and Panagariya (1983).

17. Of course, if the number of sectors with tradable goods subject to CRS is equal to the number of nonmoving factors, the usual argument can be used to show factor price equalization. See Helpman and Krugman (1985). See also the analysis in Panagariya (1983) and Tawada (1989).

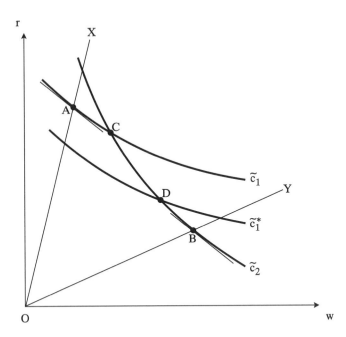

Figure 5.12

to the common capital-labor ratio of the countries. Point A is the intersection between OX and schedule $\tilde{c}_1$ and point B is the intersection between OY and schedule $\tilde{c}_2$.

Before I use this diagram to analyze the factor prices in the countries, it should be pointed out that as the world equilibrium shifts because of a redistribution of factor endowments, the output of good 1 in each country usually changes and its unit-cost schedule should be at a different location. In the present analysis, however, only the relative positions, not the absolute positions, of the schedules matter. In all the cases I analyze here the home country exports good 1, implying that it must produce more of good 1 than the foreign country. Thus schedule $\tilde{c}_1$ must be above schedule $\tilde{c}_1^*$.

I am now ready to determine the factor prices in the two countries with all possible patterns of production. Refer again to Figure 5.12. If the home country is completely specialized in the production of good 1, its production point is at A. If it is diversified, its production point is at C. If the foreign country is completely specialized in the production of good 2 its production point is at point B, or, if it is diversified its production point is at point D. In all these cases, the home country has a higher rental rate but a lower wage rate.

Suppose now that the home country is smaller. Then this analysis can be reversed and can show that under free trade the home country exports good 2 and has a lower rental rate but a higher wage rate.

5.9   International Factor Movement

Now apply the previous analysis to analyze international factor movement. In particular, assume that capital can move costlessly between the countries. Two different cases are examined, the one in which free trade prevails and the one in which commodity trade is not permitted.

The analysis provided in the previous section can be employed directly to analyze international capital movement under free trade. Again to avoid factor-proportion effects, let me for the time being assume that the two countries have the same capital-labor ratio.

Suppose that the two countries have identical factor endowments. Trade may or may not exist. If trade does not exist, the countries have the same factor prices (assuming a unique autarkic equilibrium), so capitalists in both countries do not have any incentive to transfer their capital abroad. If the price-output responses are not normal in the countries, trade will exist but the patterns of trade are not determinate. Suppose that the home country exports good 1. I explained in the previous section that the home country will have a higher rental rate under free trade (see Figure 5.12). Thus if allowed, foreign capital will flow into the home country. In other words, the country that exports good 1 is also a capital receiving country.

With good 2 as the numeraire, the final equilibrium requires equalization of the rental rates in terms of good 2. The question is whether all the capital in the country that imports good 1 will move to the host country. If the production functions satisfy the Inada conditions so that the marginal product of capital in either country goes to infinity as the capital-labor ratio in the country approaches zero, then the rental rate in the source country will rise sufficiently high when the capital-labor ratio is small. This means that the capital movement will sooner or later stop before all the capital in the source country flows out.

The situation is illustrated in Figure 5.13. Points H and H* are the two possible equilibrium points under free trade and capital movement if the two countries are identical. Point H (respectively H*), which is vertical below (respectively above) the midpoint of the diagonal, M, is the equilibrium point if the home (respectively foreign) country imports good 1 and sends out capital.

Two implications of this capital movement can be examined. First, when the home country receives foreign capital under free trade, the assumption that the price-output responses are normal and Result 5.14 imply that the home country will produce more good 1 but less good 2 if it is diversified, or will produce more good 1 if it is completely specialized in good 1. The opposite production effects will occur in the foreign country. Thus capital movement creates an excess supply of good 1 at the initial free trade price ratio. By the

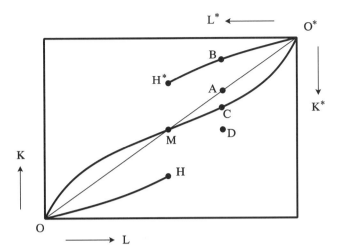

Figure 5.13

Walrasian *tâtonnement process*, the relative price of good 1 tends to fall and the home country has a higher export level of good 1 than under free trade.

Another issue is whether the wage rates in the two countries are equalized under free trade and capital movement. The answer depends on patterns of production. Suppose that the home country is the capital-receiving country. (The case in which the foreign country receives capital can be analyzed in the same way.) At point H*, as the home country is employing most of the world's capital, it is producing the capital-intensive good 1 and may also be producing good 2. On the other hand, the foreign country must be producing the labor-intensive good 2 and may or may not be producing good 1 as well. If both countries are producing good 2, then equalization of rental rates implies equalization of wage rates. (Recall that the countries have an identical, linearly homogeneous production function in sector 2.)

Suppose now that the home country is bigger so that the endowment point is at a point like point A in the diagram. I explained that in this case, the home country exports good 1 and has a higher rental rate under free trade. Thus foreign capital tends to flow in. The equilibrium point is at a point (denoted by point B) vertically above point A with equalization of rental rates. If I start with different endowment points on the upper half of the diagonal, equilibria under free trade and capital movement are at different points above the diagonal. The locus of these equilibrium points is represented by schedule O*H*.

The same analysis can be extended to the case in which the endowment point is a point on the lower half of the diagonal. The corresponding locus of equilibrium point is schedule OH. OH and O*H* are symmetric to each other about the diagonal.

Now assume that only capital movement, but not commodity trade, is allowed. Again start with the case in which the two countries have the same factor endowments. In this case, because they have the same autarkic equilibrium, they have the same factor prices. Thus capital will not move between countries, even if it is allowed.

Suppose now that the home country is bigger, with the endowment point at A in Figure 5.13. In this case, I explained earlier that with sufficiently mild scale-economies effect, the bigger country has a lower rental rate. Thus home capital tends to move out. The equilibrium occurs at a point like C. Point C is below point A, but it should be above point D that is on the right-hand side of point M.

Because trade is not allowed, both countries tend to be diversified under free capital movement. When the countries have the same rental rates in the final equilibrium, the wage rates are also equalized.

The same technique can be used to trace out the locus of equilibrium points, O*CMO. As explained, this equilibrium schedule is between the diagonal and the horizontal line through point M. Furthermore, it passes through point M because no capital movement exists if the countries have the same endowments.

The analysis can be summarized as follows.

1. The direction of capital movement depends on whether free trade is allowed. When free trade prevails, capital moves from the smaller country to the bigger country (assuming the same capital-labor endowment ratio in both countries). If free trade is not allowed, capital moves from the bigger country to the smaller country.

2. In an equilibrium under capital mobility, whether or not free trade also exists, wage rates are also equalized if good 2 is produced in both countries.

3. Free trade only, free capital movement only, and free trade and free capital movement in general all have different equilibria. Using the terminology in Wong (1986b), I conclude that commodity trade and capital mobility are complements in the price-equalization sense.

4. Under free trade, capital mobility tends to augment the volume of trade. See Markusen (1983) for the case with no initial capital movement, Panagariya (1986) for sector-specific capital, and Wong (1995b) for two countries with identical capital-labor ratio. The effect of commodity trade on the level of capital movement is ambiguous because capital flows in opposite directions with or without free trade.

5. In the special case in which the two countries have the same capital-labor ratio, the home capital moves out to the foreign country when no trade in goods is allowed. If free trade in goods is allowed, the home country has a higher rental rate and thus receives foreign capital. In other words, free trade in goods reverses the direction of capital movement (Wong, 1995b).

6. Under free trade in goods and capital movement, the bigger country exports good 1 and is a host to foreign capital (Wong, 1995b).

5.10   International Economies of Scale

So far, I have concentrated on national economies of scale. I now relax this assumption. As Ethier (1979, p. 3) argues, "advances in communications and transport have nearly fused the major industrial countries into a singular integrated economy within which former boundaries retain only residual significances as determinants of channels of technological communication." Ethier further points out that if sectors use intermediate inputs and if these inputs are tradable, then it is more likely that external effects come not only from the industries within an economy but also from industries in the rest of the world.

In this section, I explore the implications of international economies of scale. I maintain my focus on output-generated external effects, and define the sectoral production function of sector i in the presence of free trade as

$$Q_i = h_i(Q_i + Q_i^*)\widetilde{F}_i(\mathbf{v}_i), \tag{5.49}$$

where Q_i^* is the output of the sector in the foreign country (representing the rest of the world). As condition (5.49) shows, I keep the assumption of homothetic production functions. The only difference between the previous production function given by (5.11) and the present production function is function $h_i(.)$. This suggests that some of the analysis presented earlier can be applied here.[18] In particular, the relationship between the real system and the virtual system is described by

$$Q_i = h_i(Q_i + Q_i^*)\widetilde{Q}_i(\widetilde{\mathbf{p}}, \mathbf{v}). \tag{5.50}$$

I now analyze free trade. With international economies of scale, the offer-curve technique is not useful in determining an international equilibrium because foreign production affects domestic production and thus the exact location of the offer curve. One alternative technique to derive an international equilibrium is the allocation curve derived by Ethier (1979, 1982a and 1982b).

Several properties of free trade or international capital movement in the presence of international economies of scale can now be derived. I first consider free trade, which implies $p_i = p_i^*$. Because firms in the two countries

---

18. One may be tempted to make the following conclusion: Because it was shown in the previous several sections that under free trade countries tend to be completely specialized, in these cases international economies of scale reduce to national economies scale. For example, if the home country alone produces good i, $Q_i^* = 0$ in condition (5.49), which then reduces to condition (5.11). This conclusion is not correct because the analysis in the previous sections is made under the assumption of national economies of scale. With international economies of scale complete specialization is less likely.

have the same external effects, I immediately get one important property of free trade: The equalization of commodity prices implies equalization of virtual commodity prices because $p_i h_i(Q_i + Q_i^*) = p_i^* h_i(Q_i + Q_i^*)$, that is, $\tilde{p}_i = \tilde{p}_i^*$. This result, which has many useful implications, is general because it does not depend on whether the rate of VRS is constant or whether the sector is subject to IRS, CRS, or DRS.

The following three results, which rely on equalization of virtual commodity prices, are similar to those in the neoclassical framework with CRS. First, suppose that the home and foreign countries have the same capital-labor endowment ratio. With CRS in all sectors, the countries do not trade. Will they trade in the presence of variable returns to scale?

To answer this question, note that because under free trade the countries are facing the same virtual commodity prices, and because the virtual outputs are linearly homogeneous in all factors, the same capital-labor ratio implies that the countries have the same virtual output ratios, that is,

$$\frac{\tilde{Q}_2}{\tilde{Q}_1} = \frac{\tilde{Q}_2^*}{\tilde{Q}_1^*}. \tag{5.51}$$

Because the countries have the same external effects in the presence of international economies of scale, condition (5.51) implies that the countries have the same actual output ratio, that is,

$$\frac{Q_2}{Q_1} = \frac{Q_2^*}{Q_1^*}. \tag{5.51'}$$

Identical and homothetic preferences and equalization of commodity prices mean that the countries choose the same ratio of consumption goods. These conditions combined together imply that the two countries are consuming exactly what they are producing, that is, they are self-sufficient and no trade exists. This means that as long as the countries have identical capital-labor endowment ratios, whether or not they are of the same size, no trade is always a stable equilibrium if the autarkic equilibrium is stable. This result differs significantly from the one under national economies of scale.

This result may seem strange: If the countries do not trade, how do international economies of scale exist? Where do these international economies of scale come from? Helpman (1984b) suggests one answer: Even though there is no interindustrial trade, there may be intraindustry trade.[19] There is one more explanation: There may be trade in intermediate inputs and international economies of scale come from trade in intermediate inputs.

I now give up the assumption of identical capital-labor ratio in the countries so that trade may exist. I want to investigate two more properties of free

---

19. See Chapters 6 and 7 for the meaning and causes of intraindustry trade.

trade that were described by Ethier (1982b). Assume that both countries are diversified under free trade. The virtual unit cost of each sector is equal to the virtual price of the good, that is, $\widetilde{c}_i = \widetilde{p}_i$. Because the countries have the same virtual prices, they have the same virtual unit costs for each sector, that is, $\widetilde{c}_i = \widetilde{c}_i^*$. Then using the traditional arguments, I can conclude that the countries have the same free-trade factor prices. In other words, the factor price equalization theorem is valid.

I now turn to another property of free trade: the validity of the Heckscher-Ohlin theorem. To see why, suppose that the home country is capital abundant and that sector 1 is capital intensive under all relevant factor prices. Because the countries face the same real and virtual commodity prices, I can use the traditional argument to show that under free trade the home country has a higher ratio of virtual output of good 1 to that of good 2. Again because of the same external effects in the countries, the home country must also have a higher ratio of actual output of good 1 to that of good 2. With identical and homothetic preferences, the home country must export good 1.

These results, which are the same as those in a neoclassical framework, are not surprising once it is recognized that the countries are facing not just the same commodity prices but also the same virtual commodity prices.

Even though the Heckscher-Ohlin Theorem holds in the above special case, in more general cases it is difficult to predict the patterns of trade of the countries. In particular, the autarky equilibria of the countries are no longer useful to predict free-trade equilibrium. The reason is that trade shifts the external effect of sector i in a country from $h_i(Q_i)$ under autarky to $h_i(Q_i + Q_i^*)$. This change in the external effect is similar to a Hicks' neutral technological progress (technological regress if the sector is subject to DRS). This means that trade is not just an expansion of the consumption possibility frontier of a country as in the neoclassical framework, but also an expansion (or contraction) of the production possibility frontier. I can thus conclude that the law of comparative advantage may not be valid in the sense that the autarkic prices of the countries cannot be used to predict the patterns of trade or the bounds of the free-trade world price ratio.

I now make use of the preceding results to examine the relationship between commodity trade and factor mobility in the presence of international economies of scale. First of all, note that with factor price equalization, the free-trade equilibrium (assuming to be unique) and the free-trade-plus-factor-mobility equilibrium are identical. Whether the free-capital-mobility equilibrium is the same as the above two types of equilibria depends on the source of international economies of scale. If international economies of scale are absent when the countries are under autarky in commodity trade, then the equilibrium under capital mobility is different from the equilibrium under free trade. Of course, if capital mobility yields the same international economies of scale, then commodity trade and capital mobility are substitutes in the price-equalization sense.

Appendix

This appendix proves the reciprocity relations stated in Section 5.2. Differentiate both sides of $Q_i = h_i(Q_i)\widetilde{Q}_i(\widetilde{\mathbf{p}}, \mathbf{v})$ with respect to p_k to give

$$\frac{\partial Q_i}{\partial p_k} = h_i' \widetilde{Q}_i \frac{\partial Q_i}{\partial p_k} + h_i \left[\sum_j \frac{\partial \widetilde{Q}_i}{\partial \widetilde{p}_j} \frac{\partial (h_j p_j)}{\partial p_k} \right]$$

$$= h_i' \widetilde{Q}_i \frac{\partial Q_i}{\partial p_k} + h_i \left[\sum_j \frac{\partial \widetilde{Q}_i}{\partial \widetilde{p}_j} p_j h_j' \frac{\partial Q_j}{\partial p_k} \right] + h_i \frac{\partial \widetilde{Q}_i}{\partial \widetilde{p}_k} h_k. \tag{A.1}$$

In matrix form, equation (A.1) can be written as

$$\mathbf{Q_p} = \mathbf{D_\varepsilon}\mathbf{Q_p} + \mathbf{D_h}\widetilde{\mathbf{Q}}_{\widetilde{\mathbf{p}}}\mathbf{D_p}\mathbf{D_{h'}}\mathbf{Q_p} + \mathbf{D_h}\widetilde{\mathbf{Q}}_{\widetilde{\mathbf{p}}}\mathbf{D_h}$$

$$= (\mathbf{I} - \mathbf{D_\varepsilon} - \mathbf{D_h}\widetilde{\mathbf{Q}}_{\widetilde{\mathbf{p}}}\mathbf{D_p}\mathbf{D_{h'}})^{-1}\mathbf{D_h}\widetilde{\mathbf{Q}}_{\widetilde{\mathbf{p}}}\mathbf{D_h}, \tag{A.2}$$

where $\mathbf{I}$ is the identity matrix, $\mathbf{Q_p}$ is the $n \times n$ matrix of the derivatives of $\mathbf{Q}$ with respect to commodity prices, and $\mathbf{D_\ell}$ is a diagonal matrix with elements of vector ℓ; for example, $\mathbf{D_p}$ is a diagonal matrix with elements equal to commodity prices. Pre-multiply both sides of (A.2) by $(\mathbf{I} - \mathbf{D_\varepsilon})$ to give

$$(\mathbf{I} - \mathbf{D_\varepsilon})\mathbf{Q_p} = (\mathbf{I} - \mathbf{D_\varepsilon})(\mathbf{I} - \mathbf{D_\varepsilon} - \mathbf{D_h}\widetilde{\mathbf{Q}}_{\widetilde{\mathbf{p}}}\mathbf{D_p}\mathbf{D_{h'}})^{-1}\mathbf{D_h}\widetilde{\mathbf{Q}}_{\widetilde{\mathbf{p}}}\mathbf{D_h}$$

$$= [\mathbf{I} - \mathbf{D_h}\widetilde{\mathbf{Q}}_{\widetilde{\mathbf{p}}}\mathbf{D_p}\mathbf{D_{h'}}(\mathbf{I} - \mathbf{D_\varepsilon})^{-1}]^{-1}\mathbf{D_h}\widetilde{\mathbf{Q}}_{\widetilde{\mathbf{p}}}\mathbf{D_h}, \tag{A.3}$$

where it is noted that for any two non-singular matrices of the same order, $\mathbf{Y}$ and $\mathbf{Z}$, I have $\mathbf{YZ}^{-1} = (\mathbf{ZY}^{-1})^{-1}$. Let me denote $\mathbf{D_h}\widetilde{\mathbf{Q}}_{\widetilde{\mathbf{p}}}\mathbf{D_p}\mathbf{D_{h'}}(\mathbf{I} - \mathbf{D_\varepsilon})^{-1}$ by $\mathbf{A}$. Condition (A.3) gives

$$(\mathbf{I} - \mathbf{D_\varepsilon})\mathbf{Q_p} = [\mathbf{I} - \mathbf{A}]^{-1}\mathbf{A}\mathbf{D_h}\mathbf{D_p^{-1}}\mathbf{D_{h'}^{-1}}(\mathbf{I} - \mathbf{D_\varepsilon})$$

$$= \left\{[\mathbf{I} - \mathbf{A}]^{-1}[\mathbf{I} - (\mathbf{I} - \mathbf{A})]\right\}\mathbf{D_h}\mathbf{D_p^{-1}}\mathbf{D_{h'}^{-1}}(\mathbf{I} - \mathbf{D_\varepsilon})$$

$$= \left\{[\mathbf{I} - \mathbf{A}]^{-1} - \mathbf{I}\right\}\mathbf{D_h}\mathbf{D_p^{-1}}\mathbf{D_{h'}^{-1}}(\mathbf{I} - \mathbf{D_\varepsilon})$$

$$= \left[\mathbf{D_h^{-1}}\mathbf{D_p}\mathbf{D_{h'}}(\mathbf{I} - \mathbf{D_\varepsilon})^{-1}\right.$$

$$\left. - (\mathbf{I} - \mathbf{D_\varepsilon})^{-1}\mathbf{D_{h'}}\mathbf{D_p}\widetilde{\mathbf{Q}}_{\widetilde{\mathbf{p}}}\mathbf{D_p}\mathbf{D_{h'}}(\mathbf{I} - \mathbf{D_\varepsilon})^{-1}\right]^{-1}$$

$$- \mathbf{D_h}\mathbf{D_p^{-1}}\mathbf{D_{h'}^{-1}}(\mathbf{I} - \mathbf{D_\varepsilon}), \tag{A.4}$$

Because $\widetilde{\mathbf{Q}}_{\tilde{\mathbf{p}}}$ is symmetric, the term after the last equality in (A.4) is symmetric. This proves relation (1).

To prove relation (2), post-multiply both sides of (A.2) by $\mathbf{p}$. Consider first the left-hand side. A representative element of the resulting vector is $\sum_k p_k(\partial Q_i/\partial p_k)$. For the right-hand side, let me consider $\widetilde{\mathbf{Q}}_{\tilde{\mathbf{p}}}\mathbf{D}_{\mathbf{h}}\mathbf{p}$. Because $\mathbf{D}_{\mathbf{h}}\mathbf{p} = (\tilde{p}_1, \tilde{p}_2, \ldots, \tilde{p}_n)^T$, and because $\widetilde{Q}_i$ is homogeneous of degree zero in $\tilde{\mathbf{p}}$, $\widetilde{\mathbf{Q}}_{\tilde{\mathbf{p}}}\mathbf{D}_{\mathbf{h}}\mathbf{p}$ is equal to an $n \times 1$ vector of zeroes. In other words, the right-hand side of the resulting vector is a vector of zeroes. Relation (2) follows.

I now prove relation (3). By relation (1), $(\mathbf{I} - \mathbf{D}_\varepsilon)\mathbf{Q}_{\mathbf{p}}$ is symmetric. Transposing the term on the right-hand side of (A.3), I have

$$(\mathbf{I} - \mathbf{D}_\varepsilon)\mathbf{Q}_{\mathbf{p}} = \mathbf{D}_{\mathbf{h}}\widetilde{\mathbf{Q}}_{\tilde{\mathbf{p}}}\mathbf{D}_{\mathbf{h}}[\mathbf{I} - (\mathbf{I} - \mathbf{D}_\varepsilon)^{-1}\mathbf{D}_{\mathbf{p}}\mathbf{D}_{\mathbf{h}'}\widetilde{\mathbf{Q}}_{\tilde{\mathbf{p}}}\mathbf{D}_{\mathbf{h}}]^{-1}. \qquad (A.5)$$

Pre-multiply both sides of (A.5) with $\mathbf{p}^T$. A representative element of the resulting vector on the left-hand side is $\sum_i p_i(1 - \varepsilon_i)(\partial Q_i/\partial p_k)$. On the right-hand side, note that $\mathbf{p}^T\mathbf{D}_{\mathbf{h}}\widetilde{\mathbf{Q}}_{\tilde{\mathbf{p}}}$ is a vector of zeroes. This gives relation (3).

To prove other relations, differentiate both sides of $Q_i = h_i\widetilde{Q}_i$ with respect to v_j to give

$$\frac{\partial Q_i}{\partial v_j} = h_i\frac{\partial \widetilde{Q}_i}{\partial v_j} + h_i'\widetilde{Q}_i\frac{\partial Q_i}{\partial v_j} + h_i\sum_k \frac{\partial \widetilde{Q}_i}{\partial \tilde{p}_k}\frac{\partial \tilde{p}_k}{\partial v_j}$$

$$= h_i\frac{\partial \widetilde{Q}_i}{\partial v_j} + \varepsilon_i\frac{\partial Q_i}{\partial v_j} + h_i\sum_k \frac{\partial \widetilde{Q}_i}{\partial \tilde{p}_k}p_k h_k'\frac{\partial Q_k}{\partial v_j}. \qquad (A.6)$$

In matrix form, condition (A.6) can be written as

$$\mathbf{Q}_{\mathbf{v}} = (\mathbf{I} - \mathbf{D}_\varepsilon - \mathbf{D}_{\mathbf{h}}\widetilde{\mathbf{Q}}_{\tilde{\mathbf{p}}}\mathbf{D}_{\mathbf{p}}\mathbf{D}_{\mathbf{h}'})^{-1}\mathbf{D}_{\mathbf{h}}\widetilde{\mathbf{Q}}_{\mathbf{v}}, \qquad (A.7)$$

where $\mathbf{Q}_{\mathbf{v}}$ and $\widetilde{\mathbf{Q}}_{\mathbf{v}}$ are the $n \times m$ matrices of the derivatives of the corresponding output functions with respect to factor endowments. Differentiate w_j with respect to p_i to get

$$\frac{\partial w_j}{\partial p_i} = \sum_k \frac{\partial w_j}{\partial \tilde{p}_k}\frac{\partial(p_k h_k)}{\partial p_i} = \frac{\partial w_j}{\partial \tilde{p}_i}h_i + \sum_k \frac{\partial w_j}{\partial \tilde{p}_k}p_k h_k'\frac{\partial Q_k}{\partial p_i}. \qquad (A.8)$$

In matrix form, condition (A.8) reduces to

$$\mathbf{w}_{\mathbf{p}} = \mathbf{w}_{\tilde{\mathbf{p}}}[\mathbf{D}_{\mathbf{h}} + \mathbf{D}_{\mathbf{p}}\mathbf{D}_{\mathbf{h}'}\mathbf{Q}_{\mathbf{p}}]. \qquad (A.9)$$

Making use of (A.2), (A.9) reduces to

$$\mathbf{w}_{\mathbf{p}} = \mathbf{w}_{\tilde{\mathbf{p}}}\left[\mathbf{D}_{\mathbf{h}} + \mathbf{D}_{\mathbf{p}}\mathbf{D}_{\mathbf{h}'}(\mathbf{I} - \mathbf{D}_\varepsilon - \mathbf{D}_{\mathbf{h}}\widetilde{\mathbf{Q}}_{\tilde{\mathbf{p}}}\mathbf{D}_{\mathbf{p}}\mathbf{D}_{\mathbf{h}'})^{-1}\mathbf{D}_{\mathbf{h}}\widetilde{\mathbf{Q}}_{\tilde{\mathbf{p}}}\mathbf{D}_{\mathbf{h}}\right]$$

$$= \mathbf{w}_{\tilde{\mathbf{p}}}(\mathbf{I} - \mathbf{D}_\varepsilon)^{-1}\left[\mathbf{D}_{\mathbf{h}}(\mathbf{I} - \mathbf{D}_\varepsilon) + \mathbf{D}_{\mathbf{p}}\mathbf{D}_{\mathbf{h}'}(\mathbf{I} - \mathbf{D}_\varepsilon)\right.$$

$$\left.(\mathbf{I} - \mathbf{D}_\varepsilon - \mathbf{D}_{\mathbf{h}}\widetilde{\mathbf{Q}}_{\tilde{\mathbf{p}}}\mathbf{D}_{\mathbf{p}}\mathbf{D}_{\mathbf{h}'})^{-1}\mathbf{D}_{\mathbf{h}}\widetilde{\mathbf{Q}}_{\tilde{\mathbf{p}}}\mathbf{D}_{\mathbf{h}}\right]. \qquad (A.10)$$

By relation (1), $(\mathbf{I} - \mathbf{D}_\varepsilon)(\mathbf{I} - \mathbf{D}_\varepsilon - \mathbf{D_h}\widetilde{\mathbf{Q}}_{\tilde{\mathbf{p}}}\mathbf{D_p}\mathbf{D_{h'}})^{-1}\mathbf{D_h}\widetilde{\mathbf{Q}}_{\tilde{\mathbf{p}}}\mathbf{D_h}$ is symmetric. Thus I have

$$\mathbf{w_p} = \mathbf{w_{\tilde{p}}}(\mathbf{I} - \mathbf{D}_\varepsilon)^{-1}\big[\mathbf{D_h}(\mathbf{I} - \mathbf{D}_\varepsilon) + \mathbf{D_p}\mathbf{D_{h'}}\mathbf{D_h}\widetilde{\mathbf{Q}}_{\tilde{\mathbf{p}}}\mathbf{D_h}$$

$$(\mathbf{I} - \mathbf{D}_\varepsilon - \mathbf{D_p}\mathbf{D_{h'}}\widetilde{\mathbf{Q}}_{\tilde{\mathbf{p}}}\mathbf{D_h})^{-1}(\mathbf{I} - \mathbf{D}_\varepsilon)\big]$$

$$= \mathbf{w_{\tilde{p}}}\mathbf{D_h}(\mathbf{I} - \mathbf{D}_\varepsilon)^{-1}\big[(\mathbf{I} - \mathbf{D}_\varepsilon - \mathbf{D_p}\mathbf{D_{h'}}\widetilde{\mathbf{Q}}_{\tilde{\mathbf{p}}}\mathbf{D_h}) + \mathbf{D_p}\mathbf{D_{h'}}\widetilde{\mathbf{Q}}_{\tilde{\mathbf{p}}}\mathbf{D_h}\big]$$

$$\cdot (\mathbf{I} - \mathbf{D}_\varepsilon - \mathbf{D_p}\mathbf{D_{h'}}\widetilde{\mathbf{Q}}_{\tilde{\mathbf{p}}}\mathbf{D_h})^{-1}(\mathbf{I} - \mathbf{D}_\varepsilon)$$

$$= \mathbf{w_{\tilde{p}}}\mathbf{D_h}(\mathbf{I} - \mathbf{D}_\varepsilon - \mathbf{D_p}\mathbf{D_{h'}}\widetilde{\mathbf{Q}}_{\tilde{\mathbf{p}}}\mathbf{D_h})^{-1}(\mathbf{I} - \mathbf{D}_\varepsilon). \tag{A.11}$$

Because $\mathbf{Q_v} = \mathbf{w}_{\tilde{\mathbf{p}}}^T$, a comparison between (A.7) and (A.11) gives $(\mathbf{I} - \mathbf{D}_\varepsilon)\mathbf{Q_v}$ $= \mathbf{w}_{\mathbf{p}}^T$, thus proving relation (4).

To prove (v), post-multiply (A.9) by $\mathbf{p}$ to give

$$\mathbf{w_p}\mathbf{p} = \mathbf{w_{\tilde{p}}}\mathbf{D_h}\mathbf{p} + \mathbf{w_{\tilde{p}}}\mathbf{D_p}\mathbf{D_{h'}}\mathbf{Q_p}\mathbf{p}$$

$$= \mathbf{w}. \tag{A.12}$$

In deriving (A.12), I have used the fact that (a) $\mathbf{w}$ is linearly homogeneous in $\tilde{\mathbf{p}}$, and (b) by relation (2), $\mathbf{Q}$ is homogeneous of degree zero in $\mathbf{p}$, implying that $\mathbf{Q_p}\mathbf{p}$ is equal to a vector of zeroes. Relation (4) and condition (A.12) jointly give

$$\mathbf{p}^T(\mathbf{I} - \mathbf{D}_\varepsilon)\mathbf{Q_v} = \mathbf{p}^T\mathbf{w}_{\mathbf{p}}^T = \mathbf{w}^T \tag{A.13}$$

which confirms relation (5).

I now turn to relation (6). Differentiate w_j with respect to v_ℓ to give

$$\frac{\partial w_j}{\partial v_\ell} = \frac{\partial^2 g}{\partial v_j \partial v_\ell} + \sum_k \frac{\partial w_j}{\partial \tilde{p}_k} \frac{\partial (p_k h_k)}{\partial v_\ell}$$

$$= \frac{\partial^2 g}{\partial v_j \partial v_\ell} + \sum_k \frac{\partial w_j}{\partial \tilde{p}_k} p_k h_k' \frac{\partial Q_k}{\partial v_\ell},$$

which can be written alternatively in matrix form,

$$\mathbf{w_v} = g_{\mathbf{vv}} + \mathbf{w_{\tilde{p}}}\mathbf{D_p}\mathbf{D_{h'}}\mathbf{Q_v}$$

$$= g_{\mathbf{vv}} + \mathbf{w_{\tilde{p}}}\mathbf{D_p}\mathbf{D_{h'}}(\mathbf{I} - \mathbf{D}_\varepsilon - \mathbf{D_h}\widetilde{\mathbf{Q}}_{\tilde{\mathbf{p}}}\mathbf{D_p}\mathbf{D_{h'}})^{-1}\mathbf{D_h}\widetilde{\mathbf{Q}}_{\mathbf{v}}$$

$$= g_{\mathbf{vv}} + \mathbf{w_{\tilde{p}}}\big[\mathbf{D_p}^{-1}\mathbf{D_{h'}}^{-1}\mathbf{D_h}^{-1}(\mathbf{I} - \mathbf{D}_\varepsilon) - \widetilde{\mathbf{Q}}_{\tilde{\mathbf{p}}}\big]^{-1}\widetilde{\mathbf{Q}}_{\mathbf{v}}, \tag{A.14}$$

where $g_{\mathbf{vv}}$ is the Hessian matrix of the GDP function g with respect to factor endowments, and where condition (A.7) has been used. Note that from the GDP function, $g_{\mathbf{vv}}$ and $\widetilde{\mathbf{Q}}_{\tilde{\mathbf{p}}}$ are symmetric. Thus the term on the right-hand side of (A.14) is symmetric, and so is $\mathbf{w_v}$. This gives relation (6).

6 Monopolistic Competition and Intraindustry Trade in Differentiated Products

The focus of this chapter is intraindustry (sometimes called two-way, or mutual) trade in differentiated products. Intraindustry trade refers to the simultaneous export and import of goods with some common characteristics that belong to the same industry, and which have important differences among them so that they are considered to be differentiated (or heterogeneous), not homogeneous, products.

The frameworks examined so far are not suitable for analyzing intraindustry trade in differentiated products because by definition products in each industry are assumed to be homogeneous. With perfect competition and the presence of transport costs, it makes no sense for any country to have simultaneous export and import of the same commodity. To allow for intraindustry trade, I must depart from the traditional frameworks by relaxing some of their assumptions. In this chapter, I consider product differentiation and monopolistic competition, and in the next chapter, I examine models with oligopolistic firms.[1]

When product differentiation is allowed, one of the most important challenges is to determine the equilibrium number of varieties. Because consumers usually prefer more varieties to less, the assumption of constant returns must be abandoned or the number of varieties will tend to go to infinity and may not be determinate. The common approach in the literature is to assume internal economies of scale in the production of differentiated products. The presence of scale economies has two implications. First, firms want to enjoy economies of scale, meaning that the output level of each firm will not be too low, or that the number of varieties will be bounded from above. Second, no two firms will produce the same variety. If at any time there are two firms producing the same product then one of them can produce slightly more, thus lowering the average cost because of economies of scale. This enables it to sell the product at a lower price until the other firm is driven out of the market.

Internal scale economies are not compatible with perfect competition, so I have to specify the market structure in the model. The most common one assumed is monopolistic competition due to Chamberlin (1933). In such an economy, there are large numbers of existing and potential firms. Free entry and exit of firms drives the profit of firms down to zero (or close to zero, assuming identical technologies).

In this chapter, I first explain how the demand for differentiated products is derived. Then I explain the production of the homogeneous and differentiated products and the derivation of equilibrium in a closed economy. Factor accumulation in a closed economy is also explained. Next, free trade is examined, as are the effects of factor endowments on the volume and composition of

---

1. Grubel and Lloyd (1975) present other reasons for intraindustry trade.

trade. Finally, the effects of international factor movement and the relationship between international factor movement and commodity trade are discussed.

6.1 Preferences

This section explains the preferences of the consumers and derives their demands for goods. I begin with a general approach to deriving the demand for differentiated products, and then explain the two special cases: love of variety approach and ideal variety approach.

6.1.1 A General Approach

Consider a simple framework with two types of goods and two sectors. Sector 1 consists of goods of similar varieties while in sector 2 a homogeneous good is produced. For convenience, I simply call the goods in sector 1 good 1 while good 2 refers to the output of sector 2. Denote the set of all varieties of good 1 by Ω, and index the varieties by ω. Varieties may be described by different specifications or attributes (Lancaster, 1979), but following Helpman (1981) and Helpman and Krugman (1985), I consider only one dimension of attributes and assume that different varieties are represented by different points on the circumference of a circle. Let the circumference of the circle be of unit length. The varieties to be produced and made available to the economy or the world are decided by the firms, but from the consumers' point of view, the varieties supplied are given.

Consider a representative consumer, and represent his or her preferences by the utility function $u(D_1, D_2)$, where $D_2 \geq 0$ is the consumption of good 2. D_1 is in fact a subutility function that depends on the consumption of the differentiated products. Specifically, it is given by

$$D_1 = G\left[\frac{d_1(\omega)}{\overline{h}(\omega)}, \omega \in \Omega\right], \tag{6.1}$$

where $d_1(\omega) \geq 0$ is the consumption of the variety ω, and $\overline{h}(\omega) \geq 1$ is a discount factor. The role of this discount factor will be made clear later.

The utility function $u(D_1, D_2)$ is continuous, increasing, and quasi-concave in D_1 and D_2. Similarly, the subutility function $G[.]$ is continuous, increasing, and quasi-concave in the consumption of all varieties.

Choosing good 2 as the numeraire, the income of the representative consumer is denoted by I. Define I_1 as $I - D_2 \geq 0$, which is the income left to the consumer for purchasing good 1. The consumer is to choose the quantities of the consumption goods in order to maximize the utility function given by $u(D_1, D_2)$, taking the commodity prices and his or her income as given.

I conveniently decompose the utility-maximization problem of the consumer into two stages. In the first stage, taking the existing varieties, I_1, and the prices of the varieties as given, the consumer chooses the optimal varieties for consumption. In the second stage, the consumer chooses I_1, or the consumption of good 2, taking income I as given. I describe these two stages separately.

The First Stage of Utility Maximization

Denote the price of variety ω by $p(\omega)$. The budget constraint in this stage is given by

$$\sum_{\omega \in \Omega} p(\omega) d_1(\omega) \leq I_1. \tag{6.2}$$

The present problem of the consumer is

$$\max_{d_1(\omega)} G\left[\frac{d_1(\omega)}{\overline{h}(\omega)}, \omega \in \Omega\right], \tag{6.3a}$$

subject to the budget constraint in (6.2). The first-order Kuhn-Tucker conditions are

$$\frac{G_\omega}{\overline{h}(\omega)} \leq \lambda_1 p(\omega), \tag{6.4}$$

where G_ω is the partial derivative of $G[.]$ with respect to the demand for the corresponding variety, and λ_1 is the Lagrangean multiplier associated with the budget constraint in (6.2) and can be interpreted as the marginal utility of I_1.

Conditions (6.4) together with the budget constraint in (6.2) can be solved for the demand for the varieties. I denote the demand for variety ω by

$$d_1(\omega) = \theta(\mathbf{p}, I_1), \tag{6.5}$$

where $\mathbf{p}$ is the vector of the prices of all the varieties. (The demand for some of the varieties of a particular consumer may be zero.) Substituting the function in (6.5) into function $G[.]$, I obtain the demand for the differentiated products by the consumer, $D_1 = \Theta(\mathbf{p}, I_1)$.

The Second Stage of Utility Maximization

In this stage, the consumer has to allocate the given income between the differentiated goods and the homogeneous good. Substituting the function Θ into the consumer's utility function, the problem can be stated as

$$\max_{I_1, D_2} u(\Theta(\mathbf{p}, I_1), D_2) \quad \text{s.t.} \quad I_1 + D_2 \leq I. \tag{6.3b}$$

The problem given in (6.3b) can be solved for the optimal value of I_1 and D_2, both being functions of $\mathbf{p}$ and I, $I_1(\mathbf{p}, I)$ and $D_2(\mathbf{p}, I)$. Substituting function $I_1(\mathbf{p}, I)$ into function $D_1 = \Theta(\mathbf{p}, I_1)$, I obtain the demands for the varieties as functions of $\mathbf{p}$ and I.

The solution to the consumer problem is a direct application of the conventional consumer theory and techniques. It is more complicated than it appears, however, for two major reasons. First, the number of varieties is usually large. This means that the dimension of the problem is high. Second, the number of varieties is usually an endogenous variable to be determined in the framework. Without making simplification, the problem is hardly tractable. Here I introduce two approaches that are common in the trade literature.

6.1.2 The Love of Variety Approach

This approach is based on the work of Spence (1976) and Dixit and Stiglitz (1977), and was used by Krugman (1979a, 1980, 1981), Dixit and Norman (1980), and Lawrence and Spiller (1983) to explain trade in differentiated products. I now show that it can be reduced from the preceding general approach by making the following assumptions:

1. The discount factor for any variety is unity, i.e., $\overline{h}(\omega) = 1$ for all $\omega \in \Omega$.

2. All the varieties enter the function $G[d_1(\omega), \omega \in \Omega]$ in a symmetric way.

3. All consumers have identical preferences.

4. The varieties are also treated symmetrically on the production side.

I briefly explain the implications of these assumptions. If prices of all varieties are the same, then assumptions (1) and (2) imply that each consumer will purchase equal amounts of the varieties. If assumption (3) is made, all consumers have the same consumption. If the number of consumers is fixed and known, then the market demand for each variety is the product of the demand of the representative consumer and the number of consumers.

Assumption (4) is about the production side of the framework; I explain its implications in more detail later. For convenience, in deriving the equilibrium of a closed economy, I assume that all consumers have the same factor endowments so that they have the same income. However, this assumption is not crucial for our analysis because with homothetic preferences, income distribution is not important for deriving an equilibrium.

Because the varieties are treated symmetrically, very often varieties are assumed to be located at discrete points on the circumference with equal distance between any pair of adjacent varieties.

Two functional forms of the subutility function $G[.]$ are common in the literature, the CES subutility function and the additively separable subutility function.

CES Subutility Function (Dixit and Stiglitz, 1977; Dixit and Norman, 1980; Krugman, 1981; and Lawrence and Spiller, 1983)

The subutility function of the representative consumer is given by

$$G[d_1(\omega), \omega \in \Omega] = \left[\sum_{\omega} [d_1(\omega)]^{\beta} \right]^{1/\beta}, \quad \beta = \left(1 - \frac{1}{\sigma}\right), \quad \sigma > 1, \quad (6.6)$$

where σ is the elasticity of substitution. By assumption $\sigma > 1$, implying that $\beta > 0$. As shown in the appendix, the demand for variety ω is equal to:

$$d_1(\omega) = \theta(\mathbf{p}, I_1) = \frac{[p(\omega)]^{-\sigma}}{\sum_{v \in \Omega} [p(v)]^{1-\sigma}} I_1. \quad (6.7)$$

Given the demand function in (6.7), the own price elasticity of demand is equal to

$$\eta \equiv -\frac{p(\omega)}{d_1(\omega)} \frac{\partial d_1(\omega)}{\partial p(\omega)} = \sigma + \frac{(1-\sigma)[p(\omega)]^{1-\sigma}}{\sum_{v \in \Omega} [p(v)]^{1-\sigma}} - \frac{p(\omega)}{I_1} \frac{\partial I_1}{\partial p(\omega)}. \quad (6.8)$$

In evaluating the own price elasticity of demand, the income and other prices are kept constant. If the number of varieties is large, and if all the prices are not much different from each other, the second and third terms in (6.8) are negligibly small. This means that the elasticity of demand is (approximately) equal to σ. In the general equilibrium framework developed next, the assumption that the number of varieties is large is not crucial.[2]

Again making use of the demand function in (6.7), the cross price elasticity of demand for variety ω with respect to the price of another variety ω', $p(\omega')$ is

$$\frac{p(\omega')}{d_1(\omega)} \frac{\partial d_1(\omega)}{\partial p(\omega')} = -\frac{(1-\sigma)[p(\omega')]^{1-\sigma}}{\sum_{v \in \Omega} [p(v)]^{1-\sigma}} + \frac{p(\omega')}{I_1} \frac{\partial I_1}{\partial p(\omega')}.$$

If the number of varieties is large and their prices are close to each other, the cross elasticity of demand approaches zero.

That the cross elasticity of demand is small is not a comfortable result. Because the varieties are close substitutes, one would expect that the demand

---

2. Yang and Heijdra (1993), who provide an expression of the own price elasticity of demand similar to the one in (6.8), criticize the assumption that the number of varieties is large. They argue that because the number of varieties is endogenously determined, whether it is large or not should be a solution of the system, and they also point out that this assumption may lead to some misleading results. See also the reply by Dixit and Stiglitz (1993).

for a variety is very sensitive to the prices of other varieties. In other words, one would expect the cross elasticities to be large, not close to zero.[3]

I now derive the market demand. With the assumptions stated previously (symmetry between the varieties on consumption and production sides, and identical preferences), the demand function given in (6.7) also represents the demand for any variety by any consumer. Suppose that there are m identical consumers where m is given exogenously, the market demand for variety ω is given by $C_1(\mathbf{p}, I_1) = md_1(\omega)$, where $d_1(\omega)$ is given by (6.7).

If the number of varieties is large, then the production of a firm will have little effect on the income of a representative consumer. Taking the number of consumers, consumers' incomes, and the prices of other varieties as constant, the price elasticity of the market demand for variety ω is also equal to the price elasticity of an individual's demand. As a result, let η also represent the price elasticity of market demand, and by condition (6.8), $\eta = \sigma$ when the number of varieties is large. Thus η is a constant.

It is well known that a profit-maximizing firm with monopoly power will not choose an output level at which the demand is inelastic because the marginal revenue is negative. Because $\eta = \sigma$, this explains why it is assumed that $\sigma > 1$, that is, $\beta > 0$.

Additively Separable Subutility Function (Krugman, 1979a, 1980)

Instead of assuming a particular functional form, Krugman assumed an additively separable subutility function:

$$G[d_1(\omega), \omega \in \Omega] = \sum_{\omega \in \Omega} v[d_1(\omega)] \quad v' > 0, \quad v'' < 0.$$

The function $v(.)$ is differentiable, increasing, and strictly concave. Note again that the varieties enter the utility function in a symmetric way.

The first-order condition, which is similar to the one given in (6.4), can be used to solve for the demand for a variety:

$$v'(d_1(\omega)) = \lambda_1 p(\omega). \tag{6.9}$$

Condition (6.9) gives an implicit function of the demand. The market demand is again the horizontal summation of the demands of the consumers. If the number of varieties is large, each firm can take λ_1 as given. If, furthermore, the number of consumers is fixed, the price elasticity of market demand is equal to

---

3. Symmetry between varieties means that as the price of a variety goes up while the prices of all other varieties are the same, a representative consumer will increase the consumption of all other varieties by the same amount. If the number of varieties is very large, due to budget constraint the increase in the consumption of any other variety is insignificant. This explains why the cross elasticity of a variety is small.

$$\eta = -\frac{v'(d_1(\omega))}{d_1(\omega)v''(d_1(\omega))}.$$

Note that this is also equal to the price elasticity of demand by each consumer who takes his or her income as given. Another point to note is that if the marginal utility of income λ_1 is taken as given (if the number of variety is large), then the demand for each variety depends only on its own price and not on other prices. In other words, the cross elasticity of demand is zero, as in the case of a CES-type subutility function.

6.1.3 The Ideal Variety Approach

In this approach, the representative consumer has the most-preferred good or the ideal variety, $\widetilde{\omega}$, in the sense that if the consumer is presented all varieties at the same price, which is sufficiently smaller than his or her income, the first unit of good 1 he or she will purchase is the variety $\widetilde{\omega}$.[4] If the consumer purchases a variety ω different from his or her ideal choice, the utility that a single unit of variety ω yields is less than what one unit of the ideal variety yields. This is why the quantities of varieties other than the ideal one consumed have to be discounted. For simplicity, I assume that the discount factor for variety ω depends on the shorter arc distance between ω and $\widetilde{\omega}$. Denote this distance by $\delta(\omega, \widetilde{\omega})$. I then define a new variable, $h[\delta(\omega, \widetilde{\omega})] \equiv \overline{h}(\omega)$. Function $h[\delta(\omega, \widetilde{\omega})]$ is what Lancaster (1979) calls the compensation function.

Following Lancaster (1979), I assume that function $h[\delta]$ ($\delta \geq 0$) has the following properties: (1) $h[\delta] \geq 1$; (2) $h[0] = 1$; (3) $h'[0] = 0$; (4) $h'[\delta] > 0$ for $\delta > 0$; and (5) $h''[\delta] > 0$, where the primes denote derivatives.

After specifying the compensation function, I use the analysis given previously to derive the demand functions. To keep the analysis manageable, I follow Helpman (1981) and Helpman and Krugman (1985), and assume that the subutility function is given by

$$G[.] = \sum_{\omega \in \Omega} \frac{d_1(\omega)}{h[\delta(\omega, \widetilde{\omega})]}. \tag{6.10}$$

As I did before, I hypothetically decompose a representative consumer's problem into two stages. In the first stage, the consumer chooses the consumption of different varieties to maximize the subutility in (6.10) subject to the budget constraint $\sum_\omega p(\omega)d_1(\omega) \leq I_1$. Define $\widetilde{d}_1(\omega, \widetilde{\omega}) \equiv d_1(\omega)/h[\delta(\omega, \widetilde{\omega})]$ and $\widetilde{p}(\omega, \widetilde{\omega}) \equiv p(\omega)h[\delta(\omega, \widetilde{\omega})]$. Using these two variables, the first-stage of the consumer's problem becomes

---

4. This definition is slightly more general than the one in Helpman (1981) because simultaneous consumption of more than one type of variety is allowed.

$$\max_{\tilde{d}_1(\omega,\tilde{\omega})} \sum_{\omega\in\Omega} \tilde{d}_1(\omega,\tilde{\omega}) \quad \text{s.t.} \quad \sum_\omega \tilde{p}(\omega,\tilde{\omega})\tilde{d}_1(\omega,\tilde{\omega}) \le I_1. \tag{6.11}$$

It is clear from the problem in (6.11) that $\tilde{d}_1(\omega,\tilde{\omega})$ is the discounted (or compensated) consumption and $\tilde{p}(\omega,\tilde{\omega})$ is the effective price of variety ω.

The problem can be illustrated and solved graphically by Figure 6.1 for the case in which there are only two varieties, $\hat{\omega}$ and ω'. The subutility function assumed is represented by indifference curves which are straight lines inclined to the vertical axis at 45°. Line AB is one of the indifference lines. Given the income level I_1 and the prices, BC is the budget line which has a slope of $-\tilde{p}(\hat{\omega},\tilde{\omega})/\tilde{p}(\omega',\tilde{\omega})$. Without loss of generality, I assume that $\tilde{p}(\hat{\omega},\tilde{\omega}) < \tilde{p}(\omega',\tilde{\omega})$. This means that the budget line is less steep than an indifference curve. Point B gives the highest utility subject to the budget constraint. This is a corner solution, meaning that the consumer chooses to spend all of his or her income on the variety that has the lowest effective price. The discounted quantity of variety $\hat{\omega}$ demanded or the discounted quantity of good 1 demanded is the ratio of the amount of income the consumer decides to spend on the differentiated goods to the effective price of the variety $\hat{\omega}$, that is,

$$D_1 = \tilde{d}_1(\hat{\omega},\tilde{\omega}) = \frac{I_1}{\tilde{p}(\hat{\omega},\tilde{\omega})}. \tag{6.12}$$

The demand function in (6.12) is then substituted into the utility function of representative consumer.

The second stage of the consumer's problem is again described by (6.3), and it is solved for the optimal I_1 and D_2. Let me define the demand functions of I_1 and D_2 by $I_1[\tilde{p}(\hat{\omega},\tilde{\omega}), I]$ and $D_2[\tilde{p}(\hat{\omega},\tilde{\omega}), I]$. Function $I_1[\tilde{p}(\hat{\omega},\tilde{\omega}), I]$ is then substituted into (6.12) to give the demand for variety $\hat{\omega}$:

$$D_1 = \phi[\tilde{p}(\hat{\omega},\tilde{\omega}), I] \equiv \frac{I_1[\tilde{p}(\hat{\omega},\tilde{\omega}), I]}{p(\hat{\omega})h[\delta(\hat{\omega},\tilde{\omega})]}. \tag{6.12'}$$

I again assume symmetry: All consumers are alike and have the same income, except that they have different ideal varieties. The consumers are indexed by their ideal varieties, and they are distributed uniformly along the circumference of the circle.

The market demand for a particular variety is derived in the following way. In the present framework, as shown later, each variety is produced by at most one firm. The demand faced by each firm depends on two factors: the width of its market, that is, the number of consumers who have positive demands for its product, and the quantity demanded by each consumer.

Consider a firm that decides to produce a variety ω and charge a price of $p(\omega)$. I now have to determine its market demand. First note that the firm has to compete with two firms that are producing varieties close to ω. Following Helpman (1981), denote the next variety on the right-hand (left-hand)

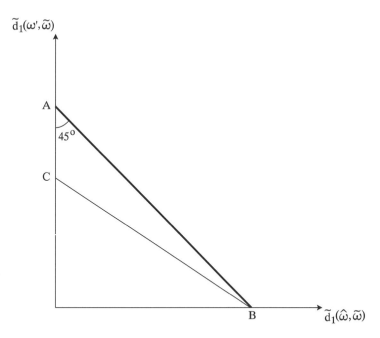

Figure 6.1

side of ω by ω_r (ω_ℓ). Further assume that the shortest arc length between ω and ω_r (ω_ℓ) is δ_r (δ_ℓ) following the approach in Helpman and Krugman (1985). I illustrate in Figure 6.2 the relationship between the variables. The diagram also shows three schedules labeled S, S_ℓ, and S_r, which represent the effective prices of the corresponding varieties, that is, $p(\omega)h[\delta(\omega, \tilde{\omega})]$, $p(\omega_\ell)h[\delta(\omega_\ell, \tilde{\omega})]$, and $p(\omega_r)h[\delta(\omega_r, \tilde{\omega})]$. These three schedules have the minimum points at ω, ω_ℓ, and ω_r, respectively. Let schedule S cut schedules S_ℓ and S_r at A_ℓ and A_r, respectively. Denote the varieties corresponding to the intersecting points by $\underline{\omega}$ and $\overline{\omega}$, as shown by the diagram. Let the shorter arc length between ω and $\underline{\omega}$ (respectively $\overline{\omega}$) be $\underline{\delta}$ (respectively $\overline{\delta}$). Specifically, these arc lengths are defined by

$$p(\omega_\ell)h(\delta_\ell - \underline{\delta}) = p(\omega)h(\underline{\delta}) \tag{6.13a}$$

$$p(\omega_r)h(\delta_r - \overline{\delta}) = p(\omega)h(\overline{\delta}). \tag{6.13b}$$

I showed that consumers purchase variety ω if and only if for them the effective price of variety ω is lower than those of ω_ℓ and ω_r. This means that, in terms of Figure 6.2, the width of the market for variety ω is from $\underline{\omega}$ to $\overline{\omega}$. Because the length of the circle's circumference is one, m is both the number and the density of consumers. Recall that the demand of a representative consumer for variety ω is equal to $d_1(\omega) = \phi\Big[p(\omega)h(\delta), I\Big]h(\delta)$. Thus the market demand for variety ω is given by

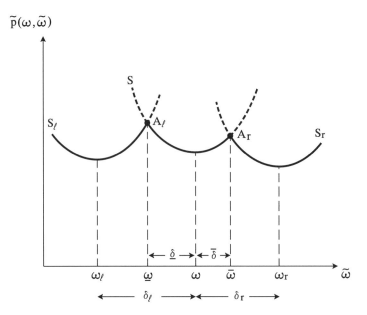

Figure 6.2

$$C_1(p(\omega), I) = m\left\{ \int_0^{\underline{\delta}} \phi\Big[p(\omega)h(\delta), I\Big]h(\delta)\mathrm{d}\delta \right.$$

$$\left. + \int_0^{\bar{\delta}} \phi\Big[p(\omega)h(\delta), I\Big]h(\delta)\mathrm{d}\delta \right\}. \tag{6.14}$$

In the present framework, I consider symmetry of the varieties on both the consumption and production sides. Following Lancaster (1979), the firms are assumed to act noncooperatively. Each firm chooses the variety to produce and the variety's price while taking the varieties and prices chosen by other firms as given. Denote the number of varieties by n. As Helpman (1981) shows, assuming identical technologies for producing the varieties, the Nash equilibrium is characterized by uniform distribution of the varieties on the circumference, and the same price charged by the firms. In terms of the earlier notation, the Nash equilibrium gives $p(\omega_\ell) = p(\omega_r) = p(\omega) = p$, $\delta_\ell = \delta_r = 1/n$ and $\underline{\delta} = \bar{\delta} = 1/(2n)$. The variety chosen by a particular firm is indeterminate.

In such a framework with symmetry, the demand elasticity for each variety in general depends on p and n, that is, $\eta = \eta(p, n)$. Helpman (1981) shows that if $u(D_1, D_2)$ is homothetic, then η is greater than one and approaches infinity as the number of varieties goes to infinity.

In most of the analysis that follows I focus on a special type of the utility function of a representative consumer:

$$u(D_1, D_2) = D_1^\alpha D_2^{1-\alpha}, \quad 1 > \alpha > 0. \tag{6.15}$$

The advantage of a Cobb-Douglas utility function as given in (6.15) is that the share of the consumer's income spent on each commodity is independent of income and prices. This means that a consumer who decides to consume variety ω has a demand for that variety given by

$$d_1(\omega) = \frac{\alpha I}{p(\omega)}.$$

With symmetry in the framework, condition (6.14) reduces to

$$C_1(p(\omega), I) = \frac{\alpha m[\underline{\delta} + \bar{\delta}]I}{p(\omega)} = \frac{\alpha m I}{n p(\omega)}. \tag{6.14'}$$

As the appendix shows, the price elasticity of the market demand is equal to

$$\eta = 1 + \frac{1}{2\varepsilon_h(1/2n)}, \tag{6.16}$$

where $\varepsilon_h = h'/(2nh)$ is the elasticity of the function $h(\delta)$ evaluated at $\delta = 1/(2n)$. As a result, the demand elasticity given in (6.16) depends only on the number of variety, but not on the price level. Because $h' > 0$ for $\delta > 0$ by assumption, I have $\eta > 1$. Furthermore, as $n \to \infty$, $\delta \to 0$ and $\eta \to \infty$. As will be seen later, this is a very useful result.

Because a representative consumer spends a given percentage of his or her income on good 2, his or her demand for good 2 is then given by

$$D_2(I) = (1 - \alpha)I.$$

In the present case with a Cobb-Douglas utility function, $D_2(I)$ is independent of the relative price of good 1. The market demand for good 2 is then given by:

$$C_2(I) = m D_2(I) = m(1 - \alpha)I. \tag{6.17}$$

6.2 Production

I now turn to the production side of the economy. Suppose that the homogeneous good 2 is produced by firms that are competitive in both factor and good markets using constant-returns technologies. Denote the unit cost function of the sector by $c_2(w, r)$ where w and r are the wage rate and rental rate, respectively. Perfect competition implies zero profit, that is,

$$1 = c_2(w, r), \tag{6.18}$$

where good 2 is the numeraire. The derivatives of the unit cost function give the labor-output and capital-output ratios of the sector:

$$a_{L2}(w,r) = \frac{\partial c_2(w,r)}{\partial w}$$

$$a_{K2}(w,r) = \frac{\partial c_2(w,r)}{\partial r}.$$

Denoting the output level of sector 2 by Q_2, the demands for labor and capital of the sector are equal to $a_{L2}(w,r)Q_2$ and $a_{K2}(w,r)Q_2$, respectively.

Sector 1 has many existing and potential firms that produce different varieties. The technologies for producing different varieties are identical and exhibit economies of scale. This ensures that no two firms will produce the same variety in equilibrium. For simplicity, assume that the technology in this sector is homothetic and that the firms are price takers in the factor markets. Thus the total cost of production for each firm can be defined as

$$TC_1 = \gamma(q_1)\bar{c}_1(w,r), \tag{6.19}$$

where q_1 is the output of the firm, and where the subscript refers to sector 1. Note that I do not have any index for the firm because in the present framework the firms are symmetric and have the same equilibrium decision. From (6.19), the marginal cost is $\gamma'(q_1)\bar{c}_1(w,r)$ and average cost is $\gamma(q_1)\bar{c}_1(w,r)/q_1$. Assume that $\gamma(q_1)$ is increasing in q_1, that is, $\gamma'(q_1) > 0$. Define ε_γ as the elasticity of function $\gamma(q_1)$. To guarantee a decreasing average cost curve, I assume that $\gamma(q_1)$ is inelastic.[5] Function $\bar{c}_1(w,r)$, which looks and behaves like a unit cost function but is not, is assumed to be increasing, differentiable, and concave in factor prices. Denote the partial derivatives of $\bar{c}_1(w,r)$ by $\bar{a}_{L1}(w,r) \equiv \partial\bar{c}_1(w,r)/\partial w$ and $\bar{a}_{K1}(w,r) \equiv \partial\bar{c}_1(w,r)/\partial r$. Thus the derived demands for labor and capital by a representative firm in sector 1 are $\bar{a}_{L1}(w,r)\gamma(q_1)$ and $\bar{a}_{K1}(w,r)\gamma(q_1)$, respectively.

Firms in sector 1 choose varieties and the prices of the varieties in a non-cooperative way. In the love of variety approach, each firm chooses a variety that has not been chosen by other firms. Because the varieties enter the utility function of a representative consumer in a symmetric way, which variety the firm chooses to produce does not matter as long as that variety is not being produced by other firms. In the ideal variety approach, the Nash equilibrium requires that the varieties produced in the economy be uniformly distributed on the circumference of the circle. In both approaches, all firms choose the same price in equilibrium.

---

5. The average cost is equal to $\gamma(q_1)\bar{c}_1(w,r)/q_1$. Differentiating it with respect to q_1, keeping factor prices constant, a decreasing average cost curve would require that $q_1\gamma'(q_1) < \gamma(q_1)$, or that $\gamma(q_1)$ is inelastic.

The market demand for each variety faced by a representative firm in sector 1, denoted by C_1, is derived in the previous section. The profit of the firm is given by $pC_1 - \gamma(q_1)\bar{c}_1(w, r)$. Taking the variety and price decisions of other firms as given, a representative firm chooses the price so that marginal revenue is equal to marginal cost. In terms of the preceding notation, the profit-maximizing condition is

$$p\left(1 - \frac{1}{\eta}\right) = \gamma'(q_1)\bar{c}_1(w, r). \tag{6.20}$$

As explained previously, the demand elasticity η is a constant in the CES-love of variety approach or it depends on n in the ideal variety approach using a Cobb-Douglas upper-tier utility function.

Assume that free entry or exit in sector 1 can be done costlessly. In equilibrium, the profit of each firm is zero, that is,

$$p = \frac{\gamma(q_1)}{q_1}\bar{c}_1(w, r), \tag{6.21}$$

where the right-hand side of (6.21) is the average cost.

6.3   A Closed Economy

Assume that the economy is endowed with given amounts of labor and capital, $\overline{L}$ and $\overline{K}$, respectively. The equilibrium conditions for the two factor markets are

$$\bar{a}_{L1}(w, r)\gamma(q_1)n + a_{L2}(w, r)Q_2 = \overline{L} \tag{6.22a}$$

$$\bar{a}_{K1}(w, r)\gamma(q_1)n + a_{K2}(w, r)Q_2 = \overline{K}. \tag{6.22b}$$

When trade in goods is not allowed, the equilibrium conditions for the two sectors are

$$q_1 = C_1(p, I) \tag{6.23a}$$

$$Q_2 = C_2(p, I), \tag{6.23b}$$

where I is the per capita income, and is given by

$$I = \frac{npq_1 + Q_2}{m}. \tag{6.24}$$

Define $Q_1 = nq_1$ which is called the aggregate output of good 1.

Equations (6.18), (6.20), (6.21), (6.22a), (6.22b), (6.23a), (6.23b), and (6.24) describe the autarkic equilibrium of the present economy. By Walras's law, one of them is redundant. The remaining seven equations are solved for the seven unknowns: w, r, n, p, q_1, Q_2, and I.

The system can be solved in a diagrammatic and simple way.[6] First, the following new variables are defined:

$$p_z = \frac{pq_1}{\gamma(q_1)} \tag{6.25a}$$

$$Z = \gamma(q_1)n \tag{6.25b}$$

$$z^s = \frac{Z}{Q_2} \tag{6.25c}$$

$$z^d = \frac{nC_1\gamma(q_1)}{C_2q_1}. \tag{6.25d}$$

Assuming that a representative consumer has a Cobb-Douglas utility function, conditions (6.14′) and (6.17) are combined to give the ratio of the demands for the two goods

$$\frac{nC_1}{C_2} = \frac{\alpha}{1-\alpha}\frac{1}{p}.$$

This implies that z^d can be written as:

$$z^d = \frac{\alpha}{1-\alpha}\frac{1}{p_z}. \tag{6.25e}$$

Using these new variables, the equilibrium conditions can be stated in the following way (repeating equation 6.18):

$$1 = c_2(w,r) \tag{6.18}$$

$$p_z = \bar{c}_1(w,r) \tag{6.26}$$

$$\bar{a}_{L1}(w,r)Z + a_{L2}(w,r)Q_2 = \bar{L} \tag{6.27}$$

$$\bar{a}_{K1}(w,r)Z + a_{K2}(w,r)Q_2 = \bar{K} \tag{6.28}$$

$$1 - \frac{1}{\eta} = \varepsilon_\gamma(q_1) \tag{6.29}$$

$$z^s = z^d. \tag{6.30}$$

Equations (6.25a), (6.25b), (6.25c), (6.25e), (6.18), and (6.26) to (6.30) can be solved for the ten unknowns: w, r, n, p, p_z, z^d, z^s, q_1, Q_2, and Z.

This new system of equations can be solved in a simple way. Equations (6.18), (6.26), (6.27), and (6.28), and variables w, r, p_z, Q_2, and Z resemble the corresponding equations and variables in the production structure in a

---

6. Similar techniques of solving the system have been used by Dixit and Norman (1980) and Helpman (1981). The present technique is closer to that in Helpman (1981).

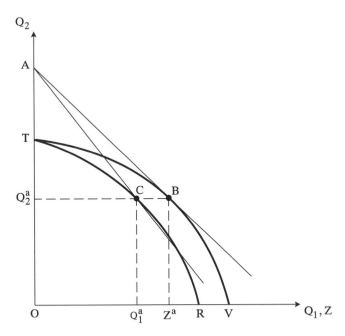

Figure 6.3

neoclassical framework, with Z interpreted as the output of sector 1 and p_z as the price of Z. With such an interpretation, I can use this system of four equations and five unknowns as an intermediate step to solving the whole system. As will be made clear later, this approach is very useful in doing comparative static experiments.

To avoid confusion, I call the system in terms of p_z and Z the *virtual system*, and the system in terms of p and Q_1 the *real system*. The virtual system behaves like a neoclassical framework, and the relationship between the variables in it has been carefully explained in Chapter 2. In particular, the relationship between Z and Q_2 can be described graphically by a *virtual production possibility frontier* (virtual PPF) that behaves like a neoclassical PPF, being downward sloping and concave to the origin. The virtual PPF is represented by schedule TV in Figure 6.3. Point B gives the equilibrium Q_2^a and Z^a. Line AB is the virtual price line that has a slope of $-p_z$ and is tangent to the virtual PPF at point B.

I can define a *virtual GDP function*: $\widetilde{g}(p_z, \overline{K}, \overline{L})$, which behaves like an ordinary GDP function. In particular, when given the equilibrium p_z^a, where the superscript "a" after a variable represents the autarkic value of the variable, I have

$$\widetilde{g}(p_z^a, \overline{K}, \overline{L}) = p_z^a Z^a + Q_2^a. \tag{6.31}$$

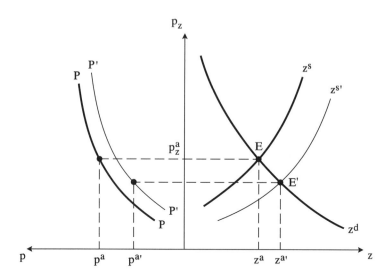

Figure 6.4

The value of the virtual GDP, in terms of good 2, is given by the vertical intercept of the virtual price line, that is, OA.

The virtual system should be contrasted with the real system, which is described by Q_2, p and Q_1. If by a choice of scale $\gamma(q_1) > q_1$ for $q_1 > 0$, then Q_1 is less than Z for any given $Q_2 > 0$. This is the case shown in Figure 6.3 in which the real PPF, TR, is below the virtual PPF except at point T where they coincide. Because for sector 1 marginal cost is generally less than p, the price line is in general not tangent to the real PPF. In the diagram, line AC is the price line with a slope of $-p^a$. The national income of the economy is given by

$$g^a = n^a p^a q_1^a + Q_2^a. \tag{6.32}$$

Compare the virtual GDP given by (6.31) and the national income given by (6.32). Using the definition of p_z and Z, it can be seen that $g^a = \tilde{g}(p_z^a, \overline{K}, \overline{L})$. In other words, the virtual price line and the real price line have the same vertical intercept, point A in Figure 6.3. Point C is the real production point, and points B and C correspond to the same output of good 2.

I now turn back to the virtual system. Recall that in this system both Z and Q_2 can be expressed as functions of p_z. This implies that $z^s = Z/Q_2$ can be expressed as a function of p_z, and this function is an increasing one. Function $z^s(p_z)$ is illustrated graphically in Figure 6.4 by schedule z^s. (Ignore the left-hand side of the diagram and schedule $z^{s\prime}$ for the time being.)

Figure 6.4 also shows schedule z^d, the relationship between p_z and z^d as given by (6.25e). This schedule is downward sloping. Condition (6.30) is depicted by the intersecting point between schedule z^s and z^d, or point E. This point gives the autarkic value of p_z, and once it is known, the equilibrium values of Z, Q_2, w, and r can be obtained in the usual way. Using the results in a neoclassical framework (explained in Chapter 2), Z (respectively Q_2) is an increasing (respectively decreasing) function of p_z. Without loss of generality, assume that sector 1 is capital intensive. Thus r (respectively w) is an increasing (respectively decreasing) function of p_z. Moreover, the magnification effects (Jones, 1965) are valid for p_z and the factor prices; for example, if $\widehat{p}_z > 0$, where the "hat" represents the rate of growth of a variable, then

$$\widehat{r} > \widehat{p}_z > 0 > \widehat{w}. \tag{6.33}$$

I now determine n and q_1. The solution can be obtained by using Figure 6.5. Schedule EE describes equation (6.29). To get the slope of schedule EE, differentiate both sides of the equation to give

$$\frac{1}{\eta^2}\frac{d\eta}{dn}dn = \frac{\gamma q_1 \gamma'' + \gamma\gamma' - (\gamma')^2 q_1}{\gamma^2}dq_1. \tag{6.34}$$

Note that $\gamma'' \overline{c}_1(w, r)$ is the rate of change of marginal cost. I assume that marginal cost is either rising or is not falling too quick with a firm's capacity so that $\gamma'' > -\gamma'/(q_1\eta)$. This implies that the fraction on the right-hand side of (6.34) is positive.[7] Under the love of variety approach, $d\eta/dn = 0$, meaning that schedule EE in Figure 6.5 is a vertical line. Under the ideal variety approach, $d\eta/dn$ is assumed to be positive and schedule EE is positively sloped.

After Z has been chosen, schedule ZZ in Figure 6.5 depicts equation (6.25b): $n = Z/\gamma(q_1)$. The intersecting point, F, between schedules ZZ and EE gives the equilibrium value of n and q_1. If there is an increase in Z, schedule ZZ shifts up and to the right, implying a higher level of q_1 and a larger n. (In the love of variety approach, schedule EE is a vertical line, meaning that the equilibrium value of q_1 is fixed.) Because Z is an increasing function of p_z, so are q_1 and n.

What is left to be determined for this closed economy is the relative price p. Differentiate both sides of (6.25a) to give

$$dp = \left[p_z\frac{q_1\gamma'(q_1) - \gamma}{q_1^2}\frac{dq_1}{dp_z} + \frac{\gamma(q_1)}{q_1}\right]dp_z. \tag{6.35}$$

---

7. Condition (6.29) can be rearranged to give

$$\frac{\gamma'}{q_1}\frac{-1}{\eta} = \frac{\gamma'}{q_1}\left(\frac{\gamma' q_1}{\gamma} - 1\right).$$

Thus $\gamma'' > -\gamma'/(q_1\eta)$ implies that $\gamma q_1 \gamma'' + \gamma\gamma' - (\gamma')^2 q_1 > 0$.

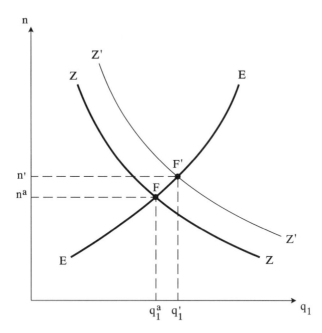

Figure 6.5

Because the average cost curve is assumed to be falling, $q_1\gamma'(q_1) < \gamma(q_1)$. Thus in (6.35) the sign of $\mathrm{d}p/\mathrm{d}p_z$ is ambiguous. If the decrease in average cost with respect to q_1 and the value of $\mathrm{d}q_1/\mathrm{d}p_z$ are significant, p may depend negatively on p_z. This creates a perverse case in which an increase in p_z raises q_1 but lowers p, implying a negative relationship between the price of each variety and the supply of the variety. Of course, under the love of variety approach, q_1 is independent of p_z, and $\mathrm{d}p/\mathrm{d}p_z > 0$ as implied by (6.35).

The possibility of such a perverse case can be illustrated in Figure 6.6 for a representative firm. Schedules labeled AC and MC are the average cost and marginal cost curves. Both the AC and MC curves are drawn under the assumption that factor prices, and hence p_z, are given. MC cuts the marginal revenue curve (labeled MR) at E (profit maximization as given by condition 6.20), which is directly below the point of tangency between AC and the demand curve labeled D (zero profit, condition 6.21). The initial equilibrium is (q_1^a, p^a). Suppose that there is an increase in p_z. The AC curve shifts up to AC$'$. Suppose that the new demand curve is at D$'$ (with zero profit). The point of tangency, F$'$, shows that the price p has fallen. For simplicity, however, I rule out this perverse case by assuming that $\mathrm{d}q_1/\mathrm{d}p_z$ is not significant (as under the love of variety approach).

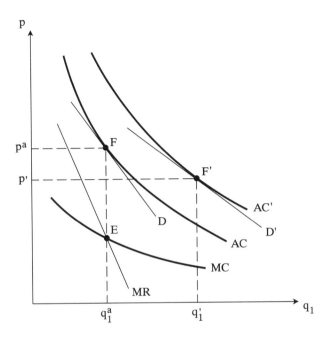

Figure 6.6

6.4 Effects of Factor Accumulation

This section examines how factor accumulation may affect production and consumption of the economy. On the production side, the effects on plant size and the number of varieties is examined. The possible change in the number of varieties has received much attention in the literature. It has been shown that in some models, when an economy gets bigger, it will produce more varieties (Krugman, 1979a; Lawrence and Spiller, 1983). The same result may or may not exist in other models.

As discussed earlier, in terms of factor endowments and variables w, r, p_z, Z and Q_2, the present framework has a production structure the same as that of a neoclassical model. To make use of this feature, I first derive the effects of increases in factor endowments on p_z, Z, and Q_2. Using the "hat" notation and the results in Chapter 2, the equations of change can be written as

$$\lambda_{L1}\widehat{Z} + \lambda_{L2}\widehat{Q}_2 = \widehat{L} + \delta_L(\widehat{w} - \widehat{r}) \tag{6.36a}$$

$$\lambda_{K1}\widehat{Z} + \lambda_{K2}\widehat{Q}_2 = \widehat{K} - \delta_K(\widehat{w} - \widehat{r}), \tag{6.36b}$$

where λ_{Li} and λ_{Ki} are the labor and capital shares, respectively, of sector i, $\delta_L = \lambda_{L1}\theta_{K1}\sigma_1 + \lambda_{L2}\theta_{K2}\sigma_2$, $\delta_K = \lambda_{K1}\theta_{L1}\sigma_1 + \lambda_{K2}\theta_{L2}\sigma_2$, and θ_{Li} and θ_{Ki} are the shares of labor and capital incomes, respectively, in sector i. I first derive how changes in factor endowments under constant p_z (or constant w and r) may affect z^s. Denote the change in z^s due to changes in factor endowments when p_z is fixed by Δz^s. So the change in z^s is equal to $dz^s = z_p^s dp_z + \Delta z^s$, where z_p^s is the partial derivative with respect to p_z when factor endowments are constant. Keeping w and r (and thus p_z) constant, conditions (6.36) can be solved for $\widehat{Z}$ and $\widehat{Q}_2$ at constant p_z, and by rearranging terms,

$$\Delta z^s = \frac{z^0(\widehat{\overline{L}} - \widehat{\overline{K}})}{|\lambda|}, \tag{6.37}$$

where z^0 is the initial value of $z^s = z^d$ and where $|\lambda| = \lambda_{L1} - \lambda_{K1} = \lambda_{K2} - \lambda_{L2}$. Because sector 1 is assumed to be capital intensive, $|\lambda| < 0$.

Let $z_p^i \equiv \partial z^i / \partial p_z$, $i = s, d$. Differentiate both sides of the equilibrium condition $z^s = z^d$ to give

$$z_p^s dp_z + \Delta z^s = z_p^d dp_z, \tag{6.38}$$

or, after rearranging terms,

$$dp_z = \frac{1}{z_p^d - z_p^s} \Delta z^s. \tag{6.38'}$$

In (6.38'), dp_z is the change in the equilibrium p_z. Using it, I can determine the change in z, which is equal to

$$dz = z_p^d dp_z = \frac{z_p^d}{z_p^d - z_p^s} \frac{z^0(\widehat{\overline{L}} - \widehat{\overline{K}})}{|\lambda|}. \tag{6.39}$$

Define $\varepsilon_z^s \equiv p_z z_p^s / z^s$ as the price elasticity of z^s. This is a measure of the response of Z/Q_2 to a change in p_z as the production point slides down the virtual PPF (with fixed factor endowments). As the virtual PPF is downward sloping, $\varepsilon_z^s > 0$. Differentiate condition (6.25e) with respect to p_z to give

$$z_p^d = -\frac{\alpha}{1 - \alpha} \frac{1}{p_z^2}. \tag{6.40}$$

Substitute the value of z_p^d given by (6.40) into (6.39) to give

$$dz = \frac{\alpha}{\alpha + A} \frac{z^0(\widehat{\overline{L}} - \widehat{\overline{K}})}{|\lambda|}, \tag{6.39'}$$

where $A \equiv (1 - \alpha) p_z z^0 \varepsilon_z^s > 0$. Condition (6.39') implies that

$$\widehat{Z} - \widehat{Q}_2 = \widehat{z}^s = \frac{\alpha}{\alpha + A} \frac{(\widehat{\overline{L}} - \widehat{\overline{K}})}{|\lambda|}. \tag{6.41}$$

Condition (6.41) and the equations of change can be solved for $\widehat{Z}$ and $\widehat{Q}_2$ (after eliminating $\widehat{w} - \widehat{r}$). After rearranging terms, I get

$$\widehat{Z} = \frac{\left[\delta_K A|\lambda| + \alpha\lambda_{K2}(\delta_L + \delta_K)\right]\widehat{L} + \left[\delta_L A|\lambda| - \alpha\lambda_{L2}(\delta_L + \delta_K)\right]\widehat{K}}{|\lambda|(\delta_L + \delta_K)[\alpha + A]} \quad (6.42\text{a})$$

$$\widehat{Q}_2 = \frac{\left[\delta_K A|\lambda| - \alpha\lambda_{K1}(\delta_L + \delta_K)\right]\widehat{L} + \left[\delta_L A|\lambda| + \alpha\lambda_{L1}(\delta_L + \delta_K)\right]\widehat{K}}{|\lambda|(\delta_L + \delta_K)[\alpha + A]}. \quad (6.42\text{b})$$

Before proceeding, let me illustrate graphically what has been obtained so far. For illustration, assume that there is an increase in the capital stock while the labor endowment is constant, that is, $\widehat{K} > 0$ and $\widehat{L} = 0$. Condition (6.37) implies that $\Delta z^s > 0$, or in terms of Figure 6.4, a rightward shift of schedule z^s. Let the new schedule be represented by the one labeled $z^{s\prime}$. The other schedule in the diagram, z^d, is not affected by the capital accumulation (see condition 6.25e).

The equilibrium is again given by the intersection point between schedules z^d and $z^{s\prime}$. This new equilibrium point, E′, shows a decrease in p_z and an increase in z. The changes in p_z and z are what equations (6.38′) and (6.39′) give, respectively. Note that the increase in z is less than what it may be should p_z not change.

Because of the increase in z and because of the expansion of the virtual PPF, there is an increase in Z and possibly a decrease in Q_2, as equations (6.42a) and (6.42b) state. In Figure 6.5, schedule ZZ, which describes condition (6.25b), shifts up and to the right. Let the new schedule be denoted by Z′Z′. Schedule EE, which comes from condition (6.29), remains stationary, cutting schedule Z′Z′ at point F′. The diagram shows that there is an increase in both the plant size and the number of varieties in sector 1.

The effect of capital accumulation on the relative price of good 1 is not so clear. First, notice that even if p_z does not change, the expansion of the virtual PPF implies an increase in Z. This shifts up schedule ZZ in Figure 6.5. Suppose that the ideal variety of preferences is represented, then schedule EE is positively sloped, meaning that the upward shift of schedule ZZ gives an expansion of the plant size in sector 1, q_1. Thus the relative price of good 1, as given by (6.25a), falls even if p_z remains constant. The left-hand side of Figure 6.4 shows schedule PP, which illustrates the relationship between p and p_z. Given these types of preferences, schedule PP shifts toward the axis of p_z. Let the new schedule be P′P′. If, however, the love of variety approach with a CES utility function is used, schedule EE is a vertical line and the plant size remains unchanged. In this case, condition (6.25a) implies that p_z is directly proportional to p, and schedule PP in Figure 6.4 is a ray from the origin and is independent of changes in schedule ZZ in Figure 6.5.

If there is a positive relationship between p_z and p, the decrease in p_z due to a capital accumulation together with the rightward shift of schedule PP implies a decrease in p as well. If the relationship between p_z and p is negative in the perverse case, the change in p is not certain. In that case, capital accumulation could make good 1 more expensive relatively.

In the preceding analysis, I considered the case in which only the capital stock grows while the labor endowment is fixed. In fact, by using (6.42a) and (6.42b), the analysis is still valid in a qualitative sense as long as $\widehat{K} \geq \widehat{L} \geq 0$ with at least one strict inequality. Thus if capital and labor grow by the same proportion, $\widehat{K} = \widehat{L} > 0$, then $\widehat{Z} = \widehat{Q}_2 = \widehat{K}$ and there is an increase in the number of varieties and the plant size of the firms in sector 1 (the same plant size under the love of variety approach).[8]

One interesting issue that can be addressed using the framework is whether the number of varieties must necessarily go up. It is clear from Figure 6.5 that the change in n depends crucially on the shift in schedule ZZ, which in turn depends on whether Z increases. To determine the latter, refer to equation (6.42a). Because $|\lambda| < 0$, one can conclude that $\widehat{Z} < 0$, and thus n *decreases*, if and only if

$$\left[\alpha\lambda_{K2}(\delta_L + \delta_K) + \delta_K A|\lambda|\right]\widehat{L} > \left[\alpha\lambda_{L2}(\delta_L + \delta_K) - \delta_L A|\lambda|\right]\widehat{K}. \tag{6.43}$$

Condition (6.43) implies that each of the following conditions is sufficient for an *increase* in Z and n: (1) $\widehat{L} = \widehat{K} > 0$ (as just analyzed) and (2) an increase in the endowment of the factor used intensively in the differentiated-product sector.

6.5   Free Trade in Goods

To analyze trade in goods, another country is introduced. The countries are labeled home and foreign, using asterisks to denote the variables of the foreign country. Assume that the countries have identical technologies and preferences (except for the ideal varieties of consumers). In the love of variety approach, consumers have identical utility functions; for example, the utility functions can be of the CES type or are additively separable as I described earlier. In the ideal variety approach, consumers in the world are indexed according to

---

8. This case is similar to the result in the case of labor force growth in Krugman's (1979) one-sector framework.

The result that no more than one firm in the world will produce the same variety depends crucially on the assumption of no transport and transaction costs. Krugman (1991) explains how the existence of fixed costs and transport costs could lead to firms in different locations producing the same variety. Wong and Yang (1994), on the other hand, introduce transaction costs to explain the relationship between the growth rate of population and the growth rate of per capita income.

their ideal varieties and they are distributed uniformly on the circumference of the circle. The consumers do have the same upper-tier utility function of the Cobb-Douglas type.

Assume that the home country is capital abundant physically. I begin with a case in which the home country is not smaller than the foreign country. Thus $\overline{K} > \overline{K}^*$ and $\overline{L} \geq \overline{L}^*$. I further assume that the factor endowments of the countries do not differ too much so that no country is completely specialized. In this case, I make direct use of the results in the previous section.

Free trade is now permitted between the countries. Assuming no transport costs, the commodity markets are fully integrated. Consumers in either country can purchase varieties from their own country and varieties from the other country. Again, because of the economies of scale in producing the differentiated products, no more than one firm in the world will produce the same variety.

Denote the number of varieties the home (respectively foreign) country produces under free trade by n (respectively n^*). Define N as the total number of varieties in the world, that is, $N = n + n^*$.

Both countries have the same production structure, which, in terms of p_z and Z, are described by equations (6.25a), (6.25b), (6.25c), (6.18), (6.26), (6.27), and (6.28). Again with symmetry of the differentiated goods on both the consumption and demand sides, both countries have the same relative price of the varieties. The commodity price equalization condition can be stated as:

$$p = p^*. \tag{6.44}$$

The consumption demands are dependent on the total number of varieties. Applying the analysis given previously, in the ideal variety approach, the market demands of the home and foreign countries for a variety are

$$C_1 = \frac{\alpha m I}{N p} \tag{6.45a}$$

$$C_1^* = \frac{\alpha m^* I^*}{N p}, \tag{6.45b}$$

where the commodity equalization condition in (6.44) has been used. Note that the demand for a variety depends on the number of varieties in the world, not on the varieties in each country.

The elasticity of market demand depends on N (in the ideal variety approach). Thus I can write $\eta = \eta(N)$. In the love of variety approach, as explained before, η is a constant. In either approach, equation (6.29) for the countries reduces to

$$1 - \frac{1}{\eta} = \varepsilon_\gamma(q_1) \tag{6.46a}$$

$$1 - \frac{1}{\eta} = \varepsilon_\gamma(q_1^*) \tag{6.46b}$$

Conditions (6.46a) and (6.46b) have a very important implication. Because the firms in both countries face the same demand elasticity, η, the conditions imply that they must have the same plant size in equilibrium, that is, $q_1 = q_1^*$.[9]

The market demand for good 2 in the countries are equal to

$$C_2 = (1 - \alpha)mI \tag{6.47a}$$

$$C_2^* = (1 - \alpha)m^*I^*. \tag{6.47b}$$

Using these market demands, the new variable z^d can be defined as:

$$z^d = \frac{N(C_1 + C_1^*)\gamma(q_1)}{(C_2 + C_2^*)q_1}, \tag{6.48}$$

where the result is that firms in both countries have the same plant size. This definition is similar to that given in (6.25d). Making use of the definition of market demands in (6.45) and (6.47), z^d reduces to

$$z^d = \frac{\alpha}{1 - \alpha} \frac{1}{p_z}, \tag{6.48'}$$

where the fact that $p = p^*$ and $q_1 = q_1^*$ has been used. The form of z^d in (6.48') is exactly the same as that of z^d in (6.25e). The last thing to specify is the market clearing conditions for goods:

$$q_1 = C_1 + C_1^* \tag{6.49a}$$

$$Q_2 + Q_2^* = C_2 + C_2^*. \tag{6.49b}$$

Condition (6.49a) states that the supply of variety by each firm is equal to the demand for that variety of the consumers in both countries, and condition (6.49b) requires the same supply of and demand for good 2 in the world. By Walras's law, one of the them is redundant in determining the equilibrium.

As discussed earlier, it is convenient to state the market clearing conditions under free trade as given by (6.49) in an alternative form:

---

9. Helpman (1981) points out that this result is also valid in a more general framework. As mentioned, in the ideal variety approach, the market demand elasticity in general depends on p and N. Thus equations (6.18), (6.26), and (6.46a) are for the production side of each country. Free trade means that the countries have the same relative price of a variety as given by condition (6.44). Thus there are three unknowns, w, r and q_1. If these three conditions are globally invertible, the countries have the same factor prices and plant size.

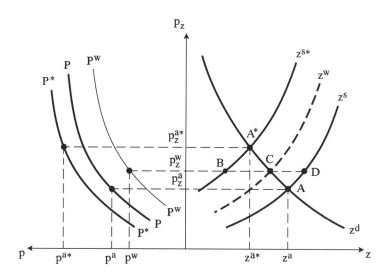

Figure 6.7

$$\varphi z^s + (1 - \varphi)z^{s*} = z^d, \tag{6.50}$$

where $\varphi = Q_2/(Q_2 + Q_2^*)$ is the share of the home country's good-2 output in the world. Condition (6.50) states that in equilibrium, z^d is a weighted average of z^s and z^{s*}. Because outputs of goods and z^d are functions of p_z, condition (6.50) states that p_z has to be chosen to satisfy the condition. Denote the equilibrium value of p_z by p_z^w.

Condition (6.50) provides a simple way to illustrate the free-trade equilibrium in Figure 6.7. In the diagram schedules z^s and z^{s*} represent the relationship between the corresponding variables and p_z for the countries as given by condition (6.25c). Similarly, the schedule labeled z^d gives the p_z-z^d relationship for the countries as given by (6.25e). Note that because of identical utility function (identical upper-tier utility function under the ideal variety approach) the two countries have the same z^d-schedule. Note also that these three schedules are not affected by trade. This means that the points at which the z^s-schedule and z^{s*}-schedule cut the z^d-schedule represent the autarkic equilibria of the countries. These points are shown as points A and A* in the diagram. Denote by p_z^a and p_z^{a*} the autarkic values of p_z in the home and foreign countries, respectively.

For any closed economy, a capital accumulation will raise the autarkic wage-rental ratio. I am now ready to establish the following results.

Result 6.1 Given no factor intensity reversal, the physical definition of factor endowment abundance is equivalent to the price definition of factor endowment abundance.

Result 6.1, which is the same as that in a neoclassical framework, it is not surprising because the present framework with differentiated products behaves (in terms of p_z and Z) like a neoclassical framework. Furthermore, this result does not depend on the sizes of the countries.

Result 6.2   The countries engage in intraindustry trade in differentiated products.

Result 6.3   The pattern of intraindustry trade is indeterminate.

Result 6.2 is also stated in equation (6.49a). Each firm in a country supplies one variety with an output level of q_1. The demand for the variety comes partly from the home country, C_1, and partly from the foreign country, C_1^*. For a variety that is produced in the home country, $q_1 - C_1$ is the home country's export, and for a variety that is produced in the foreign country, C_1 is the home country's import. As long as both countries are producing some varieties, intraindustry trade in the differentiated products exists. Result 6.3 is due to the fact that it does not matter whether a particular variety is produced in the home or foreign country because both countries have identical technologies in producing the differentiated products.

Intraindustry trade in the present framework is based on two features of the framework. First, the differentiated products are treated in a symmetric way. When the prices of the varieties are the same, each country has uniform demands for the varieties under the love of variety and the ideal variety approaches. Second, the firms producing the varieties enjoy economies of scale. This implies that no more than one firm produce each variety. Free trade thus provides an environment in which some of the varieties consumers purchase are produced in the home country and some produced in the foreign country. Intraindustry trade in the differentiated products is the result.

Figure 6.7 can be used to derive more results. First, the results in the previous section shows that when the home country has more capital but at least the same amount of labor, its z^s-schedule must be lower and to the right of the foreign z^{s*}-schedule. This is the case shown in the diagram. Thus $p_z^a < p_z^{a*}$. Second, as long as both countries are producing positive outputs of good 2, p_z^w has to be in between p_z^{a*} and p_z^a, that is,

$$p_z^{a*} > p_z^w > p_z^a. \tag{6.51}$$

Third, because the z^s-schedule is on the right-hand side of the z^{s*}-schedule, the equilibrium value of z^s is greater than that of z^{s*}. Using the definition of the z^s and the fact that all firms have the same plant size, I have

$$\frac{n}{Q_2} > \frac{n^*}{Q_2^*}. \tag{6.52}$$

Multiply both sides of (6.52) by pq_1 and rearrange terms to give[10]

$$\frac{npq_1}{Q_2} > \frac{Npq_1}{Q_2 + Q_2^*} > \frac{n^*pq_1}{Q_2^*}. \tag{6.52$'$}$$

The middle term in (6.52$'$) is the ratio of the value of world's output of good 1 to that of good 2, and because of the Cobb-Douglas utility function, it is equal to $\alpha/(1-\alpha)$. Thus the condition reduces to

$$\frac{npq_1}{Q_2} > \frac{\alpha}{1-\alpha} > \frac{n^*pq_1}{Q_2^*}. \tag{6.52$''$}$$

Condition (6.52$''$) provides bounds on the values of the ratio of the output in sector 1 to that in sector 2 in each country.

More results about free trade between the countries can be derived as follows. Because the foreign country has a higher autarkic value of p_z and because sector 1 is capital intensive, the foreign country has a lower autarkic wage-rental ratio. (See also Section 6.4.) Under free trade, the two countries face the same p_z, implying that the two countries have the same wage-rental ratio. This ratio is bounded by the autarkic wage-rental ratios of the countries. In fact, with the same numeraire, the two countries have the same free-trade wage and rental rates.[11]

Result 6.4   With diversification and no factor intensity reversal, the two countries have the same factor prices under free trade. The free-trade factor price ratio is bounded by the autarkic factor price ratios of the countries.

Result 6.4 implies that if free trade equalizes factor prices, the free-trade equilibrium is identical to an integrated equilibrium of the world with free movement of goods and factors. In other words, the equilibrium is the same as the equilibrium if the home country, while remaining closed, has factor accumulation by amounts equal to the factor endowments in the foreign country. Because the home country is capital abundant, the integration of the two markets means that the home country gains relatively more labor than capital. The analysis in the previous section implies that the home country's new z^s-schedule is on the old schedule's left-hand side. Denote this new schedule

---

10. To get condition (6.52$'$), the following condition is used: $a/b > c/d$ implies

$$\frac{a}{b} > \frac{a+c}{b+d} > \frac{c}{d},$$

where a, b, c, and d are positive numbers.

11. Factor price equalization is valid with some other more general utility functions. See footnote 9.

by z^w, which is shown by the broken schedule in Figure 6.7. The intersection point between this schedule and schedule z^d is the new equilibrium point, which is the same as the free-trade point. By applying the same analysis to the foreign country, I conclude that schedule z^w must be in between the countries' supply schedules.

I now make use of (6.52″) to derive the patterns of interindustry trade of the countries. Subtract the home country's consumption of good 2 from its production of the good to give

$$C_2 - Q_2 = (1 - \alpha)(npq_1 + Q_2) - Q_2$$

$$= (1 - \alpha)npq_1 - \alpha Q_2$$

$$> 0. \tag{6.53}$$

This means that the home country imports good 2. The budget constraint of the home country is

$$npq_1 + Q_2 = NpC_1 + C_2. \tag{6.54}$$

In (6.54), C_1 is the home country's demand for each variety, and so NpC_1 is the value of its demand for N varieties. Rearrange the terms in (6.54) to give

$$C_2 - Q_2 = p[n(q_1 - C_1) - n^*C_1]. \tag{6.54'}$$

In (6.54′), I used the fact that $N = n + n^*$. On the right-hand side of the condition, $n(q_1 - C_1)$ is the home country's export of the varieties it produces, and n^*C_1 is its imports of the varieties the foreign country produces and exports. (Remember that no two firms produce the same variety.) Thus the right-hand side of (6.54′) is the home country's net export of the differentiated goods. By (6.54), which is the country's balance of trade, the net export of the differentiated products is positive. The results are summarized as follows.

Result 6.5   The capital-abundant country imports the labor-intensive homogeneous good and is a net exporter of the capital-intensive differentiated goods.

I explained that in the absence of factor intensity reversal, the physical definition of factor abundance is equivalent to the price definition of factor abundance. Thus both the physical factor endowments and the autarkic factor prices of the countries are good predictors of the countries' intersectoral patterns of trade. Of course, as explained previously, the autarkic values of p_z in the countries can also be used to predict their intersectoral patterns of trade, but p_z is not observable, and its autarkic value is hard to estimate, even if the autarkic prices of commodities are known.

A related issue is whether the autarkic values of p can be used to predict the intersectoral patterns of trade. In other words, is the law of comparative advantage valid?

The answer to this question depends on the type of preferences. Consider first the ideal variety approach. Recall that schedules PP and P*P* on the left-hand side of Figure 6.7 illustrate the relationship between p and p_z of the home and foreign countries, respectively. I showed that if the average cost curve faced by a differentiated product firm is not falling too rapidly or under the love of variety approach, schedules PP and P*P* are positively sloped, as the diagram shows. In the case shown in the diagram, the home country has a lower autarkic value of p, that is, $p^a < p^{a*}$. Because the home country has a net export of good 1 under free trade, this seems to suggest that the law of comparative advantage is valid. But this is not correct. First, schedules PP and P*P* may be negatively sloped if the average cost in the differentiated product sector falls rapidly. Second, even if both schedules are positively sloped, their relative positions depends on the sizes of countries. If, for example, the home country is smaller even if it is still capital abundance in a relative sense, schedule PP shifts to the left. It is possible that schedule PP shifts so much to the left that the home country has a greater autarkic value of p than the foreign country does. This violates the law of comparative advantage.

Furthermore, the free-trade commodity price ratio may not have to be in the range bounded by the countries' autarkic price ratios. An example is shown in Figure 6.7. On the left-hand side of the diagram, schedules PP and P*P* represent the relationship between p-p_z of the home and foreign countries, respectively. In the case shown in the diagram, the home country has a lower autarkic price ratio, $p^a < p^{a*}$. As will be shown, under the ideal variety approach q_1 is greater under free trade than under autarky at any given level of p_z. By condition (6.25a) and the assumption that $\gamma(q_1) > q_1$, p is lower at a higher level of q_1 while p_z is fixed, meaning that schedule PP in Figure 6.7 shifts to the right under free trade. Let the new position of schedule PP be given by $P^w P^w$. This result is also true for the foreign country, meaning that P*P* also shifts to the right under trade, and its new position is the same as $P^w P^w$ because the two countries have the same plant size under free trade. If $P^w P^w$ is sufficiently close to the vertical axis, it is possible to have $p^{a*} > p^a > p^w$. This is the case shown.

The law of comparative advantage does hold if the preferences are of the love of variety and CES type. In this case, the plant size of a firm is not affected by foreign trade, and p_z is a constant multiple of p whether or not free trade exists. In Figure 6.7, schedules PP, P*P*, and $P^w P^w$ collapse to the same ray from the origin. Therefore both p and p_z are good predictors of country patterns of trade.

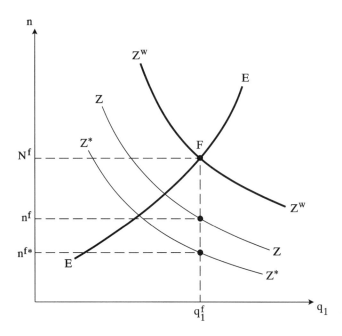

Figure 6.8

I now determine the effects of trade on the plant size and the number of varieties. In Figure 6.8, schedule EE is defined by equation (6.46a) or (6.46b) and is positively sloped. Note that η depends on the total number of varieties in the world, N. Schedule $Z^w Z^w$ illustrates the condition $N = (Z + Z^*)/\gamma(q_1)$, where Z and Z^* are obtained from the values of z^s and z^{s*} given by Figure 6.7 and the corresponding virtual PPFs of the countries. The intersecting point between the schedules, F, gives the free-trade values of N and q_1, and are denoted by N^f and q_1^f, respectively. The latter is the same for all firms in the differentiated sector in the countries. The diagram also shows schedules ZZ and Z^*Z^*, which represent the conditions $n = Z/\gamma(q_1)$ and $n^* = Z^*/\gamma(q_1)$, where Z and Z^* are the free-trade values. The values of n and n^* given by ZZ and Z^*Z^* when $q_1 = q_1^f$ are their free-trade values, n^f and n^{f*}.

It is interesting to compare N^f with the autarkic numbers of varieties in the countries, n^a and n^{a*}. Using specific models, Krugman (1979a, 1980) and Lancaster (1984) show that the number of varieties in the world under free trade is greater than what each country separately enjoys under autarky, i.e., $N^f > n^a, n^{a*}$, but using different models, Krugman (1981) and Lawrence and Spiller (1983) argue that the total number of varieties in the world is not affected by trade, that is, $N^f = n^a + n^{a*}$. In all of these cases, consumers in each country enjoy more varieties under free trade than under autarky even though the number of varieties produced in the world may decline under trade.

The results concerning the change in the number of varieties in the world are appealing and interesting. They reflect the desire of the consumers in both countries for greater varieties. More important, they suggest that the force to expand the product variety that comes from the consumers may be greater than the opposing force that comes from the firms, which tend to expand their production to enjoy the economies of scale. The economies of scale have the effect of attracting resources to a limited number of production locations.

However, do there exist other models in which the consumers in one (or both) of the countries experience a drop in the number of varieties under free trade? To analyze such a possibility, let me recall the effects of factor endowments for a closed economy analyzed in the previous section. Condition (6.42a) gives the change in Z when factor endowments increase, and no matter whether the preferences are of the love of variety type or of the ideal variety type, the change in n for the economy is positively related to the change in Z. Condition (6.42a) thus gives not only the sign of $\widehat{Z}$, but also that of $\widehat{n}$. This analysis can be applied here because it has been demonstrated that free trade between two economies can be interpreted as integration of the markets in the countries. From the consumers' point of view, free trade is the same as a growth of domestic factors. If in a closed economy a decrease in the number of varieties available to consumers is possible as factors grow, a decrease in the number of varieties for consumers is possible when free trade is allowed.

Recall that condition (6.43) is a necessary and sufficient condition for a decrease in the number of varieties for a closed economy as factors grow. By careful interpretation, this condition can be used to predict the change in the number of varieties for the consumers in a country under free trade. Because for each country free trade has the same effect on the number of varieties as an increase in factor endowments, there is an increase in the number of varieties for the consumers under trade if and only if the the value of the world Z^w is greater than the autarkic value of Z.[12]

6.6   Volumes of Trade

In the presence of intraindustry trade in differentiated products, one of the most interesting issues is about the volumes of trade. Even though the pattern of intraindustry trade is indeterminate, the volumes of trade, as will be seen,

---

12. This result is consistent with the result in a one sector model. See Krugman (1979a).

can be uniquely determined. Because of possible co-existence of interindustry trade and intraindustry trade, three different concepts of volumes of trade are explained and derived: the volume of total trade $[VT(total)]$, the volume of interindustry trade $[VT(inter)]$, and the volume of intraindustry trade $[VT(intra)]$. How these three types of volumes of trade depend on factor endowments are analyzed next.

6.6.1   The Volume of Total Trade

I explained earlier that due to the assumptions about factor abundance and factor intensity ranking of the sectors, the home country is a net exporter of the differentiated products and an importer of the homogeneous product. I also explained that with diversification of production, factor prices in the countries are equalized. I now make use of these results to explain the effects of factor endowments on the volume of total trade for the two countries analyzed earlier. To do this, let me assume that the world's factor endowments are fixed and examine how redistribution of factor endowments between the countries may affect the volume of trade. The analysis is limited to the countries of factor endowments with which factor price equalization holds.

Denote the wage and rental rates in the world under free trade by w^f and r^f, respectively. Using the factor prices, the national income levels of the countries are given by

$$g = w^f \overline{L} + r^f \overline{K} \tag{6.55a}$$

$$g^* = w^f \overline{L}^* + r^f \overline{K}^*, \tag{6.55b}$$

where $\overline{L}$ and $\overline{K}$ (respectively $\overline{L}^*$ and $\overline{K}^*$) are the home (respectively foreign) country's labor and capital endowments, respectively. From now on, I use the superscript "w" after a variable to represent that variable for the world. For example, $\overline{L}^w = \overline{L} + \overline{L}^*$ and $\overline{K}^w = \overline{K} + \overline{K}^*$ are the world's labor and capital endowments, respectively. Because in equilibrium all firms receive zero profit, I can write $g = pQ_1 + Q_2$ and $g^* = pQ_1^* + Q_2^*$, where $Q_1 = nq_1$ and $Q_1^* = n^*q_1$. Define $\psi \equiv g/g^w$ as the share of the home country's national income, where $g^w = g + g^*$. Thus $\psi^* \equiv g^*/g^w$ is the share of the foreign country's national income. Obviously $\psi + \psi^* = 1$ and both ψ and ψ^* depend on free-trade factor prices.

Slightly revising the notation used in previous chapters, define E_i (or M_i) as the home country's *value* of export (or import) of good i. Because of the possibility of intraindustry trade in the differentiated products, I have to distinguish between the home country's gross export E_1^g, which is the foreign country's consumption of these products, and its net export E_1^n. (These are of course the foreign country's gross and net imports of good 1, respectively.) Specifically, the export/import of goods of the home country are defined as:

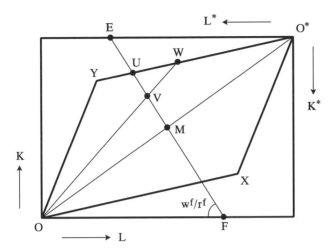

Figure 6.9

$$M_2 \equiv E_2^* = Q_2^* - \psi^* Q_2^w \tag{6.56a}$$

$$M_1 \equiv E_1^* = \psi p Q_1^* \tag{6.56b}$$

$$E_1^g = \psi^* p Q_1 \tag{6.56c}$$

$$E_1^n \equiv E_1^g - M_1 = p(\psi^* Q_1 - \psi Q_1^*). \tag{6.56d}$$

Because of balanced trade, these export levels are related to each other as follows:

$$E_1^g = E_1^* + E_2^*.$$

The volume of total trade can now be defined as the sum of the values of the countries' exports, that is,

$$VT(total) = E_1^g + E_1^* + E_2^*. \tag{6.57}$$

Because of balanced trade, $VT(total)$ can be expressed as

$$VT(total) = 2E_1^g = 2\psi^* p Q_1. \tag{6.57'}$$

Figure 6.9 shows the integrated equilibrium of the world. Given the free-trade prices, OX (= O*Y) is the world's output of good 2, while OY (= O*X) is the world's output of good 1, that is, $(n + n^*)q_1$. Because good 1 is capital intensive, OY (respectively OX) is steeper (respectively less steep) than the diagonal OO*. Point M is the mid-point of OO*, and EMF is the budget line of the countries with a slope of $-w^f/r^f$. Line OVW is any ray from origin O and is bounded by OY and OO*.

Because I require factor price equalization, I consider the effects of allocation of factor endowments between the countries represented by any point on or in the parallelgram OXO*Y. Using (6.57′), the rate of change in $VT(total)$ when the endowment point moves within parallelgram OXO*Y is equal to

$$\widehat{VT}(total) = \widehat{\psi^*} + \widehat{Q}_1, \tag{6.58}$$

where the equilibrium price p does not change. Using the definitions of ψ and ψ^*,

$$\widehat{\psi^*} = \widehat{g^*} = \frac{dg^*}{g^*} = -\frac{dg}{g^*} = -\frac{\psi}{\psi^*}\frac{dg}{g} = -\frac{\psi}{\psi^*}\widehat{g}.$$

Along ray OVW, the home country's labor and capital endowments increase at the same rate, implying that Q_1 and g also increase at the same rate, that is, $\widehat{g} = \widehat{Q}_1$. Combining these results,

$$\widehat{VT}(total) = \left(1 - \frac{\psi}{\psi^*}\right)\widehat{g}. \tag{6.58′}$$

In Figure 6.9, point V is a point on EF. Because EF passes through the mid-point of OO*, an endowment point on EF means that the countries are of the same size, that is, $\psi = \psi^*$. With an endowment point below (respectively above) EF, the home country is smaller (respectively larger) so that $\psi < \psi^*$ (respectively $\psi > \psi^*$). In other words, by condition (6.58′), at point V, $\widehat{VT}(total) = 0$. As the endowment shifts from the origin O along OW and before point V is reached, $VT(total)$ is increasing, and beyond point V, $VT(total)$ is decreasing. The maximum $VT(total)$ occurs at point V.

Now consider another movement of the endowment point. Starting from point V, let the endowment move along EF toward point U, a point on the side of the parallelgram. Because with an endowment point on line EF the two countries have the same size, when the endowment point moves from V to U, condition (6.58) reduces to

$$\widehat{VT}(total) = \widehat{Q}_1. \tag{6.58″}$$

Furthermore, the home country is getting more and more capital abundant. Thus its production of good 1 goes up, that is, producing more varieties and $\widehat{Q}_1 > 0$. Thus (6.58″) implies that $VT(total)$ is rising as the endowment point moves from point M toward point U.

By combining the results already given, combinations of endowment points that produce the same volume of total trade can be represented by iso-VT(total) curves in Figure 6.10. Curves farther away from the diagonal represent higher volumes of total trade. These curves are tangent to rays from

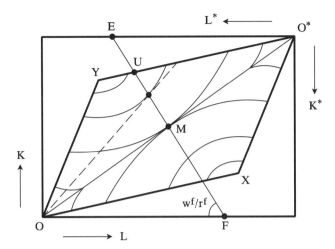

Figure 6.10

origin O at different points on EF, and are convex toward these rays.[13] The endowment point Y yields the biggest volume of total trade.[14]

The same argument can be used to derive the iso-VT(total) curves below the diagonal. Again, curves away the diagonal represent higher volumes of total trade. The curves below the diagonal are mirror image of those above the diagonal. The endowment point with the biggest volume of total trade is point X at which the home country is completely specialized in good 2.

6.6.2   The Volume of Interindustry Trade

The volume of interindustry trade is defined as the sum of the value of the home country's *net* export of good 1 and that of the foreign country's export of good 2, that is,

$$VT(inter) = E_1^n + E_2^*. \tag{6.59}$$

Using the definition of E_1^n given in (6.56d) and the trade balance, the volume of interindustry trade reduces to

$$VT(inter) = E_1^g - E_1^* + E_2^* = 2E_2^* = 2(Q_2^* - \psi^* Q_2^w). \tag{6.59'}$$

Thus the volume of interindustry trade is proportional to the foreign country's export of good 2.

---

13. See Helpman and Krugman (1985, Chapter 8) for a rigorous proof of this result.

14. Figure 6.10 shows the case in which EF cuts O*Y. In the case in which EF cuts OY, the endowment point that yields the highest volume of total trade is the point of intersection between EF and OY.

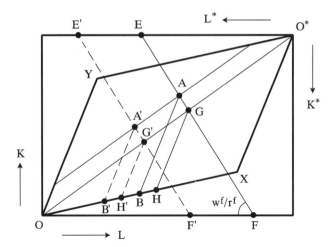

Figure 6.11

To determine how $VT(inter)$ is affected by a redistribution of factor endowments, refer to the integrated equilibrium of the world in Figure 6.11.
Suppose that the initial endowment is represented by point A. Through A,
let me construct line EF, which has a slope of $-w^f/r^f$. Let it cut the diagonal OO* at point G. Because of identical preferences of the countries (at least
with respect to the consumption of good 2), G is the consumption point of
the countries. From points A and G, draw two lines parallel to side OY of the
parallelgram, cutting side OX at B and H, respectively. It is easy to show that
BX is the foreign country's production of good 2 and HX is its consumption.
In other words, BH is the foreign country's export of good 2, and twice this
amount is the volume of interindustry trade.

Draw a line through point A and parallel to the diagonal. Suppose that the
endowment point shifts to A′, another point on this line. As before, construct
line E′F′, which is parallel to EF and cuts the diagonal at G′. The latter point
is the current consumption point of the countries. Again I draw lines A′B′ and
G′H′, which are parallel to OY, cutting side OX at B′ and H′, respectively. Using the preceding argument, two times B′H′ is the new volume of interindustry
trade.

Since by construction AA′G′G is a parallelgram, I have AA′ = GG′. Furthermore, because lines A′B′, AB, G′H′, and GH are parallel, so HH′ = BB′.
Using these results, BH = B′H′. Thus the volume of interindustry trade remains unchanged as the endowment point shifts from A to A′. I use the same
argument to show that a line parallel to the diagonal represents different endowment points with the same volume of interindustry trade. Thus
iso-VT(inter) curves are straight lines parallel to the diagonal, as Figure 6.12
illustrates.

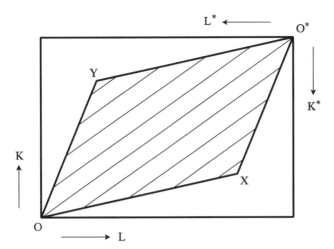

Figure 6.12

To compare the values of different iso-VT(inter) curves, suppose the endowment point A in Figure 6.11 is shifted up and along line EF. This will shift point B along OX toward origin O. Recall that twice the length of BH is the volume of interindustry trade. This implies that iso-VT(inter) lines farther away from the diagonal represent greater volumes of interindustry trade. Furthermore if point A coincides with point G, the volume of interindustry trade is zero, that is, the diagonal is the zero VT(inter) line.

6.6.3   Volume of Intraindustry Trade

I now turn to the volume of intraindustry trade, $VT(intra)$, which is defined as the volume of total trade minus the volume of interindustry trade. Thus, using (6.57′), (6.59′) and the trade balance,

$$VT(intra) = VT(total) - VT(inter) = 2E_1^g - (E_1^g - E_1^* + E_2^*) = 2E_1^*$$

$$= 2\psi p Q_1^*. \tag{6.60}$$

Again, to find the effects of redistribution of factor endowments on VT $(intra)$, I differentiate both sides of (6.60) and rearrange terms to give

$$\widehat{VT}(intra) = \widehat{\psi} + \widehat{Q}_1^*. \tag{6.61}$$

Note that condition (6.61) is similar to condition (6.58). Thus the analysis for the volume of total trade can be applied here to derive the iso-VT(intra) curves. In Figure 6.13, I construct rays such as O*W from the origin O* and line EF passing through the midpoint, M, of the diagonal. Line EF, which has a slope of $-w^f/r^f$ and cuts O*W at V, gives endowment points that

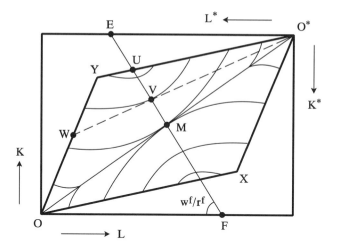

Figure 6.13

imply the same size for the countries. Using the previous argument, as the endowment point moves from O* toward W, the volume of intraindustry trade increases first, then decreases beyond point V. Alternatively, if the endowment point is on line EF, then as it moves from M toward E, $VT(intra)$ decreases monotonically. Point U where EF cuts O*Y is the endowment point with the minimum volume of intraindustry trade.[15] The same analysis applies to the endowment points in the lower half of the parallelgram OXO*Y. Based on this analysis, I can construct the iso-VT(intra) curves as shown in the diagram. They are convex toward rays from O* (respectively O) in the space above (respectively below) the diagonal, and is decreasing away from the diagonal.

6.6.4   Extent of Intraindustry Trade

The more interesting phenomenon of intraindustry trade is its extent. In the literature, it is commonly measured by the *index of trade overlap* (e.g., Hufbauer and Chilas, 1974; Grubel and Lloyd, 1975), which is defined as

$$\xi = 1 - \frac{\sum_j |E_j - M_j|}{\sum_j (E_j + M_j)}, \tag{6.62}$$

where E_j is the gross export of commodity j. In the present framework and in terms of the preceding notation, ξ is equal to

15. If alternatively EF cuts OY of the parallelgram, the endowment point with the minimum volume of intraindustry trade is at point Y.

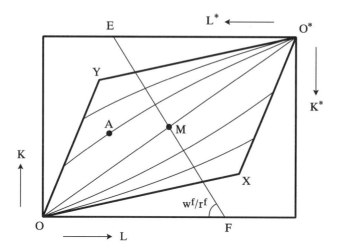

Figure 6.14

$$\xi = 1 - \frac{(E_1^g - E_1^*) + E_2^*}{E_1^g + E_1^* + E_2^*}$$

$$= \frac{2E_1^*}{2E_1^g} = \frac{\psi}{\psi^*} \frac{Q_1^*}{Q_1}. \tag{6.62'}$$

(6.62') shows that the index of trade overlap is equal to the share of intraindustry trade, that is,

$$\xi = \frac{VT(intra)}{VT(total)}. \tag{6.62''}$$

As given by (6.62'), ξ depends on two ratios, ψ/ψ^* and Q_1^*/Q_1. The effects of these two ratios can be analyzed separately. Figure 6.14 is similar to the previous diagrams showing the integrated equilibrium, with EF passing through the midpoint, M, of the diagonal. If I consider an endowment point such as A and move it along a line parallel to EF, the ratio ψ/ψ^* is constant. If A is above the diagonal and moves away from the diagonal, the home country, which is capital abundant, becomes more capital abundant. This means that the ratio Q_1^*/Q_1 decreases, and ξ decreases, too. In other words, the share of intraindustry trade increases if the endowment point moves along a line parallel to EF and toward the diagonal.

Next, move point A along a line parallel to OX. The outputs of good 1 in the countries remain constant, but if A is on the left-hand side of EF and moves toward the latter, the home country gets bigger. This means that ψ/ψ^* and ξ first increase and then decrease when point A continues to move beyond EF. Using this analysis, two conclusions can be made. First, if the endowment point is on the diagonal, $\xi = 1$: Trade is entirely intraindustry. Second, if the endowment point is on OX or O*Y, only one country produces the differentiated products, and $\xi = 0$. Trade is entirely interindustry. The iso-intraindustry-trade-share curves are given in Figure 6.14. See Helpman and Krugman (1985, Chapter 8) for the proof of the shapes of these curves.

6.7   International Factor Movement with Differentiated Products

So far I have assumed that factors are immobile internationally. I now relax this assumption and examine the effects of international factor movements. In this section, I consider only the case in which the countries allow factor movement across borders but not international trade in commodities. In the next section, I turn to the case in which commodity trade and factor movement are allowed, and I examine some issues related to their interdependence such as whether they are substitutes.

The case in which only factor movement is allowed is of interest for two reasons. First, it illustrates some of the features of international factor movement when individuals consume differentiated products. Second, it provides important information that will be used to compare international factor movement and commodity trade.

With product differentiation, the decision of factor owners about whether to move to another country becomes more complicated because the countries may have different numbers of varieties and because the number of varieties may be dependent on international factor movement. Although for each consumer the number of varieties and commodity prices are taken as given, the final equilibrium does depend on what commodities or varieties owners of the moving factors consume or repatriate. This interdependence between factor movement and varieties has to be recognized in the following analysis.

The simplest approach to analyzing international factor movement is to assume that owners of the moving factors repatriate only homogeneous products.[16] This approach is similar to the one used for the neoclassical framework with homogeneous products. In the present case without commodity trade, this approach is not appropriate because individuals consume both homogeneous and differentiated products. Thus owners of the moving factor must be allowed to repatriate differentiated products, or in the case in which they move with the factor (as in the case of labor migration) and consume in the destination country, they must be allowed to consume both homogeneous and differentiated products.

---

16. An example of using this approach is Helpman and Razin (1983).

The present analysis of the decision to move begins with the utility of the moving factor owners. In Section 6.1 of this chapter I showed that generally there are two approaches to modeling preferences. Obviously the decision of factor owners to move depends crucially on the approach. International capital movement under both approaches are analyzed in detail below.

6.7.1   Love of Variety Approach

For simplicity, I consider a CES subutility function. The demand for each variety is given by condition (6.7). In the symmetrical case, all varieties have the same equilibrium price, denoted by p. As a result, the demand of a representative consumer for each variety reduces to

$$d_1 = \frac{I_1}{np} \tag{6.7'}$$

(Recall that I_1 is the amount of the consumer's income spent on the differentiated products.) Condition (6.7') gives the subutility level from the consumption of the differentiated products

$$D_1 = \left(nd_1^\beta\right)^{1/\beta} = \frac{n^{1/(\sigma-1)}I_1}{p} = \frac{I_1}{\overline{p}}, \tag{6.63}$$

where $\overline{p} = p/[n^{1/(\sigma-1)}]$ is the effective price, which is not to be confused with $\widetilde{p}(\omega, \widetilde{\omega})$ introduced in Section 6.1. Note that because $\sigma > 1$, the effective price decreases as the number of varieties increases at a given level of p. Rearranging the terms in (6.63) gives $I_1 = \overline{p}D_1$, meaning that the budget constraint of the consumer reduces to $\overline{p}D_1 + D_2 \leq I$. Condition (6.3b), which gives the problem of the consumer in the second stage utility maximization, reduces to

$$\max_{D_1, D_2} u(D_1, D_2) \quad \text{s.t.} \quad \overline{p}D_1 + D_2 \leq I. \tag{6.64}$$

Condition (6.64) is similar to the ordinary utility maximization problem, with $\overline{p}$ interpreted as the price of good 1. This allows me to define the consumer's indirect utility function $v^\ell(\overline{p}, I)$ under this love of variety approach as the maximum utility given in (6.64). This indirect utility function behaves as the usual indirect utility function. In particular, its derivatives are

$$\frac{\partial v^\ell}{\partial \overline{p}} = -\lambda D_1 = -\lambda n^{\sigma/(\sigma-1)}d_1 < 0 \tag{6.65a}$$

$$\frac{\partial v^\ell}{\partial I} = \lambda > 0, \tag{6.65b}$$

where λ is the marginal utility of income which is assumed to be positive. Condition (6.65a) and the definition of $\overline{p}$ can be used to derive the effects of p and n on the consumer's welfare:

294   Chapter 6

$$\frac{\partial v^\ell}{\partial p} = \frac{1}{n^{1/(\sigma-1)}} \frac{\partial v^\ell}{\partial \overline{p}} = -\lambda d_1 n < 0,$$

$$\frac{\partial v^\ell}{\partial n} = -\frac{1}{\sigma-1} \frac{p}{n^{1/(\sigma-1)+1}} \frac{\partial v^\ell}{\partial \overline{p}} = \frac{\lambda p d_1}{\sigma-1} > 0.$$

In chapter 9, the indirect utility function is used to explain a consumer's decision to move and to derive the gains from trade.

Suppose that there are two countries, home and foreign, that have the same structures as described previously. Free trade is not allowed by the countries, but capital movement is permitted. The same analysis can be extended to labor mobility. To allow a comparison of capital-mobility equilibria and the free-trade equilibria derived previously, I assume that the two countries have identical technologies. Consumers in the countries have identical, homothetic preferences.

As capital moves from one country to another, the capital owners are free to consume or repatriate any bundles of commodities. To avoid any explicit commodity trade, however, assume either that the capital owners move with their capital and consume in the destination country or that they repatriate the appropriate bundles of commodities back to the source country for consumption. In the latter case, because the repatriated bundles of commodities may be different from the commodities available in the source country, it is assumed that the repatriated bundles cannot be resold in the local markets. In other words, the owners of the moving capital remit back the exact bundles of commodities they are going to consume.[17]

Suppose that every consumer in either country has one unit of capital. If the piece of capital works in the home country, an owner earns the home rental rate, r, which is used to purchase the differentiated and homogeneous products to maximize the consumer's utility. The utility level of the consumer is $v^\ell(\overline{p}, r)$. If alternatively that piece of capital works in the foreign country, the resulting utility is $v^\ell(\overline{p}^*, r^*)$. Thus we say that (1) home capital flows to the foreign country if $v^\ell(\overline{p}, r) < v^\ell(\overline{p}^*, r^*)$; and (2) foreign capital flows to the home country if $v^\ell(\overline{p}, r) > v^\ell(\overline{p}^*, r^*)$. The equilibrium condition is $v^\ell(\overline{p}', r') = v^\ell(\overline{p}^{*\prime}, r^{*\prime})$, where primes denote equilibrium values.

Consider Figure 6.15, which shows an Edgeworth box diagram. The diagram is used to explain capital mobility when the factor endowments of the countries are given by different points in the diagram. Suppose that the factor endowment is at point M, meaning that both countries have identical factor

---

17. If the owners of the moving capital are allowed to sell the bundles of commodities they remit back, they are engaging in international trade. This gives them a bigger incentive to move. Thus more capital will move than in the case in which resale of the repatriated bundles is not allowed.

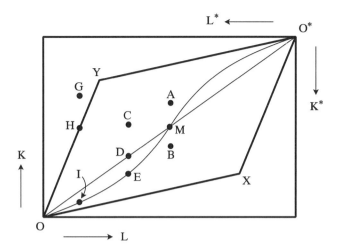

Figure 6.15

endowments. In isolation, both countries have the same autarkic prices and the same number of varieties. Thus if capital is now allowed to move, no capital mobility will exist because a capital owner gets the same utility no matter where that piece of capital works. Note that under the present approach the countries do not have to produce the same kinds of varieties. The utility of a consumer depends on the number of varieties and the quantity of each variety consumed, but not on exactly which varieties are consumed.

Suppose instead that the home country has more capital while the countries have the same amount of labor. The endowment is at a point like A, which is vertically above M in Figure 6.15. I explained earlier that capital accumulation leads to a greater number of varieties and a lower rental rate, and if the relationship between p_z and p is not perverse, then p will fall. Does such redistribution of capital between the countries affect the welfare of the capitalists in the countries? I assume that the welfare of a capitalist is affected primarily by the rental rate. This assumption means that the utility of the capitalists in the home country is now lower than that of those in the foreign country. As a result, when international capital mobility is allowed, the home country flows out to the foreign country until point M is reached. Similarly, if the endowment point is below M, such as point B, then foreign capital flows to the home country until point M is reached.

Suppose now that the endowment is at point C in Figure 6.15 so that the home country has a higher capital-labor ratio but less labor. To derive the final equilibrium, refer to Figure 6.16. Schedule HH is the relationship between n and p in the economy with different amounts of capital but the same labor endowment. As mentioned earlier, under the specified conditions, capital

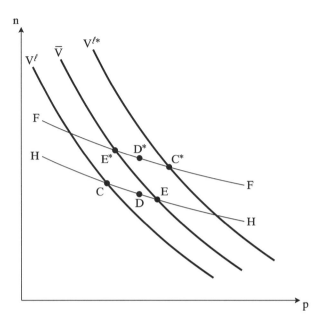

Figure 6.16

accumulation increases n but lowers p, implying a movement of a point up schedule HH toward the n-axis. Schedule FF shows the same relationship for the foreign country. Schedule FF is in general above schedule HH. To see why, suppose that the foreign country has more capital so that the countries have the same capital-labor ratio. Because the foreign country is bigger, the analysis in Section 6.4 shows that the countries have the same p but the foreign country has more varieties.

Figure 6.16 also shows the indifference curves of the capitalists. The slope of a curve is equal to

$$\frac{dn}{dp} = -\frac{v_p^\ell + \lambda dr/dp}{v_n^\ell},$$

where a subscript represents a derivative. In the absence of a perverse case and because of the assumed factor intensity ranking, $dr/dp > 0$. If it is assumed that the utility of a consumer is affected more by his or her income than by the price, then the numerator is positive. Thus an indifference curve is negatively sloped, but again because of a strong income effect, an indifference curve is steeper than schedules FF and HH.

Point C in Figure 6.15 corresponds to points C (for the home country) and C* (for the foreign country) in Figure 6.16. Schedules V^ℓ and $V^{\ell *}$ represent respectively the utility levels of capitalists in the home and foreign countries before any movement of capital. The analysis shows that $V^{\ell *} > V^\ell$. Thus if capital movement is allowed, home capital flows out. This is shown by a downward movement of point C in Figure 6.15. Sooner or later, point D is reached, which corresponds to points D and D* in Figure 6.16. At this point, both countries have the same commodity and factor prices. This is not, however, the final equilibrium because the foreign country has more varieties. Thus more home capital will flow out until a point like E in Figure 6.15 (points E and E* in Figure 6.16) is reached, and capitalists in both countries get an utility level of $\overline{V}$.

The same analysis can be applied to establish the equilibrium schedule under capital movement, OEMO*, in Figure 6.15. This schedule connects the two origins and passes through point M. It is below the diagram between OM but above the diagram between O*M.

Inflow of foreign capital in the present framework has interesting income-distributional implications. As I explained when analyzing a closed economy, capital accumulation tends to drive down the rental rate of capital. This means that an inflow of foreign capital has a negative price effect on the home capitalists. This effect is similar to the one that can be found in a neoclassical framework.

In the present framework, however, capital inflow can change the number of varieties in the economy. As condition (6.43) shows, because the differentiated-product sector is capital intensive, an inflow of foreign capital will increase the number of varieties in the economy. This benefits both the home capitalists and the home workers. For the home capitalists, if the positive effect outweighs the negative effect, an inflow of foreign capital can benefit all the residents in the home country.

In the above analysis, consumers in both countries have identical preferences. Therefore depending on the numbers and prices of varieties in both countries, capital will move either from the home country to the foreign country or from the foreign country to the home country, but not in both directions. If, however, the assumption of identical preferences assumption is dropped, then two-way movement (cross-hauling) of capital may exist. To understand this possibility, suppose that the two countries have different number of varieties and different effective prices (calculated using each country's elasticity of substitution). Then it is possible that home capital moves abroad because of more varieties there while foreign capital moves to the home country because of a lower effective price.

6.7.2   Ideal Variety Approach

I now turn to the ideal variety approach. Recall that in the first-stage of utility maximization as given by (6.11) a representative consumer chooses the optimal variety and spends the amount I_1 on this variety. The subutility level D_1 is the discounted quantity of this variety as given by condition (6.12). The second stage of the problem is then

$$\max_{D_1, D_2} \ u(D_1, D_2) \ \ \text{s.t.} \ \ \widetilde{p}(\omega, \widetilde{\omega})D_1 + D_2 \leq I. \tag{6.66}$$

Define $V^i(\widetilde{p}(\omega, \widetilde{\omega}), I)$ as the indirect utility function, which is the maximum utility given by condition (6.66). This indirect utility function has the following derivatives:

$$V_p = -\lambda d_1(\omega) < 0 \tag{6.67a}$$

$$V_\delta = -\frac{\lambda p d_1 h'}{h} < 0 \tag{6.67b}$$

$$V_I = \lambda > 0. \tag{6.67c}$$

The effects of p and I on a consumer's utility as given by (6.67a) and (6.67c) are similar to those in the traditional framework with homogeneous products. The effect of δ on the utility as given by (6.67b) means that the consumer gets a higher utility, when p and I do not change, if a variety closer to his or her ideal variety can be found.

Condition (6.67b) has an important implication on international capital movement: The decision to move abroad depends not only on prices but also on whether the factor owner can find a variety closer to his or her ideal variety. Let me again use the Edgeworth box diagram shown in Figure 6.15. Suppose that the endowment point is M so that the countries have identical factor endowments and technologies. I have shown that in the traditional framework with homogeneous products, or in the above framework with differentiated products under the love of variety approach, no factor will move between two identical countries even if it is allowed. Under the ideal variety approach, whether there is factor movement depends on the varieties produced in both countries.

As explained earlier for a closed economy, the exact locations of the varieties produced by firms are indeterminate even though the number of varieties can be determined. If I have two economies in separation, the same indeterminacy remains. This may lead to indeterminacy concerning factor movement.

Suppose that the countries produce exactly the same varieties. Then factor owners in both countries have no incentive to move. Suppose that the varieties produced in both countries are slightly different. Then some of the capital owners in each country will find that they can get a variety abroad closer to their ideal variety than all the varieties in their own country are. Thus they have an incentive to move their capital abroad even if the countries have the same rental rate and commodity prices. This is true for both countries, meaning that I now have a "two-way" international capital movement even though the net movement is zero. The volume of two-way flow increases as the varieties produced in the countries get farther apart.

If the firms in both countries are aware of the existence of international capital movement and if they take not only the prices and varieties produced by local firms as given, but also those produced by firms in another country as given, then the varieties produced in both countries under international capital mobility will be as far apart as possible. This means that the "two-way" capital movement will be maximized by the choice of variety of the firms.[18]

From now on, I focus on the net flow of capital. Using Figure 6.15, I want to show that the net capital movement under the ideal variety approach is similar to (but not necessarily the same as) the capital movement under the love of variety approach. Suppose that the endowment point is at point A, which is vertically above point M. The abundance of capital in the home country means a lower rental rate and more varieties. As explained previously, I assume that capitalists are more sensitive to their income than to the number of varieties. Thus there is a net outflow of home capital until point M is reached.

Suppose now that point C is the initial endowment point. Using the preceding argument, there is again a net outflow of home capital. As in the preceding case, point D is not an equilibrium because at this point the foreign country, being bigger, produces more varieties. Thus the foreign country still attracts a net inflow of capital. The final equilibrium is somewhere below point D, such as point E, at which the foreign rental rate is lower than the home rental rate.

The preceding analysis shows that the diagonal, except the origins and point M, do not represent equilibrium of international capital movement. Using the preceding techniques, I can construct the equilibrium schedule like (but not necessarily the same as) schedule OEMO*.

6.8 Commodity Trade and Factor Movement

I now compare commodity trade with factor mobility. I examine both their price relationship and quantity relationship.

6.8.1 Price Relationship

From the analysis in the previous section, I know that if initially only free international capital mobility but not commodity trade is allowed, the equilibrium will not be characterized by factor price equalization. Because of identical technologies, commodity prices will not be equalized either. Therefore if free trade is also allowed, flow of commodities will take place until the integrated equilibrium with equalization of commodity and factor prices

---

18. In the special case in which all capitalists in both countries have ideal varieties uniformly distributed, and so are the ideal varieties of all workers, then the varieties produced by firms in both countries will be uniformly distributed. In this case, half of the capitalists in each country will flow to the other country.

is reached. On the other hand, if the endowment point is in the factor price equalization set, free trade alone is sufficient to reach an integrated equilibrium point. Under this condition, free trade alone achieves world efficiency (as long as factor price equalization is achieved), but free capital mobility alone does not.

The more interesting case is the one in which the factor endowment point is not in the factor price equalization set. Suppose that the endowment point is at point G in Figure 6.15, which is between origin O's vertical axis and line OY. Suppose that free trade but not capital movement is allowed. Then at least one of the countries must be completely specialized: The home country may be specialized in the differentiated good, or the foreign country may be specialized in the homogeneous good. With either form of specialization, the home country has a lower rental rate under free trade. This means that in this case free trade alone is not enough to achieve world efficiency.

Suppose that international capital movement is also allowed. As long as the decision of capitalists in moving capital across countries is dominated by the income differential, home capital will move out to the foreign country. The final equilibrium is represented by either a point on OY (point H, shown in the diagram) or a point on O^*Y.[19] At this point, commodity and factor prices are equalized. In other words, both free trade and free factor movement are needed to achieved world efficiency. Using the terminology given in Chapter 3, commodity trade and factor mobility are said to be complements.

The diagram also shows the indeterminacy of factor movement. Suppose now that with the endowment point at G, initially only capital movement is allowed. Then some home capital flows to the foreign country. As explained previously, the equilibrium point, represented by point I, is a point on schedule OEMO*. Suppose that point I is in parallelgram OYO*X. If free trade is now allowed, then point I represents commodity and factor price equalization. If it is compared with point H, then it can be seen that any point between points H and I can give world efficiency under free trade and capital movement.

6.8.2   Quantity Relationship

I now turn to their quantity relationship. With factor price equalization, free trade eliminates any incentives to move factors internationally. International factor movement, however, does not eliminate free trade incentives. Thus an

---

19. To see the possibility of the second case, extend OY in Figure 6.15 to cut the L*-axis. If the endowment point is higher than point Y and close to the extended OY, home capital outflow will shift the endowment point downward until it cuts O*Y.

interesting issue is how international factor movement may affect the volume of trade.

The issue is not simple because the results depend on the initial factor endowments of the countries. Here I analyze only the effects of international factor movement on the index of intraindustry trade, because the effects on the volume of total trade, the volume of interindustry trade, and the volume of intraindustry trade can be analyzed in the same way using figures 6.10, 6.12, and 6.13. If capital movement is first allowed, as I showed earlier, the equilibrium point is usually away from the diagonal (except starting from the mid-point of the diagonal). If free commodity trade is now allowed, the index of intraindustry trade is less than unity. This index can be compared with the index of intraindustry trade if no capital mobility is allowed. The magnitude of the no-capital-mobility index depends on the initial factor endowments of the countries, however, and it can be greater or less than the cum-capital-mobility index. In general, if the factor endowment point in Figure 6.15 is far away from the diagonal, international capital movement tends to augment the index of intraindustry trade, but if the factor endowment point is close to the diagonal, international capital movement tends to diminish the index of intraindustry trade.

Appendix

Here I derive the demand function for a variety as given by condition (6.7). In the first stage, the representative consumer chooses $d_1(\omega)$ to maximize the subutility function as given by (6.6) subject to the budget constraint $\sum_\omega p(\omega)d_1(\omega) \leq I_1$, taking $p(\omega)$ and I_1 as given. The first-order condition is

$$\Psi^{(1/\beta)-1}[d_1(\omega)]^{\beta-1} = \lambda p(\omega),\tag{A.1}$$

where λ is the marginal utility of income and $\Psi = \sum_\omega [d_1(\omega)]^\beta$. Rearrange the terms in (A.1) to give

$$d_1(\omega) = [\lambda p(\omega)]^{1/(\beta-1)}\Psi^{1/\beta}.\tag{A.2}$$

Multiple both sides of (A.2) by $p(\omega)$, sum up the condition for all varieties, and make use of the budget constraint to give

$$I_1 = \lambda^{1/(\beta-1)}\Psi^{1/\beta}\sum_\nu \left[p(\nu)\right]^{\beta/(\beta-1)}.\tag{A.3}$$

Substitute (A.3) into (A.2), using the relation $\beta = (1 - 1/\sigma)$, to yield the demand function in (6.7).

I next derive the price elasticity of the market demand as given by (6.16). The following is based on Helpman (1981). Differentiate the market demand for a variety as given by (6.14). This gives

$$\frac{\partial C_1}{\partial p} = m \left\{ \int_0^{\underline{\delta}} \phi'\big[p(\omega)h(\delta), I\big]\big[h(\delta)\big]^2 d\delta + \int_0^{\overline{\delta}} \phi'\big[p(\omega)h(\delta), I\big]\big[h(\delta)\big]^2 d\delta \right\}$$

$$+ \; m\phi[., .]h(\delta)\frac{\partial \underline{\delta}}{\partial p} + m\phi[., .]h(\delta)\frac{\partial \overline{\delta}}{\partial p}, \tag{A.4}$$

where $\phi' = \partial\phi/\partial\tilde{p}$, and $p = p(\omega)$ is the price of the variety under consideration. To determine how $\underline{\delta}$ is affected by p, differentiate (6.13a) with respect to p, keeping $p(\omega_\ell)$ and δ_ℓ as given. Rearranging terms gives

$$\frac{\partial \underline{\delta}}{\partial p} = -\frac{h(\underline{\delta})}{p(\omega_\ell)h'(\delta - \delta_\ell) + ph'(\underline{\delta})}. \tag{A.5}$$

Assuming a symmetric case, $\underline{\delta} = \delta - \underline{\delta} = 1/(2n)$ and $p(\omega_\ell) = p$. Substitute these conditions into (A.5) to give

$$\frac{\partial \underline{\delta}}{\partial p} = -\frac{h(1/2n)}{2ph'(1/2n)}. \tag{A.6}$$

Similarly, by differentiating (6.13b) and rearranging terms,

$$\frac{\partial \overline{\delta}}{\partial p} = -\frac{h(1/2n)}{2ph'(1/2n)}. \tag{A.7}$$

Substituting (A.6) and (A.7) into (A.4) and making use of the symmetry properties gives

$$\frac{\partial C_1}{\partial p} = m \left\{ \frac{\phi'[., .][h(1/2n)]^2}{n} - \frac{\phi[., .][h(1/2n)]^2}{ph'(1/2n)} \right\}. \tag{A.8}$$

Assuming a Cobb-Douglas type upper-tier utility function,

$$\phi = \frac{\alpha I}{ph(1/2n)}$$

$$\phi' = -\frac{\alpha I}{p^2[h(1/2n)]^2}. \tag{A.9}$$

Substitute (A.9) into (A.8) to yield

$$\frac{\partial C_1}{\partial p} = -\alpha m I \left\{ \frac{1}{np^2} + \frac{h(.)}{p^2 h'(.)} \right\}. \tag{A.10}$$

In this symmetry case, the market demand, as given by (6.14′), is equal to

$$C_1 = \frac{\alpha m I}{np}. \tag{6.14′}$$

Using (A.10) and (6.14′), the price elasticity of the market demand for a variety is equal to

$$\eta = -\frac{p}{C_1}\frac{\partial C_1}{\partial p} = 1 + \frac{nh(.)}{h'(.)} = 1 + \frac{1}{2\varepsilon_h(1/2n)},$$

where $\varepsilon_h = h'/(2nh)$ is the elasticity of the function $h(\delta)$ evaluated at $\delta = 1/(2n)$.

In this chapter, I focus on international trade in goods and factor mobility with another type of market structure: oligopoly. Contrary to the models examined in previous chapters, the models in this chapter have only a limited number of firms in the industry concerned. The strategies of a firm in terms of its output and the price of its output have significant effects on the decision of other firms. As a result, how one firm conjectures about the reactions of the other firms is crucial in its decision making.

In the literature, two types of conjectures of the firms receive the most attention: the Cournot conjectures and the Bertrand conjectures. Both types of conjectures have been assumed and both have interesting implications about the behavior of firms and the equilibrium of the economy. There are, however, still controversies over which of these types of conjectures better describes the behavior of firms. The Cournot models are simpler to analyze and more tractable, but some pointed out that the Bertrand competition is more consistent with the observation that usually the firms, not auctioneers, set the prices.

Cournot competition and Bertrand competition have been extended to the theory of international trade, and relevant models have been constructed to explain trade. Perhaps the most important contribution of oligopoly models is the theory of intraindustry trade in identical products. In some interesting models, it has been shown that firms in different countries choose to engage in cross-hauling of an identical product and make positive profit, even though it is costly to export the product from one country to another. Because from the world's point of view intraindustry trade in an identical product between two countries in the presence of positive transport costs is a waste of resources in the world, why would firms in different countries choose to mutually penetrate into each other's market? This important question is answered in this chapter.

The existence of intraindustry trade in identical products, nevertheless, depends on several assumptions. It is thus natural to ask whether this result is robust if some of these assumptions are relaxed. Two of these assumptions are more interesting and I analyze in detail the implications of relaxing them: no arbitrage and Cournot competition.

If perfect arbitrage is allowed and if transport costs are zero, the markets in different countries are fully integrated. It is then easy to see that intraindustry trade in identical products is not necessary but one-way trade may exist. Actually, because transport costs are zero, it does not matter whether intraindustry trade exists: It is the net flow of a product that matters. Arbitrage is not perfect if transport costs are positive. The existence of transport costs thus make the market partially segmented, and it is thus interesting to determine whether intraindustry trade takes place. This is an important issue to be analyzed later in this chapter.

I next consider models that are based on Bertrand competition. To examine trade, there must be more than one market. The startling result in a multimarket Bertrand model is that although no arbitrage is allowed and transport costs are positive, no intraindustry trade exists between the segmented markets. The absence of intraindustry trade may seem surprising, but it is intuitive. The fact that the firms choose the supplies to different markets after they have chosen the prices (and after they have chosen capacity constraints) allows the firms to optimally allocate their production capacities between the markets. Such ability to shuffle their products between the markets has the effects of arbitrage. Therefore, when the firms choose the prices, they do not choose price levels that will create a price gap large enough to invite arbitrage, knowing that arbitrage is possible.

Most papers in the literature analyze trade with oligopoly using partial equilibrium frameworks. These frameworks have the advantage of focusing on one single industry in order to highlight intraindustry trade and competition between oligopolistic firms. These partial equilibrium models, however, neglect the income effect of demand and the interaction between sectors. Furthermore, because they usually do not explicitly consider factor prices, they are not helpful in analyzing international factor mobility.

In the second half of this chapter, I present a two-sector, two-factor general equilibrium model, and analyze the effects of trade on resource allocation and factor prices. One of the advantages of a general equilibrium framework is that factor prices can be analyzed explicitly. Thus in the last section, I examine different issues related to international factor mobility in the presence of oligopolistic firms in sector 1. One result is that international trade in goods and capital mobility are complements in the price-equalization sense because international trade in goods alone, international capital mobility alone, and international trade in goods plus capital mobility in general yield different equilibria, and generally movements in goods and capital are needed to achieve world efficiency. The quantitative relationship between international trade in goods and capital mobility is much more complicated, however.

7.1 Cournot Competition with No Arbitrage: The Basic Model

I now introduce the basic model of intraindustry trade in identical products that is due to Brander (1981) and Brander and Krugman (1983). The model focuses on one industry that is assumed to be sufficiently small in the economy so that all income and intersectoral effects are neglected. In such a partial equilibrium framework, the following hierarchy of notation is adopted: Variables of the foreign firm are distinguished by asterisks but those of the home firm are not, and variables of the home market are represented by lower case letters while those of the foreign market are represented by upper case letters. The model has the following features, some of which will be relaxed later:

1. There are two countries, called the home and the foreign countries. If international trade is allowed, no government regulations or restrictions exist.

2. There is one firm in each country producing a homogeneous product. If no international trade is allowed, the firm in each country is a monopolist. Homogeneity of the product is not crucial for the results derived later.

3. The firms compete in a Cournot fashion, meaning that each firm conjectures that the output of the other firm in each market is independent of its production.

4. Denote the marginal cost and fixed cost of the home firm by c and f, and those of the foreign firm by c^* and f^*, respectively. Marginal costs are assumed to be constant.

5. There is no arbitrage across countries. In other words, there is no resale of the product, and only these two firms can export the good from their own countries to the other country. The implication of this no-resale assumption is that the firms can price discriminate in the two markets, and that the prices of the good in these two markets may not be the same even though free trade is allowed. The two markets are thus said to be *segmented*.

6. The inverse demand function in the home country is denoted by $p = p(q)$, where p is the price of the commodity and q is the aggregate demand. Similarly, denote the inverse demand in the foreign country by $p^* = p^*(q^*)$ where p^* is the foreign price and q^* is the foreign demand. Use primes to denote derivatives of p and p^*. Both demand curves are downward sloping, that is, $p', p^{*\prime} < 0$.

7. Denote the output of the home firm by $x + X$, of which x is supplied to the home market and X exported to the foreign market. Denote the output of the foreign firm by $x^* + X^*$, of which x^* is the supply to the home market and X^* to its own market.

8. In shipping the good across countries in either direction, there is a nonnegative transport cost. The per unit transport cost, denoted by $\tau \geq 0$, is treated as a parameter and is exogenous to the firms. Two simplifying assumptions are made. First, no transport cost is needed to ship the good from a firm to its local market. Second, the transport cost between countries is assumed not to be sensitive to the direction of movement of the good.[1] When $\tau = 0$, the transport cost is zero, and if $\tau = p^*$ (respectively p), the transport cost is too high for any profitable export by the home (respectively foreign) firm. As shown

---

1. These assumptions can be relaxed easily.

later, however, transport cost may be prohibitive even if it is smaller than the corresponding price.

For each market, the supply of the good comes from the local firm and possibly from the other firm. This gives the following market-clearing conditions for the two markets:

$$q = x + x^* \tag{7.1a}$$

$$q^* = X + X^*. \tag{7.1b}$$

Denote the profits of the home and foreign firms by π and π^*, respectively, which are defined as

$$\pi = p(q)x + p^*(q^*)X - cx - (c + \tau)X - f \tag{7.2a}$$

$$\pi^* = p(q)x^* + p^*(q^*)X^* - (c^* + \tau)x^* - c^*X^* - f^*. \tag{7.2b}$$

Conditions (7.2) reflect the fact that the transport cost makes it more expensive for each firm to supply the good to the other market. For convenience, I use subindices to denote partial derivatives of the profit functions; for example, $\pi_x = \partial\pi/\partial x$, and so on.

The first-order conditions of the two firms for a Cournot-Nash equilibrium can be obtained by differentiating the profit conditions in (7.2) and making use of conditions (7.1) to give:

$$\pi_x = p(q) + xp'(q) - c \le 0 \tag{7.3a}$$

$$\pi_X = p^*(q^*) + Xp^{*\prime}(q^*) - (c + \tau) \le 0 \tag{7.3b}$$

$$\pi_{x^*}^* = p(q) + x^*p'(q) - (c^* + \tau) \le 0 \tag{7.3c}$$

$$\pi_{X^*}^* = p^*(q^*) + X^*p^{*\prime}(q^*) - c^* \le 0. \tag{7.3d}$$

The first-order conditions given by (7.3) is based on the Cournot conjectures made by the firms. For example, in choosing the optimal supply to the local market, x, the home firm is taking x^* and X^* as given.

The most interesting case is the one in which conditions (7.3) give an interior solution, that is, both firms are supplying positive outputs to both markets. To determine the conditions for an interior solution, I first examine the home firm's production decision. If in the absence of the home firm's production the foreign firm has chosen its optimal supply x_0^* to the home market, and if the resulting monopoly markup $(= p(x_0^*) - c)$ for the home firm is positive, then by (7.3a) the home firm's supply to the home market is positive. Similarly, if the foreign firm has chosen its optimal supply to the foreign market $(= X_m^*)$ without any home export, and if the monopoly markup for the home firm is positive $(p^*(X_m^*) > c + \tau)$, then the home firm's export is positive. Such conditions can also be applied to the foreign firm.

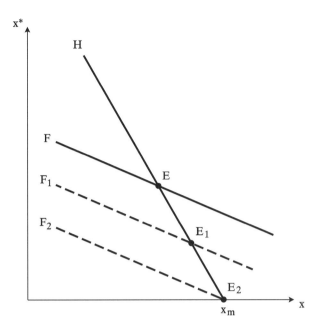

Figure 7.1

Assuming an interior solution, the inequalities in conditions (7.3) are replaced with equalities, and together with the market-clearing conditions (7.1), they are solved for q, q^* and the firms' outputs, x, X, x^*, and X^*. The analysis can be simplified by noting that, due to constant marginal costs, conditions (7.1a), (7.3a), and (7.3c) contain only three unknowns, q, x, and x^*, and thus can be solved for these variables. Similarly, conditions (7.1b), (7.3b), and (7.3d) can be solved for q^*, X, and X^*.

Because of the symmetry between the countries, the following analysis concentrates on the home market. Making use of condition (7.1a), condition (7.3a) (with equality) gives the implicit reaction function of the home firm and it is illustrated by schedule H in Figure 7.1.[2] Similarly, conditions (7.1a) and (7.3c) jointly give the implicit reaction function of the foreign firm and are illustrated by schedule F. (Ignore schedules F_1 and F_2 for the time being.)

Define $\phi = p' + xp''$ and $\phi^* = p' + x^*p''$. By Hahn's (1962) stability conditions, assume that $\phi < 0$ and $\phi^* < 0$.[3] These conditions are satisfied if p'' is negative or sufficiently small, that is, the home demand curve is not too convex

---

2. As Dixit (1986a) notes, the term "reaction function," which is also called best-reply or best-response function, is not appropriate for one-shot games. These functions, however, are still a useful mathematical technique.

3. Again, for one-shot games, the concept of stability of equilibrium is meaningless. The stability conditions derived here are, however, useful for comparative static studies.

toward the origin. Further note that these conditions imply the second-order conditions for the firms. Substitute (7.1a) into conditions (7.3a) and (7.3c) and differentiate the latter two conditions with respect to x, x^* and τ to give

$$\begin{bmatrix} \phi + p' & \phi \\ \phi^* & \phi^* + p' \end{bmatrix} \begin{bmatrix} \mathrm{d}x \\ \mathrm{d}x^* \end{bmatrix} = \begin{bmatrix} 0 \\ 1 \end{bmatrix} \mathrm{d}\tau. \tag{7.4}$$

Using conditions (7.4), the slopes of the reaction schedules in Figure 7.1 are given by

$$\left. \frac{\mathrm{d}x^*}{\mathrm{d}x} \right|_H = -\frac{\phi + p'}{\phi} < 0$$

$$\left. \frac{\mathrm{d}x^*}{\mathrm{d}x} \right|_F = -\frac{\phi^*}{\phi^* + p'} < 0.$$

The stability conditions further imply that schedule H is steeper than schedule F, as Figure 7.1 shows. The intersecting point E between schedules H and F in Figure 7.1 depicts the equilibrium point (x_s, x_s^*) that solves the first-order conditions (7.3a) and (7.3c), where the subscript "s" denotes the equilibrium value of a variable in the present framework with segmented markets.

Applying the same analysis to the foreign market, I can determine the equilibrium outputs of the firms supplied to the foreign market, (X_s, X_s^*). Again with an interior solution (under the conditions stated previously), X_s and X_s^* are positive. As a result, both firms supply positive quantities of a homogeneous good to both markets. This phenomenon is called intraindustry (two-way) trade in, or "cross-hauling" of, an *identical* product. Because the markets are segmented, the prices of the commodity in different markets may be different.

To understand the possibility and implications of intraindustry trade in identical products, consider a special case in which the two countries are symmetric with identical demand and identical marginal costs, $p(q) = p^*(q)$ and $c = c^*$. The transport cost is positive but not prohibitive so that an interior solution is obtained. Due to symmetry, in equilibrium, $x_s = X_s^*$ and $X_s = x_s^*$, implying that $p_s = p_s^*$. This special case reveals several interesting features. First, intraindustry trade exists despite the fact that it is wasteful (from both countries' point of view). Second, a comparison of conditions (7.3a) and (7.3c), and a comparison of (7.3b) and (7.3d) show that $x_s > x_s^*$ and $X_s^* > X_s$. Third, because the prices in both markets are the same, and because of the transport costs, each firm receives a smaller per unit profit from the other market than from its own market. In other words, the f.o.b. price for export is below the domestic price, a phenomenon that Brander and Krugman (1983) call "reciprocal dumping." If the prices in the markets are different, at least one, but not necessarily both, of the firms is dumping.

In determining intraindustry trade, transport cost plays an important role. From the first-order conditions in (7.3), an increase in transport cost on export has the same effect as that of an increase in a firm's marginal cost. More specifically, Cramer's rule can be used to solve the equations in (7.4) for the following derivatives:

$$\frac{dx}{d\tau} = -\frac{\phi}{\Delta} > 0$$

$$\frac{dx^*}{d\tau} = \frac{\phi + p'}{\Delta} < 0,$$

where $\Delta = p'(p' + \phi + \phi^*) > 0$. Thus an increase in τ increases domestic supply but discourages import. Graphically, this represents a shift of schedule F in Figure 7.1 downward to, say, schedule F_1. The new intersecting point E_1 depicts a greater x but a smaller x^*. As a result, an increase in τ shifts the equilibrium point down along schedule H.

If the transport cost is increased sufficiently so that schedule F shifts down to the position shown by schedule F_2 in Figure 7.1, then the equilibrium point is point E_2 at which $x = x_m$, the home firm's monopoly output under autarky, and $x^* = 0$. The corresponding value of transport cost, denoted by $\bar{\tau}^*$ and called the critical value of τ for zero foreign export, is the prohibitive transport cost. Using conditions (7.1a) and (7.3c), the critical value of τ is equal to:

$$\bar{\tau}^* = p(x_m) - c^*. \tag{7.5a}$$

Similar analysis can be used to derive the critical value of τ for the home firm below which the home export is positive:

$$\bar{\tau} = p^*(X_m^*) - c, \tag{7.5b}$$

where X_m^* is the autarkic output of the foreign firm that solves condition (7.3d) (when $X = 0$).

Without loss of generality, suppose that $\bar{\tau} < \bar{\tau}^*$. Then depending on the value of τ, intraindustry trade may or may not exist. Three cases can be identified:

1. $\tau < \bar{\tau} < \bar{\tau}^*$: Intraindustry trade exists.

2. $\bar{\tau} < \tau < \bar{\tau}^*$: One-way trade exists with the foreign firm exporting.

3. $\bar{\tau} < \bar{\tau}^* < \tau$: No trade exists.

If some of these inequalites are replaced by equalities, a firm is indifferent to trade and no trade. For example, if $\tau = \bar{\tau}$, the home firm's profit remains unchanged whether or not it exports one unit of the good to the foreign market. If

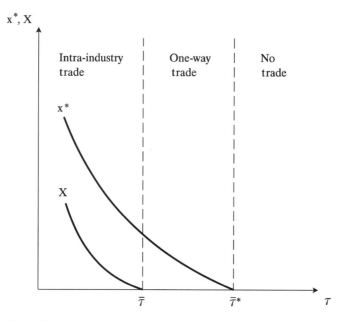

Figure 7.2

$\bar{\tau} = \bar{\tau}^*$, intraindustry trade is observed if $\tau < \bar{\tau} = \bar{\tau}^*$, and no trade is observed if $\bar{\tau} = \bar{\tau}^* < \tau$.

The results can be illustrated in Figure 7.2, which shows the dependence of the firms' exports, X and x^*, on the transport cost. As explained earlier, X and x^* are monotonically decreasing in τ. Schedules X and x^* in the diagram show the changes in the firms' exports as τ varies. The three cases to determine two-way trade are also illustrated in the diagram.

In an interesting paper, Fung (1991) argues that if the firms can collude, then no intraindustry trade will exist. If, however, the goods are differentiated, then intraindustry trade is still possible even if the firms collude.

7.2   Free Entry and Exit

Suppose now that there are $n \geq 1$ identical firms in the home country and $n^* \geq 1$ identical firms in the foreign country. If n and n^* are taken as given, the analysis in the previous section can easily be extended. First, the market-clearing conditions are

$$q = nx + n^*x^* \tag{7.6a}$$

$$q^* = nX + n^*X^*, \tag{7.6b}$$

where because of symmetry between the firms in each country they must have the same equilibrium output, meaning that I can omit the indices for the firms. The first-order conditions in (7.3) remain valid as long as q and q^* are now given by (7.6), and they can be solved for the outputs of representative home and foreign firms in terms of n, n^*, and τ. With n and n^* given as parameters, the analysis in the previous section can be used to show that *intraindustry trade still exists* if the transport cost is not significant.

Suppose that free entry and exit are allowed. The numbers of firms per country will adjust to bring the profits of the firms to zero. (I neglect the integer problem.) Assuming a positive fixed cost for each firm, the zero-profit condition can be used to solve for the equilibrium values of n and n^*, the values that will drive the profits of the firms down to zero. The endogeneity of n and n^* does not change the analysis much, except that the ability to solve the markets separately no longer exists. Because n and n^* appear in all equations, the markets are interrelated.

Will the presence of free entry and exit eliminate intraindustry trade? The answer in general is no, so long as the transport cost is insignificant and the fixed costs f and f^* are positive. To see the intuition behind this answer, suppose that the two economies are initially separated with no trade allowed. Firms in each market earn zero profit while each firm equated marginal revenue to marginal cost. Because the fixed costs are positive, zero profit implies that the market price in each country is greater than the average variable cost of a representative firm. Suppose now that free trade is allowed. To each firm in a country, the marginal revenue of the first unit sold to another country is equal to the market price. This means that as long as the market price in another country is high enough (relative to the marginal cost and transport cost), each firm will have an incentive to export to the other country. This leads to intraindustry trade.

As in the previous case, transport costs do play a role in intraindustry trade. Denote the maximum value of τ with which foreign firms are willing to export by $\bar{\tau}_n^*$, where the subscript "n" denotes the fact that the critical value of τ for the foreign firms generally depends on the number of firms in the home country. Using the same argument as before, $\bar{\tau}_n^*$ is equal to the difference between the autarkic price level in the home market and the foreign marginal cost, that is, the monopoly rent the foreign firms get by selling the first unit (with no transport cost) to the home market. This monopoly rent depends on the number of home firms. It is well known in microeconomic theory that the home autarkic price decreases with the number of identical home firms. This implies that $\bar{\tau}_n^* < \bar{\tau}^*$ for $n > 1$, where $\bar{\tau}^*$, given by (7.5a), is the critical value of $\bar{\tau}_n^*$ when $n = 1$. This means that if τ is nonprohibitive for the foreign firms to export when there are more than one home firms, then ceteris paribus it must be nonprohibitive for them to export should there be only one home firm.

7.3   Cournot Competition with Arbitrage: Zero Transport Cost

In many cases, the assumption of no arbitrage used in the previous section is not realistic because it requires no resale of the product even if the prices in the markets differ from each other significantly. In this section, I relax this assumption. To model arbitrage, suppose that there are many competitive trading companies in both countries that are able to purchase the good from the market where it is cheaper and sell it to another market where it is more expensive. The equilibrium and whether there is intraindustry trade depend crucially on the level of transport cost. In this section, consider the special case in which the transport cost is zero, that is, $\tau = 0$ while a more general case in which the transport cost is positive will be analyzed in the next section.

When the transport cost is zero ($\tau = 0$) and when arbitrage is allowed, the two markets are *fully integrated*, and they can be considered as a single market.[4] For simplicity, consider again the case in which there is only one firm in each country ($n = n^* = 1$).

Recall that q and q^* are the demands in the home and foreign markets, respectively. Denote the total outputs of the home and foreign firms by x and x^*, respectively. The market-clearing condition (for both markets as a whole) is

$$q + q^* = x + x^*. \tag{7.7}$$

In (7.7), x and x^* are the total outputs of the home and foreign firms, respectively. Because of zero transport cost and full integration of the markets, it does not matter which market the firms supply the good to. Only the total demand and the total supply matter.

Define the demand functions of the markets as $q = d(p)$ and $q^* = d^*(p^*)$, which are inverse functions of $p = p(q)$ and $p^* = p^*(q^*)$, respectively. Full integration of the markets implies equalization of prices, that is, $p = p^*$. Adding the two demands horizontally, I have $q + q^* = d(p) + d^*(p)$, which is then inverted to give the aggregate inverse demand function: $p = g(q + q^*) = g(x + x^*)$. The first-order conditions of the two firms are

$$\pi_x = g(x + x^*) + xg'(x + x^*) - c = 0$$

$$\pi_{x^*}^* = g(x + x^*) + x^*g'(x + x^*) - c^* = 0.$$

---

4. See the analysis in Markusen (1981) and Helpman and Krugman (1985, Sections 5.1 to 5.4) using different models.

Denote the equilibrium outputs of the home and foreign firms by x_1 and x_1^*. The equilibrium price is $p_1 = g(x_1 + x_1^*)$.

In terms of the properties of this equilibrium, the most important question is whether there is intraindustry trade. The answer is, when the two markets are fully integrated, intraindustry trade *is no longer needed*, although it can exist because of no transport cost. Because the price of the good must be equalized in the two markets, each firm will get the same marginal revenue, which is calculated from the integrated market, whether it supplies the output to the local market or to the other market. If a firm does not have any incentive to supply one more unit to the local market, it will not have any incentive to supply one more unit to the other market.

It is important to compare the present case with the previous case in which markets are segmented. When arbitrage between the markets with no transport costs is allowed, the firm in each country has to take into account the fact that part of each unit it supplies to the other market may be shipped back to its own market. Thus it can no longer neglect the effects on the price of its own market when it exports the good to another market, and the prices in different markets cannot move independently as in the previous case where no arbitrage is allowed.

One-way trade is still possible in the present case. At the equilibrium price, demands in the two markets are $q_1 = d(p_1)$ and $q_1^* = d^*(p_1)$. Thus the home country's export is equal to $x_1 - q_1$ (or import if it is negative). If the two countries are identical, there will be no (net) trade at all.

Another interesting question is whether the firms will produce more under trade than under autarky. Recall that x_m and x_m^* are the autarkic outputs of the firms. Let $p_m = p(x_m)$ and $p_m^* = p^*(x_m^*)$ be the autarkic monopoly prices in the two countries. In what follows, I consider the special case in which *the two countries are identical*, $x_m = x_m^*$ and $p_m = p(x_m) = p_m^*$.

When trade is allowed, the marginal revenue for each firm is the increase in revenue that the firm gets by selling one more unit of the good in the integrated market under the condition that arbitrage always equalizes the prices in both countries. Because the firms are symmetric, let me focus on the domestic firm. Its marginal revenue when the economies are first opened up is equal to

$$MR_1 = g(2x_m) + x_m g'(2x_m).$$

To see whether the marginal revenue given above is greater or smaller than the marginal cost, note that $g(2x_m) = p_m$ as each firm supplies the autarkic output to its own market. The derivative of $g(.)$ is given by

$$g'(2x_m) = \frac{1}{2d'(p_m)}. \tag{7.8}$$

Using the definitions of functions d, I have $p' = 1/d'$. Condition (7.8) implies that

$$g'(2x_m) = \frac{p'(x_m)}{2}. \tag{7.8'}$$

Noting that d' and $d^{*'}$ are negative, (7.8') implies that $0 > g' > p', p^{*'}$. I showed earlier that the first-order condition of the home firm under autarky gives $p(x_m) + x_m p'(x_m) = c$. Combining these results, I conclude that if the home firm maintains its autarkic output when trade is allowed, then $MR_1 > c$. This conclusion is also true for the foreign firm. At this point, both firms have an incentive to expand production. Because the countries are identical, $x_1 = x_1^* > x_m = x_m^*$. As intraindustry trade is not needed, allowing trade will not lead to trade, yet both firms are producing more.[5]

The procompetitive effect of trade is not surprising. In a single market, if there are two or more identical firms, each of them will produce more than what it wants to produce should all other firms not exist, that is, when it is a monopolist. Trade between two initially separated markets will integrate them together, and the competition between the firms will induce them to produce more even though in the special case of identical countries they do not trade.

7.4 Cournot Competition with Arbitrage and Positive Transport Cost

In the previous section, I indicated that with zero transport cost, the firms are indifferent to supplying the good to the local market or to the other market. Intraindustry trade is not needed although one-way trade can still exist. When transport cost is positive, arbitrage may or may not take place, and the markets are not fully integrated. Under certain conditions, intraindustry trade still exists.

Now suppose that transport cost τ is positive. In this case, I have to analyze arbitrage more explicitly. As assumed in the previous section, arbitrage is made by a large number of competitive trading companies. Note that the home and foreign firms are not prohibited from doing arbitrage, but as shown later, they will not choose to have arbitrage. To begin the analysis, first note that because arbitrage involves a transport cost of τ, arbitrage in either direction is not profitable if

$$|p - p^*| < \tau. \tag{7.9}$$

---

5. This result was first proved by Markusen (1981) using a general equilibrium framework.

To analyze arbitrage more explicitly, let me use the segmented-market case analyzed in Section 7.1 as a benchmark. For simplicity, I assume that the equilibrium in the benchmark case is unique. Recall that the equilibrium prices in this benchmark case are denoted by p_s and p_s^*. By condition (7.9), no arbitrage exists if $|p_s - p_s^*| < \tau$. This implies that (p_s, p_s^*) can be an equilibrium if they satisfy condition (7.9). This result has an interesting application. I know that if the two countries are identical and the markets are segmented, then the equilibrium prices in the markets are identical. Thus I can conclude that if the two countries are identical and if $\tau > 0$, then intraindustry trade exists, whether or not arbitrage is allowed.

Suppose now that the prices in the benchmark case do not satisfy (7.9). Without loss of generality, let me suppose that $p_s > p_s^* + \tau$. (The case in which $p_s^* > p_s + \tau$ can be analyzed in a similar way.) This means that arbitrage from the foreign market to the home market is profitable. As a result, (p_s, p_s^*) cannot be an equilibrium in the present case with arbitrage. In fact, without multiple equilibria in the benchmark case, $p - p^*$ cannot be smaller than τ because if $p - p^*$ is positive but less than τ, the firms do not have to worry about arbitrage but will widen the price gap. Thus I can state the arbitrage condition as follows:

$$p(q) = p^*(q^*) + \tau. \tag{7.10}$$

To be more explicit about arbitrage, define z as the amount of the good transferred by the trading companies from the foreign market to the home market; $z \geq 0$ as long as $p_s \geq p_s^* + \tau$. Thus the market-clearing conditions for the markets become

$$q = x + x^* + z \tag{7.11a}$$

$$q^* = X + X^* - z. \tag{7.11b}$$

Assume that in choosing their outputs the firms are fully aware of the possible existence of arbitrage. Because in the benchmark case the home price tends to be greater than the foreign price, I focus on possible arbitrage from the foreign market to the home market. The firms take into account the possibility that when they supply outputs to the foreign market, part of their supplies may be shipped to the home market by the trading companies.

Now it is necessary to find out how arbitrage may affect the firms' marginal revenues. Consider first the foreign market. Differentiate condition (7.10) with respect to X, X^* and z, using conditions (7.11a) and (7.11b). Rearrange terms to give

$$\frac{dz}{dX} = \frac{dz}{dX^*} = \frac{p^{*\prime}}{p' + p^{*\prime}}. \tag{7.12}$$

In condition (7.12), dz/dX is the fraction of the supply of an additional unit of the good by the home firm to the foreign market that will be shipped back by the trading companies under the condition that x, x^*, and X^* are kept constant. The derivative dz/dX^* can be interpreted in a similar way. Condition (7.12) shows one important result: The supplies of both firms to the foreign market have the same effects on arbitrage.

I next use condition (7.12) to derive the marginal revenue with respect to X. Differentiate revenue of the home firm, $p(q)x + p^*(q^*)X$, with respect to X, using the market-clearing conditions (7.11a) and (7.11b) and condition (7.12) to give the marginal revenue with respect to X:

$$xp' \frac{dz}{dX} + p^* + Xp^{*\prime}\left(1 - \frac{dz}{dX}\right) = p^* + \frac{p'p^{*\prime}(x+X)}{p'+p^{*\prime}}. \qquad (7.13a)$$

Using the same argument, the marginal revenue of the foreign firm with respect to X^* is equal to

$$p^* + \frac{p'p^{*\prime}(x^*+X^*)}{p'+p^{*\prime}}. \qquad (7.13b)$$

Now turn to the home market. There is an asymmetry between the markets. If, for example, the arbitrage condition (7.10) holds without any arbitrage, then a small increase in supply to the home market will slightly drive the home price down, but this will not invite arbitrage. If arbitrage initially exists, such an increase in supply to the home market will decrease or eliminate arbitrage. To be more explicit, I differentiate condition (7.10) with respect to x, x^*, and z, using conditions (7.11a) and (7.11b), to give

$$\frac{dz}{dx} = \frac{dz}{dx^*} = -\frac{p'}{p'+p^{*\prime}}. \qquad (7.14)$$

Differentiate the home firm's revenue with respect to x, using (7.14), to give the marginal revenue with respect to x when arbitrage is present

$$p + \frac{p'p^{*\prime}(x+X)}{p'+p^{*\prime}}. \qquad (7.15a)$$

Similarly the marginal revenue with respect to x^* for the foreign firm, assuming that arbitrage exists, is

$$p + \frac{p'p^{*\prime}(x^*+X^*)}{p'+p^{*\prime}}. \qquad (7.15b)$$

If arbitrage is absent, the marginal revenue of each firm is the same as that given in Section 7.1.

Using conditions (7.13), (7.15), and the preceding analysis, and assuming the existence of arbitrage, the first-order conditions of the firms are

$$\pi_x = p(q) + \frac{p'(q)p^{*\prime}(q^*)[x + X]}{p'(q) + p^{*\prime}(q^*)} - c \leq 0 \tag{7.16a}$$

$$\pi_X = p^*(q^*) + \frac{p'(q)p^{*\prime}(q^*)[x + X]}{p'(q) + p^{*\prime}(q^*)} - (c + \tau) \leq 0 \tag{7.16b}$$

$$\pi_{x^*}^* = p(q) + \frac{p'(q)p^{*\prime}(q^*)[x^* + X^*]}{p'(q) + p^{*\prime}(q^*)} - (c^* + \tau) \leq 0 \tag{7.16c}$$

$$\pi_{X^*}^* = p^*(q^*) + \frac{p'(q)p^{*\prime}(q^*)[x^* + X^*]}{p'(q) + p^{*\prime}(q^*)} - c^* \leq 0. \tag{7.16d}$$

Assume that the home country supplies a positive amount to the home market. This means that condition (7.16a) is satisfied with an equality. Using this condition and the arbitrage condition (7.10), in (7.16b) $\pi_X = -2\tau < 0$. In other words, if arbitrage exists, the home firm does not export, that is, intraindustry trade disappears.

Of course, it is necessary to determine whether arbitrage does exist. Let me turn to the foreign firm and assume that it supplies a positive amount to the foreign market. This means that condition (7.16d) is satisfied with an equality. Using this result and the arbitrage condition (7.10), condition (7.16c) reduces to $\pi_{x^*}^* = 0$. In other words, the foreign firm can supply the good to both markets in the presence of arbitrage. By condition (7.12), I can conclude that arbitrage does exist.

An intuition behind this result can now be provided. By using the arbitrage condition (7.10), and by comparing condition (7.13a) with (7.15a), and condition (7.13b) with (7.15b), it can be seen that for each firm the marginal revenue from the home market is greater than the marginal revenue from the foreign market by an amount of τ. For the home firm, supplying the good to the foreign market involves a transport cost. Thus in the presence of arbitrage it is never profitable for the home firm to supply to the foreign market. For the foreign firm, in equilibrium, supplying the good to both markets gives the same marginal revenue net of transport cost.

7.5   Bertrand Competition with a Homogeneous Product

In the previous sections, I concentrated on models of Cournot competition, that is, when firms pick output quantities of a product, leaving the prices to be chosen (for example, by an auctioneer) to clear the markets. I now turn to another form of competition between the firms: the Bertrand competition. In the Bertrand paradigm, firms first choose prices and supply the quantities according to some rules to clear the markets. When a firm chooses a price, it forms the conjecture that its choice will not affect the prices chosen by its competitors. A Bertrand-Nash equilibrium is one at which the price chosen by each firm is the optimal one when given the prices of its competitors.

In the simplest one-sector, Bertrand model with identical firms, each firm chooses the price level equal to its average variable cost. With zero fixed cost, each firm earns zero profit. The result is that the firms act as if they are competitive, even though the number of firms may be small and fixed. This result is called the Bertrand paradox because its theoretical implication is not consistent with the observation that oligopolistic firms usually earn positive profits.

There are three major ways of resolving the Bertrand paradox: the capacity constraint, dynamic price competition, and product differentiation.[6] In order to have a more direct comparison between trade with Bertrand competition and the results obtained previously, I focus on the use of capacity constraint to remove the Bertrand paradox and examine trade caused by two firms in two markets with Bertrand conjectures. This section relies on the work of Ben-Zvi and Helpman (1992).[7] The assumption of a homogeneous product is maintained.

Recall the two-market, two-firm, one-good model used in the previous sections. Adopt the same notation as before, but assume that the firms have Bertrand conjectures. The analysis begins with the assumption that the markets are segmented, that is, there is no arbitrage. The assumption of no arbitrage is made for convenience; as will be seen later, arbitrage will not exist even if it is allowed.

The Bertrand game with capacity constraint is described as follows. In the first stage, the firms choose production capacity constraints at some costs. These capacity constraints are the maximum quantities of the good the firms can supply to the markets. In the second stage, they pick prices for their outputs in the markets, and in the third stage, they determine the supplies of the good to the markets.

Ben-Zvi and Helpman (1992) show that for any prices and capacities the firms choose in the first two stages, there is a solution to the sale game. In the second stage, however, for any given capacity choice of the firms, a Nash equilibrium in the game may not exist (Kreps and Scheinkman, 1983). In the present model with subgame perfect equilibria, existence of equilibrium can be analyzed by noting that in the first stage each firm takes into account how its decision and the competitor's decision will affect the outcomes in the later stages. As long as choosing capacity constraints is costly, the firms

---

6. For more information about the Bertrand paradox in a single market, see Tirole (1989).

7. Venables (1990) also analyzes Bertrand competition between two firms with capacity constraints. His model is not so close to the present one because he assumes differentiated products.

choose capacity constraints that will lead to Nash equilibria in these three stages. Moreover, in the type of economic models that I am interested in, I can concentrate on the later two stages, assuming that the capacity constraints have been chosen by the firms that are fully aware of the outcomes in the later two stages.

Denote the equilibrium values of the price and sale variables by a subscript "e." For example, (p_e, P_e) are the prices charged by the home firm for its sales to the home and foreign markets, and (p_e^*, P_e^*) are the corresponding prices charged by the foreign firm, respectively. The following four main results are based on Ben-Zvi and Helpman (1992).

Result 7.1   In a market in which both firms supply positive quantities, the firms must charge the same price.

To show this result, suppose that both firms have positive supply in the home market and that $p_e < p_e^*$. Suppose that the home firm slightly raises its home price to $p = p_e + \varepsilon$ where ε is positive but small. According to the efficient rationing rule stated in Ben-Zvi and Helpman (1992), the home firm can still sell the same quantity to the home market, possibly causing a drop in the foreign firm's sale in the market.[8] This means that the home firm improves its profit, and the original p_e cannot be an equilibrium price. The same argument can be used to show that $p_e > p_e^*$ cannot be equilibrium home prices if the firms have positive supplies in this market.

Result 7.1 is the same as the result for a single market with Bertrand competition (Tirole, 1988).

Result 7.2   The gap between the equilibrium prices in the two markets is not greater than the per unit transport cost.

To show this result, recall that the equilibrium price in the foreign market charged by the foreign firm is P_e^*. I want to argue that it is not profitable for the home firm to charge a price of its supply to the home market greater than $P_e^* + \tau$. Suppose that the home firm does set $p > P_e^* + \tau$. In this case, the foreign firm can set its home price, that is, the price of its output sold in the home market, at $p^* = p - \varepsilon$ and can transfer one unit of the good from the foreign market to the home market. According to the efficient rationing rule, the foreign firm displaces the home firm's sale in the home market by one

---

8. The efficient rationing rule is as follows: If a firm charges a lower price than the other firm does, then it can supply as much as it wants up to the market demand. If it chooses not to supply to the market demand level, the other firm can supply up to the gap between the market demand and the first firm's supply. If both firms charge the same price, each firm can supply up to half of the market demand. This rule is called efficient because it maximizes consumer surplus.

unit. This means that the home firm loses a revenue equal to p. If the home firm sets its foreign price P equal to or greater than $p + \tau$, it is not able to sell this unit of the good because $p + \tau > P_e^* + 2\tau > P_e^*$. If the home firm sets $P < p + \tau$ in the foreign market, even if it can sell this unit of the good, the revenue from this market is not enough to cover the revenue in the home market it lost plus the transport cost. This means that it is not profitable for the home firm to choose $p > P_e^* + \tau$ in the first place. In other words, its optimal choice of the home price, when given the foreign firm's home price, must be $p \leq P_e^* + \tau$.

Result 7.2 is an interesting one because in the case of Cournot competition, arbitrage may be needed to keep the gap between the equilibrium prices in the markets not greater than the per unit transport cost. In the present case in which the firms choose prices before quantities, no arbitrage is required to keep the gap between the prices in the markets not greater than τ. The intuition behind this result is that when the firms choose prices before they choose sales, they have to anticipate what the other firm will do in the next stage. As a result, prices will not be chosen so that arbitrage is profitable, or the firms will distribute the sales between the markets to take advantage of any arbitrage opportunity and the chosen prices cannot be at equilibrium.

Result 7.3   With $\tau > 0$, there is no intraindustry trade.

To see why, suppose that there exists intraindustry trade in an equilibrium, that is, $X_e > 0$ and $x_e^* > 0$. At this point, is it profitable for the home firm to export one less unit of the good and sell it to the home market? In order to sell this unit to the home market, it can slightly lower its home price to $p_e - \varepsilon$ where ε is positive but very small. The increase in revenue is $p_e - \varepsilon - \varepsilon x_e$, where εx_e is the loss in revenue from the existing sale to the home market. By withdrawing one unit from the foreign market, it loses a revenue of $P_e - \tau$. Note that if the foreign firm maintains the initial sales (x_e^*, X_e^*), an excess demand will be created at the price $P_e = P_e^*$ in the foreign market. There is, however, no hope for the home firm to raise P_e because such a move will induce additional supply of the foreign firm to the foreign market, and the home firm's sale will drop to zero. Thus the increase in net revenue of the home firm in the transfer of the unit of the good is equal to $p_e - \varepsilon - \varepsilon x - P_e + \tau$, or approximately $p_e - P_e + \tau$ as ε can be made as small as possible. If the initial point is an equilibrium, such a reallocation of the home firm's capacity is not profitable, that is,

$$p_e - P_e + \tau \leq 0$$

or

$$p_e \leq P_e - \tau. \tag{7.17a}$$

I can apply the same argument to the foreign firm and show that

$$P_e^* \leq p_e^* - \tau. \tag{7.17b}$$

Using Result 7.1, conditions (7.17a) and (7.17b) imply

$$p_e \leq P_e - \tau = P_e^* - \tau \leq p_e^* - 2\tau = p_e - 2\tau,$$

which is a contradiction.

Result 7.3 is an interesting one because it shows that when the firms have Bertrand conjectures, intraindustry trade in identical commodities will not exist. The intuition behind this result is similar to that behind result 7.2. When the firms choose the prices, they are aware of how these prices will affect the optimal distribution of their capacities. In equilibrium they will not choose prices that will allow profitable mutual penetration of an identical good (or arbitrage) because transport cost is positive.

Result 7.4   If $\tau = 0$, the equilibrium of this three-stage Bertrand game, if it exists, coincides with that of a one-shot Cournot game with perfect arbitrage.

If $\tau = 0$, then Results 7.1 and 7.2 imply equalization of prices in the markets, that is, $p_e = p_e^* = P_e = P_e^* = p$. This means that the markets are fully integrated, and their total demand is equal to $d(p) + d^*(p)$. In equilibrium, the total demand is equal to the total capacity of the firms, that is,

$$d(p) + d^*(p) = \overline{x} + \overline{X}^*. \tag{7.18}$$

In the first stage when the firms choose the optimal capacities, they must take condition (7.18) into account. Because they choose the capacities independently and noncooperatively, the game is the same as the Cournot game in which the two firms are facing an integrated market.

7.6   Oligopoly and General Equilibrium

The previous sections examine several partial equilibrium models of trade in a homogeneous product produced by oligopolistic firms. In the rest of this chapter, I analyze trade in goods and international factor mobility using a general equilibrium framework with an oligopolistic industry. I make use of the two-factor, two-sector model of Melvin and Warne (1973) and Markusen (1981), and extend their techniques to investigate issues related to resource allocation and the relationship between commodity prices and factor prices. I also investigate the validity of the fundamental trade theorems and the relationship between international trade in goods and factor movement. This section describes the main features of such an economy under autarky.

Label the two sectors in the home economy sectors 1 and 2. Good 1 is produced by a single firm (a monopolist), but good 2 is produced by a large number of competitive firms. All firms employ two factors, labor (L) and capital (K), to produce the goods. I adopt the notation used in chapters 2 to 4. Thus the production function of sector i is $Q_i = F_i(K_i, L_i)$, where Q_i is the output, and L_i and K_i are the labor and capital employments in sector i, $i = 1, 2$. The capital-labor ratio of sector i is denoted by k_i. The production functions are continuously differentiable, linearly homogeneous and concave, with positive but declining marginal products of labor and capital. Linear homogeneity means that the production function of sector i can be written as $Q_i = L_i f_i(k_i)$, where $f_i(k_i) \equiv F_i(k_i, 1)$.

I further assume perfect price flexibility and perfect factor mobility across sectors. This implies full employment of factors. The country is endowed with exogenously given amounts of labor and capital, $\overline{L}$ and $\overline{K}$.

This framework looks very similar to the neoclassical framework, but the fact that there is a monopolist in sector 1 implies several complications that were not encountered previously. First, the monopolist may also be a monopsonist that can influence not only the price of the good but also factor prices. To simplify the following analysis, assume that the factor markets are competitive, meaning that all firms, including the monopolist, take factor prices as given. This assumption can be justified in the case in which the monopolist is one of the many firms in the economy so that its employment of the factors does not have significant impacts on factor prices.

The second and third complications in the present model, which are related to each other, are who owns the monopolistic firm and who receives the profit, if it is positive, and what the monopolist is maximizing. I avoid the ownership problem by assuming that the residents in this country have identical and homothetic preferences. This means that the aggregate consumption does not depend on income distribution. Thus it does not matter, as far as the equilibrium of the economy is concerned, who owns the monopolistic firm. I further assume that the firm maximizes the profit, instead of the utility of the owners.[9]

Define p as the relative price of good 1 in terms of good 2. The marginal revenue MR_1 in sector 1 is equal to $MR_1 = p(1 - 1/\eta)$, where η is the (positive) elasticity of market demand for good 1, while the marginal revenue in (competitive) sector 2 is the output price, which is unity. Taking factor prices as given, each firm will employ each factor up to the point at which marginal revenue product is equal to factor price. Thus perfect factor mobility implies that

---

9. The assumption that the monopolist maximizes profit instead of utility means that the owners of the firm care about their income but do not consider any effects of the firm's profit maximization on their utility through changes in the price levels. For a relaxation of this assumption, see Kemp and Okawa (1995a).

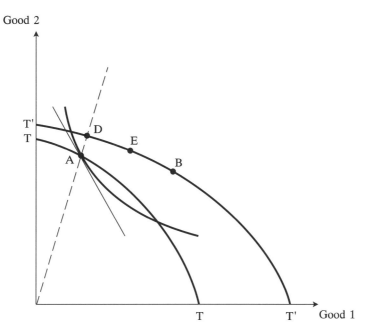

Figure 7.3

$$w = p(1 - 1/\eta)(f_1 - k_1 f_1') = (f_2 - k_2 f_2') \tag{7.19a}$$

$$r = p(1 - 1/\eta) f_1' = f_2', \tag{7.19b}$$

where w is the wage rate and r is the rental rate. Dividing condition (7.19a) by condition (7.19b), the wage-rental ratio is

$$\omega = \frac{f_1}{f_1'} - k_1 = \frac{f_2}{f_2'} - k_2. \tag{7.20}$$

Condition (7.20) is exactly the same as the corresponding condition in the neo-classical model derived in Chapter 2. This result has two implications. First, there is a one-to-one correspondence between the wage-rental ratio and the capital-labor ratio of each sector, and this correspondence can be illustrated by the ω-k diagram in Chapter 2. Second, the two sectors have the same marginal rate of technical substitution. This means that the equilibrium is at a point on the efficiency locus in an Edgeworth box diagram, and that production is efficient. The efficiency locus can be derived by the production possibility frontier (PPF) of the economy. Because both goods are produced by constant-returns technologies, the PPF is concave to the origin, as illustrated by schedule TT in Figure 7.3. Efficient production means that the production point is on the PPF, but the production point is not the point of tangency between a price line and the PPF, as I now show.

Denote the marginal rate of transformation (MRT), which is the negative of the slope of the PPF, by $MRT(y^s)$ where $y^s \equiv Q_1/Q_2$ is the ratio of the good-1 output to the good-2 output. Differentiate the production function of sector i to give $dQ_i = F_{iK}dK_i + F_{iL}dL_i$, where F_{iK} and F_{iL} are the marginal product of capital and labor, respectively. Using this result,

$$MRT(y^s) = -\frac{dQ_2}{dQ_1}\bigg|_{PPF} = -\frac{F_{2K}dK_2 + F_{2L}dL_2}{F_{1K}dK_1 + F_{1L}dL_1}.$$

Using the full employment conditions, $dK_2 = -dK_1$, $dL_2 = -dL_1$, and the factor price conditions (7.19),

$$MRT(y^s) = p(1 - 1/\eta) < p. \tag{7.21}$$

Condition (7.21) implies that at the equilibrium point the MRT is equal to marginal revenue of sector 1, and that graphically the price line is steeper than the PPF.

The relationship between factor prices and commodity prices can be derived as follows. Because of linear homogeneity of the production function, the marginal cost of good 1 is equal to the unit cost $c_1(w, r)$ (see Chapter 2). Because the monopolist is a price taker in factor markets, it takes the marginal cost as given. To maximize its profit, the monopolist chooses an output at which

$$p(1 - 1/\eta) = c_1(w, r). \tag{7.22a}$$

In sector 2, which is competitive, all firms earn zero profit in equilibrium. This implies that

$$1 = c_2(w, r). \tag{7.22b}$$

If $p(1 - 1/\eta)$ is known, conditions (7.22) are illustrated in Figure 7.4. (Ignore the broken schedule for the time being.) The schedule labeled $c_1 = MR_1$ shows the combinations of (w, r) that satisfy condition (7.22a); that labeled $c_2 = 1$ corresponds to condition (7.22b). The slope of a unit-cost schedule is equal to the reciprocal of the capital-labor ratio. The point of intersection between the two unit-cost schedules, point E, shows the values of w and r that satisfy conditions (7.22a) and (7.22b). For the sake of exposition, let me assume that sector 1 is capital-intensive at all factor prices. This means that the slope of the c_1-schedule is less steep than that of the c_2-schedule at point E, as the diagram shows. Note that if condition (7.22a) is divided by (7.22b), the result is (7.21). This result, which is a useful one, is not surprising because the MRT is equal to the ratio of marginal costs of the sectors, and with constant returns, marginal cost of each sector equals its unit cost.

Now it is necessary to derive the demand elasticity. Following Melvin and Warne (1973) and Markusen (1981), I assume that the utility function of a rep-

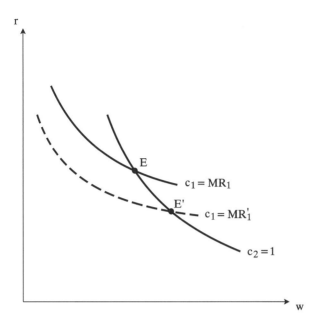

Figure 7.4

resentative consumer is of the CES type, that is, $u = [C_1^\beta + aC_2^\beta]^{1/\beta}$, where $1 > \beta > -\infty$, $\beta \neq 0$, and C_i is the consumption of good i.[10] The elasticity of substitution σ is defined as $\sigma = 1/(1 - \beta)$. Because all consumers are assumed to have identical and homothetic preferences, the utility function also represents the social utility function. When C_i is the aggregate consumption of good i, u is interpreted as the social utility level. Denote national income by $I = pQ_1 + Q_2$. Treating I as constant (because each individual treats his or her income as given), the aggregate demands for the two goods can be derived as

$$C_1 = \frac{I}{p[1 + a^\sigma p^{\beta\sigma}]} \tag{7.23a}$$

$$C_2 = \frac{a^\sigma p^\sigma I}{p[1 + a^\sigma p^{\beta\sigma}]}. \tag{7.23b}$$

Define $y^d \equiv C_1/C_2$ as the ratio of the demands. Combining (7.23a) and (7.23b), I have

$$y^d = \left(\frac{1}{ap}\right)^\sigma. \tag{7.24}$$

---

10. Many of the results in this and the following sections still hold in a slightly more general case in which the preferences are homothetic. For example, with homothetic preferences, the ratio of demands for the goods depends only on the price ratio.

The relationship between y^d and p is illustrated in Figure 7.5. Condition (7.24) implies that schedule y^d is downward sloping, touching both axes at infinity. For simplicity, I call this schedule the demand schedule because it describes the demand side of the economy, although one should be aware that it is not the same as the ordinary demand schedule for a single market.

Again treating I as constant, the demand for good 1 is differentiated with respect to p.[11] Rearranging terms gives the elasticity of demand for good 1

$$\eta = -\frac{p}{C_1}\frac{dC_1}{dp} = 1 + \frac{\beta\sigma a^\sigma p^{\beta\sigma}}{(1 + a^\sigma p^{\beta\sigma})}. \tag{7.25}$$

In condition (7.25), $\eta > 1$ if and only if $1 > \beta > 0$ or $\sigma > 1$. Because a profit-maximizing monopolist will not choose to produce at a point at which $\eta \leq 1$, I assume that $1 > \beta > 0$ or $\sigma > 1$. Differentiating η given by condition (7.25) with respect to p, I can show that $d\eta/dp > 0$.

Because η depends on p, the relationship between the supply ratio y^s and the price ratio given by condition (7.21) can be written as

$$MRT(y^s) = p\left(1 - \frac{1}{\eta(p)}\right). \tag{7.21'}$$

Differentiate both sides of (7.21') to give

$$MRT_y\, dy^s = \left[\left(1 - \frac{1}{\eta}\right) + \frac{p}{\eta^2}\frac{d\eta}{dp}\right]dp, \tag{7.26}$$

where $MRT_y \equiv dMRT/dy^s$. Concavity of the PPF implies that $MRT_y > 0$. Because η is increasing in p, the coefficient before dp in (7.26) is positive. Combining the results, I get $dy^s/dp > 0$. The relationship between y^s and p is illustrated in Figure 7.5 by the positively sloped schedule, called the supply schedule.

The autarkic equilibrium is described by the following condition

$$y^s = y^d. \tag{7.27}$$

Thus conditions (7.24), (7.21'), and (7.27) can be solved for y^s, y^d, and p. Graphically, y^s, y^d, and p can be obtained from Figure 7.5 as the intersecting point, shown as point E, between the supply and demand schedules. The analysis and the diagram show that such an equilibrium exists and is unique. After obtaining the equilibrium values of y^s and p, PPF can be used to solve for the output and consumption levels of the goods.

---

11. From the consumers' point of view, I is treated as constant. Would the monopolist regard I as constant when it evaluates the demand elasticitiy? Markusen (1981) argues that for homothetic preferences, it is immaterial whether the monopolist views I as fixed or variable.

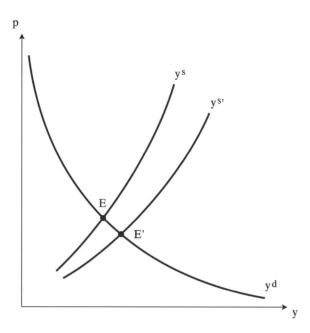

Figure 7.5

Once the autarkic price ratio is determined, the elasticity of demand for good 1, which is greater than unity, can also be determined. From condition $(7.21')$, I obtain the gap between the MRT and the price ratio. Diagrammatically, the autarkic equilibrium point is shown by point A in Figure 7.3. As explained previously, the price line is steeper than the PPF at A.

Before turning to trade and factor mobility, one more result needs to be proven.[12] Suppose that the country has a growth of its capital stock while the labor endowment is fixed. This expands the production possibility set of the economy. In terms of Figure 7.3, the PPF shifts out from TT to T'T'. Recall that sector 1 is assumed to be capital intensive. This means that schedule T'T' is beyond schedule TT in such a way that given a point like point A on TT, there is a point on T'T' such as point B that is lower than and to the right of point A, so that the slope of TT at point A is equal to that of T'T' at point B. The result may be called the Rybczynski theorem under constant MRT:

The Rybczynski Theorem under Constant MRT   Given constant MRT, an increase in the endowment of a factor increases, by a greater proportion, the output of the good which uses the factor intensively, and decrease the output of the other good.

12. This result is based on an extension of the analysis in Melvin and Warne (1973) or Markusen (1981).

This result is used to show how the equilibrium may change. For convenience, denote the MRT of the country by $MRT(y^s, \alpha)$ where α is a shift parameter. Define $MRT_\alpha \equiv \partial MRT/\partial \alpha$ and define α so that $MRT_\alpha > 0$. In the present case in which there is a growth in the capital stock and sector 1 is capital intensive, $d\alpha < 0$.

Differentiate (7.21′), *keeping p constant*, and rearrange terms to give,

$$dy^s = -\frac{MRT_\alpha}{MRT_y}d\alpha. \tag{7.28}$$

Condition (7.28) implies that with more capital stock ($d\alpha < 0$), the supply schedule shifts to the right ($dy^s > 0$ when given p). Its new position in Figure 7.5 is represented by the schedule labeled $y^{s\prime}$. On the demand side, homothetic preferences imply that the demand schedule remains unchanged. The new equilibrium is represented by the intersecting point, point E′, between the demand schedule and the new supply schedule in the diagram. By comparing points E and E′ in Figure 7.5, it can be concluded that the capital accumulation has caused a drop in p and a rise in y^s and y^d. In terms of Figure 7.3, the new equilibrium point is somewhere between point B and point D on the new PPF, where D has the same output ratio as that at point A and where point B has the same MRT as point A.

The effects of capital accumulation on factor prices can be derived using conditions (7.22a) and (7.22b), or using Figure 7.4. Because η is increasing in p, it is easy to show that $MR_1 \equiv p(1 - 1/\eta)$ is also increasing in p. In Figure 7.4, the broken line represents a new unit-cost schedule curve so that MR_1' is the new value of MR_1, $MR_1' < MR_1$. The c_2-schedule remains unchanged because good 2 is the numeraire. The new equilibrium point at which the two unit-cost schedules intersect each other represents a lower rental rate but a higher wage rate.

7.7   Trade with Oligopoly: A General Equilibrium Approach

Now introduce another country, labeled the foreign country. The foreign country has the same structure in terms of technologies and preferences as the home country. Although all individuals in the world have identical and homothetic (CES) preferences, the two countries may have different technologies or endowments. In each country there is a single producer in sector 1 while sector 2 is competitive, meaning that I now have a duopoly (in sector 1) in a general equilibrium model. Free trade between the countries is allowed. To focus the analysis on resource allocation, consider the simplest form of trade with oligopoly with the following assumptions: (1) There is zero transport cost; (2) perfect arbitrage is allowed; and (3) the firms have Cournot conjectures.

Assumptions (1) and (2) mean that the markets in the countries are fully integrated, and intraindustry trade in the same product is not needed. To include intraindustry trade, there must be market segmentation by prohibiting arbitrage or by assuming positive transport costs, but the analysis will be much more complicated. I showed earlier that if transport cost is zero and if the firms engage in Bertrand competition, the result is the same as if the firms have Cournot conjectures in the presence of perfect arbitrage.

Because the two countries have identical and CES-type preferences and because the two markets are fully integrated under free trade, I can apply the earlier techniques to derive the world demands for the goods. I use a superscript "w" to denote variables of the world, and an asterisk to denote those of the foreign country.

Condition (7.25) gives the world's elasticity of demand for good 1

$$\eta^w = -\frac{p}{C_1^w}\frac{dC_1^w}{dp} = \frac{1 + a^\sigma(1+\beta\sigma)p^{\beta\sigma}}{(1 + a^\sigma p^{\beta\sigma})}. \tag{7.25'}$$

The perceived elasticity of demand for good 1 by the home and foreign firms are respectively given by

$$\eta = -\frac{p}{Q_1}\frac{dC_1^w}{dp} = -\frac{Q_1^w}{Q_1}\frac{p}{C_1^w}\frac{dC_1^w}{dp} = \frac{\eta^w}{\theta} \tag{7.29a}$$

$$\eta^* = -\frac{p}{Q_1^*}\frac{dC_1^w}{dp} = -\frac{Q_1^w}{Q_1^*}\frac{p}{C_1^w}\frac{dC_1^w}{dp} = \frac{\eta^w}{\theta^*}, \tag{7.29b}$$

where θ and θ^* are the ratios of the home and foreign monopolistic firms' outputs to the world's total output of good 1; $\theta \equiv Q_1/Q_1^w$ and $\theta^* \equiv Q_1^*/Q_1^w$. In deriving conditions (7.29), I have used the equilibrium condition $Q_1^w = C_1^w$.

For a given PPF, there exists a one-to-one correspondence between the output of good 1 and the output ratio. Thus two functions can be defined so that

$$Q_1 = h(y^s, v) \tag{7.30a}$$

$$Q_1^* = h^*(y^{s*}) \tag{7.30b}$$

where v is a shift parameter which for the time being is ignored. Define $h_y \equiv \partial h/\partial y^s$, $h_v \equiv \partial h/\partial v$, and $h_{y*}^* \equiv dh^*/dy^{s*}$. The shift parameter is defined in such a way that $h_v > 0$. Because the PPF of each country is downward sloping, $h_y > 0$ and $h_{y*}^* > 0$.

Free-trade equilibrium can now be derived. Substitute the demand elasticities given in (7.29a) and (7.29b) into (7.21') for the countries to give

$$MRT(y^s, \alpha) = p\left(1 - \frac{\theta}{\eta^w(p)}\right) \tag{7.31a}$$

$$MRT^*(y^{s*}) = p\left(1 - \frac{\theta^*}{\eta^w(p)}\right). \tag{7.31b}$$

Conditions (7.31a) and (7.31b) are analogous to the reaction functions of two oligopolistic firms in a partial equilibrium framework derived earlier. The present conditions are more complicated, however, because there are three, not two, unknowns in the two equations, that is, y^s, y^{s*} and p. The price ratio, on the other hand, depends on the demand conditions.

Totally differentiate conditions (7.31a) and (7.31b) to give

$$\begin{bmatrix} MRT_y + \phi & -\phi^* \\ -\phi & MRT_y^* + \phi^* \end{bmatrix} \begin{bmatrix} dy^s \\ dy^{s*} \end{bmatrix}$$

$$- \begin{bmatrix} 1 - \theta(\gamma - 1/\eta^w) \\ 1 - \theta^*(\gamma - 1/\eta^w) \end{bmatrix} dp = - \begin{bmatrix} MRT_\alpha \\ 0 \end{bmatrix} d\alpha + \begin{bmatrix} -\zeta \\ \zeta \end{bmatrix} d\nu \tag{7.32}$$

where

$$\phi = \frac{pQ_1^* h_y}{\eta^w (Q_1^w)^2} > 0$$

$$\phi^* = \frac{pQ_1 h_{y*}^*}{\eta^w (Q_1^w)^2} > 0$$

$$\gamma = \frac{p}{(\eta^w)^2} \frac{d\eta^w}{dp} > 0 \quad \text{and}$$

$$\zeta = \frac{pQ_1^* h_\nu}{\eta^w (Q_1^w)^2} > 0.$$

If p in (7.32) is treated as a parameter, the condition can be solved for the effects of the shocks on the supply schedules y^s and y^{s*} of the countries ($dp = 0$):

$$\frac{\partial y^s}{\partial \alpha} = -\frac{MRT_\alpha [MRT_{y*}^* + \phi^*]}{\Delta} < 0 \tag{7.33a}$$

$$\frac{\partial y^{s*}}{\partial \alpha} = \frac{\phi MRT_\alpha}{\Delta} > 0 \tag{7.33b}$$

$$\frac{\partial y^s}{\partial \nu} = -\frac{\zeta MRT_{y*}^*}{\Delta} < 0 \tag{7.33c}$$

$$\frac{\partial y^{s*}}{\partial \nu} = \frac{\zeta MRT_y}{\Delta} > 0 \tag{7.33d}$$

where $\Delta = \phi MRT_{y*}^* + \phi^* MRT_y + MRT_y MRT_{y*}^* > 0$.

I now turn to the demand side of the countries. Facing the same price ratio and given identical and homothetic preferences, they have the same demand

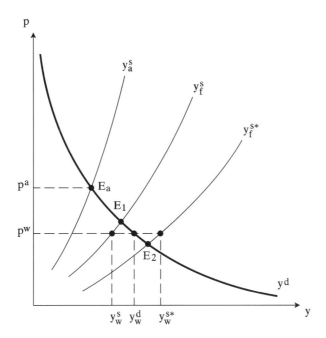

Figure 7.6

schedule y^d is shown in Figure 7.6. Bringing the supply and demand sides of the countries together, two market-clearing conditions can be stated as:

$$Q_1 + Q_1^* = Q_1^w = C_1^w \tag{7.34a}$$

$$Q_2 + Q_2^* = Q_2^w = C_2^w. \tag{7.34b}$$

By Walras's law, one of the conditions is redundant. Define $\varphi \equiv Q_2/Q_2^w = Q_2/C_2^w$ as the share of output of good 2 in the home country, while $(1 - \varphi)$ is that of the foreign country. The share φ of course depends on the equilibrium price ratio. Using (7.34b), condition (7.34a) can be rearranged to give

$$\varphi y^s + (1 - \varphi)y^{s*} = y^d. \tag{7.35}$$

Condition (7.35) means that in equilibrium y^d is a weighted average of y^s and y^{s*}. The new supply schedules are shown as y_f^s and y_f^{s*} in Figure 7.6. The equilibrium price ratio, denoted by p^w in Figure 7.6, is between the price ratios corresponding to points E_1 and E_2. The corresponding home and foreign output ratios, denoted by y_w^s and y_w^{s*}, and the world demand ratio, y_w^d, satisfy condition (7.35).

To understand how to apply this result, consider two special cases which were analyzed in Markusen (1981) using a different technique. In the first one, the two countries are identical in not just preferences but also in technologies and factor endowments. The two countries thus have the same free-trade y_f^s-schedule as shown in Figure 7.6. (For the time being, ignore the y_f^{s*}-schedule shown in the diagram but instead let the y_f^s-schedule represent both countries' supply schedules under free trade.) The equilibrium is at the point (point E_1) at which the y_f^s-schedule cuts the y^d-schedule. Under free trade, the two countries have the same output ratio, meaning that they have the same production point. How is this production point compared with the autarkic production? To answer this, recall that the supply condition is given by (7.21'). Comparing this with condition (7.29a), it can be seen that the autarkic supply schedule for both countries is given by y_a^s, which is to the left of schedule y_f^s. The autarkic point is at point E_a. Comparing E_a and E_1 shows that free trade encourages both firms in sector 1 to produce more, lowering the price of good 1. Because the countries are identical and perfect arbitrage is allowed, there is no need to have trade even though free trade is allowed. This is the procompetitive effect of free trade analyzed earlier using a partial equilibrium framework.

In the second special case, the two countries have the same technologies and the same capital-labor ratio, but the home country is bigger. Note that if trade is not allowed, scale does not matter in the present model in the sense that the countries have the same autarky price ratio. In terms of Figure 7.6, they have the same autarkic supply schedule labeled y_a^s. With CES preferences, demand elasticities are independent of the size of the country. Thus the countries have the same autarkic equilibrium point E_a.

If free trade is allowed, however, scale does matter. To analyze the effects of being bigger, the same approach can be followed as in the previous case. Suppose that the countries are initially identical. So they have the same supply schedule under free trade. Suppose now that the home country gets uniformly more labor and capital. I want to show how this may affect the countries' supply schedules.

When the home country gets uniformly bigger, its PPF shifts out proportionately. This means that for any given output level y^s, the slope of its PPF is unchanged, that is, the shift parameter α is unchanged. Because its PPF shifts out, however, output of good 1 increases at any given commodity prices. This means that as the scale of the home country expands, $dv > 0$. (Note that $h_v > 0$.)

Conditions (7.33c) and (7.33d) imply that the expansion of the home country shifts its supply schedule to the left while that of the foreign country to the right. The relative positions of their supply schedules are shown by the schedules labeled y_f^s and y_f^{s*} in Figure 7.6. Using the previous analysis, I conclude that the home country produces relatively less good 1 and so imports the good. In other words, when two countries are identical except that one is bigger uniformly, the bigger one imports the good produced by the oligopolistic firms. In an absolute term, however, the output (good 1) of the foreign oligopolist is less than that of the home oligopolist. The reason is that $y^{s*} > y^s$ implies that $MRT(y^{s*}) > MRT(y^s)$ because the home PPF is uniformly outside the foreign PPF. This means that the marginal revenue of the foreign monopolist is greater than that of the home monopolist, and using the definition of marginal revenue, $Q_1^* < Q_1$.

7.8   Validity of the Fundamental Trade Theorems

I now examine the validity of the fundamental trade theorems derived in Chapters 2 and 3.[13]

7.8.1   The Stolper-Samuelson Theorem

In the original Stolper-Samuelson theorem, commodity prices are treated as parameters and the theorem states the effects of exogenous changes in commodity prices on factor prices. In the present framework with oligopolistic firms in sector 1, it is meaningless to treat commodity prices as parameters because they are determined endogenously except in the case of a small open economy. For a small open economy, however, the single producer in the economy loses its monopoly power, and the model reduces to the neoclassical one in which the Stolper-Samuelson theorem necessarily holds.

Thus commodity prices are alllowed to be determined endogenously, and the following issue can be addressed. Suppose that there is a shock in the home country such as a growth of a factor endowment, a change in the environment of the rest of the world with which it is trading, or a change in government policy. If as a result there is an increase in the relative price of good 1, p, will the real reward of capital, which is used intensively in sector 1, rise and the real wage rate fall?

To answer this question, I adopt the notation in chapter 2 and denote the percentage increase in p by $\widehat{p}$, where $\widehat{v} \equiv dv/v$ for any variable v. Differentiate the marginal revenue in sector 1 and rearrange terms to get

$$\widehat{MR_1} = \widehat{p} + \frac{1}{\eta - 1}\widehat{\eta}. \tag{7.36}$$

I have proved that if the economy is a closed one, η is an increasing function of p. This implies that if the economy is an open one, η^w is an increasing function of the free-trade price ratio p. In the latter case, $\eta = \eta^w/\theta$, implying that $\widehat{\eta} = \widehat{\eta}^w - \widehat{\theta}$. This means that if a change in p does not affect θ too significantly, I can say that η is also an increasing function of p under free trade.

---

13. More discussion about the issues in this and the following sections is given in Wong (1993a).

With this assumption, (7.36) implies that if $\widehat{p} > 0$, then $\widehat{MR}_1 > \widehat{p}$, or if $\widehat{p} < 0$, then $\widehat{MR}_1 < \widehat{p}$.

I then turn to the relationship between a change in MR_1 and changes in factor prices. Recall that $MR_1 = c_1(w, r)$, that $1 = c_2(w, r)$, and that sector 1 is capital intensive. The traditional technique or Figure 7.4 can be employed to derive the magnification effects in terms of MR_1 and factor prices, that is, $\widehat{r} > \widehat{MR}_1 > 0 > \widehat{w}$ or $\widehat{r} < \widehat{MR}_1 < 0 < \widehat{w}$, depending on the sign of $\widehat{MR}_1$. Combining these results and the preceding ones, I conclude that if there is a shock that causes a change in p, then

$$\widehat{r} > \widehat{MR}_1 > \widehat{p} > 0 > \widehat{w}; \quad \text{or} \quad \widehat{r} < \widehat{MR}_1 < \widehat{p} < 0 < \widehat{w}.$$

Thus for a closed economy or for an open economy when θ remains fairly constant, the Stolper-Samuelson theorem holds.[14]

7.8.2   The Rybczynski Theorem

I showed earlier that if the MRT (and thus the factor prices) is constant, then in this sense the Rybczynski theorem holds.

7.8.3   The Law of Comparative Advantage and the Heckscher-Ohlin Theorem

The difficulty of proving the law of comparative advantage in the present model is that production of the duopolistic firms depends on a series of factors such as cost conditions, demand conditions, and the interaction between them. This point was made by Helpman and Krugman (1985, Chapter 5) using a partial equilibrium framework. I now show that this law in general is not valid in a general equilibrium framework. One counterexample is presented using Figure 7.7 as follows.

For simplicity, assume that the two countries have identical and homothetic (CES-type) preferences. Figure 7.7 shows the common demand schedule of the countries and the world. The supply schedules of the foreign and home countries under autarky are labeled y_a^{s*} and y_a^s, respectively, with equilibrium points at E_a^* and E_a. In this case, the foreign autarkic relative price of good 1 is higher than that of the home country. If free trade is allowed, the two supply schedules shift to y_f^{s*} and y_f^s. The shift of a supply schedule depends on the relative size of a country, the technologies and the preferences. Suppose that the home country is sufficiently larger than the foreign country. Conditions (7.33c) and (7.33d) imply that it is possible for the foreign supply schedule to lie on the right-hand side of the home supply schedule, a case illustrated

---

14. Melvin and Warne (1973) argue that when both industries are characterized by two duopolists, one firm in each industry in each country, and when both duopolists in each industry collude to maximize their joint profit, the Stolper-Samuelson theorem may not hold.

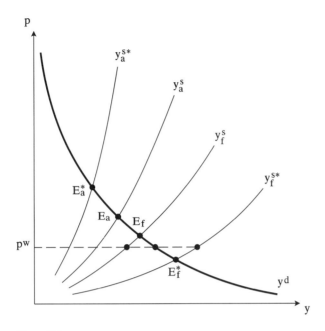

Figure 7.7

by schedules y_f^{s*} and y_f^s in Figure 7.7. The world price, p^w, which clears the markets, implies that the home country imports good 1, the good in which it has a comparative advantage. This violates the law of comparative advantage.

Another counterexample can be constructed by using the results in the previous section. Suppose that the two countries are identical except that the home country is bigger. I showed that they have the same autarkic price ratio, but when free trade is allowed, the bigger home country imports good 1.

Because the law of comparative advantage does not hold, it seems that there is no hope for the Heckscher-Ohlin theorem; however, a modified version of the theorem does hold. Let me start with the case in which the two countries have identical factor endowments, technologies, and preferences. Assume that sector 1 is capital intensive and that the preferences are of the CES-type. This means that the countries have the same autarkic equilibrium. When free trade between them is allowed, no trade will exist, as I showed earlier. In terms of Figure 7.6, under free trade the identical supply schedules of the two countries shift from the one labeled y_a^s to the right, implying a drop in p and an increase in the good-1 output.

Suppose now that the home country has an increase in its capital stock. Whether the home country will export or import good 1 depends on whether its free-trade supply schedule is on the right- or left-hand side of that of the foreign country. I showed in the previous section that there are two factors that determine the relative positions of the countries' supply schedules. The increase in the capital stock tends to push the home supply schedule to the right relative to the foreign counterpart, but being bigger means that the home supply schedule tends to be on the left-hand side of the foreign schedule.

In order to eliminate the scale effect, I gradually withdraw labor and capital from the home country by the same proportion until the production possibility frontiers of the two countries intersect at the foreign country's autarkic production point. The scale effect is thus zero, meaning that in a diagram like Figure 7.6, the home supply schedule is on the right-hand side of the foreign one. (This case is opposite to what is shown in Figure 7.6.) The world equilibrium price is at p^w, with the home country exporting the capital-intensive good 1. Thus the Heckscher-Ohlin theorem holds.[15]

If in the preceding analysis the home country has more labor endowment instead, no adjustment for their sizes is needed. In this case, the labor endowment growth will shift the home country's supply schedule to the left. The scale effect, that is, the home country being bigger, will further shift the home supply schedule to the left while the foreign supply schedule shifts to the right. Thus the home country will unambiguously import the capital-intensive good 1. In this case, labor endowment growth and its size both encourage the home country to produce relatively more of good 2 and to import good 1. The modified Heckscher-Ohlin theorem can now be stated in an oligopoly model:

The Heckscher-Ohlin Theorem with Oligopoly   A country that is bigger and is abundant in the factor used intensively in the competitive sector exports the good from the competitive sector. If two countries have the same size in the sense that the scale effect is zero, each country exports the good that uses its abundant factor intensively.

7.8.4   Factor Price Equalization Theorem

This theorem in a model of monopolistic sectors was first examined by Melvin and Warne (1973). Assuming identical technologies and (CES-type) preferences across countries, they show that if the monopolistic firms in sector 1 of the home and foreign countries cooperate and choose production to maximize their joint profit (so that they together form an international monopolist), then the factor price equalization theorem holds. The reason is that if the two firms

15. Strictly speaking, the condition that the scale effect is zero holds only in the neighborhood close to the foreign country's autarky point. This means that the result is true only if the factor endowments of the countries are not too far apart. Alternatively, labor and capital can be withdrawn (at the same rate) from the home country so that the home PPF cuts the foreign PPF at the foreign country's free-trade production point. The result is then true for any differences in the capital-labor ratios of the countries. The difficulty is that a lot of information is needed to calculate the foreign country's free-trade equilibrium point.

cooperate, then the equalization of output prices means that they have the same marginal revenue. To maximize their joint profit, the firms must produce at a point at which the common marginal revenue is equal to their marginal costs or unit costs. If the economies are diversified, sector 2 in these economies must also have the same unit cost. Assuming that the unit cost functions are globally invertible, factor prices are equalized.

Helpman and Krugman (1985, Chapter 5) consider another case. Assuming that the number of factors is equal to the number of competitive sectors in the two countries, they show that under the usual conditions such as identical technologies and diversification in the competitive side of each economy, there exist some factor endowments with which the economies have the same factor prices under free trade. The sectors with oligopolistic firms withdraw resources from the economies, thus placing additional constraints on the allocation of factors between the economies in order to have factor price equalization.

If, however, the oligopolistic firms do not collude, as is assumed here, and if the number of factors is greater than the number of competitive sectors (but is equal to the number of sectors), whether the factor price equalization theorem is still valid is not clear. This issue is addressed as follows.

Recall that the marginal revenue of good 1 for the home oligopolistic firm under free trade is $p(1 - \theta/\eta^w)$, where θ is the share of the home country's good-1 output in the world. If the home and foreign countries have the same output of good 1 under trade, then they face the same marginal revenue. In equilibrium, the marginal revenue is equated to the marginal cost, or the unit cost. Thus if the number of (competitive and oligopolistic) sectors is equal to the number of factors (with diversification), if all oligopolistic firms in each sector have the same output, and if the unit cost functions are globally invertible, factor price equalization exists.

Because factor price equalization requires the same output of good 1 in both countries, I now determine cases in which this condition is satisfied. The obvious case is the one in which the countries are initially identical, with the same factor endowments, technologies, and preferences. This case is shown in the Edgeworth box diagram in Figure 7.8. The box shows the given factor endowments in the world. Different points inside the box represent different ways of allocating the factors between the countries. If the countries have identical endowments, then the endowment point is at point M, the midpoint of the diagonal of the Edgeworth box. In this case, the countries have identical factor prices under free trade.

I now search for other cases in which factor prices are equalized. Suppose now that the endowments are represented by a point such as point A on the diagonal between points M and O*. This means that the countries have the same capital-labor ratio, but that the home country is bigger. I showed that,

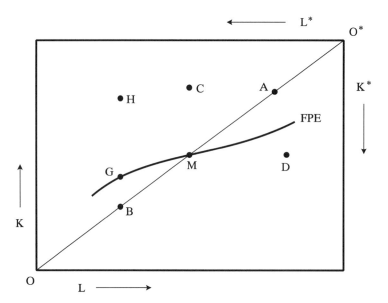

Figure 7.8

being bigger, the home country produces more good 1 than the foreign country does under free trade. This means that the home oligopolistic firm in sector 1 faces a smaller marginal revenue. Using Figure 7.4, it can be shown that the home country has a smaller rental rate (in terms of good 2) and a higher wage rate.[16] Using the same argument, I can show that if the endowment point is between M and the origin O, such as B, the home country has a higher rental rate.

Suppose now that the home country has more capital than the foreign country, while they both have the same amount of labor. The new endowment point can be a point at C that is vertically above point M in the diagram. To show that the home country must have a smaller rental rate under free trade, I must first prove that the home country produces a greater output of good 1 (capital intensive) under trade. Suppose not, that is, $Q_1 < Q_1^*$. This implies that $\theta < \theta^*$, that the home monopolist receives a higher marginal revenue than the foreign mo­nopolist does, and that at the free-trade production point $MRT > MRT^*$. By the Rybczynski theorem under a given MRT, however, an increase in the home capital stock must shift the home PPF in such a way that at the same MRT, the home production of the capital-intensive good 1 increases. This implies that if under free trade $MRT > MRT^*$, then $Q_1 > Q_1^*$. This is a contradiction. So

16. For example, in Figure 7.4, point E (corresponding to a higher marginal revenue) represents foreign factor prices while point E′ represents those in the home country.

Q_1 must be greater than Q_1^*, implying that the home MR in sector 1 is smaller than the foreign counterpart. Figure 7.4 again can be used to show that the home country has a smaller rental rate.

Consider now the case in which the home country has more labor but the same amount of capital as compared with the foreign country. The endowment point is at a point such as D. The argument can be reversed to show that the home country has a higher rental rate.

Combining these results, it can be concluded that there are some endowment points in the diagram with which the countries have factor price equalization. These endowment points are represented by the factor price equalization schedule FPE. The analysis shows that it must lie in the smaller region between the diagonal and a horizontal line passing through point M. In the neighborhood around point M, schedule FPE is positively sloped but is less steep than the diagonal. Points above (respectively below) it represent endowments of the countries so that the home country has a lower (respectively higher) rental rate. In general, schedule FPE will not be too close to the axes because one of the countries may get complete specialization.[17]

7.9   Factor Mobility and Commodity Trade

So far, I have not allowed internationl factor mobility. In this section, I relax this assumption. Using the two-country framework constructed previously, I investigate the relationship between international trade and factor mobility. In particular, I analyze whether they are substitutes or completements in the senses given in Chapters 3 and 4.

In the two-country framework, I again assume that the countries have identical technologies and (homothetic) preferences. Recall that the box diagram in Figure 7.8 shows the distribution of factor endowments between the countries. Suppose that the endowment point is given by point G, a point on the factor price equalization schedule FPE. If the countries permit free trade but not factor movement between them, factor prices are equalized. Thus no factor movement will exist even if it is allowed. This result is similar to the Mundell (1957) result.

But are international trade and factor mobility substitutes in the price-equalization sense as defined by Wong (1986a)? In other words, will either international trade in goods alone or international factor mobility alone lead to

---

17. If the foreign country gives up too much capital (point C being too close to the upper horizontal axis), it may be completely specialized in the production of good 2, the labor-intensive good.

the same equilibrium? To answer this question, let me now analyze *free international capital mobility* but not trade in goods.[18] Assume that owners of the moving factor repatriate their earnings back to their own country in terms of good 2, the numeriare.

I first have to determine the direction of movement of capital. To do that I have to compare the autarky factor prices in the countries. The analysis is given in several steps. First, suppose that the countries have identical factor endowments (in addition to identical technologies and preferences). The endowment point is at point M in Figure 7.8. The countries obviously have the same factor prices and no international capital movement is expected. Consider the second case in which both countries have the same capital-labor ratio, with the home country being small. A possible endowment point is point B. Because scale does not matter in a closed economy scale, the countries must still have the same factor prices. So again no international capital movement is expected. In the third case, the home country is capital abundant. A possible endowment point is point G. I showed earlier that for a closed economy, an increase in its capital stock will lower the rental rate and raise its wage rate. This means that being capital abundant, the home country has a lower autarkic rental rate than the foreign one.

If at point G international capital mobility is allowed, home capital will flow out to the foreign country until the rental rates in the countries are equalized. The equilibrium is represented by point B in Figure 7.8, which is a point on the diagonal and is directly below point G. The countries have the same capital-labor ratio, and thus the same wage-rental ratio. Because of identical technologies and preferences, they have the same commodity prices. Again, there is an equilibrium with equalization of commodity and factor prices.

The present analysis shows that if the endowment point is a point on schedule FPE, either free trade in goods or free capital mobility will lead to commodity and factor price equalization. This is similar to the Mundell result, but the similarity stops here. In the neoclassical model with two competitive sectors, the free-trade equilibrium is identical to the free-capital-mobility equilibrium so that when either free trade or free capital mobility is allowed, further allowing the other will have no effect. Thus in the neoclassical model, international trade and factor mobility are substitutes. In the present model *they are not*.

When the endowments of the countries are given by point G, the equilibrium under international capital mobility is point B, with the home capital moving to the foreign country. Suppose now that free trade in goods is allowed. The analysis shows that with the same capital-labor ratio but with different

---

18. The case of free international labor mobility can be analyzed in a similar way.

sizes, the countries trade. In particular, the home (smaller) country will export good 1. Under free trade, the home country will have a higher rental rate. Thus free trade will induce capital to move from the foreign country back to the home country until the equilibrium point is back to point G in Figure 7.8.

The present analysis shows that if the factor endowments are given by a point on the factor price equalization schedule FPE, then free trade alone is sufficient to achieve the world equilibrium with equalization of commodity and factor prices. If only free capital mobility is allowed, the equilibrium is a point on the diagonal and is less efficient than under free trade in goods. So international trade in goods and capital mobility are not substitutes in the price-equalization sense. This result, which is contrary to the one in the neoclassical model, can be explained intuitively. If free trade is not allowed, the two monopolists are single producers in their own markets. Free trade changes the market structure because the two monopolists have to compete in an integrated market, and they become duopolists. Thus free trade achieves something that free capital mobility alone cannot.

In the above analysis, the initial factor endowment point is assumed to be on the factor price equalization schedule FPE in Figure 7.8 so that free trade leads to equalized factor prices. Suppose now that the endowment point is not on schedule FPE. Specifically, let the endowment point be at point H, which is vertically above point G, in the diagram.

Let me first analyze free trade. Because point H is above schedule FPE, the home country has a rental rate lower than the foreign one under free trade. Thus if international capital mobility is allowed under free trade, home capital will flow out to the foreign country until point G is reached. Capital mobility then stops because commodity and factor prices are equalized. Suppose instead at the initial endowment point H free capital mobility but not free trade is allowed. Being capital abundant, the home country has a lower rental rate than the foreign one, and home capital will again flow out until point B is reached. Thus more home capital flows out in the absence of trade than in the presence of trade. As analyzed previously, if at point B free trade is allowed, some of the capital in the foreign country will flow back to the home country until point G is reached. This means that the free-trade equilibrium, the free-capital-mobility equilibrium, and the free-trade-plus-capital-mobility equilibrium *are all different*. Free trade and free capital mobility are needed to achieve the equilibrium represented by a point on the factor price equalization schedule. So they are complements in the price-equalization sense.

So far I have focused on whether factor mobility or commodity trade alone is enough to reach an efficient world equilibrium. I now examine how they may affect each other's level. For simplicity, assume that only capital mobility is allowed while labor is immobile across countries. It turns out that these effects are much more complicated than their price effects because in many cases it is not easy to predict the patterns and volume of trade.

Markusen (1983) is the first to provide a formal analysis of this issue. He considers a case in which the home and foreign countries are identical except that the foreign country is uniformly bigger. This corresponds to point B in Figure 7.8. I showed earlier that if only free commodity trade is allowed, the home country will export (capital-intensive) good 1, and that it has a higher free-trade rental rate of capital. If capital mobility is further allowed, foreign capital will flow to the home country. In other words, the home (respectively foreign) country gains (respectively loses) the factor which is used intensively in its exportable (respectively importable) sector. Assuming that such reallocation of capital will encourage the home country's volume of export, Markusen concludes that international capital movement augments the volume of trade.

In more general cases, however, the effect of capital movement on the volume of trade is difficult to predict. The reason is that the volume of trade depends on several conditions such as the interaction between the two oligopolistic firms. In some cases, capital movement could lead to a decrease in the volume of trade or even elimination of trade. Consider one example. Suppose that the home country has more capital but the same amount of labor as the foreign country. This can be represented by point C in Figure 7.8. At this point the home country has a lower rental rate of capital under free trade. This means that if capital movement is now allowed, home capital flows out until the rental rates in the countries are equalized when they have the same amount of capital, that is, point M. At M, however, the volume of trade is zero, meaning that commodity trade is wiped out by capital movement.

IV WELFARE ECONOMICS AND GAINS FROM TRADE

8   Core Theorems of the Welfare Economics of International Trade

This chapter discusses two main issues in the welfare economics of international trade. The first deals with different approaches to measuring the welfare of a multihousehold economy, and the second is about changes in welfare of an economy due to changes in economic conditions.

Measuring the "welfare" of a multihousehold economy is one of the fundamental issues in welfare economics, whether the economy is closed or open. The importance of measuring welfare arises not only because it may be affected by changes in economic environments, but also because criteria need to be developed for a criterion for comparing different government policies. Very often a shock due to a change in an economic environment or government policy makes some households better off and others worse off. In such instances, how does the economic welfare change, and what criteria can the government use when deciding on a particular policy?

To answer such questions, four major approaches to comparing the welfare levels of an economy in two economic situations are discussed. These are the Pareto approach, the social welfare approach, the social utility approach, and the compensation approach. In the last approach, there are two types of compensation, the use of lump-sum transfers or the use of consumption (or commodity) taxation.[1] The second issue analyzed here is the impact of certain shocks on the welfare of an economy and on the world. These shocks are due to government policies or changes in economic conditions in the rest of the world. The effects of these impacts in the neoclassical framework are summarized by six core welfare economics theorems in international trade theory. The theorems, which describe the welfare impacts of free trade and certain types of restricted trade, have important policy implications. It is interesting to note that all these theorems are valid under the social utility (with the assumption of no inferior goods for one of the theorems) and compensation approaches, whether compensation is made by using lump-sum transfers or consumption taxes. The analysis provided in the present chapter is interesting because these theorems are usually proved in the literature using one approach or the other.

8.1   The Pareto Approach to Welfare Comparison

Consider a fairly general framework. In an economy, here referred to as the home country, there are H households that are labeled $1, \ldots, H$. Denote the

---

1. This policy is usually called commodity taxation in the literature. I call it consumption taxation because the taxes are actually imposed on the consumption of goods and services. Sometimes commodity taxation and consumption taxation are used interchangeably. Lump-sum compensation is a very common approach in cost-benefit analysis. For closed-economy analysis, see, for example, Boadway (1974), Foster (1976), Bruce and Harris (1982), and Ng (1983).

utility function of the hth household by $u^h(\mathbf{C}^h)$ where $\mathbf{C}^h$ is the n-dimensional vector of consumption goods chosen by the household. The utility function $u^h(\mathbf{C}^h)$ is continuous, increasing, and quasi-concave. Unless stated otherwise, the households may have different preferences or endowments.

Suppose there is a shock to the economy due to a change in government policy or a change in the environment in the rest of the world the economy is trading with. Label the situation before the shock α and that after the shock β. (Autarky is considered to be a special trade situation with prohibitive tariffs.) In other words, situation α is the initial situation and situation β the final one. Variables in situation α are distinguished by a superscript α, but for simplicity and unless confusion may arise, variables in situation β do not have a similar superscript. Assume that the population, preferences, endowments, and technologies remain unchanged in the two situations. The present analysis is to compare the welfare of the economy in these two situations.

This section explains the Pareto approach. Under this approach, situation β is said to be *Pareto-superior* (or *Pareto-preferred*) to situation α (or situation β is better than situation α in the Paretian sense) if and only if

$$u^h(\mathbf{C}^h) \geq u^h(\mathbf{C}^{h\alpha}), \quad \text{for all } h = 1, \ldots, H, \tag{8.1}$$

with at least one inequality. In other words, one situation is Pareto-preferred to the other if no household is worse off while some households are better off.

The Pareto approach can be illustrated by Figure 8.1 for the simple case in which there are only two households in the economy. Schedules $\alpha\alpha$ and $\beta\beta$ are the utility possibility frontiers (UPF) corresponding to situations α and β, respectively. (Ignore schedules labeled W^1, W^2, and W^3 for the time being.) Each UPF is the locus of the two households' utility levels when income is distributed between them.[2] Point A shows the initial utility levels of the households (in situation α). If the final utility point is at point B (in situation β), both households are better off and according to the previous definition, situation β is Pareto-preferred to situation α.

The Pareto approach to welfare comparison is the fundamental one in modern welfare economics theory. It has the advantage that no interpersonal comparison of utility is required. Furthermore, the Paretian ranking of situations is transitive in the sense that if there exist three situations, α, β, and γ so that situation γ is Pareto-preferred to situation β and situation β Pareto-preferred to situation α, then situation γ is Pareto-preferred to situation α.

Strictly speaking, the Pareto approach compares the welfare levels of households at two different equilibrium points. No compensation or income redis-

---

2. The UPFs in Figure 8.1 should not be confused with a UPF formed by distributing a given basket of goods between the households. The one in Figure 8.1 can be regarded as the envelope of all those UPSs corresponding to different possible consumption baskets.

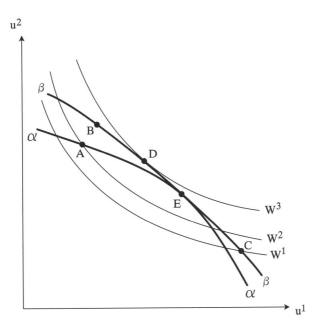

Figure 8.1

tribution is considered. This is its virtue, but is also its shortcoming. There are many real-world examples in which the inequality in (8.1) holds for some households but not for others, that is, some households are better off while some households are worse off. An example can be given for the two-household economy using Figure 8.1. Suppose that in the final equilibrium (in situation β) the utility levels of the households are represented by point C (instead of point B) in the diagram, meaning that household 1 is better off but household 2 is worse off. In such a case, the Pareto rule does not lead to any conclusive ranking. This shows that the Pareto approach to ranking situations is not complete.

In international trade, there are many examples in which the Pareto approach does not provide a definite conclusion about welfare changes. For example, consider again the traditional two-factor, two-good framework presented in Chapter 2. Suppose again that there are two households (or two groups of households). Household 1 owns a fixed amount of labor services but no capital services, and household 2 owns a given endowment of capital services but does not supply any labor services. Further suppose that the economy exports the labor-intensive good so that free trade raises the relative price of the labor-intensive good. By the Stolper-Samuelson theorem, the real income to household 1 is higher under free trade than under autarky, but the real income to household 2 is lower. In this case, free trade and autarky cannot be compared under the Pareto approach.

8.2   The Social-Welfare Approach to Welfare Comparison

Suppose that there exists a Bergson-Samuelson social welfare function $W(u^1, u^2, \ldots, u^H)$ that is defined over the set of the households' utility levels. To have a meaningful welfare function, the utility functions of the households must be of cardial measure. As explained in Chapter 2, this function gives an index of the welfare level of the economy. It is usually assumed that the function is increasing (but not necessarily quasi-concave) in the utility levels of the households.

A situation is then said to be *SW-preferred* to another one, subject to a given social welfare function, if and only if it yields a higher social welfare level. Figure 8.1 shows three iso-welfare contours labeled W^1, W^2, and W^3 in the special case in which there are only two households. The slope of a welfare contour is equal to $-(\partial W/\partial u^1)/(\partial W/\partial u^2)$. If the social welfare function is increasing in utility levels, an iso-welfare contour is negatively sloped and welfare levels increase to the northeast. For the three iso-welfare contours in the diagram, $W^3 > W^2 > W^1$. Suppose that the initial equilibrium welfare levels of the households are represented by point A in the diagram and the final equilibrium utility levels are represented by point C. Then situation α is SW-preferred to situation β because point A corresponds to a higher welfare level.

This approach, like the Pareto approach, compares the social welfare levels at initial and final equilibria. No compensation is needed. Its main advantage over the Pareto approach is that it is complete as long as the utility functions of the households are defined over the set of all consumption bundles. For example, I indicated earlier that if the final equilibrium is represented by point C in Figure 8.1, the Pareto approach does not give any conclusion. With a social welfare function, however, I would not have any difficulty in ranking point A with point C. Another advantage of the social welfare approach is that its ranking is also transitive. Moreover, a situation Pareto-preferred to another must also be SW-preferred to the latter one, although the reverse may not be true.

The main shortcoming of this approach is that there is no single definition of social welfare function. Instead, various definitions depend on what weights one gives to different households.[3] Using different social welfare functions, it is possible to reverse the ranking of two different situations.

The last point can be illustrated using the example in the previous section: Free trade raises the welfare of household 1 (the worker) but hurts household 2

---

3. There are several forms of social welfare function that are common in the literature. See, for example, Boadway and Bruce (1984, Chapter 5) for a survey of these functional forms and a discussion of the requirements for social welfare orderings.

(the capitalist). Suppose there are two social welfare functions $W^x(u^1, u^2)$ and $W^y(u^1, u^2)$. If function $W^x(u^1, u^2)$ puts a sufficiently large weight on household 1's welfare, it will rank free trade above autarky. If function $W^y(u^1, u^2)$ gives household 2's welfare a sufficiently large weight, however, it will rank autarky above free trade. Thus by using different social welfare functions, some people may prefer free trade to autarky while some other people may prefer autarky to free trade.

8.3   The Social-Utility Approach to Welfare Comparison

Another approach to comparing two situations is to assume the existence of a social utility function $u(\mathbf{C})$ where $\mathbf{C} = \sum \mathbf{C}^h$ is the aggregate consumption bundle. In Chapter 2, I mentioned several cases in which a social utility function exists. The two most common cases are the one in which households have identical and homothetic preferences and the one in which income is always redistributed optimally to maximize a social welfare function. In both cases, the utility level $u = u(\mathbf{C})$ is a good index of the aggregate welfare level of the economy.

A social utility function is usually assumed to behave like an individual's utility function: It is continuous, increasing, and quasi-concave in consumption goods. Denote the vector of commodity prices by $\mathbf{p}$, the vector of factor endowments by $\mathbf{v}$, and the transfer the country receives from abroad by b. I showed in Chapter 2 that the social utility function is used to define the minimum social expenditure function $e(\mathbf{p}, u)$ and the indirect trade utility function $V(\mathbf{p}, \mathbf{v}, b)$.

Using the preceding functions, situation β is said to be SU-preferred to situation α if and only if one of the following four conditions is satisfied:

1. $u(\mathbf{C}) > u(\mathbf{C}^\alpha)$;

2. $V(\mathbf{p}, \mathbf{v}, b) > V(\mathbf{p}^\alpha, \mathbf{v}^\alpha, b^\alpha)$;

3. $e(\mathbf{p}, u) > e(\mathbf{p}, u^\alpha)$; and

4. $e(\mathbf{p}^\alpha, u) > e(\mathbf{p}^\alpha, u^\alpha)$,

where $\mathbf{C}$ and $\mathbf{C}^\alpha$ are now the utility-maximizing consumption bundles in situations β and α, respectively. The equivalence between (1) and (2) is due to the definition of the indirect trade utility function, and the equivalence between conditions (1), (3) and (4) are due to the fact that the expenditure function is strictly increasing in the utility level. In (3), $e(\mathbf{p}, u) - e(\mathbf{p}, u^\alpha)$ is called the *compensating variation* of the economy, and in (4) $e(\mathbf{p}^\alpha, u) - e(\mathbf{p}^\alpha, u^\alpha)$ is called the economy's *equivalent variation*. Both compensating variation and

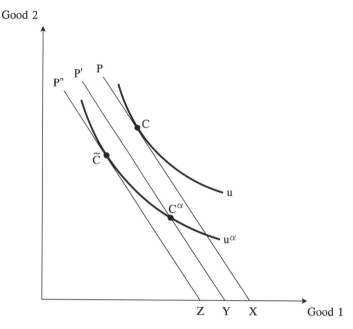

Figure 8.2

equivalent variation are exact measures of welfare changes. They differ only in the reference prices used for comparison.[4]

The compensating variation is shown in Figure 8.2. Points C^α and C are the consumption points in the corresponding situations, and u^α and u are the corresponding utility levels. Lines P, P′, and P″ represent the price lines in situation β. Lines P and P″ are tangent to the social indifference curves u and u^α at points **C** and $\widetilde{\mathbf{C}}$, respectively, while line P′ passes through point C^α. Price line P represents the national income in situation β while price line P″ gives the minimum expenditure to reach utility levels of u^α. Thus the gap between them is called the compensating variation. In terms of good 1, the compensating variation is equal to XZ in the diagram.

Consider the following condition:

$$\mathbf{p} \cdot \mathbf{C} > \mathbf{p} \cdot \mathbf{C}^\alpha. \tag{8.2}$$

Condition (8.2) implies an increase in national income of the economy evaluated using *final domestic prices*. The two terms in condition (8.2) are illus-

4. The compensating variation is more common in the trade literature. Grinols and Wong (1991), by decomposing the compensating variation, develop a convenient way of measuring welfare changes that has many applications.

trated in Figure 8.2. In terms of good 1, XY is equal to $\mathbf{p} \cdot \mathbf{C} - \mathbf{p} \cdot \mathbf{C}^\alpha$, which is positive in the case shown. Using condition (8.2), there is the following important theorem, which has been widely used in the literature:

Theorem 8.1   If condition (8.2) is satisfied, then situation β is SU-preferred to situation α.

To see why, note that by the definition of the expenditure function, $\mathbf{p} \cdot \mathbf{C}^\alpha \geq e(\mathbf{p}, u^\alpha)$. On the other hand, $\mathbf{p} \cdot \mathbf{C} = e(\mathbf{p}, u)$. Thus (8.2) implies that $e(\mathbf{p}, u) > e(\mathbf{p}, u^\alpha)$. According to condition (3), situation β is SU-preferred to situation α.

Define the consumption gain CG as

$$CG = \mathbf{p} \cdot \mathbf{C}^\alpha - e(\mathbf{p}, u^\alpha) \geq 0. \tag{8.3}$$

The consumption gain can be interpreted as the saving in expenditure for the economy to achieve the initial utility level u^α under the new prices. Its sign is due to the definition of the expenditure function. If consumption substitution is possible in the sense that the relevant indifference curve is curved as shown in Figure 8.2, and if there is a change in the domestic prices, then $CG > 0$. Alternatively, if the domestic prices do not change, or if consumption substitution is not possible, then $CG = 0$. As explained previously, $e(\mathbf{p}, u) - e(\mathbf{p}, u^\alpha)$ is the aggregate compensating variation and is a good measure of the welfare change. Using the consumption gain, the compensating variation can be disaggregated into two components:

$$e(\mathbf{p}, u) - e(\mathbf{p}, u^\alpha) = (\mathbf{p} \cdot \mathbf{C} - \mathbf{p} \cdot \mathbf{C}^\alpha) + CG,$$

that is, the compensating variation is the sum of the increase in national income as described by condition (8.2) and the consumption gain.

Note that condition (8.2) is sufficient but not necessary for a welfare improvement, but it has a very interesting implication. It states that according to the aggregate budget constraint, the consumption bundle $\mathbf{C}^\alpha$ chosen in situation α is still affordable in situation β. The fact that a different consumption bundle, $\mathbf{C}$, is chosen means that $\mathbf{C}$ yields a higher (or not lower) utility level to the economy. In other words, if a well-behaved social utility function exists, the theory of revealed preference can be applied to the economy as a whole.

Because the social utility function is defined over the set of aggregate consumption bundles, the ranking of situations in this approach is complete. Furthermore, it is transitive. Note that Theorem 8.1 does not require any particular form of the social utility function as long as it satisfies certain regularity conditions (such as monotonicity and quasi concavity).

Another important feature of the social utility approach is that Theorem 8.1 holds whether or not trade impediments are present. This is because under this approach the social utility levels are compared at the initial and final equilibrium points, and the national income level at given prices is a good index of the social utility level. This makes the approach different from the compensation approach described next.

8.4   The Lump-sum Compensation Approach to Welfare Comparison

As discussed previously, when an economy shifts from one situation to another due to a shock, it is possible (in fact very often the case) that some households gain and some other households lose. In these cases, the Pareto approach provides no conclusion. The idea of the compensation approach is to redistribute income in order to compensate the losers so that after the compensation no losers but (possibly) some gainers can be found. If no government resources are required in the compensation process, then the compensation is said to be feasible and the two situations after compensation are compared in the Paretian way. Thus the main purpose of the compensation approach is to make use of the advantage of the Pareto approach so that no interpersonal comparison is required, and at the same time it suggests a way to avoid (or reduce the degree of) the incompleteness of the Pareto approach.

There are two main methods of compensation: lump-sum transfers and consumption taxation. In this section I focus on the former way of compensation. Compensation through redistribution of income has long been suggested as a way to compare two economic situations. This approach can be traced back to the work of Kaldor (1939), Hicks (1940), Scitovsky (1941), Little (1949), and Samuelson (1950). It has been applied to the theory of international trade to prove the gains from trade by Samuelson (1939) for a small economy, and by Samuelson (1962), Kemp (1962), Kemp and Wan (1972), Grandmont and McFadden (1972), Chipman and Moore (1972), and Ohyama (1972) for gains from trade for economies of any size, and by Kemp and Wan (1976, 1986a) and Grinols (1981, 1984) for gainful formation of customs union.

Two of the mostly commonly used approaches in the theory of international trade are the Kaldor-Hicks criterion and the Samuelson criterion.[5] The Kaldor-Hicks approach is to treat the initial equilibrium (in situation α) as a reference point, and then to redistribute income among households in the final situation (situation β). Situation β is said to be *KH-preferred* to situation α if there exists at least one income redistribution in situation β to make sure that every

---

5. For a survey of these criteria, see Takayama (1972, Chapter 17), Ng (1983 Chapter 3), and Boadway and Bruce (1984, Chapters 3 and 9).

household is not worse off and that some households are better off than in situation α.[6]

The Kaldor-Hicks approach can be illustrated using the two-household model and Figure 8.1. Suppose that point A represents the initial equilibrium utility levels and point C the final equilibrium utility levels. In the final situation, the first household gains but the second household loses, meaning that no conclusion can be drawn by using the Pareto approach. Under the Kaldor-Hicks approach, income is redistributed in situation β. Graphically, this means a movement along the UPF labeled $\beta\beta$. If a point such as point B on schedule $\beta\beta$ can be found to the northeast of point A, then situation β is said to be preferred to situation α (or point A) in a Kaldor-Hicks sense.[7]

The Samuelson criterion, on the other hand, allows income redistribution in both situations. Thus situation β is said to be *Samuelson-preferred* to situation α if for any income redistribution in situation α, there exist points in situation β at which no household is worse off while some households are better off.

The Samuelson criterion can also be illustrated by Figure 8.1. Schedule $\beta\beta$ is entirely beyond schedule $\alpha\alpha$ except at point E, where they touch. Thus no matter how income is redistributed in situation α (except that represented by point E), at least one income redistribution exists in situation β so that no household is worse off but some households are better off. By the definition given previously, situation β is Samuelson-preferred to situation α.

It has been shown that the Kaldor-Hicks criterion is not consistent, because it is possible that situation β is KH-preferred to (an equilibrium in) situation α while at the same time situation α is KH-preferred to (an equilibrium in) situation β. This is called the Scitovsky paradox (Scitovsky, 1941).[8] In contrast, the Samuelson criterion is consistent. It is also transitive but the Kaldor-Hicks criterion is not. By definition, if a situation is Samuelson-preferred to another situation, it must be KH-preferred as well, although the reverse may not be true. If, however, situation β is KH-preferred to situation α no matter where the initial equilibrium point in situation α is, then situation β is also Samuelson-preferred to situation α.

The biggest disadvantage of the Samuelson criterion is that it is not complete. In the real world, it is very often not the case that the UPF corresponding to one situation is entirely beyond another. In these cases, the Samuelson

---

6. This is what is sometimes called the strong version of the Kaldor-Hicks criterion. In the weak version, what is required is that no household is worse off while possibly some households are better off. The same strong and weak versions can be given under the Samuelson approach described later.

7. If a point does not exist on schedule $\beta\beta$ that is northeast of point A, it does not mean that schedule $\alpha\alpha$ is KH-preferred to situation β.

8. For examples of Scitovsky paradoxes, see Takayama (1972, pp. 500–502).

criterion does not produce any conclusive ranking. Another difficulty of applying the Samuelson criterion is that it requires a lot of information about both situations because income redistribution in both situations is considered. The Kaldor-Hicks criterion, on the other hand, takes the initial utility levels of households as given and considers income redistribution only in the final situation. Because of the difficulty of getting a conclusive ranking under the Samuelson approach, in what follows I will use only the Kaldor-Hicks criterion to examine whether the final situation is preferred to the initial one.

In the literature, several similar but not identical lump-sum compensation schemes have been suggested. The one that introduced and used here to prove the core theorems of welfare economics in international trade is based on Wong (1991a). This scheme is slightly different from the one introduced and used by Grandmont and McFadden (1972) to prove gains from free trade and by Grinols (1981, 1984) to prove gains from customs union formation. The later scheme, which is labeled the GMG scheme, is discussed and used extensively in Kemp and Wan (1993). The differences between these schemes are discussed later.

Let the hth household be endowed with resources $\mathbf{v}^h$. For simplicity assume that $\mathbf{v}^h$ remains unchanged in situations α and β, but this assumption can easily be relaxed. Because compensation is made in situation β, it is necessary to distinguish between two equilibria, the precompensation equilibrium and the postcompensation equilibrium. In this scheme, primes denote the postcompensation values of variables while the precompensation values have no primes. For example, in situation β, $\mathbf{C}$ is the precompensation aggregate consumption while $\mathbf{C}'$ is the postcompensation consumption.

There are J firms in the economy indexed $1, \ldots, J$. The production possibility set of each firm is closed, bounded from above, and convex. Possibility of inaction and free disposal are allowed, but no externalities or variable returns are assumed. All markets are competitive.

As in Chapter 2, assume that the first $m^t \leq m$ factors are mobile internationally. Denote the inflow of foreign factors by the m^t-dimensional vector $\mathbf{k}$ (negative elements representing outflow of home capital) and their home prices by $\mathbf{r}$. Firms employ factors $\mathbf{v}$ and $\mathbf{k}$ to produce output $\mathbf{Q}$. In equilibrium, their profits are zero. This means that

$$\mathbf{p} \cdot \mathbf{Q} = \mathbf{w} \cdot \mathbf{v} + \mathbf{r} \cdot \mathbf{k}. \tag{8.4}$$

Denote the world prices of commodities by $\mathbf{p}^*$ and those of the moving factors by $\mathbf{r}^*$. The differences between domestic and world prices are due to trade taxes imposed by the home government:

$$\mathbf{t} = \mathbf{p} - \mathbf{p}^*$$

$$\mathbf{s} = \mathbf{r} - \mathbf{r}^*.$$

In situation β, the income of the hth household from the sale of its resources is $\mathbf{w} \cdot \mathbf{v}^h$. In addition, it receives a transfer of z^h from the government. Its total income is $\mathbf{w} \cdot \mathbf{v}^h + z^h$. It chooses a consumption basket to maximize its utility function subject to the budget constraint:

$$\mathbf{p} \cdot \mathbf{C}^{h\prime} \leq \mathbf{w} \cdot \mathbf{v}^h + z^h, \tag{8.5}$$

where $\mathbf{C}^{h\prime}$ is the household's postcompensation consumption.

Under this approach each household receives a transfer from the government so that it can afford its initial consumption (a negative transfer meaning a lump-sum tax). The transfer is chosen to be

$$z^h = (\mathbf{p} \cdot \mathbf{C}^{h\alpha} - \mathbf{w} \cdot \mathbf{v}^h) + \phi^h R, \tag{8.6}$$

where R is a real number to be defined later, and where ϕ^h is the share of R the household receives, $1 \geq \phi^h \geq 0$, $\sum_h \phi^h = 1$. The transfer given by (8.6) has three components: the value of the household's initial consumption evaluated using final prices, the negative of the value of its endowments evaluated using final prices, and a share of R. If the household receives shares of firms' outputs, as assumed in the Arrow-Debreu framework, these shares are included in $\mathbf{v}^h$. Different ways of sharing R among the households can be considered. One example is to divide it equally among the households, that is, $\phi^h = 1/H$ for all h.

The compensation scheme given by (8.6) is different from the GMG scheme in two ways. First, the transfer in (8.6) is based on the household's endowment, which includes any distribution from the firms, in the final situation whereas the GMG scheme includes the household's endowment in the initial situation. Second, the scheme in (8.6) distributes R among the households. As will be explained later, in the case of the gains from free trade, R is the production gain. The GMG scheme, on the other hand, does not have such a term.

Substitute the transfer z^h into (8.5) to give a new budget constraint of the hth household:

$$\mathbf{p} \cdot \mathbf{C}^{h\prime} \leq \mathbf{p} \cdot \mathbf{C}^{h\alpha} + \phi^h R. \tag{8.5$'$}$$

The role of the transfer, z^h, is clear from this new budget constraint. The first two components of z^h, $(\mathbf{p} \cdot \mathbf{C}^{h\alpha} - \mathbf{w} \cdot \mathbf{v}^h)$, guarantee that the household has sufficient income to purchase the initial consumption bundle $\mathbf{C}^{h\alpha}$ under the new prices, and the third component, $\phi^h R$, is non-negative if R is non-negative. Given the first two components of z^h, the household has a budget line passing through the initial consumption point, meaning that the initial consumption bundle is still affordable. Thus the household is not worse off, or is better off if consumption substitution exists. The increase in welfare of this household due to consumption substitution is called the *consumption gain* for this household. The sum of all households' consumption gains is the economy's consumption gain. The third component, if positive (when $R > 0$ and $\phi^h > 0$), will make sure that the household is better off even if consumption substitution is absent.

The role of the lump-sum transfer can be illustrated by using Figure 8.2, which is now reinterpreted so that it represents the consumption choice of the hth household. In this diagram, C^α is replaced by $C^{h\alpha}$ (the household's initial consumption point) and u^α is replaced by $u^{h\alpha}$ (the household's initial utility level). The price lines in the diagram represent the *final* price ratio. The minimum expenditure needed to purchase the initial consumption bundle when facing the new prices is $\mathbf{p} \cdot \mathbf{C}^\alpha$. If $R = 0$ or $\phi^h = 0$, (8.5′) implies that the new budget line of the hth household passes through the initial consumption point, meaning that the initial consumption bundle is still affordable. The household is not worse off and is better off if consumption substitution exists. If $R, \phi^h > 0$, then the household budget line shifts out to line P in the diagram, and by choosing the consumption bundle $\mathbf{C}$, the household improves its utility to a level of u.

The last thing to check is whether this lump-sum compensation scheme is feasible. Let T be the trade tax revenue, $T = (\mathbf{p} - \mathbf{p}^*) \cdot \mathbf{M}' + (\mathbf{r} - \mathbf{r}^*) \cdot \mathbf{k}'$. Using the definition of transfer given by (8.6), the net revenue of the government is equal to

$$T - \sum_{h=1}^{H} z^h = (\mathbf{p} - \mathbf{p}^*) \cdot \mathbf{M}' + (\mathbf{r} - \mathbf{r}^*) \cdot \mathbf{k} - \sum_{h=1}^{H} \left\{ \mathbf{p} \cdot \mathbf{C}^{h\alpha} - \mathbf{w} \cdot \mathbf{v}^h + \phi^h R \right\}$$

$$= (\mathbf{p} - \mathbf{p}^*) \cdot \mathbf{M}' + (\mathbf{r} - \mathbf{r}^*) \cdot \mathbf{k} - \mathbf{p} \cdot \mathbf{C}^\alpha + \mathbf{w} \cdot \mathbf{v} - R. \qquad (8.7)$$

The scheme is said to be feasible if the government's net revenue is nonnegative, that is, the expression in (8.7) is non-negative. If the scheme is feasible, then situation β is said to be *lump-sum-preferred* to situation α.

Several conditions are derived under which situation β is lump-sum-preferred to situation α. Consider a condition analogous to condition (8.2):

$$\mathbf{p}^* \cdot \mathbf{C} > \mathbf{p}^* \cdot \mathbf{C}^\alpha. \qquad (8.8)$$

Condition (8.8) states that there is an increase in national income evaluated at *final world prices*. It reduces to condition (8.2) if the economy has free trade.

In the presence of trade restrictions, world prices are not the prices households are facing. As argued by Little and Mirrlees (1969) and Bhagwati and Hansen (1973a), however, a change in national income measured in terms of world prices is a better measure of the change in the potential welfare of the economy. When compensation has to be made, it is the potential welfare of the economy, not the precompensation welfare levels of households, that matters. This means that under the present approach, condition (8.8) rather than condition (8.2) better reflects the feasibility of compensation schemes.

Theorem 8.2   For a small open economy, if condition (8.8) is satisfied, then situation β is lump-sum-preferred to situation α.

To prove this theorem, define

$$R = \mathbf{p}^* \cdot (\mathbf{C} - \mathbf{C}^\alpha),$$

which is positive by condition (8.8). The government carries out the lump-sum compensation as described by (8.6). Because the economy is small and open, income redistribution made in situation β will not affect the production of the economy, $\mathbf{Q}' = \mathbf{Q}$ and $\mathbf{k}' = \mathbf{k}$, meaning that the economy has unchanged national product, and that with balanced current account, $\mathbf{p}^* \cdot \mathbf{C}' = \mathbf{p}^* \cdot \mathbf{C}$. The hth household receives transfer z^h as defined by (8.6), and its budget constraint is given by (8.5$'$), implying that it is better off with nonsatiation. If the budget constraints of all households are summed up, then by the definition of R, I have

$$\mathbf{p} \cdot \mathbf{C}' \leq \mathbf{p} \cdot \mathbf{C}^\alpha + \mathbf{p}^* \cdot \mathbf{C} - \mathbf{p}^* \cdot \mathbf{C}^\alpha. \tag{8.9}$$

In the presence of trade restrictions and current account balance, the trade tax revenue received by the government is $\mathbf{p} \cdot \mathbf{M}' + \mathbf{r} \cdot \mathbf{k}$ where $\mathbf{M}'$ denotes postcompensation import.

This compensation scheme is feasible because the net government revenue is non-negative:

$$\mathbf{p} \cdot \mathbf{M}' + \mathbf{r} \cdot \mathbf{k} - \sum_{h=1}^{H} z^h = \mathbf{p} \cdot \mathbf{M}' + \mathbf{r} \cdot \mathbf{k} - \sum_{h=1}^{H} \left\{ \mathbf{p} \cdot \mathbf{C}^{h\alpha} - \mathbf{w} \cdot \mathbf{v}^h + \phi^h R \right\}$$

$$= \mathbf{p} \cdot \mathbf{M}' + \mathbf{r} \cdot \mathbf{k} - \mathbf{p} \cdot \mathbf{C}^\alpha + \mathbf{w} \cdot \mathbf{v} - \mathbf{p}^* \cdot \mathbf{C} + \mathbf{p}^* \cdot \mathbf{C}^\alpha$$

$$= \mathbf{p} \cdot \mathbf{C}' - \mathbf{p} \cdot \mathbf{C}^\alpha - \mathbf{p}^* \cdot \mathbf{C} + \mathbf{p}^* \cdot \mathbf{C}^\alpha$$

$$\geq 0,$$

where the last equality is due to firms' zero profit condition in (8.4), and the last inequality is due to the sum of the households' budget constraints given in (8.9).

The theorem in the case in which free trade but no factor movement exists (at least in the final situation) can be illustrated in Figure 8.3 for a two-

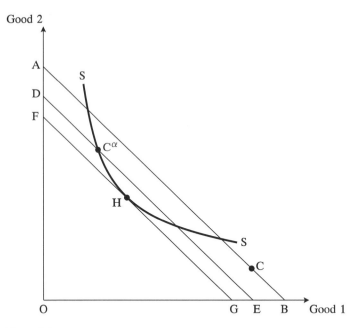

Figure 8.3

good economy.[9] In the diagram, schedule SS represents the Scitovsky contour, which is the locus of the minimum amounts of good 1, when given good 2, that is needed to be distributed among all households to make them as well off as before. If the economy is supplied with goods represented by a point above schedule SS, at least one household can be made better off without hurting other households, and if the point is below schedule SS, at least one household must be worse off.

Points $\mathbf{C}^{\alpha}$ and $\mathbf{C}$ in Figure 8.3 are the consumption points (before income redistribution) in situations α and β, respectively. AB is the price line in situation β passing through $\mathbf{C}$. Because the economy is a small open one, AB represents its consumption possibility frontier in this situation. Any point on or below AB is feasible.

FG is a price line that is tangent to contour SS. The point of tangency, point H, between FG and SS is the consumption basket that can be distributed among the households to make them as well off as before. Because in the case shown in Figure 8.3 point H is below AB, some households can be made better off in situation β without hurting other households. The gap between

9. As pointed out by Boadway and Bruce (1984), another case to which Theorem 8.2 applies is a closed economy with a linear production possibility frontier.

AB and FG is called the aggregate compensating variation. By making use of the diagram, the following theorem can be established:[10]

Theorem 8.3   For a small open economy under free trade, situation β is lump-sum-preferred to situation α if and only if the aggregate compensating variation is positive.

In Figure 8.3, line DE is a price line that passes through the initial consumption point $\mathbf{C}^\alpha$. In the case shown, line DE is below line AB. This means that condition (8.8) is satisfied. It is clear from the diagram that if condition (8.8) is satisfied, the aggregate compensating variation is positive.

It should be noted that Theorem 8.2 in general applies only to a small open economy. The difficulty of applying it to large open economies is that if an increase in national income as given by (8.8) is observed in the final situation, it is possible that income redistribution could affect both domestic and world prices so that condition (8.8) no longer holds. There are, however, some special cases in which the theorem does apply to large open economies. Some examples are given later.

8.5   The Consumption-Taxation Compensation Approach to Welfare Comparison

Dixit and Norman (1980, 1986) suggest two schemes of consumption (commodity) taxes that can be used to compensate the losers. The two schemes are similar but in fact are slightly different from each other. They are called the *Dixit-Norman (DN) scheme* and the *extended DN scheme*, respectively. Dixit and Norman (1986) also hint at a third scheme but they do not provide any proof. I elaborate it later and call it the *modified DN scheme*.

8.5.1   The Dixit-Norman (DN) Scheme

Consider again the preceding framework. In the presence of trade taxes, denote the trade tax revenue in situation α by $T^\alpha = (\mathbf{p}^\alpha - \mathbf{p}^{*\alpha}) \cdot \mathbf{M}^\alpha + (\mathbf{r}^\alpha - \mathbf{r}^{*\alpha}) \cdot \mathbf{k}^\alpha$. This revenue, if nonzero, is distributed to the households according to some exogenously given rules.[11] As assumed before, the hth household receives a share ϕ^h of the revenue, $1 \geq \phi^h \geq 0$, $\sum_h \phi^h = 1$. The budget constraint of the household in situation α is

---

10. Boadway (1974) and Foster (1976) show that when there is a divergence between consumption and production prices for a closed economy, a positive aggregate compensating variation is not necessary for a welfare improvement. Wong (1991a) extends their argument to an open economy.

11. Dixit and Norman (1980, 1986) consider only gains from free trade. The present analysis considers more general cases in which trade taxes and subsidies may be present, and the initial situation may be a trade situation.

$$\mathbf{p}^\alpha \cdot \mathbf{C}^{h\alpha} \le \mathbf{w}^\alpha \cdot \mathbf{v}^h + \phi^h T^\alpha. \tag{8.10}$$

In the final situation, or situation β, the government imposes specific taxes $(\mathbf{p}^\alpha - \mathbf{p})$ on the household consumption goods and $(\mathbf{w} - \mathbf{w}^\alpha)$ on the endowments of the households. This means that while the firms are facing domestic prices $(\mathbf{p}, \mathbf{w})$, the households are facing prices $(\mathbf{p}^\alpha, \mathbf{w}^\alpha)$. Furthermore, the households continue to receive the same amount of trade tax revenue equal to the amount they receive in situation α. Because the households do not see any changes in the prices they face and income they receive, they have the same budget constraint as given by (8.10) and they will make the same consumption choices, $\mathbf{C}^{h\alpha}$, as before, implying that they are exactly as well off as in situation α.

Under this scheme, the government collects a possible trade tax revenue $T' = (\mathbf{p} - \mathbf{p}^*) \cdot \mathbf{M}' + (\mathbf{r} - \mathbf{r}^*) \cdot \mathbf{k}$ and a consumption tax revenue equal to $(\mathbf{p}^\alpha - \mathbf{p}) \cdot \mathbf{C}^\alpha + (\mathbf{w} - \mathbf{w}^\alpha) \cdot \mathbf{v}$, where T' and $\mathbf{M}'$ are the trade tax revenue and import level in the presence of the consumption taxes, respectively. The total tax revenue (including the consumption tax revenue) less the initial trade tax revenue is equal to

$$T' + (\mathbf{p}^\alpha - \mathbf{p}) \cdot \mathbf{C}^\alpha + (\mathbf{w} - \mathbf{w}^\alpha) \cdot \mathbf{v} - T^\alpha.$$

If free trade prevails in both situations, $T' = T^\alpha = 0$. The Dixit-Norman scheme is said to be feasible, and situation β is said to be DN-preferred to situation α, if and only if the net tax revenue is nonnegative.[12]

Using the preceding definition of the scheme, the following theorem shows that condition (8.8) is again sufficient for a welfare improvement:

Theorem 8.4 Consider a small open economy with a balanced current account before compensation in the final situation, β. Situation β is DN-preferred to situation α if and only if condition (8.8) with a weak inequality is satisfied.

First consider the sufficiency part of the theorem. Because the current account is balanced before compensation in situation β, $\mathbf{p}^* \cdot \mathbf{C} = \mathbf{p}^* \cdot \mathbf{Q} - \mathbf{r}^* \cdot \mathbf{k}$, where $\mathbf{C}$ is the consumption bundle before compensation. Using this condition of balanced trade, condition (8.8) reduces to (assuming a weak inequality)

$$\mathbf{p}^* \cdot \mathbf{Q} - \mathbf{r}^* \cdot \mathbf{k} \ge \mathbf{p}^* \cdot \mathbf{C}^\alpha. \tag{8.8'}$$

Because for a small open economy facing given world prices and having fixed trade taxes, the consumption taxation compensation will not affect the produc-

---

12. In their 1980 work Dixit and Norman do not state explicitly what the government is going to do with a positive revenue. Their 1986 work is more explicit: The government throws away a positive revenue.

tion side of the economy. So conditions (8.4) and (8.8′) remain valid after the compensation. Furthermore, the postcompensation import vector is equal to $\mathbf{M}' = \mathbf{C}^\alpha - \mathbf{Q}$.

To see the feasibility of the above scheme when given condition (8.8), I show that the net tax revenue is non-negative:

$$T' + (\mathbf{p}^\alpha - \mathbf{p}) \cdot \mathbf{C}^\alpha + (\mathbf{w} - \mathbf{w}^\alpha) \cdot \mathbf{v} - T^\alpha = T' - \mathbf{p} \cdot \mathbf{C}^\alpha + \mathbf{w} \cdot \mathbf{v}$$

$$= -\mathbf{p}^* \cdot \mathbf{M}' - \mathbf{r}^* \cdot \mathbf{k}$$

$$= \mathbf{p}^* \cdot \mathbf{Q} - \mathbf{r}^* \cdot \mathbf{k} - \mathbf{p}^* \cdot \mathbf{C}^\alpha$$

$$\geq 0. \tag{8.11}$$

The first equality is due to the initial budget constraints of the households (with nonsatiation) as given by (8.10), the second one is due to the definitions of the trade tax revenue and import and the zero-profit condition (8.4), the third one is due to the definition of import, and the inequality is due to condition (8.8′).

I now turn to the necessary part of the theorem. If situation β is DN-preferred to situation α, then the compensation must be feasible, meaning that the new trade tax revenue plus the consumption tax revenue less the initial trade tax revenue is non-negative. Following the steps in proving condition (8.11), $\mathbf{p}^* \cdot \mathbf{Q} - \mathbf{r}^* \cdot \mathbf{k} - \mathbf{p}^* \cdot \mathbf{C}^\alpha \geq 0$. Because trade is balanced before compensation, condition (8.8) (with a weak inequality) exists.

Note again that Theorem 8.4 is valid generally only for a small open economy. As mentioned earlier when discussing lump-sum transfers, if the economy is a large one, then the imposition of the taxes may affect equilibrium prices and the production of the economy, and condition (8.8) may no longer hold in the presence of the taxes. There are, however, cases in which a similar theorem holds irrespective of the size of the economy. Examples will be given later.

8.5.2   The Extended Dixit-Norman (EDN) Scheme

Kemp and Wan (1986b) argue that what Dixit and Norman (1980) have shown for the DN scheme is that every household in situation β is as well off as in situation α. It is not clear whether conditions exist under which some households can be made better off. In fact, Kemp and Wan (1986b) present several numerical examples to show that there are cases in which under the DN scheme it is not possible to make any household better off without hurting other households as the economy moves from autarky to free trade. In response to this criticism, Dixit and Norman (1986) extend their original scheme. To explain this extended scheme, I first modify Theorem 8.4:

Theorem 8.4′   Consider a small open economy with a balanced current account before compensation in situation β. Suppose that the Weymark condition is satisfied. Situation β is EDN-preferred to situation α if and only if condition (8.8) with a weak inequality is satisfied.

I now prove this theorem, and in proving it I explain the extended D-N scheme and the Weymark condition. I first consider the sufficiency part. Compensation is implemented by the government in two hypothetical steps, but in actual implementation the steps are combined. In step one the government imposes the DN scheme, except that the tax revenue, if positive, is spent on commodities. Let the government's purchase be denoted by $\mathbf{G}'$. (Variables in this step are distinguished by primes.) This means that the import of goods is equal to $\mathbf{M}' = \mathbf{C}^{\alpha} + \mathbf{G}' - \mathbf{Q}'$. ($\mathbf{Q}'$ is the same as $\mathbf{Q}$ because the compensation does not affect production.) The value of the government purchase is $\mathbf{p}' \cdot \mathbf{G}'$, which is equal to the tax revenue given by (8.11). As shown earlier, in this step the households in situation β are as well off as in situation α.

In step two, Dixit and Norman (1986) make the assumption that there exists at least one commodity, either pure or Hicksian composite, such that in situation α all consumers are on the same side of the market.[13] This is called the *Weymark condition*. If this condition is satisfied, Weymark (1979) shows that the government can change the consumer prices of the goods to improve the welfare of some households without hurting the other households.[14] Let the new consumer's prices be $(\mathbf{p}^{c\prime\prime}, \mathbf{w}^{c\prime\prime})$ and the producer's prices be $(\mathbf{p}'', \mathbf{w}'', \mathbf{r}'')$, the corresponding consumption demand of the hth household be $\mathbf{C}^{h\prime\prime}$, and variables without superscript h be the aggregate variables. The budget constraint of the hth household becomes

$$\mathbf{p}^{c\prime\prime} \cdot \mathbf{C}^{h\prime\prime} \leq \mathbf{w}^{c\prime\prime} \cdot \mathbf{v}^{h} + \phi^{h} T^{\alpha}. \tag{8.12}$$

Define $\mathbf{G}''$, the new government purchase of goods, in the following way:

$$\mathbf{G}'' = \mathbf{G}' - (\mathbf{C}'' - \mathbf{C}^{\alpha})$$

$$= \mathbf{M}' + \mathbf{Q}' - \mathbf{C}''. \tag{8.13}$$

This new government purchase replaces the old. Note that because producers are facing constant world prices, their production remains the same in steps one and two. Thus condition (8.13) states that the import levels remain the same in both steps.

---

13. This means that some consumers are net buyers, none are net sellers, and the commodity is not a free good, or some consumers are net sellers, none are net buyers, and the commodity is not the only valuable good.

14. See also Dixit and Norman (1986, p. 117).

The next thing is to check the total expenditure of the government, including the purchases of goods $\mathbf{G}''$. It is equal to

$$T'' + (\mathbf{p}^{c''} - \mathbf{p}'') \cdot \mathbf{C}'' + (\mathbf{w}'' - \mathbf{w}^{c''}) \cdot \mathbf{v} - T^\alpha - \mathbf{p}'' \cdot \mathbf{G}''$$

$$= T'' - \mathbf{p}'' \cdot \mathbf{C}'' + \mathbf{w}'' \cdot \mathbf{v} - \mathbf{p}'' \cdot \mathbf{G}''$$

$$= T'' + \mathbf{w}'' \cdot \mathbf{v} - \mathbf{p}'' \cdot \mathbf{M}' - \mathbf{p}'' \cdot \mathbf{Q}'$$

$$= (\mathbf{p}'' - \mathbf{p}^*) \cdot \mathbf{M}' + (\mathbf{r}'' - \mathbf{r}^*) \cdot \mathbf{k} + \mathbf{w}'' \cdot \mathbf{v} - \mathbf{p}'' \cdot \mathbf{M}' - \mathbf{p}'' \cdot \mathbf{Q}'$$

$$= 0,$$

where the first equality is due to the households' budget constraints (with nonsatiation) given by (8.12), the second equality is due to the definition of $\mathbf{G}''$ as given by (8.13), the third equality is due to the tariff revenue, and the last equality is due to current account balance and zero-profit conditions of the firms. The necessary part of Theorem 8.4′ is proved in the same way as the one used to prove Theorem 8.4.

8.5.3   The Modified Dixit and Norman (MDN) Scheme

Dixit and Norman (1986) suggest that in situation β small poll grants can be given out while keeping the consumer's prices at $\mathbf{p}^\alpha$ and $\mathbf{w}^\alpha$ so that all households are better off. They do not give any details about this plan. Elsewhere, I have suggested (Wong 1991a) that the government distributes the entire production gain to all households (in the case of gains from trade). If the production gain is positive and if satiation is ruled out, all households are better off in situation β. I call this the modified Dixit-Norman scheme (MDN). It is no longer a pure price policy as the DN and EDN schemes are. The MDN scheme is now used to modify Theorem 8.4:

Theorem 8.4″   Consider a small open economy with a balanced current account before compensation in situation β. Situation β is MDN-preferred to situation α if and only if condition (8.8) is satisfied.

To prove the sufficiency part of this theorem, let me define R so that $R = \mathbf{p}^* \cdot (\mathbf{C} - \mathbf{C}^\alpha)$. If condition (8.8) is satisfied, R is positive. In situation β, the government imposes the consumption taxes as described, and gives the hth household an amount equal to $\phi^h(T^\alpha + R)$. The budget constraint of the hth household, which faces the initial prices, becomes

$$\mathbf{p}^\alpha \cdot \mathbf{C}^{h'} \le \mathbf{w}^\alpha \cdot \mathbf{v}^h + \phi^h(T^\alpha + R). \tag{8.14}$$

Recall that primes are used to denote the variables in situation β in the presence of the policy. Because $R > 0$, the household can do better than choosing the initial consumption bundle (with nonsatiation). What is left to show is that the policy is feasible. In fact it is, because the tax revenue less the transfers is equal to zero:

$$T' + (\mathbf{p}^{\alpha} - \mathbf{p}) \cdot \mathbf{C}' + (\mathbf{w} - \mathbf{w}^{\alpha}) \cdot \mathbf{v} - T^{\alpha} - R = T' - \mathbf{p} \cdot \mathbf{C}' + \mathbf{w} \cdot \mathbf{v}$$
$$= (\mathbf{p} - \mathbf{p}^*) \cdot \mathbf{M}' +$$
$$(\mathbf{r} - \mathbf{r}^*) \cdot \mathbf{k} - \mathbf{p} \cdot \mathbf{C}' + \mathbf{w} \cdot \mathbf{v}$$
$$= -\mathbf{p}^* \cdot \mathbf{M}' - \mathbf{r}^* \cdot \mathbf{k}$$
$$= 0,$$

where the first equality is due to the aggregation of the budget constraints (with nonsatiation) as given by (8.14); the second equality is due to the definition of tariff revenue; the third equality is due to the definition of imports ($\mathbf{M}' = \mathbf{C}' - \mathbf{Q}$) and firms' zero profit condition ($\mathbf{p} \cdot \mathbf{Q} = \mathbf{r} \cdot \mathbf{k} + \mathbf{w} \cdot \mathbf{v}$); and the last one is due to the current account balance. Note that for the present small open economy, the compensation scheme does not affect the producer's prices, implying that the production point is not affected by the compensation. The necessary part of the theorem is proved along the same line as before.

What is the significance of the MDN scheme as compared with the DN and EDN schemes? First, it does not require the Weymark condition. Second, the information the government needs in implementing the scheme is small. It needs to know whether condition (8.8) holds in order to compute the value of R. No individual information, not even the initial consumption bundle of any household, is needed. Third, it avoids the waste of resources under the DN and EDN schemes. Fourth, like the DN and EDN schemes but unlike the lump-sum transfer scheme, it does not capture consumption gains. Fifth, unlike the DN and EDN schemes, it is not a pure price policy. It involves distribution of the gain described by (8.8). Sixth, it ensures that at least some households are better off when condition (8.8) holds with a strict inequality.

It should be noted that Theorem 8.4″ (and also Theorems 8.4 and 8.4′) applies to a small open economy, because for a large economy the consumption taxes imposed by the home government may disturb the international equilibrium and condition (8.8) may be violated. There are, however, some special cases in which the theorems apply to large open economies as well. Some examples are given next.

8.6   Comparing Different Approaches to Measuring Welfare

I now compare the social utility and the compensation approaches using either lump-sum transfers or consumption taxation.

8.6.1   Social Utility versus Compensation

Social utility and compensation are the two most commonly used approaches in the theory of international trade (and also in some other fields) to compare the welfare levels of an economy in two or more situations. In the next section they are applied to derive several core theorems in the theory of international trade. Before doing that, I present a brief discussion of the similarities and differences between them, and about their merits and shortcomings.

The social utility approach is very useful and is relatively simple to use in economic analysis. Because it treats the economy as a whole as a single consumer, many results in the consumer theory can be applied easily. For example, the theory of revealed preference is applicable for the economy as a whole. In many cases, it is relatively simple to rank different policies based on the social utility levels they yield.

The compensation approach based on the Kaldor-Hicks criterion, strictly speaking, compares a situation with a given equilibrium in another situation. With the initial equilibrium point taken as given, the Scitovsky paradox can be avoided. This, however, limits the applicability of this approach. For example, if several policies are to be compared, the same initial equilibrium has to be chosen. In general, the ranking of policies are dependent on which initial equilibrium the government chooses.

The social utility and the compensation approaches have been criticized for assuming that income is redistributed (when maximizing a social welfare function is needed). In the real world, income is rarely redistributed to maximize any social welfare function or to adequately compensate any losers. Furthermore, the costs of income distribution are seldom included in the theoretical consideration of the welfare impacts of policies.

A more rigorous comparison between the social utility approach and the compensation approach needs to be more explicit about the existence of a social utility function. In Chapter 2, I mentioned that there are at least three cases in which a social utility function exists: (1) All households have identical preferences and identical endowments; (2) all households have identical and homothetic preferences; and (3) there exists a Bergson-Samuelson social welfare function and income is always redistributed to maximize the social welfare function. I evaluate these two approaches to welfare comparison in these cases.

First consider case (1) in which all households are identical in terms of preferences and endowments. In this case, the social utility function is the same as that of a household, and in equilibrium all households have the same utility level. There is an increase in the social utility level if and only if the utility level of each household increases. Therefore in this case the social-utility

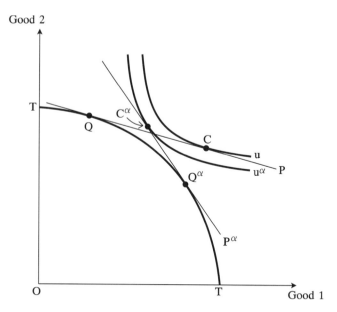

Figure 8.4

approach to welfare comparison is equivalent to the lump-sum-transfer approach. These two approaches are not equivalent to the consumption-taxation approach, however. A counterexample is given for a two-good economy using Figure 8.4.

In Figure 8.4, TT is the PPF of a small open economy under free trade. In situation α, the economy produces at Q^α, consumes at C^α, and achieves a utility level of u^α. Suppose that there is a change in the terms of trade (and a resulting change in the patterns of trade). The new price line is P, with the new production and consumption points at Q and C, respectively. In the case shown in the diagram, there is an improvement in the social utility level. Because all households are identical, they have an increase in welfare. So situation β (the new situation) is SU-preferred and lump-sum-preferred to situation α.

Suppose now that the government imposes consumption taxes so that the households face initial prices and thus choose the initial consumption bundle. Under the original Dixit-Norman approach, the aggregate demands for goods are represented by point C^α in Figure 8.4. Because this point is above the new budget line P, such a consumption tax policy is not feasible, and I cannot say that situation β is DN-preferred to situation α.[15] However, if for a small open

---

15. This case shows that if the government knows that all households are not worse off under the new prices, then there is no need to impose the compensating consumption taxes.

economy under free trade situation β is DN-preferred to situation α, then it is also SU-preferred and lump-sum-preferred to situation α as well. The reason is that if compensation by consumption taxes is feasibile, then condition (8.8) is satisfied. By using Thoerem 8.2, situation β is lump-sum-preferred (and thus SU-preferred) to situation α.

Now turn to case (2) in which all households have identical and homothetic preferences (but not necessarily the same endowments). In this case, the functional form of the social utility function is the same as that of each household. Of course, having possibly different endowments, the households may have different utility levels.

In Chapter 2 I showed that a redistribution of income would not affect the aggregate demands and thus not the equilibrium. Thus if there is an increase in the social utility level, then the aggregate consumption bundle can be redistributed among the households to make all of them better off. Similarly if in situation β income can be redistributed to make all households better off, then there must also be an increase in the social utility level. In other words, the social-utility (SU) ranking of two economic situations is equivalent to the lump-sum-compensation (LC) ranking. This case is similar to the previous case, except that in this case, generally compensation has to be made.

The same argument as the preceding one can be used to show that an increase in social utility does not imply the feasibility of a consumption tax policy, but for a small open economy under free trade, feasibility of a consumption tax policy does imply an increase in social utility level.

Now turn to case (3). The households in general have different preferences or endowments, but a Bergson-Samuelson social welfare (SW) function exists. With income redistributed optimally to maximize the SW function, a social utility function exists. The first result here is that a SU ranking does not imply a LC ranking. This point is explained for a two-household economy by using Figure 8.5. Schedules $\alpha\alpha$ and $\beta\beta$ are the utility possibility frontiers (UPF) in situations α and β, respectively. Point E^α represents the initial utility levels of the households (with optimal income distribution) and the resulting social welfare level, W^α. In situation β, by optimally distributing income, the economy reaches a higher social welfare level (and thus a higher social utility level), W. The diagram shows, however, that in situation β it is not possible to redistribute income to make both households better off (or not worse off).

If in situation α income is distributed optimally, then a LC ranking does imply the same SU ranking. The reason is that when the households are made as well off as before with some better off, the social welfare level must be higher, and the social utility level (obtained by maximizing the social welfare function) must be higher than before. This result does not depend on the size of the economy.

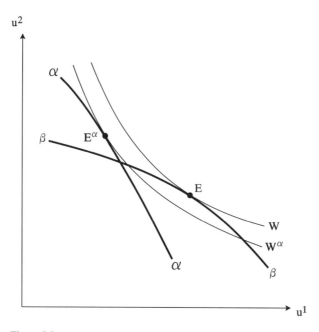

Figure 8.5

Using the preceding argument, I can also say that a SU ranking does not imply the same consumption-taxation (CT) ranking. If for a small open economy under free trade, the income in situation α is distributed optimally, then a CT ranking implies the same LC ranking, and thus the same SU ranking.

The above results are summarized by the following theorem:

Theorem 8.5   First, suppose that all households have identical preferences and identical endowments, or that they have identical and homothetic preferences. The SU ranking of two situations is equivalent to the LC ranking. These two rankings do not imply the same CT ranking, although for a small open economy under free trade, the CT ranking does imply the other two rankings. Second, suppose that all households have different preferences or endowments. The SU ranking does not imply the LC ranking or the CT ranking. If income is redistributed optimally in the initial situation, then the LC ranking implies the SU ranking; and, furthermore, for a small open economy under free trade, the CT ranking implies both the SU ranking and LC ranking.

8.6.2   Lump-sum Transfers versus Consumption Taxation

Recently, there has been interest in assessing the merits and shortcomings of these two ways of compensating the losers as the economy shifts from one situation to another. Two issues have been brought forward: efficiency and the information required in implementing the policies. A brief discussion of these two issues is provided here.

In the presence of lump-sum transfers described above, consumers and producers are facing the same prices, although these prices may be different from those before the transfers are given. Thus no domestic distortions are created, and Pareto consumption and production efficiency is maintained. When consumption taxation is imposed instead to compensate losers, wedges between consumer prices and producer prices are created. Such a distortionary policy prohibits the economy from getting the full potential benefits of the shift in the economic situation. Furthermore, there is a waste of resources when the government disposes of any tax revenue, as Dixit and Norman (1986) suggest.

The information required to implement the compensatory policies is an interesting but controversial issue. Let me consider the consumption taxation approach first. In the DN approach, the government needs to know only the final prices (assumed to be observable in the final situation) and the initial prices. In the MDN approach, the government has to be able to observe these prices and to determine the amount of gain due to an increase in national income as given by (8.8). This requires the government to have knowledge about the aggregate consumption bundles in the two situations. The latter approach needs more information than the former approach, but this is the price the government has to pay if it wants to be sure that at least some households are better off. The information requirement of the EDN approach is different. The government has to know in which markets the Weymark condition holds, and to know the amount of goods it needs to purchase in the two stages. Kemp and Wan (1993) argue that to determine the validity of the Weymark condition for some markets requires only local information, but to compute the final prices and the government purchase, the government needs more information. For a small open economy, only (global) information about domestic preferences is needed, but for a large economy (as in the general case of gains from free trade), information about the rest of the world is also needed.

In the literature, the lump-sum transfer approach is sometimes criticized for requiring the government to know the preferences of all individuals and the technologies of all firms. This is not true. As I showed, the government needs to know only the initial consumption bundles of all households and the value of the gain (as given by condition (8.8), or being equal to the sum of production gain and terms-of-trade gain as explained below). Knowing the value of the gain is less critical because the government has the option of distributing only part of the gain, but knowing the initial consumption bundles of all households is a challenge.

If the government has full information about the households' preferences, then it can compute their initial consumption points without a problem. If such information is not available, then to compensate all households may be difficult. In particular, if the government has to rely on the households to reveal their consumption patterns—and if households are aware of the fact that the government will use this information for computing the values of transfers— the government may not get the correct information. This is the incentive (in)compatibility problem. As Dixit and Norman (1986, p. 121) note, "[t]he net benefit to each individual under a lump-sum transfer scheme depends importantly on his own characteristics. He therefore has a strong incentive to manipulate his behaviour so as to mislead the planner about these characteristics and secure a larger net transfer." This argument raises several questions and issues.

1. Under what conditions can a household mislead the planner in order to secure a larger net transfer?

2. How does a household mislead, and what kind of misleading information will it give to the government?

3. What are the consequences when the households do give misleading information?

4. Are there incentive-compatible schemes through which the government can lead the households to reveal true information?

Let me provide some answers to these questions. First, to get a larger net transfer, a household must know how a transfer is related to its initial consumption bundle. The knowledge that is required includes that of the initial and final prices of the goods it consumes and is endowed with. It also may have to know the increase in national income (such as the sum of production gain and the terms-of-trade gain). The information can be huge, especially in the real world with many commodities and factors. Kemp and Wan (1989) have serious reservations about whether households can get the information required to appropriately manipulate their behavior.

Second, suppose that a household does have all the information. Wong (1993b) shows that a household will consume a good up to a point at which the marginal cost of overconsuming it is equal to the marginal benefit that it will bring through an increase in transfers. In a model with two tradable goods, the household consumes in the initial situation more of a good that will become more expensive in the final situation. However, if there are more than two goods, it is difficult to predict how the consumption pattern of a household may change, except in the special case in which its utility function is weakly separable in consumption goods.

Third, suppose that some households do mislead the government about their consumption behaviors in the initial situation. If the number of these households is small, then the initial situation is not much affected. Theorems 8.2 and 8.3 remain valid even though the lump-sum compensation scheme is not incentive compatible. If the number of households that mislead the government is large, then their behavior may significantly affect the market prices. In this case, making welfare comparisons is difficult.

There are two ways of measuring the welfare of a household in the initial situation, or there are two ways of interpreting the initial situation. If the government takes the affected initial situation as a benchmark for determining the changes in the households' welfare, then compensation can be made as described above, and given condition (8.8), the government can always make all households better off as compared with what they get in the initial situation after the households have distorted their consumption. If the government needs to use the hypothetical initial situation should all households not mislead as a benchmark, then to compensate all households is not easy because the hypothetical situation is not observable. It is, however, equally difficult for any household to claim that it is a loser. Given these difficulties, it seems to be more reasonable for the government to use the affected situation as a benchmark; then the theorems proved above remain valid.

The last question is about incentive-compatible schemes. Whether an incentive-compatible scheme exists depends on what information the government has. In general, it is difficult to design a scheme under which all households are willing to reveal their true preferences except in some special cases. Feenstra and Lewis (1991), however, consider a model in which the government knows everything including the functional form of all individuals except their endowments. Consider a small open economy that initially is under autarky or trading freely under given world prices. Suppose that there is a drop in the relative world price of the imported goods. Feenstra and Lewis (1991) show that the government can use nonlinear tariffs to make sure that all individuals truthfully reveal their endowments and are better off (or not worse off).

8.7   The Core Theorems of Welfare Economics in International Trade

I now apply the preceding analysis to derive six core theorems of welfare economics of international trade. I show that (with the additional assumption of the absence of inferior goods for one of the theorems under the social utility approach) all of these theorems are valid *whether or not a social utility function exists, or whether compensation is made using lump-sum transfers or consumption taxation.* These six core theorems are

Theorem 8.6 For any economy, large or small, free trade is better than no trade.[16]

Theorem 8.7 For a small open economy, an improvement in the terms of trade is beneficial.[17]

Theorem 8.8 For a small open economy, trade in additional commodities (including primary factors of production) is beneficial.[18]

Theorem 8.9 For any economy, large or small, natural trade is better than no trade.[19]

Theorem 8.10 For a small, tariff-ridden open economy,

1. a uniform reduction in trade taxes is beneficial (an additional assumption of no inferior goods is needed under the social utility approach);[20] and

2. free trade in goods and factors is the optimal policy.

Theorem 8.11 An expansion of an existing customs union can be mutually beneficial.

Corollary 1 Formation of a customs union can be mutually beneficial. [21]

Corollary 2 Free trade is the first-best policy for the world.

The theorems are proved and discussed in the following three sections. It is noted that because free trade is a form of natural trade, theorem 8.9 obviously covers theorem 8.6. The theorem of gains from free trade is very well known and important in the literature, however, and it deserves to be stated as a separate theorem.

8.8   Welfare of a Single Economy: The Case of Free Trade

The first three theorems (8.6 to 8.8) describe the change in welfare of a single economy when at least situation β is free trade. In shifting from situation

---

16. Samuelson (1939, 1962), Kemp (1962), Bhagwati (1968), Grandmont and McFadden (1972), Kemp and Wan (1972), Ohyama (1972), and Kemp and Ohyama (1978).

17. Kemp (1962), Krueger and Sonnenschein (1967), and Wong (1991a).

18. Wong (1983, 1991a) and Grossman (1984).

19. Kemp (1962), Ohyama (1972), and Deardorff (1980).

20. Lloyd (1974), Fukushima (1979), Diewert, et al. (1989), and Wong (1991a). Fukushima (1979) provides an alternative version of part (1) of the theorem: Because uniform (nonprohibitive) ad valorem rates of trade taxes are just as good as zero taxes (except for the cost of raising subsidy expenditures and distributing tax revenues), a uniform movement of all trade taxes toward any nonprohibitive ad valorem rate is welfare improving.

21. Kemp (1964), Vanek (1965), Ohyama (1972), and Kemp and Wan (1976, 1986a).

α to situation β, convexity of technology and profit maximization of firms imply that

$$\mathbf{p} \cdot \mathbf{Q} - \mathbf{w} \cdot \mathbf{v} - \mathbf{r} \cdot \mathbf{k} \geq \mathbf{p} \cdot \mathbf{Q}^\alpha - \mathbf{w} \cdot \mathbf{v} - \mathbf{r} \cdot \mathbf{k}^\alpha$$

or

$$\mathbf{p} \cdot \mathbf{Q} - \mathbf{r} \cdot \mathbf{k} \geq \mathbf{p} \cdot \mathbf{Q}^\alpha - \mathbf{r} \cdot \mathbf{k}^\alpha. \tag{8.15}$$

Free trade in situation β implies that $\mathbf{p} = \mathbf{p}^*$ and $\mathbf{r} = \mathbf{r}^*$. Production gain PG and terms-of-trade gain TG are defined according to the following conditions:

$$PG = (\mathbf{p} \cdot \mathbf{Q} - \mathbf{r} \cdot \mathbf{k}) - (\mathbf{p} \cdot \mathbf{Q}^\alpha - \mathbf{r} \cdot \mathbf{k}^\alpha) \tag{8.16a}$$

$$TG = \mathbf{p} \cdot \mathbf{Q}^\alpha - \mathbf{p} \cdot \mathbf{C}^\alpha - \mathbf{r} \cdot \mathbf{k}^\alpha. \tag{8.16b}$$

With the type of technology described previously, condition (8.15) implies that PG is non-negative. If production substitution is possible (when the production possibility set is strictly convex and smooth) and if domestic prices change ($\mathbf{p} \neq \mathbf{p}^\alpha$), PG is positive. The terms-of-trade gain TG is the value of initial outputs less that of initial consumption and the payment to the incoming factors, both evaluated using final prices $\mathbf{p}$. It can be positive or negative.

I now make use of PG and TG to establish a result which will be used to prove theorems 8.6 to 8.8. For an economy under free trade, whether small or large,

$$\mathbf{p} \cdot \mathbf{C} - \mathbf{p} \cdot \mathbf{C}^\alpha = \mathbf{p} \cdot \mathbf{M} + \mathbf{p} \cdot \mathbf{Q} - (\mathbf{p} \cdot \mathbf{Q}^\alpha - \mathbf{r} \cdot \mathbf{k}^\alpha) + TG$$

$$= \mathbf{p} \cdot \mathbf{M} + \mathbf{r} \cdot \mathbf{k} + PG + TG$$

$$= PG + TG. \tag{8.17}$$

In proving (8.17), the first equality is due to the definitions of $\mathbf{M}$ and TG; the second equality is due to the definition of PG, and the third is due to the current account balance. The condition shows that there is an increase in national income as described by condition (8.2) or (8.8) if $PG + TG > 0$.

In (8.17), if the economy is small, the prices are given exogenously. If the economy is large, the prices are determined endogenously. Assume that these prices exist (under the usual conditions for existence of equilibrium). It should be noted that results in (8.17) hold no matter what world prices are.

I now have to find conditions under which the term in (8.17) is positive (or non-negative). The sign of PG is known to be non-negative (positive if there is a change in prices and if PPF is strictly concave to the origin). The sign of TG is in general ambiguous, but in the following cases it is non-negative:

1. The economy is under autarky in the initial situation, $\mathbf{Q}^\alpha \geq \mathbf{C}^\alpha$ and $\mathbf{k}^\alpha = \mathbf{0}(m^t)$, implying that $TG \geq 0$.

2. A small open economy under free trade experiences an improvement in the terms of trade. The terms of trade of an economy are said to be improved if $\mathbf{p} \cdot \mathbf{Q}^\alpha - \mathbf{p} \cdot \mathbf{C}^\alpha - \mathbf{r} \cdot \mathbf{k}^\alpha > 0$, that is, $TG > 0$.[22]

3. The economy is a small open one with free trade and balance of trade in situation α, that is, $\mathbf{p}^\alpha \cdot \mathbf{Q}^\alpha - \mathbf{p}^\alpha \cdot \mathbf{C}^\alpha - \mathbf{r}^\alpha \cdot \mathbf{k}^\alpha = 0$. Now additional goods or factors are allowed to flow between countries with no policy impediments. Because the prices of the goods and factors that are tradable initially remain unchanged, $\mathbf{p} \cdot \mathbf{Q}^\alpha - \mathbf{p} \cdot \mathbf{C}^\alpha - \mathbf{r} \cdot \mathbf{k}^\alpha = 0$, which means that $TG = 0$.

Applying theorems 8.1, 8.2, and 8.4″ (or 8.4′, or 8.4) immediately gives theorems 8.6, 8.7, and 8.8 using a social utility function, and theorems 8.7 and 8.8 (for a small open economy) using either lump-sum compensation or consumption-taxation compensation. As for theorem 8.6, note that $PG + TG \geq 0$ no matter how income is redistributed under autarky or under free trade. This means that no matter how households are compensated using either lump-sum transfers or consumption taxes, there is always an increase in national welfare, satisfying condition (8.2) when the production gain is positive. The proofs of theorems 8.2 and 8.4″ can thus be extended to prove theorem 8.6 using lump-sum or taxation compensation. So theorems 8.6 to 8.8 are valid under both the social utility and the compensation approaches.

Theorems 8.6 and 8.7 can be illustrated diagrammatically for the case of a two-good economy with no international factor mobility. In Figure 8.6, TT represents the production possibility frontier (PPF) of the home country. Because in the absence of trade the country has to produce what it consumes, its PPF is also its autarkic consumption possibility frontier (CPF). Trade opportunities expand the CPF of the country. To derive its consumption possibilities, consider any production point such as Q in the diagram. Position the offer curve of the foreign country OC* so that its origin coincides with point Q. The intersecting point between a tangent to the PPF at point Q and the foreign offer curve, shown as point C, is a possible free-trade equilibrium. The free-trade CPF of the country, shown as SS in the diagram, is then the locus of points such as C when the origin of the foreign offer curve slides along TT.[23]

---

22. For a two-good economy under free trade but no international factor movement, an improvement in the terms of trade means an increase in the relative price of the exportable good. This is a special case of the statement in the text. To see this point, assume that good 1 is the exportable. By (8.16b), a positive TG means that $p_1 Q_1^\alpha + p_2 Q_2^\alpha > p_1 C_1^\alpha + p_2 C_2^\alpha$. Rearranging terms and making use of the trade balance in situation α, $p_1/p_2 > p_1^\alpha/p_2^\alpha$.

23. The free-trade CPF is not to be confused with another envelope, called the Baldwin envelope (Baldwin, 1948, 1952), which touches the foreign offer as the latter slides along the home PPF. For a large open economy, the Baldwin envelope is uniformly beyond the free-trade CPF except that they touch each other and the home PPF at the point at which the home PPF has a slope the same as that of the foreign offer curve at its origin. For a small open economy, the Baldwin envelope and the free-trade CPF are straight lines and they coincide with each other.

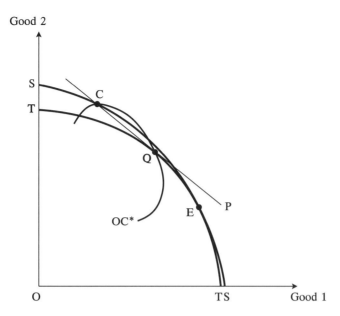

Figure 8.6

The outward shift of the CPF represents an expansion of the consumption possibility set except at point E at which the free-trade CPF touches the PPF.[24]

The expansion of the CPF, which represents the technological superiority of free trade over autarky, means that no matter what aggregate consumption bundle the country has under autarky, the country can find a consumption point under free trade by choosing the appropriate income distribution and production, so that more of each good is available to the households. This result can be illustrated in terms of utility possibility curves (UPC) such as those in Figure 8.1. Thus in that diagram, the free-trade UPC can be represented by a schedule such as $\beta\beta$ and the autarky UPC represented by a schedule such as $\alpha\alpha$. Due to the technological superiority of free trade, schedule $\beta\beta$ is beyond schedule $\alpha\alpha$ except at point E, which corresponds to point E in Figure 8.6.

The gains from trade can be evaluated using the social welfare approach. Refer again to Figure 8.1. Suppose that point A (on schedule $\alpha\alpha$) is the autarky equilibrium point and point C (on schedule $\beta\beta$) is the free-trade equilibrium point. Using the social welfare function and the illustrated iso-welfare curves, the autarkic social welfare level is W^2 and the free-trade social welfare level is W^1. Because $W^2 > W^1$, I now have a case in which *autarky is SW-preferred to free trade* in terms of the assumed social welfare function.

---

24. The slope of the PPF at point E is equal to the autarkic price ratio in the foreign country, that is, the slope of the foreign offer curve at the origin.

This illustrates that free trade is not necessarily better than autarky under the social welfare approach. It also highlights the fact that social-welfare rankings are sensitive to the assumed social welfare function. Suppose that another social welfare function is assumed that gives a much greater weight to the welfare of the first household, free trade can be SW-preferred to autarky.

It should be noted that because in Figure 8.1 schedule $\beta\beta$ is beyond schedule $\alpha\alpha$ (except at point E), if income redistribution is allowed, then under free trade a point (such as point D) on schedule $\beta\beta$ can be found that is SW-preferred to point A. In particular, the maximum social welfare level under free trade must be higher than the autarky point (except point E), and this result does not depend on the functional form of the social welfare function. In Figure 8.1, W^3 is the maximum welfare level and it is higher than the autarkic welfare level W^2. In other words, if income can be redistributed to maximize the social welfare function, free-trade social welfare must be higher (or not lower) than autarkic social welfare. This result is not surprising because free trade is SU-preferred to autarky.

The change in social utility as the economy shifts from autarky to free trade can be illustrated in Figure 8.7. The autarky equilibrium is at the point of tangency, denoted by point A, between the indifference curve labeled u^a and the production possibility frontier TT. The free-trade equilibrium consumption point of the country, shown as C^f, is at the point of tangency between a social indifference curve and the price line passing through the production point Q^f.

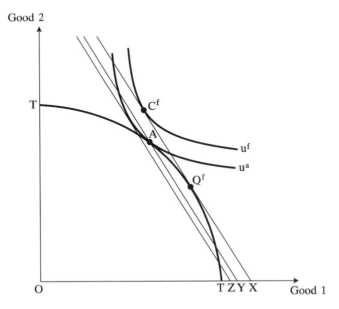

Figure 8.7

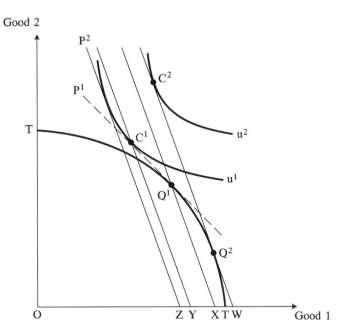

Figure 8.8

The slope of the price line is equal to the (negative) equilibrium world relative price of good 1. The free-trade social utility level is u^f. The fact that $u^f > u^a$ implies a gainful trade.

In Figure 8.7, the compensating variation measured in terms of good 1 is equal to ZX, where Z is the horizontal intercept of the world price line that is tangent to the indifference curve u^a. It is common to decompose the aggregate compensating variation of the economy. To do this, draw a world price line passing through the autarky point A, and denote its horizontal intercept by Y. The *consumption gain* is denoted by ZY, which is the increase in welfare due to a change in the prices consumers face and thus a change in consumption point, and the *production gain* is represented by YX, which is the increase in welfare due to a change in the production point.

The welfare impact of an improvement in the terms of trade for the two-economy without factor movement is illustrated in Figure 8.8. The economy initially faces an exogenously given world price ratio P^1. When the world price ratio changes to P^2, the production and consumption points shift from Q^1 and C^1 to Q^2 and C^2, respectively. Furthermore, the welfare increases from u^1 to u^2, confirming Theorem 8.7. The compensating variation is equal to ZW, which can be decomposed into the *consumption gain* ZY, the *production gain* XW, and the *terms-of-trade gain* YX.

8.9   Welfare of a Single Economy: The Case of Restricted Trade

I now turn to the case in which there is restricted trade in at least one of the situations. The two relevant theorems are 8.9 and 8.10.

8.9.1   Proving Theorem 8.9

I first focus on theorem 8.9. Recall that in Chapter 3 trade is defined to be natural if the following condition holds:

$$\mathbf{p} \cdot \mathbf{M} + \mathbf{r} \cdot \mathbf{k} \geq 0. \tag{8.18}$$

One sufficient condition for (8.18) is that no trade subsidies are imposed. Free trade is a special case of natural trade, and in this case, $\mathbf{p} = \mathbf{p}^*$, $\mathbf{r} = \mathbf{r}^*$, and condition (8.18) holds with an equality. The proof of the theorem 8.9 when a social utility function exists is given in Chapter 3. Thus in the present chapter I discuss only the case in which a social utility function does not exist and compensation is required.

For a large open economy compensation may affect the international equilibrium. For theorem 8.9, I require that condition (8.15) holds after compensation. Recalling that a prime is used to denote a variable after compensation, natural trade here implies

$$\mathbf{p}' \cdot \mathbf{M}' + \mathbf{r}' \cdot \mathbf{k}' \geq 0. \tag{8.18'}$$

Denote the sum of the production gain plus trade tax revenue by R, that is,

$$R = (\mathbf{p}' \cdot \mathbf{Q}' - \mathbf{r}' \cdot \mathbf{k}' - \mathbf{p}' \cdot \mathbf{Q}^{\alpha}) + \mathbf{p}' \cdot \mathbf{M}' + \mathbf{r}' \cdot \mathbf{k}', \tag{8.19}$$

where under autarky no factor movement exists. Production gain is non-negative. By condition (8.18'), the trade revenue is non-negative. This implies that $R \geq 0$.

Making use of the definitions of the production gain and trade revenue, and the condition that $\mathbf{Q}^{\alpha} \geq \mathbf{C}^{\alpha}$, R reduces to

$$R = \mathbf{p}' \cdot \mathbf{C}' - \mathbf{p}' \cdot \mathbf{Q}^{\alpha}$$
$$\leq \mathbf{p}' \cdot \mathbf{C}' - \mathbf{p}' \cdot \mathbf{C}^{\alpha}. \tag{8.19'}$$

Because $R \geq 0$, condition (8.19') implies that $\mathbf{p}' \cdot \mathbf{C}' \geq \mathbf{p}' \cdot \mathbf{C}^{\alpha}$. In fact, the weak inequality can be replaced by a strong inequality if the production gain is positive or the trade revenue is positive. Thus I can apply theorems 8.2 and 8.4″ to show that natural trade as defined by condition (8.18') is lump-sum-preferred and MDN-preferred to autarky.

8.9.2   Proving Theorem 8.10

I now turn to part (1) of theorem 8.10, first considering the use of lump-sum or consumption taxation compensation. Suppose that the initial specific tax rates on trading goods and moving factors are respectively given by

$$\mathbf{t} = \mathbf{p}^\alpha - \mathbf{p}^*$$

$$\mathbf{s} = \mathbf{r}^\alpha - \mathbf{r}^*.$$

Although the world prices remain unchanged, the home government lowers the tax rates to $\theta\mathbf{t}$ and $\theta\mathbf{s}$, where $1 > \theta \geq 0$. The new domestic prices are $\mathbf{p} = \theta\mathbf{t} + \mathbf{p}^*$ and $\mathbf{r} = \theta\mathbf{s} + \mathbf{r}^*$. Using the definition of the initial tax rates,

$$\mathbf{p} = \theta(\mathbf{p}^\alpha - \mathbf{p}^*) + \mathbf{p}^* = \theta\mathbf{p}^\alpha + (1-\theta)\mathbf{p}^* \tag{8.20a}$$

$$\mathbf{r} = \theta(\mathbf{r}^\alpha - \mathbf{r}^*) + \mathbf{r}^* = \theta\mathbf{r}^\alpha + (1-\theta)\mathbf{r}^*. \tag{8.20b}$$

Conditions (8.20) imply that each new domestic price is a weighted average of the initial domestic price and the world price.

As given in condition (8.15), the value of domestic outputs less the costs of inflowing factors, both evaluated using domestic prices, is always maximized. Substituting $\mathbf{p}$ and $\mathbf{r}$ given in (8.20) into (8.15),

$$\theta(\mathbf{p}^\alpha \cdot \mathbf{Q} - \mathbf{r}^\alpha \cdot \mathbf{k}) + (1-\theta)(\mathbf{p}^* \cdot \mathbf{Q} - \mathbf{r}^* \cdot \mathbf{k}) \geq \theta(\mathbf{p}^\alpha \cdot \mathbf{Q}^\alpha - \mathbf{r}^\alpha \cdot \mathbf{k}^\alpha)$$

$$+ (1-\theta)(\mathbf{p}^* \cdot \mathbf{Q}^\alpha - \mathbf{r}^* \cdot \mathbf{k}^\alpha) \tag{8.21a}$$

Reversing the position of situations α and β in condition (8.15),

$$\mathbf{p}^\alpha \cdot \mathbf{Q}^\alpha - \mathbf{r}^\alpha \cdot \mathbf{k}^\alpha \geq \mathbf{p}^\alpha \cdot \mathbf{Q} - \mathbf{r}^\alpha \cdot \mathbf{k}. \tag{8.21b}$$

Multiply both sides of (8.21b) by θ and then combine it with condition (8.21a) to give

$$\mathbf{p}^* \cdot \mathbf{Q} - \mathbf{r}^* \cdot \mathbf{k} \geq \mathbf{p}^* \cdot \mathbf{Q}^\alpha - \mathbf{r}^* \cdot \mathbf{k}^\alpha. \tag{8.22}$$

Note that in both situations (before and after the changes in taxes), the world prices stay unchanged. Assuming that the current account is balanced in both situations, condition (8.22) reduces to

$$\mathbf{p}^* \cdot \mathbf{C} \geq \mathbf{p}^* \cdot \mathbf{C}^\alpha. \tag{8.22'}$$

By theorems 8.2 and 8.4″, condition (8.22′) implies that the uniform reduction in trade taxes represents a welfare improvement when either lump-sum transfers or consumption taxation are used.

I now consider part (1) of theorem 8.10 when a social utility function exists. The tariff revenue is equal to $\mathbf{p} \cdot \mathbf{M} + \mathbf{r} \cdot \mathbf{k}$, while the national product is equal to $\mathbf{p} \cdot \mathbf{Q} - \mathbf{r} \cdot \mathbf{k}$. Using the social expenditure function $e(\mathbf{p}, u)$, the budget constraint of the economy is given by

$$e(\mathbf{p}, u) = (\mathbf{p} \cdot \mathbf{Q} - \mathbf{r} \cdot \mathbf{k}) + (\mathbf{p} \cdot \mathbf{M} + \mathbf{r} \cdot \mathbf{k}) = \mathbf{p} \cdot \mathbf{Q} + \mathbf{p} \cdot \mathbf{M}.$$

Differentiate both sides of the above condition to give

$$e_{\mathbf{p}}d\mathbf{p} + e_u du = \mathbf{p} \cdot d\mathbf{Q} + \mathbf{Q} \cdot d\mathbf{p} + \mathbf{p} \cdot d\mathbf{M} + \mathbf{M} \cdot d\mathbf{p}. \tag{8.23}$$

Using the definition of $\mathbf{M}$ ($= \mathbf{C} - \mathbf{Q} = e_{\mathbf{p}} - \mathbf{Q}$) and the fact that efficient production implies $\mathbf{p} \cdot d\mathbf{Q} - \mathbf{r} \cdot d\mathbf{k} = 0$, condition (8.23) reduces to

$$e_u du = \mathbf{p} \cdot d\mathbf{M} + \mathbf{r} \cdot d\mathbf{k}. \tag{8.23'}$$

To interpret condition (8.23′), recall that $\mathbf{t}$ is the initial tariff vector. Now treat θ as a parameter, $1 \leq \theta \leq 0$, so that

$$\mathbf{p} = \theta \mathbf{t} + \mathbf{p}^* \tag{8.24a}$$

$$\mathbf{r} = \theta \mathbf{s} + \mathbf{r}^*. \tag{8.24b}$$

The initial value of θ is unity. Thus a uniform reduction in trade taxes means a decrease in the value of θ. With θ being treated as a parameter, $d\mathbf{p} = \mathbf{t}d\theta$ and $d\mathbf{r} = \mathbf{s}d\theta$. Because $d\mathbf{M} = de_{\mathbf{p}} - d\mathbf{Q}$, condition (8.23′) reduces to

$$e_u du = (\theta \mathbf{t} + \mathbf{p}^*) \cdot d\mathbf{M} + (\theta \mathbf{s} + \mathbf{r}^*) \cdot d\mathbf{k}$$

$$= \theta \mathbf{t} \cdot d\mathbf{M} + \theta \mathbf{s} \cdot d\mathbf{k}$$

$$= \theta \mathbf{t} \cdot e_{\mathbf{pp}}\mathbf{t}d\theta + \theta \mathbf{t} \cdot e_{\mathbf{p}u}du - \theta [\mathbf{t}^T, \mathbf{s}^T] \cdot \nabla \begin{bmatrix} \mathbf{Q} \\ -\mathbf{k} \end{bmatrix} \begin{bmatrix} \mathbf{t} \\ \mathbf{s} \end{bmatrix} d\theta, \tag{8.25}$$

where the superscript "T" represents transpose of a vector, the second equality is obtained by differentiation of the balance-of-trade condition $\mathbf{p}^* \cdot \mathbf{M} + \mathbf{r}^* \cdot \mathbf{k} = 0$ using constant world prices, and ∇ is the differentiation operator with respect to $(\mathbf{p}, \mathbf{r})$. Rearranging the terms in (8.25) gives

$$(e_u - \theta \mathbf{t} \cdot e_{\mathbf{p}u})du = \theta \mathbf{t} \cdot e_{\mathbf{pp}}\mathbf{t}d\theta - \theta [\mathbf{t}^T, \mathbf{s}^T] \cdot \nabla \begin{bmatrix} \mathbf{Q} \\ -\mathbf{k} \end{bmatrix} \begin{bmatrix} \mathbf{t} \\ \mathbf{s} \end{bmatrix} d\theta. \tag{8.25'}$$

First look at the right-hand side of condition (8.25′). It is well known that the expenditure function is concave in $\mathbf{p}$ and the GDP function is convex in $(\mathbf{p}, \mathbf{r})$. Thus $e_{\mathbf{pp}}$ is negative semidefinite and $\nabla[\mathbf{Q}, -\mathbf{k}]$ is positive semidefinite. In other words, the right-hand side of (8.25′) is positive (or non-negative) if $d\theta < 0$. Turning to the left-hand side of the condition and using the definition of the trade taxes, I have

$$\theta \mathbf{t} \cdot e_{\mathbf{p}u} = \mathbf{p} \cdot e_{\mathbf{p}u} - \mathbf{p}^* \cdot e_{\mathbf{p}u}$$

$$= e_u - \mathbf{p}^* \cdot e_{\mathbf{p}u},$$

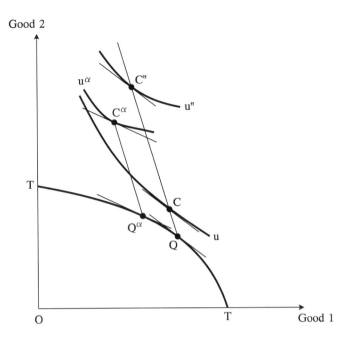

Figure 8.9

where $\mathbf{p} \cdot e_{\mathbf{p}u} = e_u$ because e_u is linearly homogeneous in prices. Thus the left-hand side of (8.25′) reduces to $\mathbf{p}^* \cdot e_{\mathbf{p}u} du$. If inferior goods are ruled out, then $e_{\mathbf{p}u}$ is positive and $\mathbf{p}^* \cdot e_{\mathbf{p}u} > 0$. Combining these results, theorem 8.10 (1) is obtained when a social utility function exists.

Given part (1) of theorem 8.10, whether a social utility function exists or compensation is available, part (2) of the theorem follows immediately, because the same analysis can be applied repeatedly until $\theta = 0$ (or θ approaches 0).

Part (1) of theorem 8.10 may not be true if inferior goods exist (Bhagwati and Kemp 1969; Riley 1970). To see the possibility of a welfare deterioration due to a uniform reduction in tariffs, consider again the two-good economy with no international factor movement. In Figure 8.9, the initial production point of the economy is at point Q^α, and the initial consumption point is at C^α, yielding a utility level of u^α. With balanced trade, the line joining Q^α and C^α represents the world price ratio, which is given exogenously. An initial tariff on the imported good 2 means that the domestic relative price of good 2 is higher than the world relative price. A reduction in the tariff rate will lower the domestic relative price of good 2, shifting the optimal production point to Q. If good 1 is inferior, the consumption point can end up at point C as shown in the diagram with a lower utility level, $u < u^\alpha$. Thus trade liberalization can hurt the economy when an inferior good is present. A careful study of the diagram shows that even in the presence of an inferior good, another consumption point on the new world price line can be found with a utility level higher than the initial one. It is because while the income consumption curve (ICC, not shown in the diagram) corresponding to the final domestic price ratio is negatively sloped in the space between the indifference curves u and u^α, it will sooner or later bend out and become positively sloped at higher utility level. This means that the ICC will cut the new world price line (the one that passes throughh Q) at a point higher than the indifference curve u^α. This point is shown as point C'' in Figure 8.9, which represents a welfare improvement, $u'' > u^\alpha$.

That a point with a higher utility can be found even in the presence of inferior goods means that part (2) of Theorem 8.10 is still valid under the social utility approach.

8.10   Welfare of the World

Turning to the welfare of a group of countries, the effect of free trade on the welfare of the world is discussed and Theorem 8.11 and its corollaries are proven.

Suppose that there are $N \geq 2$ countries, and initially there are B countries that are members of a customs union (CU), $1 \leq B < N$. Some new countries join the CU. Let the new number of member countries be A, where $B < A \leq N$ (B stands for "before" while A stands for "after"). I need to show that such an expansion of the customs union can be mutually beneficial.

Label the situation before the expansion of the customs union α and that after the expansion β. I follow the strategy in Kemp and Wan (1979, 1986a) and allow the member countries (after the expansion of the customs union) to choose appropriate trade taxes so that the economies of the nonmember countries are not disturbed. In particular, they have the same volume of trade and factor movement (with the member countries of the CU), the same prices, and thus the same welfare levels as before.

I next slightly extend the previous notation. Index the (new and old) member countries after the customs union expansion by $a = 1, \ldots, A$. I use a subscript "a" to denote the variables of the ath member country. For example, $\mathbf{C}_a^{h\alpha}$ is the consumption bundle of the hth household in the ath country in situation α, and $\mathbf{C}_a^h$ is its consumption bundle in situation β. Variables without subscripts h and a are the aggregate variables or variables common in the customs union. For example, $\mathbf{C}_a^\alpha \equiv \sum_h \mathbf{C}_a^{h\alpha}$ and $\mathbf{C}^\alpha \equiv \sum_a \mathbf{C}_a^\alpha$. Furthermore, $\mathbf{p}$ and $\mathbf{w}$ are the common commodity and factor prices in the member countries after the expansion of the customs union. There are H_a households in the ath country.

Following condition (8.16a), I define the production gain for the ath member country as follows:

$$PG_a = (\mathbf{p} \cdot \mathbf{Q}_a - \mathbf{r} \cdot \mathbf{k}_a) - (\mathbf{p} \cdot \mathbf{Q}_a^{\alpha} - \mathbf{r} \cdot \mathbf{k}_a^{\alpha}) \geq 0. \tag{8.26}$$

With convex technology and perfect competition, profit maximization of firms ensures that the production gain is non-negative (or positive if production substitution exists).

8.10.1   The Social Utility Approach

First assume that for each of the member countries there exists a social utility function. Further assume that the ath country receives an intermember-country transfer of b_a after the expansion of the CU. In the presence of the transfer, its current account balance gives

$$b_a = \mathbf{p}^* \cdot \mathbf{M}_a + \mathbf{r}^* \cdot \mathbf{k}_a, \tag{8.27}$$

where $(\mathbf{p}^*, \mathbf{r}^*)$ are world commodity and factor prices. Let T_a be the tariff revenue the ath country gets, that is,

$$T_a = (\mathbf{p} - \mathbf{p}^*) \cdot \mathbf{M}_a + (\mathbf{r} - \mathbf{r}^*) \cdot \mathbf{k}_a. \tag{8.28}$$

The new national income of the ath country can now be determined:

$$
\begin{aligned}
\mathbf{p} \cdot \mathbf{C}_a &= \mathbf{p} \cdot \mathbf{Q}_a + \mathbf{p} \cdot \mathbf{M}_a \\
&\geq \mathbf{p} \cdot \mathbf{Q}_a^{\alpha} - \mathbf{r} \cdot \mathbf{k}_a^{\alpha} + \mathbf{r} \cdot \mathbf{k}_a + \mathbf{p} \cdot \mathbf{M}_a \\
&= \mathbf{p} \cdot \mathbf{C}_a^{\alpha} - \mathbf{p} \cdot \mathbf{M}_a^{\alpha} - \mathbf{r} \cdot \mathbf{k}_a^{\alpha} + \mathbf{r} \cdot \mathbf{k}_a + \mathbf{p} \cdot \mathbf{M}_a \\
&= \mathbf{p} \cdot \mathbf{C}_a^{\alpha} - \mathbf{p} \cdot \mathbf{M}_a^{\alpha} - \mathbf{r} \cdot \mathbf{k}_a^{\alpha} + T_a + b_a, \tag{8.29}
\end{aligned}
$$

where the first equality is due to the defintion of imports; the first inequality is due to a non-negative production gain as defined in (8.26); the second equality is due to the definition of $\mathbf{M}_a^{\alpha}$; and the last equality is due to the current account balance as given in (8.27) and the value of tariff revenue as given in (8.28).

Now let the intermember transfer be $b_a = \mathbf{p} \cdot \mathbf{M}_a^{\alpha} + \mathbf{r} \cdot \mathbf{k}_a^{\alpha} - T_a$. When this transfer is substituted into (8.29), $\mathbf{p} \cdot \mathbf{C}_a \geq \mathbf{p} \cdot \mathbf{C}_a^{\alpha}$. This weak inequality is replaced by a strong inequality if the production gain is positive. In the latter case, Theorem 8.1 can be applied to conclude that the ath country is better off (or at least not worse off). Furthermore, the intermember transfers are feasible because

$$
\begin{aligned}
\sum_a b_a &= \mathbf{p} \cdot \mathbf{M}^{\alpha} + \mathbf{r} \cdot \mathbf{k}^{\alpha} - T \\
&= \mathbf{p} \cdot \mathbf{M}^{\alpha} + \mathbf{r} \cdot \mathbf{k}^{\alpha} - (\mathbf{p} - \mathbf{p}^*) \cdot \mathbf{M} - (\mathbf{r} - \mathbf{r}^*) \cdot \mathbf{k} \\
&= \mathbf{p}^* \cdot \mathbf{M} + \mathbf{r}^* \cdot \mathbf{k} \qquad\qquad [\mathbf{M} = \mathbf{M}^{\alpha},\ \mathbf{k} = \mathbf{k}^{\alpha}] \\
&= 0. \qquad\qquad\qquad\qquad\qquad\qquad [\text{balanced trade}]
\end{aligned}
$$

8.10.2   Lump-sum Compensation

Now relax the assumption of existence of a social utility function and consider compensation. First assume lump-sum transfers. Suppose that after the
expansion of the customs union, the government of the ath country gives its
hth household the following transfer:

$$z_a^h = \mathbf{p}' \cdot \mathbf{C}_a^{h\alpha} - \mathbf{w}' \cdot \mathbf{v}_a^h + \phi_a^h R_a,$$

where $R_a = PG_a$, the production gain of the ath country as given by (8.26).
Recall that the prime after a variable denotes the value of the variable after
compensation. Following the preceding analysis, it is clear that the household
is not worse off, or is better off if consumption or production substitution
exists.

In addition to the transfers, the governments of the member countries
as a whole receive a tariff revenue equal to $\mathbf{p}' \cdot \mathbf{M}^\alpha + \mathbf{r}' \cdot \mathbf{k}^\alpha$. Recall that
the nonmember countries' trade and factor movement are constantly main-
tained due to the appropriate trade taxes and income taxes (on the moving
factors to and from the nonmember countries) chosen by the member countries. The total revenue of the governments of all the member countries is
equal to $\mathbf{p}' \cdot \mathbf{M}^\alpha + \mathbf{r}' \cdot \mathbf{k}^\alpha - \sum_a \sum_h z_a^h$, and, by rearranging terms, it is non-
negative:

$$\mathbf{p}' \cdot \mathbf{M}^\alpha + \mathbf{r}' \cdot \mathbf{k}^\alpha - \sum_a \sum_h z_a^h = \mathbf{p}' \cdot \mathbf{M}^\alpha + \mathbf{r}' \cdot \mathbf{k}^\alpha - \mathbf{p}' \cdot \mathbf{C}^\alpha + \mathbf{w}' \cdot \mathbf{v} - \mathbf{p}' \cdot \mathbf{Q}'$$

$$+ \mathbf{r}' \cdot \mathbf{k}' + \mathbf{p}' \cdot \mathbf{Q}^\alpha - \mathbf{r}' \cdot \mathbf{k}^\alpha$$

$$= 0,$$

where the definition $\mathbf{M}^\alpha = \mathbf{C}^\alpha - \mathbf{Q}^\alpha$, the definitions of PG_a and z_a^h, and the
zero-profit condition have been used. Thus the compensation scheme is feasi-
ble. Note that the feasibility of the scheme applies to all the member countries
as a whole. This implies that the compensation scheme in general requires intermember transfers.

8.10.3   Consumption Taxation

I now consider consumption taxation with poll grants. As mentioned earlier,
the government of the ath member country will impose consumption taxes so
that all the households in the country are facing the pre-expansion prices. In
addition, the government distributes the production gain PG_a as defined in
(8.26) equally among all households. The sum of all tax revenues (including
tariff revenue) of all member countries is

$$\mathbf{p}' \cdot \mathbf{M}' + \mathbf{r}' \cdot \mathbf{k}' + \sum_a \sum_h \left\{ (\mathbf{p}^\alpha - \mathbf{p}') \cdot \mathbf{C}_a^{h\prime} + (\mathbf{w}' - \mathbf{w}^\alpha) \cdot \mathbf{v}_a^h - \phi_a^h PG_a \right\}$$

$$= \mathbf{p}' \cdot \mathbf{M}' + \mathbf{r}' \cdot \mathbf{k}' - \mathbf{p}' \cdot \mathbf{C}' + \mathbf{w}' \cdot \mathbf{v}$$

$$= \mathbf{r}' \cdot \mathbf{k}' - \mathbf{p}' \cdot \mathbf{Q}' + \mathbf{w}' \cdot \mathbf{v}$$

$$= 0,$$

where the first equality is due to households' budget constraints ($\mathbf{p}^\alpha \cdot \mathbf{C}_a^{h\prime} = \mathbf{w}^\alpha \cdot \mathbf{v}_a^h + \phi_a^h PG_a$, with nonsatiation), the second is due to the definition of imports, and the third is firms' zero-profit conditions. Again intermember transfers are generally required.

Now turn to the corollaries of Theorem 8.11. In the special case in which initially no customs union is formed, that is, $B = 1$, the theorem implies that the formation of a customs union can be mutually beneficial. This gives Corollary 1. For Corollary 2, Theorem 8.11 implies that a Pareto improvement can be achieved when an existing customs union is expanded, by adding one new member country at a time, until all countries join the customs union, that is, free trade in the world. This then gives the corollary.

Theorem 8.11 has two other applications. First, in proving the theorem I showed that during the expansion of an existing CU, the welfare of the rest of the world can be made unchanged if appropriate external tariffs and income taxes (on moving factors to and from nonmember countries) are chosen by the member countries. This result does not depend on whether there are already other CUs existing in the rest of the world. Thus formation of trading blocks can be mutually beneficial.

The second application is that there may exist other external tariffs and income taxes that further improve the welfare of the member countries (in the presence of inter-member transfers). In this case, however, the nonmember countries may be hurt.

9 Gains from Trade for Economies with Imperfections

In Chapter 8, I provided welfare economics analysis of Arrow-Debreu type economies, and established six core theorems. In this chapter, I consider other types of economies which depart from some of the Arrow-Debreu assumptions. In particular, the economies that I focus on have the following distortions or imperfections:

1. external economies of scale;
2. monopolistic competition with differentiated products;
3. oligopoly;
4. incomplete markets; and
5. overlapping generations.

It is well known that when some of the assumptions for the Arrow-Debreu type economies are not satisfied, the first theorem of welfare economics does not hold. When this theorem is not true, generally the six core theorems of welfare economics in international trade developed in the previous chapter are violated. This means that these six core theorems are generally not valid for each of the present five types of economies with imperfections.

In the present chapter, I take a narrower view and analyze the validity of only one of these core theorems: the gains from trade theorem. There are two reasons why my focus is on this theorem. First, it is the one that receives the most attention in the literature, and secondly, the analysis that I provide below can be extended to examine the validity of some other theorems.

The first three of the five model types have been described in detail in chapters 5 to 7. I make use of the properties of these models to show that trade may hurt an economy, and to derive conditions for a gainful trade. The last two types of models have not appeared earlier in this book, and their properties are described here. These two types of models are of particular interest because it has been shown that free trade can be Pareto inferior to autarky.

9.1 External Economies of Scale

Chapter 5 analyzes some important properties of a framework in which sectors are subject to external effects. The analysis focuses on the causes of international trade in goods and factor mobility, and their effects on income distribution and resource allocation. In this section, I explain how free trade may affect the welfare of different economies.

Chapter 8 explains that the change in the welfare of an economy during a transition from one trade situation to another can be decomposed into the production gain (PG), consumption gain (CG), and terms-of-trade gain (TG). For an economy moving from autarky to free trade, TG is zero so that I can concentrate on the first two. If a well-behaved social utility function exists and if consumption distortions are absent, then the CG is non-negative. The sign of the PG is ambiguous. If the PG is non-negative, a nonharmful free trade is guaranteed. Thus the present analysis is to find sufficient conditions under which the PG is non-negative.

9.1.1   A General Model

I begin with the m-factor, n-sector framework described in Chapter 5. I consider first the general case without explicitly mentioning the external effects. Let these effects be represented by vector $\mathbf{Z}$. Thus the production function of sector i can be written as $Q_i = F_i(\mathbf{v}_i, \mathbf{Z})$, where Q_i is the output and $\mathbf{v}_i$ is the vector of inputs. This general case reduces to the special cases of output-generated or factor-generated economies of scale, or national or international economies of scale, by including the appropriate variables in vector $\mathbf{Z}$. Following the convention in the previous chapter, the autarkic value of a variable or vector is distinguished by a superscript "a" while the free-trade value of the variable or vector has no such superscript.

In the present model, the production of the economy can be described by the GDP function defined in Chapter 5, $\breve{g} = \breve{g}(\mathbf{p}, \mathbf{v}, \mathbf{Z})$ where $\mathbf{p}$ is the vector of commodity prices and $\mathbf{v}$ is the vector of factor endowments. When $\mathbf{Z}$ is taken as given, function $\breve{g}(\mathbf{p}, \mathbf{v}, \mathbf{Z})$ has the usual properties of a GDP function in the neoclassical model. The optimal output of sector i is given by

$$Q_i = \breve{Q}_i(\mathbf{p}, \mathbf{v}, \mathbf{Z}) = \frac{\partial \breve{g}}{\partial p_i},$$

where $\mathbf{Z}$ is evaluated at the equilibrium values. The autarkic outputs are equal to $\mathbf{Q}^a = \breve{\mathbf{Q}}(\mathbf{p}^a, \mathbf{v}, \mathbf{Z}^a)$ while the free-trade outputs are equal to $\mathbf{Q} = \breve{\mathbf{Q}}(\mathbf{p}, \mathbf{v}, \mathbf{Z})$.

Result 9.1   The following is a sufficient condition for a nonharmful free trade:

$$\mathbf{p} \cdot \breve{\mathbf{Q}}(\mathbf{p}^a, \mathbf{v}, \mathbf{Z}) \geq \mathbf{p} \cdot \breve{\mathbf{Q}}(\mathbf{p}^a, \mathbf{v}, \mathbf{Z}^a). \tag{9.1}$$

To prove this result, recall that the production gain is equal to $\mathbf{p} \cdot (\mathbf{Q} - \mathbf{Q}^a)$. I now show that condition (9.1) implies a non-negative production gain. Because the present GDP function behaves like an ordinary GDP function when $\mathbf{Z}$ is fixed,

$$\mathbf{p} \cdot \breve{\mathbf{Q}}(\mathbf{p}, \mathbf{v}, \mathbf{Z}) \geq \mathbf{p} \cdot \breve{\mathbf{Q}}(\mathbf{p}^a, \mathbf{v}, \mathbf{Z}). \tag{9.2}$$

Combining conditions (9.1) and (9.2) together,

$$\mathbf{p} \cdot \mathbf{Q} = \mathbf{p} \cdot \breve{\mathbf{Q}}(\mathbf{p}, \mathbf{v}, \mathbf{Z}) \geq \mathbf{p} \cdot \breve{\mathbf{Q}}(\mathbf{p}^a, \mathbf{v}, \mathbf{Z}^a) = \mathbf{p} \cdot \mathbf{Q}^a.$$

So the production gain is non-negative. Because the consumption gain is non-negative, free trade is nonharmful. Free trade is strictly gainful if consumption gain or production gain is positive.

The intuition behind Result 9.1 is that free trade is not bad for the economy if under autarky the changes in the external effects do not lead to a decrease in the total values of outputs. Result 9.1 is similar to a result in Helpman and Krugman (1985, p, 51) except that theirs is stated in terms of factoral value-addeds of sectors. If the GDP function of the economy is known, then condition (9.1) provides an alternative way of checking whether trade is gainful.

In what follows, I focus on a special framework that was analyzed in Chapter 5 and is common in the literature. In this framework, (1) the external effects are output-generated, (2) intersectoral external effects are absent, and (3) production functions are homothetic. As explained, external economies of scale may be national or international. I analyze gains from trade under these two types of economies of scale separately.

9.1.2 National Economies of Scale

The external effects in sector i are represented by $h_i(Q_i)$, and the rate of variable returns to scale (VRS), ε_i, is the elasticity of $h_i(Q_i)$, that is, $\varepsilon_i = Q_i h_i'/h_i$. Homotheticity of the production functions allows me to analyze the properties of the economy in terms of the virtual system. For example, the virtual output of good i is related to the actual output of good i by $\widetilde{Q}_i = Q_i/h(Q_i)$, where a tilde is used to denote a variable in the virtual system. (For more details, see Chapter 5.) Define $\mathbf{D_h}$ as the $n \times n$ diagonal matrix that has a representative diagonal element given by $h_i(Q_i)$. I let h_i^a be $h_i(Q_i^a)$. Result 9.1 reduces to:

Result 9.1'   The following is a sufficient condition for a nonharmful free trade:

$$\mathbf{p} \cdot \mathbf{D_h}\widetilde{\mathbf{Q}}^a \geq \mathbf{p} \cdot \mathbf{D_h^a}\widetilde{\mathbf{Q}}^a. \tag{9.3}$$

Condition (9.3) can be compared with two conditions in the literature. Helpman (1984b, p. 336) provides a condition similar to (9.3). The difference between the present condition and Helpman's is that the latter is stated in terms of the factoral value-added of each sector while condition (9.3) is stated in terms of $\widetilde{\mathbf{Q}}$. In general, the factoral value-addeds of a sector are not observable, but if the GDP function is known, then condition (9.3) can still be used to provide a sufficient condition for a gainful trade.

In a more general framework, Grinols (1991, 1992) derives an alternative sufficient condition for a positive production gain under free trade. His analy-

sis does not require zero profit of firms (as in the case of internal economies
of scale), and he explicitly allows the existence of fixed costs of firms.
The latter assumption enables him to analyze the consequence of having some firms producing zero output in the autarkic or free-trade equilibrium.

The sufficient condition in Result 9.1′ is general. For example, it reduces to
the following famous result as a special case:

Result 9.2   If the opening of trade results in the noncontraction of every
sector that is subject to increasing returns to scale (IRS) and nonexpansion of
every sector that is subject to decreasing returns to scale (DRS), then trade is
nonharmful (Kemp and Negishi, 1970).

To prove Result 9.2, consider sector i, which is subject to IRS. If $Q_i \geq Q_i^a$,
then $h_i(Q_i) \geq h_i(Q_i^a)$. Consider sector j, which is subject to DRS. If $Q_j \leq
Q_j^a$, then $h_j(Q_j) \geq h_j(Q_j^a)$. If sector k is subject to constant returns to scale,
then $h_k(Q_k)$ is a constant. These conditions give (9.3), and by Result 9.1′, free
trade is nonharmful.

Results 9.1′ and 9.2 can be illustrated graphically. In Figure 9.1, TT is the
production possibility frontier (PPF), and Q^a is the autarkic point with the
autarkic price line P^a. Sector 1 is subject to IRS and sector 2 subject to CRS.
Under free trade, the production point shifts to Q^f. P_1^f, P_2^f, and P_3^f are three
parallel world price lines. The diagram shows a welfare improvement given
by XZ using the compensating variation measure, which can be decomposed
into the consumption gain, XY, and the production gain, YZ.

Trade may be harmful for this economy.[1] Figure 9.2 shows such a
possibility. When free trade is allowed, the production point shifts from
Q^a to Q^f, causing the welfare of the economy to drop from u^a to u^f. As
usual, the change in welfare can be decomposed into the CG (= XY) and the
PG (= YZ). In the case shown, the PG is sufficiently negative.[2] Such a possibility of losing from trade is the basis of Graham's (1923) argument for protection.

More interesting results can be obtained if small changes are considered.
Let me write $h_i = h_i^a + \Delta h_i$. Condition (9.3) reduces to

$$\sum_i p_i \widetilde{Q}_i^a \Delta h_i \geq 0. \tag{9.4}$$

---

1. For a numerical example that shows that free trade hurts an economy, see Helpman (1984b,
pp. 345–346).

2. The diagram can be used to show that Result 9.2 is only a sufficient condition for a gainful
trade. Suppose that point Q^f is sufficiently close to (but on the left hand side of) Q^a and that
the world price ratio is not too steep, then it is possible that the world price is tangent to an
indifference curve above the autarkic indifference curve, leading to an improvement in welfare.

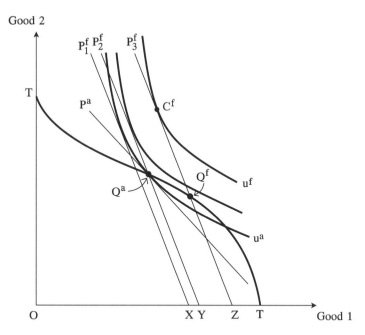

Figure 9.1

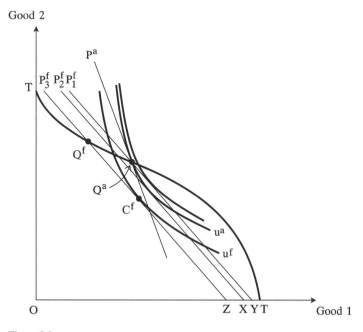

Figure 9.2

Using the definition of the rate of VRS, $\Delta h_i = (\varepsilon_i h_i^a / Q_i^a)\Delta Q_i = \varepsilon_i \Delta Q_i / \tilde{Q}_i^a$. Thus condition (9.4) reduces to

$$\sum_i p_i \varepsilon_i \Delta Q_i \geq 0. \tag{9.4'}$$

Condition (9.4′) provides another way to prove Result 9.2. If it is satisfied, then trade is not harmful.

The intuition behind (9.4′) can be provided as follows. In Chapter 5, I proved that

$$\sum_i p_i (1 - \varepsilon_i)\Delta Q_i = 0. \tag{9.5}$$

Rearranging the terms, condition (9.5) gives

$$\sum_i p_i \varepsilon_i \Delta Q_i = \sum_i p_i \Delta Q_i. \tag{9.5'}$$

The term on the right-hand side of (9.5′) is the production gain, which is non-negative if and only if condition (9.4′) is satisfied.

Another application of condition (9.4′) can be provided by choosing an arbitrary sector, for example, sector n, as a reference. By rearranging terms, the terms on the left-hand side of the condition can be written as

$$\sum_{i=1}^{n} p_i \varepsilon_i \Delta Q_i = \sum_{i=1}^{n-1}(\varepsilon_i - \varepsilon_n)p_i \Delta Q_i + \varepsilon_n \sum_{i=1}^{n} p_i \Delta Q_i$$

$$= \sum_{i=1}^{n-1} \frac{\varepsilon_i - \varepsilon_n}{1 - \varepsilon_n} p_i \Delta Q_i, \tag{9.6}$$

where the last equality in (9.6) is due to (9.5′). An important result can be obtained from (9.4′) and (9.6):

Result 9.3 If with reference to sector n all sectors with stronger IRS or weaker DRS do not contract and all sectors with weaker IRS or stronger DRS do not expand, then free trade is nonharmful (Eaton and Panagariya, 1979).

Results 9.1′ to 9.3 are more general than the way in which they are stated. First, they do not depend on whether outputs respond normally or perversely to prices, nor do they depend on whether the PPF is convex (Markusen and Melvin, 1984). Second, because the conditions in results 9.1′ to 9.3 are sufficient for a non-negative production gain, they are also sufficient conditions for a nonharmful free trade, a nonharmful improvement in the terms of trade for a small open economy, a nonharmful international factor movement under free trade, and a nonharmful expansion of an existing customs union. More-

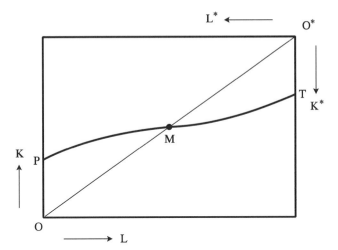

Figure 9.3

over, as Chapter 8 shows, even if a social utility function does not exist, these results are also applicable for a small open economy if costless compensation (using lump-sum transfers or consumption taxes) is allowed. Caution should be given, however, when applying these results to a large open economy because compensation may disturb the equilibrium prices and these conditions may no longer be satisfied after the compensation has been made.

More results can be obtained in some special cases. For example, consider the two-country framework described in Chapter 5 in which capital-intensive sector 1 is subject to IRS and labor-intensive sector 2 is subject to CRS. The two countries have identical technologies, and identical and homothetic preferences. Different possible factor endowments in the countries can be represented by different endowment points in an Edgeworth box diagram, the dimension of which is given by the fixed labor (horizontally) and capital (vertically) endowments in the world. An Edgeworth box diagram is shown in Figure 9.3.

Point M is the midpoint of the diagonal, and schedule PMT is the pattern-of-trade schedule derived in Chapter 5. Assuming normal price-output response in both countries, schedule PMT is bounded by the diagonal and the horizontal line through point M. In general, the sign of the slope of this schedule is ambiguous, but it is positively sloped in the small region around point M. I assume the Marshallian adjustment process explained in Chapter 5, that is, sector 1 expands if the relative market price of good 1 is higher than the relative supply price. I showed that if the endowment point is above (respectively below) schedule PMT, the home country exports (respectively imports) good 1.

Because sector 2 is subject to CRS, results 9.2 and 9.3 imply that the economy gains from trade if the production of good 1 increases. Because the countries have identical and homothetic preferences, if the home country exports good 1, and if multiple equilibria are ruled out, then its free-trade production of good 1 must be greater than its autarkic production. These results together imply that the country that exports good 1 gains from trade.

The following result can be derived from this analysis:

Result 9.4   In the present framework with national economies of scale, if the home country is not labor abundant but has more capital than the foreign country, then the home country gains from free trade but the foreign country may be hurt.

Result 9.4 applies to any endowment point inside the box diagram shown in Figure 9.3 above the diagonal and a horizontal line through point M. A corollary of Result 9.4 is:

Result 9.4′   If the two countries have the same capital-labor ratio, then the bigger country gains from free trade but the smaller country may be hurt (Markusen and Melvin, 1981; Ethier, 1982a; Tawada, 1989).

Results 9.4 and 9.4′ show how one important gains-from-trade result in the neoclassical framework is affected by the presence of IRS. In the traditional framework with constant returns, small and large countries gain but usually smaller countries gain more (welfare improvement as a percent of the autarkic welfare, using either the compensating variation or equivalent variation measure) because they tend to experience greater percentage changes in prices. Results 9.4 and 9.4′ demonstrate that smaller countries may be hurt by free trade. The reason is that a smaller country tends to contract its production of the IRS good but expands its production of the CRS good. The sign of its production gain, as a result, is ambiguous. Examples in which smaller countries lose from trade are given in Ethier (1982a), Helpman (1984b), and Tawada (1989).[3]

I now turn to a case that is not covered by Results 9.4 and 9.4′: The countries have identical factor endowments (not just identical technologies, and identical and homothetic preferences). Because the countries are identical, no-trade is an obvious equilibrium, but this equilibrium may not be (Marshallian) stable. If it is not stable, then trade exists and at least one of the countries may finally be completely specialized. The patterns of trade are not determinate.

---

3. Assuming only one factor in the model, Tawada (1989, p. 40) shows that the smaller country loses from free trade if only that country is diversified, and gains if only the large country is diversified.

By Result 9.2 or 9.3, the country that exports good 1 must gain from trade because its production of the good that is subject to IRS expands. Whether the other country also gains from trade is not certain.[4]

Chapter 5 showed that if there is one factor in the framework, then the no-trade equilibrium is necessarily not Marshallian stable and trade exists. If there are two factors, however, the no-trade point may be Marshallian stable. If the no-trade point is indeed Marshallian stable, trade would not exist (or more accurately, the no-trade point is a stable equilbrium). In this case, the countries' welfare remains at the autarkic level even if free trade is allowed.

9.1.3 International Economies of Scale

Suppose that the countries experience international economies of scale. How are the previous results affected? First, Results 9.1′ to 9.3 remain valid, so long as function $h_i(.)$ is appropriately evaluated. For example, the sufficient condition (9.3) in Result 9.1′ becomes

$$\sum_i p_i h_i(Q_i + Q_i^*)\widetilde{Q}_i^a \geq \sum_i p_i h_i(Q_i^a)\widetilde{Q}_i^a. \tag{9.3′}$$

In (9.3′), $h_i(Q_i + Q_i^*)$ is compared with $h_i(Q_i^a)$. Is it more likely that this condition is satisfied? The answer is that it depends on the economies of scale. For example, the modified Kemp-Negishi (1970) conditions become: The sufficient condition for a nonharmful trade exists when if sector i is subject to international IRS, then $Q_i + Q_i^* \geq Q_i^a$, and if sector j is subject to international DRS, then $Q_j + Q_j^* \leq Q_j^a$. This is the modified form of Result 9.2. Consequently, to see whether these types of sufficient conditions are satisfied I cannot look at the production change of just one economy. For example, if the world's total output of every good under free trade is greater than the autarkic output of the country, a case considered to be possible (or even likely), then the change in output is of the "right" sign for an IRS sector but of the "wrong" sign for a DRS sector.

To get stronger results, I turn to the two-sector model in which sector 1 is subject to IRS while sector 2 is subject to CRS. Results 9.2 to 9.3 imply that a sufficient condition for a gainful trade for an economy is that the world's free-trade output of good 1 is not less than the autarkic production of good 1 in the country.

Furthermore, as explained previously, because the economies have identical and homothetic preferences, without multiple equilibria, the economy that

---

4. See Helpman (1984b, pp. 345–346) for a numerical example in which the country that imports good 1 is hurt.

exports good 1 must produce more of good 1 than under autarky, and must then gain from trade. Whether the country that imports good 1 gains from trade is ambiguous.

I showed in Chapter 5 that in the presence of international economies of scale the Heckscher-Ohlin theorem holds whether the sectors show IRS, DRS, or CRS (see also Ethier, 1982b). This implies that the patterns-of-trade schedule coincides with the diagonal in the Edgeworth box diagram in Figure 9.3 so that an endowment point above (respectively below) it means that the home country exports (respectively import) capital-intensive good 1.

Result 9.5   In the present framework with identical technologies and international economies of scale, the country that is abundant in the factor used intensively in the IRS-sector gains from trade. The other country, however, may or may not gain.

Consider now the special case in which the countries have identical factor endowment ratio and normal price-output responses. As shown in Chapter 5, the countries do not trade. Because the economies remain closed, international economies of scale can be regarded as a Hicks-neutral technological progress in sector 1, although the extent of the technological progress depends endogenously on the outputs of good 1 in the countries. In this case, both countries gain from trade irrespective of their sizes.

More explicit conditions for a gainful trade can be derived by using the supply- and demand-price schedules derived in Chapter 5. The supply-price schedule gives the break-even price ratios, p^s, that corresponds to different output ratios, $z \equiv Q_1/Q_2$. Panels (a) and (b) of Figure 9.4 show two possible supply-price schedules. In panel (a), p^s-schedule is positively sloped, illustrating normal price effects of outputs. In panel (b), p^s-schedule is negatively sloped due to perverse price effects of outputs. The demand price, p^d, is the price ratios that lead to different consumption ratios of the goods, C_1/C_2. If preferences are homothetic, which is assumed, the demand-price schedule is negatively sloped, as shown in both panels. Autarkic equilibrium is described by the intersecting point between the schedules. Furthermore, I demonstrated in Chapter 5 that the equilibrium shown in panel (a) is both Marshallian and Walrasian stable, while that shown in panel (b) is Marshallian stable but not Walrasian stable.

When trade is permitted and when international economies of scale exist, even if no trade actually takes place, the p^s-schedule but not the p^d-schedule shifts. I now argue that the following conditions describe one possible new *production equilibrium* (superscript "a" represents an autarkic value and a prime represents the value at this equilibrium):

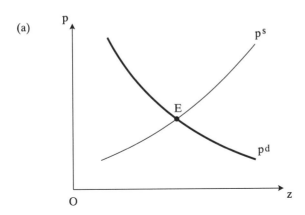

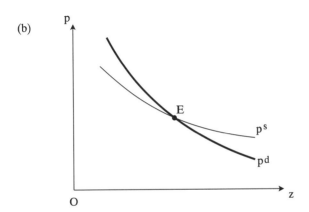

Figure 9.4

$$p'h_1(Q_1' + Q_1^{*'}) = p^a h_1(Q_1^a) \tag{9.7a}$$

$$Q_1' = h_1(Q_1' + Q_1^{*'})F_1(\mathbf{v}_1^a) \tag{9.7b}$$

$$Q_2' = Q_2^a = F_2(\mathbf{v}_2^a). \tag{9.7c}$$

Due to conditions (9.7b) and (9.7c), the economy maintains the autarkic re-source allocation. Because sector 2 is subject to CRS, its output remains un-changed. Because the foreign country generally consumes both goods under autarky, $Q_1^{*'} > 0$ and condition (9.7b) imply an increase in Q_1 even resource allocation is fixed. Condition (9.7b) implies that Q_1 and h_1 have the same percentage change. Condition (9.7a), which requires that ph_1 stays station-ary, implies that factors in sector 1 receive the autarkic factor prices. Because factors in sector 2 continue to receive the autarkic factor prices, factors have no incentive to move between sectors. Conditions (9.7a) and (9.7b) imply that firms in sector 1 receive the autarkic revenues, that is, they have the maximum (zero) profit. Thus this is a production equilibrium.

In terms of the panels of Figure 9.4, conditions (9.7a) and (9.7b) mean that any point on the p^s-schedule will shift down and to the right by the same proportion. In panel (a), the p^s-schedule shifts down, and the new intersecting point represents a lower autarkic price, a higher output of good 1 (because Q_1/Q_2 increases and because the PPF expands), and a higher national welfare. Because the two economies with identical technologies have the same supply-price schedule, in this case trade is gainful for *both economies*, irrespective of their sizes.

If the supply-price schedule is negatively sloped, the result is not so certain. When trade is permitted, the supply-price schedule may shift up or down. Loosely speaking, the analysis can be used to argue that if the supply-price schedule is flatter, it is more likely that it shifts down under trade.

In panel (b) of Figure 9.4, the autarkic equilibrium is Marshallian stable. Thus if the supply-price schedule shifts down, the equilibrium output of good 1 increases, and national welfare is higher. If the supply-price schedule shifts up instead, then p is higher while the national welfare may or may not be higher than the autarkic level.

The same analysis can be applied to analyze the case in which the autarkic equilibrium is Walrasian stable with a negatively sloped supply-price schedule. If the schedule shifts up and to the right, then trade is gainful. The preceding analysis can be summarized as follows:

Result 9.6   In the present framework when the two countries have identical factor endowment ratios, both countries gain from trade liberalization if the supply-price schedule is positively sloped (normal price-output responses), although no trade exists. If the supply-price schedule is negatively sloped (perverse price-output responses), then trade liberalization is gainful if the supply-price schedule shifts down after trade.

To illustrate some of the ideas explained above, let me provide an example. Similar examples appear in Ethier (1979) and Helpman (1984b).

Example 9.1   There is only one factor, labor. Let $Q_1 = Q_1^{0.5}L_1$, $Q_2 = L_2$, and $L = 8$. The production function of sector 1 reduces to $Q_1 = L_1^2$. The utility function is of the CES-type, with equal weight given to the consumption of each good. The supply price and demand price schedules are given by the following equations:

$$z = \left[L(p^s)^2 - p^s\right]^{-1} \tag{9.8a}$$

$$z = (p^d)^{-3}. \tag{9.8b}$$

Differentiating the expressions in conditions (9.8) and rearranging terms, the
slopes of the schedules are

$$\frac{dp^s}{dz} = -\frac{(L(p^s)^2 - (p^s))^2}{2Lp^s - 1} < 0 \tag{9.9a}$$

$$\frac{dp^d}{dz} = -\frac{p^4}{3} < 0. \tag{9.9b}$$

Both schedules are negatively sloped. Solving the two equations in (9.8), two
equilibria are developed: $(p, z, Q_1) = (0.127, 488.0, 61.98)$ and $(7.87, 0.002, 0.016)$. Call the first equilibrium A and the second one B. Conditions (9.9a)
and (9.9b) can be used to show that point A is Marshallian stable, but point B
is not.[5]

Suppose that the previous economy is permitted to trade with another, identical economy. The world equilibrium can be derived by doubling the labor
force in the economy, $L = 16$. Solving the two equations in (9.8) again, I
get two equilibria: $(p, z, Q_1) = (0.063, 4048.0, 254.0)$ and $(15.937, 0.0002, 0.004)$. Call these two new equilibria A' and B', respectively. Because the
countries are identical, if they have the same equilibrium, p and z at points
A' and B' are common in both countries, and Q_1 is the world's total output of
good 1.

The equilibria in the above example can be illustrated in Figure 9.5. Because
the supply function of good 1 is given by $Q_1 = p^{-2}$, the supply is globally
elastic. The analysis implies that trade shifts the supply-price schedule down
(to $p^{s'}$).

With respect to equilibrium A, trade leads to an increase in output of good
1 because of an increase in z and an expansion of the PPF, and a decrease in
p. The analysis implies that both countries gain. If the autarkic equilibrium
is B and it shifts to B', then there is an increase in p and a decrease in z in
both countries. Because the wage rate is unity (from the production function
of sector 2), the national income of each country is constant in terms of good
2, and an increase in p implies a decrease in welfare. Thus Helpman (1984b,
p. 341) concludes that if the autarkic equilibrium of both countries is B then it
shifts to B' and both countries lose under free trade.

Helpman's presumption that point B shifts to point B' and thus both countries lose under trade, however, is not correct if the economies adjust in a
Marshallian fashion. The reason is that point A is Marshallian stable, but point

---

5. At point A, $dp^d/dz = -0.000087$ and $dp^s/dz = -4 \times 10^{-6}$, implying that the p^d-schedule is
steeper than the p^s-schedule: This equilibrium is Marshallian stable. At point B, $dp^d/dz = -1281$
and $dp^s/dz = -1906$, meaning that the p^s-schedule is steeper than the p^d-schedule and that this
point is not Marshallian stable.

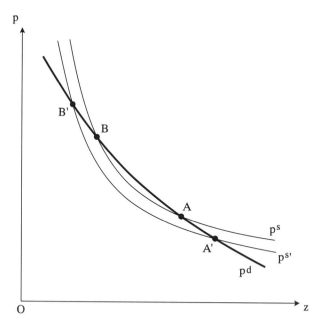

Figure 9.5

B is not. Suppose that point B is the common autarkic equilibrium point of the countries. When free trade is allowed so that the supply schedule shifts to $p^{s'}$, the autarkic price ratio is greater than the supply price, meaning that under the Marshallian adjustment rules firms in sector 1 of both countries will expand, thus increasing z. The equilibrium point in Figure 9.5 shifts down and to the left, until point A' is reached. In other words, the economies will not shift to point B'. The fall in the price ratio as represented by this free-trade equilibrium point means an increase in welfare of both countries.

9.2   Monopolistic Competition with Differentiated Products

I now analyze gains from trade for economies with monopolistic competition and differentiated products by using the framework discussed in Chapter 6. In such a framework, commodities are symmetric both on the consumption and on the production sides. In the love of variety approach, all individuals within an economy have identical preferences, but in the ideal variety approach, all individuals have different ideal varieties although the functional form of their utility functions are the same.

As I did before, I distinguish the autarkic values of variables by a superscript "a" but use no such superscript for their free-trade values. Consider the following two conditions: (1) $pnq_1 + Q_2 \geq pn^a q_1^a + Q_2^a$; and (2) $N \geq n^a$. In (1), n is the number of varieties produced in the home country under free trade and q_1 is the scale of production of a firm in the differentiated-product sector. The left-hand side of condition (1) represents the total value of outputs under free trade (evaluated at free-trade prices) while the right-hand side is the value of autarkic outputs evaluated using free-trade prices. So condition (1) states that the production gain is non-negative. In the present framework with differentiated products and monopolistic competition, this condition is not guaranteed. In (2), $N = n + n^*$ is the total number of varieties in the world under free trade. Condition (2) states that there is an increase in the number of varieties faced by the home consumers.

I will show below that these two conditions are jointly sufficient for a gainful trade. Furthermore, if the production function of sector 1 is homothetic and identical across countries, then condition (2) implies condition (1) so that (2) is sufficient for a gainful trade. For such economies, more sufficient conditions for a gainful trade can be derived.

9.2.1   Love of Variety Approach

Under this approach, individuals within and across countries have identical preferences. The utility of a representative individual is thus a good index of the welfare of a society. Let the utility function of a representative consumer be $u(D_1, D_2)$ where D_1 is a subutility with respect to the differentiated products. Assume that this subutility function is of the CES type, that is,

$$D_1 = G[d_1(\omega), \omega \in \Omega] = \left[\sum_\omega [d_1(\omega)]^\beta \right]^{1/\beta}, \quad \beta = \left(1 - \frac{1}{\sigma}\right), \quad \sigma > 1,$$

where $d_1(\omega)$ is the consumption of variety ω, and σ is the elasticity of substitution. By assumption $\sigma > 1$, implying that $\beta > 0$. With symmetry, a representative consumer selects equal amounts of all available varieties, $d_1(\omega) = d_1$ for all available ω. The subutility function reduces to $D_1 = N^{1/\beta} d_1$. Using the utility function, the consumer's indirect utility function can be written as $V^\ell(\overline{p}, I)$ where $\overline{p} = pN^{-1/(\sigma-1)}$ is the effective price of a variety, p is the market price of a variety, and I is the consumer's income (see Chapter 6). The budget constraint of the consumer is

$$I \geq pNd_1 + D_2 = \overline{p}D_1 + D_2. \tag{9.10}$$

I now prove that conditions (1) and (2) are sufficient for a gainful trade (Helpman and Krugman, 1985). Because all consumers are identical, they share the national income equally. This means that the income of a representative consumer under free trade is equal to

$$I = \frac{pnq_1 + Q_2}{m}$$

where m is the number of consumers. Thus condition (1) implies that

$$I \geq pn^a \frac{q_1^a}{m} + \frac{Q_2^a}{m}. \tag{9.11}$$

Under autarky, the consumers share the outputs of the two sectors equally, meaning that $q_1^a = md_1^a$ and $Q_2^a = mD_2^a$. Using these autarkic conditions and condition (2), (9.11) reduces to

$$I \geq pn^a d_1^a + D_2^a$$

$$= p(n^a)^{-1/(\sigma-1)} D_1^a + D_2^a$$

$$\geq pN^{-1/(\sigma-1)} D_1^a + D_2^a \qquad \text{[condition (2)]}$$

$$= \overline{p} D_1^a + D_2^a.$$

This shows that under free trade the autarkic consumption bundle is affordable and the consumer is not hurt by free trade. In fact, as long as there is a change in commodity prices or N, the consumer's welfare must be improved by free trade because a CES subutility function implies positive consumption gain.

If conditions (1) and (2) are not satisfied, whether trade is gainful can be determined by comparing the autarkic utility $V^\ell(\overline{p}^a, I^a)$ with the free-trade utility $V^\ell(\overline{p}, I)$.

9.2.2   Ideal Variety Approach

The difficulty of this appproach in showing the change in national welfare is that all individuals in an economy have different preferences or ideal varieties. In equilibrium the individuals do not have the same utility level. Therefore I have to find an appropriate index to represent the welfare level of the economy.

In the framework considered in Chapter 6, all consumers have identical utility functions except for their ideal varieties, and they have identical incomes. With a Cobb-Douglas upper tier utility function, they spend the same proportion of their income on a differentiated product. Facing the same price of the varieties, they consume the same amount of a variety even though in general they may choose different varieties. This allows me to choose an appropriate compensation function that will yield an "average" welfare of the consumers. Let $\widetilde{\sigma}$ be the "average" distance for all consumers between their ideal variety and the actual variety they choose. With symmetry in the economy, $\widetilde{\sigma} = 1/(4n)$. This provides a direct link between the number of varieties and the "average" distance. The compensation function that gives the average utility is equal to $h(\widetilde{\sigma})$. Thus if d_1 is the amount of a variety each consumer demands, the subutility level using the "average" distance is equal to $D_1 = d_1/h(\tilde{\sigma})$, with the corresponding effective price being $\tilde{p} = ph(\tilde{\sigma})$. I now define the index for the welfare of the economy as the maximum utility $u(D_1, D_2)$ by choosing D_1 and D_2 subject to the budget constraint

$$I \geq \tilde{p}D_1 + D_2 = pd_1 + D_2,$$

where I is the income of a representative consumer.[6] Denote the maximum utility by the indirect utility function $V^i(\tilde{p}, I)$. I state that trade is gainful if and only if $V^i(\tilde{p}, I) > V^i(\tilde{p}^a, I^a)$.

I now show that if conditions (1) and (2) are satisfied, trade is gainful. Divide the national income level on the left-hand side of condition (1) by the number of consumers to give the income of the representative consumer $I = (pnq_1 + Q_2)/m$. Condition (1) implies that

$$I \geq p\frac{n^a q_1^a}{m} + \frac{Q_2^a}{m}. \tag{9.12}$$

Under autarky, $n^a q_1^a = m d_1^a$ and $Q_2^a = m D_2^a$. Thus (9.12) reduces to

$$I \geq pd_1^a + D_2^a = ph(\tilde{\sigma}^a)D_1^a + D_2^a. \tag{9.12'}$$

Recall that $\tilde{\sigma} = 1/(4n)$. Thus condition (2) implies that $\tilde{\sigma}^a \geq \tilde{\sigma}$ and that $h(\tilde{\sigma}^a) \geq h(\tilde{\sigma})$. Using this result, (9.12') reduces to

$$I \geq ph(\tilde{\sigma}^a)D_1^a + D_2^a \geq ph(\tilde{\sigma})D_1^a + D_2^a = \tilde{p}D_1^a + D_2^a, \tag{9.12''}$$

which states that the autarkic consumption bundle is affordable. Thus trade does not hurt the representative consumer. If under trade commodity prices do change, the consumer must gain because the consumption gain is positive.

9.2.3 Homothetic Technologies

The sufficiency of conditions (1) and (2) for a gainful trade does not depend on homotheticity of the production function of sector 1. If homotheticity of technologies is assumed and if the countries have identical technologies, then more sufficient conditions for a gainful trade can be derived.

The first result I now derive is that in the type of economies discussed in Chapter 6 condition (2) implies condition (1). I explained in that chapter that the virtual system in terms of p_z and Z behaves like the neoclassical framework. Thus the production gain in terms of this system must be non-negative, that is,

---

6. The present index for the welfare of the economy is different from the one in Helpman and Krugman (1985, p. 184), but both of them give the same qualitative result.

$$p_z Z + Q_2 \geq p_z Z^a + Q_2^a. \tag{9.13}$$

Using the definitions of $p_z \equiv pq_1/\gamma(q_1)$ and $Z \equiv \gamma(q_1)n$, the left-hand side of (9.13) is the national income level of the economy under free trade. Rearranging terms, (9.13) reduces to

$$pnq_1 + Q_2 \geq \frac{pq_1}{\gamma(q_1)}\gamma(q_1^a)n^a + Q_2^a$$

$$= p\frac{q_1}{\gamma(q_1)}\frac{\gamma(q_1^a)}{q_1^a}n^a q_1^a + Q_2^a. \tag{9.13$'$}$$

Suppose now that condition (2) is satisfied. As mentioned in Chapter 6, under certain conditions (the love of variety approach or for the ideal variety approach with a marginal cost curve in sector 1 not falling too rapidly) if there is an increase in the number of varieties in the world under trade, the plant size of a representative firm does not fall. In fact, under the love of variety approach with CES-type preferences, the plant size of each firm remains constant. Thus $N \geq n^a$ implies that $q_1 \geq q_1^a$. This further implies that, because of declining average cost, $q_1/\gamma(q_1) \geq q_1^a/\gamma(q_1^a)$. Using this result, (9.13$'$) reduces to

$$pnq_1 + Q_2 \geq pn^a q_1^a + Q_2^a, \tag{9.13$''$}$$

which is condition (1). Thus in the present framework, an increase in the number of varieties faced by consumers (condition 2) is sufficient for a gainful trade.

I now search for conditions under which the number of varieties faced by a country increases. The first case is a small economy trading with a large economy. Because the number of varieties produced in the large economy will not be too much affected by its trading with the small economy, the latter must experience an increase in the number of varieties and thus gains from trade.

Two more conditions for a gainful trade can be derived. As shown in Chapter 6, the number of varieties increases if and only if the virtual output of sector 1, Z, increases. Furthermore, if a closed economy has an accumulation of the factor that is used intensively in the differentiated-product sector, Z increases. Combining these results and condition (2), I conclude that the economy that is scarce in the factor used intensively in the differentiated product sector gains from trade. If this economy happens to be the large economy as described in the first case, then this is an example in which free trade benefits both economies. I also showed in Chapter 6 that if a closed economy experiences an equiproportionate expansion of both factors, then the number of varieties increases. Thus if the countries have identical capital-labor ratio, then both of them gain from trade.

9.3   Oligopoly with Identical Products

This section examines the possibility of gains from trade for economies with oligopoly in two frameworks that are described in detail in Chapter 7: a partial equilibrium framework and a general equilibrium framework.

9.3.1   A Partial Equilibrium Framework

First consider the two-firm, two-country, one-product model discussed in Chapter 7. In this model, markets are segmented, and I explained that if the demands for the good in both countries are strong enough, intraindustry trade in the good exists.

I begin the welfare analysis with the home country while the same analysis can be applied to the foreign country. In the present partial equilibrium framework, I represent national welfare by the sum of consumer surplus, CS, and the profit of the domestic firm, π.[7] Denoting the inverse demand by $p(q)$ where q is the quantity demanded, consumer surplus is equal to

$$CS = \int_0^q p(v)\mathrm{d}v - pq. \tag{9.14}$$

I decompose the profit of the home firm, π, into three components: profit from the home market, π^h, profit from the foreign market, π^f, and negative fixed cost, $-f$, that is, $\pi = \pi^h + \pi^f - f$. This means that in calculating π^h and π^f, the fixed cost has been excluded. The first two components of the profit are equal to

$$\pi^h = [p(q) - c]x \tag{9.15a}$$

$$\pi^f = [p^*(q^*) - c - \tau]X, \tag{9.15b}$$

where c is the constant marginal cost, τ is the per unit transport cost, q is domestic demand, q^* is foreign demand, $p^*(q^*)$ is the foreign inverse demand, and x and X are the home firm's sale in the home and foreign markets, respectively. The home welfare is equal to

$$W = CS + \pi = CS + \pi^h + \pi^f - f. \tag{9.16}$$

---

7. To justify the use of consumer surplus and producer surplus to represent national welfare, it is usually assumed that the marginal utility of income of a representative consumer is constant and that income distribution is neglected. Another approach is to assume that consumers' welfare is measured by a separable utility function such as $u(q) + u_0$ where q is the consumption of the good under consideration, and u_0 is a variable representing the utility from the consumption of other goods. The marginal utility of income derived from this function is constant, and the inverse demand function is given by $u'(q) = p$ where the prime stands for a derivative. Note further that if a tariff is imposed on the imported good, as is considered in Chapter 11, the tariff revenue should be included in the definition of national welfare given by condition (9.16).

Furthermore, define x^* and X^* as the foreign firm's supplies to the home and foreign markets, respectively. Also define $\bar{\tau}$ (respectively $\bar{\tau}^*$) as the critical value of τ for the home (respectively foreign) firm above which the firm's export is zero. As I did, I now assume that $\bar{\tau} < \bar{\tau}^*$ unless the countries are identical. In the latter case, $\bar{\tau} = \bar{\tau}^*$. If $\tau > \bar{\tau}$, then $X = 0$ and $\pi^f = 0$. If $\tau > \bar{\tau}^*$, then $X = x^* = 0$ and $q = x$, meaning that no trade in this good between the countries exists.

Zero Transport Cost

I first look at the case in which there is no transport cost. I want to determine whether trade benefits the countries and the world. The world welfare is here defined as the sum of the welfare levels of the two countries. There is a well-known result in the theory of industrial organization that two firms competing in a Cournot way is more efficient (from the economy or world's point of view) than if only one of them produces and supplies as a monopoly. Making use of this result, I can say that the world as a whole gains when free trade is allowed because each market is now supplied by two firms instead of one firm. I can further conclude that if international compensation is possible or if the countries are identical, intraindustry trade must benefit both countries.

If international compensation is not made or if the countries are different, however, free trade may hurt one of the countries. To show this possibility, consider the following example.

Example 9.2   The home inverse demand function is given by $p = a - bq$ and the foreign inverse demand function given by $p^* = a^* - b^*q^*$. It is easy to show that under autarky the output of the home firm is $x^a = (a - c)/(2b)$, where the superscript "a" represents the autarkic value. The consumer surplus and the home profits are equal to $CS^a = (a - c)^2/(8b)$, $\pi^{ha} = (a - c)^2/(4b)$ and $\pi^a_f = 0$. The home country's national welfare is equal to $W^a = 3(a - c)^2/(8b) - f$.

Suppose now that free trade is allowed with no transport cost. Solving the first-order conditions of the firms (see Chapter 7), the productions of the firms are (superscript "f" representing the free-trade values)

$$x^f = \frac{a - 2c + c^*}{3b}$$

$$x^{f*} = \frac{a + c - 2c^*}{3b}$$

$$X^f = \frac{a^* + c^* - 2c}{3b^*}$$

$$X^{f*} = \frac{a^* - 2c^* + c}{3b^*}.$$

Using the values of these outputs, the home country's welfare under trade can be determined.

$$W^f = \frac{(2a - c - c^*)^2}{18b} + \frac{(a - 2c + c^*)^2}{9b} + \frac{(a^* - 2c + c^*)^2}{9b^*} - f.$$

The change in the welfare of the home country is equal to

$$\Delta W = W^f - W^a = -\frac{(a - c)^2}{24b} + \frac{(c - c^*)^2}{6b} + \frac{(a^* - 2c + c^*)^2}{9b^*}.$$

In general, the sign of ΔW is ambiguous. If the firms have similar marginal costs, that is, $c - c^*$ is sufficiently small, then ΔW reduces to

$$\Delta W \approx -\frac{(a - c)^2}{24b} + \frac{(a^* - c)^2}{9b^*}.$$

If a^* is sufficiently smaller than a and b^* sufficiently larger than b, then ΔW is negative, meaning that free trade hurts the home country. The intuition behind this result is that under these conditions the rent that the home firm gets from selling its output to the foreign market is small but the home firm is sufficiently hurt by the competition from the foreign firm as free trade is allowed by both governments.

Conversely, if a^* is sufficiently larger than a and b^* sufficiently smaller than b, then the home country gains from free trade. Because the autarkic welfare of the home country is $3(a - c)^2/(8b) - f$, $(a - c)^2/b$ is a measure of the size of the country. The results can be used to argue that a small country must gain from trade while a large one may be hurt (see the previous section for another result concerning the gains from trade for a small and a large countries.)

Positive Transport Cost

Now allow the existence of a positive transport cost. Let me begin by analyzing the effects of a change in τ on the home welfare. Assuming that the home country has a positive import of the good from the foreign firm, differentiate CS given by (9.14) with respect to τ to give

$$\frac{dCS}{d\tau} = p\frac{dq}{d\tau} - p\frac{dq}{d\tau} - qp'\frac{dq}{d\tau} = -qp'\frac{dq}{d\tau}. \tag{9.17}$$

In Chapter 7 I showed that when $x^* > 0$, an increase in τ lowers the total supply. Thus $dCS/d\tau < 0$. If τ is so high that $x^* = 0$, then CS is not affected by τ, that is, $dCS/d\tau = 0$.

The effect of transport cost on π^h is obtained by differentiating condition (9.15a):

$$\frac{\mathrm{d}\pi^h}{\mathrm{d}\tau} = xp'\frac{\mathrm{d}q}{\mathrm{d}\tau} + (p-c)\frac{\mathrm{d}x}{\mathrm{d}\tau}. \tag{9.18}$$

In Chapter 7 I showed that if $x^* > 0$, then $\mathrm{d}x/\mathrm{d}\tau > 0$ and $\mathrm{d}q/\mathrm{d}\tau < 0$. Condition (9.18) implies that $\mathrm{d}\pi^h/\mathrm{d}\tau > 0$. If $x^* = 0$ when τ is too high, then π^h is independent of τ.

Following the same procedure as previously discussed, differentiate (9.15b) to give

$$\frac{\mathrm{d}\pi^f}{\mathrm{d}\tau} = X\left(p^{*\prime}\frac{\mathrm{d}q^*}{\mathrm{d}\tau} - 1\right) + \left[p^* - c - \tau\right]\frac{\mathrm{d}X}{\mathrm{d}\tau}. \tag{9.19}$$

If $\tau < \bar{\tau}$ so that $X > 0$, I can use the results in Chapter 7 to get $\mathrm{d}X/\mathrm{d}\tau < 0$ and

$$p^{*\prime}\frac{\mathrm{d}q^*}{\mathrm{d}\tau} = \frac{(p^{*\prime})^2}{\Delta^*}, \tag{9.20}$$

where $\Delta^* = p^{*\prime}(p^{*\prime} + \Phi + \Phi^*)$, $\Phi = Xp^{*\prime} + p^{*\prime\prime}$ and $\Phi^* = X^*p^{*\prime} + p^{*\prime\prime}$. Assuming Hahn's stability conditions, $\Phi < 0$ and $\Phi^* < 0$. Thus $\Delta^* > 0$ and $p^{*\prime}\mathrm{d}q^*/\mathrm{d}\tau > 0$. Condition (9.20) implies that

$$\left(p^{*\prime}\frac{\mathrm{d}q^*}{\mathrm{d}\tau} - 1\right) = -\frac{p^{*\prime}(\Phi + \Phi^*)}{\Delta^*} < 0. \tag{9.20'}$$

By condition (9.20'), condition (9.19) implies that if $X > 0$ then $\mathrm{d}\pi^f/\mathrm{d}\tau < 0$. If, however, $\tau \geq \bar{\tau}$ so that $X = 0$, then $\mathrm{d}\pi^f/\mathrm{d}\tau = 0$.

Using these results, the effect of the transport cost on the home welfare is given by:

$$\frac{\mathrm{d}W}{\mathrm{d}\tau} = \frac{\mathrm{d}CS}{\mathrm{d}\tau} + \frac{\mathrm{d}\pi^h}{\mathrm{d}\tau} + \frac{\mathrm{d}\pi^f}{\mathrm{d}\tau}$$

$$= -x^*p'\frac{\mathrm{d}q}{\mathrm{d}\tau} + (p-c)\frac{\mathrm{d}x}{\mathrm{d}\tau} + X\left[p^{*\prime}\frac{\mathrm{d}q^*}{\mathrm{d}\tau} - 1\right] + \left[p^* - c - \tau\right]\frac{\mathrm{d}X}{\mathrm{d}\tau}. \tag{9.21}$$

In general, the sign of $\mathrm{d}W/\mathrm{d}\tau$ is ambiguous. Let me focus on two special cases. First, suppose that τ is greater than $\bar{\tau}$ but it is equal to or slightly less than $\bar{\tau}^*$. This means that $X = 0$ and $x^* \approx 0$. The expression in (9.21) is approximately equal to

$$\frac{\mathrm{d}W}{\mathrm{d}\tau} \approx (p-c)\frac{\mathrm{d}x}{\mathrm{d}\tau} > 0. \tag{9.22}$$

Condition (9.22) implies that when the transport cost is close to prohibitive with $X = 0$ and $x^* \approx 0$, a small increase in the transport cost benefits the home country. The reason is that an increase in transport cost will discourage foreign firm's export to the home country but encourage home firm's supply to the local market. This result implies that if the transport cost τ is initially equal to or greater than $\bar{\tau}^*$, then no trade exists. If τ is slightly lower, the foreign firm starts exporting to the home market and the home country is hurt. This result is an important one for us. Suppose that the transport cost is slightly less than prohibitive for the foreign firm. Trade is initially prohibited by either government. Suppose that trade is then allowed. This is like a small decrease in τ from $\bar{\tau}^*$, and the result implies that free trade hurts the home country. A corollary of this result is derived in Brander and Krugman (1983). They show that *if the countries are identical*, then the *world's* welfare (and also the welfare of each country) increases with the transport cost when the latter is close to prohibitive. Note that when the countries are identical, $\bar{\tau} = \bar{\tau}^*$, and condition (9.22) is applicable for both countries.

Now consider the second special case. Suppose that the two countries are identical and τ is sufficiently small. Then

$$-x^* p' \frac{dq}{d\tau} + X p^{*\prime} \frac{dq^*}{d\tau} = 0$$

and

$$(p-c)\frac{dx}{d\tau} + (p^* - c)\frac{dX}{d\tau} = (p-c)\frac{d(x+X)}{d\tau} = (p-c)\frac{d(x+x^*)}{d\tau} < 0,$$

where I showed in Chapter 7 that $d(x+x^*)/d\tau < 0$. Using these results, I have $dW/d\tau < 0$.

By combining these results I can illustrate the dependence of the home welfare on transport cost by the schedule labeled W in Figure 9.6.[8] Note that W^a is the home autarkic welfare level, and W_0^f is the country's welfare under free trade with no transport cost. As explained earlier, W^a may be greater than W_0^f because the country may be hurt by free trade.

I now turn to foreign welfare. For this case there is an expression similar to that in (9.21):

$$\frac{dW^*}{d\tau} = -X p^{*\prime} \frac{dq}{d\tau} + (p^* - c^*)\frac{dX^*}{d\tau} + x^* \left[p' \frac{dq}{d\tau} - 1 \right]$$

$$+ \left[p - c^* - \tau \right] \frac{dx^*}{d\tau}. \tag{9.23}$$

If $0 \le \tau < \bar{\tau}$ so that intraindustry trade exists, the previous analysis applies to the W^*. If the countries are different and if $\bar{\tau} \le \tau < \bar{\tau}^*$, the foreign firm exports but the home firm does not. Therefore the foreign market is not affected by a small change in transport cost. The foreign firm, however, gains from a

---

8. If the countries are not identical, the schedule for W may not be negatively sloped when τ is small.

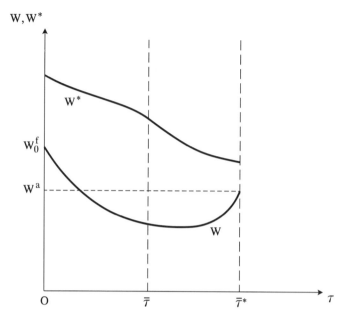

Figure 9.6

reduction in τ because it penetrates deeper into the home market. Thus I can conclude that the foreign welfare is negatively related to τ. Using these results, I can show the change in W^* with respect to τ in Figure 9.6. Note that W^* is negatively related to τ when the latter is slightly less than either critical value, $\bar{\tau}$ or $\bar{\tau}^*$. These results suggest that if the countries are not identical, the world's welfare may not fall with a decrease in τ when τ is slightly smaller than the critical value.[9]

9.3.2 A General Equilibrium Framework

I now turn to the general equilibrium, integrated-market model with a home and a foreign oligopolistic firms analyzed in Chapter 7. In this model, good 1 is produced by a firm in each of the countries and good 2 is produced by competitive firms. I first analyze the home country. In Figure 9.7, TT represents the PPF of the home economy. Under autarky, the firm in sector 1 is a monopolist. A possible autarkic equilibrium is represented by point A in the diagram. Because no firm is assumed to have any monopsony power in factor markets, the production point is on the PPF. I explained that at point A the price line is tangent to the indifference curve labeled u^a but is steeper than the PPF. When good 2 is chosen as the numeraire, the marginal revenue of sector 1 is equal to

---

9. Hwang (1984), using a conjectural variation approach, shows that if the firms are identical and if they collude to a certain degree, then free trade is Pareto inferior to autarky.

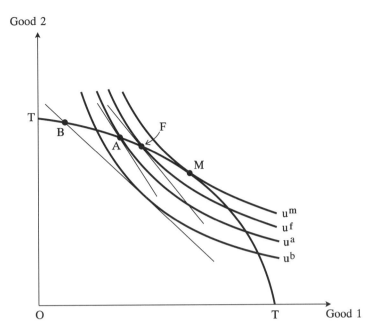

Figure 9.7

the MRT, which is the magnitude of the slope of the PPF. It is well known that the inefficiency of the monopolistic home firm implies an underproduction of good 1. The optimal point is at M at which the indifference curve u^m is tangent to the PPF.

In the Markusen (1981) case in which the home and foreign countries are identical, allowing free trade benefits both countries. This case is shown in Figure 9.7. With the possibility of trade and the threat of import competition, home and foreign firms in sector 1 produce more, even though no trade takes place. The equilibrium is at point F, which represents a higher output level of good 1. Point F, as compared with point A, has a smaller price ratio but a greater marginal revenue, and yields a higher utility level, u^f, than the autarkic utility level. The benefit of this procompetitive effect of free trade to both countries is obvious from the diagram.

In other cases, however, free trade does not necessarily benefit a country. Suppose instead that the countries are not identical and the production point for the home country under free trade is point B in Figure 9.7, with the line passing through it representing the free-trade price line. This line is tangent to an indifference curve with a lower utility level, showing that free trade has hurt this economy.

Because point B corresponds to a lower output of good 1, it may be conjectured that a necessary condition for a deterioration of welfare under trade is a decrease in the output of good 1. Equivalently, a sufficient condition for an increase in welfare is an increase in the output of good 1. This conjecture, in fact, is true and can be proved formally as follows. (This result is due to Helpman and Krugman, 1985.)

Because preferences are convex, the consumption gain as defined in the previous chapter is non-negative. The present proof thus concentrates on finding conditions under which production gain is non-negative. Denote the output of good i by Q_i, $i = 1, 2$. Let the autarky value of a variable be denoted by a superscript "a" while its value under trade has no superscript. Because the marginal revenue of sector 1, MR_1, is numerically equal to the MRT, convexity of the production possibility set implies that

$$MR_1(Q_1 - Q_1^a) + (Q_2 - Q_2^a) \geq 0. \tag{9.24}$$

Because of a downward sloping demand curve in sector 1, $p > MR_1$. Thus if $Q_1 - Q_1^a > 0$, then

$$p(Q_1 - Q_1^a) + (Q_2 - Q_2^a) > MR_1(Q_1 - Q_1^a) + (Q_2 - Q_2^a). \tag{9.25}$$

Note that the left-hand side of (9.25) is the production gain. Combining conditions (9.24) and (9.25) together, I have

$$p(Q_1 - Q_1^a) + (Q_2 - Q_2^a) \geq 0,$$

meaning that production gain is non-negative and that trade is nonharmful.

Several more results in the present framework can be derived easily.

1. Consider a closed economy in which good 1 is produced by a monopolist while sector 2 is competitive. Preferences of individuals are identical and homothetic of the CES type. Suppose that the economy is replicated n times with n identical oligopolistic firms in sector 1. The above analysis can be used to show that the per capita utility is an increasing function of n. In the limiting case in which n approaches infinity, sector 1 becomes perfectly competitive and per capita utility reaches a maximum.

2. Consider two countries, home and foreign. The home country has n identical firms producing good 1 when sector 2 is competitive. The foreign country is an m/n-replication of the home country, meaning that there are m firms in sector 1. If free trade is allowed between the countries, their markets are integrated and the world is an $(m + n)/n$-replication of the home country or an $(m + n)/m$-replication of the foreign country. Result (1) implies that both countries gain from trade (Kemp and Okawa, 1995b).

3. Under free trade, both the home and foreign countries as described in (2) have the same per capita utility. Result (1) implies that the smaller country gains more from trade than the bigger country does.

9.4   Pareto-Inferior Trade When Markets Are Incomplete

I now turn to another type of distortion: market incompleteness. This distortion arises when uncertainty is present and when individuals lack sufficient instruments to reach an ex ante optimal allocation of resources.

With uncertainty and incomplete markets, examples have been constructed to show that free trade may harm a country (Turnovsky, 1974; Batra and Russell, 1974; and Pomery, 1984). Because market incompleteness is a type of distortion, these examples are not too surprising. What is striking is that, as shown by Newbery and Stiglitz (1984) and Shy (1988), free trade may be Pareto inferior to autarky. To fully appreciate the examples by Newbery, Stiglitz, and Shy, note that in the models considered in Chapter 8 and in this chapter, when individuals are heterogeneous in terms of preferences and factor endowments, free trade usually is beneficial to some and harmful to some. Furthermore, Helpman and Razin (1978, p. 137), basing themselves on Hart's (1975) finding that the opening of additional securities markets in a closed economy can harm every individual, have argued that free trade in commodities only might be preferred by all countries to free trade in both goods and securities. These examples apparently turn the gains-from-trade theorem upside down, and have led Grinols (1987, p. 58) to conclude that "neither the free trade equilibrium nor the autarkic equilibrium need be a Pareto optimum. Either could Pareto dominate the other."

The work of Kemp and Wong (1995b, 1995c) shows, however, that the pessimism caused by these examples about the gainfulness of trade is unfounded. They point out that in all of these examples, the government of the country that is hurt by free trade has not adequately compensated losers. If costless compensation can be made, Kemp and Wong argue, then there always exists a feasible lump-sum compensation scheme that makes every individual not worse off, with some individuals better off if consumption gain or production gain is positive.

In this section, I briefly explain the meaning of incomplete markets, and then provide a simple example to show that uncompensated free trade is Pareto inferior to autarky. In the next section, I will show the compensation scheme that the government can use to make free trade beneficial.

9.4.1   The Meaning of Incomplete Markets

Consider a closed, pure-exchange economy with H households and I goods. There are two periods, 0 and 1. Variables in period 0 are known but there are S mutually exclusive states of nature in period 1. Define $\mathbf{I} = (1, \ldots, I)$ and $\mathbf{S} = (1, \ldots, S)$. Denoting the consumption of the ith good by the hth household if state s in period 1 exists by C_{is}^h and let $\mathbf{C}_s^h = (C_{1s}^h, \ldots, C_{Is}^h)$

and $\mathbf{C}^h = (\mathbf{C}^h_1, \ldots, \mathbf{C}^h_S)$. The hth household's preferences are assumed to be represented by the utility function $u^h(\mathbf{C}^h)$ and its endowments in period 1 if state s exists are $\mathbf{v}^h_s$. The utility function is assumed to be differentiable and quasi-concave. No consumption is done in period 0.[10]

Consider first the special case in which no transactions of any type between the households are allowed. Then each household has to consume what it is endowed with. In general this is not Pareto efficient. Suppose that the restrictions on transactions are slightly relaxed. After a state has been realized, the households are allowed to trade among themselves freely. This gives ex post Pareto optimality. It is not Pareto optimal in an ex ante sense, however, because in period 0, being risk averse, each household wants to hedge against risks in period 1, which generally requires trading of goods in different states.[11] I now consider two cases in which ex ante Pareto optimality can be reached.

Existence of Future Markets

Suppose that in period 0 future markets of all goods in all states exist so that each household can decide, subject to its budget constraint, the amount of each good in each state it wants to buy or sell. Perfect foresight is assumed. Treating goods in different states as different goods, there are altogether IS goods, IS prices, and IS markets. Taking the prices of goods as given, the household chooses the optimal consumption bundle to maximize its utility:

$$\max u^h(\mathbf{C}^h) \quad \text{s.t.} \quad \sum_i \sum_s p_{is} C^h_{is} \leq \sum_i \sum_s p_{is} v^h_{is}, \tag{9.26}$$

where p_{is} is the price of good i in state s. Note that the budget is not necessarily balanced for each state. The first-order conditions are:

$$\frac{\partial u^h}{\partial C^h_{is}} - \lambda^h p_{is} \leq 0 \quad \text{for all} \quad i \in \mathbf{I}; \ s \in \mathbf{S}, \tag{9.27}$$

where λ^h is the household's marginal utility of income. Condition (9.27) has an important implication. For any two households, the hth and the jth, if they consume the same two goods, the ith and the kth, in any state s, then

$$\frac{\partial u^h/\partial C^h_{is}}{\partial u^h/\partial C^h_{ks}} = \frac{\partial u^j/\partial C^j_{is}}{\partial u^j/\partial C^j_{ks}}. \tag{9.28a}$$

Similarly, if the hth and the jth households consume the same good ith in any two states, s and t, the following condition holds:

---

10. The assumption that there is no consumption in period 0 is to make the analysis simpler but it can easily be relaxed.

11. See Laffont (1989, Chapter 5).

$$\frac{\partial u^h / \partial C_{is}^h}{\partial u^h / \partial C_{it}^h} = \frac{\partial u^j / \partial C_{is}^j}{\partial u^j / \partial C_{it}^j} \tag{9.28b}$$

for all $i, k, \in \mathbf{I}$; $s, t \in \mathbf{S}$.

Condition (9.28a) means that in any state, two households have the same marginal rate of substitution between any two goods they consume, and (9.28b) states that the households have the same marginal rate of substitution between a good in state s and the good in state t, if they consume the good in both states. It is well known that conditions (9.28) are the necessary conditions for economic efficiency. Thus the economy reaches an ex ante Pareto optimality, assuming that the second-order conditions hold.

That ex ante Pareto optimality is reached in the presence of the future markets is not surprising because by interpreting any good in different states as different goods, the framework is the same as the Arrow-Debreu model. Note that if the households consume all goods in all states, condition (9.28a) represents $S(I-1)$ independent equations and condition (9.28b) represents $(S-1)$ independent equations.

Because condition (9.28a) implies ex post Pareto optimality, I conclude that ex ante Pareto optimality implies ex post Pareto optimality. This means that even if after a state is realized all markets are reopened, no transactions will take place.

Existence of Security Markets

Now I consider another case in which security markets, but not future markets, exist. Suppose that in period 0 there exists M mutually independent securities that each household can buy or sell. The seller of the mth security pays the consumption bundle $\mathbf{a}_s^m = \{a_{is}^m\}$ per unit to the buyer in period 1 if state s occurs, $s \in \mathbf{S}$.[12] Suppose further that $M = S$, that is, the number of securities is the same as the number of states. Let $\mathbf{M} = (1, \ldots, M)$, and denote the purchase of security m by the hth household by z_m^h (negative for sale of security m).

In period 0, no future markets exist, but households are allowed to buy or sell securities. In period 1 after a state is realized, and after they have received the payments for securities they bought or made the payments for the securities they sold, households are allowed to exchange goods. Households have perfect foresight of commodity prices before a state is realized, but they do not necessarily have the same belief about the probability of occurance of each state.[13]

---

12. For any good i, the $S \times M$ matrix $\{a_{is}^m\}$ has full column rank.

13. See Radner (1972).

Given this sequence of markets, M security markets in period 0 and I commodity markets in each state in period 1, the problem of the hth household is

$$\max u^h(\mathbf{C}^h) \quad \text{s.t.} \quad \sum_m r_m z_m^h \leq 0$$

$$\mathbf{p}_s \cdot \mathbf{C}_s^h \leq \mathbf{p}_s \cdot (\mathbf{v}_s^h + \sum_m z_m^h \mathbf{a}_s^m) \quad \text{for all } s \in \mathbf{S}, \tag{9.26'}$$

where $\mathbf{p}_s = (p_{1s}, \dots, p_{Is})$ and r_j is the price of the jth security. The first-order conditions of the household are

$$\frac{\partial u^h}{\partial C_{is}^h} - \lambda_s^h p_{is} \leq 0 \tag{9.29a}$$

$$\sum_i \sum_s \lambda_s^h p_{is} a_{is}^m - \phi^h r_m \leq 0 \tag{9.29b}$$

$$\text{for all } s \in \mathbf{S}, \; i \in \mathbf{I}, \; m \in \mathbf{M},$$

where ϕ^h is a Lagrangean multiplier and λ_s^h is the marginal utility of income of the hth household if state s occurs. Assuming that the hth and the jth households consume positive amounts of all goods, conditions (9.29) give:[14]

$$\frac{\partial u^h / \partial C_{is}^h}{\partial u^h / \partial C_{ks}^h} = \frac{\partial u^j / \partial C_{is}^j}{\partial u^j / \partial C_{ks}^j} \tag{9.30a}$$

$$\frac{\sum_i \sum_s a_{is}^m (\partial u^h / \partial C_{is}^h)}{\sum_i \sum_s a_{is}^n (\partial u^h / \partial C_{is}^h)} = \frac{\sum_i \sum_s a_{is}^m (\partial u^j / \partial C_{is}^j)}{\sum_i \sum_s a_{is}^n (\partial u^j / \partial C_{is}^j)}. \tag{9.30b}$$

$$\text{for all } i, k \in \mathbf{I}; \; s \in \mathbf{S}; \; m, n \in \mathbf{M}.$$

Condition (9.30a), representing $S(I-1)$ independent equations, is similar to (9.28a). Condition (9.30b) represents $(M-1) = (S-1)$ independent equations. Altogether, there are $IS - 1$ independent equations in conditions (9.30a) and (9.30b). For each household, the IS marginal utility variables of the IS goods can be regarded as unknowns. Thus these $IS - 1$ equations can be solved for $IS - 1$ unknown marginal rates of substitution. By arranging terms, $(M-1)$ conditions similar to those given by (9.28b) can be obtained. As a result, for any two households and any pair of goods they consume in any state, they have the same marginal rate of substitution between the two goods, and

---

14. This assumption is made just for simplicity. Alternatively, let I^s, $s \in \mathbf{S}$, be the number of goods both households consume if state s occurs. The households should have the same marginal rate of substitution between any goods in any states they consume.

(with the second-order conditions are satisfied) ex ante Pareto optimality is achieved (Arrow, 1964).

That the above economy achieves ex ante Pareto optimality depends crucially on the assumption that the number of independent securities M is equal to the number of states S in period 1. If, however, $M < S$, the Pareto optimality conditions (9.28) cannot be guaranteed. In this case, it is said that the markets are incomplete.[15]

An economy with incomplete markets behaves quite differently from an Arrow-Debreu economy. Not only is a competitive equilibrium in general Pareto suboptimal, it is also possible that a competitive equilibrium does not exist.[16] Furthermore, it has been shown that the existence of an addition security may hurt every individual (Hart, 1975).

9.4.2   Pareto Inferior Free Trade with Incomplete Markets

I now provide an example to show that free trade can be Pareto inferior.[17] Suppose that in the pure exchange economy there are two commodities and two price-taking households (or two homogeneous and equi-populated classes of price-taking households). In period 0, there are no future markets or security markets. In period 1, there are two states, $s = 2$. The hth household has a utility function given by

$$v^h(\mathbf{C}_1^h) + \beta^h v^h(\mathbf{C}_2^h) \qquad \beta^h > 0, \quad h = 1, \, 2,$$

where $\mathbf{C}_s^h$ is the consumption vector of the household in state s, $s = 1, 2$.

Initially the economy does not trade with other countries. Exchange in goods between the households in each state is allowed. The equilibrium condition in state s, $s = 1, 2$, is:

$$\sum_{h=1}^{2} \mathbf{C}_s^h = \sum_{h=1}^{2} \mathbf{v}_s^h.$$

The parameters β^1 and β^2 play no part in the determination of equilibrium prices.

Figure 9.8 depicts four possible one-state equilibria, two alternative equilibria for each state. Therefore there are four possible two-state equilibria:

---

15. For more details about incomplete markets, see Laffont (1989, Chapter 6) and Geanakoplos (1990).

16. The earlier approach to prove existence of equilibrium when markets are incomplete is to impose an arbitrary ceiling on the demand correspondences (Radner, 1972). Geanakoplos and Polemarchakis (1986), and Kemp and Wong (1995b, 1995c) instead assume that the payments of all securities are given in terms of one single good (such as gold). For generic existence of equilibrium with incomplete markets, see Husseini et al. (1990).

17. This example is due to Kemp and Wong (1995b).

Good 2   Household 2

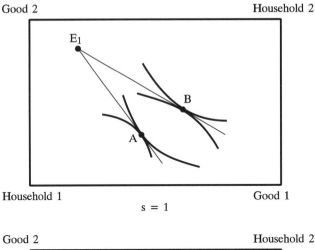

Household 1   Good 1
                        s = 1

Good 2   Household 2

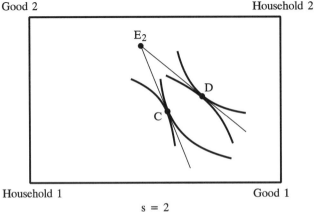

Household 1   Good 1
                        s = 2

Figure 9.8

(A, C), (A, D), (B, C), and (B, D). In (B, C) the first household is better off in the first state and worse off in the second state than in (A, D). The opposite is true of the second household. Because the equilibria are independent of β^1 and β^2, these parameters can be chosen arbitrarily. Choose β^1 small enough and β^2 large enough so that both households prefer (B, C) to (A, D). And suppose that, for whatever reason, (B, C) is the autarkic equilibrium.

Later, the country is given the opportunity to trade at a given world price sufficiently close to (but not identical to) that of the equilibrium (A, D). Then, clearly, some trade takes place. Moreover, both households are worse off under free trade than under autarky. This means that the autarkic equilibrium is Pareto-preferred to the free-trade equilibrium.

It should be noted that in the preceding example the economy has multiple equilibria, however, harmful free trade does not depend on the existence of multiple equilibria. Other examples with unique equilibria have been constructed to show that free trade could be Pareto inferior to autarky (Newbery and Stiglitz, 1984; Shy, 1988).

9.5   Gain from Compensated Trade with Incomplete Markets

Now assume that costless compensation using lump-sum transfers is available to the government of the economy considered in Section 9.4. I want to show that the government can find feasible compensation schemes to make sure that no household is worse off under free trade than under autarky.

Let me first refer back to the example provided in Section 9.4. Consider Figure 9.9. If in state 1 the second household transfers an amount $E_1 E_1'$ of the first good to the first household and if in state 2 the first household reciprocates by

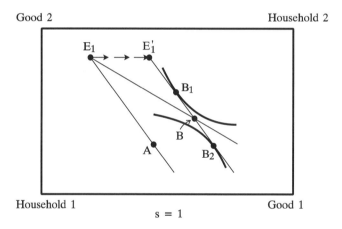

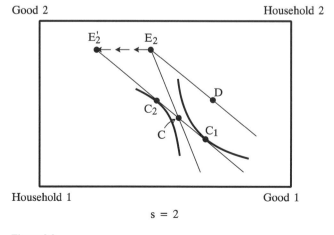

Figure 9.9

transferring $E_2 E_2'$ of the same good to the second household, then both households benefit; indeed they find themselves in a new *compensated* free-trade equilibrium that each prefers to autarky. This two-way transfer is a sufficiently good substitute for the missing security market so that compensated free-trade is gainful.

Taking one step more, it can be easily verified that, whatever the two-state autarkic equilibrium, there is a scheme of compensation which ensures that free trade is gainful. Thus, in this example, the traditional proposition is preserved. For compensation to ensure a gainful trade in less special circumstances, see Kemp and Wong (1995b, 1995c).

9.6   Pareto-Inferior Trade with Overlapping Generations

I now examine gains from trade in another class of models. The model considered here is the traditional two-factor, two-sector framework except that the economy grows over time with overlapping generations (OG). The consumption loan model constructed by Samuelson (1958) has captured the interest and fascination of economists about OG models. Although statically an OG model looks exactly the same as a typical Arrow-Debreu type general equilibrium model, it has been discovered that the model has certain nontraditional and nonintuitive features. For example, it is recognized that in such a model a competitive equilibrium may not be Pareto optimal (so that the first theorem of welfare economics may not hold), and that money may have positive value.[18]

When a competitive equilibrium of a OG model is not Pareto optimal, it is not entirely surprising to find that free trade with no government intervention may be harmful. Kemp and Long (1979), Binh (1985), and Serra (1991) have constructed examples to show that autarky is Pareto-preferred to free trade. These examples cast doubt on the robustness of the gainfulness of free trade and of the validity of the other core welfare economics theorems proved in the previous chapter.

Kemp and Wong (1995a) show, however, that for a class of economies with overlapping generations, there can always be found one or more policies that can fully compensate those who otherwise would have been harmed by free trade. Thus free trade can be made Pareto superior to autarky. In fact, Kemp and Wong (1995a) demonstrate that these policies can also be used to ensure a welfare improvement (or not welfare deterioration) if there is an improvement in the terms of trade for a small open economy, if there is an enlargement of

---

18. See Geanakoplos (1987) for a survey and discussion of different issues about overlapping-generations models.

a small country's set of tradable goods and factors, or if a customs union is formed.

In this section, I briefly describe an OG model and show that without adequate government policies, free trade can be Pareto inferior to autarky. In the next section, I explain government policies that can ensure a gainful free trade.

The model has two goods, consumption and investment. The consumption good is capital intensive under all possible factor prices. In period t, the amounts of capital K_t and labor L_t are given. Denote the outputs of consumption and investment goods by Q_{ct} and Q_{it}, respectively, and the prices of consumption and investment goods by p_t and q_t, respectively. Later, it will be convenient to choose the investment good as the numeraire and set $q_t = 1$ for all t. The economy is characterized by concave, linearly homogeneous and continuously differentiable sectoral production functions, and the absence of any static distortions. The gross domestic product (GDP) function is then defined by

$$g(p_t, q_t, K_t, L_t) = \max_{Q_{ct}, Q_{it}} \left\{ p_t Q_{ct} + q_t Q_{it} : \Gamma(Q_{ct}, Q_{it}, K_t, L_t) \leq 0 \right\}, \quad (9.31)$$

where $\Gamma(\cdot)$ is the production possibility set. Technologies are stationary over time.

Each individual lives for two periods. In the first period, the young individual works and earns an income given by the wage rate, w_t. In addition, that person may receive a transfer of b_t^y from the government (negative for a transfer to the government). The income is devoted partly to consumption and partly to saving. In the next period, the old individual retires but receives an income from earlier saving and possibly a transfer from the government, b_{t+1}^o. A subsidy τ_{t+1} on saving may be provided by the government. Denoting the per unit payment to capital service by r_{t+1}, each unit of saving yields a return of $(r_{t+1} + \tau_{t+1})$ in period $t + 1$. With perfect foresight, there is no difference between expected and realized values of variables in period $t + 1$.

To focus the analysis on capital formation, assume that the population has a zero net growth rate so that, in each period, the same number of individuals are born and die. Because the labor force remains constant, it can be normalized so that $L_t = 1$ for all t. The population in any period is then 2, the sum of young and old people.

Denote the demand for the consumption good of the young individual in period t by c_t^y, saving by s_t and the demand for consumption when the individual is old in period $t + 1$ by c_{t+1}^o. The individual's budget constraints are (with nonsatiation)

$$p_t c_t^y + s_t = w_t + b_t^y \quad (9.32a)$$

$$p_{t+1} c_{t+1}^o = (r_{t+1} + \tau_{t+1}) s_t + b_{t+1}^o \quad (9.32b)$$

where the investment good is now chosen as the numeraire. Denote the utility of an individual born in period t by a utility function $u(c_t^y, c_{t+1}^o)$ that is increasing, continuously differentiable, and strictly quasi-concave. The bequest motive is neglected. Moreover, preferences are uniform across generations. The benefits and feasibility of the compensation scheme to be introduced later do not require the existence of a steady state and thus do not require uniform preferences.[19] The individual born in period t chooses (c_t^y, s_t, c_{t+1}^o) to maximize $u(c_t^y, c_{t+1}^o)$ subject to the budget constraints in (9.32).

Denote the individual's indirect utility function by $v(w_t + b_t^y, p_t, r_{t+1} + \tau_{t+1}, p_{t+1}, b_{t+1}^o)$. By the envelope theorem, the saving function is equal to

$$s_t = s(w_t + b_t^y, p_t, r_{t+1} + \tau_{t+1}, p_{t+1}, b_{t+1}^o) = \frac{\partial v/\partial r_{t+1}}{\partial v/\partial b_{t+1}^o}.$$

The capital stock used in period t depreciates completely in one period.[20] The capital stock in the next period comes from the production of the investment good in period t, Q_{it}, less any possible export of the good, E_{it}, and plus any possible foreign capital inflow in period $t+1$, κ_{t+1} (κ_{t+1} being negative for domestic capital outflow), that is,

$$K_{t+1} = Q_{it} - E_{it} + \kappa_{t+1}. \tag{9.33}$$

Denoting the export of the consumption good in period t by E_{ct}, the equilibrium conditions for the commodity markets are

$$c_t^y + c_t^o + E_{ct} = Q_{ct} \tag{9.34a}$$

$$s_t + E_{it} = Q_{it}. \tag{9.34b}$$

In view of equations (9.33) and (9.34b), in equilibrium I have

$$K_{t+1} = s_t + \kappa_{t+1}. \tag{9.33'}$$

For the time being, assume that the government refrains from intervening, so that $b_t^y = b_{t+1}^o = \tau_{t+1} = 0$. With positive demand for each good, production is diversified. This implies that, locally, factor prices depend on the relative price of the consumption good but not on factor endowments. A steady state is defined as a state in which the growth of the capital stock is zero, that is, $K_{t+1} = K_t$. Because the labor force is constant over time, because preferences

19. In fact the validity of the propositions in this section does not depend on the factor intensities of sectors or require the assumptions of constant population and steady technologies.

20. I make the simplifying assumption that a capital stock depreciates completely in one period because I want to avoid the need to analyze what individuals do with their capital before they die.

are identical across generations, and because the technologies are stationary, in a steady state variables like prices are also stationary; for example, $p_{t+1} = p_t = p$ for all t.

The indirect utility function of a representative individual in any steady-state equilibrium, whether or not the economy is closed, reduces to

$$v(w, p, r, p, 0) \equiv v(w + 0, p, r + 0, p, 0).$$

Using (9.31)–(9.34), the dependence of utility on the relative price is given by

$$\frac{dv}{dp} = \lambda^y \left(\frac{dw}{dp} - \frac{w}{p} + \frac{s}{r} \frac{dr}{dp} \right). \tag{9.35}$$

Because the GDP function is linearly homogeneous in commodity prices and also in factor endowments, $w = pg_{\ell p} + g_{\ell q}$, $r = pg_{kp} + g_{kq}$ and $Q_i = g_{\ell q} + kg_{kq}$, where subindices of g represent partial derivatives. Substitute these relations into (9.35) and rearrange terms to give[21]

$$\frac{dv}{dp} = \frac{\lambda^y}{p} \left[\left(K - \frac{s}{r} \right) g_{kq} + (s - Q_i) \right]. \tag{9.35'}$$

Because the consumption good is capital intensive, $g_{kq} < 0$.

Consider first a closed economy so that $E_{ct} = E_{it} = \kappa_t = 0$. In a steady state, $s = Q_i = K$; hence (9.35') reduces to

$$\frac{dv}{dp} = \frac{s^a \lambda^y}{p^a} \left(1 - \frac{1}{r^a} \right) g_{kq}, \tag{9.35''}$$

where the superscript "a" denotes the autarkic value. The golden rule path is defined to be that steady-state path along which the utility of each individual is at a maximum. Let the corresponding relative price of the consumption good be p^*. The first-order condition for a golden rule path is that, at p^*, $dv/dp = 0$ or, by (9.35''), that $r = 1$. This rule implies that the interest rate, which is defined as $r - 1$, is equal to zero. (Note that in the present framework the rate of growth of population is zero.)

I now provide an example to show that in the framework free trade can be Pareto inferior, hurting all the individuals in the economy. A competitive steady-state equilibrium need not be on a golden rule path. Suppose that there exists an autarkic steady state and that the steady-state price of the consumption good is slightly smaller than the golden rule price, that is, $p^a < p^*$. Because the consumption good is capital intensive, the assumption that $p^a < p^*$ implies that the autarkic rental rate is less than unity, $r^a < 1$. Substituting the

---

21. Because $g_{\ell p} \equiv dw/dp$ and $w = pg_{\ell p} + g_{\ell q}$, $dw/dp - w/p = -g_{\ell q}/p$. Because $g_{kp} \equiv dr/dp$ and $r = pg_{kp} + g_{kq}$, $dr/dp = (r - g_{kq})/p$. Substitute these results into (9.35). Because $Q_i = g_{\ell q} + Kg_{kq}$, equation (9.35') then follows.

value of r^a into condition (9.35″) and because $g_{kq} < 0$, I get $\mathrm{d}v/\mathrm{d}p > 0$ in a sufficiently small region around the autarkic price.

Suppose now that, at the beginning of period $t = t'$, free trade is allowed with the rest of the world. The rest of the world is in a steady state, with the price of the consumption good equal to p^w. Suppose further that the economy is a small one, taking world prices as given, and that p^w is slightly smaller than the economy's autarkic price ratio, that is, $p^w < p^a$. Because the economy is a price taker, it will move to the new steady state with $p = p^w$ in one period.

To evaluate the welfare effects of free trade on this economy, I must examine the change in the steady-state utility of a representative individual, and that of a representative individual during the transitional period, that is, period t'. First, look at the change in steady-state welfare. Because $\mathrm{d}v/\mathrm{d}p > 0$, a fall in the price of the consumption good under free trade will lower the steady-state utility level of a representative individual. This means that free trade hurts all individuals who are born in or after period t'. Moreover, free trade is detrimental to the individuals who were born in period $t' - 1$ and who are old during the transitional period t', because the income of the latter group comes entirely from the rental rate of capital, which falls under free trade.

9.7 Gain from Compensated Trade with Overlapping Generations

In the previous example of Pareto inferior trade with overlapping generations, no compensations have been given. One may conjecture that a compensation scheme like the one used for the incomplete-market model can be employed to ensure that trade is gainful for the present overlapping-generations economy. This conjecture is in general not true.

The difficulty of getting a gainful trade for the present model by using compensations is that the present model is a dynamic one. What the economy can achieve and what the government can do in any period depends on what the economy has done in the past, not just the environment in the rest of the world in that period. Although the previous analysis suggests that the government can use compensation to ensure a static gainful trade at the time when trade is allowed, there is no guarantee that the ability to get gainful trade in future periods exists.

To see this point more clearly, suppose that in the period when free trade first exists, the government does use a compensation scheme to ensure that all individuals in that period are not worse off, or better off if consumption gain or production gain is positive. Being better off does not mean that an individual in period t will save as much as what he or she would do under autarky. Suppose that all individuals choose to save very little. If international capital movement is prohibited even though free trade in goods is allowed, then in period $t + 1$ the economy will have a smaller amount of capital than it would have under autarky. This represents a shrinkage of the production possibility set (PPS). If the shrinkage is significant, then the government may not be able to fully compensate all the individuals in period $t + 1$ and beyond.

Government policies that ensure a gainful trade do exist. Kemp and Wong (1995a) suggest four policies under which an economy can experience an improvement of its welfare: (1) when it moves from autarky to free trade, whether it is a large or small economy; (2) when its terms of trade improve if it is small; (3) when more goods or factors are allowed to trade if it is small; and (4) when it forms a customs union with other countries. The four policies in case (1) are described as follows. (To save space, I omit the details of the last three cases but they can be found in Kemp and Wong, 1995a.)

International Capital Movement

Suppose that free trade in goods and free international capital movement are allowed. The foreign capital owners earn an income according to the domestic rental rate and repatriate their income out of the economy. As explained in Chapter 2, the firms together with the capital owners jointly maximize the gross national product (GNP) of the economy. This allows me to define the GNP function

$$\tilde{g}(p_t, r_t, s_{t-1}) = \max_{Q_{ct}, Q_{it}, \kappa_t} \left\{ p_t Q_{ct} + Q_{it} - r_t \kappa_t : \right.$$

$$\left. \Gamma(Q_{ct}, Q_{it}, s_{t-1} + \kappa_t) \leq 0 \right\}, \qquad (9.36)$$

where for convenience, $q_t (= 1)$ and L_t are dropped as arguments from the GNP function. In (9.36), s_{t-1} is the private saving already chosen in the previous period. In the presence of international capital movement, the GDP function defined by (9.31) can be replaced by

$$g(p_t, s_{t-1} + \kappa_t) = \max_{Q_{ct}, Q_{it}} \left\{ p_t Q_{ct} + Q_{it} : \Gamma(Q_{ct}, Q_{it}, s_{t-1} + \kappa_t) \leq 0 \right\}. \quad (9.31')$$

As explained in Chapter 2, the GDP function and the GNP function are related to each other in the following way:

$$\tilde{g}(p_t, r_t, s_{t-1}) = g(p_t, s_{t-1} + \kappa_t) - r_t \kappa_t.$$

Denote the value of a variable under autarky by a "hat," while its value under free trade does not have a hat. Define

$$\bar{\kappa}_t \equiv \hat{s}_{t-1} - s_{t-1}. \qquad (9.37)$$

The interpretation of variable $\bar{\kappa}_t$ is that if the economy receives an amount of capital inflow equal to $\bar{\kappa}_t$ in period t, it gets the same amount of capital stock in that period as under autarky. Using the GNP function, I define the production gain of the economy as it moves from autarky to free trade as

$$P_t = p_t Q_{ct} + Q_{it} - r_t \kappa_t - (p_t \widehat{Q}_{ct} + \widehat{Q}_{it} - r_t \overline{\kappa}_t). \tag{9.38}$$

The production gain as given by (9.38) can be interpreted as follows. If the economy chooses an inflow of foreign capital equal to $\overline{\kappa}_t$, its capital stock remains the same as that under autarky. This means that the autarkic production point $(\widehat{Q}_{ct}, \widehat{Q}_{it})$ must still be feasible. Because the economy actually chooses an inflow of foreign capital equal to κ_t and the production point (Q_{ct}, Q_{it}), by (9.36), its national income must not be lower than what it gets by choosing $(\widehat{Q}_{ct}, \widehat{Q}_{it}, \overline{\kappa}_t)$. This implies that the production gain is nonnegative.

Under this policy, no saving subsidy is needed. The lump-sum transfer given by the government to the young generation in period t is denoted by b_t^y and that to the old generation in the same period is b_t^o. They are given by

$$b_t^y = p_t \widehat{c}_t^y + \widehat{s}_t - w_t + P_t/2 \tag{9.39a}$$

$$b_t^o = p_t \widehat{c}_t^o - r_t \widehat{s}_{t-1} + P_t/2. \tag{9.39b}$$

As conditions (9.39) show, the young and old generations in each period share the production gain equally, although other ways of sharing the production gain are possible.

To see the role of these transfers, substitute them into the individuals' budget constraints given by (9.32) to give:

$$p_t c_t^y + s_t \le p_t \widehat{c}_t^y + \widehat{s}_t + P_t/2 \tag{9.40a}$$

$$p_t c_t^o \le r_t s_{t-1} + p_t \widehat{c}_t^o - r_t \widehat{s}_{t-1} + P_t/2. \tag{9.40b}$$

Condition (9.40a) is only one of the two budget constraints of the young generation in period t (the second budget constraint being for period $t + 1$). I assume that similar lump-sum transfers are given in the next and future periods. Thus a condition similar to condition (9.40b) applies to the individual in period $t + 1$ when he or she is old. If the production gain is nonnegative (under the conditions mentioned previously), then it can be seen from conditions (9.40) that the autarkic consumption bundle $(\widehat{c}_t^y, \widehat{c}_t^o)$ is still affordable to the young individual in period t (including the consumption quantity when the individual is old in the next period) when the autarkic saving is chosen. Therefore the individual is not worse off. In fact, the individual is better off if the consumption gain or the production gain is positive.

Finally, I need to show that the lump-sum transfer scheme is feasible for any period. This is indeed the case, because the net expenditure of the government in period t is zero:

$$b_t^y + b_t^o = p_t \widehat{c}_t^y + \widehat{s}_t - w_t + p_t \widehat{c}_t^o - r_t \widehat{s}_{t-1} + P_t \qquad \text{[condition (9.39)]}$$

$$= p_t \widehat{c}_t^y + \widehat{s}_t - w_t + p_t \widehat{c}_t^o - r_t \widehat{s}_{t-1} + p_t Q_{ct} + Q_{it} - r_t \kappa_t$$

$$- (p_t \widehat{Q}_{ct} + \widehat{Q}_{it} - r_t \overline{\kappa}_t) \qquad \text{[condition (9.38)]}$$

$$= p_t Q_{ct} + Q_{it} - w_t - r_t \widehat{s}_{t-1} - r_t \kappa_t + r_t \overline{\kappa}_t \qquad \text{[condition (9.34)]}$$

$$= p_t Q_{ct} + Q_{it} - w_t - r_t (s_{t-1} + \kappa_t) \qquad \text{[condition (9.37)]}$$

$$= 0. \qquad \text{[zero profit]}$$

Public Saving

Suppose that international capital movement is not allowed. As mentioned previously, there is no guarantee that under free trade the individuals will save sufficiently so that the economy has enough of resources to yield a positive production gain. Public saving plus a compensation scheme as described below can be used to ensure a gainful trade.

I now explain how the government uses lump-sum transfers and public saving to provide the economy a capital stock under free trade not less than that under autarky.

With no international capital mobility, the production gain reduces to

$$P_t = p_t Q_{ct} + Q_{it} - (p_t \widehat{Q}_{ct} + \widehat{Q}_{it}). \tag{9.38'}$$

If the amount of capital stock under free trade in period t is not less than that under autarky in the same period, then the production gain is not negative.[22]

This policy (under free trade) in period t consists of two parts. The first part is the lump-sum transfer scheme as described by conditions (9.39) with the production gain given by (9.38'). The second part is public saving, h_t, which is defined as

$$h_t = \max [\widehat{s}_t - s_t, 0]. \tag{9.41}$$

According to (9.41), the public saving is zero if the private saving under free trade is not less than that under autarky, $s_t \geq \widehat{s}_t$. If the free-trade private saving falls short of the autarkic private saving, then the government supplements the private saving with public saving so that the capital stock in the next period is the same as that under autarky.

The policy guarantees that the production gain is non-negative, and thus that all individuals are not worse off under trade (better off if consumption gain or

---

22. Note that in the present context, immiserizing growth is not possible because there is no domestic, static distortion, and because the economy shifts to free trade.

production gain is positive). Feasibility of this and the following two policies are described in Kemp and Wong (1995a).

Saving Subsidy

An alternative policy for the government to ensure that the capital stock under free trade in goods but no capital movement in any period is not less than the autarkic capital stock is to use saving subsidy. This policy also has two parts. The first part consists of lump-sum transfers as described by (9.39), and the second part is the saving subsidy. The saving subsidy is so chosen that the private saving under free trade and in the presence of the lump-sum transfers is not less than the autarkic level. I explained earlier that when the capital stock under free trade in any period is the same as the autarkic level, the production gain as defined by (9.38′) is non-negative. The implication is that the autarkic saving and consumption for any individual are still feasible under free trade.

Consumption Taxation

The fourth policy for the government to avoid a harmful trade is to use consumption taxes. The purpose of this policy is similar to that of consumption taxation policy explained in the previous chapter. The government uses taxes on consumption goods and saving so that all individuals under free trade are facing autarkic prices in any period. As a result, under free trade the individuals will choose the autarkic saving and consumption bundles, and they are not worse off. In fact, I can follow the procedure described in the previous chapter, and allow the government to distribute any positive government revenue to the individuals as poll grants. If the government revenue to be distributed is positive, the individuals are better off.

V TRADE POLICIES

10 Theory of Distortions and Optimal Policy Intervention

It is well known that in an Arrow-Debreu type general equilibrium framework, a competitive equilibrium is Pareto efficient. The agents in an economy, while making decisions to maximize their own objective functions, jointly determine an equilibrium at which all the necessary conditions for an optimal point of the economy are satisfied. This result, which is called the first theorem of welfare economics, has a very strong policy implication: Government interventions cannot improve upon a competitive equilibrium in a Pareto sense.

The world is more complicated than the Arrow-Debreu framework, however, and for various reasons, the agents in an economy, when maximizing their own objectives, do not lead the economy to a point with Pareto efficiency. In this case, the economy is said to be distorted.

When distortions exist, government intervention may be desirable, and in fact the distortions mean that welfare of the economy can be improved if removal of the distortions is possible and relatively costless. The more important question is, how should the government intervene?

One should be aware of two dangers in government intervention. First, the government, with a goal to improve national welfare, may not be using the first-best or optimal policy. Second, the government may be influenced too much by interest groups and lobbying activities so that the government uses the wrong policies to satisfy the objective functions of these groups at the expense of other groups in the economy.

The purpose of this chapter is to present the theory of distortions and optimal government intervention, and to apply the theory to suggest policies to improve the welfare of economies with several well-known types of distortion. The theory can be used to give useful guidelines to government planners who are interested in applying the appropriate policies to improve national welfare, and to point out the cost of using inappropriate policies.

This chapter begins with a planner's problem in which the planner is supposed to be able to allocate resources to maximize an objective function. The planner's problem is compared with a market equilibrium of an economy, and through such comparison, distortions that exist in the economy may be identified. This is the first step a planner can take before any appropriate policies are determined. The principle of optimal policy intervention gives the guideline for adopting the appropriate policies. There may be circumstances under which the appropriate policies cannot be adopted and the distortions in the economy cannot be entirely removed. This leads to the theory of second best and piecemeal policy recommendations. In some cases, second-best policies can be suggested. The theory of distortion is related to a phenomenon called immiserizing growth which means that growth can be welfare deteriorating if distortions exist in the economy. I examine several cases and the conditions for immiserizing growth. The last two sections of this chapter examine the optimal policies and their effects in two types of economies analyzed in chapters 5 and 6: external economies of scale, and monopolistic competition and differentiated products. Two important topics that will not be covered in the present chapter but will be discussed in great detail in the following two chapters are trade policies in the presence of international goods trade and capital movement and strategic trade policies.

The theory of distortion and optimal policy intervention presented in this chapter have been developed by many people over a long period of time. Sometimes it is difficult to identify the source or originator of the ideas and results. It should be mentioned that the work of Meade (1955, especially chapters 9 to 18) should get special attention and respect because it contains much analysis that was later further developed and elaborated in the 1960s and 1970s. For useful surveys of work of different generations, see Bhagwati (1968b, 1971), Negishi (1972), Chacholiades (1978, Chapters 20 and 21), Dixit and Norman (1980, Chapter 6), Woodland (1982, Chapter 11), Bhagwati and Srinivasan (1983a, Chapters 16 to 25), Ng (1983), Corden (1984), Krueger (1984), Baldwin (1984), and Boadway and Bruce (1984).

10.1 A Planner's Problem

A useful approach to analyzing distortions in an economy is to start with a planner's problem. In this approach, it is assumed that the government has effective and costless ways to allocate resources and make production and distribution decisions. The problem of the government is to choose the optimal production and distribution to maximize an objective function that represents the national welfare of the economy. The solution is then compared with a market equilibrium in which consumers and producers make their optimal decisions of consumption and production in the absence of any government intervention. If the market equilibrium coincides with the solution of the planner's problem, the economy is said to be distortion free and no government intervention is needed because the markets, guided by "invisible hands," can by themselves pick the optimal point. If the market equilibrium is not the same as the solution to the planner's problem, that is, the value of the objective function in the market equilibrium is less than the maximum value, distortions are said to exist. The market equilibrium is then compared with the planner's problem in order to find out where and what the distortions are. This will help suggest the right government policies to correct the distortions so that the economy can reach the optimal point.

Even though the solution to a planner's problem gives the optimal point of an economy, economists have the tendency to avoid relying on government interventions and control of resource allocation in the markets. If the "invisible hands" can guide markets to achieve the optimal point, any government interventions are discouraged. If distortions are present, it is usually argued that government interventions should be kept at a minimum. One of the main reasons for such an "anti-government-intervention" attitude is that solving the planner's problem requires a huge amount of information. Much of this information resides in the markets and the agents (consumers and firms). To collect all the required information is probably prohibitively costly, and very often the agents do not have the right incentives to supply the true information to the government.[1]

I now explain the planner's problem in achieving the optimal point of an economy. The economy under consideration in the present section is called the home country. It is the m-factor, n-sector competitive, constant-returns economy described in Chapter 2, but the analysis given here is not limited to this framework and can be applied to solve problems for other types of economies.

I assume that the objective function of the economy is represented by a "well-behaved" social utility function $u(\mathbf{C})$, where $\mathbf{C}$ is the n-dimensional vector of consumption goods. The production function of the ith sector, $i = 1, \ldots, n$, is given by $Q_i = F_i(\mathbf{v}_i)$ where Q_i is the output level and $\mathbf{v}_i$ is the m-dimensional vector of inputs. The economy is trading with a foreign country. Denote the n-dimensional vector of the foreign country's export supply functions by $\mathbf{E}^*$. The willingness of the foreign country to trade is described by the set $\Theta^*(\mathbf{E}^*) \leq 0$. The function $\Theta^*(\mathbf{E}^*) = 0$ is the offer surface of the foreign country and is assumed to be differentiable.

The problem of the planner is

$$\max_{\mathbf{C},\mathbf{Q},\{\mathbf{v}_i\},\mathbf{E}^*} u(\mathbf{C}) \quad \text{s.t.} \quad \mathbf{E}^* \geq \mathbf{C} - \mathbf{Q};$$

$$F_i(\mathbf{v}_i) \geq Q_i;$$

$$\Theta^*(\mathbf{E}^*) \leq 0;$$

$$\sum_i v_{ij} \leq v_j;$$

$$\text{for all } i = 1, \ldots, n; \; j = 1, \ldots, m.$$

1. However, this "anti-government-intervention" attitude has been criticized. For example, no matter how well the markets can achieve efficiency, they usually cannot adequately solve the equity problem, and some sort of government intervention to redistribute income is usually unavoidable when equity is an important goal of the government. Although in this chapter I follow the tradition and focus mainly on efficiency, I can point out that one approach to analyzing the equity problem is to use the Bergson-Samuelson social welfare function explained in Chapters 2 and 8.

To solve this problem, define the following Lagrangean function

$$\mathcal{L} = u(\mathbf{C}) + \sum_i \phi_i \left(E_i^* + Q_i - C_i \right) + \sum_i \alpha_i \left[F_i(\mathbf{v}_i) - Q_i \right] - \beta \Theta^*(\mathbf{E}^*)$$

$$+ \sum_j w_j \left(v_j - \sum_i v_{ij} \right),$$

where ϕ_i, α_i, β, and w_j are Lagrangean multipliers. The first-order conditions are

$$\frac{\partial \mathcal{L}}{\partial C_i} = u_i - \phi_i \leq 0 \qquad (10.1a)$$

$$\frac{\partial \mathcal{L}}{\partial E_i^*} = \phi_i - \beta \Theta_i^* \leq 0 \qquad (10.1b)$$

$$\frac{\partial \mathcal{L}}{\partial Q_i} = \phi_i - \alpha_i \leq 0 \qquad (10.1c)$$

$$\frac{\partial \mathcal{L}}{\partial v_{ij}} = \alpha_i F_{ij} - w_j \leq 0, \qquad (10.1d)$$

where $u_i \equiv \partial u / \partial C_i$, $\Theta_i^* \equiv \partial \Theta^* / \partial E_i^*$, and $F_{ij} \equiv \partial F_i / \partial v_{ij}$. For goods i and k, which are consumed, produced, and traded in equilibrium, conditions (10.1a), (10.1b), and (10.1c) (using equality) can be combined together to give

$$\frac{u_i}{u_k} = \frac{\Theta_i^*}{\Theta_k^*} = \frac{\alpha_i}{\alpha_k}. \qquad (10.2)$$

Similarly, if factors j and ℓ are employed in sectors i and k to produce positive outputs, condition (10.1d) can be used to give

$$\frac{F_{ij}}{F_{i\ell}} = \frac{F_{kj}}{F_{k\ell}}. \qquad (10.3)$$

Conditions (10.2) and (10.3) are two necessary conditions for an optimal point. The second-order conditions are assumed to be satisfied.

Let me examine more closely these necessary conditions and find out some economic intuition about the solution to the problem. In (10.2), the ratio of u_i to u_k is the *marginal rate of substitution* between the goods, which is denoted by DRS_{ik} ("D" for domestic). Differentiation of the given set $\Theta^*(\mathbf{E}^*) = 0$ for goods i and k gives

$$\frac{\Theta_i^*}{\Theta_k^*} = -\frac{dE_k^*}{dE_i^*},$$

which is the quantity of export of good k the foreign country is willing to supply for each unit of *import* of good i it gets. Because one country's import is the other country's export, Θ_i^*/Θ_k^* can also be interpreted as the maximum quantity of good k the home country can get back for each unit of good i it gives up through trade. Because of this interpretation, this ratio is called the *foreign marginal rate of transformation* and denoted by FRT_{ik}.

To interpret the third ratio in condition (10.2), note that Lagrangean multiplier α_i is the shadow price of $F_i(\mathbf{v}_i)$. If good i is produced, $F_i(\mathbf{v}_i) = Q_i$. Thus α_i/α_k is the ratio of the shadow price of good i to that of good k when both of them are produced, and in equilibrium it is numerically equal to the rate of change of production of good k with respect to good i. This is what is called the *(domestic) marginal rate of transformation* between the goods. Let me denote it by DRT_{ik}. In a two-good economy, DRT is (the negative of) the slope of the production possibility frontier (PPF).

Thus condition (10.2) can be written in an alternative form:

$$DRS_{ik} = FRT_{ik} = DRT_{ik}. \qquad (10.2')$$

Condition (10.2′) requires that for any pair of goods that are consumed, produced, and traded, the three marginal rates must be equal. The intuition behind this condition is that DRS_{ik} is the amount of good k consumers have to get back for consumption in order to be willing to give up one unit of good i, and that at an optimal point this ratio must be equal to the amount of good k the economy can get back either through domestic production transformation or trade for each unit of good i it gives up.

Now turn to condition (10.3). The ratio on each side of the equation is the *marginal rate of technical substitution* between factors j and ℓ in a sector. Denote the marginal rate of technical substitution between factors j and ℓ in sector i by $MRTS_{j\ell}^i$. It is well known that if condition (10.3) is satisfied, production is efficient and occurs at a point on the efficiency locus in an Edgeworth box diagram, or at a point on the PPF in the commodity space. Thus condition (10.3) can be written in an alternative form given as follows:

$$MRTS_{j\ell}^i = MRTS_{j\ell}^k. \qquad (10.3')$$

10.2   Optimality of a Competitive Equilibrium

Now consider a competitive equilibrium in the $m \times n$ framework. Assume that the economy is trading freely with the foreign country under *given foreign prices*. I compare the conditions of a competitive equilibrium derived in these chapters with the solution to the planner's problem given previously.

Begin with the factor markets. Taking factor prices as given, firms in sector i, $i = 1, \ldots, n$, employ each factor up to the point at which the price of the factor is equal to the value of marginal product of the factor. Thus the ratio of the prices of any two factors is equal to the ratio of the factors' marginal products in the sector. The latter ratio is the marginal rate of technical substitution between the factors in the sector. Because all firms face the same set of factor prices, there is equalization of the marginal rates of technical substitution between any two pair of factors in any two sectors with positive employment of the factors. Thus in a competitive equilibrium, condition (10.3) for the solution of a planner's problem is satisfied.

Now analyze the commodity markets. In the presence of a social utility function, the economy behaves like a consumer. Utility maximization implies that the marginal rate of substitution between two goods with positive consumption is equal to the price ratio, that is, for goods i and k,

$$DRS_{ik} \equiv \frac{u_i}{u_k} = \frac{p_i}{p_k}. \tag{10.4a}$$

On the production side, because firms employ factors efficiently, and because technologies are subject to constant returns, production occurs at a point at which the marginal rate of transformation is equal to the price ratio, that is, at which a price hyperplane is tangent to the PPF. For goods i and k with positive outputs,

$$DRT_{ik} = \frac{p_i}{p_k}. \tag{10.4b}$$

Because the home country is facing given world prices, from the home country's point of view, the offer surface of the foreign country is a hyperplane. In the special case with two tradable goods, the foreign offer curve is a straight line. Thus the foreign marginal rate of transformation between goods i and k that are being traded is equal to the foreign price ratios, that is,

$$FRT_{ik} = \frac{p_i^*}{p_k^*}, \tag{10.4c}$$

where an asterisk denotes a foreign variable. Furthermore, free trade between the countries implies equalization of commodity prices, that is,

$$\frac{p_i}{p_k} = \frac{p_i^*}{p_k^*}. \tag{10.4d}$$

Combining conditions (10.4a) to (10.4d) together gives optimality condition (10.2) (or (10.2')), which is obtained from the planner's problem:

$$DRS_{ik} = FRT_{ik} = DRT_{ik}.$$

In other words, both necessary conditions for an optimal point are satisfied. With the second-order conditions and a unique equilibrium assumed, I conclude that a competitive equilibrium for the present economy under free trade coincides with the optimal point in the planner's problem so that no government intervention is needed. This conclusion is consistent with one of the core theorems of welfare economics in international trade proved in Chapter 8: Free trade is the optimal policy for a small open economy.

A closer look at this result will show that it is not surprising. It is well known that for a closed Arrow-Debreu type economy, a competitive equilibrium is Pareto efficient. In the present economy, I assume a social utility function instead of examining the consumption behavior of each individual. The necessary conditions for an optimal point as given by (10.2) and (10.3) are the same as those for a Pareto efficient point.[2] This means that the theorem can be used to explain why a competitive equilibrium yields an optimal point for a closed economy.

When the economy trades freely with another country, the economy has two different ways to transform one good to another: through production by domestic firms and through trade. In a planner's problem, the planner chooses the transformation of one good to another in a way that yields a higher return to consumers. In equilibrium, these transformations of two traded goods with positive domestic production must be the same. This is what condition (10.2) implies.

In a competitive equilibrium, domestic consumers and producers are guided by signals in the markets, that is, prices. If foreign prices are given, then the foreign rates of transformation are fixed. When free trade prevails, domestic prices are equal to the given foreign prices. Thus domestic consumers and producers respond to foreign prices. In particular, utility maximization implies that marginal rate of substitution is equated to the foreign price ratio, and profit maximization implies that domestic factors are employed efficiently and that the domestic marginal rate of transformation is equal to the foreign price ratio.

In proving the optimality of a competitive equilibrium, I require that firms in all sectors face the same factor prices. In Chapter 2, I introduced a model with sector-specific factors. Without perfect sectoral mobility, the prices of these sector-specific factors in different sectors may be different. In such a model, the efficiency of a competitive equilibrium can be analyzed as follows. I mentioned in that chapter that there are two approaches to interpreting the model. If the sector-specific factors in different sectors are regarded as different factors, then the fact that their prices in different sectors are different poses no problem to the efficiency of resource allocation. In another approach, sector specificity of factors is a short-run phenomenon, and in the long run factors move perfectly between sectors. Thus inefficiency is at best a short-run problem. If possible, the only thing the government needs to do is to speed up the movement of factors between sectors.

---

2. For the conditions for Pareto efficiency, see any advanced microeconomics book, for example, Varian (1992, pp. 225–227).

10.3   Types of Distortions

In the preceding model, the necessary conditions for an optimal point are satisfied in a competitive equilibrium. There are, however, cases in which some of these conditions do not hold, that is, some of the equalities in conditions (10.2) and (10.3) are replaced by inequalities. Depending on where an inequality occurs, the following types of distortions can be classified as follows.

1. $DRS_{ik} = DRT_{ik} \neq FRT_{ik}, MRTS_{j\ell}^i = MRTS_{j\ell}^k$.
2. $DRS_{ik} = FRT_{ik} \neq DRT_{ik}, MRTS_{j\ell}^i = MRTS_{j\ell}^k$.
3. $DRS_{ik} \neq DRT_{ik} = FRT_{ik}, MRTS_{j\ell}^i = MRTS_{j\ell}^k$.
4. $DRS_{ik} = DRT_{ik} = FRT_{ik}$, while factor markets are distorted.

Type (1) distortion, which is called an *external or foreign distortion*, occurs when the ratio of domestic prices is not the same as the foreign marginal rate of transformation. An example of a foreign distortion is that the economy has external monopoly power and is trading freely with other countries. The failure to extract this monopoly power means that the economy is not pursuing an optimal policy. I will analyze this type of distortion and the type of government policies needed to achieve Pareto optimality in the next chapter.

Distortions of types (2) to (4) are called *internal or domestic distortions*. Type (2) occurs, for example, when production externality occurs, and type (3) can be due to consumption externality. Type (4) distortion exists in the factor markets, and usually results in a production point below the efficient PPF. For example, if the marginal rates of technical substitution are different in different sectors, then factors are not allocated efficiently, that is, the production point is not on the efficiency locus or on the efficient PPF. Very often, factor market distortions result in unemployment of factors.

Factor market distortions can exist in several forms.[3] The first is a constant differential between the wages in different sectors (Hagen, 1958; Johnson, 1966; Bhagwati and Srinivasan, 1971; Jones, 1971b; Batra, 1971a, 1971b; Herberg and Kemp, 1971; Neary 1978b; and Schweinberger, 1979). An example is the persistent gap between rural wages and urban wages in most less developed countries. Such wage differential may or may not be distortionary, depending on its cause. For example, suppose that initially the rural and urban wage rates are equalized, but there is a shock so that the urban wage rate

---

3. For surveys of different forms of factor market distortions, see Magee (1973, 1976), and Bhagwati and Srinivasan (1983a, chapters 21–23.)

becomes higher. Rural workers are free to move to the urban area to earn a higher wage rate, but the costs of migration keep the wage rates from becoming equalized. If the costs of migration cannot be reduced by any government policies, then the wage differential in this case is not distortionary. If the wage differential is due to the actions of labor unions in the urban area or legislation, then it is distortionary.

The existence of a wage differential means that the feasible PPF, which is the locus of all maximum outputs when given the wage-differential constraint, is below the efficient PPF and may not be concave to the origin. What is more, the price line in general is not tangent to the feasible PPF.

The second form of factor market distortions is the existence of sector-specific sticky wages (Harris and Todaro, 1970; Bhagwati and Srinivasan, 1974; Srinivasan and Bhagwati, 1975; Corden and Findlay, 1975). The Harris-Todaro model is widely used in the literature. In this model, the wage rate in the urban area is fixed, perhaps due to the action of a powerful urban labor union. When this wage rate is substantially higher than the rural wage rate, rural workers flow to the urban area. Equalization of wage rates is prevented due to the existence of unemployment in the urban area, and to the fact that rural workers compare the rural wage rate to the expected wage rate in the urban area. Again workers are not allocated efficiently and unemployment (in the urban area) exists.

The third form of factor market distortions is an economy-wide sticky wage (Haberler, 1950; Lefeber, 1971; Brecher, 1974a, 1974b). An example of this form of distortion is an economy-wide minimum wage restriction. If all sectors are subject to the same wage floor, and if factors are perfectly mobile between sectors, then the economy is featured by equalization of marginal rates of technical substitution. The existence of the minimum wage, if binding, would cause unemployment.

For each type of distortion, Bhagwati (1971) distinguishes between whether it is endogenous or government policy imposed. A distortion is endogenous if it is due to some imperfections in the system, or market imperfections, under a policy of laissez-faire. A distortion is policy imposed if it is the result of economic policies.

The four distortions represent a departure of the economy from the optimality conditions. There are, however, other kinds of frameworks that may have other types of distortions. In the later part of this chapter I examine in detail two other kinds of framework to illustrate the use of government policies: external economies of scale and monopolistic competition with differentiated products.[4]

---

4. Other forms of distortions may exist in other types of economies. See Boadway and Bruce (1984, Chapter 4) for a discussion.

10.4   Optimal Policy Intervention

Suppose distortions in the economy exist so that some of the optimality conditions given by (10.2) and (10.3) do not hold in a market equilibrium. I now
examine what the government can do to improve national welfare. Without allowing the government to directly control resource allocation, the policies I
focus on are taxes, subsidies, and sometimes quantitative restrictions. When
tax and subsidy policies are imposed, it is assumed that subsidy expenditures
are financed by lump-sum taxes imposed on individuals, and that tax revenues
are distributed to individuals in a lump-sum fashion.

In order to illustrate the principle of optimal policy intervention, I consider
one type of distortion: consumption externality. Other types of distortions and
the corresponding optimal policies are discussed in later sections.

Suppose that good 1 is something like telephone, television, computer software, and other communication networks so that the utility one can get from
consuming the good depends not only on the quantity of the good but also
on the number of consumers and the total consumption of the good. When
a representative consumer increases his or her consumption of the good, the
consumer also increases (indirectly) the utility of all consumers. If the number
of consumers is large, however, each of them will neglect the indirect effect
because the increase in one's consumption is only a negligible fraction of the
total consumption. Such a consumption externality, which is called network
externality, is similar to the external effects analyzed in Chapter 5. See, for
example, Katz and Shapiro (1985).

The existence of the consumption externality thus creates a divergence between the social marginal utility (SMU) and the private marginal utility (PMU)
of good 1. The SMU of good 1 is given by the derivative of the social utility
function and is denoted by u_1. The PMU of good 1, denoted by PMU_1, is
what a consumer perceives, ignoring the positive effect, and is less than u_1.
To simplify the analysis, let $PMU_1 = \psi u_1$, where $0 < \psi < 1$. Further assume
that ψ is a constant, although qualitatively the present result does not depend
on whether it is a constant.

Consumers make their consumption decision based on the PMU of the
goods. Because consumption externality exists for good 1 only (by assumption), the consumption equilibrium can be described by the following equations

$$\frac{\psi u_1}{u_2} = \frac{p_1}{p_2} \tag{10.5a}$$

$$\frac{u_i}{u_k} = \frac{p_i}{p_k}, \quad i, k = 2, \ldots, n. \tag{10.5b}$$

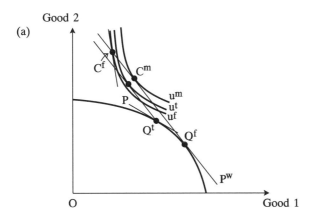

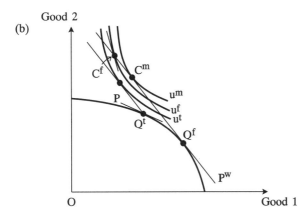

Figure 10.1

I now assume that the economy trades freely with the rest of the world, and that it takes all foreign prices as given. This means that $p_i = p_i^*$. Because no other distortions exist in the economy, (10.5a) and (10.5b) imply the following conditions:

1. $DRS_{12} > DRT_{12} = FRT_{12}$;
2. $DRS_{ik} = DRT_{ik} = FRT_{ik}$, for all $i, k = 2, \ldots, n$;
3. $MRTS_{j\ell}^i = MRTS_{j\ell}^k$, for all $i, k = 1, \ldots, n, j, \ell = 1, \ldots, m$.

To illustrate conditions (1) to (3), consider the traditional two-good framework shown in Figure 10.1. These conditions imply that the production point is on the PPF of the economy, and is at a point of tangency between a world price line and the PPF. This is point Q^f in both panels of the diagram. Because of the present consumption distortion, however, the consumption point is not at a point where the world price line touches an indifference curve. The consumption point, C^f, is on the world price line and at a point on an indifference curve with a slope of $p_1^*/(\psi p_2^*)$. The resulting utility level is equal to u^f.

A comparison of conditions (1) to (3) with (10.2) and (10.3) shows that only one of the optimality conditions is not satisfied. The problem of the government is to find out the appropriate tax/subsidy policy to improve national welfare. Usually there exist more than one welfare-improving policies but often only one of them is the first-best. When there is more than one way of correcting a prevailing distortion in an economy, the following result can be stated:

Principle of Optimal Policy Intervention   In the presence of distortions, optimal policy intervention requires a tax/subsidy policy addressed directly to offsetting the source of the distortion.

The principle of optimal policy intervention has been pointed out and illustrated with special examples in many papers, but probably the two best-known ones are Johnson (1965) and Bhagwati (1971). The first paper focuses mainly on domestic distortions and the government responses, while the second one synthesizes the developments in the 1950s and 1960s, and establishes the general theory of distortions.

This principle can be illustrated by using the present economy with a consumption distortion. As explained earlier, the source of the distortion is consumption externality, which is characterized by underconsumption of good 1. According to the principle, a subsidy is required to be imposed on good 1 to encourage consumers to buy more. I now prove that a specific consumption subsidy of $(1 - \psi)p_1^*$ on good 1 is needed to correct the present distortion.

In the presence of the subsidy, the consumer price of good 1, that is, the net cost of each unit of good 1 to the consumers, is $p_1^* - (1 - \psi)p_1^* = \psi p_1^*$. Consumers make decisions based on prices. This means that the utility maximizing condition (10.5a) is replaced by

$$\frac{\psi u_1}{u_2} = \frac{\psi p_1^*}{p_2^*},$$

or,

$$\frac{u_1}{u_2} = \frac{p_1^*}{p_2^*}. \tag{10.6}$$

Using condition (10.6), $DRS_{12} = DRT_{12} = FRT_{12}$. By assumption, there are no distortions in the factor markets. Thus all the optimality conditions are satisfied, meaning that the market equilibrium in the presence of the consumption subsidy is identical to the optimal point. This is shown in both panels of Figure 10.1 by point C^m at which the free-trade world price line touches an indifference curve.

There are, however, other possible policies to correct the present distortion. Now consider the effects of some trade policies. Let good 1 be the exportable. To correct the present consumption externality, the government can use a specific export tax of $(1 - \psi)p_1^*$ on good 1. In equilibrium, the domestic price of good 1 is equal to $p_1^* - (1 - \psi)p_1^* = \psi p_1^*$. Under this policy, not only consumers, but also producers, are facing this new price of good 1 in the home market.

In the presence of the export tax, consumers choose the point at which condition (10.6) is satisfied. Because firms face domestic prices instead of foreign prices, however, the production point is at a tangency between a domestic price line and the PPF in Figure 10.1, Q^t. The important implication of the present export tax is that although it corrects the inequality between DRS and FRT $(= p_1^*/p_2^*)$, it also creates an inequality between DRT and FRT. Now $DRS = FRT \neq DRT$. Because the original distortion is replaced by another distortion, this policy cannot be a first-best policy.

The trade tax or subsidy that corrects the inequality between DRS and FRT could in fact hurt the economy. Such a possibility is illustrated in Figure 10.1. Panel (a) shows the case in which the export tax improves national welfare, while in panel (b), the economy is hurt by such an export tax.

Three further results can be established. First, the government can impose a tariff of $(1/\psi - 1)p_2^*$ on the imported good 2 instead of the export tax. The same equilibrium as that under the export tax is achieved. This result, which is due to Lerner (1936), is called *symmetry between an import tax and an export tax*: An export tax has the same effects on the economy as a tariff of the same ad valorem rate.[5]

The second result is that *an export tax on good 1 is equivalent to a consumption subsidy and a production tax of the same rate on good 1*. To see why, note that an export tax with an ad valorem rate of $(1/\psi - 1)$ on p_1 lowers the domestic price faced by consumers and producers to ψp_1^*. On the other hand, a consumption subsidy on good 1 lowers the price of the good for the consumers and a producer tax lowers the revenue received by the producers in the sector. Thus a consumption subsidy and a production tax of ad valorem rate of $(1/\psi - 1)$ on p_1 produce the same effect as the export tax. The same argument can be used to show that a tariff is equivalent to a consumption tax and a production subsidy of the same ad valorem rate on the imported good.

---

5. The analysis shows that in the presence of the export tax, $p_1 = \psi p_1^*$, $p_2 = p_2^*$, and $p = \psi p^*$. Thus the ad valorem export tax rate (applied to the domestic price) on good 1 is $t_e = (1/\psi) - 1$. Suppose now that a tariff on imported good 2 instead of an export tax on good 1 is imposed. Let the ad valorem tariff rate be $t_i = (1/\psi) - 1$. Then $p_1 = p_1^*$ and $p_2 = (1 + t_i)p_2^* = p_2^*/\psi$. Combining these results gives $p = \psi p^*$, which is the same condition as before.

The third result is that if good 1 is instead the importable, then under certain conditions *an import subsidy is as good as a consumption subsidy.*[6] Suppose that the government imposed an import subsidy on good 1 with a specific rate of $(1 - \psi)p_1^*$. In equilibrium, the domestic price of good 1 faced by consumers is $p_1^* - (1 - \psi)p_1^* = \psi p_1^*$, which is lower than the world price. This policy thus corrects the consumption externality. For the producers, however, this case is different from the preceding one with good 1 as the exportable. As Alam (1988) and Casas (1991) point out, because domestic producers can choose between selling their outputs to the domestic market and selling them to the world markets, and because the import subsidy causes a drop in the domestic price of good 1, domestic firms prefer to sell their outputs to the world markets. The result is *two-way trade in an identical product.* If no transport costs exist, then the import subsidy has no effect on the production side of the economy, implying that it is equivalent to a consumption subsidy and is the first-best policy. Alternatively, an export subsidy on good 2 is the same as a production subsidy and is not effective in correcting the present consumption distortion. In the presence of an export subsidy, consumers will purchase good 2 from abroad.

It is common to assume that a trade subsidy is just a negative trade tax.[7] As I just showed, this is not correct. It is known that a tariff is regarded as a consumption tax plus a production subsidy. If an import subsidy can be considered as a negative tariff, it would be the same as a consumption subsidy plus a production tax. In the presence of an import subsidy, however, the firms would try to avoid the tax burden by selling their outputs abroad. As long as such sales to foreigners are not prohibited, two-way trade exists and an import subsidy has the effect of a consumption subsidy. Similarly, if an export subsidy can be regarded as a negative export tax, it is the same as a consumption tax plus a production subsidy. Under this policy consumers would try to avoid the consumption tax by buying directly from abroad, and two-way trade will exist.

The nonsymmetry between a trade tax and a trade subsidy is due to two factors: First, firms or consumers have an incentive to evade the taxing effect of a trade subsidy by selling to or buying from abroad; and second, the government does not prohibit such evasion.

So far I have compared the national welfare level under free trade in the presence of a distortion and a situation with a correcting policy. I now take a

---

6. In writing this and the following two paragraphs, I benefited from a correspondence with Murray C. Kemp and a conversation with Neil Bruce.

7. For example, Chacholiades (1978, p. 443) says that "since subsidies are merely negative taxes, what has been said in relation to export and import taxes necessarily holds for export and import subsidies as well."

slightly different approach under which I can get more results. Differentiate the social utility function to give

$$du = \mathbf{MU} \cdot d\mathbf{C}, \tag{10.7}$$

where $\mathbf{MU} = (u_1, \ldots, u_n)$. I then differentiate the trade account balance equation $\mathbf{p}^* \cdot \mathbf{C} = \mathbf{p}^* \cdot \mathbf{Q}$ to give

$$\mathbf{C} \cdot d\mathbf{p}^* + \mathbf{p}^* \cdot d\mathbf{C} = \mathbf{Q} \cdot d\mathbf{p}^* + \mathbf{p}^* \cdot d\mathbf{Q}. \tag{10.8}$$

For simplicity, ignore factor market distortions. This means that the production point is on the PPF of the economy, and the combination of different possible production points can be described by $\Gamma(\mathbf{Q}) = 0$. Differentiate this equation to give

$$\sum_{i=1}^{n} \Gamma_i d Q_i = 0. \tag{10.9}$$

Combine (10.8) and (10.9), substitute them into (10.7), and rearrange terms to give (Bhagwati et al., 1969)

$$du/\lambda = \sum_{i=1}^{n} \left\{ (u_i/\lambda - p_i^*)dC_i + (Q_i - C_i)dp_i^* + (p_i^* - \alpha\Gamma_i)dQ_i \right\}, \tag{10.10}$$

where $\lambda > 0$ is the marginal utility of income, and α is a positive constant. $\alpha\Gamma_i$ is interpreted as the marginal cost of sector i.

Condition (10.10) gives the effects of small changes in C_i, p_i^*, and Q_i on national welfare. To illustrate how this condition can be applied, consider again the present model with consumption distortion. Because the economy is a small open one, $dp_i^* = 0$ for all i. If producers are facing world prices, profit maximization and convex technology imply that at the production point, a world price line is tangent to the PPF, that is, $p_i^* = \alpha\Gamma_i$. On the consumption side, consumers equate u_i/λ to p_i^* for all goods except good 1. The presence of consumption externality for good 1 means that $\psi u_1/\lambda = p_1^*$, implying that $u_1/\lambda - p_1^* > 0$. Using this analysis, condition (10.10) reduces to

$$du = (u_1 - \lambda p_1^*)dC_1. \tag{10.10'}$$

As long as $u_1 > \lambda p_1^*$, a policy such as a consumption subsidy on good 1 that increases the consumption of the good without destroying the equality of other optimality conditions is beneficial. This immediately leads to the following result:

Result 10.1 In the presence of only one distortion, gradual reduction in the "degree" of the distortion brings successive welfare improvement until the distortion is removed.

In (10.10′), as long as $u_1 > \lambda p_1^*$, an increase in consumption subsidy in good 1, which in turn encourages the consumption of good 1, increases national welfare. I note further that assuming that the second-order condition holds, social utility reaches a maximum when $du = 0$, that is, $u_1 = \lambda p_1^*$. The optimal specific subsidy rate is $(1 - \psi)p_1^*$.

Condition (10.10) can also be used to analyze the effects of a trade tax or subsidy. I showed that a trade policy that corrects the inequality between DRS and FRT could be welfare worsening. The question is, does there always exist a welfare-improving trade policy in the presence of a consumption distortion? The answer is yes, and the proof comes again from condition (10.10′). Suppose that initially free trade prevails. At this point, $p_i^* = \alpha \Gamma_i$ for all i and $u_i = \lambda p_i^*$ for all $i = 2, \ldots, n$. Therefore a marginal change in utility is given by condition (10.10′). A small trade tax or subsidy will have second-order effects on production of all goods and consumption of all goods except good 1, but how it affects welfare depends on how it affects the economy's consumption of good 1. Thus a small export tax on good 1, which encourages the domestic consumption of the good, is welfare improving.[8]

The theory of optimal policy intervention in the presence of distortions is dual to the theory of noneconomic objectives. Suppose now that a market equilibrium of a competitive economy coincides with the optimal point of the planner's problem, that is, the economy is distortion free. The government wants to achieve a certain noneconomic objective such as a minimum production level of a sector that is higher than the production level in a competitive equilibrium. To achieve this objective the government must move the economy away from its competitive equilibrium by constraining the values of certain variables. This amounts to deliberately introducing distortions into the economy, and some of the optimality conditions are violated. The problem is to find the least costly way to achieve the noneconomic objective. By applying the principle of optimal policy intervention, the optimal (or least-costly) way is to "choose that policy intervention that creates the distortion affecting directly the constrained variable" (Bhagwati, 1971, p. 77; see also Bhagwati and Srinivasan, 1969).

10.5   Theory of Second Best and Piecemeal Policy Recommendations

In the previous section, it is assumed that it is costless to impose the policies that correct the distortions present in the economy. I now drop this assumption.

---

8. Bhagwati and Ramaswami (1963) and Johnson (1965) wonder whether there exists a welfare-improving tariff in the presence of a domestic distortion. Kemp and Negishi (1969) point out that a welfare-improving tariff can always be found. A similar result is in Meade (1955).

I again consider the above model with consumption externality. Denote the maximum social utility level (at the optimal point) by u^1 and the cost (in terms of a numeraire good) of implementing the consumption subsidy described by h^1. Thus the net national income under the "first-best" policy, evaluated using international prices, is $e(\mathbf{p}^*, u^1) - h^1$, where $e(\mathbf{p}^*, u)$ is the social expenditure function.

Suppose for the time being that the cost of implementing the "first-best" policy is prohibitive, that is, h^1 is sufficiently large. This implies that imposing such a policy (a consumption subsidy in the economy considered earlier) is never beneficial for the economy and the "first-best" policy is actually not the first-best. The second-best policy of the government, assuming for the time being zero cost of implementation, is then to maximize social utility subject to the usual constraints plus the existing distortion that is too costly to remove. In the present model, the planner's problem is described as follows:

$$\max_{\mathbf{C},\mathbf{Q},\mathbf{E}^*} u(\mathbf{C}) \quad \text{s. t.} \quad \mathbf{E}^* \geq \mathbf{C} - \mathbf{Q};$$

$$\Gamma(\mathbf{Q}) \leq 0;$$

$$\Theta^*(\mathbf{E}^*) \leq 0;$$

$$\frac{\psi u_1}{u_2} = \frac{\Gamma_1}{\Gamma_2}.$$

Note that for simplicity I ignore the factor markets, assuming that factors can be employed efficiently. The last constraint reflects the consumption externality so that consumers value the consumption of good 1 less than the society does. I define the following Lagrangean function

$$\mathcal{L} = u(\mathbf{C}) + \sum_i \phi_i (E_i^* + Q_i - C_i) - \alpha\Gamma(\mathbf{Q}) - \beta\Theta^*(\mathbf{E}^*) + \mu\left(\frac{\psi u_1}{u_2} - \frac{\Gamma_1}{\Gamma_2}\right).$$

The first-order conditions are

$$\frac{\partial \mathcal{L}}{\partial C_i} = u_i - \phi_i + \mu\psi \frac{u_2 u_{1i} - u_1 u_{2i}}{u_2^2} \leq 0 \tag{10.11a}$$

$$\frac{\partial \mathcal{L}}{\partial E_i^*} = \phi_i - \beta\Theta_i^* \leq 0 \tag{10.11b}$$

$$\frac{\partial \mathcal{L}}{\partial Q_i} = \phi_i - \alpha\Gamma_i - \mu\frac{\Gamma_2\Gamma_{1i} - \Gamma_1\Gamma_{2i}}{\Gamma_2^2} \leq 0. \tag{10.11c}$$

Let me define $Z_i \equiv (u_2 u_{1i} - u_1 u_{2i})/u_2^2$ and $Y_i \equiv (\Gamma_2\Gamma_{1i} - \Gamma_1\Gamma_{2i})/\Gamma_2^2$. For goods i and k that are consumed, produced and traded, these first-order conditions (with equality) are combined to give

$$\frac{\phi_i}{\phi_k} = \frac{\Theta_i^*}{\Theta_k^*} = \frac{u_i + \mu\psi Z_i}{u_k + \mu\psi Z_k} = \frac{\alpha\Gamma_i + \mu Y_i}{\alpha\Gamma_k + \mu Y_k}. \tag{10.12}$$

Condition (10.12) is identical to the optimality condition (10.2) if one of the following conditions holds

1. $\mu = 0$.

2. $Z_i/u_i = Z_k/u_k$ and $Y_i/\Gamma_i = Y_k/\Gamma_k$ for all goods i and k that are consumed and produced domestically.

Condition (1) can be ruled out because it would imply that the constraint $\psi u_1/u_2 = \Gamma_1/\Gamma_2$ is not binding (or is just binding). A case in which condition (2) holds is that $Z_i = Z_k = Y_i = Y_k = 0$. This implies that (a) u_1/u_2 is independent of the consumption of any good, and (b) Γ_1/Γ_2 is independent of the production level. One possibility for (a) to happen is that goods 1 and 2 must be perfect substitutes in consumption, but this violates the assumption that only good 1 has consumption externality. Similarly, (b) requires that goods 1 and 2 are perfect substitutes in production, that is, having the same production function. Another possibility for (a) to hold, as Lloyd (1973, 1974) points out, is that goods 1 and 2 as a group and all other goods as another group are separable in both consumption and production. In general, however, condition (2) is not satisfied.

Making use of the analysis, the following results can be obtained:

Result 10.2 If one of the optimality conditions cannot be satisfied, in general all other optimality conditions are no longer desirable in the second-best solution.

Result 10.3 It is not true that a situation with more optimality conditions satisfied is superior to a situation with less optimality conditions satisfied.

Result 10.4 In the presence of more than one distortion, a gradual reduction in the degree of one of the distortions does not necessarily imply a successive improvement in welfare. (Results 10.2 to 10.4 are due to Lipsey and Lancaster, 1956–1957.)

Result 10.5 Distortions cannot be ranked uniquely with each other (Bhagwati, 1971).

Results 10.1 to 10.5 have many applications in the theory of international trade.[9] For example, consider a small open economy with no domestic distortions. If the economy trades freely with the rest of the world, it can achieve the

---

9. Results 10.2 to 10.3 are negative results. For other developments in the theory of second best, see Negishi (1972) and Ng (1983).

highest utility level. Suppose, however, that some nonprohibitive trade taxes (negative for subsidies) are imposed. These taxes thus create policy imposed distortions.

If there is only one distortion due to a trade tax, then by Result 10.1, a gradual reduction in the magnitude of the tax rate is welfare improving. If, however, there are two or more trade taxes, then Results 10.3 and 10.4 imply that a gradual reduction in, or complete elimination of, any one tax rate while all other tax rates are held constant could lower welfare.

This example suggests that in the presence of more than one distortion in an economy, if all the distortions cannot be removed at the same time, then results 10.1 to 10.5 do not provide any recommendation of what policies the government should take to improve national welfare. Because of the negative implications of these results in general frameworks, there has been interest in finding conditions and policies under which the welfare of an economy can be improved despite the assumption that not all distortions can be eliminated at once. This is the idea of piecemeal policy recommendations.[10]

In Chapter 8, I examined two cases in which piecemeal welfare-improving policies exist. In the first case, there is a small open economy with no domestic distortions but trade taxes. I showed that if all the taxes cannot be removed at once, then a gradual uniform reduction in the tax rates is welfare improving until all the tax rates are zero. In another case in which the world welfare is concerned, some countries impose trade taxes (possibly nonuniform taxes) on the goods from other countries. I showed that if not all trade taxes imposed by all countries can be removed at the same time, then an expansion of an existing customs union (or the formation of a new customs union) can be mutually beneficial.

By making use of condition (10.10), one more piecemeal policy can be suggested. Consider again a small open economy with trade taxes but no domestic distortions. Because consumers and producers face the domestic prices, the marginal utilities of goods are proportional to the prices, that is, $u_i/\lambda = p_i$. Similarly, firms set marginal costs at the price levels, that is, $\alpha \Gamma_i = p_i$. Because the economy has no external monopoly power, $dp_i^* = 0$ for all i. Substitute these conditions into (10.10) and rearrange terms to give

$$du/\lambda = \sum_{i=1}^{n} \left[(p_i - p_i^*) dM_i \right],$$
(10.13)

---

10. See Woodland (1982, pp. 341–347) for an excellent survey of piecemeal trade policies. See also Hatta (1977a, 1977b) and Fukushima (1979) for the conditions under which a fall in the highest or a rise in the lowest tariff rate would improve the welfare of a small, tariff-ridden economy.

where $M_i \equiv C_i - Q_i$ is the import (negative for export) of good i. Note that $\sum_i (p_i - p_i^*) M_i$ is the trade tax revenue. Thus (10.13) states that if there is a shock when given fixed prices so that the tax revenue increases, then there is an improvement in welfare.

A stronger condition for a welfare-improving trade policy is that it causes an increase (respectively decrease) in the volumes of import or export of those goods that are subject to trade taxes (respectively subsidies). An alternative condition was derived by Bertrand and Vanek (1971). Let t_i be the ad valorem trade tax rate on the foreign price of good i, $p_i = (1 + t_i) p_i^*$. An alternative form of condition (10.13) is

$$\mathrm{d}u/\lambda = \sum_{i=1}^{n} t_i p_i^* \mathrm{d} M_i, \tag{10.13$'$}$$

Differentiating the balance-of-trade condition, $\mathbf{p}^* \cdot \mathbf{M} = 0$, and noting that foreign prices are fixed, I get $\mathbf{p}^* \cdot \mathrm{d}\mathbf{M} = 0$. Substitute this condition into (10.13$'$) to give

$$\mathrm{d}u/\lambda = \sum_{i \neq k} (t_i - t_k) p_i^* \mathrm{d} M_i. \tag{10.13$''$}$$

Let good k be the good with the highest tariff rate, that is, $t_k \geq t_i$ for all i with some inequalities. Condition (10.13$''$) states that small changes in trade taxes would be welfare improvement if the imports (respectively exports) of all goods other than good k decrease (respectively increase).

So far I have concentrated on the second-best policy, assuming that implementing the "first-best" policy is prohibitively costly. I now drop this assumption so that h^1 is not too large, and analyze whether the "first-best" policy should be given up. For simplicity, assume again that there is only one distortion, although this assumption is not crucial for the following result. This distortion cannot be eliminated in the planner's second-best problem. I denote the maximum utility level in the second-best problem by u^2, and let the cost of implementing the policies required to reach the second-best point in a market mechanism be h^2. Therefore the national income in the presence of the second-best policy, evaluated using international prices, is $e(\mathbf{p}^*, u^2) - h^2$.

Should the government choose the "first-best" policy or the second-best policy? Obviously, the answer depends on the magnitudes of $e(\mathbf{p}^*, u^1) - h^1$ and $e(\mathbf{p}^*, u^2) - h^2$: The second-best policy, instead of the "first-best" policy, should be adopted if and only if $e(\mathbf{p}^*, u^2) - h^2 > e(\mathbf{p}^*, u^1) - h^1$. By definition, $u^1 > u^2$. This implies that $e(\mathbf{p}^*, u^1) > e(\mathbf{p}^*, u^2)$. Therefore a necessary condition that the second-best policy is imposed is that $h^1 > h^2$; for example, h^1 is sufficiently large. There are, however, many cases in which the opposite condition exists: $h^2 > h^1$. The reason is that the second-best policy usually requires intervention in many markets, and there is no direct relationship between the distortions initially existing in the economy and the nature of intervention in each market (tax or subsidy). For example, in the present model with a consumption distortion in market 1, a consumption subsidy on this good is needed. If this subsidy is not to be imposed, how do we know whether a production or consumption tax or subsidy is needed in all markets other than market 1? To answer this question the whole system of the economy needs to be solved.

10.6   Immiserizing Growth

A country grows if one of its sectors experiences a technological progress or if its factor endowments expand. With more advanced technologies or more factors in the economy, the country's production possibility frontier (PPF) shifts out. This means that the original production point is still an element of the country's new production possibility set, and therefore it is supposed that the growth of the country would bring with it an increase in national welfare. Bhagwati (1968b, 1971) states the following result:

Result 10.6   For each kind of distortion, growth may be immiserizing.

Result 10.6 states that if distortions exist in an economy, growth may worsen national welfare. To see such a possibility, consider the following well-known examples in the literature.[11]

The Free Trade Case

Figure 10.2 shows the case of a large open economy that trades freely with the rest of the world.[12] $T^\alpha T^\alpha$ is its initial PPF, with the economy producing at point Q^α. Line P^α represents the world price line and the economy consumes at point C^α, yielding a social utility level of u^α. A growth of the economy, which may be due to a technological progress or an accumulation of factors,

---

11. Many examples of immiserizing growth have been presented in the literature, and it is not possible to go over all of them here. The reader who is interested in the possibility of immiserizing growth in the presence of factor market distortions can see, for example, Bhagwati (1968a, 1973), Batra and Pattanaik (1970), and Batra and Scully (1971).

12. Whether an economy can be harmed by its growth under free trade has long been a classical question. Edgeworth (1894) already notes the possibility that growth may cause a deterioration of the external terms of trade and a decrease in the welfare of an economy. Mill (1909) provides an analysis of such a possibility. This possibility became a point of focus again during the post-war dollar shortage debate (Hicks, 1953), and Johnson (1954, 1955) derives conditions under which growth can deteriorate the terms of trade of a country. Bhagwati (1958) derives the conditions for immiserizing growth and shows that these conditions do not require market instability. For a more recent treatment of immiserizing growth, see Kemp (1969, pp. 104–113); and Bhagwati and Srinivasan, (1983a, Chapter 25).

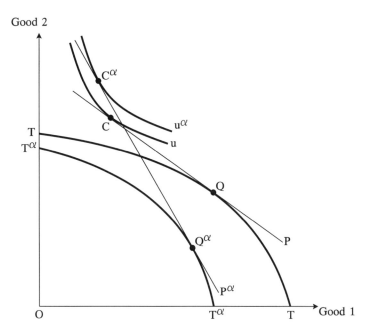

Figure 10.2

shifts the PPF out to TT. Suppose that the new world price line is given by P. The point where it touches the new PPF is the post-growth production point, Q. Through trade, the economy consumes at point C, yielding a social utility level of u. In the case shown, $u < u^\alpha$, illustrating an immiserizing growth.

A Tariff-Ridden Economy

Johnson (1967a) first notes that immiserizing growth can occur even if the economy is small. Suppose that an economy that has no external power is protected by a fixed, nonprohibitive tariff on its imported good 2. In Figure 10.3, $T^\alpha T^\alpha$ represents the economy's PPF before growth. The production point Q^α occurs at the point of tangency between the domestic price line P and the pre-growth PPF. The corresponding consumption point C^α lies on the world price line P^w and is a point of tangency between a social indifference curve and a domestic price line. This gives a pre-growth social utility level of u^α. A growth of the economy expands the PPF out to TT. With the world prices and the tariff rate unchanged, suppose that the production point shifts up to point Q. The corresponding consumption point is at C and the social utility level is u. In the case shown, the growth causes a drop in national welfare, $u < u^\alpha$.

These two cases seem to be quite different from each other, but they do share one important feature: the economies in both cases are distorted. In the first case, a large open economy adopts a free-trade policy. The fact that it has external monopoly power means that under free trade a foreign distortion

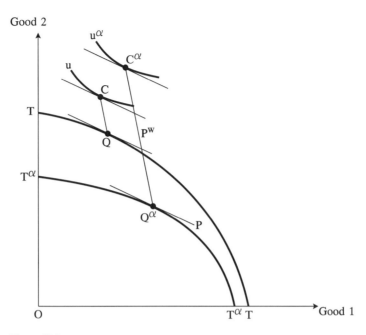

Figure 10.3

exists. In the second case, the optimal policy for the small open economy is free trade. The nonprohibitive tariff is a policy-imposed distortion. Because of the existence of a distortion in each of these two cases, immiserizing growth is possible. This illustrates Result 10.6.

Before deriving a general condition for immiserizing growth, the intuition behind these two cases is first given. Call the pre-growth situation α, and the post-growth situation β. Distinguish the pre-growth values of variables by a superscript α, while variables in situation β have no such superscripts. The welfare effect of growth is given by the difference between the utility levels of the economy before and after growth, that is, $u - u^{\alpha}$.

Because of the existence of a distortion, an economy does not reach its maximum utility level. Use a "tilde" to represent the maximum utility level of the economy under consideration. Thus $\tilde{u}^{\alpha}$ and $\tilde{u}$ are the maximum pre-growth and post-growth utility levels, respectively.

The welfare effect of growth is now given by

$$u - u^{\alpha} = (\tilde{u} - \tilde{u}^{\alpha}) + \left[(\tilde{u}^{\alpha} - u^{\alpha}) - (\tilde{u} - u)\right]. \tag{10.14}$$

Let me analyze the terms on the right-hand side of (10.14). Because growth represents an expansion of the production possibility set, the post-growth maximum utility level must be higher than (or at least as high as) the pre-growth maximum utility level. So $\tilde{u} > \tilde{u}^{\alpha}$. The term $\tilde{u}^{\alpha} - u^{\alpha}$ is the decrease in welfare due to the presence of distortions, and is called the pre-growth cost of distortions. Similarly, $\tilde{u} - u$ is the post-growth cost of distortions. Condition (10.14) thus states that growth is not immiserizing if the post-growth cost of distortions is not more than the pre-growth cost of distortions. A slightly stronger and obvious condition for a welfare-improving growth is that there are no distortions after the growth.

A more useful way of measuring the welfare effects of growth is to use the indirect trade utility (ITU) function of the economy, $V(\mathbf{p}, \mathbf{v}, b)$. Consider, for example, an increase in the endowment of factor v_j. The effect on the economy's welfare is obtained by totally differentiating the ITU function while keeping the endowments of all other factors constant, that is,

$$
\frac{dV}{dv_j} = \frac{\partial V}{\partial v_j} + \sum_i \left(\frac{\partial V}{\partial p_i} \frac{\partial p_i}{\partial v_j} \right) + \frac{\partial V}{\partial b} \frac{\partial b}{\partial v_j}
$$

$$
= \lambda \left\{ w_j + \sum_i \left(E_i \frac{\partial p_i}{\partial v_j} \right) + \frac{\partial b}{\partial v_j} \right\}, \tag{10.15}
$$

where E_i is the export level of good i. In condition (10.15), dV/dv_j is proportional to the sum of the terms inside the braces, which is interpreted as the shadow price of factor j. Thus growth due to an accumulation of a factor is immiserizing if and only if its shadow price is negative.

Condition (10.15) can now be applied in several cases. First, consider a small open economy under free trade. I showed that free trade is the economy's optimal policy and thus the economy is distortion free. Free trade and given world prices mean that $\partial p_i / \partial v_j = 0$ for all i. I further assume that the transfer b is constant. (For example, it is zero under free trade and no international transfer or factor movement.) The welfare effect of an accumulation of factor j is

$$
\frac{dV}{dv_j} = \lambda w_j > 0,
$$

which means that growth must be beneficial and the welfare effect is proportional to the market price of the factor. This result is not surprising because free trade is the economy's first-best policy.

Now consider the free-trade case of immiserizing growth. Because this is a large open economy, $\partial p_i / \partial v_j \neq 0$, and because no international transfer exists, $\partial b / \partial v_j = 0$. Condition (10.15) then reduces to

$$
\frac{dV}{dv_j} = \lambda \left\{ w_j + \sum_i \left(E_i \frac{\partial p_i}{\partial v_j} \right) \right\}. \tag{10.16}
$$

In (10.16), $\sum_i E_i (\partial p_i / \partial v_j)$ is the terms-of-trade gain (TG) due to an increase in factor j (see Chapter 8). This term is positive if there is an improvement in the terms of trade (TOT). Condition (10.16) then states that in this case, growth is not immiserizing if there is an improvement in the TOT. An alternative interpretation of this condition is that the source (a necessary condition) for an immiserizing growth is a deterioration of the TOT.[13]

Now consider the Johnson case of a tariff-ridden, small open economy. The tariff revenue of the economy is $b = (\mathbf{p} - \mathbf{p}^*) \cdot \mathbf{M}$. Under fixed world prices and tariffs, domestic prices are independent of factor accumulation, that is, $\partial p_i / \partial v_j = 0$ for all i. Condition (10.15) then reduces to

$$\frac{dV}{dv_j} = \lambda \left\{ w_j + \frac{\partial b}{\partial v_j} \right\} = \lambda \left\{ w_j + \sum_i (p_i - p_i^*) \frac{\partial M_i}{\partial v_j} \right\}. \tag{10.17}$$

Condition (10.17) states that an increase in the endowment of factor j is not immiserizing if the tariff revenue does not fall.

Consider now a 2×2 model and refer to Figure 10.3. Line $C^\alpha Q^\alpha$ defines the pre-growth trade triangle and line CQ defines the post-growth trade triangle. In the case shown in the diagram, growth shrinks the trade triangle and tariff revenue. Further conditions for immiserizing growth can be obtained from the diagram. Suppose for illustration that growth is due to capital accumulation. Because domestic prices are fixed, the line joining point Q and Q^α is the Rybczynski line for capital. In the case shown, good 2 is capital intensive so that capital accumulation encourages the production of good 2 but discourages that of good 1. In the absence of inferior goods, the consumption point C must give a lower utility level than the pre-growth utility level if and only if point Q is on the left-hand side of the world price line P^w, or if and only if the world price line is steeper than the Rybczynski line. This is the case shown in the diagram. I explained in Chapter 2 that the slope of the Rybczynski line for capital is equal to

$$\left. \frac{dQ_2}{dQ_1} \right|_{R_K} = -\frac{Q_2/L_2}{Q_1/L_1}.$$

Thus immiserizing growth occurs if and only if

$$p^* > \frac{Q_2/L_2}{Q_1/L_1}. \tag{10.18}$$

Because good 2 is the imported good, $p_2 = p_2^*(1 + t)$, where t is the given ad valorem tariff rate. So $p^* = p(1 + t)$. Substitute this condition into (10.18) and rearrange terms to give a necessary and sufficient condition for immiserizing growth in the Johnson case (Martin, 1977):

$$1 + t > \frac{\theta_{L1}}{\theta_{L2}}, \tag{10.18'}$$

---

13. For more conditions for immiserizing growth in the free-trade case, see Bhagwati and Srinivasan (1983a, pp. 256–258).

where θ_{Li} is the labor share in sector i, that is, good 2 is capital intensive.[14]

Although in the Johnson case trade is restricted by given tariffs, condition (10.15) can be used to analyze the cases in which trade is restricted by quotas. Suppose that the domestic government can capture the quota premia through quota auction, implying that the international transfer is equal to $b = \sum_i (p_i - p_i^*) M_i$. Note that if the trading of a good, which is exported or imported, is not subject to any quantitative restriction, its domestic price is the same as its foreign price. If the prevailing quotas are fixed, the effect of a factor accumulation on the total quota premium is equal to

$$\frac{\partial b}{\partial v_j} = \sum_i M_i \frac{\partial p_i}{\partial v_j}. \tag{10.19}$$

Condition (10.19) is applicable whether export or import quotas (or a combination) exist, or whether some or all of the trading goods are subject to the quantitative restrictions; for example, if good k is not subject to any trade restrictions, $p_k = p_k^*$ and $\partial p_k / \partial v_j = 0$. Substituting (10.19) into (10.15) and noting that $E_i + M_i = 0$ for all i,

$$\frac{dV}{dv_j} = \lambda w_j,$$

which means that an increase in the endowment of any factor under given quotas must be welfare enhancing (Alam, 1981; Miyagiwa, 1993).

Several remarks about this result can be made. Although Alam (1981) and Miyagiwa (1993) prove it for a two-good model, it in fact holds no matter how many trading goods the model has, or how many goods are subject to quantitative restrictions. Second, this result holds even if factors are sector specific because specific-factors models are just special cases of the present more general model. Third, this result is true even if nontraded goods are present. (The quota for a nontraded good is zero.) Fourth, this result is no longer true if the government does not get the quota premia, that is, if the quotas are voluntary export restraints. Fifth, this result is not true if trade is restricted by a combination of tariffs and quotas. Sixth, this result may or may not be true if the economy is subject to variable returns to scale (Chao and Yu, 1991).[15]

The theory of immiserizing growth has several applications. First, I note that natural trade represents an expansion of the consumption possibility frontier

---

14. Bertrand and Flatters (1971) also derive conditions for immiserizing growth in the Johnson case.

15. Chao and Yu (1991) show that under variable returns to scale (VRS) and a fixed import quota, growth due to technological progress is not immiserizing if the sector that grows is subject to not a smaller degree of VRS than the other sector, but that growth can be immiserizing if the growing sector is subject to a smaller degree of VRS.

of the economy. This is similar to an expansion of the production possibility frontier of a closed economy due to growth. Thus I can apply the analysis to conclude that in the absence of domestic distortions, natural trade is better than no trade. This is the result I obtained in Chapter 8.

Second, growth of the economy due to factor accumulation is opposite to withdrawal of factors from the economy. Directly unproductive, profit-seeking (DUP) activities such as lobbying use up some of the resources available in the economy. If the DUP activities do not directly contribute to national welfare, then their effects can be analyzed by reversing the analysis of the theory of immiserizing growth. For example, in the presence of distortions, DUP activities may be welfare improving. This result applies equally to emigration of factors.

As mentioned earlier, growth due to the accumulation of a factor is immiserizing if and only if the shadow price of the factor is negative. Thus it is now not surprising to see that DUP activities may be welfare improving if they intensively use a factor whose shadow price is negative. (For more details, see Bhagwati and Srinivasan, 1983a, Chapters 25 and 30.)

10.7   External Economies of Scale

In this section, I examine a framework characterized by external economies of scale and apply the theory of distortions and the principle of optimal policy intervention to analyze the welfare effects of policies. The features of the present model are described in Chapter 5, and the notation introduced in that chapter is followed here.

10.7.1   Employment Subsidy in a General Model

I begin with the general model in which the production function of sector i, $i = 1, \ldots, n$, is given by

$$Q_i = F_i(\mathbf{v}_i, \mathbf{Z}), \tag{10.20}$$

where Q_i is the sectoral output level, $\mathbf{v}_i$ is the input vector, and $\mathbf{Z}$ represents the external effects. The production function is differentiable in all arguments, and is concave and linearly homogeneous in all inputs represented by $\mathbf{v}_i$. Firms treat $\mathbf{Z}$ as constant, behaving competitively.

I begin with a closed economy. To a firm, the *private marginal product* (PMP) of the jth factor is equal to

$$PMP_{ij} = \frac{\partial F_i}{\partial v_{ij}}, \tag{10.21}$$

which is evaluated when $\mathbf{Z}$ is taken as fixed.

The *social marginal product* (SMP) of factor j in sector i, on the other hand, is equal to the total impact of a marginal unit of the factor on the whole sector's output, that is,

$$SMP_{ij} = \frac{\partial F_i}{\partial v_{ij}} + \sum_h \left(\frac{\partial F_i}{\partial Z_h} \frac{\partial Z_h}{\partial v_{ij}} \right). \tag{10.22}$$

Distortion in the present framework is due to the ignorance of the external effects by the firms. A comparison of conditions (10.21) and (10.22) reveals the consequence of distortion: a gap between social marginal product of a factor and its private marginal product. Applying the principle of optimal policy intervention explained earlier, the first-best policy is to impose a specific subsidy of s_{ij} on the employment of factor j in sector i, where s_{ij} is given by

$$s_{ij} = p_i \sum_h \left(\frac{\partial F_i}{\partial Z_h} \frac{\partial Z_h}{\partial v_{ij}} \right), \tag{10.23}$$

where the values of all variables, including the commodity price p_i, are equilibrium values. In the presence of the subsidy, the effective price of the jth factor in sector i is

$$w_j = p_i \frac{\partial F_i}{\partial v_{ij}} + s_{ij}$$

$$= p_i \left[\frac{\partial F_i}{\partial v_{ij}} + \sum_h \left(\frac{\partial F_i}{\partial Z_h} \frac{\partial Z_h}{\partial v_{ij}} \right) \right]. \tag{10.24}$$

In condition (10.24), the first term on the right-hand side comes from the private marginal product of the factor and is the factor price paid by the firms, and the second term represents the subsidy. A comparison of conditions (10.22) and (10.24) reveals the role of the subsidy: It ensures that each factor receives according to its social marginal product, not its private marginal product.

10.7.2   Production Subsidy with Output-Generated Externality

In the rest of this chapter, I focus on the special case in which the external effects are output-generated. This will allow me to obtain more intuition about optimal policy intervention and to get more results. Assume that the production function of sector i is given by

$$Q_i = F_i(\mathbf{v}_i, Q_i)$$

$$= h_i(Q_i) \widetilde{F}_i(\mathbf{v}_i),$$

and as before, assume that the production function is homothetic in factor inputs. As explained in Chapter 5, the social marginal product of factor j in sector i is equal to

$$SMP_{ij} = \frac{h_i(Q_i)}{1 - \varepsilon_i} \frac{\partial \widetilde{F}_i}{\partial v_{ij}}, \qquad (10.25)$$

where $\varepsilon_i \in (-\infty, 1)$ is the rate of variable returns to scale. Following the analysis in the previous section, an employment subsidy is needed to encourage firms to employ factors up to the point at which factors are paid according to their social marginal products. Because the production function is homothetic, consider an employment subsidy of $s_i p_i h_i (\partial \widetilde{F}_i / \partial v_{ij})$, where

$$s_i = \frac{\varepsilon_i}{1 - \varepsilon_i}. \qquad (10.26)$$

Note that the rate s_i is only sector specific but not factor specific. This means that all factors in sector i receive the same subsidy rate s_i.

In the presence of the subsidy given by (10.26), the reward of factor j in sector i is equal to

$$w_j = \left[1 + s_i\right] p_i h_i(Q_i) \frac{\partial \widetilde{F}_i}{\partial v_{ij}}$$

$$= \frac{p_i h_i(Q_i)}{1 - \varepsilon_i} \frac{\partial \widetilde{F}_i}{\partial v_{ij}}. \qquad (10.27)$$

In condition (10.27), $p_i h_i(Q_i) \left[\partial \widetilde{F}_i / \partial v_{ij}\right]$ is what one unit of factor j receives from firms, and the rest of its income comes from the government. This condition and condition (10.25) imply that the factor receives the value of its social marginal product.

Because all factors in a sector receive the same subsidy rate, this policy is equivalent to a production subsidy policy. Thus instead of the employment subsidy, a production subsidy of ad valorem rate of s_i can be given to the firms in sector i. With the subsidy, the price faced by the firms, which is called the producer's price, p_i^p, is equal to

$$p_i^p = (1 + s_i) p_i = \frac{p_i}{1 - \varepsilon_i}, \qquad (10.28)$$

where p_i is the consumer's price. Firms make production decision based on p_i^p, not on p_i. Because firms consider only the private marginal product of factors, they pay factors according to the value of their private marginal product evaluated using the producer's price, meaning that the reward of factor j is

$$w_j = p_i^p PMP_{ij} = \frac{p_i h_i(Q_i)}{1 - \varepsilon_i} \frac{\partial \widetilde{F}_i}{\partial v_{ij}},$$

which is the same as the one given by (10.27).

Using the producer's prices, it is easy to determine the effects of the policy on production. For simplicity, consider a two-factor, two-sector framework. Recall that the marginal rate of transformation is related to producer's price ratio in the following way

$$\frac{dQ_2}{dQ_1} = -\frac{1 - \varepsilon_1}{1 - \varepsilon_2} \frac{p_1^p}{p_2^p}. \tag{10.29}$$

Condition (10.29) is derived in Chapter 5 except that prices are replaced by producer's prices. Using the definition of p_i^p, condition (10.29) reduces to

$$\frac{dQ_2}{dQ_1} = -\frac{p_1}{p_2}. \tag{10.29'}$$

Condition (10.29′) implies that with the subsidies, a price line is tangent to the PPF at the production point.

The implications of this policy for a closed economy are illustrated in Figure 10.4. Without loss of generality, I assume that $\varepsilon_1 > \varepsilon_2$. TT is the PPF of the economy, and in the absence of any policy intervention, the autarkic equilibrium is at point A. The price line P^a represents the autarkic price ratio. To improve national welfare, the government imposes the subsidies as given by (10.26). Point B depicts the optimal point at which the social indifference curve of a level of u^b is tangent to the PPF. The price line P represents the price ratio faced by consumers while the price line P^p represents that faced by producers. The present social utility level is higher than that in the absence of any policy intervention, $u^b > u^a$.

Some remarks about this result can be made. First, the optimal point shown in Figure 10.4 occurs at a concave portion of the PPF. This is not necessarily true. Figure 10.5 shows an economy in which both sectors are subject to strong increasing returns to scale so that the entire PPF is convex to the origin. Appropriate subsidies will shift the production point from the autarkic point A to the optimal point B.

The second remark is that condition (10.29′) is only a necessary condition for optimality, not a sufficient one. If firms adjust their outputs in a Marshallian way as described in Chapter 5, (10.29′) does give at least a local maximum. Consider Figure 10.6. Point A is the autarkic point, and at points D, B, and C condition (10.29′) is satisfied. The difference between these three points is that point C represents the global maximum, point B is a local maximum, and point D is a local minimum.[16] If in the presence of the subsidies the production point shifts from point A to point B (respectively point D), then there is an

---

16. There is at least one local minimum between points B and C. I ignore it because it is not related to the present analysis.

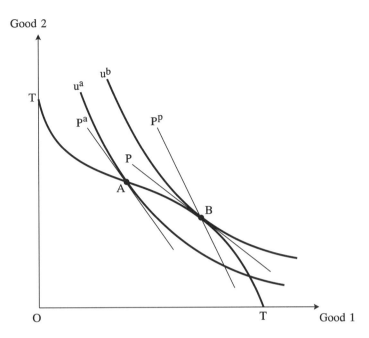

Figure 10.4

improvement (respectively a deterioration) in national welfare. At which of these two points would the economy end up?

If firms adjust their outputs according to the rules suggested by Mayer (1974c), Chang (1981), and Ide and Takayama (1991, 1993), then the answer is point B. By lowering the supply price faced by the firms in a sector, a production subsidy encourages these firms to expand. Because by assumption $\varepsilon_1 > \varepsilon_2$, firms in sector 1 receive relatively more subsidy than firms in sector 2, and thus have greater incentives to expand. So the production point shifts from the no-intervention point A to the right and down until point B is reached. National welfare reaches a higher level.

The analysis implies that the production point will shift to the first local maximum. There is, however, no guarantee that the global maximum is reached unless the first local maximum happens to be the global maximum, as in the case illustrated in Figure 10.4. To determine the global maximum, much more information is needed.

The third remark is that the adjustment to the first local maximum does not depend on whether the price-output responses are normal or perverse. The autarkic equilibrium is required to be Marshallian stable. Figure 10.7 shows two cases. In panel (a), the price-output responses are normal because the supply-price schedule is positively sloped, but in panel (b), the price-output responses

464   Chapter 10

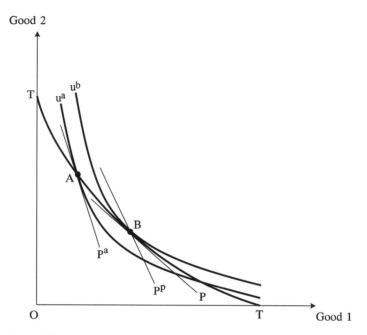

Figure 10.5

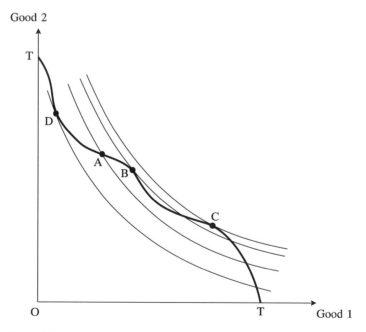

Figure 10.6

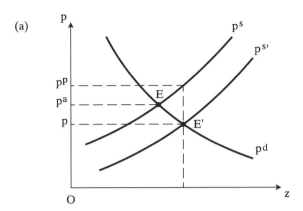

(a)

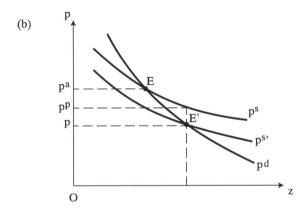

(b)

Figure 10.7

are perverse. In both cases, however, the autarkic equilibria are Marshallian stable.

I now determine the effects of the subsidy program on output levels using Figure 10.7. By condition (10.28), the producer price ratio is related to the consumer price ratio in the following way:

$$p^p \equiv \frac{p_1^p}{p_2^p} = \frac{1 - \varepsilon_2}{1 - \varepsilon_1} \frac{p_1}{p_2} = \frac{1 - \varepsilon_2}{1 - \varepsilon_1} p. \tag{10.30}$$

Because by assumption $\varepsilon_1 > \varepsilon_2$, condition (10.30) implies that $p < p^p$. In both panels of Figure 10.7, which shows the consumer price ratio, schedule p^s shifts down to $p^{s\prime}$ due to the subsidy policy so that the latter schedule describes the value of p that corresponds to p^p as given by (10.30). The intersection between schedules $p^{s\prime}$ and p^d (the demand price) depicts the equilibrium point E'. In both cases, there is an increase in the output of good 1.

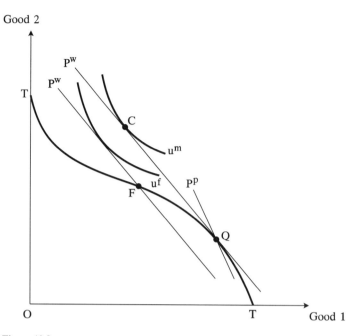

Figure 10.8

10.7.3   Optimal Policy for a Small Open Economy

I now consider a small open economy that trades freely under given world relative price of good 1, p^w. In Figure 10.8, production of the economy is depicted by point F. Through export of good 1 and import of good 2, the economy reaches a social utility level of u^f. Production subsidies that are given by (10.26) shift the production point to Q at which a world price line $\mathrm{P^w}$ is tangent to the PPF. $\mathrm{P^p}$ denotes the producer's price line. Foreign trade allows the economy to consume at point C, the point of tangency between the world price line and a social indifference curve. As a result, the economy reaches a utility level of u^m. As explained, imposing these production subsidies is the first-best policy.

In the case shown in Figure 10.8, the economy is diversified in production under free trade. Consider an economy with sufficiently strong increasing returns in both sectors so that the supply-price schedule is downward sloping. See panel (b) of Figure 10.7. If free trade under given world prices is now allowed, the demand-price schedule becomes a horizontal line corresponding to the world price ratio, p^w. The production pattern depends on the values of p^a and p^w. Consider first the case in which $p^w < p^a$. According to the adjustment mechanism described, firms in sector 1 will experience a loss as free trade is allowed, and will lower their production until the economy is completely specialized in good 2. This case is shown in Figure 10.9. Point A is the autarkic

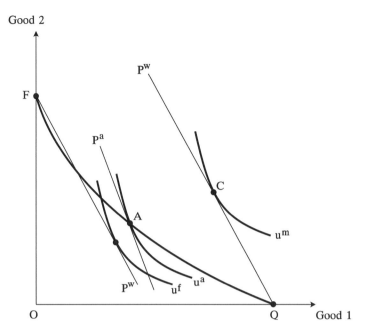

Figure 10.9

equilibrium point with a corresponding social utility level of u^a. Point F is the free-trade production point and P^w is a world price line. In the case shown, free trade hurts the economy, that is, the free-trade utility level u^f is less than u^a. (Of course, welfare improvement under free trade is possible. The reader can modify the diagram to show a gainful trade.)

As explained, the optimal policy is a production subsidy. Assuming that the government imposes a production subsidy at the time free trade is allowed, and the rate of the subsidy needed is slightly greater than $p^a - p^w$.[17] Firms in sector 1 are induced to produce more until the economy is completely specialized in good 1. This is the production point Q in Figure 10.9. The resulting utility level is the optimal one, u^m.

Consider now the second possibility that the world relative price of good 1 is greater than the autarkic relative price, that is, $p^w > p^a$. In this case, the economy will be completely specialized in good 1 even without any government intervention. This production pattern is the optimal one for the economy and no government intervention is needed.

_____

17. In fact, the government can lower the subsidy as more of good 1 is produced because the supply price of good 1 falls with its output. Specifically, denote the supply price of good 1 at a certain level of good 1 by p^s. If $p^s < p^w$, no production subsidy is needed because firms in good 1 are willing to expand their outputs even in the absence of any policy intervention. If $p^s > p^w$, a production subsidy of a specific rate slightly greater than $p^s - p^w$ is needed to encourage production of good 1.

10.8   Monopolistic Competition and Differentiated Products

I now turn to monopolistic competition and differentiated products. The model used here is the one introduced in Chapter 6, but for simplicity, I consider only the love of variety approach.

In the presence of monopolistic competition, one obvious distortion in the economy is the inefficient production of each of the firms. A firm equates the marginal cost to marginal revenue, and sets a price higher than the marginal cost. Thus some sort of production subsidy can be suggested for improving national welfare. At the same time, the number of varieties yields utility to consumers. Because the number of varieties is determined endogenously, it is not clear whether the equilibrium number of varieties is the optimal one from the economy's point of view. As a result, it is not immediately obvious what kind of policies is needed to achieve the optimal point for the economy.

The approach taken in this section is to first consider a planner's problem in which a planner is allowed to choose the optimal plant size of each firm and the optimal number of varieties. I then compare this planner's problem with a market equilibrium as analyzed in Chapter 6 in order to determine the policies for the government.

10.8.1   A Planner's Problem

I use the framework analyzed in Chapter 6. There are two factors, labor and capital, and two sectors labeled 1 and 2. Sector 1 consists of differentiated goods while good 2 is a homogeneous good. For simplicity, sector 1 is assumed to be capital intensive. There are m consumers in the economy, which is closed.

The first thing to be decided is the appropriate function that can be used to measure national welfare. Under the love of variety approach, all consumers have the same preferences that are described by the following utility function $u(D_1, D_2)$, where D_i is the demand for good i. D_1 is a subutility function of the consumption of the differentiated products. Under the Spencer, Dixit, and Stiglitz (S-D-S) approach, all goods are symmetric on the production and consumption sides, and the subutility function is assumed to be of the CES type, that is,

$$D_1 = \left(n d_1^\beta\right)^{1/\beta} = n^{1/\beta} d_1, \tag{10.31}$$

where n is the number of varieties, d_1 is the consumption of each type of variety, and $\beta = (1 - 1/\sigma)$, $\sigma > 1$. I showed that if the number of varieties is large, the elasticity of market demand, η, is equal to σ, that is, $\eta = \sigma$. Denote the marginal utility of good i by u_i, $i = 1, 2$.

Because all consumers are assumed to have the same income and they face the same prices, they must choose the same bundle of consumption goods.

Thus they have the same utility level, and such a level is a good measure of the national welfare.

It is assumed that the technology of the firms in sector 1 is homothetic and exhibits increasing returns to scale. Following the notation in Chapter 6, I denote the total cost of producing each variety of good 1 by $\gamma(q_1)\bar{c}_1(w, r)$, where q_1 is the output of each firm in sector 1, and w and r are the wage and rental rates, respectively. Function $\bar{c}_1(w, r)$, which looks like a unit cost function but is not, is continuously differentiable, concave, and linearly homogeneous in factor prices. Define $\varepsilon_\gamma \equiv \gamma' q_1/\gamma$ as the elasticity of $\gamma(q_1)$. To guarantee a decreasing average cost curve, assume that ε_γ is less than unity. Define $Z \equiv n\gamma(q_1)$. Sector 2 is competitive with constant-returns technology. Define Q_2 as the output of the sector.

I explained in Chapter 6 that the analysis about the production side of the economy can be simplified by focusing first on the *virtual system* given in terms of Z and Q_2. It was shown that the virtual system behaves like a neoclassical framework. I thus denote the virtual production possibility set (PPS) by $\tilde{\Gamma}(n\gamma(q_1), Q_2) \leq 0$, which gives all feasible combinations of Z and Q_2. The virtual PPS of the present economy is convex. I showed that a competitive production equilibrium occurs at a point of tangency between the virtual PPS and a line with a slope of $-p_z$. Denote the partial derivatives of $\tilde{\Gamma}(n\gamma(q_1), Q_2)$ by $\tilde{\Gamma}_1$ and $\tilde{\Gamma}_2$.

Market clearing is described by the following conditions:

$$d_1 = q_1/m \tag{10.32a}$$

$$D_2 = Q_2/m. \tag{10.32b}$$

Using conditions (10.31) and (10.32), the utility function of a representative consumer can be written as $u(n^{\sigma/(\sigma-1)}q_1/m, Q_2/m)$. The planner's problem is to maximize this utility function subject to the resource constraint: $\tilde{\Gamma}(n\gamma(q_1), Q_2) \leq 0$. Define the following Lagrangean function:

$$\mathcal{L} = u(n^{\sigma/(\sigma-1)}q_1/m, Q_2/m) - \phi\tilde{\Gamma}(n\gamma(q_1), Q_2),$$

where ϕ is the Lagrangean multiplier. Assuming an interior solution, the first-order conditions with respect to q_1, n and Q_2 are

$$\frac{\partial \mathcal{L}}{\partial q_1} = \frac{u_1 n^{\sigma/(\sigma-1)}}{m} - \phi\tilde{\Gamma}_1\gamma' n = 0 \tag{10.33a}$$

$$\frac{\partial \mathcal{L}}{\partial n} = \frac{u_1 \sigma n^{1/(\sigma-1)}q_1}{m(\sigma-1)} - \phi\tilde{\Gamma}_1\gamma = 0 \tag{10.33b}$$

$$\frac{\partial \mathcal{L}}{\partial Q_2} = \frac{u_2}{m} - \phi\tilde{\Gamma}_2 = 0. \tag{10.33c}$$

These conditions can be simplified as follows. Divide (10.33a) by (10.33b) and rearrange terms to give

$$1 - \frac{1}{\sigma} = \frac{\gamma' q_1}{\gamma}. \tag{10.34}$$

Similarly, divide (10.33b) by (10.33c) to give

$$\frac{\sigma}{\sigma-1}\frac{u_1}{u_2}q_1 n^{1/(\sigma-1)} = \frac{\tilde{\Gamma}_1}{\tilde{\Gamma}_2}\gamma. \tag{10.35}$$

Conditions (10.34) and (10.35) are two necessary conditions for optimal allocation of resources and efficient production. Assume that the government can pick the global maximum at which conditions (10.34) and (10.35) are satisfied.

10.8.2   Optimal Subsidy

Suppose that the government cannot directly control resource allocation. In this case, are there any policies, such as taxes or subsidies, that the government can use to bring the economy to the planner's optimal point in a market equilibrium? Note that in the present framework, production decisions of the firms consist of choosing the output level and (indirectly) the number of varieties. In the absence of government interventions, it is possible that in a market equilibrium the output level of a differentiated product and the number of varieties are suboptimal. For this reason, two necessary conditions for optimality are needed.

It is well known that a firm with monopoly power tends to underproduce and overcharge. A production subsidy is effective in inducing the monopolistic firm to increase its output. Therefore in the present framework, the policy that immediately comes to one's mind is a production subsidy on the firms in the differentiated-product sector. Such a policy can induce the firms to produce more. Because each firm earns zero profit in the long run, however, with free entry and exit in the sector, a production subsidy may lead to more or less varieties produced. It is not clear what the appropriate production subsidy is.

I now suggest a subsidy that can lead the economy to an equilibrium the same as the one discussed in the planner's problem. Suppose that the government gives a subsidy to each firm in sector 1 equal to $\gamma(q_1)s$ where the value of s is to be derived later. With the subsidy, the profit of a firm in that sector is

$$\pi = pq_1 - \gamma(q_1)\big[\bar{c}_1(w, r) - s\big],$$

where $p = p(q_1)$ is the inverse demand function. The firm chooses a variety that is currently not produced by other firms, and an output of the variety that will maximize its profit. Taking s and factor prices as given, its first-order condition with respect to output is

$$p + p'q_1 = p\left(1 - \frac{1}{\eta}\right) = \gamma'(q_1)\left[\bar{c}_1(w, r) - s\right], \tag{10.36}$$

where η is elasticity of market demand for the firm's output. Free entry and exit implies that in equilibrium the profit of a firm is zero, that is,

$$pq_1 = \gamma(q_1)\left[\bar{c}_1(w, r) - s\right]. \tag{10.37}$$

Substitute (10.37) into (10.36) to give

$$1 - \frac{1}{\eta} = \frac{\gamma'(q_1)q_1}{\gamma(q_1)}. \tag{10.38}$$

It is shown in Chapter 6 that if there is a large number of varieties, the elasticity of market demand is equal to σ. Thus condition (10.38) is the same as one of the necessary conditions, (10.34), in the planner's problem.

The intuition behind the result can be explained as follows. Because $\eta = \sigma$, condition (10.34) derived in the planner's problem is the same as the first-order condition of a firm even in the absence of any government intervention (see Chapter 6). This condition then implies the same output level of each variety both in the planner's problem and in a market equilibrium in the presence of the subsidy.

I now explain how the government chooses the value of s in order to satisfy the second necessary condition. Recall that a line of slope $-p_z$ is tangent to the virtual PPS at the virtual production point. Thus $p_z = \tilde{\Gamma}_1/\tilde{\Gamma}_2$, and condition (10.35) can be written in an alternative way:

$$\frac{\sigma}{\sigma - 1}\frac{u_1}{u_2}q_1 n^{1/(\sigma-1)} = p_z \gamma. \tag{10.35'}$$

In equilibrium, the consumers choose the consumption bundle to equate the marginal rate of substitution to the effective price ratio, that is,

$$\frac{u_1}{u_2} = \bar{p} = \frac{p}{n^{1/(\sigma-1)}}. \tag{10.39}$$

Substitute (10.39) into (10.35') to give

$$\frac{\sigma}{\sigma - 1}\frac{p}{n^{1/(\sigma-1)}}q_1 n^{1/(\sigma-1)} = p_z \gamma,$$

or, after simplifying the terms,

$$p = \frac{\sigma - 1}{\sigma}\frac{p_z \gamma}{q_1}. \tag{10.35''}$$

Substituting (10.38) into (10.35'') and making use of the definition that $p_z = \bar{c}_1(w, r)$, I get

$$p = \gamma'(q_1)\bar{c}_1(w, r). \tag{10.40}$$

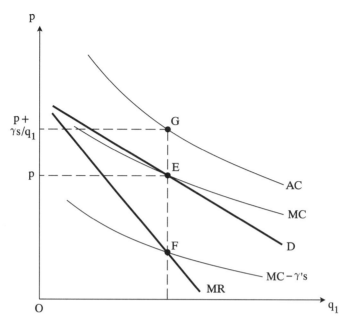

Figure 10.10

Condition (10.40) is now the second condition for an optimal market equilibrium. It has a very nice interpretation. It states that at the optimal point, the price of a variety is equal to the marginal cost, $\gamma'(q_1)\bar{c}_1(w, r)$. This means that at the optimal point, the firm produces as if it is competitive.

The remaining issue is what subsidy the government needs in order to satisfy condition (10.40). To address this issue, I refer back to the firm's first-order condition given by (10.36). By comparing this condition and (10.40), the optimal value of s is seen as

$$s = -\frac{p'q_1}{\gamma'} = \frac{p}{\gamma'\sigma}. \tag{10.41}$$

Using condition (10.41), the amount of subsidy the government gives to a representative firm in sector 1 is equal to $\gamma s = p\gamma/(\gamma'\sigma)$.

The optimal policy and the resulting equilibrium can be illustrated in Figure 10.10. Schedule D is the demand curve for the variety of a representative firm. Point E is the equilibrium point at which the marginal cost curve, MC, cuts the demand curve. In the presence of the above subsidy, the perceived marginal cost curve for the firm is the lower one labeled MC$-\gamma'$s. The firm chooses the production point at which this curve cuts the marginal revenue curve MR. Point E is below the average cost curve labeled AC. The gap between the price and the average cost is the per unit subsidy equal to $\gamma s/q_1$. With the subsidy, the firm makes zero profit.

The economy considered above is a closed one. I now turn to an open economy. As I did in the preceding section, I assume that the present economy is a small one that cannot influence the price levels in the foreign country it is trading with.

It is easy to conjecture that without external monopoly power to affect foreign prices, the present economy will have no incentive to restrict trade and so the subsidy policy described above remains the first-best policy. This conjecture, however, is not true because there is a big difference between the present economy and the economy with external effects analyzed in the preceding section. Even though the price levels in the foreign country are fixed, the firms in the differentiated product sector in the home country and those in the foreign country that sell their products to the home country do have monopoly power. When the home firms are competing not only with the foreign firms but also with each other, they fail to capture the monopoly rent that they will be able to get should they act jointly. This calls for government trade intervention in addition to what was described above.

The government trade intervention can be imposed on two fronts. First, the government can limit the inflow of foreign products with tariffs (Venables, 1982; Flam and Helpman, 1987a; Gros, 1987). A tariff raises the prices of foreign products in the domestic market. This helps the domestic firms in competing with foreign firms and improves the external terms of trade of the economy.

On the other side, the home government can impose export subsidies. An export subsidy will help a domestic firm compete with foreign firms in the foreign market, but the subsidy also has the detrimental effect of deteriorating the terms of trade. Thus the net welfare effect of an export subsidy is ambiguous, and an export tax may be needed instead (Flam and Helpman, 1987a).[18]

Further discussion about the use of tariffs and export subsidies can be found in the following two chapters, where I explain how these policies may affect the external terms of trade of an economy and how they may help domestic firms capture more monopoly rents.

---

18. Flam and Helpman (1987a) also analyze an R&D subsidy and an output subsidy.

In this chapter, I investigate the effects of different policies for a country in the presence of international trade in goods or factor mobility. These policies include taxes and subsidies on the trading goods and moving factors, and also on the choice between capital and labor mobility. I assume the existence of a well-behaved social utility function, and use the social utility level as a criterion for ranking policies.

Throughout this chapter, it is assumed that only the government of the country under consideration (the home country) may impose impediments or stimuli on the trading goods or moving factors. The government of the foreign country always allows free goods trade and free capital movement, and does not retaliate even if it is hurt by the policies of the home country. The discussion of retaliation and trade wars is postponed until Chapter 12.

In most of this chapter, I use a two-factor, two-good framework similar to the one introduced in Chapter 4, and examine international trade in goods and capital movement. In this framework, the two countries may have different factor endowments, different preferences, or different technologies. Keeping the dimension of the framework low allows me to investigate in more detail the interactions between trade in goods and capital movement. The dimension of the present framework should not be considered a handicap, however, because the techniques introduced earlier provide me tools to extend the present framework easily.

11.1 Effects of Protection

In this section, I investigate the effects of trade taxes or subsidies and income taxes or subsidies on moving capital imposed by the home country. I use the two-factor, two-sector, and two-country framework and the notation described in Chapter 4. Choosing good 2 as the numeraire, p and r are, respectively, the price of good 1 and the rental rate in the home country, and the inflow of foreign capital is denoted by κ (negative for outflow of home capital). I denote the specific trade tax or subsidy imposed by the home government on good 1 by t, and the specific tax or subsidy on the income of owners of moving capital by s.[1] Assuming that the home government can effectively eliminate the type of two-way trade in the presence of export or import subsidy described in Chapter 10, trade subsidies are regarded as negative trade taxes.

Recall that the indirect trade utility (ITU) function of the home country can be denoted by $V(p, \kappa, b)$, where b is the transfer the country receives from

---

1. The choice of numeraire affects whether an optimal tax or subsidy should be imposed on a particular moving good or factor. The sign of the total tax revenue is independent on the choice of numeraire. See Bond (1990).

abroad. To simplify the notation, the given factor endowments of the home country have been deleted as arguments from the ITU function. As explained, the export supply of good 1 of the country is given by $E_1 = E_1(p, \kappa, b) = (1/\lambda)\partial V(p, \kappa, b)/\partial p$ where $\lambda > 0$ is the marginal utility of income. I use subscripts to denote the partial derivatives of $E_1(p, \kappa, b)$; for example, $E_{1b} = \partial E_1/\partial b$.

By the notation in Chapter 4, $C_1 = C_1(p, I)$ is the Marshallian demand for good 1 of the home country, and $I = g(p, \kappa) + b$ is the country's national income. The marginal propensity to consume good 1 is denoted by $m_1 \equiv p\partial C_1/\partial I$. Assuming no inferior goods, $0 < m_1 < 1$. Noting that export of good 1 is equal to production less consumption, I have

$$E_{1\kappa} = \frac{\partial Q_1}{\partial \kappa} - \frac{\partial C_1}{\partial I}\frac{\partial I}{\partial \kappa} = \frac{\partial Q_1}{\partial \kappa} - \frac{m_1 r}{p} \tag{11.1a}$$

$$E_{1b} = -\frac{\partial C_1}{\partial I} = -\frac{m_1}{p}. \tag{11.1b}$$

In deriving (11.1a), I use $\partial g/\partial \kappa = r$. In (11.1b), note that when given p and κ the production of the home country remains unchanged.

In equilibrium, the home and foreign prices are related by $p = p^* + t$ and $r = r^* + s$. A positive s represents an income tax (respectively subsidy) if κ is positive (respectively negative), and similarly a positive t represents a trade tax (respectively subsidy) if the home country imports (respectively exports) good 1. Therefore $-tE_1$ is the import or export tax revenue, and $s\kappa$ is the income tax revenue. The transfer b received by the home country is the sum of these two tax revenues plus income earned by home capital working abroad less income earned by foreign capital working at home:

$$b = -(r - s)\kappa - tE_1. \tag{11.2}$$

With no inferior goods, and because $t < p$, $0 < (1 - tm_1/p) < 1$ for $t < 0$. Substitute $r = r(p, \kappa)$ into condition (11.2). The implicit function theorem can be used to invert condition (11.2) to give $b = b(p, \kappa, s, t)$. This function allows the definition of a new export function of the home country: $\mathcal{E}_1(p, \kappa, s, t) \equiv E_1(p, \kappa, b(p, \kappa, s, t))$. If taxes are absent, this export function is the same as the one used in Chapter 4. As shown in Chapter 4, it is more convenient to work with function $\mathcal{E}_1$ than with function E_1. Again use subscripts to denote the partial derivatives of $\mathcal{E}_1$ and b, that is, $\mathcal{E}_{1j} \equiv \partial \mathcal{E}_1/\partial j$ and $b_j \equiv \partial b/\partial j$, $j = p, \kappa, s, t$.[2]

---

2. Caution should be given when interpreting the derivatives of $E(p, \kappa, b)$ and those of $\mathcal{E}_1(p, \kappa, s, t)$. For example, in evaluating the price effect on export of good 1, E_{1p}, variables κ and b are kept constant, while in evaluating $\mathcal{E}_{1p}$, κ, s and t are kept constant.

Using (11.2), the partial derivatives of b are equal to

$$b_p = -r_p \kappa - t\mathcal{E}_{1p} \tag{11.3a}$$

$$b_\kappa = s - r - r_\kappa \kappa - t\mathcal{E}_{1\kappa} \tag{11.3b}$$

$$b_s = \kappa - t\mathcal{E}_{1s} \tag{11.3c}$$

$$b_t = -E_1 - t\mathcal{E}_{1t} \tag{11.3d}$$

Using the derivatives of b given in (11.3), the following partial derivatives of function $\mathcal{E}_1(p, \kappa, s, t)$ are

$$\mathcal{E}_{1p} = \gamma\left[E_{1p} + m_1 r_p \kappa / p\right] \tag{11.4a}$$

$$\mathcal{E}_{1\kappa} = \gamma\left[E_{1\kappa} + m_1(r + r_\kappa \kappa - s)/p\right] \tag{11.4b}$$

$$\mathcal{E}_{1s} = -\gamma m_1 \kappa / p \tag{11.4c}$$

$$\mathcal{E}_{1t} = \gamma m_1 E_1 / p, \tag{11.4d}$$

where $\gamma = 1/(1 - m_1 t/p)$. Assuming the absence of inferior goods and with $t > 0$, $\gamma > 1$. Thus from condition (11.4c), $\mathcal{E}_{1s} < 0$ if and only if $\kappa > 0$, and from condition (11.4d), $\mathcal{E}_{1t} > 0$ if and only if $E_1 > 0$. An application of condition (11.4b) is that if the home country is diversified (so that $r_\kappa = 0$) and has no income tax of foreign capital (so that $s = 0$), and if there are no inferior goods, then the sign of $\mathcal{E}_{1\kappa}$ is the same as that of $\partial Q_1/\partial\kappa$, that is, positive if and only if good 1 is capital intensive.[3]

I define a similar export function for the foreign country, $E_1^* = \mathcal{E}_1^*(p^*, \kappa^*, s^*, t^*)$. For the time being, I write $s^* = t^* = 0$.

The equilibrium of the present framework is described by the following conditions:

$$p = p^* + t \tag{11.5a}$$

$$r = r^* + s. \tag{11.5b}$$

$$\mathcal{E}_1(p, \kappa, s, t) + \mathcal{E}_1^*(p^*, \kappa^*, 0, 0) = 0 \tag{11.5c}$$

$$\kappa + \kappa^* = 0 \tag{11.5d}$$

When the two policy parameters s and t are given, conditions (11.5a), (11.5b), (11.5c), and (11.5d), together with the two rental rate functions $r = r(p, \kappa)$ and $r^* = r^*(p^*, \kappa^*)$ can be used to solve for the six variables p, p^*, κ, κ^*, r and r^*.

---

3. I derived this result in Chapter 4 for the special case when $s = t = 0$. In that case, because $t = 0$, the absence of inferior goods is not a condition for this result.

Substitute the value of p^* in (11.5a) and that of κ^* in (11.5d) into (11.5b) and (11.5c), and then differentiate the latter two conditions. Rearranging terms, I get

$$
\begin{bmatrix} -(\mathcal{E}_{1p} + \mathcal{E}^*_{1p*}) & -(\mathcal{E}_{1\kappa} - \mathcal{E}^*_{1\kappa*}) \\ r_p - r^*_{p*} & r_\kappa + r^*_{\kappa*} \end{bmatrix} \begin{bmatrix} dp \\ d\kappa \end{bmatrix} = \begin{bmatrix} \mathcal{E}_{1t} - \mathcal{E}^*_{1p*} & \mathcal{E}_{1s} \\ -r^*_{p*} & 1 \end{bmatrix} \begin{bmatrix} dt \\ ds \end{bmatrix}. \tag{11.6}
$$

For simplicity, let Θ denote the matrix on the left-hand side of condition (11.6). Its determinant is given by

$$
|\Theta| = -(\mathcal{E}_{1p} + \mathcal{E}^*_{1p*})(r_\kappa + r^*_{\kappa*}) + (\mathcal{E}_{1\kappa} - \mathcal{E}^*_{1\kappa*})(r_p - r^*_{p*}). \tag{11.7}
$$

As explained in Chapter 4, if p adjusts according to a *tâtonnement* process and if capital moves in response to international rental rate differential, the equilibrium is stable if the following conditions are satisified:

$$
-(\mathcal{E}_{1p} + \mathcal{E}^*_{1p*}) + (r_\kappa + r^*_{\kappa*}) < 0 \tag{11.8a}
$$

$$
|\Theta| > 0. \tag{11.8b}
$$

Using condition (11.6) and Cramer's rule, the effects of the policy parameters on p and κ are given by (partial derivatives being denoted by subscripts):

$$
p_t = \frac{1}{|\Theta|} \left[(\mathcal{E}_{1t} - \mathcal{E}^*_{1p*})(r_\kappa + r^*_{\kappa*}) - r^*_{p*}(\mathcal{E}_{1\kappa} - \mathcal{E}^*_{1\kappa*}) \right] \tag{11.9a}
$$

$$
p_s = \frac{1}{|\Theta|} \left[\mathcal{E}_{1s}(r_\kappa + r^*_{\kappa*}) + (\mathcal{E}_{1\kappa} - \mathcal{E}^*_{1\kappa*}) \right] \tag{11.9b}
$$

$$
\kappa_t = \frac{1}{|\Theta|} \left[r^*_{p*}(\mathcal{E}_{1p} + \mathcal{E}^*_{1p*}) - (r_p - r^*_{p*})(\mathcal{E}_{1t} - \mathcal{E}^*_{1p*}) \right] \tag{11.9c}
$$

$$
\kappa_s = -\frac{1}{|\Theta|} \left[(\mathcal{E}_{1p} + \mathcal{E}^*_{1p*}) + \mathcal{E}_{1s}(r_p - r^*_{p*}) \right]. \tag{11.9d}
$$

Conditions (11.5a), (11.9a), and (11.9b) can be combined to give the effects of the policy parameters on p^*:

$$
p^*_t = p_t - 1 = \frac{1}{|\Theta|} \left[(\mathcal{E}_{1t} + \mathcal{E}_{1p})(r_\kappa + r^*_{\kappa*}) - r_p(\mathcal{E}_{1\kappa} - \mathcal{E}^*_{1\kappa*}) \right] \tag{11.9e}
$$

$$
p^*_s = p_s. \tag{11.9f}
$$

Conditions (11.9a) to (11.9f) show that the effects of the policy parameters on the prices and capital movement are in general ambiguous. Interesting results can be obtained in the special case in which *both countries are diversified*. In this case, the rental rate of capital in each country depends only on the price ratio but not capital movement, meaning that $r_\kappa = r^*_{\kappa*} = 0$. Using this result, the determinant of Θ reduces to

$$|\Theta| = (\mathcal{E}_{1\kappa} - \mathcal{E}_{1\kappa*}^*)(r_p - r_{p*}^*).$$ (11.7′)

With diversification in both countries, the stability conditions as given by (11.8) reduce to

$$\mathcal{E}_{1p} + \mathcal{E}_{1p*}^* > 0$$ (11.8a′)

$$(\mathcal{E}_{1\kappa} - \mathcal{E}_{1\kappa*}^*)(r_p - r_{p*}^*) > 0$$ (11.8b′)

As given by condition (11.7′), $|\Theta|$ is positive if in both countries either the trade and income taxes are small (t and s are low), or the marginal propensity to consume good 1 is sufficiently small. Under these conditions $\mathcal{E}_{1\kappa}$ is approximately equal to $\partial Q_1/\partial \kappa$, and by the Samuelson reciprocity the latter is equal to $\partial r/\partial p$. The same result holds for the foreign country. Thus $|\Theta|$ is approximately equal to $(r_p - r_{p*}^*)^2 > 0$.

Using the determinant of Θ given in (11.7′), the price effects of the taxes given in (11.9) reduce to

$$p_t = -\frac{r_{p*}^*}{r_p - r_{p*}^*}$$ (11.10a)

$$p_t^* = -\frac{r_p}{r_p - r_{p*}^*}$$ (11.10b)

According to (11.10), if both countries are diversified, then the effects of a trade tax on prices in the presence of international capital movement depend crucially on the factor intensity rankings of the sectors. For example, if sector 1 is capital intensive in both countries, $r_p, r_{p*}^* > 0$, and if r_p is greater (respectively smaller) than r_{p*}^* then both p and p^* decrease (respectively increase) as t goes up.

This result can be explained intuitively. Under diversification in both countries, the rental rates are affected only by commodity prices but not by capital movement. This means that both the home and foreign price ratios have to adjust in such a way that they cause the same change in the home and foreign rental rates in order to clear the capital market.

For the case in which sector 1 is capital intensive in both countries, the price effects of the trade tax on good 1 are illustrated in Figure 11.1. Schedules HH and FF represent the p–r relations in the home and foreign countries, respectively, before the change in t. For simplicity, assume that initially there is free trade in goods and capital movement, $t = s = 0$. The diagram shows the diversification parts of the schedules. The intersecting point of the schedules, point W, represents the initial equilibrium of the world, with the common (in both countries) pre-tax equilibrium price equal to p_o. The slope of schedule HH equals r_p and that of schedule FF equals r_{p*}^*. Panel (a) shows the case in which $r_p > r_{p*}^* > 0$ and in the case shown in panel (b), $r_{p*}^* > r_p > 0$.

(a)

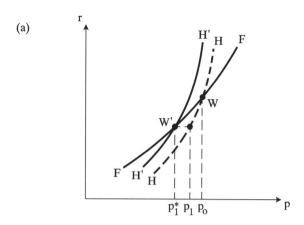

(b)

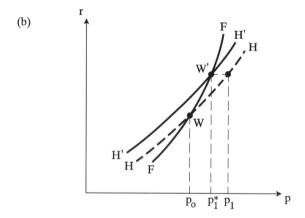

Figure 11.1

An increase in t shifts schedule HH horizontally to the left by an amount equal to the specific trade tax rate. The new schedule is denoted by H′H′. The new intersecting point W' shows the new world equilibrium, with the domestic and foreign price ratios changing to p_1 and p_1^*, respectively. In panel (a), because $r_p > r_{p*}^* > 0$, both p and p^* drop, with p^* dropping more than p, thus confirming conditions (11.10). In panel (b), $r_{p*}^* > r_p > 0$, and both p and p^* rise with p rising by a greater amount. These two panels also reveal one more feature of the effect of the tax policy: If the countries are initially diversified with positive outputs of both goods, then after a small trade tax the countries will remain diversified (Inada and Kemp, 1969).

The effects of the trade tax in the presence of international capital movement can be compared with those when capital is immobile internationally. If capital mobility is ruled out, then an imposition of a tariff by a country with external monopoly power generally raises the domestic relative price of the importable but lower the foreign price of the good. If the sum of the domestic marginal propensity to import and the foreign elasticity of import demand is greater than unity, then the domestic relative price of the importable falls. The latter result is called the *Metzler paradox* (Metzler, 1949).[4] When international capital movement is allowed, the effects of a tariff on the commodity prices are governed also by other factors such as the slopes of the country p–r schedules when both countries are diversified. For example, in panel (a) of Figure 11.1, if the home country imports good 1, then the Metzler paradox exists.

Continuing to assume that both countries are diversified, the price effects of a capital income tax can be derived. Substituting $r_\kappa = r_{\kappa*}^* = 0$ into (11.9b) and (11.9f) and rearranging terms give

$$p_s = p_s^* = \frac{1}{r_p - r_{p*}^*}. \tag{11.11}$$

According to condition (11.11), p_s and p_s^* are both positive (respectively negative) if and only if $r_p > r_{p*}^*$ (respectively $r_p < r_{p*}^*$). The reason for this result is that if both countries are diversified, p and p^* have to adjust to satisfy conditions (11.5a) and (11.5b).

The result given by (11.11) is illustrated in Figure 11.2 for the case in which sector 1 is capital intensive in both countries. In the diagram, schedules HH and FF are, respectively, the diversification portions of the p–r schedules of the home and foreign countries before the change in the tax on the moving capital owners' income. Again assume that initially there is free trade in goods and international capital movement, $t = s = 0$. The world equilibrium is at the point of intersection between the schedules, point W, giving the pre-tax price ratio and the rental rate at p_o and r_o, respectively. An increase in s shifts schedule HH down to H'H', with the vertical gap between schedules HH and H'H' equal to the specific income tax. The intersecting point W' between schedules FF and H'H' depicts the new world equilibrium. In panel (a) in which $r_p > r_{p*}^* > 0$, the international price ratio of good 1 goes up to p_1, confirming condition (11.11). The diagram also shows that both rental rates go up, too, with $r_1 > r_1^*$ because of the tax. Panel (b) of Figure 11.2 shows the case in which $r_{p*}^* > r_p > 0$.

The effect of a trade policy on capital movement is given by (11.9c). In general, the sign of κ_t is ambiguous. It is noted that if both countries are

---

4. See Chacholiades (1978, pp. 474–480) for a discussion.

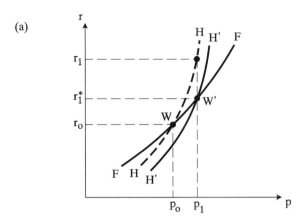

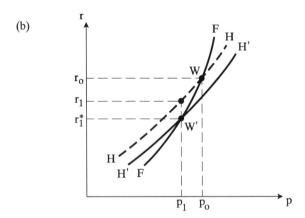

Figure 11.2

diversified $r_\kappa = r_{\kappa^*}^* = 0$. If, furthermore, r_p is sufficiently close to $r_{p^*}^*$, then (11.9c) reduces to

$$\kappa_t = \frac{r_{p^*}^*(\mathcal{E}_{1p} + \mathcal{E}_{1p^*}^*)}{|\Theta|},$$

which, due to the stability condition given by (11.8a′) and (11.8b′), is positive if and only if $r_{p^*}^*$ is positive. Thus if sector 1 is capital intensive in both countries, a trade tax on good 1 (a tariff if the home country imports good 1 or an export subsidy if it exports good 1) will attract foreign capital. This is consistent with the common concept of tariff-jumping foreign direct investment. It should be noted, however, that because in the present framework capital moves internationally in response to the rental rate differential, the effect of trade restrictions on capital movement is much more complicated than what is seen in the concept of tariff-jumping foreign investment. Thus, if sector 1 is instead labor intensive in both countries, then an increase in trade restriction would encourage domestic capital to flow out ($\kappa_t < 0$). In other words, the direction of movement of capital depends crucially on the factor intensity rankings. In Chapter 13, I consider other models that are more suitable to examine the phenomenon of tariff-jumping direct investment.

Condition (11.9d) gives the effect of the income tax s on capital movement. In the case in which both countries are diversified, r_p is sufficiently close to r_{p*}^*, condition (11.9d) reduces to

$$\kappa_s = -\frac{\mathcal{E}_{1p} + \mathcal{E}_{1p*}^*}{|\Theta|} < 0.$$

This means that an income tax would discourage the inflow of foreign capital.

The effects of the trade tax policy on trade are measured by the changes in the home country's export of good 1

$$\frac{dE_1}{ds} = \mathcal{E}_{1p}p_s + \mathcal{E}_{1\kappa}\kappa_s + \mathcal{E}_{1s}$$

$$\frac{dE_1}{dt} = \mathcal{E}_{1p}p_t + \mathcal{E}_{1\kappa}\kappa_t + \mathcal{E}_{1t}.$$

Using conditions (11.9a) to (11.9d), the effects of protection on trade are given by

$$\frac{dE_1}{ds} = -\frac{\mathcal{E}_{1s}\mathcal{E}_{1\kappa*}^*A + (\mathcal{E}_{1p}\mathcal{E}_{1\kappa*}^* + \mathcal{E}_{1\kappa}\mathcal{E}_{1p*}^*) + \mathcal{E}_{1s}\mathcal{E}_{1p*}^*B}{|\Theta|} \qquad (11.12a)$$

$$\frac{dE_1}{dt} = \frac{\mathcal{E}_{1\kappa}r_p\mathcal{E}_{1p*}^* + \mathcal{E}_{1\kappa*}^*r_{p*}^*\mathcal{E}_{1p} - \mathcal{E}_{1t}\mathcal{E}_{1\kappa*}^*A - \mathcal{E}_{1p*}^*(\mathcal{E}_{1t} + \mathcal{E}_{1p})B}{|\Theta|}, \qquad (11.12b)$$

where $A = (r_p - r_{p*}^*)$ and $B = (r_k + r_{k*}^*)$. The signs of these effects can be determined in certain cases. For example, in (11.12a), if both countries are diversified and have no inferior goods, if $\mathcal{E}_{1p}$ and $\mathcal{E}_{1p*}^*$ are both positive, and if r_p is sufficiently close to r_{p*}^*, then an increase in an income tax would increase the home country's export supply of good 1 if and only if sector 1 is labor intensive in both countries. Note that if both countries are diversified and have no inferior goods, $\mathcal{E}_{1\kappa}r_p$ and $\mathcal{E}_{1\kappa*}^*r_{p*}^*$ in (11.12b) are always positive. If it is further given that $\mathcal{E}_{1p}$ and $\mathcal{E}_{1p*}^*$ are positive, and if r_p is sufficiently close to r_{p*}^*, then $dE_1/dt > 0$, that is, an increase in export subsidy encourages export supply of good 1 (or an increase in tariff discourages import demand for good 1). This can be regarded as the normal response of export to the trade subsidy. If these conditions are not satisfied, perverse responses are possible.

11.2 Optimal Protection

In this section, I explain the optimal policies of the home country, assuming that the foreign country remains passive. Based on the analysis given in the previous section p and κ can be expressed as functions of s and t, that is, $p = p(s, t)$ and $\kappa = \kappa(s, t)$. I then further write $b = b(p(s, t), \kappa(s, t), s, t)$. Substitute these functions into the home indirect trade utility function to yield a new function for the home welfare $\tilde{V}(s, t)$:

$$\tilde{V}(s, t) \equiv V(p(s, t), \kappa(s, t), b(p(s, t), \kappa(s, t), s, t)).$$

The derivatives of function $\tilde{V}$, denoted by subscripts, are

$$\tilde{V}_s = V_p p_s + V_\kappa \kappa_s + V_b(b_p p_s + b_\kappa \kappa_s + b_s)$$

$$= \lambda\big[E_1 p_s + s\kappa_s + \kappa - (r_p p_s + r_\kappa \kappa_s)\kappa - t(\mathcal{E}_{1p} p_s + \mathcal{E}_{1\kappa}\kappa_s + \mathcal{E}_{1s})\big]$$

$$\tilde{V}_t = V_p p_t + V_\kappa \kappa_t + V_b(b_p p_t + b_\kappa \kappa_t + b_t)$$

$$= \lambda\big[E_1 p_t - E_1 + s\kappa_t - (r_p p_t + r_\kappa \kappa_t)\kappa - t(\mathcal{E}_{1p} p_t + \mathcal{E}_{1\kappa}\kappa_t + \mathcal{E}_{1t})\big],$$

where conditions (11.3c) and (11.3d) have been used. Totally differentiating the equilibrium conditions (11.5a), (11.5c), and (11.5d), and making use of this result, the partial derivatives of function $\tilde{V}$ reduce to

$$\tilde{V}_s = -\lambda\big[E_1^* p_s^* - s\kappa_s - \kappa + (r_p p_s + r_\kappa \kappa_s)\kappa - t(\mathcal{E}_{1p^*}^* p_s^* - \mathcal{E}_{1\kappa^*}^*\kappa_s)\big] \quad (11.13a)$$

$$\tilde{V}_t = -\lambda\big[E_1^* p_t^* - s\kappa_t + (r_p p_t + r_\kappa \kappa_t)\kappa - t(\mathcal{E}_{1p^*}^* p_t^* - \mathcal{E}_{1\kappa^*}^*\kappa_t)\big]. \quad (11.13b)$$

I now derive the optimal policies for the home country in several cases, beginning with the general case.

11.2.1 Goods Trade and Capital Movement

The problem of the home government in the present case is to choose the optimal values of s and t to maximize $\tilde{V}(s, t)$. By making use of the derivatives as given by (11.13), the first-order conditions of the problem are:

$$E_1^* p_s^* - s\kappa_s - \kappa + (r_p p_s + r_\kappa \kappa_s)\kappa - t(\mathcal{E}_{1p^*}^* p_s^* - \mathcal{E}_{1\kappa^*}^*\kappa_s) = 0 \quad (11.14a)$$

$$E_1^* p_t^* - s\kappa_t + (r_p p_t + r_\kappa \kappa_t)\kappa - t(\mathcal{E}_{1p^*}^* p_t^* - \mathcal{E}_{1\kappa^*}^*\kappa_t) = 0. \quad (11.14b)$$

The maximization problem can be illustrated by Figure 11.3.[5] Each of the iso-welfare contours, which comes from function $\tilde{V}(s, t)$, shows different combinations of s and t that give the same welfare level. For example, the iso-

5. See Neary (1993) for an alternative approach.

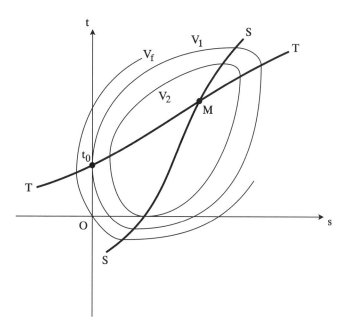

Figure 11.3

welfare contour that passes through the origin gives the welfare level V_f of the home country under free trade and capital movement. The welfare levels in the diagram increase toward the optimal point M; for example, $V_2 > V_1$.

Condition (11.14a) is represented by schedule SS in Figure 11.3, which is the locus of points at which the slopes of the iso-welfare contours are zero. Differentiate $\widetilde{V}_s = 0$ and rearrange terms to give the slope of schedule SS:

$$\left.\frac{dt}{ds}\right|_{SS} = -\frac{\widetilde{V}_{ss}}{\widetilde{V}_{st}}.$$

If $\widetilde{V}(s,t)$ is (locally) strictly concave, $\widetilde{V}_{ss} < 0$ at least in the neighboring area around the optimal point. Thus the slope of SS is positive if and only if $\widetilde{V}_{st}$ is positive.

Condition (11.14b) is represented by schedule TT, which is the locus of points at which the slopes of the iso-welfare contours are infinite. Totally differentiate $\widetilde{V}_t = 0$ and rearrange terms to give the slope of schedule TT:

$$\left.\frac{dt}{ds}\right|_{TT} = -\frac{\widetilde{V}_{ts}}{\widetilde{V}_{tt}}.$$

If $\widetilde{V}(s,t)$ is (locally) strictly concave, $\widetilde{V}_{tt} < 0$ at least in the neighboring area around the optimal point. Thus the slope of TT is positive if and only if $\widetilde{V}_{ts}$ is positive.

The optimal point with the highest welfare W_m is at a point of intersection between schedules TT and SS in Figure 11.3. This optimal point can be reached by using the first-best policy, which consists of the optimal tax-cum-subsidy on the trading goods and moving capital.

When only one of s and t can be chosen optimally, the maximum utility the home government gets generally is less than W_m, as Figure 11.3 shows. For example, suppose that the home government can levy a tax on the traded good 1 but not on the moving capital. The optimal tariff rate is then given by condition (11.14b). In terms of Figure 11.3, if s is constrained to be zero, then the optimal value is equal to t_0, with the home country achieving a welfare level of V_1.

If, however, an income tax on the moving capital is not possible, choosing an optimal trade tax is only a third-best policy. As Brecher (1983) argues, the second-best policy is a combination of t and either production or consumption tax-cum-subsidy. To see the intuition behind Brecher's results, let me suppose that the home government has chosen the optimal value t_0. See Figure 11.3. Now if a production or consumption tax-cum-subsidy can be imposed, a wedge between production and consumption prices can be created so that the home government can indirectly affect the domestic rental rate, and thus the movement of capital to further improve its welfare. These two policy instruments, trade tax and consumption or production tax, should dominate trade tax only. Similarly, if s but not t can be chosen, then a production or consumption tax-cum-subsidy, if possible, can be used as a second instrument to improve the country's welfare.[6] By the theory of second best, t plus a consumption or production tax cannot be ranked uniquely vis-à-vis s plus a consumption or production tax. To get more insight of the above analysis, I examine the following three special cases that appear frequently in the literature.

11.2.2   Pure Goods Trade

This is the textbook case with no international capital mobility, $\kappa = s = 0$. Condition (11.14b) reduces to

$$E_1^* p_t^* - t\mathcal{E}_{1p^*}^* p_t^* = 0, \tag{11.15}$$

or, after rearranging terms,

$$t = \frac{E_1^*}{\mathcal{E}_{1p^*}^*}, \tag{11.15'}$$

---

6. Brecher's results can be derived using the present framework by slightly modifying the indirect trade utility function. In the definition of the function, this requires a divergence between production price ratio and the consumption price ratio.

which is the formula for the optimal specific trade tax. In particular, if the home country imports good 1 (so $E_1^* > 0$) and the foreign export supply increases with p^*, the optimal tax is positive. If I divide both sides of (11.15') by p^*, I have

$$\frac{t}{p^*} = \frac{E_1^*}{p^* \mathcal{E}_{1p^*}^*}, \tag{11.15''}$$

which is the optimal ad valorem tariff rate. The term on the right-hand side of (11.15'') is the reciprocal of the elasticity of foreign export supply.

11.2.3   Constant Commodity Prices and Free Goods Trade

Suppose now that domestic and foreign commodity prices are fixed and that $t = 0$. I want to determine the effects of capital movement on the home welfare and on the optimal restriction of capital movement. First note that when domestic commodity prices are fixed and no trade taxes exist, national welfare can be written as

$$dV = \lambda \big[sd\kappa + \kappa ds - \kappa dr \big]. \tag{11.16}$$

Consider first the case in which there is no income tax on the moving capital. Condition (11.16) reduces to

$$dV = -\lambda \kappa dr. \tag{11.17}$$

If capital movement is treated as an exogenous variable (as in the case in which capital moves sluggishly across countries), the welfare effect of capital inflow can be obtained from (11.17):

$$\frac{dV}{d\kappa} = -\lambda \kappa \frac{dr}{d\kappa}. \tag{11.17'}$$

This means that an inflow of foreign capital is beneficial if and only if $\kappa > 0$ and the capital movement drives down the domestic rental rate (Berry and Soligo, 1969). The reason for this result is that if the domestic rental rate falls, the home country pays less to the owners of foreign capital that has already been invested in the home country.

There are two cases in which inflow of foreign capital does not change domestic welfare. In the first case, there is no capital movement initially, that is, $\kappa = 0$. This means that a marginal capital inflow does not affect national welfare because foreign capital owners take away what their capital has contributed (Grubel and Scott, 1966; Wong, 1986a). Second, the economy is a small open one with diversification in production and free trade. Because of the one-to-one correspondence between commodity prices and factor prices, the domestic rental rate and thus domestic welfare are independent of the level

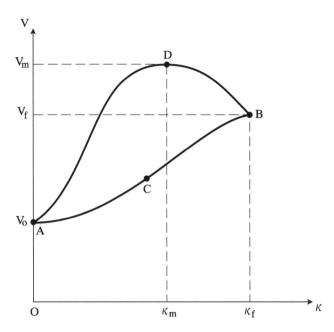

Figure 11.4

of capital movement. Thus national welfare is independent of the level of capital movement (Kenen, 1971).

11.2.4   The Pure Capital Mobility Case

Now consider another special case in which capital is allowed to move internationally but trade in goods is ruled out. For example, MacDougall (1960) considers a one-good framework, while in the framework of Wong (1986b) there exists more than one good. For simplicity, I examine the MacDougall model, but the analysis can easily be extended to a higher dimensional framework using the techniques in Wong (1986a).

By (11.17′), if the domestic rental rate drops monotonically with foreign capital inflow, an increase in κ (from zero) cannot hurt. This can be illustrated in Figure 11.4. In the diagram, schedule ACB shows the increase in national welfare as foreign capital flows in. As the analysis shows, schedule ACB is rising monotonically except at the no-capital-flow point A at which the schedule's slope is zero. Point B corresponds to the free capital movement point at which $r = r^*$ and after κ_f has moved in. National welfare increases from V_o to V_f.

In the above case, the domestic government allows foreign capital owners to be paid the market rental rate. Suppose now that the government imposes an income tax s on foreign capital earning so that the owners of the foreign capital working in the home country receive an income the same as foreign rental rate.[7] Condition (11.16) reduces to

$$\frac{dV}{d\kappa} = \lambda \left[s - \kappa \frac{dr^*}{d\kappa} \right], \tag{11.18}$$

where $r = r^* + s$ has been used. It is reasonable to assume that $dr^*/d\kappa > 0$. When $\kappa = 0$, the welfare effect of a capital inflow is

$$\left. \frac{dV}{d\kappa} \right|_{\kappa=0} = \lambda s > 0.$$

Thus, in the presence of an income tax, an inflow of foreign capital is beneficial when κ is small. This is, of course, due to the tax revenue foreign capital has generated. At the free capital mobility equilibrium point at which $\kappa = \kappa_f$ and $s = 0$, the welfare effect of capital inflow is

$$\left. \frac{dV}{d\kappa} \right|_{\kappa=\kappa_f} = -\lambda \kappa \frac{dr^*}{d\kappa} < 0.$$

The dependence of national welfare on capital inflow is represented by schedule ADB in Figure 11.4. Schedules ACB and ADB have two common points, at A and B, because national welfare does not depend on whether an income tax is imposed when there is no capital inflow ($\kappa = 0$ at point A) or when the income tax is zero ($s = 0$ at point B). Schedule ADB is rising when κ is small and falling when κ is close or equal to κ_f. The schedule reaches a maximum at a point before point B. Schedule ADB is above schedule ACD except at points A and B, because the former includes an income tax imposed by the home government on foreign capital inflow.

The analysis and schedule ADB suggest an optimal policy for the home country. By setting $dV/d\kappa$ in (11.18) to zero, the first-order condition for a maximum welfare is

$$s_m = \kappa_m \frac{dr^*}{d\kappa}, \tag{11.19}$$

where subscript m represents the value of a variable corresponding to the optimal point. Condition (11.19) gives the formula for an optimal income tax. Alternatively, condition (11.19) can be written as

---

7. Of course, if foreign capital owners receive an income in the home country exactly the same as what they receive in the foreign country, they have no incentive to move their capital to the home country. The home government can attract foreign capital inflow by making their after-tax income slightly more than the foreign rental rate.

$$r_m = r_m^* + \kappa_m \frac{dr^*}{d\kappa} = \frac{d(r^*\kappa)}{d\kappa}. \qquad (11.19')$$

Condition (11.19′) shows that the optimal point occurs when the domestic rental rate r is equal to the rate of change of $r^*\kappa$ with respect to κ. This shows the analogy between the home country and a monopsonist. As the only capital-receiving country in this model, the home country acts like a monopsonist, choosing the amount of foreign capital inflow at which the domestic rental rate is equal to foreign capital's marginal expense ($= r^* + \kappa dr^*/d\kappa$), but paying foreign capital the foreign rental rate. In Figure 11.5, the equilibrium occurs at the point of intersection between the marginal expense (ME) curve and the domestic rental rate curve labeled r. The specific income tax rate is equal to the gap between the marginal expense curve and the r^* curve.

So far it has been assumed that the home country is a capital receiving country, $\kappa \geq 0$. Now assume that the home country is a source country, that is, $\kappa < 0$. For convenience, define $\tilde{\kappa} = -\kappa > 0$.

When domestic capital goes to the foreign country and works there, it earns the foreign rental rate r^*. I assume that the owners will repatriate this income back to the home country. This means that the home country receives a transfer of $b = -r^*\kappa = r^*\tilde{\kappa}$. The welfare effect of capital outflow is equal to

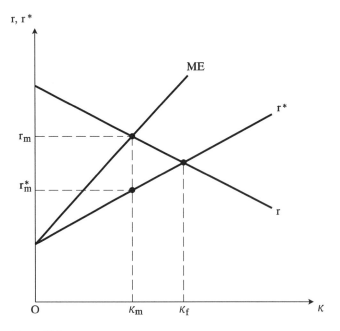

Figure 11.5

$$\frac{\mathrm{d}V}{\mathrm{d}\widetilde{\kappa}} = \lambda \left[\left(r^* - r\right) + \widetilde{\kappa}\frac{\mathrm{d}r^*}{\mathrm{d}\widetilde{\kappa}} \right]. \tag{11.20}$$

To see how capital outflow affects national welfare, evaluate $\mathrm{d}V/\mathrm{d}\widetilde{\kappa}$ at the no-capital-flow point

$$\left. \frac{\mathrm{d}V}{\mathrm{d}\widetilde{\kappa}} \right|_{\widetilde{\kappa}=0} = \lambda\left(r^* - r\right).$$

Because domestic capital flows voluntarily, I assume that $r^* > r$ when $\widetilde{\kappa} = 0$. This condition implies that an outflow of capital is beneficial to the home country even at the autarkic point. The reason is that when initially there is no capital movement, the benefit of domestic capital out-flow (the foreign rental rate) is greater than the cost (the domestic rental rate).

I now turn to the free capital mobility equilibrium point at which $r^* = r$ and when domestic capital $\widetilde{\kappa}_f$ has moved out of the economy. The welfare effect of an outflow of an additional unit of domestic capital is

$$\left. \frac{\mathrm{d}V}{\mathrm{d}\widetilde{\kappa}} \right|_{\widetilde{\kappa}=\widetilde{\kappa}_f} = \lambda\left[\widetilde{\kappa}\frac{\mathrm{d}r^*}{\mathrm{d}\widetilde{\kappa}}\right] < 0,$$

where the sign is due to the assumption that $\mathrm{d}r^*/\mathrm{d}\widetilde{\kappa} < 0$.

The effects of capital outflow on the welfare of this source country are illustrated by schedule ACB in Figure 11.6. The schedule is rising when $\widetilde{\kappa}$ is small, and is falling when $\widetilde{\kappa}$ is close or equal to the free capital mobility level $\widetilde{\kappa}_f$.

The analysis suggests that under free capital movement policy, the source country tends to invest too much abroad (Kemp, 1962; Ruffin, 1984). Thus a restriction on capital outflow is desirable from the country's point of view. Setting the derivative in (11.20) to zero,

$$r_m = r_m^* + \widetilde{\kappa}_m\frac{\mathrm{d}r^*}{\mathrm{d}\widetilde{\kappa}},$$

which is the domestic rental rate at the optimal point. The optimal restriction is also illustrated in Figure 11.7. The home country, being the only capital send-ing country, has monopoly power. The foreign rental rate curve is analogous to the average revenue curve of a monopolist. The marginal revenue MR curve in the diagram is derived from $r^* + \widetilde{\kappa}\mathrm{d}r^*/\mathrm{d}\widetilde{\kappa}$. The domestic rental rate is similar to the marginal cost for a firm because r is a measure of the cost of sending out capital. The optimal point occurs at the point at which schedule r cuts the marginal revenue schedule MR.

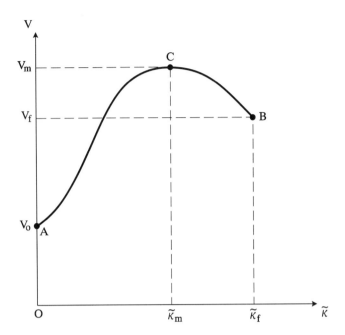

Figure 11.6

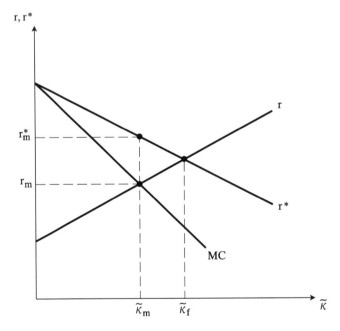

Figure 11.7

11.3 Can Optimal Taxes Be Negative?

It has long been noted that in the neoclassical framework with two tradable goods and internationally immobile factors, under certain conditions the optimal tariff for an economy on the importable good may be negative (Graaf, 1949–1950). Kemp (1969) argues that if the foreign offer curve is concave toward its own imported-good axis, the optimal tariff is positive. If, however, the foreign offer curve is not concave, an optimal subsidy may be needed. He lists four cases in which the foreign offer curve is not concave. First, the foreign country imposes a tariff; second, there are strongly increasing returns abroad; third, there are factor market imperfections abroad; and fourth, there are strong income-distribution effects. In each of these cases, foreign offer curves may not be single valued. Similarly, multiple equilibria in the country with an active government can also lead to a negative optimal tariff (Riley, 1970).

When the traditional framework is extended to a multisector one, generally more cases for negative optimal taxes can be found. When more than two goods are tradable, maximizing national welfare would require a vector of optimal trade taxes for the domestic country, and in general there is no reason to believe that the optimal trade tax vector contains only positive (or nonnegative) elements. Both Feenstra (1986) (assuming three trading goods) and Itoh and Kiyono (1987) (assuming a continuum of goods) show the existence of cases in which export subsidies are welfare improving.

One feature of a multigood framework is that whether a particular good should be taxed or subsidized is no longer unique, and not just the magnitude of the tax on the good but also its sign depend on the normalization of domestic prices (see Kemp 1969 and Bond 1990). The reason is simple. On the one hand homogeneity of the framework means that domestic prices are unique up to a multiple scale, and on the other hand, whether a particular good should be taxed or subsidized depends on the difference between the optimal domestic price and the foreign price (as well as the patterns of trade). For a good that is imported, if under one system of normalization the optimal domestic price of a particular good is higher than the foreign one, then the good should be taxed. It is possible, however, that under another system of normalization its optimal domestic price is lowered than its foreign price, meaning that it should be subsidized.

The point can be illustrated by using an example in the present model with international capital mobility. Suppose that at the optimal point after the home country has chosen the optimal policy, the prices and rental rates in the foreign country are given by $(p_1^*, p_2^*, r^*) = (1, 1, 1)$. With good 2 chosen as the numeraire, the corresponding prices in the home country are $(p_1, p_2, r) = (0.5, 1, 0.8)$. The optimal tax vector of the country is $(t_1, t_2, s) = (-0.5, 0, -0.2)$. Further suppose that the trade vector of the home country is $(E_1, E_2, \kappa) = (3, -2, 1)$, that is, the country is exporting good 1, importing good 2, and is a host to foreign capital. Note that the current account (evaluated at world prices) is balanced. Basing on the patterns of trade, the home government is imposing a positive export tax on good 1 and a subsidy on the income earning by foreign capital in the home country. The trade revenue collected by the home government is equal to $-t_1 E_1 + s\kappa = 0.5(3) - 0.2(1) = 1.3$.

Suppose now that good 1 instead is chosen as the numeraire. The domestic prices become $(1, 2, 1.6)$. Homogeneity of the system means that the new prices give exactly the same equilibrium as the one under the initial prices. The optimal taxes for the home country are $(0, 1, 0.6)$, and the resulting tax revenue is $-t_2 E_2 + s\kappa = 2.6$. This means that the home government has to tax both the imported good 2 and the inflowing foreign capital. By such a change in the numeraire, the optimal policy of the home country would require a switch of the tax on good 1 from positive to zero, that on good 2 from zero to positive, and that on foreign capital from negative to positive.

Despite the fact that a particular commodity should be taxed or subsidized is not unique, the *sign of the tax revenue* is independent on the choice of numeraire. This point is illustrated by the preceding example. (The tax revenue changes from 1.3 to 2.6 as good 1 instead of good 2 is chosen as the numeraire.) This result led Bond (1990) and L. Young (1991) to focus on the sign of tax revenue under the optimal policy of the home government. For example, by extending the result in a two-good framework, L. Young (1991) shows that if the foreign offer surface is strictly concave down then optimal home tariff revenue is positive.

11.4   An Alternative Approach to Analyzing Protection

This section presents another approach to welfare maximization. The major feature of the present approach is its emphasis on how national welfare is affected by the volume of trade and the level of capital movement. This approach is useful to show how the government should choose the volume of trade and the level of capital movement to reach the highest welfare level for the economy.

Recall the Meade's direct utility function derived in Chapter 2. In the present two-factor, two-sector framework, it can be defined as

$$U(E_1, E_2, \kappa) = \max_{(C_1, C_2, Q_1, Q_2)} \left\{ u(C_1, C_2) - \beta \Gamma(Q_1, Q_2, \kappa) \right.$$

$$\left. - \sum_{i=1}^{2} \left[\alpha_i (E_i - Q_i + C_i) \right] \right\}, \quad (11.21)$$

where $u(C_1, C_2)$ is the social utility function, and $\Gamma(Q_1, Q_2, \kappa) \leq 0$ is the production possibility set. The first-order conditions for the maximization problem in (11.21) are (assuming an interior solution):

$$u_i = \alpha_i \quad i = 1, 2 \tag{11.22a}$$

$$\alpha_j - \beta \Gamma_j = 0 \quad j = 1, 2, \tag{11.22b}$$

where $u_i = \partial u / \partial C_i$ and $\Gamma_j = \partial \Gamma / \partial Q_j$. Let $\Gamma_\kappa = \partial \Gamma / \partial \kappa$. Using the envelope theorem, the derivatives of the direct utility function are

$$\frac{\partial U}{\partial E_i} = -\alpha_i = -u_i < 0$$

$$\frac{\partial U}{\partial \kappa} = -\beta \frac{\partial \Gamma}{\partial \kappa} = -\alpha_2 \frac{\Gamma_\kappa}{\Gamma_2} = u_2 \frac{\partial Q_2}{\partial \kappa} = u_2 r > 0,$$

where $\partial Q_2 / \partial \kappa$ is evaluated along the production possibility frontier when Q_1 is fixed, and it is equal to r, the rental rate in terms of good 2.

Suppose that the level of export of good 2 the home country makes is related to its level of export of good 1 and the amount of capital inflow. This relationship can be denoted by the function $E_2 = \overline{E}_2(E_1, \kappa)$. This function depends on how the home country trades with the foreign country, that is, whether the countries are imposing taxes or subsidies on goods and capital movement. I will be more explicit about this function later.

Substituting function $\overline{E}_2(E_1, \kappa)$ into the utility function $U(E_1, E_2, \kappa)$, define a new welfare function $W(E_1, \kappa) \equiv U(E_1, \overline{E}_2(E_1, \kappa), \kappa)$. Again, function W depends on how good 2 is exchanged for good 1 and foreign capital.

Because this section focuses mainly on the optimal policy of the home country, let me denote the offer surface of the foreign country by $\Theta^*(E_1^*, E_2^*, \kappa^*) = 0$, where κ^* is the amount of capital it receives (or negative of the amount of capital it sends out). Assuming nonvanishing derivatives, invert the foreign offer surface to give $E_2^* = \Phi^*(E_1^*, \kappa^*)$. To simplify the notation, define $\Phi_1^* \equiv \partial \Phi^* / \partial E_1^*$ and $\Phi_{\kappa^*}^* \equiv \partial \Phi^* / \partial \kappa^*$. Note that $-\Phi_1^*$ (respectively $\Phi_{\kappa^*}^*$) is the slope of the offer surface when taking κ^* (respectively E_1^*) as given.

Because the home country chooses the optimal policy, it should exploit the foreign offer surface. Using the equilibrium conditions, $\overline{E}_2(E_1, \kappa) = -\Phi^*(-E_1, -\kappa)$. Furthermore, it is easy to show that

$$\frac{\partial \overline{E}_2}{\partial E_1} = \frac{\partial E_2^*}{\partial E_1^*} = \Phi_1^*$$

$$\frac{\partial \overline{E}_2}{\partial \kappa} = \frac{\partial E_2^*}{\partial \kappa^*} = \Phi_{\kappa^*}^*.$$

The foreign budget constraint is assumed to be satisfied:

$$p^* E_1^* + E_2^* = r^* \kappa^*. \tag{11.23}$$

The derivatives of $W(E_1, \kappa)$, which are represented by subscripts, are

$$W_1 = \frac{\partial U}{\partial E_1} + \frac{\partial U}{\partial E_2} \frac{\partial \overline{E}_2}{\partial E_1}$$

$$= -u_1 - u_2 \Phi_1^*$$

$$= -u_2(p + \Phi_1^*) \tag{11.24a}$$

$$W_\kappa = \frac{\partial U}{\partial \kappa} + \frac{\partial U}{\partial E_2} \frac{\partial \overline{E}_2}{\partial E_\kappa}$$

$$= u_2(r - \Phi_{\kappa^*}^*), \tag{11.24b}$$

where the last equality in (11.24a) is due to the fact that at the equilibrium point the price ratio is equal to the marginal rate of substitution. Note that because good 2 is chosen as the numeraire, u_2 is equal to the marginal utility of income, λ.

The intuition behind the two derivatives given by (11.24) is clear. In (11.24a), p is the marginal cost in terms of good 2 of exporting one more unit of good 1, while $-\Phi_1^*$ is the marginal benefit because it is the amount of good 2 the foreign country is willing to give up for each unit of good 1 received. Similarly, in (11.24b), $r - \Phi_{\kappa^*}^*$ is the net marginal benefit of foreign capital inflow.

I now examine the optimal policy for the home government. Its problem is

$$\max_{E_1, \kappa} W(E_1, \kappa).$$

The first-order conditions of this problem are

$$W_1(E_1, \kappa) = 0 \tag{11.25a}$$

$$W_\kappa(E_1, \kappa) = 0. \tag{11.25b}$$

By making use of the partial derivatives given by (11.24) and rearranging terms, the first-order conditions reduce to

$$p = -\Phi_1^* \tag{11.26a}$$

$$r = \Phi_{\kappa^*}^*. \tag{11.26b}$$

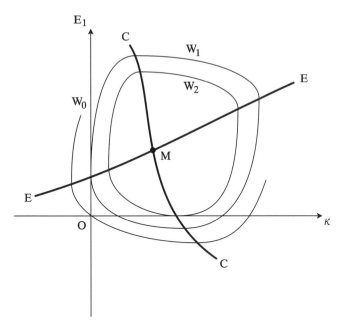

Figure 11.8

Both conditions in (11.26) imply that at the optimal point, the slope of the foreign offer surface is equal to the corresponding price. This is just a simple illustration of the optimality conditions derived in Chapter 10: equalization of domestic and foreign marginal rates of transformation and marginal rate of substitution. The domestic price ratio is the domestic marginal rate of substitution and domestic marginal rate of transformation while the slope of the foreign offer surface is the foreign marginal rate of transformation.

The maximization problem of the home country and the first-order conditions are illustrated in Figure 11.8. The diagram shows three iso-welfare contours corresponding to different welfare levels. The contour that goes through the origin gives the welfare level W_0 under autarky in goods trade and capital movement. In the case shown in the diagram, $W_2 > W_1 > W_0$, and there is a peak in welfare level at point M.

The first-order condition (11.25a), which gives the optimal value of E_1 when given a particular value of κ, is represented by schedule EE. Schedule EE is also the locus of the points at which the iso-welfare contours have infinite slopes. The slope of schedule EE is

$$\frac{\mathrm{d}E_1}{\mathrm{d}\kappa}\bigg|_{\mathrm{EE}} = -\frac{W_{1\kappa}}{W_{11}}.$$

Similarly, the first-order condition in (11.25b) is illustrated by schedule CC, which is also the locus of points at which the iso-welfare contours have zero slopes. The slope of schedule CC is

$$\left.\frac{dE_1}{d\kappa}\right|_{CC} = -\frac{W_{\kappa\kappa}}{W_{\kappa 1}}.$$

The optimal point M occurs at the point of intersection between schedules EE and CC.

More conditions for the optimal policy can be derived. First, differentiate the budget constraint of the foreign country as given by (11.23), keeping capital movement fixed, that is, $d\kappa^* = 0$. This gives

$$p^* dE_1^* + E_1^* dp^* + dE_2^* = \kappa^* r_{p*}^* dp^*.$$

Rearranging terms yields

$$\Phi_1^* = \frac{dE_2^*}{dE_1^*} = -p^* - \frac{E_1^* - \kappa^* r_{p*}^*}{\mathcal{E}_{1p*}^*}. \tag{11.27a}$$

Condition (11.27a) is the (negative) slope of the foreign offer surface when capital movement is fixed (but may be nonzero).[8]

Second, differentiate the foreign budget constraint in (11.23), keeping E_1^* constant. Then,

$$\Phi_{\kappa^*}^* = \frac{dE_2^*}{d\kappa^*} = r^* + \frac{(E_1^* - \kappa^* r_{p*}^*)\mathcal{E}_{1\kappa^*}^*}{\mathcal{E}_{1p*}^*} + \kappa^* r_{\kappa^*}^*. \tag{11.27b}$$

The slopes of the foreign offer surface given by (11.27) can be substituted into the first-order conditions (11.26). Recall that the taxes on capital movement and good 1 are given by $s = r - r^*$ and $t = p - p^*$. The first-order conditions and conditions (11.27) then imply the following formulas for the optimal taxes:

$$t_m = \frac{E_1^* - \kappa^* r_{p*}^*}{\mathcal{E}_{1p*}^*}$$

$$s_m = \frac{(E_1^* - \kappa^* r_{p*}^*)\mathcal{E}_{1\kappa^*}^*}{\mathcal{E}_{1p*}^*} + \kappa^* r_{\kappa^*}^*.$$

In the special case in which the home country is small so that foreign prices are independent of trade and capital movement, the slopes of foreign offer surface reduce to $\Phi_1^* = -p^*$ and $\Phi_\kappa^* = r^*$. This further implies that the optimal taxes are zero.

---

8. By differentiating the foreign budget constraint with respect to p^* and rearranging terms, it can be shown that Φ_1^* is alternatively equal to $\mathcal{E}_{2p*}^*/\mathcal{E}_{1p*}^*$, where $E_2^* = \mathcal{E}_2^*(p^*, \kappa^*)$.

11.5   Capital Movement under Optimal Goods Trade

In the previous three sections, I followed the steps of Kemp (1966) and Jones (1967) and analyze how the home country chooses the optimal taxes (or alternatively chooses the optimal amounts of goods trade and capital movement). It is assumed that the world equilibrium can be achieved quickly so that the home country is picking the equilibrium that yields the highest domestic welfare. This requires that goods and capital flow costlessly and rapidly across countries.

International capital movement can be very sluggish, however. This leads to an alternative approach to the present welfare analysis. Capital movement is treated as an exogenous variable, and I ask how a change in the amount of capital that flows across countries may affect the welfare of the countries.

Such a question has been asked frequently in the literature. For example, Uzawa (1969), Bhagwati (1973), Brecher and Diaz Alejandro (1977), Markusen and Melvin (1979), Minabe (1981), Grossman (1984), and Neary and Ruane (1988) present cases in which an exogenous capital movement may hurt a small, tariff-ridden economy. On the other hand, Brecher and Choudhri (1982) examine the Singer-Prebisch proposition (Singer, 1950; Prebisch, 1959) and show that foreign direct investment from developed countries to less developed countries may hurt the latter.

Also interesting is the case in which capital movement initially does not exist but then is allowed while goods trade prevails. This is just like opening up a market that is originally closed to the rest of the world. Wong (1983), examining a small open economy, observes that free goods trade plus either labor mobility or capital mobility is preferred to just goods trade or just movement of that factor. Grossman (1984), using a social utility function, shows that when free goods trade exists, allowing movement of factors benefits a small open economy. Wong (1991a) extends this proposition to the case in which a social utility function does not exist, but compensation through lump-sum transfers or commodity taxation are allowed.

Because free goods trade is the optimal policy for a small open economy (when free capital movement is allowed or when no capital movement exists), one may conjecture that if an economy, independent of its size, always adopts an optimal goods trade policy, exogenous capital movement would be beneficial to the economy. Markusen and Melvin (1979) show that this conjecture is not correct. Grossman (1984) presents an intuitive counterexample to illustrate the fact that capital movement under an optimal goods trade policy could be detrimental. Consider the two-factor, two-sector framework in which all the assumptions for the factor price equalization theorem are satisfied. Initially, there is goods trade but no factor movement between two countries, both of which have monopoly power. Commodity and factor prices are equalized. The home country now imposes an optimal tariff (assumed to be positive under the conditions stated previously). This raises the domestic price of the importable and the domestic rental rate if the importable is capital intensive. If capital movement is now allowed, foreign capital will flow in until rental rates are equalized. At this equilibrium, if the countries are diversified, then commodity prices are also equalized. Neglecting multiple equilibria, the home country has the same welfare level as that under free trade. This means that capital movement under an optimal goods trade policy can hurt (at least ultimately).

In this section, I develop a general theory of the impact of capital movement on a country that is choosing an optimal goods trade policy. I argue that as long as capital flows in the "right" direction, it must benefit the country.

Using the partial derivatives of $W(E_1, \kappa)$, the total effects of a marginal capital movement on the welfare of the home country are

$$\frac{dW}{d\kappa} = \frac{\partial W}{\partial E_1} \frac{dE_1}{d\kappa} + \frac{\partial W}{\partial \kappa}, \tag{11.28}$$

where $dE_1/d\kappa$ is the change in the equilibrium export of good 1 by the home country due to a marginal change in κ. Because in this section I assume that the home country always chooses the optimal goods trade policy, by the first-order condition, $\partial W/\partial E_1 = 0$. Thus condition (11.28) reduces to

$$\frac{dW}{d\kappa} = \frac{\partial W}{\partial \kappa}. \tag{11.28'}$$

In other words, the total effect of capital movement is the same as the partial effect as long as the volume of trade is always chosen optimally. If I make use of the partial derivative of function W, the welfare effect of capital movement becomes

$$\frac{dW}{d\kappa} = u_2 \left(r - \frac{\partial E_2}{\partial \kappa} \right), \tag{11.28''}$$

where it is recalled that $\partial E_2/\partial \kappa$ is the volume of export of good 2 the home country is willing to have when it receives one additional unit of foreign capital at a given level of E_1. With nonsatiation so that $u_2 > 0$, condition (11.28'') thus states that an additional inflow of foreign capital benefits the home country if and only if $r > \partial E_2/\partial \kappa$.

Capital does not flow internationally in response to the difference between r and $\partial E_2/\partial \kappa$, however. In particular, if capital always flows from a country where the rental rate is lower to a country where the rental rate is higher, then the direction of its movement may not be beneficial from the home country's point of view. For example, if $r < \partial E_2/\partial \kappa$ and $r > r^*$, then foreign capital will tend to flow in and this capital inflow will be detrimental to the home country. Similarly, if $r > \partial E_2/\partial \kappa$ and $r < r^*$, then domestic capital will flow out, hurting the home country. Assuming that capital flows in response to rental rate differential, it is said that there is a *diversion in capital movement* if either one of the following conditions holds: (1) $\partial E_2/\partial \kappa > r > r^*$; and (2) $r^* > r > \partial E_2/\partial \kappa$. In other words, capital movement is diverted if, from the home country's point of view, it flows in the "wrong" direction. This result can be summarized by the following proposition:

Welfare-Enhancing Capital Movement under Optimal Goods Trade   For a country facing a passive foreign country, if goods trade is always chosen optimally and if there is no diversion in capital movement, then a small additional international capital movement is beneficial.

The advantage of this proposition is that it is applicable even if initially international capital movement is present. However, the proposition is not of much use unless conditions can be found that determine whether capital movement diversion is present.

Depending on what the owners of the moving capital receives, two cases can be distinguished and analyzed: the case in which they earn the foreign rental rate r^*, and the case in which they earn the home rental rate r. The first case is more applicable when the home country sends out capital and the foreign country imposes no income tax or subsidy, or when the home country receives foreign capital and imposes an income tax or subsidy so that owners of the moving capital receive (marginally more than) the foreign rental rate. The second case is more applicable when the home country receives foreign capital and does not impose any income tax or subsidy.

11.5.1   Moving Capital Receiving r^*

First look at the case in which the moving capital receives r^*. The foreign country trades at its price p^* and receives (or sends out) capital at its rental rate r^*. So its budget constraint is $p^*E_1^* + E_2^* = r^*\kappa^*$, which is the same as condition (11.23). Thus, using the analysis in the previous section, I can show that the dependence of E_2 on E_1 and κ remains the same as that given by conditions (11.27), that is,

$$\frac{\partial E_2}{\partial E_1} = \Phi_1^* = -p^* - \frac{E_1^* - \kappa^* r_{p*}^*}{\mathcal{E}_{1p*}^*}$$

$$\frac{\partial E_2}{\partial \kappa} = \Phi_{\kappa^*}^* = r^* + \frac{(E_1^* - \kappa^* r_{p*}^*)\mathcal{E}_{1\kappa^*}^*}{\mathcal{E}_{1p*}^*} + \kappa^* r_{\kappa^*}^*.$$

As mentioned, an optimal policy on goods trade requires the home government to impose a tax on good 1 given by $t_m = (E_1^* - \kappa^* r_{p*}^*)/\mathcal{E}_{1p*}^*$. As a result, the total (as well as partial) effect of capital movement on the home welfare is

$$W_\kappa = u_2 \Big[(r - r^*) - t_m \mathcal{E}_{1\kappa^*}^* + \kappa r_{\kappa^*}^* \Big],$$ (11.29)

where the optimal tariff formula has been used.

To avoid capital movement diversion W_κ and $(r - r^*)$ must have the same sign. Condition (11.29) thus gives the following sufficient conditions for no capital movement diversion: (1) $t_m \mathcal{E}_{1\kappa^*}^* - \kappa r_{\kappa^*}^* \leq 0$ if $r > r^*$; and (2) $t_m \mathcal{E}_{1\kappa^*}^* - \kappa r_{\kappa^*}^* \geq 0$ if $r < r^*$. These conditions show that whether international capital movement is beneficial to the home country under an optimal goods trade policy depends not only on the direction of capital movement but also on other factors such as the optimal tax and factor intensity ranking. In particular, if the foreign country is diversified so that $r_{\kappa^*}^* = 0$, and if the optimal trade policy of the home country is a tax, then capital inflow (respectively outflow) is beneficial if the foreign importable sector is capital (respectively labor) intensive.[9] Another sufficient condition for no capital movement diversion is that the foreign country is diversified and the optimal trade tax rate for the home country is zero (as in the case of a small open economy). In this case, condition (11.29) reduces to $W_k = u_2(r - r^*)$, and capital movement must be beneficial.

11.5.2 Moving Capital Receiving r

I now turn to the case in which the owners of the moving capital receive the rental rate in the home country. The budget constraint of the foreign country can be written as[10]

$$p^* E_1^* + E_2^* = r\kappa^*.$$ (11.30)

Differentiating condition (11.30), keeping either κ^* or E_1^* constant, will give the dependence of E_2 on E_1 or κ:

$$\frac{\partial E_2}{\partial E_1} = \frac{\partial E_2^*}{\partial E_1^*} = -p^* - \frac{E_1^*}{\mathcal{E}_{1p^*}^*} + \frac{\kappa r_p}{\mathcal{E}_{1p}}$$ (11.31a)

$$\frac{\partial E_2}{\partial \kappa} = \frac{\partial E_2^*}{\partial \kappa^*} = r + \frac{E_1^* \mathcal{E}_{1\kappa^*}^*}{\mathcal{E}_{1p^*}^*} - \frac{\kappa r_p \mathcal{E}_{1\kappa}}{\mathcal{E}_{1p}} + \kappa r_\kappa.$$ (11.31b)

---

9. For example, assume that $r > r^*$ and that the home country exports good 1. An optimal tax means that $t_m < 0$. An inflow of foreign capital is beneficial if $\mathcal{E}_{1\kappa^*}^* > 0$. (With diversification, $r_{\kappa^*}^* = 0$.) As I discussed in Chapter 4, with diversification $\mathcal{E}_{1\kappa^*}^* > 0$ if and only if the foreign sector 1 is capital intensive. Other cases can be analyzed in a similar way.

10. The foreign country's budget constraint can be derived as follows. Because the home country imposes a tax or subsidy on good 1 but nothing on moving capital, its budget constraint is $pE_1 + E_2 = r\kappa + tE_1$ where $-tE_1$ is the tax revenue. Substituting the equilibrium conditions $E_i + E_i^* = 0$, $i = 1, 2$, $\kappa + \kappa^* = 0$ and $p = p^* + t$ into the home budget constraint will give the foreign budget constraint.

Condition (11.31a) gives the optimal tax imposed on good 1:

$$t_m = \frac{E_1^*}{\mathcal{E}_{1p^*}^*} - \frac{\kappa r_p}{\mathcal{E}_{1p}}. \tag{11.32}$$

The total and partial effects of capital movement on the welfare of the home country are

$$\frac{dW}{d\kappa} = u_2 \left[r - \frac{\partial E_2^*}{\partial \kappa^*} \right] = -u_2 \left[\frac{E_1^* \mathcal{E}_{1\kappa^*}^*}{\mathcal{E}_{1p^*}^*} - \frac{\kappa r_p \mathcal{E}_{1\kappa}}{\mathcal{E}_{1p}} + \kappa r_\kappa \right].$$

Recall that the optimal tariff as given by (11.32) is under the condition that κ is treated as fixed. Thus this condition gives the optimal trade policy of the home country when some of the factors working in the domestic economy are foreign owned (Bhagwati and Tironi, 1980; Bhagwati and Brecher, 1980; Brecher and Bhagwati, 1981). The first term on the right-hand side of condition (11.32) gives the optimal tariff for the home country when no foreign capital is working in the economy, and the second term measures the effect on the tariff due to the presence of foreign capital and also the payment to this capital. For example, suppose that the home country is a small open economy so that $\mathcal{E}_{1p^*}^*$ is infinitely large. Without the presence of foreign capital, the optimal tariff is zero. If $\kappa > 0$ and if foreign capital owners receive the home rental rate, then the optimal tariff for a small open economy is

$$t_m = -\frac{\kappa r_p}{\mathcal{E}_{1p}}. \tag{11.32'}$$

With diversification at home, t_m is positive if and only if sector 1 is labor intensive, that is, $r_p < 0$ (assuming that $\mathcal{E}_{1p} > 0$). The intuition behind this result is clear. A positive (respectively negative) t increases the home price ratio p, and, by the Stolper-Samuelson theorem, lowers the payment to the foreign capital working in the home economy if $r_p < 0$.

11.6 Capital Movement for a Large Open Economy under Free Trade in Goods

In this and the following sections, I examine how capital movement may affect the welfare of the home country when it does not have an optimal goods trade policy. The volume of trade is not optimal from the home country's point of view, and the partial welfare effect of capital movement may be different from its total effect. As a result, even if capital movement is not diverted so that partial welfare effect is positive, the total welfare effect may be negative and international capital movement may be detrimental to the home country.

In this section, I focus on a large open economy that allows free goods trade. Even though free trade in goods leads to equalization of commodity prices, $p = p^*$, the rental rates in the countries, however, may be different when capital moves only sluggishly. The following two cases are analyzed separately: the moving capital receives the home rental rate r; and the moving capital receives the foreign rental rate r^*.

11.6.1 The Moving Capital Receives r

In this case, the foreign budget constraint is given by (11.30): $p^* E_1^* + E_2^* = r\kappa^*$, and the home country faces the values of $\partial E_2/\partial E_1$ and $\partial E_2/\partial \kappa$ as given by (11.31). Using the latter two expressions, the partial derivatives of the home welfare function are:

$$W_1 = u_2 \left[\frac{E_1^*}{\mathcal{E}_{1p^*}^*} - \frac{\kappa r_p}{\mathcal{E}_{1p}} \right]$$

$$W_\kappa = -u_2 \left[\frac{E_1^* \mathcal{E}_{1\kappa^*}^*}{\mathcal{E}_{1p^*}^*} - \frac{\kappa r_p \mathcal{E}_{1\kappa}}{\mathcal{E}_{1p}} + \kappa r_\kappa \right]$$

Note that W_1 is no longer necessarily zero because of the absence of an optimal trade policy. The expression of W_κ is the same as that in the previous section because in both cases the moving capital receives the home rental rate. The total welfare effect is equal to

$$\frac{dW}{d\kappa} = W_1 \frac{dE_1}{d\kappa} + W_\kappa. \tag{11.33}$$

In (11.33), $dE_1/d\kappa$ is the change in the equilibrium home export of good 1 as one unit of foreign capital is transferred to the home country. In terms of the E_1–κ framework developed in Chapter 4, it is equal to the slope of schedule GT in the framework. As shown in Chapter 4, it is given by

$$\left. \frac{dE_1}{d\kappa} \right|_{GT} = \frac{\mathcal{E}_{1p} \mathcal{E}_{1\kappa^*}^* + \mathcal{E}_{1\kappa} \mathcal{E}_{1p^*}^*}{\mathcal{E}_{1p} + \mathcal{E}_{1p^*}^*}. \tag{11.34}$$

If both countries are diversified and $\mathcal{E}_{1p}$ and $\mathcal{E}_{1p^*}^*$ are positive, then schedule GT is positively sloped if and only if sector 1 is capital intensive in both countries.

The previous section shows that if there is no capital movement diversion, then $(r - r^*)$ and W_κ have the same sign. In particular, if the home country is a host country and pays foreign capital the home rental rate, $r > r^*$. Thus if capital movement diversion is absent, an inflow of foreign capital is beneficial if W_1 and $dE_1/d\kappa$ have the same sign. An example of this sufficient condition for an welfare-enhancing capital inflow is that a decrease in the export level of good 1 at any given capital movement level is beneficial (that is, $W_1 < 0$)

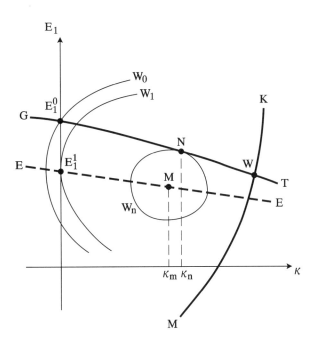

Figure 11.9

and that an inflow of capital does lower the export level of good 1 (that is, $dE_1/d\kappa \leq 0$).

An illustration of the last sufficient condition is given by Figure 11.9. Schedule GT shows the locus of the equilibrium levels of E_1 under free goods trade at different levels of capital movement while schedule KM shows the locus of the equilibrium capital movement level at a different export level. The vertical intercept E_1^0 of schedule GT shows the home export level of good 1 under free trade but no capital movement. The corresponding welfare level of the home country is indicated by the iso-welfare contour labeled W_0. The diagram also shows the optimal goods trade locus EE, which shows the home optimal export levels of good 1 at different levels of κ. That schedule KM is on the right-hand side of the vertical axis means that under free goods trade foreign capital tends to flow in. The final world equilibrium under free goods trade and capital movement is represented by point W.

The diagram shows the case in which schedule EE is below schedule GT, meaning that within this relevant range, the home country wishes to lower the export level (for example by using an export tax). With no capital movement, the optimal export level is E_1^1, which is lower than the free-trade export level E_1^0. Thus the partial effect $W_1 < 0$. In the case shown, schedule GT is negatively slope, indicating that an inflow of foreign capital lowers the export level.

Given all these conditions, inflow of foreign capital improves the home welfare.

Of course, that W_1 and $dE_1/d\kappa$ have the same sign is only sufficient but not necessary for a welfare-enhancing inflow of foreign capital. Note that the slope of an iso-welfare contour is equal to $-W_\kappa/W_1$. Thus by making use of (11.33), it can be shown that a necessary and sufficient condition for a welfare-enhancing inflow of foreign capital is

$$\frac{dE_1}{d\kappa}\bigg|_{GT} \gtrless -\frac{W_\kappa}{W_1} \quad \text{if } W_1 \gtrless 0.$$

With schedule KM far to the right of the vertical axis, the home country can set a ceiling on the level of capital inflow to reach a constrained optimal (under free goods trade). The first-order condition for this constrained optimal is $dW/d\kappa = 0$, which implies a tangency between schedule GT and an iso-welfare contour. This constrained optimal is depicted by point N with a capital inflow level of κ_n. The constrained optimal point N and the corresponding capital flow level κ_n can be compared with the optimal point M and κ_m. It is easy to see from Figure 11.9 that the sign of $\kappa_n - \kappa_m$ is ambiguous. If the iso-welfare contour is concave toward the optimal point,[11] then $\kappa_n > \kappa_m$ if and only if schedule GT is negatively sloped at point N (the case shown in Figure 11.9).

More conditions for welfare-enhancing capital movement can be obtained by making use of the slope of schedule GT given by (11.34) and the partial derivatives of function $W(E_1, \kappa)$. Thus

$$\frac{dW}{d\kappa} = u_2 \left\{ \left[\frac{E_1^*}{\mathcal{E}_{1p^*}^*} - \frac{\kappa r_p}{\mathcal{E}_{1p}} \right] \left[\frac{\mathcal{E}_{1p}\mathcal{E}_{1\kappa^*}^* + \mathcal{E}_{1\kappa}\mathcal{E}_{1p^*}^*}{\mathcal{E}_{1p} + \mathcal{E}_{1p^*}^*} \right] \right.$$
$$\left. - \left[\frac{E_1^*\mathcal{E}_{1\kappa^*}^*}{\mathcal{E}_{1p^*}^*} - \frac{\kappa r_p\mathcal{E}_{1\kappa}}{\mathcal{E}_{1p}} + \kappa r_\kappa \right] \right\}$$
$$= u_2 \left\{ \frac{(E_1^* + \kappa r_p)(\mathcal{E}_{1\kappa} - \mathcal{E}_{1\kappa^*}^*)}{\mathcal{E}_{1p} + \mathcal{E}_{1p^*}^*} - \kappa r_\kappa \right\}. \tag{11.35}$$

Suppose that initially diversification and no capital movement exist. Then a small inflow of foreign capital will benefit the home country if both countries' exportable sectors are labor intensive.[12] Alternatively, a small inflow of for-

11. In other words, the set $\left\{(E_1, \kappa) : W(E_1, \kappa) \geq W_1\right\}$ is convex where W_1 is the welfare level of the contour tangent to the vertical at E_1^1.

12. By condition (11.35), a welfare-enhancing capital inflow when initially $\kappa = 0$ requires that $E_1^*(\mathcal{E}_{1\kappa} - \mathcal{E}_{1\kappa^*}^*) > 0$. For example, if the home country exports good 1 (that is, $E_1^* < 0$), the home sector 1 and the foreign sector 2 need to be labor intensive (that is, $\mathcal{E}_{1\kappa} < 0$ and $\mathcal{E}_{1\kappa^*}^* > 0$).

eign capital will hurt the home country if both countries's exportable sectors are capital intensive.

11.6.2   The Moving Capital Receives r^*

I now turn to the case in which the moving capital is paid the foreign rental rate r^*. As mentioned previously, this case is more applicable if the home country is a source country of capital and receives the foreign rental rate, or if the home country as a host country pays only (marginally above) the foreign rental rate to the inflowing foreign capital. Using the above analysis, the partial derivatives of function $W(E_1, \kappa)$ are

$$W_1 = u_2 \left[\frac{E_1^*}{\mathcal{E}_{1p*}^*} + \frac{\kappa r_{p*}^*}{\mathcal{E}_{1p*}^*} \right]$$

$$W_\kappa = u_2 \left[(r - r^*) - \frac{E_1^* \mathcal{E}_{1\kappa*}^*}{\mathcal{E}_{1p*}^*} - \frac{\kappa r_{p*}^* \mathcal{E}_{1\kappa}}{\mathcal{E}_{1p*}^*} + \kappa r_{\kappa*}^* \right].$$

Based on these derivatives and the slope of schedule GT given by (11.34), the total welfare effect of capital movement is

$$\frac{\mathrm{d}W}{\mathrm{d}\kappa} = u_2 \left\{ (r - r^*) + \left[\frac{E_1^* + \kappa r_{p*}^*}{\mathcal{E}_{1p*}^*} \right] \left[\frac{\mathcal{E}_{1p} \mathcal{E}_{1\kappa*}^* + \mathcal{E}_{1\kappa} \mathcal{E}_{1p*}^*}{\mathcal{E}_{1p} + \mathcal{E}_{1p*}^*} - \mathcal{E}_{1\kappa*}^* \right] + \kappa r_{p*}^* \right\}$$

$$= u_2 \left\{ (r - r^*) + \frac{(E_1^* + \kappa r_{p*}^*)(\mathcal{E}_{1\kappa} - \mathcal{E}_{1\kappa*}^*)}{\mathcal{E}_{1p} + \mathcal{E}_{1p*}^*} + \kappa r_{\kappa*}^* \right\}. \tag{11.36}$$

Condition (11.36) gives several sufficient conditions for an increase in welfare due to an inflow of foreign capital or an outflow of domestic capital. For example, suppose that $r < r^*$ so that home capital tends to flow out. If initially there is no or little capital movement, and if the foreign countries is diversified and if the exportable sectors in both countries are capital intensive, then an outflow of home capital benefits the home country.[13]

11.7   Capital Movement for a Small, Protected Economy

I now turn to a small open economy that is facing exogenously given world prices. The economy is protected by either a tariff with a fixed rate, or a quota with a fixed level. The previous chapter shows that the effect of an accumulation of a factor on national welfare is given by

---

13. If the foreign country is diversified, $r_{\kappa*}^* = 0$. By condition (11.36), $\mathrm{d}W/\mathrm{d}\kappa < 0$ if $(E_1^* + \kappa r_{p*}^*)$ and $(\mathcal{E}_{1\kappa} - \mathcal{E}_{1\kappa*}^*)$ have different signs. For example, This condition is satisfied if κ is sufficiently small, if the foreign country exports good 1, and if both the foreign sector 1 and the home sector 2 are capital intensive.

$$\frac{\mathrm{d}V}{\mathrm{d}\kappa} = \frac{\partial V}{\partial \kappa} + \frac{\partial V}{\partial p}\frac{\partial p}{\partial \kappa} + \frac{\partial V}{\partial b}\frac{\partial b}{\partial \kappa}$$

$$= \lambda\left\{r + E_1\frac{\partial p}{\partial \kappa} + \frac{\partial b}{\partial \kappa}\right\}. \tag{11.37}$$

Condition (11.37) can now be interpreted as the effects of a capital inflow on the welfare of the home country. The reason is that the formula that was derived in the previous chapter for the welfare effect of a factor accumulation applies to the welfare effect of capital inflow, except that the transfer b has to be measured appropriately. As I explained in Section 11.1 of this chapter, the transfer is equal to $b = (s - r)\kappa - tE_1$.

The welfare effect of an inflow of an exogenous amount of foreign capital is analyzed in two cases: tariff and quota. First consider a tariff of a fixed rate. This implies that the domestic prices are fixed, $\partial p/\partial \kappa = 0$ and that under diversification the domestic rental rate is fixed. The effect of capital inflow on the transfer is given by condition (11.3b), that is, $b_\kappa = s - r - r_\kappa\kappa - t\mathcal{E}_{1\kappa}$. Substitute these results into (11.37) to give

$$\frac{\mathrm{d}V}{\mathrm{d}\kappa} = \lambda\left(s - r_\kappa\kappa - t\mathcal{E}_{1\kappa}\right). \tag{11.38}$$

Consider only the case in which the economy is diversified, $r_\kappa = 0$. If no income tax is present, then condition (11.38) implies that an inflow of foreign capital improves national welfare if and only if the trade tax revenue increases. This result is similar to the one in the previous chapter for the welfare effect of a factor accumulation. Substitute the effect of capital inflow on the export level of good 1 as given by (11.4b) into (11.38) to give

$$\frac{\mathrm{d}V}{\mathrm{d}\kappa} = \lambda\left\{s\left(1 + \frac{t\gamma m_1}{p}\right) - t\gamma\frac{\partial Q_1}{\partial \kappa}\right\}. \tag{11.38'}$$

If no income tax is assumed and if no inferior goods are present (so $\gamma > 0$), then foreign capital is beneficial if and only if $\partial Q_1/\partial \kappa$ is negative, or if and only if sector 1 (assumed to be the importable if tariff is imposed, or the exportable if an export subsidy is imposed) is labor intensive. Alternatively, foreign capital inflow is immiserizing if and only if sector 1 is capital intensive. This result has been derived by many people such as Uzawa (1969), Bhagwati (1973), Hamada (1974), Brecher and Diaz Alejandro (1977), and Neary and Ruane (1988). Minabe (1981) obtains a similar result for the welfare effect of an outflow of domestic capital. Although in the present framework I assume perfect capital mobility between the sectors in a country, the analysis also applies to sector-specific capital. (See the condition for the welfare effect of factor accumulation given in Chapter 10.) Thus condition (11.38') can be applied to show that with a tariff but in the absence of an income tax, an inflow of the type of capital specific to the importable (respectively exportable) is immiserizing (respectively welfare-enhancing) (Srinivasan, 1983).

I now turn to capital inflow in the presence of a fixed quota ($E_1 = \overline{E}_1$). In this case, the domestic price is no longer fixed. Assuming that the government gets the quota premium, the transfer is equal to $b = (s - r)\kappa - (p - p^*)E_1$. The effect of an inflow of capital (with $\kappa \geq 0$) on transfer is equal to

$$\frac{\partial b}{\partial \kappa} = s - r - \kappa \frac{dr}{d\kappa} - E_1 \frac{\partial p}{\partial \kappa}.$$

Substitute this condition into (11.38) to give

$$\frac{dV}{d\kappa} = \lambda \left(s - \kappa \frac{dr}{d\kappa} \right). \tag{11.39}$$

Thus with $\kappa \geq 0$, foreign capital inflow is beneficial in the presence of a quota if $dr/d\kappa < 0$ (Dei, 1985; Miyagiwa, 1991).

11.8   Choosing between Capital Mobility and Labor Mobility: The Ramaswami Case

Thus far, the analysis concentrates on international movement of capital while labor is immobile between the countries. As emphasized before, capital and labor are two symmetric inputs in the production processes, and thus if they are treated in the same way in terms of repatriation of income, they may be treated symmetrically in terms of movement between countries. This means that the welfare analysis presented above can be applied to the case when labor is mobile internationally but capital is not.[14] This does not mean, however, that international capital mobility and international labor mobility would have the same welfare impacts on the countries.

In this and the next sections, I discuss two cases in which international capital mobility is compared with international labor mobility in terms of the home country's welfare: the Ramaswami case and foreign investment in a duty-free zone.[15]

Suppose that the home country has the options of allowing domestic capital outflow and permitting foreign labor inflow. In each of these options, the home country can impose optimal taxes on the moving factor. The question is which of the two factor mobility policies the home country prefers.

To make the problem manageable, the model can be simplified by assuming that there is only one homogeneous good in the home and foreign countries.

---

14. There are many asymmetric issues between international capital mobility and international labor mobility. Some of these issues are discussed in detail in Chapters 13 and 14.

15. For two other cases, see Wong (1983) and Suzuki (1989).

There is thus no need to have trade in goods, and the impacts of international factor movement on the terms of trade can be ignored. I further assume that the countries have identical technology, and that the common production function for the sector, denoted by $F(K, L)$, is strictly increasing, concave, twice differentiable, and linearly homogeneous in factor inputs. In order to have the desired patterns of factor movement, I assume that the home country versus the foreign country is capital abundant in the sense that it has a higher capital-labor ratio. Assuming a passive foreign country and using the preceding analysis, I can easily derive for the home country the monopolistic policy of home capital outflow and the monopsonistic policy of foreign labor inflow.

Even with the assumption of a single good and identical technology, it seems that the given information is still not sufficient to give a definite ranking of the two factor movement policies. For example, the ranking may depend on the technology or the functional form of the production function. Using a remarkable argument, however, Ramaswami (1968) derives the strong yet unintuitive result that monopsonistic labor inflow always dominates monopolistic capital outflow, irrespective of the functional form of the production function.

Denote the given capital and labor endowments of the home country by $\overline{K}$ and $\overline{L}$, respectively.[16] Foreign variables are distinguished by asterisks. The home country is capital abundant, that is,

$$\frac{\overline{K}}{\overline{L}} > \frac{\overline{K}^*}{\overline{L}^*}.$$

The allocation and movement of factors can be illustrated by the box diagram in Figure 11.10. The size of the box represents the given world endowments of labor (measured horizontally) and capital (measured vertically). Point E is the endowment point. That it is above the diagonal shows the capital abundance in the home country. I assume symmetry between capital mobility and labor mobility so that workers who move from one country to another repatriate their earnings back to the source country and consume there. The two curves that pass through point E and are denoted by Q_E and Q_E^* are isoquants of the countries with the output levels given by

$$Q_E = F(\overline{K}, \overline{L})$$

$$Q_E^* = F(\overline{K}^*, \overline{L}^*).$$

Because the production function is linearly homogeneous, the distance measured along the diagonal from each origin (O or O*) also represents the output

---

16. The following analysis is based mainly on Calvo and Wellisz (1983) and Bhagwati and Srinivasan (1983b).

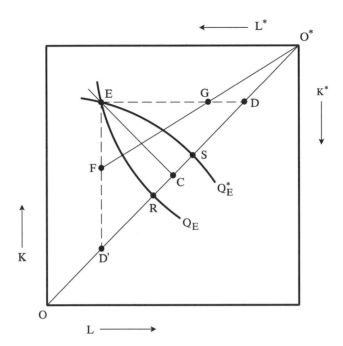

Figure 11.10

level. With nonsatiation, the welfare level of each country is strictly increasing in the national income in terms of the good.

Note that any point on the diagonal represents the same capital-labor ratio and thus the same factor prices (because of identical technology) in the countries. This means that the world equilibrium under free factor mobility must be at a point on the diagonal. For example, if free labor mobility but not capital mobility is allowed, the equilibrium is point D, with ED of foreign labor working in the home country. Similarly, if free capital mobility but not labor mobility is allowed, ED′ of home capital will move to the foreign country.

Point D (for labor mobility) or D′ (for capital mobility) represents the gross domestic products (GDPs) of the countries. To get their national income levels, construct line EC whose slope is the (negative) common wage-rental ratio under free capital or labor mobility. Length OC (respectively O*C) represents the home (respectively foreign) country's national income and welfare. Because this wage-rental ratio must be in between the autarkic wage-rental ratios in the countries (because of decreasing marginal products), point C must be in between points R and S. This means that both countries must gain from free factor mobility.

Now turn to the ranking of factor mobility policies with optimal taxation. A vigorous analysis can be broken down into the following steps.

Step 1 Suppose that an arbitrary amount $c =$ EF in Figure 11.10 (EF $<$ ED$'$) of the home capital moves to the foreign country while labor movement between the countries is prohibited. The slope of FO* gives the new capital-labor ratio in the foreign country. Denote the current foreign rental and wage rates by r^* and w^*, respectively, where $r^* = F_K(\overline{K}^* + c, \overline{L}^*)$ and $w^* = F_L(\overline{K}^* + c, \overline{L}^*)$, and where subscripts for $F(\overline{K}^* + c, \overline{L}^*)$ represent the marginal products of capital and labor. Let $e =$ EG in Figure 11.10 be the amount of foreign labor working with the home capital in the foreign country. The current national income of the home country is

$$y_1 = F(\overline{K} - c, \overline{L}) + r^*c, \tag{11.40}$$

where $F(\overline{K} - c, \overline{L})$ is the GDP and r^*c is the repatriation of the home capital working in the foreign country. Linear homogeneity of the production function means that $F(c, e) = r^*c + w^*e$. Using this result, the home national income is equal to

$$y_1 = F(\overline{K} - c, \overline{L}) + F(c, e) - w^*e. \tag{11.40$'$}$$

Step 2 Consider an alternative home policy. Instead of allowing home capital outflow, the home country allows an inflow of foreign labor equal to $e =$ EG and pay the incoming worker a wage rate of w^* which is equal to that in step 1. The total home output is $F(\overline{K}, \overline{L} + e)$ and the national income is

$$y_2 = F(\overline{K}, \overline{L} + e) - w^*e. \tag{11.41}$$

Concavity of the production function implies that $F(\overline{K}, \overline{L} + e) \geq F(\overline{K} - c, \overline{L}) + F(c, e)$. Thus by comparing conditions (11.40$'$) and (11.41),

$$y_2 \geq y_1.$$

In fact, if the production possibility set is strictly convex, then there is always efficiency gain when two production techniques with different capital-labor ratios are combined together. So $y_2 > y_1$.

Step 3 The labor inflow policy described in step 2 is not necessary the optimal one. Suppose that the home country chooses the optimal income tax on the incoming workers, and denote the resulting national income level by y_3. Thus $y_3 \geq y_2$. Combining these results, $y_3 \geq y_1$. In fact, the last inequality can be replaced by an equality if there is efficiency gain in step 2 or the labor policy in step 2 is not optimal.

I have shown that monopsonistic labor inflow dominates monopolistic capital outflow. In fact, the amount of capital outflow considered in step 1 does not have to be the optimal amount. This implies that for any amount of capital outflow ($EF < ED'$), there exists a labor inflow policy that dominates the capital outflow policy. These results indicate that from a country's point of view, it is better to exploit foreign factor working in the domestic economy than to allow outflow of domestic factor.[17] Because capital and labor are symmetric, and so are the home and the foreign countries, the analysis can be applied to show that from the foreign country's point of view, monopsonistic capital inflow dominates monopolistic labor outflow (if the home country is passive).

Other policies can also be examined. First, as analyzed in previous sections, a quantitative restriction on the outflow of capital can give the same welfare (ignoring income distributional effects) to the home country as the monopolistic capital outflow policy, because with a quota domestic capital owners get the rent. Second, home welfare rises monotonically with inflow of foreign labor when foreign workers earn and repatriate the home wage rate until free labor mobility equilibrium is reached. This means that a quota on foreign labor inflow is inferior to free labor mobility. Third, Bhagwati and Srinivasan (1983b) suggest a perfectly discriminatory policy on the inflowing foreign labor. Under this policy, each unit of labor that enters the home country and works there is paid (marginally greater than) the prevailing foreign wage rate, w^*. Because the foreign wage rate rises with more labor movement, a foreign worker that moves to the home country will be paid more than all those foreign workers that moved earlier. Denoting the amount of foreign labor outflow by variable e, the wage rate is the marginal product of labor, that is,

$$w^* = F_L(\overline{K}^*, \overline{L}^* - e) = -F_e(\overline{K}^*, \overline{L}^* - e),$$

where the subscripts represent partial derivatives. Labor movement stops at the free labor movement point D in Figure 11.10 when wage rates are equalized. Let the amount of labor that has moved be $e^w = ED$. The total payment to the foreign workers working in the home country is

$$\int_0^{e^w} w^* \mathrm{d}e = -\int_0^{e^w} F_e(\overline{K}^*, \overline{L}^* - e) \mathrm{d}e = F(\overline{K}^*, \overline{L}^*) - F(\overline{K}^*, \overline{L}^* - e^w).$$

$$(11.42)$$

Because $F(\overline{K}^*, \overline{L}^* - e^w)$ is the income of the capitalists and remaining workers in the foreign country, condition (11.42) implies that the foreign country's national income is equal to $F(\overline{K}^*, \overline{L}^*)$ which is the foreign national income under autarky. In other words, this perfectly discriminatory policy of the home

---

17. Monopsonistic labor inflow may be dominated by monopolistic capital outflow if there is a third factor (Kuhn and Wooten, 1987) or if there is unemployment in the home country (Brecher and Choudhri, 1987).

country leaves the foreign country as well off as under autarky, and the home country has captured the entire world gain from labor movement.

Noting that a perfectly discriminatory policy may be difficult to implement in reality, Jones, et al. (1986) propose yet another policy for the home country that produces the same welfare effect as a perfectly discriminatory labor policy. Their policy is to tax the incoming foreign workers and use a subsidy to attract foreign capital to flow in. The labor income tax and capital income subsidy are set at the levels so that all inflowing foreign factors receive (marginally greater than) their autarkic rewards. The home country continues to receive foreign factors until (nearly) all foreign factors have migrated to the home country. This is called an (almost) complete 'buy-out' policy. With (nearly) all foreign factors working in the home country, the total world output is the same as that under free factor mobility. Because all foreign factors receive their autarkic rewards, the home country has captured all the world gain from factor mobility. So this policy gives the same welfare impact on the home country as the perfectly discriminatory labor inflow policy.[18]

Combining these results, the following ranking of policies in terms of the home country (ignoring income distributional effects) can be stated:

complete 'buy-out' = perfectly discriminatory labor inflow

$\geq$ monopsonistic labor inflow

$\geq$ monopolistic (using tax or restriction) capital outflow

$\geq$ free factor mobility $\geq$ restriction on labor inflow,

where "$\geq$" means "is preferred to" and "=" means "has the same welfare effect as."

11.9   Choosing between Capital Mobility and Labor Mobility: Duty-Free Zones

There has been controversy in the literature about where an exogenous amount of foreign capital should be located when a country is planning to form a duty-free zone (DFZ).[19] Consider a small open economy (the home country) that is protecting its importable industry with a tariff. Label the domestic economy of the country the domestic zone (DZ). The exogenous amount of foreign capital can be introduced into the DZ. This is called the *capital inflow policy*.

18. If the home country has a technological superiority, then a partial, or in some cases complete, buy-out of foreign factors may still be optimal. See Jones and Easton (1989).

19. A duty-free zone is sometimes called a free trade zone, an export processing zone, or a special economic zone.

Alternatively, the home country can form a DFZ, draw the same amount of foreign capital to the DFZ, and allow domestic labor to flow out to the zone to work with the foreign capital. This is called *labor outflow policy*. The problem of whether the foreign capital should be located in the DZ or in the DFZ can be alternatively regarded as a choice between capital inflow or labor outflow.[20]

Hamada (1974), which provides the first vigorous analysis of the effects of DFZ, said that labor outflow (with the foreign capital in the DFZ) is superior to (or can hurt less than) capital inflow (into the DZ). Although they agree with Hamada (1974) that foreign investment necessarily hurts the tariff-ridden economy no matter where it is located, Hamilton and Svensson (1982, p. 63) argue that, "*in contrast* [original emphasis] to Hamada's result, our conclusion was that a given amount of capital imported into (duty-) free zone decreases welfare (of the host country) more than the same amount of capital imported directly into the domestic zone."

Thus Hamilton and Svenssion conclude that capital inflow is superior to labor outflow, contrary to Hamada's ranking. This discrepancy is clearly puzzling. To resolve this puzzle, Wong (1986c) provides a thorough analysis on the effects of DFZ and factor mobility and finds that the ranking of these two policies depends on the kind of good produced in the DFZ, the kind of good used for repatriation, and whether the repatriation is taxed or subsidized. The discrepancy between Hamada's and Hamilton and Svensson's results is due to the different assumptions they make regarding these three factors.

Wong's analysis can be summarized as follows. Suppose the home country imports the capital-intensive good 2. With a non-prohibitive tariff on the imported good 2 or a subsidy on the exporting good 1, the home price ratio of good 1 p is less than the world price ratio p^*. Incomplete specialization of the economy is assumed.

First consider allowing the exogenous amount of foreign capital working in the DFZ, using the existing technologies in the DZ. Assume further that good i, $i = 1, 2$, is produced in the DFZ; factor services are paid and repatriated in terms of good i; and no tax or subsidy is imposed on factor income repatriation. This means that a certain amount of domestic labor moves to the DFZ, works with the foreign capital, and repatriates the wage in terms of good i back to the DZ. The equilibrium exists when the wages rate in terms of good i in the two zones are equalized. Because of the use of identical technologies, the DFZ and sector i in the DZ have the same equilibrium capital-labor ratio and the same rental rate.

Now hypothetically redraw the boundary so that the DFZ becomes part of the DZ. Because of identical technology and capital-labor ratio, production in

---

20. This terminology is due to Hamilton and Svensson (1983).

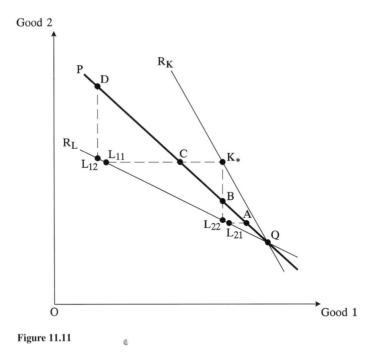

Figure 11.11

the DFZ is not disturbed, and domestic factors and the foreign capital earn the same rewards as before. Thus there is the first result: Capital inflow is equivalent to labor outflow if the good produced in the DFZ is used for repatriation in the absence of taxation.

This result can be illustrated graphically by Figure 11.11. Point Q is the production point before any factor movement and the formation of a DFZ. Line PQ represents the domestic price line and is tangent to the production possibility frontier (the latter not shown). When a certain amount of foreign capital flows into the DZ, the production point shifts up along the Rybczynski line R_K to point K_*. By the analysis given in Chapter 2, the national income of the home country is a point on the domestic price line and its exact location depends on which good is used for repatriation. Thus, point B (respectively C) is the national income point if good 2 (respectively 1) is repatriated, with K_*B (respectively K_*C) representing the income repatriated.

If a DFZ is formed and foreign capital is located there, domestic labor will flow out, shifting the production point of the DZ up along the Rybczynski line R_L. Using the analysis, the exact location of the new production of the DZ can be obtained easily. Thus, if good 2 (respectively 1) is produced in the DFZ and repatriated without tax or subsidy, the new production is at L_{22} (respectively L_{11}) because national income must be at point B (respectively C), the same as that under the corresponding capital inflow policy.

So far, I have explained two pairs of policies that produce the same welfare effect. These two policies can also be ranked with each other. Because the given world relative price of good 1 is higher than the home relative price due to the tariff, a national income point *higher* on the domestic price line PQ in Figure 11.11 represents a *lower* national welfare level. Because point C is higher than point B, the factor mobility policy under which the importable (good 2) is produced and used for repatriation without tax is superior to the policy under which good 1 is produced and used for repatriation without tax. Combining these results produces the following ranking:

$$L_{22} = K_{*2} \geq K_{*1} = L_{11},$$

where L (respectively K) represents the labor outflow (respectively capital inflow) policy, the first subscript represents the type of good being produced, the second subscript represents the type of good used for repatriation. When capital works in the DZ, it does not matter which good it is producing, so the first subscript in the capital inflow policy is represented by an asterisk. Note that for simplicity I use L_{ij} to represent a particular labor policy and L$_{ij}$ to represent the GDP point of the corresponding labor policy in Figure 11.11.

Suppose now that income repatriated by domestic workers working in the DFZ in terms of good 2 (respectively 1) back to the DZ or that income repatriated by foreign capitalists working in the DZ in terms of good 1 (respectively 2) out of the country is subject to a tax (respectively subsidy) the same as the trade tax rate. Such a tax or subsidy will eliminate any possible arbitrage using income repatriation done by the moving factor owners due to the price differential between the DZ and the rest of the world. As a result, moving factor owners and the home country will be indifferent to which good they use for repatriation. Combining these results gives the following ranking:

$$L_{22} = L_{21S} = K_{*1T} = K_{*2} \geq K_{*2S} = K_{*1} = L_{11} = L_{12T},$$

where a third subscript is added to denote a tax (T) or a subsidy (S) that is imposed on income repatriation.

I next consider the case in which, without the above compensatory taxes or subsidies, good i is produced in the DFZ but workers repatriate good j $(i \neq j)$. Consider first the case when good 1 is produced in the DFZ. If workers are required to repatriate good 1, as assumed before, equilibrium is represented by point L$_{11}$ in Figure 11.11. I now relax this repatriation constraint. Because good 2 is cheaper in the DFZ (or more expensive in the DZ), workers will prefer their income in terms of good 2 (thus avoiding the tariff). This means that the effective wage rate at point L$_{11}$ is higher than that in the DZ, thus drawing more workers to move out to the DFZ. The equilibrium production point of the DZ will be at a point such as L$_{12}$ on the Rybczynski line R_L, and the corresponding national income point will be at D. On the other hand, if instead good 2 is produced in the DFZ but workers are required to repatriate good 1, less labor will move to the DFZ than without this repatriation constraint. This means that the equilibrium production point of the DZ will be a point on R_L such as L_{21}, with a corresponding national income point at A. Recalling that national income points higher on the the domestic price line yield lower national welfare levels, the analysis immediately gives the following ranking: $L_{21} \geq L_{22}$ and $L_{11} \geq L_{12}$. Thus I have established the following result:

$$FT \geq RT \geq L_{21} = L_{22T} \geq L_{22} = L_{21S} = K_{*1T} = K_{*2} \geq K_{*2S}$$

$$= K_{*1} = L_{11} = L_{12T} \geq L_{12} = L_{11S}, \tag{11.43}$$

where I have included the policies of free trade (FT) and restricted trade with no factor mobility (RT). The first two inequalities are well-known results from the analysis in the previous sections.

The ranking in (11.43) can be applied to explain the seemingly conflicting policy rankings in Hamada (1974) and Hamilton and Svensson (1982). Hamada assumes that good 2 is produced in the DFZ and that factor income repatriation is taxed, and concludes that labor outflow is superior to capital inflow, that is, $L_{22T} \geq K_{*2S}$. On the other hand, Hamilton and Svensson, by showing that under certain conditions good 1 is produced in the DFZ and assuming that no restrictions on factor income repatriation, arrive at the conclusion that capital inflow is superior to labor outflow, that is, $K_{*1} \geq L_{12}$. According to condition (11.43), both of them are right, the discrepancy between their conclusions being due to the different assumptions they make.

12 Strategic Trade Policies

This chapter examines trade policies in the presence of a small number of players: a limited number of firms or a limited number of governments. Because the number of players is small, the action taken by one player may have significant effects on other players. Throughout this chapter, it is assumed that the governments are fully aware of the relationship between players' actions in choosing the optimal policies.

In this chapter, two models are examined. In the first, there are oligopolistic industries in which there are only a few producers. This model was examined in detail in Chapter 7. In the extreme case, there is one firm in the industry in each of the countries under consideration. Interactions between the firms affect not only the production of the firms, but also trade between the countries and the countries' welfare. Here I examine the effects of several trade policies on production, consumption, trade, and welfare.

In the second model there are two governments that actively choose optimal policies to maximize their objective functions. The focus of analysis in this type of model is the interactions between governments, not between firms in different countries. The industries under consideration may or may not be competitive.

I begin with an extension of the partial equilibrium, oligopoly model described in Chapter 7. Assuming that the other trading country always allows free trade, the optimal policies for a country are derived and their effects are determined. This model is useful because it is simple, can be used to examine some very common strategic trade policies, and reduces to other models that have appeared in the literature. In the second part of this chapter, I drop the assumption that the foreign government is passive in order to analyze the interactions between two governments. I analyze the equilibrium and consequences of trade wars, and suggest alternatives to trade wars.

12.1 Optimal Policies in the Presence of Oligopolistic Industries

I begin with the partial equilibrium, oligopoly model of intraindustry trade explained in Chapter 7. Recapitulating the main features of the model, there are two countries labeled the home and foreign countries, each with one firm in an industry of a homogeneous product. The markets in both countries are segmented as described in Chapter 7, and the firms engage in Cournot competition. In the absence of government intervention, intraindustry trade generally exists. Using the earlier notation, denote the outputs supplied by the home (respectively foreign) firm to the home and foreign markets by x and X (respectively x^* and X^*), respectively. The home (respectively foreign) firm has a constant marginal cost, c (respectively c^*), and a constant fixed cost, f (respectively f^*). Because intercountry transport costs play no important role in this chapter, I simply assume that they are zero.

The demands in the home and foreign markets are denoted by q and q^*, respectively. In equilibrium,

$$q = x + x^* \tag{12.1a}$$

$$q^* = X + X^*. \tag{12.1b}$$

Denote the inverse demand function of the home and foreign markets by $p(q)$ and $p^*(q^*)$, respectively. Assuming twice differentiability of the functions and using primes to denote the derivates of these inverse demand functions, I assume that $p' < 0$ and $p^{*\prime} < 0$.

In setting policies, the home government is assumed to be a Stackelberg leader vis-à-vis the firms: It chooses policies in the first move and then the firms make production decisions.[1] Three policies are considered: *a home sale subsidy* with a specific rate of r, *an export subsidy* with a specific rate of s, and *an import tax* with a specific rate of t.[2] A negative tax is considered here to be a subsidy and vice versa.[3] Even though I am considering one single industry, the possibility of intraindustry trade implies that export and import taxes could be imposed simultaneously. In the presence of these policies, the profit functions of the firms are given by

$$\pi = xp(q) + Xp^*(q^*) - c(x + X) - f + rx + sX \tag{12.2a}$$

$$\pi^* = x^*p(q) + X^*p^*(q^*) - c^*(x^* + X^*) - f^* - tx^*. \tag{12.2b}$$

To obtain a subgame perfect equilibrium, I first solve the game's second stage. Each firm chooses its output to maximize its profits, taking the outputs of the other firm and the policy parameters as given. Using subindices to denote partial derivatives, the first-order conditions (with an interior solution) are

$$\pi_x = p(q) + xp'(q) - c + r = 0 \tag{12.3a}$$

$$\pi_X = p^*(q^*) + Xp^{*\prime}(q^*) - c + s = 0 \tag{12.3b}$$

$$\pi_{x^*}^* = p(q) + x^*p'(q) - c^* - t = 0 \tag{12.3c}$$

$$\pi_{X^*}^* = p^*(q^*) + X^*p^{*\prime}(q^*) - c^* = 0. \tag{12.3d}$$

---

1. One justification for allowing the government to take the first move is that policies effectively constrain the decision making of the firms (e.g., the firms have to pay the taxes imposed by the government), and that the government wants to keep its credibility so that whatever policies it announces in the first stage are irreversible.

2. Many papers in the literature examine one strategic policy at a time, but a few papers do derive the optimal policies to tackle simultaneously more than one distortion: Examples are Dixit (1984, 1988), Cheng (1988), and Krishna and Thursby (1991).

3. In the previous two chapters, I mentioned that an import subsidy is not necessarily the same as a negative tariff because it can create a two-way trade. In the present model, two-way trade exists even before any policy is imposed.

Because marginal costs are constant, the system of equations in (12.3) can be disaggregated into two subsystems. Given r, t, and the inverse demand function $p(q)$, conditions (12.1a), (12.3a), and (12.3c) can be solved for x, x^* and q. Similarly, given s and $p^*(q^*)$, conditions (12.1b), (12.3b), and (12.3d) can be solved for X, X^* and q^*. The dichotomy of the system implies that x and x^* depend only on r and t while X and X^* depend only on s.

Before solving the first stage of the game, it is necessary to analyze how the outputs are dependent on the policy parameters. First consider the home market. Define $\phi = p' + xp''$ and $\phi^* = p' + x^*p''$. Hahn's (1962) stability conditions require that ϕ, $\phi^* < 0$. These two conditions are satisfied if the home demand curve is not too convex toward the origin, which is assumed.

Differentiate (12.3a) and (12.3c) to give

$$\begin{bmatrix} \phi + p' & \phi \\ \phi^* & \phi^* + p' \end{bmatrix} \begin{bmatrix} dx \\ dx^* \end{bmatrix} = \begin{bmatrix} -dr \\ dt \end{bmatrix}.$$

By Hahn's stability conditions and p', $p^{*\prime} < 0$, all the elements in the above matrix are negative. Using Cramer's rule, I can solve for

$$dx = -\frac{(\phi^* + p')dr + \phi dt}{\Delta} \tag{12.4a}$$

$$dx^* = \frac{\phi^* dr + (\phi + p')dt}{\Delta}, \tag{12.4b}$$

where $\Delta = (p')^2 + p'\phi + p'\phi^* > 0$. Thus the dependence of the outputs on the policy parameters are $\partial x/\partial r > 0$, $\partial x/\partial t > 0$, $\partial x^*/\partial r < 0$, and $\partial x^*/\partial t < 0$. As expected, both home sale subsidy and import tax have positive total effects on domestic production but negative effects on foreign export. The two conditions in (12.4) can be added up to give

$$dq = \frac{-p'dr + p'dt}{\Delta}, \tag{12.4c}$$

which implies that $\partial q/\partial r > 0$ and $\partial q/\partial t < 0$. The effects of a tariff on the outputs can be illustrated in Figure 12.1. Schedules hh and ff are the reaction curves of the home and foreign firms for the home market under free trade, respectively. Using Hahn's stability conditions, both schedules are negatively sloped, with schedule hh being steeper. Point N is the free-trade Nash equilibrium. Condition (12.3c) shows that an increase in t has the same effect as an increase in the foreign firm's marginal cost, and it shifts the foreign firm's reaction curve downward to $f'f'$, for example. The new equilibrium point is M, which represents an increase in the home firm's output but a decrease in that of the foreign firm.

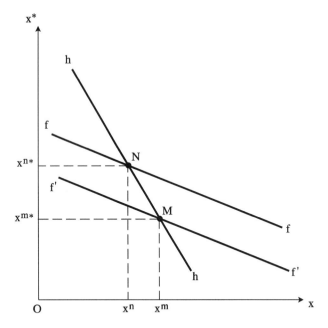

Figure 12.1

I now turn to the dependence of X and X^* on the export subsidy s. Define $\Phi = p^{*\prime} + Xp^{*\prime\prime}$ and $\Phi^* = p^{*\prime} + X^*p^{*\prime\prime}$. Again, by Hahn's stability conditions, Φ, $\Phi^* < 0$, which is satisfied if the foreign demand curve is not too convex toward the origin. Differentiate conditions (12.3b) and (12.3d) to give

$$\begin{bmatrix} \Phi + p^{*\prime} & \Phi \\ \Phi^* & \phi^* + p^{*\prime} \end{bmatrix} \begin{bmatrix} dX \\ dX^* \end{bmatrix} = \begin{bmatrix} -ds \\ 0 \end{bmatrix}.$$

Using Cramer's rule,

$$\frac{\partial X}{\partial s} = -\frac{\phi^* + p^{*\prime}}{\Delta^*} > 0 \qquad (12.5a)$$

$$\frac{\partial X^*}{\partial s} = \frac{\Phi^*}{\Delta^*} < 0 \qquad (12.5b)$$

$$\frac{\partial q^*}{\partial s} = -\frac{p^{*\prime}}{\Delta^*} > 0 \qquad (12.5c)$$

where $\Delta^* = (p^{*\prime})^2 + p^{*\prime}\Phi + p^{*\prime}\Phi^* > 0$.

Using the comparative static results, I now solve the first stage of the game. As was done in Chapter 9, national welfare is defined as the sum of consumer surplus, $CS(q)$, the profit of the home firm, π, and the net tax revenue, $tx^* - rx - sX$, that is,

$$W = CS(q) + \pi + tx^* - rx - sX,$$

$$= CS(q) + xp(q) + Xp^*(q^*) - c(x + X) - f + tx^*. \tag{12.6}$$

where $CS(q) = \int_0^q p(v)dv - p(q)q$. Because the equilibria of the home and foreign markets are independent of each other, the home sale subsidy and import tariff policies for the home market and the export subsidy policy for the foreign market are analyzed separately.

12.2   Policies for the Home Market

For the home market, the home government chooses r and t to maximize national welfare W, taking the equilibrium of the foreign market as given. In the present problem, analytically the welfare function can be maximized by choosing x and x^*.[4] In order to do this, I first have to find out the relationship between the policy parameters and outputs. First, keep x^* constant, that is, $dx^* = 0$. Using this assumption, the comparative-static condition (12.4b) gives the combinations of r and t that jointly keep x^* constant:

$$dr = -\frac{\phi + p'}{\phi^*}dt.$$

Substitute this condition into (12.4a) and rearrange terms to yield

$$dx = dt/\phi^*. \tag{12.7a}$$

Thus the rate of change in t that is needed when x increases marginally while x^* stays unchanged is equal to $t_x = \phi^*$. Using the same approach, $dx = 0$ can be set in (12.4a) and $dr = -\phi dt/(\phi^* + p')$ obtained. Substitute this result into (12.4b) and rearrange terms to give

$$dx^* = \frac{1}{\phi^* + p'}dt. \tag{12.7b}$$

Thus $t_{x^*} = \phi^* + p'$.

Differentiation of the home welfare function given by (12.6) with respect to x and x^*, using (12.7a) and (12.7b), gives the first-order conditions:

---

4. To see this point, denote the first-order conditions of the firms by $g(x, x^*, r) = 0$ and $g^*(x, x^*, t) = 0$, and the home welfare that comes from the home market by $V(x, x^*, r, t)$. Using the implicit function theorem, the firms' first-order conditions can be solved to give $x = x(r, t)$ and $x^* = x^*(r, t)$. Differentiation of the home welfare function to give $dV = [V_x x_r + V_{x^*} x_r^* + V_r]dr + [V_x x_t + V_{x^*} x_t^* + V_t]dt$. Alternatively, solve the firms' first-order conditions to give $r = r(x, x^*)$ and $t = t(x, x^*)$. Differentiation of the home welfare function gives $dV = [V_r r_x + V_t t_x + V_x]dx + [V_r r_{x^*} + V_t t_{x^*} + V_{x^*}]dx^*$. Mathematically both approaches are equivalent.

$$\frac{\partial W}{\partial x} = -qp' + (p - c) + xp' + x^*\phi^* = (p - c) + (x^*)^2 p'' = 0 \qquad (12.8a)$$

$$\frac{\partial W}{\partial x^*} = -qp' + xp' + t + x^*(\phi^* + p') = t + x^*\phi^* = 0. \qquad (12.8b)$$

Setting the derivatives in (12.8) to zero gives the first-order conditions for welfare maximization. To analyze (12.8a), first consider a closed economy or an economy with zero import. With $x^* = 0$, the condition reduces to $p = c$, which is the famous condition for a competitive output of a domestic monopoly in a closed economy. The same condition also holds under trade in the special case in which the home demand is linear, that is, $p'' = 0$ (Dixit, 1988; Cheng, 1988). Using condition (12.8a) and the home firm's first-order condition (12.3a), the optimal home sale subsidy rate is:

$$\tilde{r} = -xp' + (x^*)^2 p'', \qquad (12.9a)$$

which is positive if x^* is sufficiently small or if the demand curve is not too curved.

Assuming an interior solution (with respect to x^*), condition (12.8b) gives the optimal tariff:

$$\tilde{t} = -x^*\phi^* = -x^*(p' + x^*p'') > 0. \qquad (12.9b)$$

The sign of $\tilde{t}$ as given by (12.9b) comes from the stability condition. In some cases, however, the optimal tariff is prohibitive. To determine these cases, substitute the foreign firm's first-order condition given by (12.3c) and (12.8a) into (12.8b) to give

$$\frac{\partial W}{\partial x^*} = c - c^* + 2x^*p'. \qquad (12.10)$$

If $c < c^*$, meaning that the home firm is more cost efficient, then by (12.10) the optimal value of x^* is zero and a prohibitive tariff is optimal (Dixit, 1984).

More implications of a nonprohibitive tariff, as given by (12.9b), can be obtained as follows. Suppose that initially free trade is allowed by both countries, that is, $r = s = t = 0$. Differentiate the welfare function given by (12.6) with respect to t, evaluating at the free-trade point, to yield

$$\left.\frac{\partial W}{\partial t}\right|_{FT} = -qp'\frac{\partial q}{\partial t} + \pi_{x^*}\frac{\partial x^*}{\partial t} + x^*, \qquad (12.11)$$

where the subscript "FT" means free trade. Condition (12.11) gives the welfare effect of a small tariff. To understand the role of this tariff, the three terms on the right-hand side of (12.11) are respectively called the *consumption effect*, the *profit-shifting* (or *rent-shifting*) *effect*, and the *revenue effect* of a tariff.

The consumption effect, which shows the tariff's effect on consumer surplus, is negative because by (12.4c) a small tariff decreases total supply in the home market. This is the consumption cost of a tariff analyzed in previous chapters. The revenue effect, of course, describes how a small tariff increases the government revenue.

To understand the profit-shifting effect, recall that a tariff increases the home firm's sale to the domestic market but decreases that of the foreign firm. Therefore the effects of a small tariff on the portions of both firms' profits from the home market are evaluated at ($r = t = 0$)

$$\frac{\mathrm{d}\pi}{\mathrm{d}t} = \pi_x x_t + \pi_{x*} x_t^* = \pi_{x*} x_t^* = x p' x_t^* > 0 \tag{12.12a}$$

$$\frac{\mathrm{d}\pi^*}{\mathrm{d}t} = \pi_x^* x_t + \pi_{x*}^* x_t^* = \pi_x^* x_t = x^* p' x_t < 0, \tag{12.12b}$$

where $\pi_x = \pi_{x*}^* = 0$ due to profit maximization. A comparison of (12.12a) and (12.11) shows that the profit-shifting effect of a tariff is just its (positive) effect on the profit of the home firm. Condition (12.12b) shows that the tariff has a negative effect on the foreign firm's profit. Therefore a tariff has the effect of "shifting" (part of) the foreign firm's profit to the home firm, hence the term "profit-shifting."[5] This term, which appears frequently in the literature, should be used with the following two points in mind. First, an increase in the profit of the home firm does not have to be at the expense of the foreign firm. In maximizing its national welfare, the (selfish) home government does not care whether the foreign firm gets more or less profit. There are other policies that may increase both the home and the foreign firms' profits so that no profit is being shifted. Second, even in the present case in which the foreign firm experiences a drop in its profit, the decrease in its profits may be less or greater than the increase in the home firm's profit. This means that profit is not just shifted, but may also be lost or created. Nevertheless, the profit-shifting effect of a tariff in the present model is important, and distinguishes it from the tariff in competitive economies. An important point to note is that there are no terms-of-trade effects in the present framework because the home firm, being a monopoly firm in the domestic market, should have captured all potential gains due to changes in the product price.[6]

The three effects of a small tariff raise the issue of whether its net effect is positive and desirable. To address this issue, substitute the comparative-static

---

5. The profit-shifting effect can be illustrated by Figure 12.1. If iso-profit curves of the firms are added to the diagram, it is easy to note that point M represents a higher profit for the home firm and a lower profit for the foreign firm than point N.

6. Of course, if there are more than one home firms, they will fail to capture all potential gains from changes in the product price, and an optimal tariff will have a terms-of-trade effect.

terms given by (12.4b) and (12.4c) into (12.11) and rearrange terms to give

$$\frac{\partial W}{\partial t}\bigg|_{FT} = \frac{p'(\phi q + \phi^* x^*)}{\Delta} > 0. \tag{12.11'}$$

This means that the profit-shifting and revenue effects of a small tariff outweigh its negative consumption effect. This suggests the use of a positive tariff.[7]

The present framework can be used to study two special cases in the literature. In the first case, there is a domestic monopoly in the home market that faces a perfectly elastic foreign supply. Hence there are no strategic interactions between the home firm and foreign firms. If there is free trade, the home firm has no monopoly power and has to take the foreign price as given. A tariff could restore some of its monopoly power because the tariff allows it to charge a higher price and get more profit.[8] The increase in the home firm's profit comes exclusively from domestic consumer surplus, and because the economy is too small to affect the world price or to shift foreign profits, the optimal tariff is zero.

In the other special case of the present model, the home economy has either zero production or a competitive domestic industry so that a downward sloping home excess demand curve can be defined. A foreign monopolist is supplying a homogeneous product to the home market. In this case, a small tariff is beneficial because of an increase in tariff revenue that comes from the profit of the foreign firm and that outweighs the (increase in) consumption cost. The optimal tariff is positive under these circumstances (see Katrak, 1977, De Meza, 1979, and Brander and Spencer, 1981).

When domestic production is absent, two more results can be derived. First, if the foreign monopolist has a constant marginal cost, a first-best policy for the home country is to put a price ceiling on the foreign import, the ceiling being (slightly greater than) the marginal cost. The foreign firm will produce up to the point at which the marginal cost curve cuts the demand curve. Then the home economy gets all the economic rent and the foreign firm receives zero profit from selling its output to the home market. Even if the foreign firm's

---

7. Sometimes an optimal tariff is imposed in the absence of a home sale (or production) subsidy. I can differentiate the national welfare function given by (12.6) and rearrange terms to get

$$\tilde{t}\bigg|_{r=0} = \frac{qp'(\partial q/\partial t) - \pi_{x^*}(\partial x^*/\partial t) - x^*}{\partial x^*/\partial t},$$

which is the same as the condition for the optimal tariff in Brander and Spencer (1984, equation (21)). Of course, it is not the first-best policy.

8. Depending on the world price and the tariff rate, an increase in protection may increase domestic production or increase the monopolist's profit or both (see Bhagwati, 1965; and Helpman and Krugman, 1989, Chapter 3).

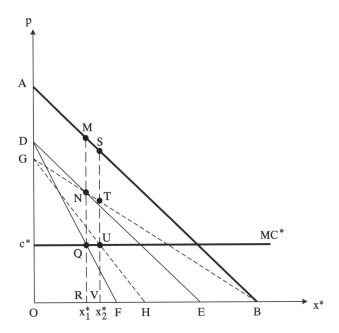

Figure 12.2

marginal cost is rising, the home government can still extract all the economic rent from the foreign firm by putting various price ceilings on different units of import, or by putting a flat price ceiling and a lump-sum tax on foreign import (see Helpman and Krugman, 1989, pp. 51–53).

One interesting issue is how specific tariffs are compared with ad valorem tariffs. In a framework in which firms (and consumers) are price takers, a specific tariff and an ad valorem tariff have the same effects as long as they drive the same wedge between domestic and external prices. In contrast, in a framework with foreign monopoly power, *for any given specific tariff, there exists a Pareto superior (or noninferior) ad valorem tariff*.[9]

To prove this statement, consider Figure 12.2. For illustration, I assume a linear home (excess) demand curve, but the result holds for any demand curve that is not too convex toward the origin. In the diagram, AB is the demand curve. I first consider a specific tariff. The effective demand curve for the foreign firm is DEB, which represents its after-tax per unit revenue. (The vertical gap between AB and DE is the specific tariff rate.) DF is the positive portion of its effective marginal revenue curve. Marginal cost, c^*, is assumed to be constant although the same result holds for any marginal

---

9. Hwang, et al. (1994) consider the choice of export subsidy in the presence of government revenue constraint, and argue that a specific subsidy is superior to an ad valorem subsidy.

cost that is not decreasing too rapidly. The equilibrium point is at Q, with a home import of x_1^*. RM is the domestic price, of which MN is the per unit tariff. Suppose that the government imposes an ad valorem tariff instead of the specific tariff so that if the foreign firm maintains its original export, the same tariff revenue is generated. In terms of the diagram, the new effective demand curve is represented by GNB, which cuts the effective demand curve (under the initial specific tariff) at point N. The new marginal revenue curve is GH, which cuts the marginal cost line at U. As a result, the foreign export increases to x_2^*. The intuition for this result is that the tariff is now expressed as a fixed percentage of the price. So by lowering its price, the foreign firm can pay less tariff for each unit of export. The result is a fall in the market price and an increase in the firm's profit. This represents a Pareto improvement. First, the home consumers benefit from a drop in the price. Second, if the foreign firm does not change its production, its profit remains unchanged. Because it chooses to increase its production to x_2^*, it must get a higher (or not lower) profit. Third, the home government collects more tariff revenue. To show the last point, note that the tariff revenue is equal to $\bar{t}px^*$ where $\bar{t}$ is the ad valorem tariff rate that would give the same tariff revenue as before if the foreign firm keeps the same export level. Because x^* increases, and because marginal revenue is positive, px^* must also increase, that is, the tariff revenue goes up.[10]

If the optimal ad valorem tariff is different from the one constructed earlier, national welfare can be even higher. If the optimal ad valorem tariff is smaller than the one assumed previously, then it is preferred to the optimal specific tariff by home consumers, the home government, and the foreign firm.

12.3   Policies for the Foreign Market

I now turn to the optimal policy for the foreign market, that is, choosing s to maximize national welfare, taking the equilibrium of the home market as given. Differentiate function W with respect to s to give the first-order condition:

$$\frac{\partial W}{\partial s} = -s \frac{\partial X}{\partial s} + \pi_{X^*} \frac{\partial X^*}{\partial s} = 0. \tag{12.13}$$

Rearrange the terms in (12.13) and make use of (12.5a) and (12.5b) to give the optimal export subsidy $\tilde{s}$:

---

10. The Pareto superiority of an ad valorem tariff remains unchanged if competitive domestic firms exist, because their profits are zero and are unaffected by any tariffs. If, however, the domestic firms originally earn positive profits because of imperfect competition, they may be hurt by an increase in the foreign export.

$$\tilde{s} = \frac{\pi_{X^*} X_s^*}{X_s} = -\frac{X p^{*\prime} \Phi^*}{\phi^* + p^{*\prime}} > 0. \tag{12.14}$$

Condition (12.14) suggests that an export subsidy can improve national welfare.

The role of an export subsidy in the present framework is interesting. Recall that in the neoclassical two-sector framework with competitive industries, a small import/export tax is in general beneficial because it improves a country's terms of trade. The reason that an export subsidy is beneficial in the present framework is entirely different. It is noticed from the definition of the home firm's profit function (12.2a) that an export subsidy has the same effect as a decrease in the marginal cost of the home firm. This gives the home firm an advantage in competing with the foreign firm in the foreign market. Similar to what a tariff does, an export subsidy shifts foreign profit towards the home firm. To see the profit-shifting effect of an export subsidy, evaluate the welfare effect as given by (12.13) at the free-trade point ($s = 0$):

$$\left. \frac{\partial W}{\partial s} \right|_{FT} = \pi_{X^*} \frac{\partial X^*}{\partial s} = \frac{X p^{*\prime} \Phi^*}{\Delta} > 0. \tag{12.13$'$}$$

Condition (12.13$'$) shows that a small export subsidy is welfare improving. The term $\pi_{X^*} X_s^*$ represents the profit-shifting effect and is analogous to a similar term for an import tariff, given by the second term on the right-hand side in (12.11).

There is, however, one big difference between a tariff and an export subsidy: With a tariff, the home government also receives part of the foreign firm's profit in the form of tariff revenue, while with an export subsidy, the government has to shoulder the subsidy expenditure burden.

The profit-shifting effect of the optimal export subsidy in the present framework can be illustrated graphically. Suppose that initially there is no export subsidy, that is, $s = 0$. Equations (12.3b) and (12.3d) give the reaction functions of the firms, which are illustrated by curves HH (home) and FF (foreign) in Figure 12.3. These two curves intersect at point N, and by Hahn's stability conditions HH is steeper than FF. The profit function of the home firm can be illustrated by iso-profit curves in Figure 12.3. The curves labeled π^n and π^s are two of the curves, where $\pi^s > \pi^n$. Note that although this diagram and Figure 12.1 look similar, they are different. The present diagram represents the foreign market and the previous one describes the home market.

Point S at which the iso-profit curve π^s touches the foreign reaction curve FF is the Stackelberg equilibrium with the home firm acting as a leader. The home firm wants to reach this point. One way is to convince the foreign firm that the home firm is committed to an output of X^s, not X^n. If the foreign firm is convinced, it will react with a production of X^{s*}.

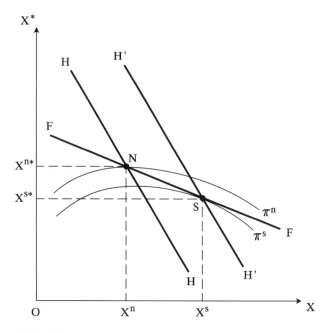

Figure 12.3

Such a precommitment of the home firm is not credible, however, because with perfect information the foreign firm knows the reaction curve of the home firm HH. If it chooses an output of X^{n*}, then the optimal response of the home firm is X^n. No matter what output the home firm states it will choose, the foreign firm just sticks to its Nash equilibrium output X^{n*} and the home firm will choose an output of X^n to maximize its profit subject to the foreign firm's choice. So the equilibrium is at point N and the home firm cannot play a Stackelberg leadership role.

The export subsidy helps the home firm do what it cannot do by itself. I showed that the export subsidy encourages the home firm's export. In terms of Figure 12.3, its reaction curve shifts to the right. If it shifts to H′H′ as shown in the diagram, the new Cournot-Nash equiliibrium is at point S (at which H′H′ cuts FF). In the presence of the export subsidy, a committment by the home firm that it is choosing a production of X^s is credible, and the foreign firm is willing to choose an output of X^{s*}. Point S is just the Stackelberg point with the home firm acting as a leader when no export subsidy is imposed. This means that with the export subsidy, the home firm acts as if it were a Stackelberg leader.[11] As condition (12.6) shows, the part of the home welfare

---

11. Because of the subsidy, the profit of the home firm in the presence of the subsidy is even more than what it gets if it can act as a Stackelberg leader before the export subsidy is imposed.

that comes from the foreign market is equal to the part of the home firm's profit that comes from the foreign market less any subsidy. This means that the iso-profit curves in Figure 12.3 (in the absence of export subsidy) also represent the iso-welfare contours of the economy (with or without export subsidy). Thus point S is the optimal point for the home country.

The role of an export subsidy analyzed in the present model of intraindustry trade is exactly the same as that in an alternative model that is very popular in the literature. Suppose that neither the home nor the foreign country consume the product.[12] Instead, both the home and foreign firms export their outputs to a third country. The Cournot-Nash equilibrium can be derived in the same way as discussed previously, and an export subsidy can be used again to improve national welfare (see Spencer and Brander, 1983; and Brander and Spencer, 1985). Because of the absence of domestic consumption, an export subsidy is the first-best policy for the home country.

12.4   Some Extensions

In the preceding sections, I used a duopoly model of intraindustrial trade to analyze the effects of several policies. In this section, I extend the above model in several directions.

12.4.1   Increasing Returns

So far, I have assumed that both firms have constant marginal costs. It is a convenient assumption because it allows me to derive the equilibria of the home and foreign markets separately. Now let me assume the existence of either static or dynamic increasing returns so that the marginal cost of a firm is a declining function of the firm's output.

It is clear from the analysis in Chapter 7 that increasing returns qualitatively do not affect the presence of intraindustry trade, but they do remove the dichotomy of the system because a firm's supply to one market affects the firm's marginal cost and thus the equilibrium in another market. The derivation of the equilibria in the markets becomes more complicated but the essence of the analysis remains unchanged.

In terms of policies, the main motive for the two trade policies, tariff and export subsidy, is to shift the foreign firm's profit to the home firm by encouraging the production of the home firm and discouraging that of the foreign firm. In the presence of increasing returns, the profit-shifting effects of these

---

12. Although in Brander and Spencer (1985) no consumption in the two countries is assumed, I have shown that if the firms' marginal costs are constant, their export decisions do not depend on whether there is domestic consumption.

two policies are even stronger. By producing more, the home firm can lower its marginal cost while the opposite is true for the foreign firm (Krugman, 1984).

12.4.2 Multiple Firms

Suppose now that there are $n > 1$ identical home firms and $n^* > 1$ identical foreign firms. I want to determine how the presence of multiple firms may affect the policies analyzed previously. The model is the same as the one in Chapter 7.

I begin with the second stage of the game in which all firms take the home government's policies as given and compete in a Cournot fashion. Marginal costs of the firms are constant, and the foreign government adopts a free trade policy. By symmetry, all domestic firms have the same equilibrium production, and so do the foreign firms. Using the earlier notation, the market-clearing conditions are

$$q = nx + n^*x^* \tag{12.15a}$$

$$q^* = nX + n^*X^*. \tag{12.15b}$$

Differentiating the first-order conditions of a representative home firm—conditions (12.3a) and (12.3b)—and those of a representative foreign firm—conditions (12.3c) and (12.3d)—and rearranging terms, the following comparative-static conditions are obtained:

$$\begin{bmatrix} dx \\ dx^* \end{bmatrix} = \frac{1}{\Lambda} \begin{bmatrix} n^*\phi^* + p' & -n^*\phi \\ -n\phi^* & n\phi + p' \end{bmatrix} \begin{bmatrix} -dr \\ dt \end{bmatrix},$$

where $\Lambda = p'(p' + n\phi + n^*\phi^*) > 0$. Solving these conditions, I can show that an increase in r or t increases x but decreases x^*. Furthermore, the total supply to the home market depends positively on an increase in r but negatively on an increase in t, while an increase in t improves the home firms' profits but hurts the foreign firms' profits.

The same procedure can be used to derive the effects of an export subsidy:

$$\begin{bmatrix} dX \\ dX^* \end{bmatrix} = \frac{1}{\Lambda^*} \begin{bmatrix} n^*\Phi^* + p^{*\prime} & -n^*\Phi \\ -n\Phi^* & n\Phi + p^{*\prime} \end{bmatrix} \begin{bmatrix} -ds \\ 0 \end{bmatrix}$$

$$= \frac{1}{\Lambda^*} \begin{bmatrix} -(n^*\Phi^* + p^{*\prime}) \\ n\Phi^* \end{bmatrix} ds,$$

where $\Lambda^* = p^{*\prime}(p^{*\prime} + n\Phi + n^*\Phi^*) > 0$. It can be shown that an increase in s encourages home production but discourages foreign production. Furthermore, the export subsidy increases the total supply to the foreign market, and improves a representative home firm's profit but hurts a representative foreign firm's profit.

Let me turn to optimal policies. First consider a home sale subsidy and a tariff. Because the home and foreign markets are segmented, I can again use the techniques explained earlier and choose x and x^* to maximize $W \equiv CS(q) + n(\pi - rx - sX) + tn^*x^*$. Following the same procedure as earlier, I differentiate W with respect to x and x^*. Making use of the first-order conditions of the firms, the optimal policies for the home markets are:

$$\tilde{r} = -xp' + n^*(x^*)^2 p''$$

$$\tilde{t} = -x^*(p' + n^*x^*p'').$$

Again, $\tilde{r}$ and $\tilde{t}$ are positive if the demand curve is not too curved. As was the case in the previous section, a tariff has a positive profit-shifting effect, a positive revenue effect, and a negative consumption effect. Unlike the previous case, however, when there is more than one domestic home firms acting non-cooperatively, they will not maximize their joint profit and they will not take into full account the effects of their output on the external price. Thus, they tend to overproduce from the economy's point of view, and the tariff has a positive terms-of-trade effect as well.

The export subsidy can be analyzed in a similar way. Differentiating the national welfare function with respect to s, using the first-order conditions of the firms, and rearranging terms,

$$\tilde{s} = \frac{Xp^{*'}[(n-1)p^{*'} - n^*\Phi^*]}{n^*\Phi^* + p^{*'}}. \tag{12.16}$$

The sign of $\tilde{s}$ as given by (12.16) is in general ambiguous, but I can say that it is positive if n is sufficiently small. The reason for the ambiguity is that if there are two or more home firms, they fail to capture the full effect of their outputs on the external prices. From the home country's point of view, they are overexporting. An export subsidy has two opposing effects: It shifts foreign profits to the home firms, and it encourages the home firms to export more. The first effect is known to be positive but the second is negative because it deteriorates the external terms of trade. If the number of home firms is sufficiently large, the second effect outweighs the first one and the economy needs an optimal export tax (Dixit, 1984).

12.4.3 Free Entry and Exit

So far it has been assumed that the number of firms in each country is fixed. This can be regarded as a short-run situation. Unless there are entry barriers such as legal or technical ones, new firms will enter the market in the long run if they can earn positive profits. On the other hand, if protectionist policies imposed by the home government drive down foreign firms' profits, some of those with negative profits will leave the market.

I now turn to a long-run model with free entry and exit. Neglecting the integer problem, I assume that the number of firms in each country is determined endogenously such that the profit of a representative firm is driven down to zero.

Our present concern is how free entry and exit may change the optimal policies analyzed previously. This issue was first analyzed by Venables (1985) for the case of segmented markets. His argument is presented here.

Consider again the multifirm model. Define the demand function of the home market as $q = g(p)$ where $g'(p) = 1/p'(q)$. Similarly, the foreign demand function is defined to be $q^* = g^*(p^*)$ where $g^{*\prime}(q^*) = 1/p^{*\prime}(q^*)$. The market clearing conditions are given by (12.15a) and (12.15b). Again use r, s, and t to denote the home sale subsidy, export subsidy, and import tariff imposed by the home government. The foreign government permits free trade.

When the number of firms in each country is determined endogenously, the dichotomy of the system under the present policies breaks down. When n and n^* can vary, they serve as the links between the home and foreign markets. For example, an increase in tariff will increase domestic firms' profits but lower those of the foreign firms, and if this changes the number of firms, the supplies to the home and foreign markets change. Thus the two markets must be solved simultaneously to determine the equilibrium values of n and n^* and the equilibrium output of each firm.

Venables (1985) suggests a clever way of analyzing an equilibrium. Instead of determining the numbers of firms, he focuses on the equilibrium prices. In this way he avoids the need of determining n and n^* explicitly.

Solve the first-order conditions of a representative home firm (12.3a) and (12.3b) to express its outputs in terms of the prices:

$$x = -g'(p)(p - c + r) \tag{12.17a}$$

$$X = -g^{*\prime}(p^*)(p^* - c + s) \tag{12.17b}$$

It should be noted that although mathematically the home firm's outputs are expressed as functions of market prices (and policy parameters), economically each firm takes other firms' outputs, not market prices, as given.

Substitute (12.17a) and (12.17b) into the representative home firm's profit function to give the firm's optimal profit

$$\tilde{\pi} = -g'(p - c + r)^2 - g^{*\prime}(p^* - c + s)^2 - f = 0. \tag{12.18a}$$

In (12.18a), I set the optimal profit to zero under the condition of free entry and exit (ignoring the integer problem). The optimal profit is expressed as a function of p and p^* and is illustrated in Figure 12.4 by the schedule labeled HH. Schedule HH is negatively sloped if a higher level of p or p^* represents more profit for a representative home firm. In the special case in which both

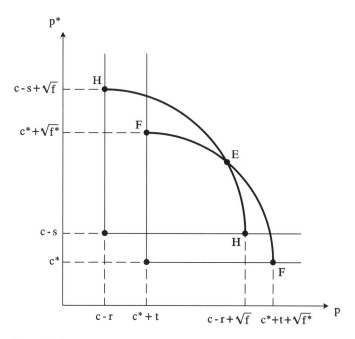

Figure 12.4

demand curves are linear, g' and $g^{*\prime}$ are constants and the slope of HH is equal to

$$\frac{\mathrm{d}p^*}{\mathrm{d}p}\bigg|_{HH} = -\frac{g'(p-c+r)}{g^{*\prime}(p^*-c+s)} < 0.$$

If, furthermore, the two demand functions are the same, $g(p) = g^*(p)$ and by choice of units $g' = g^{*\prime} = -1$, HH is a circle with a radius of $\sqrt{f}$ and a center at $(c-r, c-s)$. This is the case shown in Figure 12.4. The diagram does not show the part of the curve for $p < c - r$ or $p^* < c - s$ because these parts represent negative profits of the home firms from the corresponding market.

The same technique can be used to derive the optimal profit function of a representative foreign firm:

$$\tilde{\pi}^* = -g'(p-c^*-t)^2 - g^{*\prime}(p^*-c^*) - f^* = 0. \tag{12.18b}$$

This function is represented by schedule FF. Again in the special case in which the demand curves are linear, the slope of schedule FF is equal to

$$\frac{\mathrm{d}p^*}{\mathrm{d}p}\bigg|_{FF} = -\frac{g'(p-c^*-t)}{g^{*\prime}(p^*-c^*)} < 0.$$

If, furthermore, $g' = g^{*\prime} = -1$, schedule FF is a circle with a radius of $\sqrt{f^*}$ and a center at (c^*+t, c^*). The diagram shows the case in which schedule HH

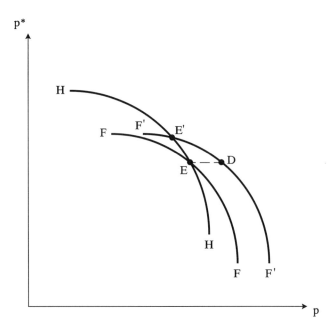

Figure 12.5

cuts schedule FF at point E from above. This happens due to the assumption that each schedule is affected more strongly by an increase in the local price than by the same increase in the other price. This is an important feature of the present model.

Now the welfare effects of two trade policies—import tariff and export subsidy—can be derived. First, suppose there is an increase in t. This shifts schedule FF in Figure 12.5 to the right, and the new schedule is shown by $F'F'$ in the diagram. The new intersecting point shows an interesting result: a decrease in p and an increase in p^*. Thus a tariff has a perverse effect on the domestic price (similar to the Metzler effect).

The reason for this perverse effect of a tariff is due to free entry and exit of firms. To understand the intuition behind it, first consider the foreign firms. Because of the tariff, if p^* does not change, the domestic price has to go up by an appropriate amount to maintain a zero profit for a representative foreign firm. The increase in p is shown by ED in Figure 12.5.[13] At point D, however, the profit of a home firm is positive. This attracts new home firms. The resulting increase in production will drive down the profit of foreign firms, causing some of them to leave the markets. The changes in the numbers

---

13. If p^* is held constant and if the domestic demand is linear, then condition (12.18b) implies that the domestic price has to go up by the amount of the tariff in order to maintain the profit of a representative foreign firm zero.

of firms in the countries must leave one price higher and one price lower than before because the domestic profit schedule has not changed. Suppose that p^* falls and p rises. To restore zero foreign profit, p must have risen more than the increase in tariff. With these changes in prices, however, the home firms must have positive profits because of the assumption that each firm's profit is affected more by the local price. This contradicts the zero profit condition, meaning that p^* must rise and p must fall to reach a new equilibrium.

How does the tariff affect home welfare? With the home firms earning zero profits, national welfare is defined in the following way:

$$W = CS(p) - nsx + n^*tx^*, \tag{12.19}$$

where consumer surplus is now expressed as a function of domestic price, $CS(p)$. Note that because the profit of a domestic firm is zero in equilibrium, it does not appear in (12.19). First assume that $s = 0$. Because an increase in t drives down the domestic price, it improves consumer surplus. If the tariff revenue had no social value, then the optimal tariff would be prohibitive. If the tariff revenue does have social value, a prohibitive tariff is in general not optimal because it produces zero revenue. In this case, the optimal tariff is positive but less than prohibitive.

I now turn to an export subsidy, assuming that tariff is zero. In terms of Figure 12.6, an increase in s shifts schedule HH down to H'H'. The new equilibrium point E'' represents a fall in p but a rise in p^*. The changes in prices due to an export subsidy are contrary to what is expected in a traditional framework. The decrease in domestic price benefits consumers, but the subsidy expenditure hurts the government revenue. Venables (1985) shows that if the demand schedules are linear, a small subsidy is beneficial.

The argument for export subsidy in Venables' model depends crucially on the assumption that the markets are segmented. Once this assumption is relaxed, an export subsidy could deteriorate national welfare (Horstmann and Markusen, 1986; Markusen and Venables, 1988).

When markets in the two countries are integrated, two important consequences arise. First, intraindustry trade in identical products is no longer needed. Second, if firms in both countries produce an identical product under free trade, trade policies could drive firms in one of the countries out of the market. To see the second point, suppose that at the initial free-trade equilibrium, the home country imposes an export subsidy. This raises the profits of the home firms but hurts those of the foreign firms. Some foreign firms will leave the market while some new home firms will enter. This process can continue until all foreign firms are out of the market.

Because of the two points mentioned, Horstmann and Markusen (1986) and Markusen and Venables (1988) both assume that the products of the home

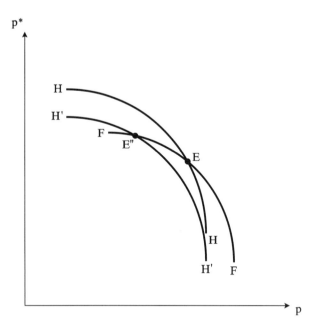

Figure 12.6

firms and those of foreign firms are imperfect substitutes.[14] This has two implications on the welfare effects of export subsidies. First, the profit-shifting effect of an export subsidy, even if it exists, is much weaker than before. Second, an export subsidy has a negative terms-of-trade effect, as in a traditional framework. In the model in Horstmann and Markusen (1986), the welfare effect of an export subsidy is negative, while in Markusen and Venables (1988) the welfare effect of an export subsidy is ambiguous.

In Horstmann and Markusen (1986), the export subsidy has a further adverse effect: inefficient entry of firms. Because the subsidy increases the profits of existing firms in the home country, new firms enter the market. Because each new firm has to incur a fixed cost, and in their model fixed costs are sunk costs, addition of new firms wastes resources.

12.5   Further Arguments against Export Subsidies

There has been a lot of interest in the literature in analyzing strategic trade policies, and much of the attention has been on export subsidies. Several reasons can be used to explain this interest. First, it is believed that some gov-

---

14. Markusen and Venables (1988) do allow the possibility that home and foreign products are perfect substitutes as a special case.

ernments are aggressively using policies to promote their exports, and these policies seem to be responsible for the rapid and impressive growth of their economies. Second, unless there are distortions, nonconvexity of technologies or preferences, or multiple goods, export subsidies are not compatible with a welfare maximizing government in the traditional framework (see Chapters 10 and 11). Trade with oligopolistic industries provides a sound theoretical rationale for the use of export subsidies. These models raise a lot of theoretical interest. Third, export subsidies are consistent with the common notion that they help domestic exporting firms capture larger market shares in foreign markets, and this should be good for the firms (and presumably also good for the economy).

Further theoretical analysis shows that the results based on strategic use of exports subsidies are usually sensitive to the underlying assumptions of the models used. This was shown in the previous section, and I have presented cases in which export taxes instead of subsidies should be used. In this section, more arguments against the use of export subsidies are discussed.[15]

12.5.1 Price Competition

I now consider an alternative type of competition between firms—price competition (or called Bertrand competition). I focus on the role of export subsidies and consider a simple model. There are two firms, one in each country, producing two goods that are imperfect substitutes. No consumption of the goods in either country is assumed so that the firms export their outputs to a third market. This model is similar to the one used in Sections 12.1 to 12.3 and also to the one in Brander and Spencer (1985) except that the strategic variable is price, not quantity. Eaton and Grossman (1986) show that the optimal export subsidy in the present model is negative, that is, an export tax, not an export subsidy, should be used to improve national welfare. Their argument is presented here.

Denote the demands for the output by home foreign firms in the third market by $q(p, p^*)$ and $q^*(p, p^*)$, respectively, where p and p^* are the prices set (for the third market) by the home and foreign firms, respectively. As before, subscripts are used to denote partial derivatives; e.g., $q_p \equiv \partial q/\partial p$. I assume that $q_p < 0$ and $q^*_{p^*} < 0$, that is, each demand curve is downward sloping.

The profit function of the home firm is now equal to $\pi(p, p^*, s) = (p - c + s)q(p, p^*)$ where s is the specific export subsidy (or export tax if it is negative). Similarly, the profit function of the foreign firm is $\pi^*(p, p^*) = (p^* - c^*)q^*(p, p^*)$. Taking s as given, the firms choose prices in a Bertrand

---

15. See Grossman (1986), Dixit (1986b), Bhagwati (1988), and Haberler (1990) for nontechnical discussions against the use of strategic export subsidies. Three other recent surveys are given in Krishna and Thursby (1990), Vousden (1990), and Chang and Katayama (1992).

fashion to maximize their profits. The first-order conditions of the firms are given by

$$\pi_p \equiv q_p(p - c + s) + q(p, p^*) = 0 \qquad (12.20a)$$

$$\pi_{p^*}^* \equiv q_{p^*}^*(p^* - c^*) + q^*(p, p^*) = 0. \qquad (12.20b)$$

Conditions (12.20) give the reaction functions of the firms, and together they are solved for the Bertrand-Nash equilibrium prices, $p = p(s)$ and $p^* = p^*(s)$.

To find out how the equilibrium prices are dependent on s, totally differentiate the first-order conditions to give

$$\begin{bmatrix} \pi_{pp} & \pi_{pp^*} \\ \pi_{p^*p}^* & \pi_{p^*p^*}^* \end{bmatrix} \begin{bmatrix} dp \\ dp^* \end{bmatrix} = \begin{bmatrix} -q_p ds \\ 0 \end{bmatrix}, \qquad (12.21)$$

where

$$\pi_{pp} = q_{pp}(p - c + s) + 2q_p$$

$$\pi_{pp^*} = q_{pp^*}(p - c + s) + q_{p^*}$$

$$\pi_{p^*p}^* = q_{p^*p}^*(p^* - c^*) + q_p^*$$

$$\pi_{p^*p^*}^* = q_{p^*p^*}^*(p^* - c^*) + 2q_{p^*}^*.$$

For stability of the equilibrium, I assume that (see the appendix): (1) $\pi_{pp} < 0$, $\pi_{p^*p^*}^* < 0$; and that (2) either (a) $0 < q_{p^*} + q_{pp^*} < -(q_p + q_{pp})$ and $0 < q_p^* + q_{p^*p}^* < -(q_{p^*}^* + q_{p^*p^*}^*)$ or (b) $0 > q_{p^*} + q_{pp^*} > q_p + q_{pp}$ and $0 > q_p^* + q_{p^*p}^* > q_{p^*}^* + q_{p^*p^*}^*$. Condition (1) ensures that the first-order conditions of the firms give maxima. Condition (2a) implies that $0 < \pi_{pp^*} < -\pi_{pp}$ and $0 < \pi_{p^*p}^* < -\pi_{p^*p^*}^*$, and (2b) implies that $0 > \pi_{pp^*} > \pi_{pp}$ and $0 > \pi_{p^*p}^* > \pi_{p^*p^*}^*$. If the products supplied by the firms are (ordinary) substitutes [respectively complements] so that $q_{p^*} > 0$, $q_p^* > 0$ [respectively $q_{p^*} < 0$, $q_p^* < 0$], and if q_{pp^*} and $q_{p^*p}^*$ are sufficiently small, condition (2a) [respectively (2b)] is satisfied. Conditions (12.21) are solved to give

$$p_s = -\frac{q_p \pi_{p^*p^*}^*}{\Omega}$$

$$p_s^* = \frac{q_p \pi_{p^*p}^*}{\Omega},$$

where $\Omega = \pi_{pp}\pi_{p^*p^*}^* - \pi_{pp^*}\pi_{p^*p}^*$. Based on conditions (1) and (2a) or (2b), $\Omega > 0$. Furthermore, $p_s < 0$ and $\text{sign}(p_s^*) = -\text{sign}(\pi_{p^*p}^*)$. If $q_{p^*p}^*$ is sufficient small, then $\pi_{p^*p}^* \approx q_p^*$. Therefore $p_s^* < (\text{respectively} >) 0$ if the goods are substitutes (respectively complements).

In the first stage, the home government chooses an export subsidy to maximize national welfare, which is defined as follows:

$$W(s) = \pi[p(s), p^*(s), s] - sq[p(s), p^*(s)].$$

The first-order condition is

$$\frac{dW}{ds} = \pi_p p_s + \pi_{p^*} p_s^* + \pi_s - [q + sq_p p_s + sq_{p^*} p_s^*]$$

$$= (p - c)q_{p^*} p_s^* - sq_p p_s = 0. \tag{12.22}$$

In deriving dW/ds, note that $\pi_p = 0$ because p is always chosen optimally, and that $\pi_{p^*} = (p - c + s)q_{p^*}$. Solving (12.22), the optimal export subsidy, $\widetilde{s}$ is:

$$\widetilde{s} = \frac{(p - c)q_{p^*} p_s^*}{q_p p_s} = -\frac{(p - c)q_{p^*} \pi_{p^* p}^*}{q_p \pi_{p^* p^*}^*} < 0. \tag{12.23}$$

Note that the sign of $\widetilde{s}$, given by (12.23), does not depend on whether the goods are (ordinary) substitutes or complements. With Bertrand competition, the optimal policy of the home government is an export tax.

Figure 12.7 illustrates the case in which the firms' outputs are substitutes. Schedule HH shows the reaction curve of the home firm as given by (12.20a) and schedule FF shows that of the foreign firm as given by (12.20b). Slopes of the schedules are equal to

$$\left.\frac{dp^*}{dp}\right|_{HH} = -\frac{\pi_{pp}}{\pi_{pp^*}} > 0 \tag{12.24a}$$

$$\left.\frac{dp^*}{dp}\right|_{FF} = -\frac{\pi_{p^* p}^*}{\pi_{p^* p^*}^*} > 0. \tag{12.24b}$$

Furthermore, by the stability conditions, schedule HH is steeper than schedule FF. The diagram also shows two iso-profit curves of the home firm labeled by the corresponding profits π^n and π^s, with $\pi^s > \pi^n$ (s stands for Stackelberg and n for Nash). Curve π^s touches schedule FF at point S.

If the home firm can act as a leader and can credibly be precommitted to a price of p^s, then the foreign firm's optimal price is p^{s*}, allowing the home firm to earn a profit of π^s. Because such precommittment is not credible, however, the equilibrium is at the intersecting point between schedules HH and FF.

As is the case in Section 12.3, the home government can help the domestic firm and thus the economy by using a policy to shift the home firm's reaction curve to H'H', cutting schedule FF at S, which is the new Nash equilibrium point. In the present case, however, the policy that shifts schedule HH to the

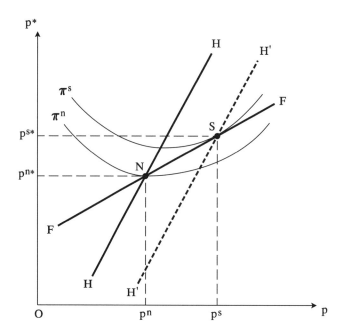

Figure 12.7

right is an export tax, not an export subsidy, as can be seen from the second-order differentiation condition (12.21).[16] The diagram shows one more feature of this export tax policy: both the home and foreign firms gain from the policy.

If the goods are complements instead, the slopes of schedules HH and FF, as given by condition (12.24), are negative. Condition (12.23) shows that the optimal policy of the home government is still an export tax.

The Bertrand case as analyzed by Eaton and Grossman illustrates several points. First, the results about the use of policies could be very sensititve to the underlying assumptions of a model, such as whether the firms compete in a Cournot or Bertrand fashion. When the nature of the competition between the firms is not known, imposing a strategic policy based on one model can be devastating. Second, compare Figure 12.3 with Figure 12.7. In Figure 12.3, the reaction curves are negatively sloped and an export subsidy is needed for welfare improvement. Using the terminology of Bulow et al. (1985), the goods are said to be "strategic substitutes." In Figure 12.7, the reaction curves are positively sloped and an export tax is required instead. The goods are then

---

16. By (12.21), if p^* is held constant, then the change in p caused by an export subsidy is $\left. \mathrm{d}p/\mathrm{d}s \right|_{\mathrm{d}p^*=0} = -q_p/\pi_{pp} < 0$.

said to be "strategic complements." Eaton and Grossman (1986, pp. 393–394 fn 10) summarize these results as follows: "For Cournot and Bertrand competition among (ordinary) substitutes, optimal policy involves subsidizing exports if the goods are strategic substitutes and taxing exports otherwise. If the goods instead are (ordinary) complements, then the opposite correspondence between strategic substitutes and complements and optimal policy obtains."

12.5.2   The Choice of Technology

Several authors have examined the possibility that firms choose profit-maximizing technologies while taking into account the (possible) imposition of export subsidies; for example, see Spencer and Brander (1983) and Hwang et al. (1993). Spencer and Brander (1983) analyzes how two rival firms compete not only in quantities of production but also in the choice of technologies. Hwang et al. (1993), as Carmichael (1987), Gruenspecht (1988) and Choi (1995) do, note that there are cases in which home firms have an opportunity of acting first before the home government sets a policy. The advantage of taking the first move thus allows the firms to affect the government policy parameters. Hwang et al. (1993) examines the choice of technology by home firms before an export subsidy is chosen, and argue that in such a case an export subsidy could hurt the home economy.

To see the possibility raised by Hwang et al. (1993), consider again the model used previously in which a home firm and a foreign firm produce an identical product and compete only in a third market. I now allow the home firm to choose, at a cost, the level of technology. The technology is reflected by marginal costs, and once the technology is chosen, the marginal cost is fixed. To represent the cost of technology, let me rewrite the "fixed" cost of the home firm as $f(c)$. This cost is no longer fixed in the sense that it depends on the technology parameter c chosen by the firm. Assume that $f'(c) < 0$ and $f''(c) > 0$. Once c has been chosen, the "fixed" cost is truly a fixed cost. For simplicity, assume that the foreign firm's choice of technology is independent of the home export subsidy policy and that the foreign government is inactive.

The game is described as follows. In the first stage, the home firm chooses technology, c. In the second stage, the home government chooses an export subsidy, and in the third stage, the home and foreign firms compete in a Cournot fashion. It is clear that the last two stages of the present game, when c can be treated as a parameter, are the same as the first and second stages of the Cournot game described earlier.

The notation used before can be modified slightly. Denote by q and q^*, respectively, the exports of the home and foreign firms to the third market, which has an inverse demand given by $p = p(q + q^*)$, where p is the common price of the product. The profit functions of the home and foreign firms are

$\pi(q, q^*, s, c) = qp(q + q^*) - cq + sq - f(c)$ and $\pi^*(q, q^*; c^*) = q^*p(q + q^*) - c^*q^* - f^*$.

The Cournot-Nash equilibrium in the third stage can be solved in the same way as before. The firms' outputs can be denoted by $q = q(s, c)$ and $q^* = q^*(s, c)$. The effects of the home export subsidy were derived earlier [conditions (12.5a) and (12.5b)]: $q_c = -q_s < 0$ and $q_c^* = -q_s^* > 0$.

The home country's national welfare is defined by $W(s; c) = \pi(q(s, c), q^*(s, c), s, c) - sq(s, c)$. In the second stage, the home government chooses s to maximize $W(s; c)$, taking c as given. Denote the solution by $s = s(c)$, which is positive.

Now turn to the first stage of the game. The home firm chooses c to maximize its own profit $\pi[q(s(c), c), q^*(s(c), c), s(c), c]$. Denote the profit-maximizing marginal cost by c^3, where the superscript reflects the present three-stage game. Let the equilibrium be described by the triplet (c^3, s^3, q^3).

To understand the implications of the choice of technology, let me pause for a moment and consider another game in which no subsidy is going to be imposed. This is a two-stage game in which the home firm chooses c in the first stage and both firms compete with Cournot conjectures in the second stage. To avoid confusion, I distinguish the variables in this game by "hats." The home and foreign firms' profits are represented by $\widehat{\pi}(\widehat{q}, \widehat{q}^*, \widehat{c})$ and $\widehat{\pi}^*(\widehat{q}, \widehat{q}^*, \widehat{c})$, respectively. In the second stage, as before, both firms choose the optimal outputs in a Cournot fashion: $\widehat{q}(\widehat{c})$ and $\widehat{q}^*(\widehat{c})$. In the first stage, the home firm chooses $\widehat{c}$ to maximize its profit $\widehat{\pi}(\widehat{q}(\widehat{c}), \widehat{q}^*(\widehat{c}))$. Let the optimal marginal cost be c^2, and let the equilibrium be represented by $(c^2, 0, q^2)$ where 0 in the triplet represents no export subsidy.

The total cost of production for the home firm is $TC = cq + f(c)$. Treating the output level $q = q^2$ as given, TC is represented by curve AB in Figure 12.8,[17] which is assumed to be convex downward. The value of c, denoted by c^e and called *efficient technology*, solves $q + f'(c) = 0$ and minimizes TC corresponding to a given q.

In the two-stage game without export subsidy, however, the home firm will not choose the efficient technology, c^e, in the first stage. It knows that in the second stage it competes with the foreign firm in a Cournot fashion. Thus it has an incentive to choose a more productive technology (or a smaller value of c) in order to boost up its second-stage production level. In other words, as shown in Figure 12.8, $c^2 < c^e$.

In the three-stage game, the home government imposes in the second stage an export subsidy that depends on the marginal cost chosen by the home firm

17. The approach of treating q as a parameter is for convenience because q is determined endogenously, but this approach does emphasize the direct relationship between c and the total cost. See Spencer and Brander (1983) for an application of this approach.

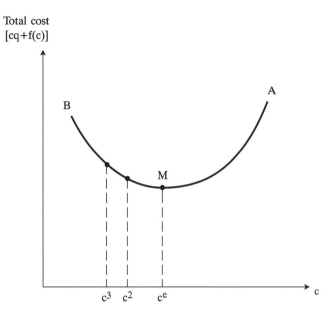

Total cost
$[cq+f(c)]$

Figure 12.8

in the first stage. As analyzed by Hwang et al. (1993), there are cases in which the subsidy is negatively related to the marginal cost picked by the home firm. In these cases, in the first stage the home firm, anticipating that the amount of export subsidy imposed in the next stage depends on its technology, has an incentive to choose a marginal cost lower than what it might choose in the two-stage game. In other words, $c^3 < c^2$.

I now turn to welfare analysis, comparing the home country's welfare in a three-stage game with that in a two-stage game. Imagine that the economy starts out as a two-stage game with its equilibrium at $(c^2, 0, q^2)$, and that the game then shifts to a three-stage one with the equilibrium correspondingly shifting to (c^3, s^3, q^3). Hypothetically, let me break this shift into three different steps and explain the implication of each step.

1. *Overinvestment Effect*—from $(c^2, 0, q^2)$ to $(c^3, 0, q^2)$. As the output level is hypothetically frozen, the home firm chooses a lower marginal cost. In terms of Figure 12.8, c^2 is less than the efficient level. Now c^3 is even less efficient. Thus, using the cost curve at $q = q^2$ in the diagram, I conclude that the overinvestment effect is negative in the sense that the home firm chooses a less efficient technology to produce the same output.

2. *Scale Effect*—from $(c^3, 0, q^2)$ to $(c^3, 0, q')$. Assuming that the home firm has chosen c^3, let its optimal output (without export subsidy) be q'. This means that with c^3 but without any subsidy, q' yields a higher profit than q^2

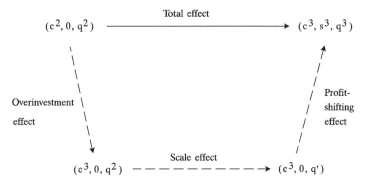

Figure 12.9

(although c^2 and q^2 produce a even higher profit). In the absence of subsidy, national welfare is equal to the profit of the home firm. The scale effect is thus positive.

3. *Profit-Shifting Effect*—from $(c^3, 0, q')$ to (c^3, s^3, q^3). Now let the home government choose the optimal export subsidy first, and then let both firms choose their optimal outputs according to the rules given. Because in this step the home firm's technology has already been chosen and is fixed, I can apply the analysis in Section 12.3 and argue that the export subsidy improves welfare (see also Brander and Spencer, 1985).

The analysis shows that the export subsidy produces a negative overinvestment effect, a positive scale effect, and a positive profit-shifting effect. These three effects are illustrated in Figure 12.9. The sign of the total effect is ambiguous. Hwang et al. (1993) presents an example in which an export subsidy deteriorates national welfare. In their example, the demand function is linear: $p = 5 - 0.02(q + q^*)$ and $f(c)$ is quadratic: $f(c) = 200c^2 - 400c + 200$. National welfare without export subsidy is 60.1 whereas that with export subsidy is only 53.4.

12.5.3 Several Oligopolistic Industries

Each of the models examined so far has a single industry with oligopolists. Thus there is only one export subsidy to consider. Suppose that there is more than one oligopolistic, exporting industry. How would the existence of these industries affect the analysis developed earlier? Should the home government still subsidize the exports of these industries?

When there are n oligopolistic industries, $n > 1$, they usually interact in more than one way. For example, their outputs may be imperfect substitutes in consumption, or they all require some inelastically supplied factors as inputs. The latter point was analyzed by Dixit and Grossman (1986).

Consider a very simple model in which all these products are produced by one input, labor. There is only one domestic firm in each industry. Denote the output of firm i by q_i, which is exported to another market (possibly the foreign market). Exhibiting constant returns, the production function of firm i requires a_i units of labor per one unit of output. With the output of a competing foreign firm in industry i denoted by q_i^*, the inverse demand is given by $p_i(q_i + q_i^*)$. (Neglect substitutability in consumption of goods from different industries.) If the wage rate is w, the profit function of firm i is $q_i p_i(q_i + q_i^*) - wl_i + s_i q_i$, where $l_i = a_i q_i$ is the labor input and s_i is the specific subsidy on good i. Being a price taker in the labor market and competing in a Cournot fashion, the first-order condition of the firm is

$$p_i + q_i p_i' = wa_i - s_i. \tag{12.25}$$

Condition (12.25) is similar to the profit-maximizing condition previously discussed. Denote the (fixed) aggregate supply of labor by $\bar{l}$. Therefore the resource constraint is

$$\bar{l} = \sum_i l_i. \tag{12.26}$$

National welfare W is represented by national income because there is no domestic consumption of these goods or because domestic consumption of these goods, if it exists, is not affected by export subsidies—the segmented market and constant marginal cost argument. Thus national welfare is defined as the sum of the income of the workers employed in these industries and the profits of these firms less the subsidy payments:

$$W = w\bar{l} + \sum_i \left[q_i p_i(q_i + q_i^*) - wl_i + s_i q_i \right] - \sum_i s_i q_i$$

$$= \sum_i \left[q_i p_i(q_i + q_i^*) \right]. \tag{12.27}$$

The problem of the government is to choose s_i, $i = 1, 2, \ldots, n$, to maximize national welfare given by (12.27), subject to the resource constraint (12.26). Let me define the Lagrangean function as $\mathcal{L} = \sum_i \left[q_i p_i(q_i + q_i^*) \right] + w(\bar{l} - \sum_i l_i)$. Note that because w is the shadow price of labor, it is equal to the Lagrangean multiplier. The first-order condition for sector i is

$$\frac{\partial \mathcal{L}}{\partial s_i} = q_i p_i'(q_{is} + q_{is}^*) + p_i q_{is} - wa_i q_{is}$$

$$= q_i p_i' q_{is}^* - s_i q_{is}$$

$$= 0, \tag{12.28}$$

where $q_{is} \equiv \partial q_i / \partial s_i$ and $q_{is}^* \equiv \partial q_i^* / \partial s_i$. Note that $q_i p_i' q_{is}^*$ when evaluated at the free trade point ($s = 0$) is the familiar profit-shifting effect. Rearrange the terms in (12.28) to give the optimal export subsidy on sector i:

$$\tilde{s}_i = \frac{q_i p_i' q_{is}^*}{q_{is}}, \tag{12.28'}$$

which is analogous to the optimal export subsidy for one strategic export sector given by (12.14). Assuming normal output responses, that is, $q_{is} > 0$ and $q_{is}^* < 0$, I have $\tilde{s}_i > 0$.

Theoretically, the subsidies as given by (12.28') should be imposed on the sectors, but there are several practical problems. First, the government may be under a budget constraint and it may be too costly to raise enough revenue to support such a subsidy project. Second, because of the labor endowment constraint, subsidizing all sectors will not increase the outputs of all sectors. Third, in the special case in which all sectors are identical, subsidizing the sectors equally as suggested by condition (12.28') will not change the output of any sector. Thus in this symmetric case, or if the government treats the sectors equally because of lack of information, free trade is the optimal policy.[18]

12.5.4 Imperfect Information

The theory of policy intervention derived so far requires that the governments know all the relevant information. Although this is a convenient assumption in theoretical work, in the real world this is not true. A lack of information may hinder the government in choosing the right policy or the optimal value of a policy parameter. This difficulty is true for most policies and for all types of market structures.

If a particular industry is competitive with a large number of firms, then to choose a particular policy such as an optimal tariff, the government needs to collect sufficient data about the market such as demands and supplies. In this case, advanced econometric techniques can be used to reveal a lot of information about the markets. Because a firm has insignificant effects on a competitive market, the government only has to focus on the market but does not have to worry about the characteristics of any particular firm.

It is very much different if the industry is oligopolistic and has a small number of firms. Because there are only a few firms in the industry, the information needed by the government is often firm-specific. This poses new difficulties. In

---

18. Dixit and Grossman (1986) show that if there is a government budget constraint so that only some of the industries can be subsidized, those with the greatest profit-shifting effects should be subsidized.

many cases, some of the information needed to determine the optimal policy may be crucial in choosing the right policy.

Dixit (1990) identifies three sources of imperfect information: unobservable outcomes, moral hazard, and adverse selection. For each of these three sources, he examines the difficulties of choosing the optimal policies. Dixit shows that in many cases, a competitive equilibrium does not exist, and there are many cases in which the competitive equilibrium is a constrained optimal, requiring no government intervention.

To choose the right policy, the government has to know the sources of imperfect information and then consider the appropriate intervention, if needed. Knowing the source of imperfect information does not mean that the correct policy parameters can be determined. I now consider some examples that are related to the use of export subsidies.

In the preceding analysis, I considered a one-shot game. The result can be extended to a multiperiod model. Suppose that in the first period the domestic firm spends resources on research and development (R & D) in order to improve its productivity in the future. If no export subsidy is given, the firm will choose the optimal amount of R & D expenditure to maximize benefits over costs. If an export subsidy is present, then the domestic firm will consider how its R & D expenditure may affect the export subsidy. In maximizing its own profit, the firm may choose an amount of R & D expenditure that is suboptimal from the economy's point of view. For example, suppose that a government subsidizes those firms that are facing severe foreign competition, or those firms that get small or negative profits. In these cases, the amount of subsidy depends on how poorly a firm performs, and the firm thus has an incentive to spend less effort and perform less impressively in order to get more subsidy.

Another problem of carrying out the export subsidy policy is that if the government does not have the right information about the technology of a domestic firm, the firm has no incentive to give the correct information to the government. In particular, if the firm knows that the information it supplies will be processed by the government to compute the rate of an export subsidy, it has every incentive to give the wrong information. More specifically, if the subsidy rule is known to the firm, it will provide the kind of information that will maximize its cum-subsidy profit. The resulting subsidy that is based on the information given by the firm is generally suboptimal, and in some cases, the subsidy actually hurts the economy (Wong, 1991b).

The lack of perfect information thus means that there exists a gap between what the government should do according to the theory and what they do in practice. For example, in the case of Bertrand competition analyzed by Eaton and Grossman (1986), the domestic government chooses an export subsidy or tax in the first stage, and the firms compete by announcing their prices in a Bertrand fashion in the second stage. Carmichael (1987) and Gruenspecht (1988) note that in some cases, firms state their prices first, then the government chooses the export subsidy rate according to some rules, *taking as given the prices stated by the firms*. In this case, the firms have the incentive to state their prices at the levels in order to get more subsidy.

Example 12.1   This example, which comes from Wong (1991b), shows the difficulty of choosing the right export subsidy rate in the absence of perfect information, as well as the possibility that the export subsidy policy described may in fact immiserize the economy. The home and foreign firms have an identical, constant marginal cost, c. With no consumption demand in either country, the firms compete in the third country, which has a linear demand: $p = a - b(X + X^*)$. If there is no intervention, then the Cournot output of each firm is $(a - c)/(3b)$, and the home welfare, which is the same as the firm's profit, is $(a - c)^2/(9b)$.

Suppose now that the home government imposes an export subsidy. With a linear demand, the subsidy rule as given by (12.14) reduces to

$$\tilde{s} = \frac{bX^s}{2}, \tag{12.29}$$

where X^s is the home firm's export if the firm can act as a Stackelberg leader without any subsidy. Suppose that the home government can estimate b. Suppose further that the home government knows the value of X^s, or the marginal cost of the firms so that it can compute X^s. Simple calculation shows that $X^s = (a - c)/(2b)$. Using this result, $\tilde{s} = (a - c)/4$, and the corresponding national welfare, which is the home firm's profit less the export subsidy, is $(a - c)^2/(8b)$. With the subsidy, national welfare is greater than that without export subsidy. This result follows the theoretical analysis.

Suppose that the government knows the above framework but not the value of c, and so it cannot compute X^s. The government may have to rely on the home firm to supply the information about X^s. If the home firm tells the truth about its marginal cost, then the home government can achieve the same equilibrium as described in the previous paragraph.

If, however, the home firm is aware of the fact that the information it gives to the government affects the amount of subsidy it is going to receive, it has an incentive to lie. If it knows that the subsidy rule is given by (12.29), then it will incorporate the rule in its profit maximization problem. Using the first-order condition of the firm, the information it chooses to give the government is $X^s = (a - c)/b$, instead of $X^s = (a - c)/(2b)$. Alternatively, if $a < 2c$, then the home firm can claim that its marginal cost is $2c - a$ instead of the true value of c. As a result, condition (12.29) implies that the export subsidy is $(a - c)/2$. By lying to the government, the home firm gets more profit, but the national welfare in this case is 0. The economy gets less than what it can get in the absence of export subsidy.

In Example 12.1, the economy is hurt by the export subsidy. This is because the government uses the wrong information in computing the subsidy rate. If $a < 2c$, then the home firm can claim to have a marginal cost of $2c - a$, which is consistent with a Stackelberg output of $(a - c)/b$. Perhaps one may say that because the government knows that the home firm has an incentive to lie, it can discount the information supplied by the firm. If the home firms knows that the government is going to discount its information, it can further inflate the information. The matter of fact is that it is difficult for the home government to check whether the home firm has lied, or how big the lie is. Whether the government can successfully improve welfare may depend on who can outsmart whom.

12.5.5   Political Economy and DUP Activities

One of the most convincing arguments against the use of strategic trade policies is the presence of interest groups in democratic societies and their lobbying and rent or revenue-seeking activities. Because these activities are made for the sake of improving these agents' profits, but are not included in the production of goods and services that enter directly the utility function of the society, they are called "directly-unproductive profit-seeking" (DUP) activities (Bhagwati, 1982a).

Following Bhagwati (1989), two types of DUP activities can be distinguished: *downstream* activities—those that seek import quota premia (Krueger, 1974) and those that seek tariff revenue (Bhagwati and Srinivasan, 1980)—and *upstream* activities—those that lobby for or against the imposition of certain policies. The costs of these two types of DUP activities should be included when one evaluates the welfare impacts of policies.

The downstream DUP-theoretic costs are important but are often neglected in the trade literature. There has not been much work done on estimating the significance and sizes of these costs, and in theoretic work, assumptions about their sizes differ. Sometimes, they are assumed to be as big as the quota premia (Krueger, 1974). In some extreme cases, however, they can be negative, meaning that these DUP activities, which represent withdrawal of resources from the economy, can in fact improve national welfare. These extreme cases occur because the protection, which is taken as given, may have distorted the economy so much that the factors used in lobbying have negative shadow prices. This is possible theoretically. Unfortunately, there are not enough empirical studies to indicate how likely these cases are. It is generally believed that these DUP costs are positive, but are less than the existing quota premia and tariff revenues.

The upstream DUP-theoretic costs should also be included in policy evaluation. Two types of costs can be identified: the costs of the resources spent on lobbying, and the costs in terms of national welfare due to the imposition of the wrong policies. The latter type of costs arises because once the policy choice is influenced by lobbying, very likely the policy that the government chooses is not the one that will improve national welfare most, but the one that is lobbied for by the most powerful interest groups.

Estimating the magnitudes of the upstream DUP costs has theoretical problems. One may attempt to use the free-trade equilibrium point as a reference, and then estimate the costs of withdrawal of resources from the economy and add to them the costs of a policy in terms of the shrunken production possibility frontier. The problem of this approach, as Bhagwati (1989) notes, is that in such a system in which a policy is endogenously determined by lobbying activities, it is no longer meaningful to use the free-trade point as a reference.

Although the impacts of the upstream activities cannot be meaningfully measured by using the free-trade point as a reference, it is reasonable to compare one policy regime with another, as Bhagwati (1989) argues. In the case of strategic policies, two policy regimes are particularly interesting. The first one is characterized by a passive government that is influenced by different interest groups. In the second regime, there is a government that vigorously and credibly implements free trade policies. In the first regime, upstream DUP activities exist and the trade policies are endogenously determined. In the second regime, the free-trade policy is set by the government, and as long as it is believed that this policy cannot be changed by lobbying, no upstream DUP activities exist. In fact, in the latter regime, because of no quota premia or tariff revenue, there are no downstream activities either. Thus, as suggested by Krugman (1987b), when lobbying for policies may exist, free trade "may be the best policy that the country is likely to get."

12.6   Nonequivalence of Tariffs and Quotas

Tariffs and quotas are two most common and obvious ways of restricting the inflow of foreign goods. It has been thought that they have the same effects on the local economies, and that for every tariff a quota that has the same effects (perhaps except for the tariff revenue) can be found. In other words, they are equivalent.

The question of whether they are equivalent was first analyzed by Bhagwati (1965, 1968d). He defines the tariff rate that the government imposes on the incoming foreign goods as the *explicit tariff rate*. He then considers no tariff but a quota that is set at the import level the same as that under the explicit tariff. The quota is auctioned off competitively so that the government captures

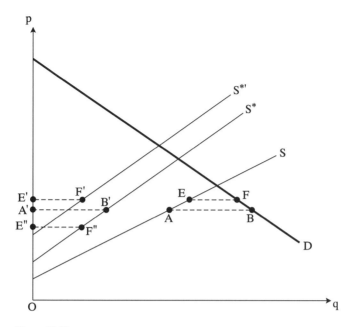

Figure 12.10

the quota premium. The quota drives a wedge between the domestic price and the foreign price. He then defines the *implicit tariff rate* based on price wedge under the quota. Whether the tariff and the quota are equivalent is the same as whether the explicit and implicit tariff rates are the same.[19]

Bhagwati shows that they are equivalent under the following three conditions: First, the domestic firms are competitive; second, the foreign firms are competitive; and third, there is perfect competition among quota-holders. To see their equivalence, consider Figure 12.10. The schedule labeled D represents the home demand, schedule S the supply from domestic firms, and schedule S* the competitive supply from abroad. Under free trade, the equilibrium price is given by OA' at which the gap between demand and domestic supply, given by AB, is equal to the foreign supply given by A'B'. The home government now imposes a specific tariff equal to E'E''. The result does not depend on whether the tariff is specific or ad valorem. The cum-tariff foreign supply curve can be represented by schedule S*': The vertical gap between S* and S*' is equal to the tariff rate. In the new equilibrium, the domestic price is OE' with the import equal to EF = E'F' = E''F''. The tariff revenue is represented by rectangle E'F'F''E''. Suppose now that a quota equal to EF is imposed instead. To clear the domestic market, the price rises to OE'. The

19. See Anderson (1988) for a recent survey and an extensive discussion of the use of quotas.

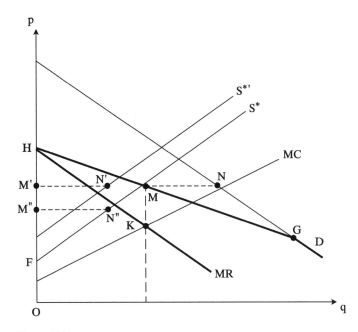

Figure 12.11

foreign producer's price is only OE″, which is the minimum price at which foreign firms are willing to supply EF. The gap between OE′ and OE″ is the per-unit quota premium. Because there is competition in quota bidding, the government is able to capture the quota premium that is the same as the tariff revenue in the previous case. The implicit specific tariff rate is E′E″, which is equal to the explicit specific tariff rate. So the tariff and the quota are equivalent.

In an interesting paper, Levinsohn (1989) examines the equivalence between tariffs and quotas when the market is imperfectly competitive and open to foreign direct investment (FDI). He shows that if the optimal tariff in the absence of FDI is not less than the gap between the marginal cost of the foreign firm and that of the foreign subsidy in the home market, then the optimal cum-FDI tariff is equivalent to the cum-FDI quota.

The equivalence between tariff and quota breaks down if any of the above conditions does not hold. To see why, suppose the first condition is violated: There is a domestic monopolist. (For the other two cases, see Bhagwati, 1965.) Figure 12.11 illustrates this case. Schedule NGD is the domestic demand and schedule S* is the competitive foreign supply. The domestic monopolist, however, does not have a supply schedule and its marginal cost is represented by schedule MC. Suppose now that a specific tariff is imposed. The cum-tariff foreign supply schedule is represented by schedule S*′, which is vertically

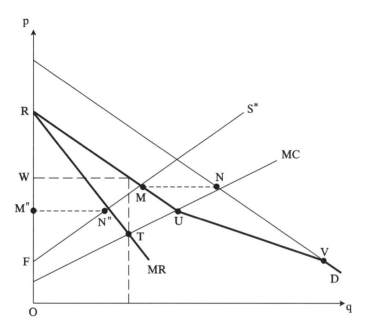

Figure 12.12

above schedule S*, the vertical gap between the schedules being the specific
rate. Taking the foreign supply as given, the home monopolist perceives the
demand for its output as represented by the kinked, thick line HGD in Figure 12.11. The corresponding marginal revenue is the line labeled by MR in
the diagram. The intersecting point between lines MC and MR, point K, gives
the firm's output. The domestic price is OM$'$ and the corresponding import is
MN = M$'$N$'$ = M$''$N$''$.

Now suppose that a quota of size MN is imposed instead of a tariff. This
case is illustrated by Figure 12.12. The perceived demand of the home monopolist is given by the thick kinked line RUVD. For comparison, the diagram also
shows the original import level MN (= M$''$N$''$). To derive the home monopolist's perceived demand, suppose that the domestic price is above OM$''$, with
the quota being binding so that the part of the perceived demand curve RU is
to the left of the market demand with a horizontal distance between them being equal to MN. If the domestic price is below OM$''$ but above OF, the quota
is not binding so that the perceived demand for the home firm becomes line
UV, which is the residual of the demand after the foreign import. When the
price is smaller than OF so that the foreign supply is zero, the perceived demand is the same as the market demand. In the present case, only the part of
the demand when the quota is binding is relevant, that is, line RU. The corresponding marginal revenue is the line labeled MR which cuts the marginal

cost line MC at point T. The latter point shows the profit-maximizing output and the corresponding market price OW. As shown by the diagram, the output of the home monopolist is lower than that in the tariff case while the market price is higher. The per unit quota premium, which is the implicit specific tariff, is WM'', which is greater than the explicit tariff rate. Thus quota and tariff are not equivalent.

Bhagwati's result can be interpreted as follows. With a tariff, the home monopolist competes with the foreign firms, taking the cum-tariff foreign supply curve as given. The presence of foreign firms makes the home firm's effort to raise price difficult, implying that its present price is less than what it wants to charge when trade is not allowed. When trade restriction is replaced by a quota of the same size as the import level under the tariff, some of its price-raising power (that is, its monopoly power) is restored. Figure 12.12 shows exactly this result: It wants to raise the price to OW, which is greater than the domestic price under a tariff ($= OM'$ shown in Figure 12.11).

12.7 Voluntary Export Restraints and Oligopolistic Firms

The preceding analysis shows that in the presence of imperfect competition quotas can affect significantly the nature of competition among firms. The previous section examines the case in which there is a domestic monopolist. In this section I consider the effects of quotas when there are oligopolistic firms in the two countries. The results depend crucially on how the firms compete. Two cases are examined: Cournot competition and Bertrand competition.

12.7.1 Cournot Competition

Consider the two-firm case analyzed in Section 12.1. Figure 12.13 shows the reaction curves H_1H_2 of the home firm and F_1F_2 of the foreign firm. Under free trade, the Nash equilibrium is at point N, the intersecting point of the reaction curves. The home economy's importation from the foreign firm is x^{n*}, with the home firm producing x^n.

Suppose now that the home government imposes a quota equal to x^{n*}, or that the foreign firm declares that it "voluntarily" restrains its export to the level of x^{n*}. In order not to consider any quota revenue explicitly, assume that any quota revenue the government receives is spent somewhere else in the economy with insignificant effects on this industry. In the presence of the quota, the foreign firm's reaction function becomes the kinked schedule MNF_2, as the part of the original reaction curve, F_1N, is no longer relevant. The new Nash equilibrium is still at point N at which the home and foreign reaction curves cut each other.

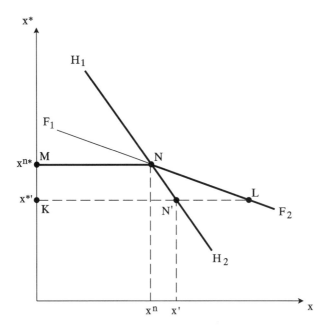

Figure 12.13

Suppose now that the quota is at a lower level such as $x^{*\prime}$. The foreign firm's reaction curve becomes $\text{KN}'\text{LF}_2$, and the new Nash equilibrium is at N'. The same analysis can be applied to other quota levels lower than x^{n*}, and for each of these quotas, the Nash equilibrium is a point on the home reaction curve. This means that if the quota is lowered gradually from the free-trade import level, the Nash equilibrium shifts down along the home firm's reaction curve. Furthermore, a lower quota gives a lower profit to the foreign firm but a higher profit to the home firm. So a quota has a profit-shifting effect similar to that of an import tariff analyzed in Section 12.1, except perhaps for the revenue.

Are tariff and quota equivalent in this case? Surprisingly, with Cournot competition, they are (Hwang and Mai, 1988). To show why, consider first the case of a tariff. As analyzed using the model explained in Section 12.1 and Figure 12.1, a tariff shifts the foreign firm's reaction curve F_1F_2 down. Let its cum-tariff reaction curve (not shown in the diagram) cut the home firm's reaction curve at point N', with the supplies of the home and foreign firms equal to x' and $x^{*\prime}$, respectively. Suppose now that a quota of $x^{*\prime}$ is imposed instead. I showed that the cum-quota reaction curve of the foreign firm is $\text{KN}'\text{LF}_2$, with the new Nash equilibrium at N'. Thus both policies give the same outputs of the firms, and the explicit tariff rate is the same as the implicit tariff rate.

The equivalence of tariffs and quotas in the present case is not surprising if the nature of competition is recognized. Whether there is a tariff or quota, the home firm takes the output of the foreign firm as given. Thus whether the policy is a tariff or a quota is not important to the home firm in the sense that if the foreign firm produces the same output under either policy (such as $x^{*\prime}$), the home firm will react with the same output (such as x'). Thus if both policies induce the foreign firm to produce the same output, the home firm will react with the same output, leading to the same market price.

Sometimes it is asked whether "voluntary" export restraints (VER) "self-imposed" by a foreign firm are indeed voluntary. It is clear that the answer to this question depends on the level of the VER. With Cournot competition, if the level of the VER is equal to or greater than the free-trade level, it is not effective and the foreign firm gets the same profit as under free trade (Mai and Hwang, 1988). If the VER is at a lower level, the foreign firm is hurt and it cannot be voluntary.

12.7.2   Bertrand Competition

I now turn to another type of competition, the Bertrand competition. As shown later, a VER affects the present strategic variable, price, in a way very much different from how it affects the strategic variable in the previous cases, quantity.

I adopt the Bertrand-competition model previously analyzed except that the market under consideration is the home market, which demands for the outputs supplied by a home firm and a foreign firm. Denote the demand for the home firm's output by $x(p, p^*)$ and that for the foreign firm's output by $x^*(p, p^*)$ where p and p^* are the home and foreign firms' choice of prices, respectively. I only consider the case in which the firms' outputs are imperfect substitutes,[20] requiring that the demand for a firm's output depends negatively on the firm's price but positively on the rival's price. Under free trade, I represent the profits of the home and foreign firms by $\pi(p, p^*)$ and $\pi^*(p, p^*)$, respectively. In Figure 12.14, the home firm's reaction curve is represented by schedule H_1H_2 and that of the foreign firm by schedule F_1F_2.

Suppose that a quota $\overline{m} \geq 0$ is imposed on the foreign import. The quota constraint can be written as $x^* \leq \overline{m}$. I first consider the case when it is just binding, that is, $\overline{m} = x^*(p, p^*)$. This constraint is represented by schedule V_1V_2 in Figure 12.14. The position of this schedule depends on the value of $\overline{m}$. The slope of this schedule is

---

20. The case in which the firms' products are complements can be analyzed in a similar way.

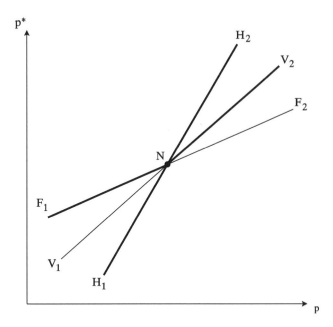

Figure 12.14

$$\left.\frac{\mathrm{d}p^*}{\mathrm{d}p}\right|_{V_1V_2} = -\frac{x_p^*}{x_{p^*}^*}. \qquad (12.30)$$

Comparing the slope of schedule V_1V_2 with those of schedules H_1H_2 and F_1F_2 given by (12.24) shows that if $x(p, p^*)$ and $x^*(p, p^*)$ have small second-order partial derivatives and if their first-order derivatives are close to each other,[21] then at point N

$$\left.\frac{\mathrm{d}p^*}{\mathrm{d}p}\right|_{H_1H_2} > \left.\frac{\mathrm{d}p^*}{\mathrm{d}p}\right|_{V_1V_2} > \left.\frac{\mathrm{d}p^*}{\mathrm{d}p}\right|_{F_1F_2} > 0.$$

This is the case shown in Figure 12.14.

Suppose that a VER equal to the free-trade import is imposed by the home government or by the foreign firm. This means that schedule V_1V_2 corresponding to this VER passes through the free-trade point N, as shown. The space below (respectively above) this schedule means that the VER is (respectively is not) binding. If the VER is not binding, the foreign firm's reaction curve remains to be its reaction curve under free trade. If it is binding, schedule V_1V_2 becomes its effective reaction curve. As a result, the reaction curve

---

21. This means that $x_p \approx x_p^*$ and $x_{p^*} \approx x_{p^*}^*$. Using this assumption and condition (12.24), it can be shown that the slope of schedule H_1H_2 is approximately $-2x_p^*/x_{p^*}^*$ and that of schedule F_1F_2 is approximately $-x_p^*/(2x_{p^*}^*)$.

of the foreign firm in the presence of the VER is the kinked, thick curve F_1NV_2 in the diagram.

To determine the equilibrium, an analysis is needed to show how the home firm chooses its price. Two cases, which are based on Harris (1985) and Krishna (1989), can be examined.

The Home Firm as a Price Leader

Harris (1985) makes the assumption that the foreign firm is responsible for not exceeding the VER and must choose p^* corresponding to p so that the VER constraint is not violated. This turns the foreign firm into a price follower because it has to know what price the home firm has chosen before it can set its price. This allows the domestic firm to take the first move to set the price p, knowing that the foreign firm will take this as given and react.[22] This case can be illustrated by Figure 12.15. For convenience, I show the effective reaction curve F_1NV_2 of the foreign firm under the VER and that of the home firm H_1H_2 under free trade. The diagram also shows the iso-profit curve labeled π^s of the home firm, which touches NV_2 at point S. It is clear that point S is the Stackelberg point, with the home firm acting as a price leader.[23] It is easy to conclude from this diagram that the VER has the following effects:

1. Equilibrium prices set by the home and foreign firms are higher than the free-trade level even though the foreign firm exports the same level as before. The reason for this is similar to the one in the Bhagwati case of a domestic monopoly and competitive foreign supply. The home firm, knowing that the foreign firm cannot export more than the VER level, can charge a higher price without worrying about more export by the foreign firm. When the home firm sets a higher price, the foreign firm has an incentive to charge more as well. As a result, the VER serves as a facilitating practice (Krishna, 1989), allowing both firms to collude indirectly and charge higher prices.

---

22. To understand why the domestic firm can take the first move, note that in the Bertrand model analyzed earlier, I emphasized that any of the firms cannot make a credit precommitment in terms of the price. In the present case, the home firm can make such a credit precommittment because it knows that once it has chosen the Stackelberg price, the foreign firm cannot choose the (lower) Nash price or the VER is violated.

23. Note that the home firm's declared price may not be time consistent, because once the foreign firm has responded, the home firm has an incentive to revise its price. For example, point S in Figure 12.15 is the Stackelberg point, with the home firm choosing p^h in the first move and the foreign firm choosing p^{h*} as a follower in the second move. If p^{h*} is the foreign firm's reaction, however, the home firm has an incentive to choose a domestic price represented by point M. In order to be willing to be a price follower, the foreign firm must be convinced that the price set by the home firm in the first move is irreversible. To make its first move credible, the home firm can do something such as advertisements to show that it will stick to the price it chooses. Alternatively, the home government may provide sufficient supervision so that once the home firm has announced its price in the first move, it cannot revise it.

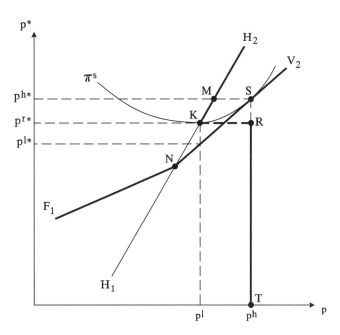

Figure 12.15

2. The home firm may produce less than before. In the special case in which the firms are identical and if schedule NV_2 is less steep than 45°, the output and market share of the home firm both decline.

3. The profit of the foreign firm is higher than before. This is due to the fact that the foreign firm sells the same quantity but charges a higher price. This result has the implication that VER *at the free-trade level* can be voluntary. However, it does not mean that the present analysis can be used to conclude that the VERs observed in the world are necessarily voluntary because these VERs are usually set at levels lower than free-trade levels. As Harris (1985) points out, VERs at sufficiently low levels hurt the foreign firm and are not voluntary.

Both Firms Set Prices Simultaneously

Krishna (1989) suggests another game between the two firms, that is, both of them set the prices simultaneously. One startling result of her analysis is that under some rationing rules, a pure-strategy Nash equilibrium does not exist. (A mixed-strategy Nash equilibrium, not surprisingly, does exist.) As in the previous case, a VER provides an opportunity for the firms to raise prices as if they collude.

To show a Nash equilibrium (or the lack of one), first note that the foreign firm's reaction remains F_1NV_2. The more difficult part of the analysis is to derive the reaction curve of the home firm. Schedule H_1NH_2, which is the home firm's reaction curve under free trade, is no longer its reaction curve under the VER. Recall that if the prices chosen by the firms are represented by a point below schedule V_1V_2 in Figure 12.14, there will be an excess demand in the home market for the foreign good because the VER is binding. Krishna assumes that arbitrage is allowed and is costless. Consumers who are lucky enough to get the foreign good will have incentives to resell it in the domestic market until the market clears. The equilibrium price is the one represented by a point on the VER-binding curve V_1V_2. For example, suppose that the foreign firm has chosen a price smaller than p^{h*} while the home firm chooses p^h (Figure 12.15). The excess demand for the foreign good leads to resale of the foreign good received by some lucky consumers, until the resale price of the foreign good reaches p^{h*}. This result is the same as if the foreign firm has chosen p^{h*}. As she notes, this is one of many possible rationing rules and it is crucial for the effects of a VER explained below.

The home firm's reaction curve can now be derived. First denote by p^{r*} the foreign price that corresponds to the lowest point of the home firm's iso-profit curve π^s, as shown in the Figure 12.15. If the foreign firm has chosen a price less than p^{r*}, the best response of the home firm is p^h because the rationing rule and costless arbitrage will push the equilibrium foreign price to p^{h*}. The consequence is represented by point S in Figure 12.15 and the home firm gets a profit of π^s. If the price chosen by the foreign firm is greater than p^{r*}, then the VER is not binding and there is no excess demand for the foreign good. Thus the best response of the home firm is the price represented by schedule KH_2 which is part of its free-trade reaction curve. If the foreign firm chooses p^{r*}, the home firm is indifferent to p^l and p^h. Combining these results, it can be concluded that the home firm's reaction curve under VER consists of the vertical line RT and schedule KMH_2.

Making use of Figure 12.15, the following results can be obtained:

1. A pure-strategy Nash equilibrium does not exist.

2. A mixed-strategy Nash equilibrium does exist, with the foreign firm setting a price at p^{r*}, and the home firm employing a mixed strategy, setting the price at p^h with a probability of α and at p^l with a probability of $(1 - \alpha)$, $1 > \alpha > 0$. The probability is so chosen that given the home firm's mixed strategy, p^{r*} maximizes the foreign firm's expected profit. (For more details about α, see Krishna (1989).)

3. The profit of the home firm at the Nash equilibrium is the same as that when it plays as a price leader. Furthermore, the foreign firm gains from the VER because it sells the same quantity as before but charges more. As in the Harris case, the VER *at the free-trade level* can be voluntary while VERs at lower levels may hurt the foreign firm.

Here, the home and foreign goods are assumed to be substitutes so that $x_{p*} > 0$ and $x_p^* > 0$. Krishna (1989) also considers the case of complements so that $x_{p*} < 0$ and $x_p^* < 0$, and shows that the VER at the free-trade level has no effect. This result is similar to the case in which the firms compete in a Cournot fashion.

12.8   Retaliation and Trade War with Competitive Industries

Thus far I have assumed that the foreign country is not active in choosing its optimal policy, and have concentrated on the strategies of oligopolistic firms. In this and the following sections, I examine the interactions between two governments and allow both of them to choose the optimal trade policies. I first consider the traditional two-sector framework with perfect competition in all markets. Without loss of generality, assume that the home country exports good 1. I begin with the analysis provided by Johnson (1953–1954).

Assuming that the technologies and preferences are continuous and strictly convex and that domestic distortions are absent so that the offer curves are continuous and strictly concave toward the axis representing the import of a country, Johnson notes that if a government takes the tariff imposed by another government as given, it has an incentive to impose its own tariff. Denote the tariff imposed by the home government by t and that by the foreign government by t^*. (In this model, it does not matter whether the tariffs are specific or ad valorem.) As a result, Johnson derives the reaction curves of the home and foreign governments, which are illustrated by schedules HH' and FF', respectively, in Figure 12.16 (assuming that the home country exports good 1). Generally the following properties of schedule HH' can be noted (similar results for schedule FF'): (1) Its horizontal intercept represents the home country's optimal tariff when the foreign government is inactive, and this tariff is positive. (2) It moves continuously down from point H so that the home country's reaction is a single-valued function of t^*. (3) It passes through some point A to the left of the vertical intercept of schedule FF'. (4) Its vertical intercept represents the value of t^* that is prohibitive so that world trade is eliminated. (5) Because of (3), OH > OF. (6) It may take any shape that fulfils these conditions. And (7) because a country is hurt more by a higher foreign tariff, the home welfare drops along schedule HH' in the direction toward H.

The intersecting point between HH' and FF', point N, represents the Nash equilibrium, (t^n, t^{n*}). Figure 12.16 shows the case in which point N is lower than point H and is to the left of point F'. In this case, the Nash tariff rate for either country is smaller than what the country wants to impose before retaliation. Properties (1) to (3) of schedule HH' and the corresponding properties

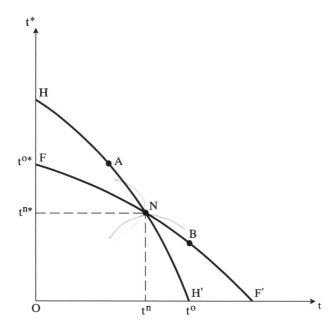

Figure 12.16

of schedule FF′ imply the existence of a Nash equilibrium with positive rates. Nash equilibrium may not be unique.

Turning to welfare, without retaliation an optimal tariff improves the welfare of a country. With retaliation, the change in welfare is not so certain. Figure 12.17 shows the offer curves of the home and foreign countries, OC and OC*, respectively. Point F is the equilibrium point under free trade, and the schedules labeled U_f and U_f^* are the home and foreign countries' trade indifference curves representing their utility levels under free trade.

Given strict concavity of the offer curves, each country wants to shift its offer curve toward the origin if the other country is inactive. Thus a Nash equilibrium with positive tariff rates for the countries is a point in the space bounded by the two offer curves. This space is disaggregated into three regions labeled α, β and γ. With respect to the welfare levels of the countries as compared with theirs under free trade, the following results can be derived:

1. At the Nash equilibrium, at least one of the countries is hurt. It is because free trade is Pareto efficient for the world.

2. If the Nash equilibrium is at a point in region α, the home country gains from this trade war. The home country's gain is less than what it can get if

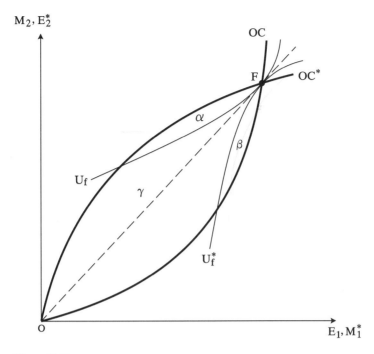

Figure 12.17

the foreign country does not retaliate. If the Nash equilibrium is at a point in region β, the foreign country gains. If it is at a point in region γ, both countries are hurt.[24]

3. If the world price ratio under a trade war is sufficiently close to the free trade price ratio, both countries are hurt. In terms of Figure 12.17, this means that the equilibrium point is close to the price line from the origin to the free-trade point, that is, the dotted line in the diagram. In this case neither country gains any (significant) improvement in the terms of trade but both must bear the costs of protection.

4. If the countries are identical, both of them must be hurt. This follows from (1) because at least one of them is hurt, or from (3) because the world price ratio under the trade war must be the same as that under free trade.

Very often the Nash equilibrium in a trade war is compared with the prisoners' dilemma. It is not quite correct to do so, however, because it is possible that one of the countries gains from a trade war (although not as much as it can have in the absence of retaliation). Only when the Nash equilibrium is at

---

24. Kennan and Riezman (1988) argue that under certain conditions, a larger country tends to win in a trade war.

a point in region γ will both countries be hurt. In this case, both countries can improve their welfare if they can commit to free trade, or if some world organizations (such as the GATT) negotiate for bilateral or multilateral trade liberalization and give effective supervision. If commitment cannot be made and if multilateral trade liberalization is not reached, both countries are stuck with lower welfare levels.

Now consider another type of trade restriction: import or export quota. I begin with the case in which the home country imposes tariffs while the foreign country chooses quotas, with quotas being auctioned off competitively so that the foreign government gets the quota premium. I showed earlier that if with competitive industries only one country is restricting trade while the other country allows free trade, then tariffs are equivalent to quotas. I now examine whether the equivalence still holds when both governments are active.

Assuming a noncooperative game between the governments, I first derive the reaction function of the home country which exports good 1. Let the optimal tariff rate of the home country in the absence of retaliation be t^0 and let the corresponding export level of the home country be E_1^0. Denote the import quota imposed by the foreign country by $\overline{Q}$. If $\overline{Q} > E_1^0$, the quota is not binding and the home country's reaction is t^0. If $0 < \overline{Q} \le E_1^0$, it is binding, and the effective offer curve of the foreign country is the truncated part of its free-trade offer curve when the home country's export is equal to or less than $\overline{Q}$, plus a line corresponding to a fixed volume of trade, $E_1 = \overline{Q}$. Taking this offer curve as given, the home country can determine the optimal tariff. In general, the home country reacts to a decrease in the foreign country's quota with a higher tariff, but as long as the quota is positive, the home country's reaction will not be prohibitive. Combining these results, I can show in Figure 12.18 the home country's reaction by curve HKN plus the horizontal axis beyond point N. The reaction curve is a straight line when $\overline{Q} > E_1^0$. When $\overline{Q}$ is smaller, the curve generally is downward sloping. Point N represents the prohibitive tariff.

I now turn to the foreign country's reaction. When given any cum-tariff offer curve of the home country, the foreign country chooses a point on this curve that gives the highest foreign welfare. If the quota is binding, the foreign government gets the premium, or if the quota is not binding, the foreign government gets no premium. The foreign reaction curve consists of curve FN plus the part of the horizontal axis beyond point N in Figure 12.18. Curve FN has a very important property: When the quota is positive, FN is on the left-hand side of HN. To see why, take any nonprohibitive tariff of the home country t' and let the reaction of the foreign country be $\overline{Q}'$. As explained previously, the foreign government must have chosen a binding quota in order to

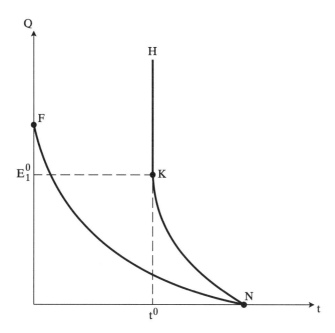

Figure 12.18

get the quota premium. Given $\overline{Q}'$, the home country will raise the tariff at least slightly higher in order to make the quota not binding so that it can capture the tariff revenue. If the home country's reaction is t'', then $t'' > t'$.

The Nash equilibrium can be represented by any point on the horizontal axis at or beyond point N, with no trade. Thus both countries return to autarky in a Nash equilibrium. This equilibrium has two properties: Tariff and quota are not equivalent, and both countries are hurt by the trade war. Furthermore, for the foreign country, tariff dominates quota.

Because the home country and the foreign country are symmetric, the analysis can be applied to show that if the foreign country chooses tariffs while the home country chooses quotas, the Nash equilibrium involves no trade. Now turn to the case in which both countries choose quotas. In this case, the Nash equilibrium is again autarky for both countries. To see why, note that if a country imposes a quota and if it is binding, the other country has an incentive to impose a slightly smaller quota in order to capture the quota premium. Thus if trade exists, it cannot be a Nash equilibrium (see Rodriguez, 1974; Tower, 1975).

If, however, both tariff and quota are used by both countries, the equilibrium is very much different. Copeland (1989) shows that with "well-behaved" offer curves, tariffs of the countries higher than the tariff-tariff Nash equilibrium (that is, at a point to the north-east of point N in Figure 12.16) with the quotas set at the corresponding levels represent a Nash equilibrium. To see why, suppose that the home tariff is set at $t' > t^n$ and the foreign tariff at $t^{*\prime} > t^{n*}$. The home country also sets an import quota while the foreign country sets an export quota so that the quotas are just binding. In terms of Figure 12.16, if tariffs are the only policy instruments, the home country wishes to lower its tariff so that it can import more, but in the presence of a binding foreign quota, tariff reduction is not effective in increasing import. This means that given the foreign tariff and quota, the home country is at its highest utility, and a quota cannot be used to improve welfare. The same argument can be applied to show that at this point the foreign country has no incentive to change its policies.

12.9   Retaliation and Trade War with Oligopolistic Industries

I now examine trade war in the presence of oligopolistic industries. With a change in the market structure, the trade policies chosen by the governments are different. I consider two cases, both of which are extension of the cases studied earlier.

12.9.1   Export Subsidy versus Export Subsidy

Suppose that the home and foreign firms supply identical products to a third market. For simplicity, assume that no domestic consumption of the product in either country exists. Denote the specific export subsidies imposed by the home and foreign governments by s and s^*, respectively. Taking these subsidies as given, the home and foreign firms compete with Cournot conjectures. Let the Nash equilibrium outputs of the firms be denoted by functions $q(s, s^*)$ and $q^*(s, s^*)$. For each country, national welfare is defined as the profit of its firm less the subsidy expenditure. This allows me to write the welfare functions of the countries as $W(s, s^*)$ and $W^*(s, s^*)$. Because a home export subsidy hurts the foreign firm's profit, it hurts the foreign welfare. Similarly, a foreign export subsidy hurts the home welfare.

Both welfare functions are represented by iso-welfare curves in Figure 12.19. W_0 is the home country's welfare under free trade, and the corresponding iso-welfare curve passes through the origin. Based on the preceding analysis, generally it is concave downward, with the space above (respectively below) it representing lower (respectively higher) home welfare levels. Similarly, the iso-welfare curve representing the foreign free-trade welfare is labeled W_0^* and passes through the origin, with the space to the right (respectively left) of it representing lower (respectively higher) foreign welfare levels.

The diagram also shows that the iso-welfare curves W_0 and W_0^* cut each other only once at the origin. This reflects the fact that when the two firms compete for a third market in the absence of any policies, they overproduce,

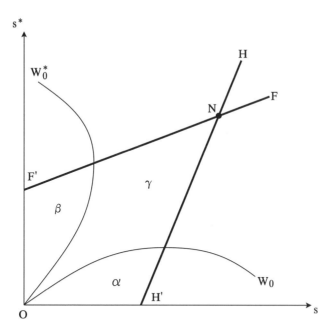

Figure 12.19

because the firms do not cooperate in their production decision and thus do not maximize the joint profit. When both governments impose export subsidies to encourage the production of their own firms, they deteriorate the joint profit of the firms, and thus their joint welfare. Therefore when both of the countries impose export subsidies, at least one of them is hurt.[25]

The locus of highest points of the home iso-welfare curves is the reaction curve of the home government (taking s^* as given), HH′. Its horizontal intercept, H′, is its optimal export subsidy with an inactive foreign government. Similarly, the locus of the points of the foreign iso-welfare curves with an infinite slope is the foreign government's reaction curve (taking s as given), FF′. Its vertical intercept, F′, gives its optimal export subsidy with an inactive home government. The intersecting point of the reaction curves, point N, is the Nash equilibrium.

A comparison of Figure 12.19 and Figure 12.17 shows that this case is similar to the trade war with tariffs. Several results can be mentioned (assuming that both countries impose positive export subsidy in equilibrium). First, at least one country loses (relative to free trade). Second, the space bounded by schedules FF′ and HH′ and the axes in Figure 12.19 can be divided into three

---

25. The analysis implies that if the governments can cooperate in choosing policies, the optimal policy to maximize their joint welfare is taxes on their firms' exports.

regions: α (below curve W_0), β (to the left of curve W_0^*), and γ. If the Nash equilibrium is in region α (respectively β), the home (respectively foreign) government wins. Third, if the countries are identical, both lose (Brander and Spencer, 1985).

12.9.2   Export Subsidy versus Import Tax (Countervailing Duty)

Now consider another type of trade war. In the model described in Section 12.1, the home and foreign firms supply their product to the home market. I argued that the optimal policy for the home economy is a home sale (or production) subsidy and an import tariff. Similarly, the foreign government has an incentive to impose an export subsidy. Denote the specific rates of these policies by r, t, and s^*, respectively.

Now consider a game in which both governments impose the appropriate policies noncooperatively in the first stage, and in the second stage firms compete with Cournot conjectures, taking the policies as given. The game is solved backward. In the second stage, the outputs of the firms are functions of the policy parameters. Taking these functions into account and taking s^* as given, the optimal home sale subsidy and optimal tariff are given by the expressions in (12.9a) and (12.9b), respectively. Even though s^* does not appear explicitly in these expressions, conditions (12.9a) and (12.9b) give the reaction functions of the home government. The dependence of the home tariff on s^* is illustrated by schedule HH' in Figure 12.20. To understand the slope of this schedule, note that while s^* works to lower the per unit cost of the foreign firm, t is to increase it. If there is an increase in s^*, the foreign firm earns more profit, the profit-shifting effect described earlier could be bigger, and the home government tends to impose a bigger tariff. So schedule HH' tends to be positively sloped. Point H' gives the optimal tariff t^o when the foreign government allows free trade. Dixit (1988) shows that with a linear home demand function, the slope of the home reaction curve is positive but less than unity.

Now turn to the foreign government. The optimal export subsidy is given by an expression similar to the one in (12.14) (with the roles of the countries reversed). This is the reaction function of the foreign government, and is illustrated by schedule FF' in Figure 12.20. Point F' shows the optimal foreign export subsidy s^{o*} when the home government is inactive. To determine the slope of this schedule, note that the optimal export subsidy maximizes foreign national welfare, or the foreign firm's profit (after paying the tariff) less the subsidy expenditure. Suppose that there is an increase in t. Then the foreign government tends to lower the export subsidy because a smaller subsidy encourages the foreign firm to produce less and thus to pay less tariff. In general, however, the slope of schedule FF' is ambiguous. Sohn (1993)

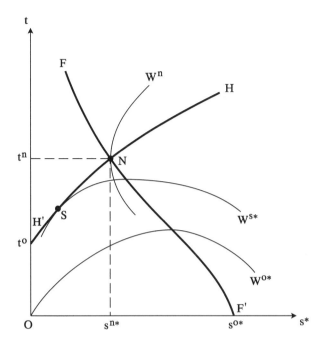

Figure 12.20

shows that if the home demand is linear, the slope of the foreign reaction curve is negative.

When both governments are active, the Nash equilibrium is shown by point N in Figure 12.20. The policies under this equilibrium are denoted by s^{n*} and t^n. Based on the assumptions about the slopes of the reaction curves, the trade war leads to an increase in the home tariff but a decrease in the foreign export subsidy as compared with what each country would impose if the other country is inactive.

The present model can be used to examine the use of countervailing duties by the home government in response to foreign subsidies.[26] With respect to countervailing duties, focus is given to the reaction of the home government or to the slope of the home reaction curve. For the case of a linear home demand, its slope is positive but less than unity (Dixit, 1988). This means that for every dollar increase in the foreign export subsidy, the home government reacts with an increase in tariff of less than one dollar. Alternatively, countervailing duty is referred to the amount of tariff the home government imposed in response to a discrete change in the foreign export subsidy. The change in the foreign export subsidy that is of particular interest is from 0 to s^{n*}. In terms of Figure 12.20,

---

26. See, for example, Dixit (1988), Collie (1991), and Sohn (1993).

the corresponding change of the home tariff is from t^o to t^n. Therefore $t^n - t^o$ is regarded as the countervailing duty imposed by the home government.[27]

I now examine the effects of a foreign export subsidy on the home country's welfare. The analysis in Section 12.1 shows that if the home country is passive in choosing policy, it is hurt by a foreign export subsidy. An interesting issue is whether the home country is still hurt if it always chooses the optimal home sale subsidy and tariff. To address this issue, let me focus on the part of the home welfare that comes from the home market and write its function as

$$W(r, t, s^*) = CS(q) + \pi(x, x^*, r) + tx^* - rx,$$

where $\pi(x, x^*, r)$ is the part of the home firm's profit that comes from the home market, and where $x = x(r, t, s^*)$ and $x^* = x^*(r, t, s^*)$ are the firms' Nash outputs. When the home government chooses r and t optimally, $\partial W / \partial r = \partial W / \partial t = 0$. Using these conditions, the effect of s^* on the home welfare is

$$\frac{dW}{ds^*} = \frac{\partial W}{\partial s^*} = -qp'q_{s^*} + \pi_{x^*}x_{s^*}^* + \tilde{t}x_{s^*}^* - \tilde{r}x_{s^*}. \tag{12.31}$$

Because t can be interpreted as an increase in foreign firm's effective marginal cost but s^* as a decrease, $x_{s^*} = -x_t$ and $x_{s^*}^* = -x_t^*$. The optimal home production subsidy and tariff are given by (12.9a) and (12.9b): $\tilde{r} = -xp' + (x^*)^2 p''$ and $\tilde{t} = -x^*\phi^*$. Using these results and the comparative-statics conditions in (12.4a) and (12.4b) gives (Collie, 1991):

$$\frac{dW}{ds^*} = x^* > 0. \tag{12.31'}$$

Condition (12.31') suggests that if the home government always chooses the optimal home sale subsidy and tariff, foreign export subsidy is beneficial. Based on this result, I can represent the welfare levels of the home country by different iso-welfare contours in Figure 12.20. For example, the schedule that passes through the Nash equilibrium point N represents the home Nash welfare level W^n. The home welfare level increases toward the right.

The positive effect of foreign export subsidy on home welfare under the specified conditions can be explained as follows. If the foreign export subsidy is increased by one dollar, the home government can increase the tariff by exactly one dollar. Because the foreign firm receives the same net subsidy as before, its production decision is not affected, but the home economy must be better off because of the increase in tariff revenue. If the home government chooses the optimal tariff and home sale subsidy corresponding to this new foreign export subsidy, the home welfare must be increased further (or not be decreased).

Making use of the home government's reaction curve, Collie (1991) analyzes a three-stage game: First, the foreign government chooses the optimal export subsidy, and then the home government chooses production subsidy and tariff, with the firms competing in a Cournot fashion in the last stage. He shows that the optimal foreign export subsidy is zero if the home demand is linear, but positive if the home demand is nonlinear.[28] In Figure 12.20, point S is the Stackelberg point, with the foreign government imposing an export subsidy in the first move. (Point S is at point t^o if the home demand is linear.) The corresponding foreign welfare level is W^{s*} and is illustrated by the corresponding iso-welfare contour.

The diagram also shows the foreign iso-welfare contour that corresponds to the free-trade welfare level W^{o*}. In the case shown, the trade war benefits the home country but hurts the foreign country if they play Nash, although the welfare effects are less significant if the foreign country can take the first move.

12.10   Alternatives to Trade Wars

The previous two sections analyze three types of trade wars between two trading countries. In the first two types, retaliation of the foreign country leads to at least one of the countries being hurt. In some extreme cases, both countries are hurt. In the third type of trade war, under certain conditions, generally one country gains and the other one loses.

The prisoners' dilemma in trade wars has received a lot of attention in the literature because of the striking result that both countries that are free to choose their optimal policies end up losing. This result seems to suggest some kind of "irrationality" in the system because both governments do not choose nonintervention even though if both of them do they get higher welfare levels. This "irrationality" is due to two features of the models; first, it is a one-shot game, and second, the two governments act noncooperatively.

I now examine how trade wars and their outcomes may be avoided by changing these two features of these models. In other words, this section ana-

---

28. In fact, if the home demand curve is nonlinear, the sign of the optimal foreign export subsidy depends on the sign of a term (variable Z in Collie, 1991), which contains the third derivative of the inverse demand function. In general the sign of this term is ambiguous but is assumed to be positive, which is sufficient for stability of equilibrium.

lyzes repeated games and bargaining between two governments. Foreign trade for each country does not end in one period but is repeated over time (probably indefinitely), and in many cases governments do negotiate.

In the following analysis, I pay most attention to the first type of trade war because it is good enough to illustrate the features of repeated games and government negotiation, but I explain how the results may change in the other two types of wars.

12.10.1 Repeated Games

Consider a trade war of the first type. Suppose that the governments are to choose tariffs, which dominate quotas, in each of the periods up to period T. The governments remain noncooperative. Would the governments still be protectionist in any of the periods?

If in the one-shot game one government (but not both) wins in the sense that its Nash welfare is higher than its free-trade welfare, one can expect that the trade war is repeated up to period T because the country that gains does not want free trade. Now let me focus on the case in which both countries lose in the one-shot game, the prisoners' dilemma. As is well known in the theory of repeated games, the answer to the question depends on whether T is finite or infinite, and on the magnitude of the discount rates of the governments. If T is finite, the result is the same as that of the one-shot game, that is, each government is protectionist and in the Nash equilibrium both governments are hurt as compared with free trade. To see why, I solve the game backward and analyze period T first. Because what the governments chose in the previous periods does not affect their welfare in this period, they maximize their present per-period welfare. The equilibrium in this period is the same as that in the one-shot game, that is, both governments are protectionist. In period $T - 1$, the governments also choose the same protectionist strategies. The same argument can be carried out to conclude that the governments are protectionist in each of these periods.

If T is infinite, and if the discount rate of each government is not too small (that is, they are close to unity so that they do not discount the future welfares too heavily), then the best strategy of each government is a trigger strategy: in the first period, it is noninterventionist, and in the next and future periods, it is noninterventionist unless the other country is interventionist in any previous periods (see Tirole, 1988, pp. 245–247). This is also known as the "tit-for-tat" strategy (Axelord, 1981).[29]

In theory, tit-for-tat is a simple strategy, but in reality, it is not. There are several difficulties in applying this strategy as a policy guideline in the real world. First, there are many policies that directly affect foreign trade but they

---

29. See Brander (1986) for an elaboration of this strategy.

are usually disguised by other names and motives, for example, import restrictions in the form of health and environmental regulations. Second, there are policies that are given the names of domestic policies but which do affect the competitiveness of domestic firms; for example, R & D and worker training subsidies. Third, in the Axelord theory, there are only two players. In the real world, there are more than two players. A tit to retaliate against a tat from a trading partner can have averse effects on another partner. Should this tit be considered as a tat by the latter partner? As a result, "in the real world it is not easy to identify clearly which policy is 'tit' and which policy is 'tat' " (Brander, 1986, p. 42). "Indeed, in a protectionist climate such as today's, tats are likely to be found readily and charged against successful rivals and the Axelord strategy likely to be captured by those who seek protectionism" (Bhagwati, 1989, p. 40).

12.10.2 Trade Negotiations

I now turn to government negotiation in the model of tariff-tariff war. Several models have been suggested in the literature. They differ not only in the assumptions of the models but also in their implications and results. What I describe now is a synthesis of some of these models. The main feature of the present model is its allowance of intercountry transfer. Such a transfer is responsible for the existence of free trade in equilibirium. I use the dual approach that allows me to derive the equilibrium easily.

The negotiation is described as follows. Representatives of the two governments first get together to determine a transfer. If the representatives agree on a transfer, a binding agreement is signed and free trade is allowed. The representatives are rational so that when they negotiate for the transfer, they are aware of how the transfer may affect the final free-trade equilibrium. Full information is thus assumed. If they cannot agree on a transfer, the negotiation collapses and a trade war occurs.

Using the two-sector general equilibrium model described in Chapter 2, denote the indirect trade utility (ITU) function of the home country by $V(p, b)$, where p is the relative price of good 1 and b is the transfer (in terms of good 2) it receives from the foreign country. (If the foreign country is to get a transfer, b is negative.) Similarly, the foreign country's ITU function is $V^*(p^*, b^*)$. Because of free trade, both countries face the same price ratio. To simplify the notation, I have dropped the given factor endowments in each country from the country's ITU function.

The next step is to determine the threat point (or conflict point). There has been disagreement in the literature as to where the threat point should be. The location depends on the assumption about what governments would do should the negotiation break down. Here I take the assumption of Mayer (1981) and

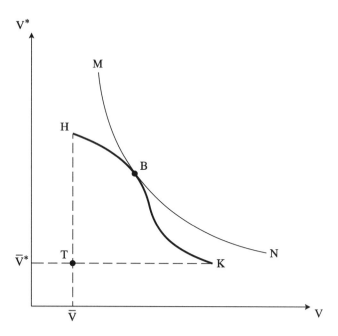

Figure 12.21

Riezman (1982) that if the negotiation breaks down, a trade war results. Let the utility levels of the countries at the Johnson-Nash equilibrium (if exists) be $\overline{V}$ and $\overline{V}^*$. The threat point is shown in Figure 12.21 (point T).

I now determine the feasible (negotiation) set. Because free trade exists after a transfer is made, the equilibrium is Pareto efficient and must occur at a point on the contract curve, that is, the locus of tangency points between the trade indifference curves of the countries. Efficiency is due to the fact that negotiation must extract all possible gains from trade. Therefore the feasible set in Figure 12.21 is the combination of utility levels of the countries that correspond to the levels on the contract curve and are higher than the threat-point levels. It is shown by schedule HK. The equilibrium must be a point on this schedule.

Using the Nash bargaining approach, the equilibrium is given by the solution of the following problem:[30]

$$\max_{b}\ [V(p,b) - \overline{V}][V^*(p^*,b^*) - \overline{V}^*]$$

$$\text{s. t.}\ \ p = p^*;\ b = -b^*. \tag{12.32}$$

---

30. See Chan (1988) for a discussion of the Nash bargaining theory and its use in analyzing trade negotiations.

The first-order condition for an interior solution is

$$(V_p p_b + V_b)[V^*(p^*, b^*) - \overline{V}^*] + (V_{p^*}^* p_b - V_{b^*}^*)[V(p, b) - \overline{V}] = 0, \quad (12.33)$$

where p_b is the effects of a transfer on the world relative price. I showed in Chapter 2 that $V_b = \lambda$, marginal utility of income of the home country, and $V_p = \lambda E_1$, export of good 1. Similarly, for the foreign country, $V_b^* = \lambda^*$ and $V_{p^*}^* = \lambda^* E_1^* = -\lambda^* E_1$, where the equilibrium condition of the good-1 market have been used. Using these conditions, the first-order condition reduces to

$$\lambda(E_1 p_b + 1)[V^*(p^*, b^*) - \overline{V}^*] - \lambda^*(E_1 p_b + 1)[V(p, b) - \overline{V}] = 0,$$

or,

$$\frac{V(p, b) - \overline{V}}{\lambda} = \frac{V^*(p^*, b^*) - \overline{V}^*}{\lambda^*}. \qquad (12.33')$$

Condition (12.33′) shows how the countries share the gain from free trade by using a transfer.

This result has a nice graphical interpretation. The slope of the feasible set, which is the rate of change of the foreign utility level with respect to the home utility level, is equal to

$$\left.\frac{dV^*}{dV}\right|_{\text{HK}} = \frac{dV^*/db}{dV/db} = -\frac{\lambda^*}{\lambda}.$$

The function in the Nash bargaining problem in (12.32) is described by different contours, and the slope of a contour is equal to

$$\left.\frac{dV^*}{dV}\right|_{\text{contour}} = -\frac{V^*(p^*, b^*) - \overline{V}^*}{V(p, b) - \overline{V}}.$$

Thus the equilibrium is represented by a point of tangency, point B in the diagram, between schedule HK and a welfare contour that is shown as MN.

In this model, the equilibrium is free trade (with transfer). If intercountry transfers are not allowed, Mayer (1981) and Riezman (1982) show that the equilibrium may not be free trade, with both countries imposing tariffs. In fact, in Mayer's model, if free trade does not exist, then one of the tariffs is negative.

12.11   Strategic Choice between Capital Mobility and Labor Mobility

In the previous chapter, I showed that in the Ramaswami model, a country prefers the optimal inflow of a scarce factor to the optimal outflow of its abundant factor, and that the first-best policy of a country is a perfectly discriminatory inflow of a scarce factor or an (almost) complete buy-out of all foreign factors. In deriving these results, it is assumed that only the home country is active in choosing the optimal policies while the other country always allows free factor mobility.

The case in which both countries strategically choose the optimal factor mobility policy was first investigated by Cheng and Wong (1990). In this section, I briefly explain their model and results. In particular, I investigate whether Ramaswami's ranking is still valid for the two countries that actively choose the optimal factor mobility policy. The game is explained as follows: In the first stage, both countries choose the type of factor (only one factor) to be permitted to flow across the border, and in the second stage, they choose the optimal restrictions on the moving factor. Both countries act noncooperatively in the sense that each of them take the policy of the other country as given when choosing its optimal policy.

I adopt the Ramaswami model used in the previous chapter. There is a homogeneous good produced by two factors, labor and capital. The home and foreign countries have identical production function: $Q = F(K, L)$ where Q is the output. This production function exhibits constant returns and continuity, and has positive but declining marginal products. The home country's factor endowments are $\overline{L}$ and $\overline{K}$. The foreign country's variables are denoted by asterisks. Without loss of generality, the home country is assumed to have a higher capital-labor ratio. All markets are competitive and factors are paid (before any taxes) its marginal product.

The game is solved backward. Because capital and labor are symmetric, first consider capital mobility. Denote the amount of home capital flowing to the foreign country by c. (Negative c represents capital flow in an opposite direction.) A Nash equilibrium is derived under capital mobility.

To restrict factor movement, a country can use either an income tax or a quota. First suppose that both countries use income taxes. Denote the specific tax rates imposed by the home and foreign governments on the income of the moving capital by t and t^*, respectively. Because home investors who do not move their capital earn the domestic marginal product, F_K, while home investors with their capital in the foreign country earn an after-tax income of $F_{K^*} - t - t^*$, the equilibrium condition of capital movement is

$$F_K(\overline{K} - c, \overline{L}) + t = F_{K^*}(\overline{K}^* + c, \overline{L}^*) - t^*. \tag{12.34}$$

In (12.34), the right-hand side represents what the home country receives for each unit of capital it sends out. By differentiating (12.34), I can show that capital movement c is discouraged by higher taxes.[31]

The home government's problem is to choose t, taking t^* as given, to maximize its national income. Assume that a Nash equilibrium, if it exists, is

---

31. Totally differentiating (12.34) and rearranging terms gives $(F_{KK} + F_{K^*K^*})dc = dt + dt^*$.

unique. This implies that when t^* is given, there is a one-to-one correspondence between t and c. Thus I assume that the home government chooses c to maximize national income, that is,

$$\max_{c} F(\overline{K} - c, \overline{L}) + c(F_{K^*}(\overline{K}^* + c, \overline{L}^*) - t^*),$$

taking t^* as given. Making use of the equilibrium condition (12.34), the optimal home tax $\tilde{t}$ is equal to

$$\tilde{t} = -cF_{K^*K^*}. \tag{12.35}$$

Taking t^* as given, (12.34) and (12.35) are solved for the reaction function of the home country. Condition (12.35) shows that if home capital does flow out, the optimal home tax rate is positive. Graphically, the reaction function can be represented by a curve such as schedule HH$'$ in Figure 12.16. The sign of the slope of schedule HH$'$ is in general ambiguous because the slope depends on the third derivatives of the production function. Condition (12.35) can be used to show that if the optimal capital movement is small, then schedule HH$'$ is negatively sloped (see Cheng and Wong, 1990). The horizontal intercept of the schedule gives the optimal tax rate, t^0, imposed by the home government when the foreign government allows free capital mobility. This is the tax we derived in the previous chapter when $t^* = 0$.

The reaction curve of the foreign government can be derived in a similar way, and is illustrated by a curve like schedule FF$'$ in Figure 12.16. The vertical intercept of the schedule represents the optimal foreign tax rate, t^{0*}, when the home government chooses to have no capital mobility restrictions. The intersecting point between HH$'$ and FF$'$, point N, stands for a Nash equilibrium under capital mobility.[32] For the sake of analyzing the first stage, I assume that the Nash equilibrium is unique. Denote the corresponding national income levels of the home and foreign countries by I_k and I_k^*, respectively.

Suppose now that the foreign country chooses quota only while the home country continues to set income tax rate. What is the new equilibrium? The argument explained in the case of trade war earlier can be used to show that the Nash equilibrium is autarky. The reason is that no matter what income tax the home country has chosen, the foreign country has an incentive to choose a quota smaller than the existing level of capital movement. Given the foreign country's quota, the home country has an incentive to choose a more severe tax in order to capture the tax revenue. This means that if there is a capital movement, it cannot be a Nash equilibrium. The same argument can be used to show that autarky is the Nash equilibrium if both countries use quota. Thus I conclude that for each country, income tax is a dominant strategy.

---

32. For the existence of a Nash equilibrium, see Cheng and Wong (1990).

Table 12.1
Pay-off matrix with different policy combinations

	Home country's options	
Foreign country's options	Labor mobility only	Capital mobility only
Labor mobility only	P_l	0
	P_l^*	0
Capital mobility only	0	P_k
	0	P_k^*

Nash equilibrium under labor mobility can be derived in the same way. I also assume that it is unique. Denote the corresponding national income levels of the home and foreign countries by I_l and I_l^*, respectively.

The pay-offs of the countries under a factor mobility policy are defined as the countries' national income levels less the corresponding autarkic levels. For example, $P_i = I_i - I_a$, $i = l, k$, where I_a is the home country's autarkic national income. The pay-offs under different policy combinations are shown in Table 12.1. In each cell, the upper value is the home country's national income and the lower value is that of the foreign country. Note that if one country chooses labor mobility only while the other country choose capital mobility only, then no factor moves across border and the countries' national incomes are the autarkic ones, that is, the pay-offs are zero.

What factor mobility the countries choose depends on the pay-offs. For example, if $P_l > P_k$, then the home country prefers labor mobility only to capital mobility only. Depending on the relative magnitudes of these pay-offs, four cases can be identified:

1. *the Ramaswami case*: $P_l > P_k$ and $P_l^* < P_k^*$;
2. *the counter-Ramaswami case*: $P_l < P_k$ and $P_l^* > P_k^*$;
3. *the capital-unanimity case*: $P_l < P_k$ and $P_l^* < P_k^*$; and
4. *the labor-unanimity case*: $P_l > P_k$ and $P_l^* > P_k^*$;

Using some numerical examples, Cheng and Wong (1990) show that depending on the production function and the factor endowments of the countries, all four cases are possible. This means that when both countries choose the policies strategically, it is no longer true that a country prefers the inflow of a scarce factor to the outflow of its abundant factor. In fact, it is possible that both countries prefer the outflow of its abundant factor to the inflow of the scarce factor (the counter-Ramaswami case). In some other cases, both countries prefer the movement of the same factor so that the Ramaswami ranking is violated for one of the countries.

Some of features of the table can be mentioned. First, no matter which of these four cases we have, there are two Nash equilibria, one with labor mobility only and one with capital mobility only. The reason is that when a country chooses the movement of a factor, then the optimal reaction of the other country is to allow the movement of the same factor. For example, labor mobility only for both countries is always a Nash equilibrium even if both countries prefer capital mobility only (the capital-unanimity case). This result, which may seem strange, is due to the fact that the countries choose policies in a noncooperative way and there is no way for them to coordinate in choosing a policy. (Using the same argument, autarky is also a Nash equilibrium.)

As a result, it is possible that for at least one country the "wrong" factor moves. Thus in the Ramaswami or counter-Ramaswami case, no matter which factor moves, one of the countries must find it undesirable. For example, if labor moves (from the foreign to the home country) in the Ramaswami case, the home country likes it but the foreign country prefers the inflow of its scarce factor, home capital. In the capital-unanimity or labor-unanimity case, there is one Nash equilibrium at which for both countries the "wrong" factor moves.[33]

Appendix

This appendix shows the stability conditions under Bertrand competition between n identical home firms and n^* identical foreign firms. Let (p^e, p^{*e}) be the equilibrium prices. Denote the rate of change of variable by a "dot" and assume that the prices adjust according to the following conditions

$$\dot{p} = k(p^e - p) \tag{A.1}$$

$$\dot{p}^* = k^*(p^{*e} - p^*), \tag{A.2}$$

where k and k^* are positive constants. For convenience, define $y \equiv p^e - p$ and $y^* \equiv p^{*e} - p^*$. Differentiate the first-order conditions of a representative home firm and a representative foreign firm given by (12.20a) and (12.20b) to get

$$nq_{pp}\dot{p}^e + n^*q_{pp^*}\dot{p}^* + (n+1)q_p\dot{p}^e + n^*q_{p^*}\dot{p}^* = 0$$

$$nq^*_{p^*p}\dot{p} + n^*q^*_{p^*p^*}\dot{p}^{*e} + nq^*_p\dot{p} + (n^*+1)q^*_{p^*}\dot{p}^{*e} = 0,$$

which can be rearranged to give

$$\dot{p}^e = -\theta\dot{p}^* \tag{A.3}$$

$$\dot{p}^{*e} = -\theta^*\dot{p}. \tag{A.4}$$

---

33. Cheng and Wong (1993) examine the policies when both factors may move.

where

$$\theta = \frac{n^*(q_{p^*} + q_{pp^*})}{(n+1)q_p + nq_{pp}}$$

$$\theta^* = \frac{n(q_p^* + q_{p^*p}^*)}{(n^*+1)q_{p^*}^* + n^*q_{p^*p^*}^*}.$$

The second-order conditions for the firms' maxima are assumed: $q_{pp} + 2q_p < 0$ and $q_{p^*p^*}^* + 2q_{p^*}^* < 0$. Define a new variable Z where

$$2Z = ky^2 + k^*(y^*)^2. \tag{A.5}$$

Condition (A5) shows that $Z \geq 0$ and is zero at the equilibrium point. Differentiate Z with respect to time to give

$$\dot{Z} = ky(\dot{p}^e - \dot{p}) + k^*y^*(\dot{p}^{*e} - \dot{p}^*)$$

$$= -(ky)^2 - (k^*y^*)^2 - kk^*yy^*(\theta + \theta^*), \tag{A.6}$$

where the adjustment conditions in (A.1) and (A.2), and conditions (A.3) and (A.4) have been used. Thus the equilibrium is stable if $\dot{Z} < 0$ when $Z > 0$ and $\dot{Z} = 0$ when $Z = 0$. It is obvious from (A.6) that the sign of $\dot{Z}$ depends on the sign of yy^* and those of θ and θ^*. I now show that either one of the following conditions is sufficient for stability:

1. $0 < n^*(q_{p^*} + q_{pp^*}) < -n(q_p + q_{pp})$, and $0 < n(q_p^* + q_{p^*p}^*) < -n^*(q_{p^*}^* + q_{p^*p^*}^*)$.
2. $0 > n^*(q_{p^*} + q_{pp^*}) > n(q_p + q_{pp})$, and $0 > n(q_p^* + q_{p^*p}^*) > n^*(q_{p^*}^* + q_{p^*p^*}^*)$.

Let me show condition (1) first. Because $q_p, q_{p^*}^* < 0$, condition (1) implies that $0 < -\theta, -\theta^* < 1$. If $yy^* < 0$, then condition (A.6) implies that $\dot{Z} \leq 0$. So I have to worry about the case in which $yy^* > 0$. Suppose that it is. Then because θ and θ^* are smaller than unity in magnitude,

$$\dot{Z} < -(ky)^2 - (k^*y^*)^2 + 2kk^*yy^*$$

$$= -(ky - k^*y^*)^2.$$

So $\dot{Z} \leq 0$ and the equilibrium is stable. Next consider condition (2), which implies that $1 > \theta, \theta^* > 0$. If $yy^* > 0$, then $\dot{Z} \leq 0$. Suppose instead that $yy^* < 0$. Thus,

$$\dot{Z} < -(ky)^2 - (k^*y^*)^2 - 2kk^*yy^*$$

$$= -(ky + k^*y^*)^2.$$

Again $\dot{Z} \leq 0$ and the equilibrium is stable.

VI SPECIAL TOPICS

13 The Multinational Corporation

A multinational corporation (MNC, also called multinational or transnational firm, or multinational or transnational enterprise) is a firm that has plants in different countries. The first plant is called the parent firm, and the country in which it is located is the source country. A foreign plant can be solely owned by the parent firm, or it can be an affiliate or a majority-owned affiliate, depending on the percentage of the equity of the foreign firm the parent firm owns. In the case of the United States, the percentage for an affiliate owned by a parent firm is 10 percent or more, and that for a majority-owned affiliate is over 50 percent. When a parent firm invests in a foreign country by setting up a plant, the process is called foreign direct investment (FDI, or direct foreign investment).

This chapter focuses on the phenomenon of MNCs, providing a critical review of some of the more important theories in the literature as well as a simple, unified model to analyze some of these issues. The literature on MNC theory has grown rapidly for several decades. Ronald Findlay (1978, p. 2), once commented on the literature of MNC: "While the literature on multinational corporations has grown even faster than its subject, most of it is of a descriptive or polemical nature, and analytical formulations of their activities, including the transfer of technology, are quite scarce." A complete investigation of the issues is not possible here, but some of the more important ones are discussed in this chapter.

13.1 Some Basic Concepts

The first thing to point out is that the theory of international capital movement (ITM) developed earlier is not sufficient to explain the phenomenon of MNC. It is fair to say that the theory of ITM focuses on the movement and renting of physical capital, and its purpose is to explain the causes and effects of this movement on resource allocation, consumption, production, trade, income distribution, and welfare. The phenomenon of MNC represents something that has not been covered by that theory, and thus calls for new analysis.

One of the first persons to suggest a new approach toward direct investment and international operation of firms was Stephen Hymer (1960) who compared direct investment with portfolio investment. Although the latter is driven by the gaps between the real interest rates among countries, he points out five features of direct investment that distinguish it from portfolio investment (Hymer, 1960, pp. 10–23):

1. In the 1950s U.S. firms that invested abroad also borrowed abroad. The phenomenon is not specific to U.S. MNCs in that period, but is true for many firms from all countries today.

2. Direct investment and portfolio investment can move in opposite directions. For example, in the period before 1914, the United States accumulated direct investment while it was still a large importer of portfolio capital.

3. It is observed that most of the investing activities were done by nonfinancial firms. This suggests that capital that moves across countries is not financial, and that these investments may also be made for some motivation other than to capture higher returns.

4. Direct investment has always shown a marked industrial distribution. For example, the direct investments of the United States appear to be persistently associated with the same industries in all other countries. If direct investment is caused solely by interest-rate differential, it should concentrate on a few countries where the interest rates are higher.

5. Cross investment often occurs within industries.

Hymer (1960) suggests that the main reason for direct investment is control. This is the official way of defining direct investment and distinguishing it from portfolio investment: If the investor owns a certain percentage of the equity of a firm in the host country it is officially a direct investment. That percentage, which could be 10, 25, 51, or 100 percent, varies from one country to another, and from one time to another, but the exact percentage is not important in theoretical work because the important thing in theory is that an investor has sufficient control over the affiliate.

As Kindleberger (1969) points out, however, economists are interested in control insofar as it affects behavior. Therefore, to understand the phenomenon of foreign direct investment and MNC, it is necessary to examine what the investors want to control and the effects of that control. This is the starting point of our analysis. Hymer (1960) suggests two motives or types of direct investment. The first type, which he calls direct investment, type 1, "has to do with the prudent use of asset," that is, the investor seeks control over the enterprise in order to ensure the safety of his investment. Direct investment of type 2 is made with the purpose of maintaining or expanding a firm's market power.

An MNC is a firm with plants in several different countries. Thus the basic issue to be addressed here is why a firm chooses to set up such plants. This question is not as trivial as it may appear. As Hymer (1960) correctly points out, operating in a foreign country involves new costs due to differences in the cultures and the legal, economic, and political systems in the source and host countries. Therefore the firm must possess some advantages relative to local firms in order to overcome these costs and compete.

To explain why a firm chooses to set up a plant in a foreign country, the necessity for the firm must first be explained. In the traditional microeconomics textbook a firm is something that brings "optimal" amounts of relevant factors of production together in order to produce an output for the sake of a profit. Coase (1937) suggests that a firm is something more than a place where factors meet and produce. Since then many theories of the firm have been proposed, and each of them can be used to derive a theory of MNC. This explains why it is so difficult to have a general theory of MNCs. Most of these theories do share one common feature: In the perfect competition paradigm, there is no role for a firm. This feature is reflected by the following two points. First, information is not perfect in the real world. A firm has some information that other firms may not have. A good example is technological information. The more technological information a firm has, the better position it is in when competing in the markets. A firm that wants to preserve its position in the market wants to keep its technological information top secret. Such information affects not only the firm's production but also its sale or license of technology. Second, the firm is not a price taker. This is mainly due to the firm's possession of technological information and possibly other advantages that gives the firm some monopoly power. Because the firm's profit depends positively on the advantages it possesses, it has an incentive to accumulate advantages. As I will show later, a firm has an incentive to use market-oriented strategies to expand its monoploy power.

13.2   Ownership Advantages

In the modern theory of MNC, a firm is an organization that possesses some firm-specific advantages. These advantages are used by the firm in competing with other firms, and they dictate what actions the firm can and will take. Thus the starting point of the present analysis is to examine what types of advantages the firm may have. Ownership advantages relevant to this analysis may be grouped into four types: technological advantage, consumer recognition advantage, market advantage, and input advantage.

Technological Advantage

This advantage is the type of information a firm owns privately and uses directly in its production process, thus the name "technological." It is commonly called technology, production technique, know-how, and knowledge. Three different types of technological advantage can be distinguished. First is the information to create, develop, and produce new products. The second type of technological advantage is something that is used to improve the production process of existing products. For example, it is the advantage that would enable a firm to increase the productivity of factors and inputs, to lower the cost of production, and to increase the quality of a product. The third type of technological advantage is the organizational skills and management techniques used to manage workers, to administer the organization hierarchy, and to control the working environment.

Technological advantage is intangible and durable, and it can hardly be measured or observed. The most important feature of this advantage is that they are like a public good to the firm (Johnson, 1970). This means that once technological advantages are achieved, the firm can increase the use of them without having to pay any additional costs (or if additional costs are needed, they are not significant.) This feature of technological advantage is particularly important as the firm sets up a new plant either in its own country or abroad. This implies economies of scale in using the technological advantage as the firm becomes multinational. The public-good nature of technological advantage is important when the firm tries to sell or license technology to other firms.

Technological advantage is usually accumulated by the firm through research and development (R & D), experience gained by the managers, training of workers, learning from other firms, and the technologies that are licensed and purchased from other firms.

Consumer Recognition Advantage

This is another firm-specific advantage that helps tilt consumers' preferences in the firm's favor. Examples are the firm's good will, brand name, trademark, and consumers' trust of the prices and quality of the firm's products. A firm that has this advantage can expect certain degree of loyalty from consumers and thus relatively more stable sales when market demand fluctuates.

Consumer recognition advantage has two important properties: It can spill over to new products, and, in many cases, is transferable geographically. For example, a firm developing a new product that is similar to its existing products can market the product by appealing to consumer loyalty and trust for existing products. This could help the sale of the new product.

As a firm goes multinational and invests in a new country, the good will, brand name and consumer loyalty it earns in its own market may be useful in the host country. For example, this occurs when McDonald'sPSregistered opens a new restaurant in China. Although the degree of usefulness depends on many factors such as the distance and cultural differences between the two countries, it is very possible that consumers may already know something about the quality of the firm's products. When setting up a new subsidiary in the host country, it is even easier for a firm to build up consumers recognition if the firm is already exporting its products to the country.

Although consumer recognition can be transferred to another country, it is usually market-specific. In other words, a firm's product is often more trusted by the consumers in its home market than by the consumers in the host country. For that reason, consumers in a market often trust the products which have been around for a long time and discriminate against products from other countries.[1] Thus for a MNC that invests in a new country and is competing with local products that are close substitutes, consumer recognition (or the lack of) could be a handicap or a disadvantage.

Consumer recognition advantage has the nature of a partial public good. This means that when the firm invests in a new country, it does not have to pay additional costs when it exploits this advantage in the host country. But in general the firm cannot capture the full effect of this advantage when it introduces a new product or an existing product to a new market.

Market Advantage

This advantage has two major types. The first is the firm's knowledge of the markets it serves, such as knowledge about the consumer preferences, strategies and other information about its competitors, availability of input suppliers, and details about the economic, legal, and political systems.

The second type of market advantage is the firm's ability to deliver its output from its plants to consumers in efficient and effective ways. The degree of the firm's market advantage depends on how successfully it lowers its costs of distribution through different levels of wholesale and retail sales, increases its monopoly power by differentiating its products, and appeals to more customers.

Market advantage is usually market-specific: It is associated with particular markets and may not be used in another market. This feature of the advantage is important in the theory of MNC. As a firm sets up a new plant in a new market, it lacks the market advantages of existing firms. Also, as compared with local firms, it also lacks good knowledge of the culture and political, legal, and economic systems, meaning that the newcomer has a market disadvantage in the host country.

Input Advantage

A firm has an advantage over its competitors if it has special access to raw material or intermediate inputs. The access may be due to the firm's control of some raw material (such as minerals) or due to contracts with the material's owner (such as a government). Such control over intermediate inputs could be the result of vertical integration.

This type of advantage also includes the possession of some intermediate inputs that have inelastic supply. For example, a firm has a certain number of experienced managers and skillful engineers and workers. The experience and

---

1. Furthermore, the preferences of patriotic consumers may be biased toward national products and away from foreign products. Local firms can also appeal to patriotism in marketing their products.

skill embodied in these people are usually firm-specific: They are very useful to a particular firm but considerably less to other firms. In some cases, special productive machines or tools owned by a firm but not by its rivals can provide an advantage.

Because capital markets are usually not perfect, a firm that can raise capital at lower costs or that keeps a significant amount of retained earnings can have a competitive edge. This is especially true if a firm invests abroad. When investing abroad, the firm has two options for raising capital, borrowing in its country or in the host country. Larger firms generally can get more favorable terms from banks when borrowing.

Access to raw materials and intermediate inputs is tangible and usually observable. It is also transferable from one country to another. The public-good nature of this advantage, if any, is very limited. For example, when a firm transfers some of the managers currently working in the parent firm to a subsidiary newly set up in another country, it may not be possible to train new managers within a short time to replace them in the parent firm. In the short run, this type of input supply is inelastic. This means that the transfer of managers to subsidiaries is at the expense of the parent firm, and an MNC must take this cost into account when choosing to invest abroad.

When the firm wishes to invest in another country, it tries to bring its ownership advantages with the investment. How much of an advantage it can bring to and use in the host country depends on the extent of the public-good nature of the advantages, and on the extent of its market specificity. If the advantage is market specific, such as a market advantage and to a less extent consumer recognition advantage, then very little of it can be brought across country borders. In fact, in the host country, the lack of an advantage means that the firm has a disadvantage as compared with local firms. Lack of knowledge of the cultural, legal, economic, and political systems of the host country is often emphasized in the literature. If an advantage has a perfect public-good nature and is not market specific, such as some types of technological advantage, the use of it by the firm's subsidiary in another country does not affect the use of it by the parent firm. If an advantage is not market specific but has little public-good nature, such as trained managers and engineers, then the firm can bring that advantage to another country, but such transferrence could diminish the use of them by the parent firm.

Identifying different types of ownership advantages helps explain a paradox (Hymer, 1960; Kindleberger, 1969). It is observed that multinational corporations not only bring financial capital for investment, but also borrow heavily from the financial markets in the host country. I argued earlier that capital markets are generally not perfect. The imperfection of capital markets has two consequences. First, the opportunity cost of the retained earnings of a firm is less than the cost of borrowing from a domestic market. Because of this gap in costs, a firm with significant retained earnings has an advantage (a type of input advantage) when it wants to expand. Second, for the subsidiaries, it may be cheaper to borrow in the host country than in the source country because, ceteris parabus, banks usually trust firms in the local market more than firms in another country. Combining these two points, it is not surprising to find that a multinational firm first uses its retained earnings. Beyond a certain point, it will raise financial capital from the market in the host country.

I can now make use of the analysis on firm-specific ownership advantages to explain a firm's decision to investing. At the present time, the focus is on investment in the manufacturing sector, and on firms that are horizontally integrated, although some of the analysis can be applied to investment in other sectors and for vertically integrated firms.

Consider an industry with a homogeneous product. There are two countries, the source and the host. There is a firm in the source country labeled P that can produce the product to be exported to the host country, go multinational, or do both. There is a local firm labeled H in the host country producing the same product. The focus of analysis is on the production of firm P and its foreign investment. Thus it can be assumed that conditions in the countries are such that firm H never finds it profitable to invest in the source country or to export its products to the source country.

Begin with firm P and consider three types of inputs: R (for R & D), which includes those types of technological and consumer recognition advantages that are not market specific and have public-good nature; M (for managers and retained earning), which includes the input advantage that are not market specific but have no public-good nature; and L (for labor), which the firm does not own but can hire from the market in which the plant is located. Factor L also includes financial capital raised in the market. In a more general model, the three variables can be vectors of inputs, but for simplicity a general model is not developed here. Denote the amounts of the two advantages owned by firm P by $\overline{R}$ and $\overline{M}$, respectively. At least in the short run, $\overline{R}$ and $\overline{M}$ are assumed to be fixed.

The production function of the parent firm P is given by

$$Q^* = F(R^*, M^*, L^*), \tag{13.1}$$

where Q^* is the output of firm P in source country while R^*, M^* and L^* are the quantities of the inputs firm P uses. Because of the public-good nature of factor R, the firm can use the full amount of the factor even if it is going to a subsidiary in another country. This means that $R^* = \overline{R}$. Factor M, however, lacks this public-good nature, and must be shared by firm P and its subsidiary if the firm invests abroad.

To facilitate the analysis on foreign direct investment, I make the following two assumptions. First, assume that there is no demand for this product in the source country. This assumption, which allows me to focus the analysis on the host market, implies that the output of firm P, Q^*, is exported to the host country. The cost of this assumption is that it excludes the possibility that the firm in the host country may also export to and invest in the source country. This cost is a small price to pay as I am developing a simple theory of the multinational corporation, but this assumption is relaxed by Chan and Wong (1994), who explicitly analyze intraindustry trade and investment.

The second assumption made is that firm P's production function is of the Leontief type

$$Q^* = \overline{R}\big[\min(M^*, L^*)\big]. \tag{13.1'}$$

This assumption will greatly simplify the analysis given later.

Suppose now that firm P is considering setting up a new subsidiary in the host country. To invest there, it has to bring with it its advantages, factors R and M. As explained previously, the public-good nature of factor R means that the parent plant's use of the factor is not affected by such an investment. This is, however, not true for the use of factor M, which lacks this public-good nature. Given a perfectly inelastic supply of the factor (at least in the short run) and denoting the amount of factor M the subsidiary uses in the host country by M, the amount of this factor left for the parent plant in the source country is $M^* = \overline{M} - M$.

As explained previously, the subsidiary of firm P has market and consumer recognition disadvantages as compared with a local firm in the host country. These disadvantages are represented in the present model by a less efficient production function. More specifically, I assume that the production function of firm P's subsidiary in the host country is

$$Q = \alpha \overline{R}\big[\min(M, L)\big], \tag{13.2}$$

where α is a positive constant, $0 < \alpha < 1$, Q is the output of the subsidiary, and M and L are the subsidiary's inputs. Note that the public-good nature of factor R allows the subsidiary to use the same amount of the factor without affecting the parent firm's use of it. The amount of factor M is what firm P brings to the host country and can be interpreted as the level of foreign direct investment. The variable α reflects the extent of the firm P's disadvantages. For simplicity assume that its value is independent of the level of investment or production.

There is a firm labeled H in the host country producing an identical product. Possessing a fixed amount $\overline{r}$ of factor R and $\overline{m}$ of factor M, the firm employs an amount ℓ of labor to produce an output level q as given by the following production function:

$$q = f(\ell, \overline{m}; \overline{r}). \tag{13.3}$$

The production function is concave, strictly increasing, and twice differentiable in $\overline{m}$ and ℓ. Because in the present analysis the amounts of factors R and M possessed by firm H play no role, they are dropped from the production function. To focus the analysis on the market of the host country, I assume that firm H has no intention of investing in the source country and exporting its product.[2] Thus its output is its supply to the host market.

Denote the inverse demand of the host market by $p = p(Q^* + Q + q)$ where p is the price of the good and $Q^* + Q + q$ is the total supply. Assume that the demand curve is downward sloping and is not too convex to the origin. Using the production functions given by (13.1′) and (13.2), the total supply is $\overline{R}(\overline{M} - M) + \alpha \overline{R}M + q = \overline{R}[\overline{M} - (1 - \alpha)M] + q$. The inverse demand function can be written as $p = p[\overline{R}(\overline{M} - (1 - \alpha)M) + q]$. Assume that if firm P exports to the host country, its per unit revenue is only $p - t$, where t represents the transport cost plus the tariff (if any) the host government imposes.

13.3   Choosing between Export and Foreign Direct Investment?

In this section, I examine the following two actions of firm P: first, to produce goods and export its outputs to the host country, and second, to invest in the host country and supply the local market with the output of its subsidiary. In the present model, export by the firm refers to the sale of the firm's output abroad, and does not include the export of the services of the firm's advantages.

One of the earliest MNC theories was developed by Aliber (1970) who, assuming economies of scale, uses the size of a country and the bias of exchange risk determination to explain how a firm chooses between export, foreign investment, and licensing, and to explain whether a country is likely to be a host country or a source country. Others have examined the export-invest decision by focusing on the costs of export and the costs of invest. For example, Hirsch (1976) states that a firm chooses to invest abroad over export if the cost of production in the host country (including the costs of control and marketing) is less than the cost of production in the source country (including the costs of marketing and the disadvantages due to producing in a foreign environment). Dunning (1977, 1981) refers to the advantage of a country in attracting foreign investment as the country's locational advantage.

---

2. Recall that I assume the source country has no demand for the product. Firm H may have the option of investing in the source country and then exporting its product to the host country. I assume that its technology is not superior enough so that this option is not profitable for it.

In analyzing the export-invest decision of a firm, most papers share the common assumption that export and foreign investment are two mutually exclusive options. So in satisfying a foreign market, a firm either exports or invests. (The option of licensing is analyzed later.) Aliber (1970, p. 22) makes this point clear by saying that "one decision faced by a firm with a patent is whether to satisfy the foreign market by exploiting the patent domestically and exporting or whether to exploit the patent abroad. A second decision is whether to exploit the patent within the firm or to sell or license the patent." Krugman (1983), Smith (1987), Dei (1990), Horstmann and Markusen (1992), and Motta (1992) are explicit in considering the choice of a firm between export and foreign investment. In the models they develop, the conditions in the source and host countries are such that it is never profitable for a firm to export and invest at the same time. (In the singular case, a firm is indifferent to exportation and investment.)

In the real world, simultaneous export to and direct investment in the host countries by MNCs do occur. Lipsey and Weiss (1981) examine fourteen industries in forty-four countries other than the United States, and conclude that the exports of the United States to these countries depend positively on the sales of the U.S.-owned affiliates in these countries. Lipsey and Weiss (1984), using firm level data, draw a similar conclusion.

In Helpman's (1984c) model with monopolistic competition and differentiated products, the locational advantage of a country comes from the costs of factors of production. If free trade leads to factor price equalization, firms do not have any incentive to invest abroad. If factor prices are not equalized by free trade, firms may have an incentive to locate its production in another country. Because of internal economies of scale, a firm will produce a variety in only one location. Because preferences in the two countries are symmetric and homothetic,[3] production in only one location implies that a firm investing and producing abroad will ship its output back to the source country.

In other papers, the relationship between export and foreign investment is less clear. For example, Markusen (1984) states that the parent firm and the subsidiary in two separate countries produce positive amounts of a good. Whether the country with the parent firm exports or imports the good depends on technologies, among other things. In Vernon's (1966) product cycle model, a country that has investment abroad may export and import a good in different stages of the same product cycle.[4] Kojima (1978) also observes a strong relationship between export and investment, but the relationship varies between two different models of direct investment. In the U.S. model, he argues,

---

3. In the love of variety approach, the countries have identical preferences.

4. Strictly speaking, the country exports and imports different goods because the goods have different quality in different stages of the product cycle.

U.S. outward direct investment comes from the industries in which the United States has a comparative advantage. This means that the investment is made by firms that are already exporting. An increase in investment tends to suppress these firms' exports and so the investment is anti-trade-oriented. In contrast, Japanese outward direct investment is trade-oriented, because it comes from those industries in which Japan has a comparative disadvantage and thus encourages importation by Japan.

These observations suggest that exportation and investment are not two mutually exclusive options for a firm, and it is not appropriate to ask which action a firm will choose, because it may choose both.

Vertical integration is one way to explain simultaneous export and investment by a firm (Helpman, 1985; Ethier, 1986a). For example, suppose that an MNC produces an intermediate input in its country and at the same time sets up a plant in a host country to carry out the downstream production. This means that the MNC invests and exports its intermediate inputs to its subsidiary at the same time. In the extreme case, the subsidiary's production is supplied to the market in the host country and there is no export back to the source country (Ethier, 1986a). There are, however, other cases of vertical integration that may give a negative correlation between export and investment. For example, the production of the intermediate input by the MNC is located abroad while the final product is produced and consumed in the source country. Then investment co-exists with importation.

By assuming increasing marginal costs for the parent plant in the source country and for the subsidiary in the host country, Horst (1971, 1973) develop a simple model to explain the possibility of co-existence of exportation and foreign investment by a MNC. His model does not explain what the marginal costs depend on, however, nor does it distinguish between different types of ownership advantages.

In this section, I make use of the model presented earlier to provide a more sophisticated explanation of the export or invest decision of an MNC. Consider a one-shot game in which firm P in the source country and firm H in the host country make decisions and take action at the same time in a Cournot fashion. I begin with firm H, which takes the total production of firm P (including that of its subsidiary) and factor prices as given. Denote the exogenously given wage rate in the host country by w and the fixed cost for firm H by z. Its problem is to choose the optimal output level to maximize its profit π, that is,

$$\max_{q} \pi \equiv pq - w\ell - z.$$

The first-order condition of this problem is

$$\pi_q = (p + qp') - w/f_\ell = 0, \tag{13.4}$$

where the subscripts denote partial derivatives. Condition (13.4) can be differentiated to give

$$\pi_{qq}\mathrm{d}q + \pi_{qM}\mathrm{d}M = 0,\tag{13.5}$$

where the second-order derivatives of function π are equal to

$$\pi_{qq} = (2p' + qp'') + wf_{\ell\ell}/f_{\ell}^3 < 0$$

$$\pi_{qM} = -\overline{R}(1-\alpha)(p' + qp'') > 0,$$

where the signs of these second-order derivatives are due to the assumptions that the demand curve is negatively sloped and not too convex to the origin and that $f_{\ell\ell} < 0$. The condition that $\pi_{qq} < 0$ satisfies the second-order condition of the firm's problem. Note that in the present model there is a one-to-one correspondence between firm P's investment in the host country and its total production (including that of its subsidiary). This allows me to invert condition (13.4) to give the reaction function of firm H:

$$q = \phi(M).\tag{13.6}$$

Its reaction function as given by condition (13.6) can be illustrated by schedule HH' in Figure 13.1. Its vertical intercept represents firm H's output when no investment comes from the source country. Its slope can be obtained by rearraning condition (13.5) to give

$$\left.\frac{\mathrm{d}q}{\mathrm{d}M}\right|_{HH'} = \phi'(M) = -\frac{\pi_{qM}}{\pi_{qq}} > 0.\tag{13.7}$$

To explain the slope of firm H's reaction function, note that the present model is similar to the usual duopoly model, with each firm taking the output of the other firm as given. Under the usual conditions, firm H will react negatively to the total output of firm P, $Q^* + Q$. Because of the market and consumer recognition disadvantages, the total output of firm P falls as it invests in the host country. Thus firm H's output reacts positively to firm P's investment.

I now turn to firm P. Denote its fixed cost in the source country by Z^*, and let the wage rate in the source country be w^*. The firm is a price taker in the labor market. For simplicity, let me assume that its fixed cost in the host country is zero. Because it may produce in both countries, its joint profit is equal to

$$\Pi = (p - t)Q^* + pQ - w^*L^* - wL - Z^*.\tag{13.8}$$

Making use of its production functions in the two countries as given by (13.1') and (13.2), its joint profit can be written as

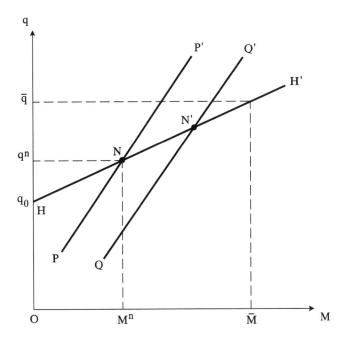

Figure 13.1

$$\Pi = \overline{R}(p - t)(\overline{M} - M) + \alpha \overline{R} p M - w^*(\overline{M} - M) - wM - Z^*. \qquad (13.8')$$

The firm chooses the optimal value of $M \geq 0$, which is regarded as the level of foreign direct investment, to maximize its joint profit. The first-order condition is

$$\Pi_M = -(1 - \alpha)\overline{R}\left\{ p + \overline{R}\left[\overline{M} - (1 - \alpha)M\right]p'\right\} + w^* + \overline{R}t - w \leq 0. \quad (13.9)$$

Condition (13.9) can now be used to determine the conditions under which firm P chooses to invest and export at the same time. First, suppose that M approaches zero. Let the corresponding reaction of firm H be $q_0 = \phi(0)$ and define $p_0 = p(\overline{R}\,\overline{M} + q_0)$ (see Figure 13.1). Π_M can be evaluated at this point:

$$\Pi_M\big|_{M \to 0} = -(1 - \alpha)\overline{R}\left[p_0 + \overline{R}\,\overline{M}\,p_0'\right] + w^* + \overline{R}t - w, \qquad (13.10)$$

where $p_0' = p'(\overline{R}\,\overline{M} + q_0)$. If $\Pi_M\big|_{M \to 0} > 0$, then the firm will find it profitable to invest at least a little in the host country. On the other hand, suppose that M approaches $\overline{M}$, that is, firm P invests its entire capacity in the host country. Define $\overline{q} = \phi(\overline{M})$ and $\overline{p} = p(\alpha \overline{R}\,\overline{M} + \overline{q})$. The value of Π_M at this point is:

$$\Pi_M\big|_{M \to \overline{M}} = -(1 - \alpha)\overline{R}\left[\overline{p} + \alpha \overline{R}\,\overline{M}\,p'\right] + w^* + \overline{R}t - w, \qquad (13.11)$$

where $\overline{p}' = p'(\alpha \overline{R}\,\overline{M} + \overline{q})$. If $\Pi_M|_{M\to\overline{M}} < 0$, then the firm will choose to lower its investment by at least a small amount. Making use of conditions (13.10) and (13.11), the condition for simultaneous export and investment can be stated as:

$$(1-\alpha)\overline{R}\left[\overline{p} + \alpha\overline{R}\,\overline{M}\overline{p}'\right] > w^* + \overline{R}t - w > (1-\alpha)\overline{R}\left[p_0 + \overline{R}\,\overline{M}p_0'\right]. \quad (13.12)$$

Let me provide some intuition behind the above result in order to show why the present firm may choose to export and invest at the same time. In condition (13.9) to (13.12), $w^* + \overline{R}t - w$ is the marginal cost of exporting per unit of factor M (producing at home) less the marginal cost of investing (producing abroad). This can be interpreted as the benefit of investing the marginal unit of factor M abroad, because w, the foreign wage rate, is the cost the firm has to pay for the investment while $w^* + \overline{R}t$, the home wage rate plus the tariff, is the cost it saves by not exporting. In (13.9), $-(1-\alpha)\overline{R}\Big\{ p + \overline{R}\big[\overline{M} - (1-\alpha)M\big]p'\Big\}$ is the drop in the revenue if the last unit of factor M is allocated abroad instead of at home, and the change in marginal revenue is due to the fact that factor M is less productive abroad than at home (recalling that $\alpha < 1$). Thus condition (13.9) states that firm P allocates factor M until the increase in the benefit of a marginal unit factor M due to a lower marginal cost abroad is equal to the drop in the revenue due to foreign investment. The same argument can be applied to conditions (13.10) and (13.11). For example, $-(1-\alpha)\overline{R}\big[p_0 + \overline{R}\,\overline{M}p_0'\big]$ is the drop in the revenue when the first unit of factor M is invested abroad, and if the drop in the revenue is smaller than $w^* + \overline{R}t - w$, then $\Pi_M|_{M\to 0} > 0$ and such investment is profitable.

I now derive more properties about the production of firm P. Assuming a positive foreign investment, totally differentiate its first-order condition given by (13.9) to yield:

$$\Pi_{MM}dM + \Pi_{Mq}dq + \Pi_{Mt}dt = 0, \qquad (13.13)$$

where

$$\Pi_{MM} = (1-\alpha)^2\overline{R}^2\Big\{2p' + \overline{R}p''\big[\overline{M} - (1-\alpha)M\big]\Big\} < 0;$$

$$\Pi_{Mq} = -(1-\alpha)\overline{R}\Big\{p' + \overline{R}p''\big[\overline{M} - (1-\alpha)M\big]\Big\} > 0;$$

$$\Pi_{Mt} = \overline{R} > 0.$$

The signs of these second-order derivatives are due to the assumption that the demand curve is not too convex to the origin. The second-order condition requires that $\Pi_{MM} < 0$.

Assuming a positive amount of foreign investment, firm P's first-order condition given by (13.9) can be inverted to give the firm's reaction function:

$$M = \Phi(q, t). \tag{13.14}$$

This function is illustrated by schedule PP$'$ in Figure 13.1. Its slope is equal to

$$\left.\frac{\mathrm{d}q}{\mathrm{d}M}\right|_{\mathrm{PP}'} = -\frac{\Pi_{MM}}{\Pi_{Mq}} > 0.$$

Now consider the production of both firms at the same time. Solving their first-order conditions given by (13.6) and (13.14), I get the Nash equilibrium in terms of the exogenous variable t: $M^n(t)$ and $q^n(t)$. Graphically, the Nash equilibrium is given by the intersecting point N between schedules HH$'$ and PP$'$.

13.4 Tariff-Jumping FDI

It is widely believed that a tariff imposed by an importing country can have positive effects on the direct investment by the producing firm, and many emirical studies have confirmed this belief.[5] Many attempts have been made to model this phenomenon. In what follows I briefly discuss some of these attempts and explain how successful they are.

Early work to examine the effects of tariffs on capital movement is made by using the type of general equilibrium framework analyzed in chapters 2 and 11. More well-known examples are Mundell (1957), Hamada (1974), and Brecher and Diaz Alejandro (1977). In such a framework, a rise in the tariff on an imported good will, in the absence of the Metzler paradox, increase the domestic price of the good. Assuming that the importable sector is capital-intensive, the Stolper-Samuelson theorem predicts that the rental rate of capital will go up. If international capital movement is allowed but no capital movement exists, then foreign capital now tends to flow in. Thus the tariff is directly responsible for the inflow of foreign capital.

The above result depends crucially on the assumed absence of the Metzler paradox and the factor intensity ranking. If the Metzler paradox is present, or if the imported sector is labor intensive, then an increase in tariff will tend to drive out some of the domestic capital, that is, instead of having foreign capital to jump over the tariff barrier to come in, domestic capital jumps over the tariff barrier to go abroad.

In the specific-factors model, a tariff could cause cross-hauling of capital movement as analyzed in chapter 4. To see this possibility, suppose that the host country imposes a tariff and that Metzler's paradox does not exist, meaning that the price of the importable in the host country increases. As explained

---

5. See Caves (1982, pp. 40–43) for a discussion of some of these studies. The results in Ray (1989) are less conclusive.

in chapters 2 and 4, the rental rate of importable-sector capital increases but that of the exportable-sector capital drops. Thus, for the host country, the importable-sector capital tends to receive capital from the rest of the world while capital in its exportable sector tends to flow out.

Smith (1987) and Motta (1992) provide another framework to explain the effect of a tariff on FDI. They do not, however, consider the opportunity costs of foreign investment. Thus in their model, a firm will either invest or export. This means that if a tariff causes direct investment, then the parent firm will cease exporting the product to the host country.[6]

The preceding model can be used to provide an alternative theory of tariff-jumping FDI. Assuming that firm P has a positive amount of investment in the host country, combine conditions (13.5) and (13.13) together to give

$$
\begin{bmatrix} \Pi_{MM} & \Pi_{Mq} \\ \pi_{qM} & \pi_{qq} \end{bmatrix} \begin{bmatrix} dM \\ dq \end{bmatrix} = - \begin{bmatrix} \Pi_{Mt} \\ 0 \end{bmatrix} dt. \tag{13.15}
$$

Define Δ as the determinant of the matrix on the left-hand side of (13.15). Using the second-order derivatives of the firms' profit functions,

$$
\Delta = (1-\alpha)^2 \overline{R}^2 \left\{ \left[(3p' + qp'') + \overline{R} \, p'p'' \left(\overline{M} - (1-\alpha)M \right) \right] \right.
$$
$$
\left. + \left[2p' + \overline{R} \, p'' \left(\overline{M} - (1-\alpha)M \right) \right] w f_{\ell\ell}/f_\ell^3 \right\}.
$$

The Routh-Hurwitz stability conditions require that $\Pi_{MM} + \pi_{qq} < 0$ and $\Delta > 0$. These conditions are satisfied if p'' is not significant.

I explained earlier that t is the per unit cost of export, which includes transport cost and the cost due to trade restriction. This means that an increase in protection by the host country can be measured by an increase in t. Therefore, to determine the effects of trade restrictions, I solve condition (13.15) to give

$$
\frac{dM}{dt} = -\frac{\pi_{qq}\Pi_{Mt}}{\Delta} > 0 \tag{13.16a}
$$

$$
\frac{dq}{dt} = \frac{\pi_{qM}\Pi_{Mt}}{\Delta} > 0. \tag{13.16b}
$$

Thus an increase in tariff will encourage both domestic production—the protectionist effect, and direct investment of firm P—tariff jumping. These effects can be illustrated in Figure 13.1. If q is held constant, then the effect of an increase in t on M is given by $-\Pi_{Mt}/\Pi_{MM} > 0$, thus shifting the reaction curve PP' of firm P to the right. Let the new reaction curve be QQ'. The new equilibrium point N' represents more direct investment of firm P and more production by firm H.

---

6. In the Smith-Motta model, a tariff can cause a disinvestment.

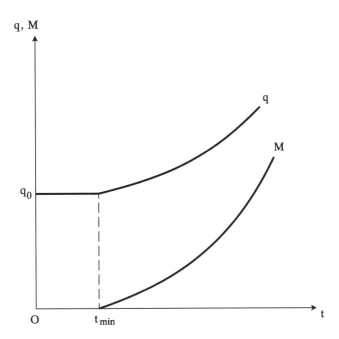

Figure 13.2

The rightward shift of schedule PP′ due to an increase in the tariff is what the literature emphasizes. The present model shows two more features of tariff-jumping FDI. First, an increase in FDI does not necessarily mean a cessation of export by firm P. Second, an increase in firm P's FDI lowers its aggregate supply to the host market, encouraging more production of firm H and thus more FDI.

The effects of t on domestic production and foreign investment can be illustrated in Figure 13.2. Although q and M have different units, I put the two schedules in the same diagram in order to compare their changes. There may be a positive tariff rate, denoted by t_{min}, below which foreign investment is zero. Specifically, t_{min} is the value of t at which $\Pi_M = 0$ when $M = 0$, and from condition (13.10), it is equal to

$$t_{min} = \frac{(1 - \alpha)\overline{R}\left[p_0 + \overline{R}\,\overline{M}\,p_0'\right] - w^* + w}{\overline{R}}.$$

The investment is positive when $t > t_{min}$. Thus when $t \geq t_{min}$, an increase in t encourages both M and q.[7]

---

7. In Figure 13.2, schedule q is a horizontal line when $t < t_{min}$, meaning that in this region the tariff has no protective effect. It is due to the fact that firm P has a Leontief-type production function and that there is no demand in the source country. If these assumptions are relaxed, there is a positive protective effect of a tariff in the absence of foreign direct investment.

13.5   To Invest or to License: The Theory of Internalization

So far I have concentrated on the export and investment options of the MNC. The theory of FDI will not be complete if I do not consider the third option: to license. In this section I explain how a parent firm chooses to exploit the host market, either to invest or to license its technology. This is what Aliber (1970) calls the second decision of a MNC.

Because the existence of a MNC shows that it prefers investment to licensing, economists have been searching for the conditions under which such a preference may occur.[8] Aliber's (1970) argument based on the foreign-exchange advantages of firms is one of the earliest attempts to explain the choice between direct investment and licensing. The more convincing theory to explain this choice of a MNC is the theory of internalization. This theory in slightly different versions appears in many papers, but Buckley and Casson (1970) are probably the first one to formally state and explain this theory. Rugman (1981) then greatly generalizes this theory, calling it the general theory of MNC. Dunning (1977, 1981) incorporates the theory into his eclectic paradigm and popularizes it. Markusen (1984) and Helpman (1984c, 1985), using the theory of internalization, establish two rigorous models of multinational corporations. Ethier (1986a) endogenizes internalization by determining what technology a firm chooses in the first stage of the game. Horstmann and Markusen (1987a) explain how a firm chooses between licensing and investment when licensing may affect the firm's reputation. An interesting study by Caves et al. (1983) investigates how the licensors and licensees share the monopoly rent of technologies the licensors own.

The theory of internalization of a firm can be traced to Coase's (1937) theory of the firm, which argues that the firm is an effective way of lowering the costs of transaction. As explained later, licensing a technology may involve huge transaction costs. This is the main reason why a market of technology seldom exists, and the firm that owns this technology can internalize the market and invests abroad, producing the product itself. Coase's theory thus implies that internalization can save the world's resources.

A common version of the theory of internalization can be summarized as follows. A firm possesses some ownership advantages (such as technological advantage) that have public-good nature but are not firm-specific so that licensing them to another firm does not affect its own use of them. Because

---

8. It is possible but not common that a firm invests and licenses out its technology at the same time.

most of these advantages are so intangible that they can hardly be measured or observed, however, it is difficult to establish a market for these advantages. It may be very costly for the owner to convince the potential buyer of the strength of these advantages and what returns these advantages can bring. Without being convinced, the potential licensee may not be willing to pay the price the owner wants. Furthermore, because the advantages are difficult to observe, it may also be very costly to write a clear, enforceable contract of licensing, and to monitor the actions of the two partners as stated in the contract. These are some of the transaction costs in Coase's theory, and are the reasons why a price mechanism is not cost efficient. Furthermore, the licensor may worry that it will lose its monopolistic ownership of the piece of technology when the licensee copies it or uses it in a way not allowed in the contract. To avoid these costs, the firm can choose to internalize the transaction by setting up a subsidiary to carry out the production. The firm then sets internal prices of these advantages to determine their costs and the profitability of the subsidiary. As long as the benefits (over the costs of licensing) of internalizing the use of these advantages and other benefits (e.g., those from a stronger market power) outweigh the disadvantages of operating in an unfamiliar environment, going multinational is a good move.[9]

Most of the papers on the theory of internalization have not formalized the choice between licensing and direct investment. It is usually assumed, implicitly or explicitly, that licensing is too costly and direct investment is the better alternative, thus bypassing the analysis on this important decision of a firm. In Markusen (1984) and Helpman (1984c, 1985), licensing is not an option for an MNC. The first models of licensing versus direct investment are provided by Ethier (1986a) and Horstmann and Markusen (1987a).[10]

I now make use of the model developed in the previous sections to explain the choice between licensing and direct investment for firm P. Given the factor prices in the countries and the per unit tariff or transport cost t, denote the profit of firm P and that of firm H when firm P forms a subsidiary in the host country by Π_0 and π_0, respectively. These are the firms' profits if firm P decides to invest in (and export to) the host country.

Suppose now that firm H is considering licensing the technology of firm P. Licensing is here defined as the acquisition of firm P's factor R by firm H. Recall that factor R has a public-good nature so that the use of it by firm H does not affect firm P's use of it.

---

9. Several good surveys of the theory of internalization are in Hood and Young (1979), Rugman (1980), Dunning (1981), Caves (1982), Buckley (1985), Cantwell (1991), and Hennart (1991).

10. Ray (1989), assuming that firms from the rest of the world choose between direct investment and licensing in the United States, suggests several reduced-form equations for FDI.

I assume that if firm P does decide to license, it will not invest in the host country at the same time. This can be one of the conditions of the licensing contract as required by firm H in order to protect itself, or it may be due to the fact that firm P does not find it profitable to invest.[11] Second, if firm H acquires firm P's technology, it will use this technology, not its own, to produce. In other words, firm H will not set up two plants. This may be due to the fact that firm H's technology is much inferior.[12]

Technology licensing depends on whether firm H knows perfectly the amount of technology firm P has, the value of $\overline{R}$. Consider two cases: (1) Firm H has perfect information about firm P's technology; and (2) Firm H has imperfect information about firm P's technology. Case (1) is considered first.[13] Suppose that firm H receives firm P's technology so that its production function becomes

$$\overline{q} = \overline{R}\{ \min[\overline{m}, \ell]\},$$

where $\overline{R}$ is the amount of factor R it acquires and $\overline{m}$ is the amount of factor M it has. For simplicity, assume that firm H cannot use its own factor R, perhaps because it is not compatible with firm P's factor R. Firm P does use the entire amount of factor M that it owns, $\overline{M}$, for production in the source country. Its output is equal to

$$\overline{Q}^* = \overline{R}\left\{ \min\left[\overline{M}, L^*\right]\right\}.$$

Define $\overline{p}$ as $\overline{p} \equiv p\left[\overline{R}(\overline{M} + \overline{m})\right]$, which is the price of the commodity when firm P licenses its technology.

To find out whether such technological transfer from firm P to firm H is profitable for both firms, and to determine the license fee, the profits of firms H and P *before any license fee*, denoted respectively by $\overline{\pi}$ and $\overline{\Pi}$, must first be determined. These before-fee profits are:

$$\overline{\pi} = \overline{p}\,\overline{R}\,\overline{m} - w\overline{m} - z$$

$$\overline{\Pi} = (\overline{p} - t)\overline{R}\,\overline{M} - w^*\overline{M} - Z^*.$$

---

11. There are observed cases in which firms license, export, and invest directly at the same time. Contractor (1985, pp. 22–23) describes the ibuprofen case in which Boots first licensed Upjohn to produce and sell ibuprofen in the United States, itself exported the product to the United States, and finally invested to produce it in Louisiana. For simplicity, the present analysis does not go so far to investigate this possibility.

12. In the study of 257 licensing agreements, Caves et al. (1983) found that these agreements usually have market restriction, production location restriction, and/or technology flowback requirement.

13. See Rodriguez (1975a), Brecher (1982), and Grossman and Helpman (1991a, Section 7.4) for other models of licensing in which technology is known.

Note that because the amounts of factor M of the two firms own are fixed, if firm H uses firm P's technology, the outputs and profits of the firms are then fixed. Denote the royalty paid by firm H by b.

No matter what the license fee is, $\bar{\pi} + \bar{\Pi}$ is the total profit of the firms with licensing. Because $\pi_0 + \Pi_0$ is their total profit when firm P chooses not to license but to invest, if $\bar{\pi} + \bar{\Pi} < \pi_0 + \Pi_0$, then there is no way to find a licensing contract satisfactory to both firms. Therefore $\bar{\pi} + \bar{\Pi} > \pi_0 + \Pi_0$ is a necessary condition for licensing. I assume that this condition is satisfied.

In the present framework, it is reasonable to consider only non-negative values of b. In other words, for convenience I exclude the possibility that the licensor (firm P) pays the licensee (firm H). I now analyze two cases in which the license fee is determined. In the first case, firm H makes a "take-it-or-leave-it" (TIOLI) offer. The minimum offer that will make firm P not worse off as compared with not licensing is equal to

$$b = \max\left[\Pi_0 - \bar{\Pi}, 0\right].\tag{13.17}$$

To understand condition (13.17), suppose that $\Pi_0 > \bar{\Pi}$, then firm H has to give a transfer of $\Pi_0 - \bar{\Pi}$ to firm P to compensate for the latter's loss. If $\Pi_0 \leq \bar{\Pi}$, then no transfer is needed. Given the value of the license fee as defined by (13.17), if $\bar{\pi} - b > \pi_0$, then firm H is better off and for both firms licensing is preferred to foreign direct investment.[14]

I now consider another way of determining the license fee: through Nash negotiation between the firms. Because direct investment by firm P is the alternative to licensing, (π_0, Π_0) is the threat point. In the Nash bargaining problem, b is chosen to maximize

$$\max_{b} (\bar{\pi} - \pi_0 - b)(\bar{\Pi} - \Pi_0 + b).$$

The first-order condition is

$$-(\bar{\Pi} - \Pi_0 + b) + (\bar{\pi} - \pi_0 - b) = 0,$$

which gives the transfer

$$b = \frac{(\bar{\pi} - \pi_0) - (\bar{\Pi} - \Pi_0)}{2}.\tag{13.18}$$

The transfer given by (13.18) ensures that both firms get the same payoff.

Note two features of this bargaining problem. First, if $\bar{\pi} + \bar{\Pi} > \pi_0 + \Pi_0$, then the two firms can find a mutually beneficial interfirm transfer so that

---

14. Of course, if I allow the possibility that b can be negative, and if $\bar{\pi} + \bar{\Pi} > \pi_0 + \Pi_0$, then at least one license fee can be found to make both firms better off.

both prefer licensing to foreign investment. This result is different from a corresponding one in Horstmann and Markusen (1987a). In their model, if both firms have perfect information, firm P must prefer foreign investment to licensing. Second, the sign of equilibrium b can be positive or negative. This means that firm P may have to pay to firm H to compensate for the latter's loss. As mentioned earlier, however, in the present problem it is more reasonable to assume that b is positive.

I now turn to case (2) in which firm H does not have perfect information about firm P's technology. Because firm P knows perfectly the technology it has, there is an asymmetry in information. The present problem is then similar to the problem of adverse selection because firm H has to make a decision based on its estimation of the value of firm P's technology. Because firm H has imperfect information about firm P's technology, the above bargaining problem between the two firms does not work. I thus consider only the case of a TIOLI offer firm H makes to firm P. For simplicity, I assume that firm H is risk neutral, but the analysis can easily be extended to the case in which it is risk averse.

To simplify the following analysis, assume that firm H believes that there are two possible values of firm P's technology, R_H and R_L, where $R_H > R_L$. Firm H, which does not know the value of $\overline{R}$, has a belief that the probability of R_H is ρ and that of R_L is $(1 - \rho)$. Denote the profits (not including the license fee) of firms H and P when $\overline{R} = R_H$ by π_H and Π_H, and their profits when $\overline{R} = R_L$ by π_L and Π_L, respectively. It is reasonable to assume that $\pi_H > \pi_L$ and $\Pi_H > \Pi_L$, meaning that both firms have higher profits if the technology of firm P is more. Define $\vartheta = \rho\pi_H + (1 - \rho)\pi_L$ as the expected profit of firm H in the presence of licensing.

As before, define

$$b_i = \max\left[\Pi_0 - \Pi_i, 0\right], \qquad i = H, L.$$

The transfer b_i, $i = H, L$, is the minimum transfer firm H has to give to firm P in order to induce the latter to license its technology. Because $\Pi_H > \Pi_L$, $b_L \geq b_H$, that is, firm H needs to pay more for the technology if the technology is lower.

Firm H's strategy depends on the relative magnitudes of firm P's profits with and without licensing. First consider the special case in which $\Pi_H > \Pi_L \geq \Pi_0$. This means that for firm P, licensing dominates direct investment in the absence of any transfer. Therefore no licensing fee is needed, $b_i = 0$. A sufficient condition for licensing is that the expected payoff of firm H, $\vartheta - \pi_0$, is positive so that firm H is willing to license.

Consider now the case in which $\Pi_0 > \Pi_L$. What kind of offer would firm H make that firm P would accept? Obviously, the answer depends on the expected payoff of firm H and the actual technology of firm P. For example, if the offer is b_H and if $\overline{R} = R_L$, then firm P will not accept the offer and chooses to invest. Firm H is fully aware of this consequence when choosing the offer.

Now examine exactly what firm H is willing to offer. First, suppose that the offer is b_L. Because the offer is enough to cover firm P's loss, no matter what its technology is, firm P will accept this offer. So the expected payoff of firm H is equal to $\vartheta_L = \vartheta - b_L - \pi_0$, where ϑ is the firm's expected profit. Suppose instead that the offer is b_H. Whether firm P will accept this offer depends on its technology. If $\overline{R} = R_H$, it accepts the offer and the payoff of firm H is $\pi_H - b_H - \pi_0$. If $\overline{R} = R_L$, the offer is not accepted and firm H's payoff is 0. Thus the expected payoff of firm H when the transfer is b_H is $\vartheta_H = \rho[\pi_H - b_H - \pi_0]$.

The analysis can be used to state the strategies of firm H: First, it gives a transfer of b_L if $\vartheta_L > \vartheta_H$ and $\vartheta_L > 0$; and second, it gives a transfer of b_H if $\vartheta_H > \vartheta_L$ and $\vartheta_H > 0$. If the condition in either (1) and (2) is satisfied, licensing is preferred to foreign investment by firm H.

Because firm H has to make a decision about licensing before the information about firm P's technology is revealed, it is possible that it makes an error in terms of whether it should license. Two types of errors can be distinguished. A Type I Error occurs when firm H rejects licensing but should have accepted it, while a Type II Error is committed if firm H accepts licensing but should have rejected it.

I want to argue that in the present framework, firm H will never commit a Type I Error, but there are conditions under which a Type II Error occurs. Consider first a Type I Error. Note that if firm H rejects licensing, it must be either $0 > \vartheta_L > \vartheta_H$ or $0 > \vartheta_H > \vartheta_L$. In either case, ϑ_L and ϑ_H are negative. Because $\vartheta_H = \rho[\pi_H - b_H - \pi_0]$, I have $\pi_H - b_H - \pi_0 < 0$, meaning that firm H receives a negative payoff if $\overline{R}$ turns out to be R_H. Next note that ϑ_L can be written as

$$\vartheta_L = \rho(\pi_H - \pi_L) + \pi_L - b_L - \pi_0.$$

Because $\pi_H > \pi_L$, if $\vartheta_L < 0$, then $\pi_L - b_L - \pi_0 < 0$, meaning that firm H receives a negative payoff if $\overline{R}$ turns out to be R_L. Therefore no matter what the value of $\overline{R}$ is, firm H will never regret that it has rejected licensing.

I now derive the condition under which firm H could commit a Type II Error. Suppose that $\vartheta_L > \vartheta_H$ and $\vartheta_L > 0$. Firm H decides to license and offer a transfer of b_L which firm P accepts no matter what $\overline{R}$ is. Note that ϑ_L can be written as

$$\vartheta_L = (1 - \rho)(\pi_L - \pi_H) + \pi_H - b_L - \pi_0.$$

Thus when $\vartheta_L > 0$ and because $\pi_L < \pi_H$, $\pi_H - b_L - \pi_0 > 0$. This means that no error in licensing has been committed if $\overline{R} = R_H$. However, Type II Error does exist if $\overline{R} = R_L$ instead and if $\pi_L - b_L - \pi_0 < 0$.

Consider now the case in which $\vartheta_H > \vartheta_L$ and $\vartheta_H > 0$. In this case, firm H offers a transfer of b_H to firm P. If $\overline{R} = R_H$, then because $\vartheta_H > 0$, firm H receives a positive payoff. If $\overline{R} = R_L$, then firm P will not accept the offer and will invest instead. Firm H's payoff is zero. In either case, a Type II Error will not exist.

13.6   Quid Pro Quo Direct Investment: The Political-Economy Context

In the 1980s, the wave of protectionism was quite strong in certain industries in some countries. One example is the automobile industry in the United States. In light of the import competition in the automobile industry that began from the end of 1970s, the U.S. government has been showing an inclination of protecting the domestic automobile industry. One outcome of such protectionist mood in the country is the voluntary export restraints (VER) on cars from Japan. The first VER was imposed in 1981 with a ceiling of 1.68 million cars per year.

I explained earlier that such trade restrictions may lead to foreign direct investment. Bhagwati (1985a, 1985b), however, suggests that foreign direct investment can exist in response to protectionist threat as well. This type of direct investment, which he christens quid pro quo direct investment, is made by an exporting firm with the purpose of defusing the protectionist threat in the future.

Wong (1989a, 1989b) provides some evidence that suggests the existence of this type of direct investment. He first notes that after the VER on the import of Japanese cars started, it has gradually been relaxed in an absolute term. The import ceiling reached 2.3 million cars per year in 1987 and was then kept fairly constant. Yet the second half of the 1980s witnessed a huge wave of investment from many Japanese automakers in the United States. This wave started with the investment of Honda in Ohio in 1978, which began production in 1982. Honda was followed by Nissan (production began in 1983), Toyota (a joint venture with General Motors with production beginning in 1984), Mazda (1987), Toyota as a separate subsidiary, solely-owned in 1988, Mitsubishi (1988), Fuji Heavy Industries (1989), and Isuzu (1989). The wave of investment from these firms does not seem to be consistent with the theory of tariff-jumping direct investment.

Wong (1989a, 1989b) also compares the profit rates of investment from different countries in different industries. He notes one special feature of the Japanese investment in "other manufacturing," which includes motor vehicles and equipment, in the United States. This industry experienced negative rates of return in each of the years from 1980 to 1986.[15] The poor performance of Japanese investment in this sector seemed to be an exception, because the investment from other countries in the same industry and Japanese investment in most other industries made profits in most of these years. Yet Japanese equity capital kept flowing in at surprisingly high rates of growth: 50.6 percent in 1984 (over the previous year), 29.6 percent in 1985, and 26.5 percent in 1986. Such growth rates, which again are not compatible with tariff-jumping foreign investment, can be explained in terms of the theory of quid pro quo direct investment.

Salvatore (1991) provides another evidence of quid pro quo direct investment. He compares the number of nontariff trade barriers in all manufacturing industries in the United States and inflow of foreign direct investment in U.S. manufacturing, and notices the positive correlation between them. He further examines the levels of nontariff barriers imposed by the United States and foreign direct investment in the following three industries: color television sets, automobiles, and steel. These are three of the most protective industries that received significant foreign direct investment in the previous years.[16]

Bhagwati et al. (1987) provide the first formal analysis of quid pro quo FDI using a two-period model. A firm in the source country exports its product to the host country in both periods, but is facing a quota to be imposed by the importing government in the second period. The quota depends negatively on the level of investment by the firm in the first period. The firm, trying to maximize the sum of the discounted profits in the two periods, chooses to invest in the first period at a level higher than what it might be in the absence of any protectionist threat. Dinopoulos (1989) examines the relationship between quid pro quo FDI and market structure, while Wong (1989b) and Dinopoulos (1992) endogenize the protectionist threat. The welfare effects of policy responses in the source and host countries are examined by Wong (1989b) and Dinopoulos and Wong (1991).[17] Salvatore (1991) has a simple model to explain the relationship between FDI, trade protection, and protectionist threat. A more recent analysis is provided by Grossman and Helpman (1994).

In what follows, I extend the model developed in the previous sections and adopt the approach in Wong (1989b) to provide a theory of optimal protectionist threat and quid pro quo FDI. The first step of the extension is to add a second period and an additional agent in the host country: the labor union.

15. The rates of return of Japanese investment in "other industries" was −7.1 percent in 1980, and fell to −12.8 percent in 1983 before it rose to −6.1 percent in 1986.

16. Ray (1989), using pooled time-series and cross-sectional data, does not find any dependence of FDI in the United States on trade protection. Because the FDI numbers and trade protection data used in his regression are for different time periods, however, interpretation of his results is difficult and it is not clear how much his results are related to the tariff-jumping and quid pro quo FDI hypotheses.

17. See Bhagwati et al. (1992) for further discussion of quid pro quo FDI.

There is an inelastic supply of industry-specific labor in the industry under consideration in the host country, $\bar{n}$. The demand for labor in this industry comes from firm H and (possibly) the subsidiary of firm P. All these workers, whether employed or unemployed, are members of the labor union.

Suppose that the wage rate in the host country is fixed throughout the two periods. Further suppose that in period 1 when the tariff rate is at t_1 the exogenous wage rate w is binding, that is, it is above the level for clearing the labor market, implying unemployment. D‹ ‛ e $u \equiv \bar{n} - L - \ell(q, w)$ as the number of unemployed workers, where L is the demand for labor of firm P's subsidiary, and $\ell(q, w)$ is firm H's demand for labor. Both of the demands for labor depend on, among other things, the level of trade protection.

In period 1, the future tariff rate is unknown. The labor union, facing the existing unemployment, lobbies for raising the tariff rate to t_2. As demonstrated in the previous sections, an increase in the tariff rate has two positive effects on domestic employment. First, firm P's export is discouraged, thus lowering its supply, driving up the price of the good, and encouraging the production of firm H. Second, firm P may increase its investment in the home country, thus increasing its demand for local labor. The tariff rate t_2 is defined to be at the level at which $\bar{n} = L + \ell(q, w)$, or $u = 0$, that is, full employment is reached.

The political process of changing the tariff rate is a long one. In period 1, as the labor union lobbies for a higher tariff rate, no one is certain of whether a new tariff rate or the existing one will be imposed in period 2. This uncertainty as perceived by the labor union and firm P can be represented by the probability of imposing t_2, θ.

The probability of imposing t_2 is affected by the intensity of the lobbying effort of the labor union. Following Findlay and Wellisz (1982), let the cost of lobbying be $C = C(\theta, u)$. This cost function depends on two factors: the probability of a higher trade protection, and the existing unemployment. The derivative $C_\theta \equiv \partial C / \partial \theta$ is called the marginal cost of lobbying, where the subscript represents a derivative. Assume that to obtain a higher probability of t_2, the labor union has to pay a higher cost of lobbying, meaning that $C_\theta > 0$. Two more assumptions can be made about the marginal cost of lobbying. First, as the labor union tries to increase the probability of t_2, it is getting more and more costly to increase the probability by one more unit. This means that $C_{\theta\theta} > 0$. Second, the marginal cost of lobbying is lower at a higher unemployment level. The justification is that if unemployment is severe, it is easier for the labor union to make its case and influence the lawmakers to impose a higher tariff rate. In other words, at a higher unemployment rate, it is less costly to increase the probability of t_2 by one more unit. This means that $C_{\theta u} < 0$.

The benefit of lobbying, B, is measured by the discounted expected total income of the workers that are unemployed in period 1 but employed in period 2 if the tariff rate is increased to t_2. For simplicity, let the labor union's discounted rate be unity. Thus I define

$$B = w\theta u = w\theta(\bar{n} - L - \ell(q, w)).$$

Now consider the following game. There are two stages in each of the two periods. In stage 1 of period 1, firm P chooses the production (and export) level and the level of direct investment in the host country, and firm H chooses production. The level of unemployment is then revealed. In stage 2, the labor union lobbies for protection and chooses the optimal protectionist threat. Assume that investment by firm P is sluggish so that once it chooses its investment, it remains constant throughout the two periods. In stage 1 of period 2, the government of the host country decides whether to increase the tariff rate to t_2 or to keep the original t_1. In stage 2, firm P, its subsidiary, and firm H choose production in a Cournot fashion. For simplicity, assume that the endowments and technologies of the two firms and the demand function remain constant in the two periods.

In order to allow a tariff rate to be effective in improving local employment after firm P has chosen its investment, the rigidity of the production function of firm P must be dropped. This of course will complicate our analysis. Because the previous sections have explained the criteria the two firms use in choosing their production, I can omit the details of the analysis and concentrate on the reactions of the firms.

Begin with the second stage of period 2. Because firm P has already chosen the level of investment (in stage 1 of period 1), M is treated as a parameter. Denote the reaction functions (in terms of output levels) of firm P and its subsidiary in the host country by $Q^*(q, M, t)$ and $Q(q, M, t)$. The reaction function of firm H is $q = q(Q^* + Q)$. Note that firm H's reaction depends directly on firm P's total output, but indirectly it also depends on the tariff rate. Following the same line, the corresponding demands for labor by the firms are: $L^*(Q^*, M, t)$, $L(Q, M, t)$ and $\ell(q)$, respectively. Note that because the wage rates in the country do not play a role here, they are dropped from the corresponding labor demand functions.

When these reactions function are solved together, the Nash equilibrium output functions of the firms is: $\widetilde{Q}^*(M, t)$, $\widetilde{Q}(M, t)$ and $\widetilde{q}(M, t)$. Note that in deriving these functions, I assume that the firms compete in terms of output and investment in a Cournot fashion. Similarly, the reduced-form demands for labor by these firms can also be derived: $L^*(\widetilde{Q}^*(M, t), M, t) \equiv \widetilde{L}^*(M, t)$, $L(\widetilde{Q}(M, t), M, t) \equiv \widetilde{L}(M, t)$, and $\ell(\widetilde{q}(M, t)) \equiv \widetilde{\ell}(M, t)$. Assume that factor M and labor are complements in the sense that $\widetilde{L}_M > 0$ and $\widetilde{\ell}_M > 0$. (Recall that the output reaction of firm H depends on firm P's investment.) The price of the good in the host country is equal to $p(\widetilde{Q}^*(M, t) + \widetilde{Q}(M, t) + \widetilde{q}(M, t)) \equiv$

$\widetilde{p}(M, t)$. Denote the profits of firms P and H by $\widetilde{\Pi}(M, t)$ and $\widetilde{\pi}(M, t)$, respectively. The profits of the firms depend on the investment of firm P in period 1 and the tariff rate. It is reasonable to assume that given any investment level, firm P's profit is hurt by a higher tariff rate, that is, $\widetilde{\Pi}(M, t_1) > \widetilde{\Pi}(M, t_2)$ if $t_2 > t_1$ for all M.

I now turn to stage 1 in period 2. Using the labor demands already described, the tariff rate, t_2, that is required to produce full employment can be determined. This tariff rate solves the following full-employment condition:

$$\bar{n} = \widetilde{L}(M, t_2) + \widetilde{\ell}(M, t_2).$$

The tariff rate can be expressed as a function of M, that is, $t_2 = t_2(M)$. Because there is so much uncertainty in the political process that before this stage is reached, however, no one is sure whether t_2 will be imposed. Assume that if t_2 is not imposed, the initial tariff rate t_1 is kept in period 2.

In stage 2 of period 1, the labor union lobbies, taking the existing unemployment (and thus the investment of firm P) as given. Because in this period the tariff rate is t_1, the number of unemployed workers is equal to

$$u(M, t_1) = \bar{n} - \widetilde{L}(M, t_1) - \widetilde{\ell}(M, t_1).$$

Assume that $u_M < 0$, that is, direct investment of firm P in the host country reduces unemployment.

The cost of lobbying is $C(\theta, u(M, t_1))$ while the benefit of lobbying is $B = w\theta u(M, t_1)$. Assume that the labor union chooses the optimal trade protection, the probability of imposing t_2, in order to maximize the net benefit of lobbying:[18]

$$\max_{\theta} N(\theta, M) \equiv w\theta u(M, t_1) - C(\theta, u(M, t_1)).$$

The first-order condition is

$$N_\theta = wu - C_\theta = 0. \tag{13.19}$$

Condition (13.19) can be inverted to give the protectionist threat as a function of the investment level of firm P:

$$\theta = \theta(M; t_1). \tag{13.20}$$

This protectionist threat function is illustrated by schedule AB in Figure 13.3. To determine the slope of this schedule, first derive the second-order derivatives of the net benefit of lobbying:

---

18. Wong (1989b) also analyzes the case in which the labor union chooses both a higher tariff rate and its probability in the second period.

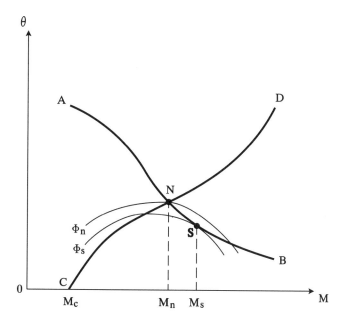

Figure 13.3

$$N_{\theta\theta} = -C_{\theta\theta} < 0 \qquad\qquad (13.21a)$$

$$N_{\theta M} = -(w - C_{\theta u}u_M)(\tilde{L}_M + \tilde{\ell}_M) < 0. \qquad\qquad (13.21b)$$

The signs of $N_{\theta\theta}$ and $N_{\theta M}$ are due to the assumptions about the signs of the terms on the right-hand side of (13.21) made earlier. Note that the second-order condition for the labor union's lobbying problem is that $N_{\theta\theta} < 0$. Therefore the slope of schedule AB in Figure 13.3 is equal to

$$\frac{d\theta}{dM}\bigg|_{AB} = -\frac{N_{\theta M}}{N_{\theta\theta}} < 0. \qquad\qquad (13.22)$$

I now turn to the first stage in period 1. In this stage, the two firms compete in a Cournot fashion. Because firm H takes firm P's outputs as given, I can focus on the latter's decision. As explained above, firm P's profit depends on its investment level and the tariff rate, $\tilde{\Pi}(M, t)$. For simplicity, assume that its discount rate is unity. Thus the problem of firm P can be stated as the maximization of the sum of the expected discounted profits in the two periods subject to the optimal protectionist threat function given by (13.20), that is,

$$\max_M \Phi(M, \theta) = \tilde{\Pi}(M, t_1) + \theta\tilde{\Pi}(M, t_2(M)) + (1 - \theta)\tilde{\Pi}(M, t_1)$$

$$\text{s.t. } \theta = \theta(M). \qquad\qquad (13.23)$$

The problem can be illustrated in Figure 13.3. First, function $\Phi(M, \theta)$ can be described by iso-profit curves in the diagram. Two possible curves are shown and labeled Φ_n and Φ_s. As I explained previously, at any given level of investment, firm P's profit decreases with the tariff rate, that is, $\widetilde{\Pi}(M, t_1) > \widetilde{\Pi}(M, t_2)$. This means that firm P's profit drops as the probability of trade restriction in period 2 increases. In terms of the diagram, $\Phi_s > \Phi_n$. Thus the solution to the problem in (13.23) is given by the point of tangency (point S in Figure 13.3) between an iso-profit curve (the one labeled Φ_s in the diagram) and the protectionist threat schedule AB. The profit Φ_s is the highest profit firm P can get subject to the given protectionist threat schedule AB. Let the corresponding direct investment of firm P be M_s.

To bring out the concept of quid pro quo FDI, compare the preceding game with another game described as follows. Suppose that there is only one stage in period 1 so that firm P's investment and production, firm H's production, and the labor union's lobbying all take place at the same time. Firm P's problem is to maximize its sum of expected discounted profits in the two periods, taking the protectionist threat, instead of the protectionist threat function in (13.20), as given. The reaction function of firm P can be described by schedule CD in Figure 13.3, which is the locus of the highest points of iso-profit curves. The intersecting point, N, between this schedule and the protectionist threat schedule AB is the equilibrium point of this game.

Schedule CD defines two more investment levels. First, its horizontal intercept gives the investment level M_c in the absence of any protectionist threat when it is known with certainty that the tariff rate remains at t_1 in period 2. The amount M_c includes the investment that exists due to the theory (such as tariff-jumping) already given. Of course, M_c can be zero. In this case, schedule CD cuts the origin or vertical axis. Second, the intersecting point N between schedules AB and CD, the Nash equilibrium point in the above one-shot game, defines the investment level M_n. This is the optimal amount of direct investment firm P has when it takes the protectionist threat as given. The amount $M_n - M_c$ is the additional investment firm P, acting in a Nash fashion, has in the presence of protectionist threat. Using the terminology in Wong (1989b), it is thus called *protection-threat-responding* direct investment.

In the first game analyzed in this section, the firms take action before the labor union lobbies. Thus firm P can choose a greater level of investment with the purpose of defusing the protectionist threat. It can be seen that the increase in investment causes a drop in the probability of a stricter protection. The amount of investment, $M_s - M_n$, is thus called quid pro quo, or *protection-threat-defusing*, direct investment.

13.7 Multinational Corporation and Market Power

In the preceding sections, a multinational corporation is treated as an organization that allocates resources to maximize the profit it receives. The opportunities to go abroad allow it to allocate resources across countries, and such opportunities are used to increase its profit further. However, many theories of MNC in the literature treat it as not just an organization but also an organism. An organism is something that feeds itself and something that grows. "There is a variety of theories about the firm, but the essence, at least in a number of theories, is growth. . . . In growing [firms] may well go abroad; in going abroad, they grow abroad" (Kindleberger, 1969, p. 6).

When firms grow domestically and abroad, they expand their monopoly power, which then allows them to capture more profit. Thus according to the market power theory of MNC, firms invest abroad because they want to secure their market power, which includes its monopolistic power on the output side and its monopsonistic power on the input side. This is what Hymer (1960) called direct investment of Type 2. "The control of the foreign enterprise is desired in order to remove competition between that foreign enterprise and enterprises in other countries" (Hymer, 1960, p. 25). Cantwell (1991, p. 21) summaries this theory as follows: "MNCs are believed to invest in foreign operations to reduce competition and increase barriers to entry in their industry, and by increasing the degree of monopoly power they may even (in the longer run) have an adverse effect on the efficiency of foreign plants." Dunning (1983) provides historical evidence of how MNCs used their product, quality, pricing, and investment strategies to enhance their monopoly power.

Growth and market power are thus two key elements of the strategies of a firm. To sustain a high rate of growth, a firm needs to capture a bigger market power, and to get more market power, a firm grows.

There are several methods that a firm can use to expand its market power and lower competition. Probably the most common and well-known methods analyzed in the literature are merger, joint venture, pricing-quantity-quality policy and preemptive investment. Merging of two firms has the direct effect of reducing the number of firms in the industry, and joint venture is to combine two or more potential firms into one.[19] Pricing-quantity-quality policy and preemptive investment can be used to deter entry of new firms. These strategies tend to increase the concentration of the industry and monopoly power of the firms.

The preemptive investment motive of a MNC was first analyzed with a formal model by Horstmann and Markusen (1987b). They begin with a firm

---

19. Merger and joint venture can be due to other factors such as technological complementarity.

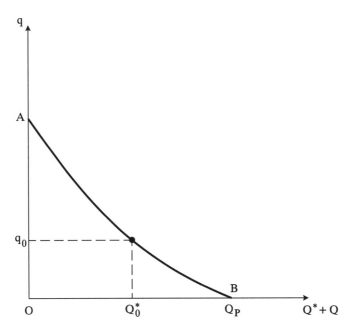

Figure 13.4

that chooses to export its product to another country. In the market in the importing country there are many potential producers but initially the market is too small to support any of them so that the exporting firm is the only supplier. As the demand in that market grows over time, a point is reached at which the market is big enough to support one domestic producer. Shortly before this point is reached, however, the exporting firm switches to investment in the importing country instead of exportation. This makes the investment by the potential domestic firm not profitable. Thus the investing firm remains to be a monopolist.

The essence of the Horstmann-Markusen hypothesis can be illustrated by our present model. In Figure 13.4, the horizontal axis represents $Q^* + Q$, which is the total production of the parent and subsidiary's plants of firm P, and the vertical axis stands for the (possible) output of a representative firm in the importing country (firm H). I assume that initially firm P exports but does not invest in the host country and that the local market is too small for any local firm. This means that $Q = q = 0$. To consider a more general model than before, let me drop the assumption that the production function of firm P is of the Leontief type. This implies that it can increase its output even though the amount of factor M is fixed.

Suppose that the demand in the host country grows. This has two direct effects. First, firm P increases its output. Second, sooner or later a point of

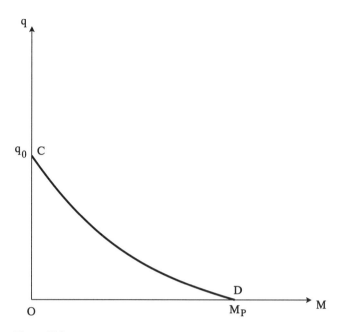

Figure 13.5

time, X, is reached so that given the export of firm P, firm H wants to have a positive output. In terms of Figure 13.4, this point is reflected by a reaction schedule AB of firm H. Under usual conditions, this schedule is downward sloping. Let firm P's prevailing export be Q_0^*. Firm H thus wants to produce an output of q_0. In such a case, there are two firms supplying the same output, one in the source country and one in the host country.

To show a preemptive direct investment of firm P, suppose that there is a positive relationship between the firm's total output, $Q^* + Q$, and its investment, M. The conditions for such a positive relationship will be discussed later. For the time being, I make use of this relationship to derive the reaction schedule of firm H in terms of M, as shown by schedule CD in Figure 13.5. Initially, firm P's investment in the host country is zero, and firm H's optimal output is q_0.

To deter the entry of firm H, firm P can invest in the host country at a level of M_P, which corresponds to a total output of Q_P (the sum of Q^* and Q). The reaction of firm H is then a zero output. Horstmann and Markusen (1987b) show that such a preemptive investment is worthwhile if the home market can support one firm but not two firms.[20]

---

20. Note that the choice for the MNC in the Horstmann and Markusen model is either export *or* invest. In the present model, the MNC may choose both.

Note that in the present model, the preceding theory depends on the positive relationship between the total output of firm P and its investment in the home country. Some sufficient conditions for this relationship are that (1) firm P's production function has some flexibility so that with a given amount of factor M it can increase its total output (by using more of other factors); (2) the market and consumer recognition disadvantages are not significant, that is, α is close to or equal to unity; and (3) there are no transport costs. Horstmann and Markusen (1987b) assume (2) and (3) explicitly ($\alpha = 1$), and (1) implicitly.

Even though the Horstmann-Markusen hypothesis is intuitive, it does raise two questions. First, if the local firm has as much information and knowledge about the market and its rival as firm P does, why cannot the local firm take the first preemptive investment and try to discourage any investment from firm P? Second, their paper does not compare investment with other strategies as a preemptive move. For example, because firm H reacts only to the market condition such as the price, firm P may increase its export, drive down the price, and thus discourage firm H from entering. This is the usual dumping argument. With dumping, firm P can save at least the plant-specific fixed cost. Can dumping be better than preemptive investment? This seems to be an open question.

Another option that may be available to firm P but is not considered in Horstmann and Markusen (1987b) is to invest in the form of a joint venture between firm P and a potential entrant. In the present model, firm P may export and have a joint venture with a local firm at the same time. Joint ventures are in fact a common form of foreign direct investment. There are of course many possible reasons for forming a joint venture. In the present case, one reason is to avoid having two firms in the host market. As mentioned previously, this is a way in which firm P maintains its market power.

13.8   Technology Transfer and Diffusion

To obtain a competitive edge, a firm would like to acquire more ownership advantages. I have distinguished four different types of ownership advantages. In this section I focus on the technological advantage. Three types of technological advantage can be distinguished: (1) the advantage that allows a firm to create, develop and process new products; (2) the technology that allows a firm to improve factor efficiency and output quality; and (3) the technology that allows a firm to manage and administer the organization. To acquire a technological information, a firm can conduct research and development, or it can imitate through learning, licensing, or purchase of advanced technologies. All of the three types of technological advantages of firms can be transferred from one firm to another, or from one country to another. Due to the public-good nature of these advantages, the use of them by their owners (the firms) does not preclude other firms from using them.

A technology cycle can be divided into several stages: invention, innovation, technology transfer or diffusion, adaption and development, and in the final stage, a public information. Invention is the creation and development of new products. Innovation "takes the invention to the point of being placed on the market" (Caves, 1982, p. 196). It also includes the design of a mass production process, that is, the development of a production function. Technology transfer or diffusion refers to the transmission of a piece of technological information from one firm to another firm. In this section, I make a distinction between international technology transfer that exists between firms in different countries and technology diffusion that exists between firms in the same country. Note that the process of setting up a subsidiary in the host country by the MNC is by itself a technological transfer, but in the present section I am more interested in how technologies are spilled over to local firms. Because technologies very often have some firm or location specificity, it is usually necessary for the firm that receives the information to adapt, modify, or further develop the technologies to suit their needs and the needs of a new market. Technology transfer, technology diffusion, adaption, and development can be repeated many times until finally a sufficient number of firms acquired this information and it is nearly costless for other firms to get it. The information is then in the public domain. In this stage, this technological information is no longer an advantage to the firm that owns it.

When a firm spends money on research and development to invent a new product or to innovate a new technology, it usually has in mind what will happen down the road. In particular, it estimates how fast other firms can successfully imitate, and how fast the information will be in the public domain. The expected rate of "depreciation" is a factor a firm will take into account when choosing the optimal amount of research and development.[21]

In this section, the discussion focuses on the relationship between technology transfer and diffusion, trade, and foreign direct investment. It has long been believed that countries that trade extensively with others have more opportunities to learn from those countries with higher technologies as compared with countries that have little foreign trade. One interesting theory proposed to explain this phenomenon is the *contagion theory* (Findlay, 1978).[22] According to this theory, technology is like a contagious disease: It will spread out farther and more quickly if there are more personal contacts. "The basis of the

---

21. This is the basis of the appropriability theory of the MNC. See Magee (1977) for a discussion.

22. As mentioned in Findlay (1978), this theory was first developed by Kenneth Arrow and Kelvin Lancaster.

analogy is the fact that technical innovations are most effectively copied when there is personal contact between those who already have the knowledge of the innovation and those who eventually adopt it" (Findlay, 1978, p. 3). Foreign trade is a channel through which people in different countries make contacts, and through which people in one country get to know about the products of the other countries. This theory further implies that direct foreign investment is an even more effective way of technology transfer. In this case, foreign firms that have technological advantages come to town, and the personal contacts between these firms and local firms are more frequent and closer than when the firms are located in foreign countries. Empirically, the contagion theory is supported by the evidence from the Hong Kong manufacturing industry (Chen, 1983) and the Mexican manufacturing industry (Blomström and Persson, 1983).

There are other reasons to explain why foreign trade and direct investment can facilitate the transfer and diffusion of technologies. First, it is the *demonstration effect*. No matter how hard a foreign firm tries to guard the secrecy of its technology, it definitely wants to demonstrate how its products work. This sends important information to other firms that such products exist and work, and that there are demands for such products at the existing prices. The products may also reveal other information about their structures and its production. Another effect is the *competition effect*. When a foreign firm produces a better product that attracts customers, other firms are threatened. To survive, they have to upgrade the quality of their products.

Foreign subsidiaries can also be a source of technological information. The reason is that foreign subsidiaries may conduct R & D for the technologies to modify the innovation done by the parent firms and to adapt the products to the local markets. The technologies developed by the foreign subsidiaries may be extremely valuable to local firms because the technologies are more specific to the local markets. Now that the subsidiaries are in the local economy, learning from them would be easier than should they be in foreign countries.

One of the earliest work on the effects of innovation and technology transfer is Vernon's (1966) product cycle model. He divides a product cycle into three stages: the new product stage, the maturing product stage, and the standardized product stage. He argues that countries such as the United States are suitable places for new products to emerge. As compared with developing countries and some other developed countries, the United States has a higher average income, higher unit labor costs, and better communication between the potential markets and the potential suppliers of the markets. In the first stage, new products are unstandardized and there is a need for swift and effective communication between producers and customers. This calls for the production to be located in the United States.

As the product becomes more mature, a certain degree of standardization usually takes place. More firms are producing similar products and the market gets more competitive. Close and swift communication with the customers is not so needed, and the cost of production becomes more and more important in competition. At this stage, the U.S. producers have to decide whether to transfer their production plants to other developed countries or even to some developing countries. If they do decide to move, they bring the technologies with them.

As the product gets standardized, the cost of production becomes a very important factor for a firm in choosing the sites of its production plant. Vernon then suggests that firms that produce this product could move to less-developed countries, of course bringing the technologies with them.

The Vernon model of product cycle has important implications about not just the patterns of trade, but also the movement of international production. Because in the maturing product and standardized product stages, cost is a big concern and being close to the customers is less needed, location becomes a very important factor in production.

By formalizing some of the ideas in Vernon (1966), Krugman (1979b) provides an interesting model to explain the effects of innovation and technology transfer between North and South. Assuming that only the North produces new products, technology transfer means the transfer of the information about producing the new products to the South. Further assuming an exogenous rate of innovation in the North and that the South always takes a constant time to learn to manufacture a new product, Krugman (1979b) shows that in the steady state there is a constant technology gap between North and South. If capital can move freely internationally, technological progress in the North will attract capital from the South.

Krugman's model has generated a new interest in innovation, technology transfer, and the product cycle theory. For example, Feenstra and Judd (1982) endogenize the level of technology transfer and examine the welfare effects of an export tariff on technology transfer, an import tariff on goods, and an export tariff on goods. Flam and Helpman (1987b) construct a model of vertical product differentiation and technology transfer, and examine the effects of income distribution on the patterns of intraindustry trade. Grossman and Helpman (1991a, 1991b, 1991c), and Segerstrom, Anant, and Dinopoulos (1990) endogenize the rate of innovation in the North and the rate of technology transfer (imitation) in the South. Assuming that development of new products is done by a monopolized firm in the North, and that imitation is done by a planner in the South, Jensen and Thursby (1986) study the strategic interactions between the North and the South. Lai (1994) extends the Grossman-Helpman model by introducing human capital and skilled labor as a second factor, and studies the effects on world income distribution.

Two major features common to the above papers can be discussed. First, the production side of these models is similar to the Dixit-Stiglitz model of monopolistic competition and product differentiation that I described in Chapter 6. Innovation by the firms in the North usually involves the development of new products. The South, which lacks the technological know-how to produce these new products, tries its best to learn and imitate. It is commonly assumed in these papers that the South has lower costs of production so that once it gets the new-product technology, it can compete with the firms in the North. An interesting related point is that the assumption of economies of scale in production (a crucial one in the Dixit-Stiglitz model) is absent in some of these papers. To guarantee that a new product is being produced only by its innovator, at least in the short run, it is assumed that the South does not have the technology, or that other firms in the North are prohibited from producing similar products, perhaps due to patent protection.

Another common feature of the above papers is that foreign direct investment (FDI) is absent in their models. This is in sharp contrast to Vernon's theory, which puts FDI as the central element of the shift in production and technology from developed to developing countries. In Vernon's product cycle theory, usually multinational corporations are responsible for international transfer of new-product technologies. Krugman and others, while recognizing the importance of international technology transfer, do not explicitly specify the channels of technology transfer. This assumption is relaxed in an extended model by Dollar (1986).

Perhaps the first model to analyze the effects of foreign direct investment on technology transfer was Findlay (1978). He nicely combines the contagion theory and the catching-up theory originally developed by Thorstein Veblen and Alexander Gerschenkron. Veblen and Gerschenkron postulated that the rate of international technology transfer is higher if the technology gap between the advanced country and the backward country is greater as long as the technology of the latter is above a certain level. A minimum technological level in the backward country is needed for it to be able to absorb advanced technology transfer from the advanced country. Findlay (1978) then develops a simple theory of direct investment and technology transfer.

To briefly explain Findlay's model and results, let $A(t)$ and $B(t)$ be the technological levels in the advanced and backward countries at time t, respectively, and let $K_f(t)$ and $K_d(t)$ be the amounts of foreign-owned and domestic-owned capital stocks in the backward country. Define

$$x \equiv \frac{B(t)}{A(t)}$$

$$y \equiv \frac{K_f(t)}{K_d(t)}.$$

Findlay then postulates that

$$\frac{\dot{B}}{B} = f(x, y)$$

where the dot denotes a derivative with respect to t and

$$\frac{\partial f}{\partial x} < 0, \quad \text{and} \quad \frac{\partial f}{\partial y} > 0.$$

The sign of $\partial f/\partial x$ is due to the Veblen-Gerschenkron theory, and that of $\partial f/\partial y$ comes from the contagion theory. The rate of growth of technology in the advanced country is assumed to be exogenously given.

Findlay does allow the capital stocks in the backward country to be endogenous. He assumes that the rate of growth of the domestic-owned capital stock is a decreasing function of $B(t)/A(t)$ and an increasing function of $K_f(t)/K_d(t)$. Assuming that the accumulation of foreign-owned capital stock comes from the foreign firms' net retained profits, he shows that the rate of growth of this capital stock is a decreasing function of $B(t)/A(t)$ but is independent of $K_f(t)/K_d(t)$. Combining these results,

$$\dot{x} = \phi(x, y) \tag{13.24a}$$

$$\dot{y} = \psi(x, y). \tag{13.24b}$$

The system is in a steady state when $\dot{x} = 0$ and $\dot{y} = 0$.

The system can be illustrated and solved by Figure 13.6, which is adopted from Findlay (1978). The schedules, TT and KK, show the loci of x and y, which give $\dot{x} = 0$ and $\dot{y} = 0$, respectively. Findlay shows that schedule TT is upward sloping while schedule KK is downward sloping. The slopes of the schedules satisfy the stability conditions. The intersecting point, S, between the schedules gives the steady-state values of x and y, that is, (x^*, y^*). The arrows show the directions of adjustment of x and y in the four regions, I, II, III and IV. If point A in region I is the initial point, then a possible adjustment path to the steady state point is shown in the diagram. As shown, the (x, y) point may enter regions II and III before it reaches the steady state point.

The Findlay model has some interesting implications. At the steady state, the technological levels in both countries are growing at the same rate, meaning that there is a constant gap between the countries' technologies. Similarly, in the steady state, there is a constant ratio between the foreign-owned and domestic-owned capital stocks in the backward country. Second, suppose that the advanced country has a jump in technology. This pushes the (x, y) point in Figure 13.6 from the steady-state point S down to a point like A. As explained, the point can swirl a little before again reaching the steady-state. This means

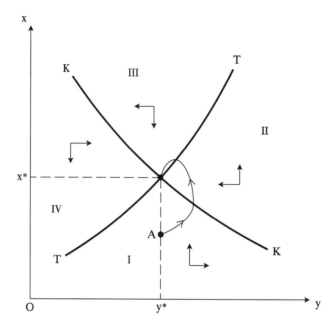

Figure 13.6

that the backward country may experience a temporary increase in foreign investment relative to the domestic capital. This result can be compared with the one in Krugman (1979b). In the Krugman model with a fixed amount of world capital, a jump in technology in the North can attract capital from the South. This means that if the South is originally a host to capital from the North, it will see a drop in the investment from the North when there is a jump in technology in the North, a result opposite to the corresponding one in Findlay.

Findlay's contagion theory was extended by Das (1987). Das (1987) makes the simple assumption that the rate of technology spillover in the host country depends on the output level of the subsidiary of an MNC. Further assuming that the subsidiary of a MNC in the host country is a dominant firm with the local firms acting competitively, he derives explicitly the optimal time paths of output and profit of the MNC subsidiary. He also shows that because of technology spillovers, the MNC subsidiary produces less than what it would do in the absence of technology spillover.

14 International Labor Migration

In the previous chapter, I examined some of the features of multinational firms and showed that foreign direct investment is something more than international movement of capital services. In the present chapter, I turn to international labor mobility, and similarly argue that international labor migration is something more than international movement of labor services.

14.1 Features of International Labor Migration

The first question to answer in this chapter is why a separate chapter on international labor migration is needed. The main reason is that chapters 2 to 12, which examine international movement of factor services, are not sufficient to analyze some of the issues related to international labor migration, which involves not just international movement of labor services. To render labor services and earn income in a different country, the owners of labor services have to move to the host country. It is the movement of these people, not just the movement of their services, that makes international labor migration so different from international capital movement or foreign direct investment.

The simultaneous movement of labor services and their owners means that the following three different types of international labor migration can be distinguished: permanent migration, temporary migration, and brain drain. Because migration is usually restricted by host countries (in some cases by source countries as well), the fourth type of migration—illegal—can also be distinguished.

14.1.1 Permanent Migration

The migration of an individual to another country is regarded as permanent if the migrant has no intention of moving back to the source country during his or her life time. In this case, the source country loses not only labor services originally provided by the migrants, but also these people and their offsprings.

When migration is voluntary, the migrants must expect an improvement in their welfare in the host country. What is less obvious is the change in the welfare of the host and source countries. To analyze how the host and source countries are affected by international labor migration I first have to determine whether the welfare of the migrants should be included in the welfare of the host or source country.

Let me first look at the host country. After an immigrant has landed, the welfare of the immigrant is naturally considered part of national welfare. Because consideration of the effects of immigration is usually needed when immigration policy is determined and immigrants have not yet been approved, however, it is more reasonable to focus on the welfare of the original residents in the host country.

From the viewpoint of the host country, when the welfare of immigrants is not included in its national welfare, permanent immigration is similar to inflow of labor services with workers repatriating their income out of the country. Thus the welfare economics analysis in chapters 8 and 11 can be applied to show that a country that is initially under autarky gains from trade and factor mobility. The analysis can be applied to show that in the absence of trade, or for a small open economy, international labor immigration, whether permanent or temporary, benefits the host country.

The welfare effects of international migration on the source country are very much different. Let me disaggregate the original residents of the country into two groups: the emigrants and the nonemigrants (or those left behind). Consider first the approach in which the emigrants are still regarded by the source government as its nationals so that their welfare still counts. When migration is voluntary, the emigrants must be better off. Because emigration is permanent, the emigrants' consumption is done in the host country, and probably all their income is spent in the host country (excluding any possible remittance). If free trade in all consumption goods with no transport costs exists, however, it does not matter where the consumption is made, and this case is then similar to the case of international labor services with full remittance of labor income. There is one exception, though. If the government wants to impose lump-sum transfers on the emigrants for the purpose of making all individuals (including emigrants or nonemigrants) not worse off, then problems arise because emigrants are residing in other countries. Such policies are discussed in Section 14.4.

Now consider the alternative approach under which the government of the source country cares about only the welfare of those left behind. How might emigration affect the welfare of those left behind? This is the main issue analyzed in the next two sections. The main conclusion is that under certain conditions those left behind are hurt by the loss of labor.

If emigration does hurt those left behind, then the government has two policy options to protect their welfare. First, it can restrict or even prohibit any emigration. This policy may not be feasible in some countries because emigration is regarded as one of the rights of people. The second option is to impose taxes on emigration. Such proposals and the difficulties of imposing them will be discussed in Section 14.4.

14.1.2   Temporary Migration

This is the case when workers move temporarily to another country and work there with a belief that there is a positive probability that they will go back to the source country in the future. Two types of temporary migration can be distinguished: voluntary and involuntary. Temporary migration is voluntary if after staying in the host country for a period of time the migrant chooses to return to the source country. Such return can be a planned one in the sense that at the time of moving to the host country, the migrant knows that he or she is going to stay in the host country temporarily and will return later. For example, with no uncertainty and perfect foresight, it is feasible for a migrant to make such a plan. Alternatively, the return of the migrant can be state-contingent, that is, the migrant will choose to return if some states occur but will choose to stay if some other states occur.

Involuntary temporary migration exists when the migrant is allowed by the host government to stay for a limited amount of time and after that the migrant is forced to return to the source country. The migrant usually is fully aware of the departure constraint when making the decision of whether to migrate. Thus involuntariness refers to the departure, not the arrival (of course, subject to an application for a visa and work permit and things like that). A well-known case is the so-called guest worker (*Gartarbeiter*) system in Germany and other countries. A detailed discussion of this system is provided in Section 14.5.

One important issue in the presence of temporary migration is that inflow of foreign workers can be a commercial policy instrument of the government of the host country. I consider two cases. In the first case, the host government allows immigration of foreign workers to help a domestic industry during a good economic situation, that is, when there is a strong demand for the industry's output. In the second case, immigration of foreign workers is used to help a domestic industry at a time when import competition is high.

14.1.3   Brain Drain

Brain drain is the outflow of skilled workers. Usually, it is the case in which residents in a source country spend their earlier years on receiving education and training in their country and then migrate to another country as skilled workers. Therefore brain drain is the simultaneous outflow of workers and human capital.

Education is a long process and can be divided into several stages: elementary, secondary, college, and university. Attention has also been paid to the cases in which some residents receive basic education in the source country but higher education in a host country. After getting higher education, the graduates may stay and work in the host country.

Brain drain, like emigration of unskilled workers, generally has adverse welfare effects on those left behind, and thus this problem can be analyzed by using the techniques used for analyzing emigration. The problem of brain drain becomes more interesting in the cases in which human capital formation is considered explicitly and determined endogenously. In sections 14.8 and 14.9, I examine two channels through which unskilled workers can acquire skill.

14.1.4   Illegal Immigration

In the real world, nearly all countries have restrictions on the inflow of foreign migrants, and some also have restrictions on the outflow of domestic residents. As long as the (economic, political, and social) incentives to move are significant, some will attempt to move illegally.

Illegal migration is usually considered a problem of the host country, partly because most countries have quantitative restrictions on the inflow of migrants, and partly because the illegal migrants have economic, political, and social consequences in the host country. A discussion of some of the issues about illegal migration is presented in the last section.

14.2   Emigration and the Welfare of Those Left Behind

In this section I analyze permanent migration from the viewpoint of a source country, focusing on the effects of emigration on the welfare of those left behind. I begin with a simple two-factor, one-sector model of the source country. Such a model excludes international trade in goods, but a more complicated model with international movement of goods will be examined later.

Call the two homogeneous factors labor and capital. In Figure 14.1, the schedule labeled MP_L represents the marginal product of labor in the source country when the capital stock is fixed. I assume that the (potential) emigrants do not demand for their own services so that the location of the MP_L schedule is not affected by emigration. It is further assumed that the schedule is negatively sloped, meaning that the marginal product of labor is decreasing. Let the initial labor endowment be L^0. With full employment and competitive markets, the market-clearing wage rate is w^0. As shown in the diagram, the corresponding wage bill is equal to the sum of the areas labeled d and e. Because the area under the marginal product curve is the total product, the total income of the capitalists is equal to the sum of the areas a, b, and c.

Suppose now that some labor flows out, with the amount of labor left behind equal to L^t. This means that the emigrated labor is equal to $L^e = L^0 - L^t$. With perfect flexibility, the wage rate rises to w^1, as shown in the diagram. The rise in the wage rate means that emigration improves the welfare of the remaining workers but hurts that of the capitalists. If I avoid the issue of income distribution, or if the government has costless schemes of redistributing income, then I can focus on the effect of emigration on the total income of those left behind, that is, the capitalists and the remaining workers.

The total income of those left behind before the emigration is equal to $a + b + c + d$, and their final income is $a + b + d$. A comparison of these two incomes shows that those left behind as a whole lose, with the loss being

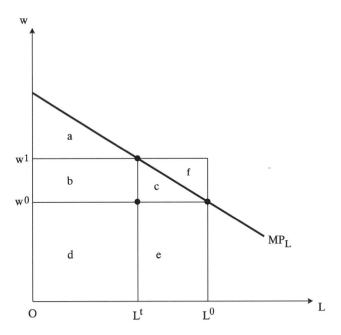

Figure 14.1

equal to the triangle c. This is the famous Harberger triangle. The diagram shows that emigration causes a drop in domestic output in the source country equal to $c + e$. The area e is what the emigrants initially earn. Thus the net loss to those left behind is area c (Berry and Soligo, 1969).[1]

The result that emigration may hurt those left behind seems to be contradictory to the result obtained in chapters 8 and 11 that international factor movement benefits both the source and host countries. There is no contradiction, and the difference between these two results can be explained in two ways. First, let me hypothetically reverse the emigration process, and imagine that the source country is initially endowed with a labor force equal to L^t and a corresponding wage rate of w^1. Now "foreign" labor equal to $L^0 - L^t$ flows in. The total labor force in the economy becomes L^0 and the wage rate drops to w^0. The income of the foreign workers, given by the area e, is repatriated. The analysis in Chapter 11 shows that the gain for the economy is equal to the area c. A welfare gain for the population L^t in this reversed process means a welfare loss to those left behind in the emigration process.

Another way of reconciling the difference between the detrimental effect of emigration on those left behind and the beneficial effects of international

---

1. See Wong (1986a), Quibria (1988), and Tu (1991) for extensions. Bhagwati and Rodriguez (1975) and Razin and Sadka (1992) provide two good surveys.

factor movement is to include the welfare of the emigrants in the welfare of the source country. In this case, information on the income of the emigrants is needed. Assuming that they migrate in response to the wage differential between the countries, the wage rate earned by them in the host country must be at least w^1, or they will not move. Let their wage rate be w^1.[2] The income of emigrants is equal to $f + c + e$. This means that national welfare of the source country is equal to $a + b + c + d + e + f$, and that the source country (including the emigrants) as a whole gains.

The analysis can be used to point out one more effect of emigration. If the average product of labor, AP_L, is greater than the marginal product of labor, MP_L, then emigration also raises AP_L. Because of this result, it is tempting (but incorrect) to conclude that those left behind benefit from emigration. Average product of labor is not a measure of the welfare of those left behind, and it is not the same thing as per capita income. The latter is the ratio of income to all residents in the economy, including workers and capitalists (see Bhagwati and Rodriguez, 1975 for more discussion).

Now consider a more general, higher dimensional model in which international trade in goods exists. Recall the m-factor, n-sector framework as explained in Chapter 2. Its GDP function is given by $g(\mathbf{p}, \mathbf{v})$, where $\mathbf{p}$ is the vector of commodity prices and $\mathbf{v}$ is the vector of factor endowments. Denote the initial factor endowments before migration by $\mathbf{v}^0$. Disaggregate the factor endowments into two components: $\mathbf{v}^e$, which includes the factors the emigrants bring with them, and $\mathbf{v}^t = \mathbf{v}^0 - \mathbf{v}^e$, which represents the remaining factors. The present analysis allows simultaneous emigration of two factors or more; that is, brain drain, which is emigration of two factors, labor and human capital. For the time being, assume that the economy is a small open one and that all goods are tradable. The commodity prices, which are not affected by international factor movement, are denoted by $\mathbf{p}^w$.

Before the emigration, the factor prices, $\mathbf{w}^0$, minimize the total factor payment and are given by $g(\mathbf{p}^w, \mathbf{v}^0) = \mathbf{w}^0 \cdot \mathbf{v}_b^0$ (see Chapter 2). After emigration, let the factor prices be given by $\mathbf{w}^1$, where $g(\mathbf{p}^w, \mathbf{v}^t) = \mathbf{w}^1 \cdot \mathbf{v}^t$. This is the total income of those left behind.

I now want to determine whether those left behind have been hurt. Because the commodity prices remain constant, the unit cost constraints must be satisfied both before and after the emigration, that is, $c_i(\mathbf{w}^0) \geq p_i^w$ and $c_i(\mathbf{w}^1) \geq p_i^w$ where $c_i(\mathbf{w})$ is the unit cost function for sector i, $i = 1, \ldots, n$. By the definition of the GDP function, I have

$$\mathbf{w}^1 \cdot \mathbf{v}^t \leq \mathbf{w}^0 \cdot \mathbf{v}^t. \tag{14.1}$$

---

2. Note that because labor movement is assumed to be sluggish and given exogenously, the foreign wage rate may be more than w^1. In this case, the following result is even stronger.

For the time being, consider only the case in which $\mathbf{w}^1 \neq \mathbf{w}^0$. Other cases in which the factor prices remain constant will be examined later. Assuming that the production possibility set is strictly convex, the weak inequality in (14.1) can be replaced by a strict inequality:

$$\mathbf{w}^1 \cdot \mathbf{v}^t < \mathbf{w}^0 \cdot \mathbf{v}^t. \tag{14.1'}$$

Denote the indirect trade utility (ITU) function of those left behind by $V^t(\mathbf{p}, \mathbf{v}, b)$, where b is the transfer received by those left behind. Before the emigration, factor endowments are $\mathbf{v}^t + \mathbf{v}^e$ and the payments to those who emigrate later are $\mathbf{w}^0 \cdot \mathbf{v}^e$, which equals $-b$. Thus the pre-emigration welfare of those left behind is $V^t(\mathbf{p}^w, \mathbf{v}^t + \mathbf{v}^e, b)$. After emigration, the remaining factor endowments are $\mathbf{v}^t$ while transfer is zero. This means that the postemigration welfare of those left behind is $V^t(\mathbf{p}^w, \mathbf{v}^t, 0)$. These two welfare levels are now compared.

The right-hand side of (14.1') represents the income of those left behind before emigration while its left-hand side represents that after emigration. Because commodity prices remain unchanged and welfare is strictly increasing in income (with no satiation), (14.1') implies that

$$V^t(\mathbf{p}^w, \mathbf{v}^t, 0) < V^t(\mathbf{p}^w, \mathbf{v}^t + \mathbf{v}^e, b), \tag{14.2}$$

that is, those left behind are hurt by the emigration.

The result is proved under the assumption that all goods are tradable. I now want to see whether it still holds if nontradable goods are present. Let me partition $\mathbf{p}$ so that $\mathbf{p}_t$ represents the prices of tradable goods which are fixed at $\mathbf{p}_t^w$, and that $\mathbf{p}_n$ represents the prices of the non-tradable goods. Let the pre-emigration prices of the nontradable goods be $\mathbf{p}_n^0$. If, hypothetically, the prices of nontradable goods are frozen, condition (14.2) implies that

$$V^t(\mathbf{p}_t^w, \mathbf{p}_n^0, \mathbf{v}^t, 0) < V^t(\mathbf{p}_t^w, \mathbf{p}_n^0, \mathbf{v}^t + \mathbf{v}^e, b). \tag{14.2'}$$

Of course the prices of the nontradable goods are determined endogenously. Denote their postemigration prices by $\mathbf{p}_n^1$, which in general are different from $\mathbf{p}_n^0$. To determine $\mathbf{p}_n^1$, I make use of a theorem in Chapter 2 which states that the autarkic commodity prices minimize the ITU function. Because the tradable goods are fixed, this theorem implies that

$$V^t(\mathbf{p}_t^w, \mathbf{p}_n^1, \mathbf{v}^t, 0) \leq V^t(\mathbf{p}_t^w, \mathbf{p}_n^0, \mathbf{v}^t, 0). \tag{14.3}$$

The weak inequality in (14.3) can be replaced by a strict inequality if satiation is ruled out and if $\mathbf{p}_n^0 \neq \mathbf{p}_n^1$, that is,

$$V^t(\mathbf{p}_t^w, \mathbf{p}_n^1, \mathbf{v}^t, 0) < V^t(\mathbf{p}_t^w, \mathbf{p}_n^0, \mathbf{v}^t, 0). \tag{14.3'}$$

Note that $V^t(\mathbf{p}_t^w, \mathbf{p}_n^1, \mathbf{v}^t, 0)$ is the welfare of those left behind after the emigration. Combining conditions (14.2′) and (14.3′), I have

$$V^t(\mathbf{p}_t^w, \mathbf{p}_n^1, \mathbf{v}^t, 0) < V^t(\mathbf{p}_t^w, \mathbf{p}_n^0, \mathbf{v}^t, 0) < V^t(\mathbf{p}_t^w, \mathbf{p}_n^0, \mathbf{v}^t + \mathbf{v}^e, b). \qquad (14.4)$$

Condition (14.4) states that those left behind are hurt by emigration even if nontradable goods are present (Rivera-Batiz, 1982).[3]

Note that the detrimental effect of emigration on the welfare of those left behind is often cited in the brain drain literature (for example, Johnson, 1967b; Hamada, 1977). As seen from the preceding analysis, this result is quite general and covers the emigration of any factors, meaning that even emigration of unskilled labor can hurt those left behind.

The analysis about the welfare effects of permanent emigration has an important implication. Because permanent emigrants have adverse effects on the aggregate income of those left behind in the source country, there is no way to redistribute the income among the remaining people to make all of them at least as well off as before. Similarly, there is no way to use commodity taxation to avoid hurting at least some of those left behind.[4]

14.3 Emigration with Constant Factor Prices

I have shown that emigration usually hurts those left behind as long as domestic factor prices or the prices of the nontraded goods change. I now examine the welfare effects of emigration in the following cases in which factor prices may not be disturbed by the outflow of factors.

If factor prices are not affected by emigration, the weak inequality in (14.1) should be replaced by an equality. This implies that condition (14.2) should have an equality sign. Thus when all goods are tradable, emigration does not affect the welfare of those left behind. The same result holds if nontradable goods are present but their prices and factor prices are not affected by emigration.

14.3.1 Infinitesimal Movement

Suppose that in the source country the number of emigrants is lowered with a corresponding increase in L^t. In terms of Figure 14.1, the decrease in the number of emigrants means that the postemigration wage drops and gets closer to the initial one, and the loss of those left behind (the Harberger triangle c)

---

3. This result was first proved by Rivera-Batiz (1982) using a framework with one tradable and one nontradable sector. His result was extended by Djajić (1986) and Kuhn and Wooton (1991).

4. See Brecher and Choudhri (1990) for a formal proof.

is smaller. In the limit when the number of emigrants approaches zero, the Harberger triangle approaches zero, meaning that a marginal emigration has no effect on factor prices and on the welfare of those left behind (Grubel and Scott, 1966; Wong, 1986a). In fact, a marginal movement of factors has no welfare effect on other people in both countries, whether or not the owners of these factors move permanently. The reason is that at the margin the emigrants take away what they have contributed.

14.3.2   Equal Number of Tradable Goods and Factors

I showed in Chapter 2 that if the number of goods traded and produced locally is equal to the number of factors plus nontraded goods, then factor prices depend on the prices of traded goods but not on the amounts of factors in the economy. This means that emigration (or immigration) would not affect factor prices and prices of the nontradable goods in the economy, and the welfare of those left behind will not be disturbed. A famous example is the 2×2 framework. Consider a small open economy facing given world prices of its two tradable goods. Emigration would not affect domestic factor prices and the welfare of those left behind of this economy (Kenen, 1971).

This result points out the danger of using the theorem of composite good to justify the assumption of a one-good framework. Suppose that the usual 2×2 economy with two tradable goods is used. If the prices of the two goods are fixed in the world markets, it is possible to aggregate the two goods into one composite good. This case does not reduce to the one-good framework described in the previous section. In the previous one, the marginal product of labor is decreasing (the neoclasscial assumption) whereas in the present case, factor prices are independent of factor endowments.

14.3.3   Emigration of Constant Fractions of All Factors

Consider again the small open economy with all tradable goods. Suppose that the outflowing factor services are a fixed proportion of the original factor endowments, that is, $\mathbf{v}^e = \beta \mathbf{v}^0$ where β is a positive constant less than unity. Then the factor prices do not change. In this case, the total income and thus welfare of those left behind are not affected by emigration.

One special case is that all residents in the source countries are identical with the same preferences and factor endowments. If the size of the economy does not matter, as in the case with constant returns and perfect competition, emigration does not affect the remaining part of the economy. Thus emigration has no effect on those left behind.

An interesting example is provided by Galor (1986). Using an overlapping generations model with identical individuals in each country, he shows that an exogenous emigration does not affect the steady state factor prices in the source country and thus does not affect the welfare of those left behind.[5]

14.3.4   Unemployment

So far it has been assumed that the economies have perfect price flexibility and full employment of factors. Suppose that in the source country, there is a binding minimum wage rate set by a labor union or by wage legislation. To analyze the consequences of a minimum wage rate, consider again the economy illustrated by Figure 14.1. The initial supply of labor force is L^0. The wage rate is exogenously set at a level w^1, which is above the level that clears the market. As a result, labor unemployment equal to $L^0 - L^t$ exists.

At this point, assume that employment of labor is decided in a Harris-Todaro process (Harris and Todaro, 1970).[6] Every day, a random drawing is made to decide who will be employed. Thus the probability of being employed for each worker is L^t/L^0, and the expected wage rate is $w^1 L^t/L^0$.

Suppose now that an amount L^e of workers move permanently out of the country, where $L^0 - L^t > L^e > 0$. The wage rate may or may not be affected by emigration. I consider two cases, as Bhagwati and Hamada (1974) do. In the first case, the minimum wage rate remains unchanged. As a result, the departure of the emigrants improves the unemployment situation but unemployment is not completely removed. Because the wage rate is not changed, the national income remains fixed, but emigration does have income distribution effects. First, the number of unemployed workers is smaller than before. Second, in the beginning of each day, the expected wage rate for each worker is higher although the total wage bill is unchanged. In this sense, the welfare of those left behind is improved.

I now turn to the second case. Because the wage rate in the host country is higher than the prevailing wage rate in the source country, the permission of emigration may lead to international emulation: The domestic labor union may request a higher minimum wage rate. If the wage rate does go up, emigration has both the *direct effect* of outflow of domestic workers and the *indirect effect* due to an increase in the minimum wage rate.

An increase in the wage rate above w^1 is detrimental to national income. This point can also be shown by using Figure 14.1, where the output of the economy is given by the area below the marginal product schedule. Thus the total effect of emigration on the total welfare of those left behind may be negative even if unemployment is present.

---

5. If emigration is not restricted in Galor's model, all residents in the source country will flow out and the result holds in an empty way.

6. The Harris-Todaro process has also been used to analyze brain drain in the presence of unemployment by Bhagwati and Hamada (1974), McCulloch and Yellen (1975), Rodriguez (1975b), and Hamada and Bhagwati (1976).

There are, however, cases in which emigration is favored by a government in the presence of unemployment if the social net benefits created by the unemployed is negative. For example, unemployed workers receive unemployment benefits from the government and are a drain in the government budget. Another case is that unemployment is widespread and has caused social unrest and social problems.

14.4   Government Policies in the Presence of Permanent Emigration

The previous section shows that the outflow of permanent workers, whether they are skilled or unskilled, hurts those left behind. This leads to the suggestion that the emigrants, who gain from their flight to another country with higher wage rates, have to compensate those left behind for the latter's loss. Two major types of taxes for the source country have been suggested.

The first is the Soviet-type exit tax imposed on emigrants before they leave the country. In this case, this tax is a financial obligation the emigrants have to fulfill before they are allowed to move out. A similar tax is imposed by China lately on those who want to go abroad for study. The Chinese tax is imposed in the form of a guarantee fee, the purpose of which is for the student to guarantee that he or she will return back after the graduation, or the fee will be forfeited.

In the absence of a perfect capital market, the Soviet and Chinese taxes have deterrent effects, because people have to meet certain conditions before they can migrate. In addition to deterring migration, such taxes are used to recover at least part of what the country has invested in the emigrants in the form of education. This argument, which is more applicable in the case of brain drain (the outflow of skilled workers), has some merit in countries like the Soviet Union or China where education is heavily subsidized by the government.

Bhagwati (1972b), on the other hand, suggests that a tax be imposed on the income of the permanent emigrants. The difference between this tax and the Soviet-type exit tax is that it is levied after the departure, not at the time of departure, of the emigrants and on the income actually earned by the emigrants. The purpose of this tax is to compensate those left behind for their losses. In terms of Figure 14.1, for the emigration of $L^0 - L^t$, the minimum tax required for compensation is given by area c. In the special case of a linear marginal product schedule, this area is a triangle, being equal to half of the increase in income of the emigrants when the latter earn w^1 in the host country.[7]

This tax does raise some legal problems. Because it is levied on the earned income of the emigrants, it is paid when the emigrants are working in other

---

7. See Bhagwati (1976b) and Hamada (1977) for more details about this tax.

countries. How can the government of a source country levy a tax on a resident in another country? The suggestion is that the host country collects the tax revenue and hands it over directly to the source country, or to an international agency such as the United Nations to be distributed to different source countries. This means that a host country has to use two tax scales, one on its own initial citizens and one on its new citizens who migrated from other countries. This policy may not be feasible constitutionally in some countries (such as the United States) or not be feasible politically (see Bhagwati, 1976b; and Bhagwati and Partington, 1976 for more discussion).

In the literature, it is usually assumed (explicitly or implicitly) that when an emigration tax is levied, the amount of emigration is not significant and is given exogenously. This assumption is reasonable if migration is under a quota system and is regulated by host countries. If emigration is to be determined endogenously, then to assess the appropriate emigration tax, one has to take into account the fact that emigration may be affected by the tax. In this case, what tax to be imposed on the emigrants is not so clear.

I now try to provide an answer to the question of levying taxes on endogenous emigrants. The analysis consists of two parts. The first examines how the emigration tax may affect emigration. Figure 14.2 shows the given world labor endowment and the distribution of labor between the source and host countries, with O^S and O^H representing the origins of the source and host countries, respectively. With the labor endowment in the world fixed, the source country initially has L^0 and the host country has L^{0*}. The schedules labeled MP_L and MP_L^* represent the marginal products of labor in the source and host countries, respectively. For illustration, the schedules are assumed to be straight lines and are independent of migration. The initial wage rates in the two countries, w^0 and w^{0*}, are given by HA and HG, respectively, in the diagram.

In the absence of any taxes, the final equilibrium point is E, with a wage rate equal to w^1 and an amount of labor equal to L^1 remaining in the source country. Suppose now that the Bhagwati tax is imposed. First, for the time being assume that *emigration is independent of the tax*. This tax can be represented by a specific income tax on the emigrants given by ED, where D is the midpoint of the gap, EB, between the initial and final wage rates in the source country. As explained previously, those left behind are fully compensated, although emigration does have an income distributional effect.

With the (specific) Bhagwati tax, however, the after-tax wage rate for the emigrant is given by L^1D, which is less than the prevailing wage rate in the source country. If the emigrants are aware of the presence of the tax, the assumption that emigration is independent of the tax is no longer valid. To determine the equilibrium when the tax policy is known to the emigrants, let me assume a fixed specific tax rate and construct line DC, which is parallel

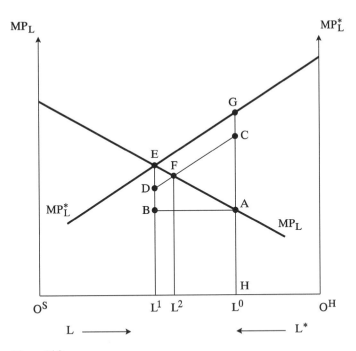

Figure 14.2

to schedule MP_L^*. Line DC shows the dependence of the after-tax wage rate on emigration. The equilibrium in this case, shown as point F, is given by the intersecting point between DC and schedule MP_L, with labor equal to L^2 remaining in the source country. This means that only labor of an amount equal to $L^0 - L^2$ emigrates to the host country. Because the corresponding wage rate is less that w^1, the chosen tax rate is more than half of the gap between the wage rate and the initial one, meaning that those left behind are *overcompensated* by this tax.

I now turn to the determination of an emigration tax under endogenous emigration so that those left behind are adequately compensated (but not overcompensated). Because the number of emigrants is dependent on the income tax, I shall treat the labor endowment of those left behind, L^t, as a variable to be determined endogenously.

Let the production function of the source country be $F(K, L)$ and that of the host country be $F^*(K^*, L^*)$. With no international capital movement, and because factor endowments are given, $K = \overline{K}$ and $K^* = \overline{K}^*$. The initial labor endowment in the source country is also given, and following the preceding notation, it is denoted by L^0. The production functions are concave, differentiable, and linearly homogeneous. Denote the income of those left behind before the emigration by y^0, which is equal to

$$y^0(L^t) = F_K(\overline{K}, L^0)\overline{K} + F_L(\overline{K}, L^0)L^t. \tag{14.5}$$

When emigration exists, the source country imposes a specific income tax on the emigrants. To get an equilibrium labor outflow equal to $(L^0 - L^t)$, the income tax is set at $F_{L^*}^*(\overline{K}^*, \overline{L}^* + L^0 - L^t) - F_L(\overline{K}, L^t)$, where $F_{L^*}^*(\overline{K}^*, \overline{L}^* + L^0 - L^t)$ is the wage rate in the host country. The product of this income tax rate and the number of emigrants, $L^0 - L^t$, is the tax revenue. The income of those left behind in the presence of this tax revenue is

$$y^t(L^t) = F_K(\overline{K}, L^t)\overline{K} + F_L(\overline{K}, L^t)L^t$$

$$+ \left[F_{L^*}^*(\overline{K}^*, \overline{L}^* + L^0 - L^t) - F_L(\overline{K}, L^t)\right](L^0 - L^t)$$

$$= F(\overline{K}, L^t) + \left[F_{L^*}^*(\overline{K}^*, \overline{L}^* + L^0 - L^t) - F_L(\overline{K}, L^t)\right](L^0 - L^t). \tag{14.6}$$

The government of the source country chooses the income tax rate, or alternatively, the number of emigrants, so that the income of those left behind remains unchanged, that is, $y^0(L^t) = y^t(L^t)$. Denote the corresponding level of emigration by $\widetilde{L}^t$, which solves the following equation:

$$y^0(\widetilde{L}^t) = y^t(\widetilde{L}^t). \tag{14.7}$$

After $\widetilde{L}^t$ has been determined, the tax rate can be obtained from the wage rates in the countries.

The problem and existence of such a value of emigration $\widetilde{L}^t$ can be illustrated in Figure 14.3. The schedules labeled y^0 and y^t show the loci of the corresponding income levels. The location and shape of the schedules can be derived as follows. First, when $L^t = L^0$, that is, when no emigration occurs, no compensation is needed, that is, $y^0(L^0) = y^t(L^0)$. Second, when $L^t = L^1$, which is the value of L^t that equates the two wage rates, the corresponding tax rate is zero. Without any compensatory tax, those left behind are hurt. At this point, because the tax revenue is zero, $y^t(L^1) < y^0(L^1)$.

Next let me determine the slopes of the schedules. Differentiate $y^0(L^t)$ as given by (14.5) with respect to L^t to give

$$\frac{\mathrm{d}y^0}{\mathrm{d}L^t} = F_L(\overline{K}, L^0) > 0.$$

Thus the y^0 schedule is a positively sloped straight line. Similarly, I differentiate $y^t(L^t)$ with respect to L^t to give

$$\frac{\mathrm{d}y^t}{\mathrm{d}L^t} = F_L - (F_{L^*L^*}^* + F_{LL})(L^0 - L^t) - (F_{L^*}^* - F_L), \tag{14.8}$$

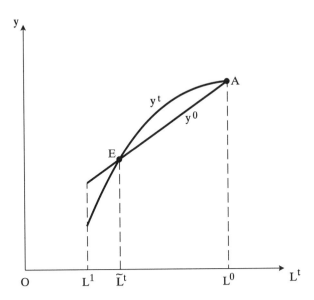

Figure 14.3

where all derivatives are evaluate at L^t. When $L^t = L^0$, the slope reduces to

$$\left. \frac{\mathrm{d}y^t}{\mathrm{d}L^t} \right|_{L^t=L^0} = F_L(\overline{K}, L^0) - \left[F_{L^*}^*(\overline{K}^*, L^*) - F_L(\overline{K}, L^0) \right]. \tag{14.8$'$}$$

Condition (14.8$'$) shows that at $L^t = L^0$, the slope of schedule y^t may be positive or negative, but because $F_{L^*}^*(\overline{K}^*, L^*) > F_L(\overline{K}, L^0)$, it is less than the slope of schedule y^0. Because of continuity of functions, there exists at least one value of $\widetilde{L}^t$ that solves (14.7).

This analysis has an important implication for the use of lump-sum transfers to provide a Pareto-improving international factor movement. When a compensatory tax on the emigrants can be imposed and the tax revenue can be collected by the government of the source country, a lump-sum scheme exists to provide a Pareto improvement during emigration (Kemp, 1993).

14.5 External Effects

It has long been recognized that a worker can produce external effects on the productivity of other workers (Gruebel and Scott, 1966; Johnson, 1967b). The external effects come from the interactions among the workers in the form of intellectual communications, demonstration effects, interpersonal competition and technology spillover. External effects among workers can be positive or negative, depending on how in a given environment workers interact. In the present analysis, I consider a positive external effect, meaning that workers working together are more productive than working separately under the same conditions such as the same ratio of labor to other inputs.[8]

I now examine how the presence of external effects of employment may affect these results. I again begin with the one-sector model. There are many identical, competitive firms in the economy. To capture these external effects, I assume that the production function of the ith firm is given by

$$Q^i = F(K^i, h(L)L^i), \tag{14.9}$$

where superscript "i" represents the firm's variable, and L is the labor employment in the economy; $L = \sum_i L^i$. Function $h(L)$ reflects the external effects and is assumed to be differentiable. Assuming positive external effects, the function has the following properties: first, $h(1) = 1$; and second, $h'(L) > 0$ for $L \geq 1$.

The external effects are considered to augment labor employment, and as given by (14.9), they are similar to a labor-augmenting technological progress.[9] Thus $h(L)L^i$ is the effective labor employment. The production function is assumed to be continuous (or differentiable), concave, and linearly homogeneous in K^i and $h(L)L^i$.

The effects captured by function $h(L)$ are ignored by the firms and individuals, meaning that they all take L and thus $h(L)$ as given. As a result, this case is similar to the Marshallian externality analyzed in Chapter 5. Firms are competitive and individuals are price takers.

Assuming that the firms are identical, the aggregate production function can be obtained by summing up the outputs of the firms to give

$$Q = \sum_i Q^i = \sum_i F(K^i, h(L)L^i) = F\left(\sum_i K^i, h(L) \sum_i L^i\right)$$

$$= F(K, h(L)L). \tag{14.10}$$

Cost minimization under perfect competition gives the following employment conditions:

---

8. The literature pays more attention to positive external effects among workers. For example, Lucas (1988) and Azariadis and Drazen (1990) emphasize these external effects in economic development and Miyagiwa (1991) investigates the role of these effects in brain drain.

9. Two differences between the present formulation and that in Lucas (1988) can be noted. First, Lucas considers only the aggregate production function; so he does not examine the production choice of a firm. Second, he assumes a Cobb-Douglas production function. With this production function, labor-augmenting, capital-augmenting, and neutral technological progresses are not distinguishable. Similar ways of representing external effects of employment can also be found in Azariadis and Drazen (1990) and Miyagiwa (1991), but none of them considers the behavior of firms. Note that an alternative production function can be considered: $h(L)F(K^i, L^i)$. Interested readers can derive a similar analysis using this function.

$$w = h(L)F_L(K^i, h(L)L^i) = h(L)F_L(K, h(L)L) \tag{14.11a}$$

$$r = F_K(K^i, h(L)L^i) = F_K(K, h(L)L), \tag{14.11b}$$

where F_K and F_L represent the derivatives of $F(.,.)$ with respect to K and $h(L)L$, respectively. The production function and the employment conditions given by (14.11) have two important implications. First, as emphasized in the literature, for $L > 1$ the wage rate is higher than $F_L(K^i, h(L)L^i)$. Function $h(L)$ gives the external effects on the wage rate. Second, the ith firm earns zero profit, because

$$wL^i + rK^i = h(L)L^i F_L(K^i, h(L)L^i) + K^i F_K(K^i, h(L)L^i) = Q^i.$$

As condition (14.11a) shows, a change in employment has two effects on the wage rate: a change in the aggregate employment and thus a change in the value of $h(L)$ and a change in $F_L(K^i, h(L)L^i)$. Both the firms and individuals ignore the first effect, treating $h(L)$ as a constant. The change in w with respect to labor employment is illustrated by schedule PP in Figure 14.4. The slope of schedule PP can be obtained by differentiating (14.11a) with respect to L:

$$\frac{dw}{dL} = h'(L)F_L(K, h(L)L) + (1 + \varepsilon)[h(L)]^2 F_{LL}(K, h(L)L), \tag{14.12}$$

where ε is the elasticity of $h(L)$ and is analogous to the rate of variable returns to scale defined in Chapter 5. As explained, I here consider only positive external effects, implying that $\varepsilon > 0$. By assumption, $F_{LL} < 0$. This means that schedule PP is downward sloping if and only if $(1 + \varepsilon)[h(L)]^2 F_{LL}(K, h(L)L) < -h'(L)F_L(K, h(L)L)$. I assume that the external effects are not significant so that PP is downward sloping.

To determine the welfare effects of emigration, I have to find out the social marginal product of labor, SMP_L. It is equal to:

$$SMP_L = F_L\big[h(L) + Lh'\big] = (1 + \varepsilon)h(L)F_L. \tag{14.13}$$

The social marginal product of labor is illustrated by schedule SS in Figure 14.4. Assuming that the external effects are not significant, schedule SS is negatively sloped. By comparing conditions (14.11a) and (14.13), and because $\varepsilon > 0$, $SMP_L > w$, that is, schedule SS is above schedule PP. The relative positions of these schedules have an important implication: Although the external effects make the wage rate greater than the partial derivative $F_L(K^i, h(L)L^i)$, the workers are in fact underpaid because the firms are ignoring the external effects. In other words, at the margin the workers are getting less than what they have contributed. The gap between the social marginal product of labor and the wage rate represents a distortion in the economy.

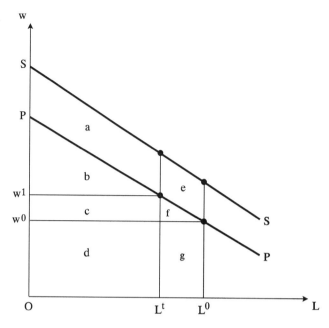

Figure 14.4

I now examine how this distortion may affect the effects of emigration analyzed in the previous sections. In Figure 14.4, L^0 is the initial labor endowment in the economy. Now an amount $L^0 - L^t$ of labor moves out of the economy. The wage rate, which is determined by schedule PP, rises from w^0 to w^1. How does emigration affect the welfare of those left behind?

To answer this question, first note that the area under schedule SS, not the area under schedule PP, gives the output. Thus the output before emigration is equal to $a + b + c + d + e + f + g$. Area g is the initial income of the workers who later emigrate, meaning that the total income of those left behind before emigration is $a + b + c + d + e + f$. After the emigration of $L^0 - L^t$, the income of those left behind is equal to $a + b + c + d$. This gives a loss to those left behind equal to $e + f$. Area f is the Harberger triangle analyzed above. In the present case, there is an additional loss of those left behind given by area e. This is due to the fact that the marginal emigrant receives before emigration less than what that person has contributed.

The presence of the external effects has three important implications. First, if the amount of emigration is decreased so that L^t gets closer to L^0, then triangle f and area e decrease, and in the limit triangle f becomes zero and area e is a line between schedules SS and PP. What this means is that even a marginal emigration is harmful because the emigrants take away (their social marginal product) more than what they have received. The Grubel-Scott-Wong effect no longer holds.

Second, even if the income of the emigrants is included in national welfare, emigration may still be harmful. To determine this effect, the income of the emigrants has to be known. Suppose that the emigrants also earn a wage rate of w^1 in the host country and that there is no cost of emigration. For simplicity, assume that schedule PP between L^t and L^0 is a straight line. Then the income of the emigrants in the host country is $2f + g$, and the total income of those left behind and emigrants is $a + b + c + d + 2f + g$. The change in national welfare is equal to $f - e$. Thus if the external effects are sufficiently large so that $e > f$, then emigration is harmful even if the emigrants are still considered to be nationals.

Third, because in the presence of external effect the loss of those left behind is greater than area f, the Bhagwati tax, which is equal to half of the increase in the income of the emigrants, is not enough to compensate those left behind. In fact, in the case in which $e > f$ and when emigrants' wage rate is equal to w^1, there is no way to compensate those left behind without hurting the emigrants.

So far, the analysis is restricted to a one-sector model. If more sectors are allowed in the model, the external effects of employment can have resource allocational implications. For example, consider a two-sector model in which the external effects of employment are more significant in sector 1 than in sector 2. Then, because firms ignore these effects, firms in sector 1 may underemploy labor to a greater extent than firms in sector 2, creating an underproduction of good 1. Furthermore, firms in different sectors may have different marginal rates of technical substitution, meaning that the production point may not be on the production possibility frontier.[10] In this case, appropriate employment subsidies in both sectors will be welfare improving.

14.6   Temporary Migration and Guest Workers

I now turn to temporary migration. In this case, migrants stay in the host country only for a limited length of time and after that there are constraints which represent a positive probability that they will move back to their home country. Legally they are still the citizens of the host country. Economically, it is reasonable to assume that for both the source and host countries, the welfare of the immigrants is considered part of the national welfare of the source country, not that of the host country.

---

10. The production point is on the production possibility frontier if the external effects of employment affect the production functions in a Hicks-neutral fashion.

When migration is temporary, it is sometimes assumed that income of the migrants is remitted back to the source country so that their income is included in the latter country's national income. This assumption is of course a first approximation, because the migrants physically live in the host country during their stay, and they must spend at least part of their income on consumption in the host country, although evidence suggests that temporary workers on average remit a bigger share of their income back to the source country than permanent workers do.[11]

Where the migrants consume may not matter if between the source and host countries free trade in all goods exists with no transport costs. If trade restrictions or transport costs are present, however, choosing to consume in the host country instead of in the source country by these workers can have effects on resource allocation, prices, and thus welfare. In this case, if the countries want to determine the welfare effect of migration, the differentials between the prices in the countries must be taken into consideration.

In terms of the departure of a migrant back to the source country, temporary migration can be voluntary or involuntary. First let me analyze voluntary temporary migration, meaning that after a period of time, a migrant voluntarily returns back to the source country. The return can be planned or state-contingent. In the latter case, the return takes place because of the occurrence of some states but will not take place if some other states occur. For simplicity, I only consider a planned return because the following analysis can also be applied to a state-contingent return.

A successful analysis of voluntary temporary migration requires an intertemporal model with at least two periods because return takes place at a date later than the date at which planning and migration take place. For a planned return, no uncertainty perfect foresight can be assumed.

The easier way to explain planned temporary migration is to assume that in the first period the wage rate is higher in the host country than in the source country, and in the second period the wage rate is higher in the source country so that the migrants return. This means, however, that the wage rate in at least one country is not a constant in these periods. In the literature, more attention is paid to those cases in which both countries are in steady states so that the wage rates in both countries are stationary (but not necessarily equal). With stationary wages in both countries, can planned temporary migration occur?

11. One interesting note about the behavior of the temporary workers is due to Galor and Stark (1990). Assuming that native and foreign workers have identical preferences, they argue that because temporary workers face a positive probability of returning in the near future (next period) back to the source country where the wage rates are lower, these workers have higher saving rates than native workers do. If in the next period it turns out that the temporary workers stay in the source country, they are richer than the domestic workers.

One model that explains planned temporary migration is provided by Djajić and Milbourne (1988). The fundamental feature of their model is that workers in the source country have strong preferences toward consuming in the source country. Thus a bundle of goods can yield a much higher utility to a worker if consumed in the source country than if consumed in the host country. The source country in their model is a small one, facing a much higher wage rate in the host country. Thus workers in the source country choose to work in the host country, earn a higher wage rate, save part of the income, and return to the host country later.

In Section 14.8 and 14.9, I present two other models in which planned temporary migration can exist. These two models involve other features, learning by doing and education, and can be used to endogenize other types of migration such as permanent migration and brain drain.

I now turn to involuntary temporary migration. A migrating worker who is allowed to work in a host country for a limiting amount of time is sometimes called a guest worker. The term "guest" reflects the temporariness of the stay of these workers in the host country, and, to a certain extent, the fact that they are being invited by the host country, and that the system is being controlled by the host country. The latter point is important because in such a system the host country specifies the length of and conditions for the stay of the guest workers.

Many countries have guest workers systems, but these systems differ from each other in many ways. The one that draws the most attention of economists is the one instituted in West Germany. The German system, which is called the *Gastarbeiter* system, is designed to allow and administer the inflow of temporary workers into the economy from countries such as Turkey, Greece, Italy, Yugoslavia, Portugal, and Spain. These workers are recruited by offices abroad and are initially given the permission to come and work for one year in a designated employment. The permit can be renewed, and after five years it could lead to permanent residency.

What makes the German system different from other guest worker systems is that it had minimal political and quantitative restrictions. It was established in the 1960s and early 1970s at a time when the German economy was under full employment and shortage of workers.[12] As mentioned by Bhagwati et al. (1984), the German system can be described by several features:

1. No prior limits were imposed on the number of foreign workers to be allowed in annually.

---

12. More restrictions were imposed on the inflow of foreign workers after 1973 when the domestic marcoeconomic situations in Germany became difficult.

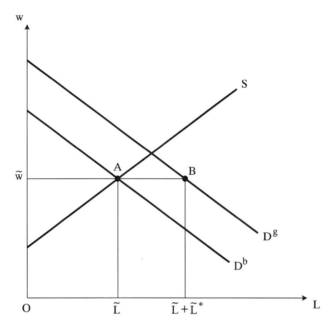

Figure 14.5

2. Provided there was no objection from unions and the local authorities, firms could recruit workers from foreign countries.

3. In principle, German law forbade the recruitment of foreign workers except at identical wages with native German workers in identical jobs.

These features of the German *Gastarbeiter* system can be described by a demand-determined model of international labor migration (Piore, 1979; Bhagwati et al. 1984). To illustrate this model, consider the domestic labor market as illustrated by Figure 14.5. Schedule D^g is the demand for labor of an industry, which, in a competitive sector, is given by the marginal product of labor. (Ignore schedule D^b for the time being.) Schedule S denotes the supply of national labor. Suppose that the domestic wage rate is set at $\tilde{w}$, which is lower than the equilibrium level but significantly higher than the foreign one. The corresponding supply of labor is equal to $\tilde{L}$. The diagram shows that at this wage rate there is an excess demand for labor given by AB. To satisfy the excess demand, firms import guest workers in amounts equal to $\tilde{L}^* = $ AB. At point B, the labor market is in equilibrium.[13]

The demand-determined model has two implications. First, a small change in the supply condition of foreign workers (e.g., foreign wages) does not affect

---

13. Djajić (1989a) examines the choice between work and leisure of a guest worker when migration is temporary. Martin (1994) provides further evaluation of the German system.

the inflow of foreign workers. Second, a change in the demand condition, for example, a shift of the labor demand curve, will directly affect the inflow of foreign workers. The positive relationship between the rate of change in labor demand and the rate of change in foreign worker inflow for the German *Gastarbeiter* system from 1964–1965 to 1971–1972 was confirmed by Bhagwati et al. (1984).

The main weakness of the demand-determined model of international labor migration is that it does not explain how the local wage rate $\tilde{w}$ and the national labor employment are determined. One way of endogenizing the wage rate is to use the idea of implicit contract between the firms and the native workers as proposed by Ethier (1985). He argues that designing and signing a contract on the wage rates (and possibly the employment levels) takes time, and once it is signed, it is binding and rigid. In many cases, the firms and workers have to agree on a contract on wage rates before the state of nature is revealed. If the economic situation turns out to be good, excess demand for labor is created, and such excess demand can be satisfied by an import of foreign workers. Ethier (1985) distinguishes between the European model in which the employment level specified in the contract is rigid, and the U.S. model in which the specified employment level is state dependent.

I now use the Ethier argument to formalize the Bhagwati-Shatz-Wong demand-determined model of international labor migration described above. Consider a competitive industry in the source country. For simplicity assume that the firms in the industry face an exogenously given world price of their output, p. Denote the employment of native and foreign workers by L and L^*, respectively. I assume that native and foreign workers are perfect substitutes so that in the host country they are paid the same wage rate.[14] Holding other industry-specific inputs fixed, the sectoral (short-run) production function is given by $F(L + L^*)$. I assume that $F' > 0$ and $F'' < 0$.

The problem is divided into two stages. In the first stage, the firms jointly sign a contract with the native workers (or the union representing them) on the wage rate, which is state-invariant. For simplicity assume that the labor union has no monopoly power in setting a wage rate, and that the supply of labor is state-invariant, responding only to the wage rate stated in the contract. In the second stage, the state of nature is revealed. If there is an excess demand for labor, firms will hire foreign workers. It is assumed that in signing the contract with native workers in the first stage, the firms do not know which state will occur in the next stage but are fully aware of what they will do when a state occurs.

---

14. I assume that native workers and foreign workers are perfect substitutes because of feature (3) of the *Gastarbeiter* system. Ethier (1985) assumes that native and foreign workers are imperfect substitutes so that in the host country they receive different wage rates. In his model, a change in the wage rate in the source country may affect the inflow of the guest workers.

There are only two states of nature denoted by g (for good) and b (for bad), with the probability of state g being equal to ρ, $1 > \rho > 0$. Use a superscript g or b to denote the value of a variable in a particular state. For example, p^g and p^b are the given world price of the good in states g and b, respectively, with $p^g > p^b$.

The problem is solved by considering the second stage first. Suppose that state i, $i = g, b$, occurs. For a representative firm, the number of native workers, ℓ, and the wage rate, w, have already been decided in the previous stage and are taken as given. The problem of the firm is then to choose the optimal number of foreign workers, $\ell^* \geq 0$, to maximize its profit, which is given by $p^i F(\ell + \ell^{*i}) - w(\ell + \ell^{*i}) - z$ where z is the state-invariant fixed cost. The first-order condition of this problem is

$$p^i F'(\ell + \ell^{*i}) - w \leq 0, \qquad i = g, b. \tag{14.14}$$

Condition (14.14) gives the number of foreign workers employed by the firm in state i, and the sum of these foreign workers employed by all firms is the inflow of foreign workers. If the firm does choose foreign workers in state i, the inequality in (14.14) is replaced by an equality.

I now turn to the first stage, in which the state of nature is unknown. The firm, which is assumed to be risk-neutral, is to choose the labor contract to maximize its expected profit, that is,

$$\max_{\ell} \left\{ \rho \left[p^g F(\ell + \ell^{*g}) - w(\ell + \ell^{*g}) - z \right] + (1 - \rho) \left[p^b F(\ell + \ell^{*b}) \right. \right.$$

$$\left. \left. - w(\ell + \ell^{*b}) - z \right] \right\}.$$

The first-order condition is

$$\rho \left[p^g F'(\ell + \ell^{*g}) - w \right] + (1 - \rho) \left[p^b F'(\ell + \ell^{*b}) - w \right] \leq 0. \tag{14.15}$$

Combining conditions (14.14) and (14.15), it can be concluded that condition (14.14) must have an equality for any of the states (if the firms are to choose any workers): No matter what state occurs, the optimal employment policy of the firm is to hire labor up to the point at which the wage rate is equal to the value of marginal product of labor.

An examination of conditions (14.14) and (14.15) shows that the above model can determine only the total employment in each state, that is, $\ell + \ell^{*g}$ and $\ell + \ell^{*b}$. In countries such as Germany in which a guest worker system exists, firms are required to hire domestic workers first before foreign workers are recruited. If this requirement is strictly enforced, then the employment of domestic workers, ℓ, must be the supply of native workers at the prevailing wage rate.

The last thing to determine is the equilibrium wage rate. An equilibrium can be explained with the aid of Figure 14.5. Schedules D^g and D^b are the values of marginal product of labor schedules in states g and b, respectively. In the diagram, $\tilde{w}$ is the wage rate that clears the labor market without immigration if state b occurs. The question is whether $\tilde{w}$ is the wage rate chosen by the firms.

Because the number of foreign workers working in the host country is non-negative, equilibrium means that the wage rate cannot be above $\tilde{w}$, because if the bad state occurs, native workers will be in excess supply. However, can the equilibrium wage rate be lower than $\tilde{w}$? The answer is no because as explained earlier firms are required to hire domestic workers first. Thus $\tilde{w}$ is the equilibrium wage rate. This means that the domestic firms employ no foreign workers in the bad state but imports foreign workers equal to AB in the good state.

The model has an interesting implication. An improvement in the good state, that is, an upward shift of schedule D^g, will result only in more inflow of foreign workers but not in a change in the employment of native workers. An improvement in the bad state, that is, an upward shift of schedule D^b, will increase the employment of native workers and the wage rate but decrease the inflow of foreign workers by the same amount as the increase in the employment of native workers.

The message of the model is that inflow of foreign workers can be a commercial policy of the government. This is an interesting phenomenon observed in some countries in the past several decades. In this case, foreign workers are allowed to flow in when the domestic industry is experiencing a good time. They are needed to alleviate the domestic shortage of labor. There are other cases, however, in which foreign workers are introduced by a government to help a domestic industry which is experiencing a bad time.

Labor immigration being a policy option for a government is first analyzed with rigorous models by Bhagwati (1982b). He argues that when a domestic labor-intensive industry experiences an import competition (that is, a decrease in the price of imported foreign goods), a government can use either a tariff or an inflow of foreign workers to maintain the initial production level of the industry. He studies several models and concludes that for a small open economy, inflow of foreign labor in general dominates a tariff. Similar arguments for using immigration as a commercial policy in the presence of import competition are also provided by Sapir (1983) and Dinopoulos (1983).

Bhagwati's argument for the Heckscher-Ohlin-Samuelson model for a small open economy under free trade can be briefly presented as follows. In Figure 14.6, point Q_1 is the initial production point, and the price line P_1 is the

Good 2

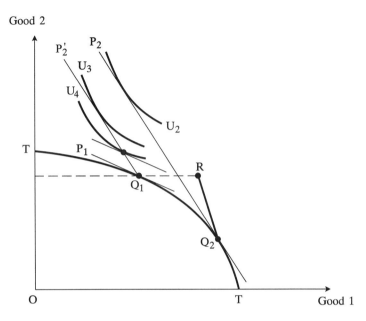

Figure 14.6

initial world price line. The economy imports good 2, which is labor intensive. Suppose that there is a decrease in the relative world price of good 2.
In the absence of any friction, the economy's production point shifts to Q_2,
with the new price line given by P_2. The result is an improvement of the
welfare of the economy. Let the new social utility level be U_2. However, import competition hurts the domestic good-2 industry. Suppose that because
of political pressure or other reasons the government wishes to protect the
good-2 industry and maintain its initial production level. Three policies can
be considered.[15]

The first policy is a tariff that raises the domestic price ratio to the initial
one. This policy shifts the production point back to its original point, Q_1. The
resulting social utility level is U_4. A better policy is a production subsidy
to keep the same production and the same protection effect as those under
a tariff. Because the consumers are still facing the world prices, they can
reach a higher utility level, $U_3 > U_4$. The first-best policy, however, is to
allow free trade and inflow of foreign workers (assuming that the foreign
wage rate is sufficiently low). Under this policy, domestic firms are still facing
world prices. Inflow of foreign workers shifts the production point up and to

---

15. Other policies are also available. For example, the government can subsidize employment
in sector 2. This policy is inferior to production subsidy, however, and I ignore it in the present
analysis.

the left along the Rybczynski line Q_2R. When point R is reached, the initial production level of good 2 is maintained. After payment to foreign workers (in the absence of income taxes), line P_2 is the national income line, or the budget line for the nationals. This gives a social utility level of U_2, the same as that under free trade.

14.7   The Problem of Brain Drain

Brain drain refers to emigration of skilled workers. Outflow of these workers means not just a shrinkage of the labor force in the source country, but also a loss of human capital that these workers bring with them to other countries. For many countries, especially less developed countries (LDC) where human capital is regarded as scarce, brain drain is considered to be a big economic problem and a focus of government policy makers.

The analysis shows that in the neoclassical framework, outflow of any factors, including unskilled and skilled workers, is in general detrimental to those left behind in the source country. Brain drain of course has the same negative effect on those left behind. Apparently, however, some people regard the outflow of skilled workers as a more serious phenomenon than the outflow of unskilled workers.

Two reasons may be offered to explain such a concern. First, in many LDCs, there is widespread unemployment of unskilled workers. Outflow of some of these workers may have zero or small social costs to the countries (see the analysis in Section 14.3). Skilled workers, or human capital, are regarded as scarce, and brain drain means a loss of human capital. Second, brain drain is related to the education and training process in a source country. In many LDCs, education is subsidized by the governments. Public subsidization of education can be regarded as an investment in human capital of the country. Emigration of educated people thus means the loss of returns to such an investment, and this loss is in addition to the adverse effect on the welfare of those left behind. Moreover, the possibility that skilled workers can migrate to developed countries (DC) where wage rates are higher represents an incentive to get education and may distort the equilibrium under education.[16]

The analysis in the early part of this chapter shows that if the human capital of the skilled workers is taken as given, the analysis can be applied to examine the welfare effects of brain drain and draw similar conclusions. Here I focus on the sources and reasons for brain drain. In the following two sections, I explain two processes in which unskilled workers become skilled workers: learning by

---

16. See Bhagwati and Hamada (1974) for further discussion.

doing and education. Before that, I explain one source of brain drain pointed out by Kwok and Leland (1982).

Suppose that some unskilled (or semi-skilled) workers in the source country go to another country, called the host country, to study. In the host country, these workers acquire skill through education. After graduation, they have to decide whether to return home. Firms in the host country have perfect information about the productivity of these workers, and thus they are willing to pay the workers according to their marginal products. Firms in the source country, however, lack perfect information and are willing to pay only the expected, or average, productivity of those who return.

Denoting the wage rate in the host country by w^*, there exists a constant $0 < \phi < 1$ so that these graduates prefer to return to the source country if and only if what they receive in the source country is not less than ϕw^*. The variable ϕ reflects the degree of preference a graduate has toward working and consuming in the source country. For example, if ϕ is large (close to unity), the degree of such preference is low, and the wage rate in the source country a graduate is able to receive has to be close to w^* before he or she is willing to return to the source country.

Brain drain depends crucially on the value of ϕ. If ϕ is sufficiently large, the most productive graduates will not return home because ϕw^* is greater than the average productivity of the returning workers, which is what firms in the source country are willing to offer. In fact, if ϕ is sufficiently close to unity, all graduates except those with the lowest productivity will not return home. Those with the lowest productivity will be offered the same wage rate by firms in both countries and they are indifferent between staying and returning. On the other hand, if ϕ is sufficiently low so that ϕw^* is smaller than the average productivity of the graduates, all of them will return home. If ϕ is not too low so that some graduates do return home, they must have lower productivities than those who stay behind.[17]

Using the same argument, Katz and Stark (1984) show that with imperfect information, only the not-so-bright students and not-so-skilled workers in the source country will go abroad for study and work because the schools and firms in the host country cannot observe perfectly the productivity of these individuals.[18] Lien (1987) extends the Kwok and Leland model by introducing signals that graduates in the host country can send when they consider returning home.

Because of the biases in the international movement of unskilled and skilled workers due to asymmetrical information, government intervention has been

---

17. Strictly speaking, there is emigration of unskilled or semi-skilled workers in Kwok and Leland (1982).

18. See the reply in Kwok and Leland (1984).

suggested. Kwok and Leland (1982) show that subsidies imposed by the host country can attract more graduates to return. Lien (1993), however, points out that such subsidies could induce more and better students to study abroad and thus improve the average ability of the graduates. Thus the net effect of the subsidies on the number of returning students is ambiguous.

14.8   Learning by Doing and International Migration

Learning by doing is an important channel through which workers acquire skill. Because the amount of experience workers obtain depends on the activities in different sectors, modeling learning by doing is one way of endogenizing the rate of technological progress in the economy. More important, it is one way of extending the Solow-Swan type growth model. The work of Arrow (1962), which was followed by papers such as Sheshinski (1967), provides an approach to incorporating learning by doing in a growth model. Because learning by doing is a source of dynamic economies of scale, Kemp (1974) analyzes how it may provide a rationale for protecting an infant industry. Later work such as Krugman (1987c), A. Young (1991) and Ishikawa (1992) discusses the relationship between learning by doing and trade.

Yet very little work has been done to analyze international labor migration with learning by doing. I now provide a simple model to analyze the interrelationship between learning by doing and international migration. Furthermore, the model is used to endogenize the decision of potential emigrants concerning the timing of emigration and the length of staying in the host country: whether to stay temporarily and permanently.

Consider an overlapping generations model similar to the one described in Chapter 9. That model is now modified to explain voluntary and involuntary temporary migration, permanent migration and brain drain. Consider a representative individual in the home country who lives for two periods. In the first period, the individual works and through working acquires experience. This experience will make the individual more productive when he or she works in the next period. There is only one good in the model that can be used for consumption and investment. Taking the classical assumption that workers do not save or borrow, there is another group of individuals in the economy who save and invest. For simplicity, I assume that people who save do not emigrate and that their saving is not affected by emigration of the workers.

Suppose that there exist two countries. Because of possible "cross-hauling," it is not appropriate to call them the source and host countries. Let me label them the home and the foreign countries. I first describe the home country and analyze labor migration from the home to the foreign country. Denote the output of the good in period t by Q_t. I assume that the experience a worker gets in period t is a function of the output level: $E_{t+1} = E(Q_t)$, where E_{t+1}

is the experience measured in the unit of effective labor (EL). The experience
E_{t+1} is used to improve the worker's productivity in period $t+1$. The experience function satisfies the following properties: $E(0)=1$ and $E'(Q_t)>0$ for $Q_t>0$. This means that a worker without experience has one unit of EL, and a worker with an experience E_{t+1} can provide E_{t+1} units of EL.

There are N_t workers born in period t. For simplicity I assume that in the absence of migration the population remains constant so that $N_t = N$. Thus in period t, there are N young workers and N old workers. In the absence of migration, the effective labor force in period t is $L_t = N + NE(Q_{t-1}) = N[1+E(Q_{t-1})]$. Let the capital stock in period t be K_t, which is assumed to be independent of emigration, if any. The production function is denoted by $Q_t = F(K_t, L_t)$.

In period t, a young worker supplies 1 unit of EL and earns a wage rate of w_t. Without saving or borrowing, the income is spent on consumption, c_t^y. In period $t+1$, the worker supplies $E(Q_t)$ units of EL and earns w_{t+1} for each unit of EL. The income, $E(Q_t)w_{t+1}$, is also spent on consumption, c_{t+1}^o. With no saving, the worker's budget constraints are:

$$c_t^y \leq w_t \tag{14.16a}$$

$$c_{t+1}^o \leq E(Q_t)w_{t+1}. \tag{14.16b}$$

I assume that the worker has perfect foresight so that there is no difference between his or her perceived wage rate and the actual wage rate in period $t+1$.

Assuming that the utility function of a representative worker, $u(c_t^y, c_{t+1}^o)$, is strictly increasing, continuous, and quasi-concave, the worker chooses the optimal consumption bundle to maximize his or her utility. Denote the worker's indirect utility function by $v[w_t, E(Q_t)w_{t+1}]$. By the envelope theorem, the derivatives of the indirect utility function are

$$\frac{\partial v}{\partial w_t} = \lambda_t^y > 0 \tag{14.17a}$$

$$\frac{\partial v}{\partial w_{t+1}} = \lambda_{t+1}^o E(Q_t) > 0 \tag{14.17b}$$

$$\frac{\partial v}{\partial Q_t} = \lambda_{t+1}^o E'(Q_t)w_{t+1} > 0, \tag{14.17c}$$

where $\lambda_t^y > 0$ and $\lambda_{t+1}^o > 0$ are the worker's marginal utility of income in periods t (when young) and $t+1$ (when old), respectively.

The model described so far can be used to analyze involuntary temporary emigration or guest workers. In such a case, workers in the beginning of period t are allowed to move to the foreign country and work there until the end of the

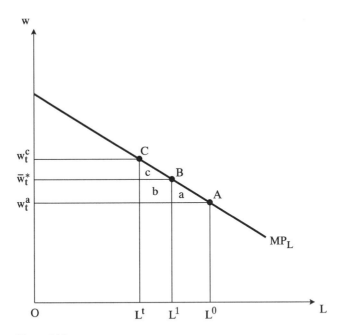

Figure 14.7

period when they return to the home country. In period $t + 1$, the guest workers work in the home country. Workers who choose to work abroad in period t not only earn an income of w_t^*, but also gain an experience that is related to the production level in the foreign country. Denoting the foreign output by Q_t^*, the experience that workers from the home country gets is $E(Q_t^*)$. Thus a representative worker's indirect utility level is $v[w_t^*, E(Q_t^*)w_{t+1}]$. Temporary migration will be chosen if and only if $v[w_t^*, E(Q_t^*)w_{t+1}] > v[w_t, E(Q_t)w_{t+1}]$.

To see how temporary emigration in the present case is different from the one considered previously, let me focus on a simple case in which the home country is a small one. Then w_t^* and Q_t^* are taken as given and are denoted by $\overline{w}_t^*$ and $\overline{Q}_t^*$. Using a superscript "a" to denote the autarkic value of a home variable, I assume that $\overline{w}_t^* > w_t^a$ and $\overline{Q}_t^* > Q_t^a$, the second inequality being due to the small size of the home country. The choice of a young worker between staying at home and working abroad is illustrated and derived by Figure 14.7. The diagram shows the downward sloping marginal product of labor schedule, MP_L. The pre-emigration labor force is L^0. If workers move in response to wage differential, as in the static framework considered previously, an amount of home labor $L^0 - L^1$ will move out until $w_t = \overline{w}_t^*$ as shown by point B. In the present model, however, at point B home workers still have an incentive to move out because $\overline{Q}_t^* > Q_t$. The intuition is that by working abroad even if the foreign wage rate is the same as, or even slightly lower than, the domestic wage rate, the home workers can get more experience and earn more when they return home in the next period. Thus at point B young domestic workers still want to move out until a point such as point C is reached and the wage rate is w_t^c. If w_{t+1} can be taken as given, the equilibrium point is given by the following condition

$$v[\overline{w}_t^*, E(\overline{Q}_t^*)w_{t+1}] = v[w_t^c, E(F(K_t, L_t^t))w_{t+1}],$$

where L_t^t is the remaining labor force in the home country in period t. In general, w_{t+1} is determined endogenously. One way of doing this is to consider a steady state in which $w_{t+1} = w_t^c$.

In the present framework, those left behind are hurt by emigration. The static welfare cost is still present. Furthermore, there are two additional effects that could make emigration more damaging. First, emigration goes beyond the static equilibrium point B in Figure 14.7. The total static welfare loss in period t as shown in the diagram is equal to $a + b + c$, whereas if only $L^0 - L^1$ moves out, then the loss is a. Second, with the outflow of workers in period t, the home country produces a smaller output and the remaining workers earn less experience. This hurts the supply of EL in the next period. On the other hand, the guest workers that return from abroad bring with them the experience they earn in the foreign country. This improves the supply of EL. The net effect of emigration on the supply of EL in period $t + 1$ is ambiguous.

In the case considered earlier, guest workers are allowed to emigrate only when they are young, and when they get older they are forced to return home. I now drop this assumption, allowing workers in the home country to choose where to work in both periods. This means no restrictions on migration imposed by any government. Workers in the home country face the following options:

1. permanent emigration, working abroad when young and old; and

2. temporary emigration, working abroad when young, and working at home when old;

3. brain drain, working at home when young, and working abroad when old;

4. no migration, working at home when young and old.

To simplify the analysis, assume stationary wage rates in both countries, that is, $w_t = w_{t+1} = \overline{w}_t$ and $w_t^* = w_{t+1}^* = \overline{w}_t^*$. Constancy of the wage rates may be because the countries have reached steady states, or because within the relevant range of periods the wage rates remain fixed and because emigration is not significant enough to affect wage rates. With this assumption, the utility of a representative worker is $v[\overline{w}_t, E(Q_t)\overline{w}_t]$. Let the prevailing home and foreign output levels in period t be $\overline{Q}_t$ and $\overline{Q}_t^*$, respectively. Treating Q_t and w_t as parameters, the utility level of a representative worker before emi-

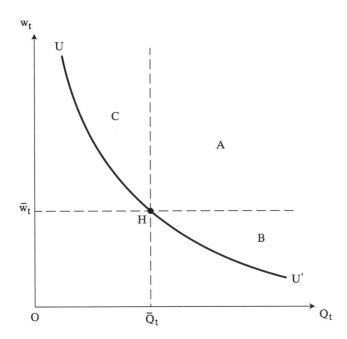

Figure 14.8

gration can be represented by schedule UU′ in Figure 14.8. Point H represents $(\overline{Q}_t, \overline{w}_t)$. Using the partial derivatives of $v[w_t, E(Q_t)w_{t+1}]$ given by (14.17), the slope of schedule UU′ is:

$$\left.\frac{\mathrm{d}w_t}{\mathrm{d}Q_t}\right|_{\mathrm{UU'}} = -\frac{\lambda^o_{t+1}E'\overline{w}_t}{\lambda^y_t + \lambda^o_{t+1}E} < 0.$$

Workers choose the options that give them the highest utility.

Now drop the assumption that the home country is a small one but for the time being let me consider only the decision of home workers. Because utility is increasing in a direction away from the origin, if the foreign output and wage $(\overline{Q}^*_t, \overline{w}^*_t)$ is in the space above (respectively below) schedule UU′, a representative worker in the home country will move (respectively not move) to the foreign country. When and for how long the worker will move depends on the exact location of the point $(\overline{Q}^*_t, \overline{w}^*_t)$. Let the vertical line and horizontal line through H divide the space above schedule UU′ in Figure 14.8 into three regions labeled A, B, and C.

I now show that if $(\overline{Q}^*_t, \overline{w}^*_t)$ is in region A, B, or C, a representative worker will respectively choose option 1, 2, or 3.

1. *Permanent emigration*   In region A, $\overline{w}^*_t > \overline{w}_t$ and $\overline{Q}^*_t > \overline{Q}_t$. Given these conditions, a representative worker has two reasons to move in period t: to

earn a higher wage and to get more experience. In period $t + 1$, the worker wants to stay in the foreign country because of the higher wage rate there.

2. *Voluntary temporary emigration*   Now $\overline{w}_t^* < \overline{w}_t$ and $\overline{Q}_t^* > \overline{Q}_t$ in region B. A representative worker is willing to go abroad when young, despite the lower foreign wage rate, because of greater experience he or she can get abroad. When old, however, the worker prefers to return home and to work there because of a higher home wage rate.

3. *Brain drain*   In region C, $\overline{w}_t^* > \overline{w}_t$ and $\overline{Q}_t^* < \overline{Q}_t$. This case is opposite to the case in (2). The worker chooses to work at home when young in order to gain more experience. When old, the worker moves to the foreign country to earn a higher wage rate.

In the preceding analysis, I was interested in the decision of the marginal individual. If this individual does choose to move, the initial equilibrium will be disturbed. The total amount of migration will depend on how the two economies are affected by migration.

Suppose now that migration in both directions is allowed so that workers in both countries can move to the other country. In Figure 14.9, an indifference curve of a representative home worker labeled U^h and that of a representative foreign worker labeled U^f are shown. The home indifference curve passes through the home point H, $(\overline{Q}_t, \overline{w}_t)$, and the foreign indifference curve passes through the foreign point F, $(\overline{Q}_t^*, \overline{w}_t^*)$. Depending on the relative positions of points H and F and the slopes of the indifference curves, three possible cases are shown in panels (a) to (c) in the diagram. (Other cases can be analyzed in a similar way.) In all these cases, point F is above indifference curve U^h, meaning that a representative home worker has an incentive to work in the foreign country in at least one period. As analyzed previously, the type of migration of the home worker depends on the exact location of point F. On the other hand, point H may or may not be above curve U^f, implying that a representative foreign worker may or may not migrate. More details are given as follows.

In panel (a), point F is above and to the right of point H. Thus a representative home worker wishes to move to the foreign country permanently while a representative worker in the foreign country has no incentive to move to the home country in any period. In panels (b) and (c), point F is above but to the left of point H, meaning that a representative home worker wants to migrate when he or she is old. This is brain drain. In panel (b), point H is below curve U^f. Thus a representative foreign worker does not want to move to the home country in any period. In panel (c), however, point H is above curve U^f so that a representative foreign worker will move to the home country when young but return back when old, that is, temporary migration. In this case,

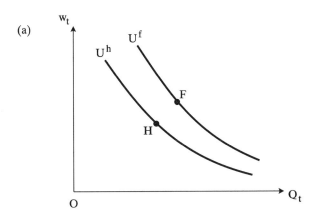

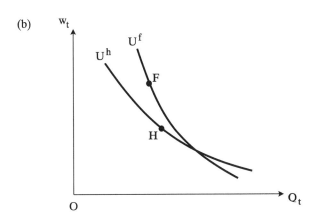

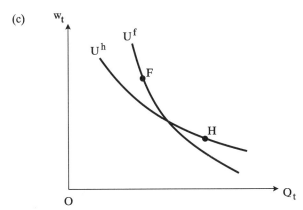

Figure 14.9

workers in both countries move in opposite directions, and I have a case of "cross-hauling" of workers.

14.9   Education, Human Capital Formation, and International Migration

In this section, I turn to another channel through which an individual acquires skill and human capital: education. Human capital became an important focus of interest when economists such as Kenen, Keesing, and Baldwin regarded it as an important input in the U.S. economy and used it to explain the Leontief paradox. Although their work is mainly static in nature and treats human capital in an economy as exogenously given, Findlay and Kierzkowski (1983) provide a rigorous model to explain the formation of human capital through education and show that a certain form of the Heckscher-Ohlin theorem is valid. The focus of their paper is international goods trade, not international labor migration.

One of the earliest works on human capital formation and international migration is Bhagwati and Hamada (1974) which was described earlier. They consider two types of workers and two binding minimum wage rates in the two labor markets. This creates unemployment of both types of workers. Unskilled labor can become skilled labor through education. The cost of education is fully subsidized by the government so that the equilibrium in the education process is that the two types of workers have the same expected wage rates. Bhagwati and Hamada (1974) allows emigration of skilled workers only, the phenomenon of brain drain.

The permission of emigration of skilled workers of course would encourage more unskilled workers to get education. This could be costly to the government. Thus even though there is unemployment in the skilled worker market in the source country, the possibility of brain drain could hurt those left behind. Bhagwati and Hamada also point out that due to international emulation, the permission of emigration of skilled workers may lead to a rise in the minimum wage rate of skilled workers, and this could hurt national income.

Bhagwati and Hamada (1982) provide another model of education and international migration. In this model, which is an extension of the closed-economy model of education by Atkinson (1973), individuals in an economy are endowed with different levels of ability. An individual can increase his or her earning by receiving education. The resulting earning is a function of the individual's ability and the amount of time spent on education. In a two-country model, education is provided in both countries. These two countries may have different education technologies, different wage rates, and different tax schedules.

An individual faces two choices. First, the person has to choose the optimal amount of time to maximize the sum of the discounted stream of after-tax income levels, depending on where the individual receives education and works. If education is to be received abroad, the cost of migration has to be taken into account. Then the individual compares the maximum sums of the discounted streams of after-tax income in these countries and decides whether to migrate. It is assumed that if the individual chooses to receive education abroad, then he or she will stay in the foreign country after graduation. In the Bhagwati-Hamada model, it is shown that emigration hurts those left behind. On the policy side, Bhagwati and Hamada analyze three different types of policies: income tax on nonmigrants, education subsidy, and income tax on migrants.[19]

The Atkinson model of education is later extended by Djajić (1989b) to analyze the role of qualitative and quantitative restrictions on international migration, and by Miyagiwa (1991) to examine scale economies in education.

Markusen (1988) provides another approach to human capital formation and international labor migration. There are two sectors. Good Y is competitive with constant returns technology, and good X is produced with sector-specific capital and a composite index of skilled labor services. Each individual is endowed with one unit of labor to produce good Y, but can choose to become a skilled labor in order to work in sector X by paying a price. The amount of skill the individual can get after training is fixed, but he or she can choose the type of skill to get. In a Nash equilibrium, each individual chooses a type of skill that no other individuals have chosen. Firms in sector X view the available types of skill as given but choose to employ the optimal amount of each type of skill. In such a model, there are external economies of scale of the sector in terms of capital and total supply of skill while firms perceive that their technologies exhibit constant returns in terms of capital and the amount of each type of skill when holding the number of types of skill constant. Each individual again has two choices: whether to become a skilled worker and whether to migrate.[20] Markusen shows that free trade in goods and free migration can lead to factor price equalization, but a smaller economy tends to experience emigration, making it even smaller. This calls for government support of sector X using production subsidy, but education subsidy could be welfare worsening.

Shea and Woodfield (1993) provide another model of education and international labor migration. Assuming that skilled workers can either work or

---

19. Strictly speaking, emigration in the Bhagwati and Hamada (1982) model is outflow of unskilled workers.

20. In fact, if the individual decides to become a skilled worker, there is the third choice: what type of skill to get. Because the available types of skill enter the production function of sector X symmetrically, the individual just chooses one type of skill currently no other people have chosen.

teach, and assuming fixed student-staff ratio and graduation rate, they derive the steady state of an economy. They then examine the optimal immigration policy for a host country, and show that immigration of skilled workers is beneficial but immigration of unskilled workers is not.

Another education process is suggested by Lucas (1988) and Azariadis and Drazen (1990). Such a process can be analyzed nicely in the overlapping generations model described in the previous section. Suppose again that there is a group of individuals in the economy who work but do not save. Individuals can accumulate human capital through education when young, and the human capital acquired improves their productivity when old. Through their lives, individuals can decide where to work and where to get education. Thus four options a worker faces can be described as follows.

1. *permanent emigration*   working and studying abroad when young, and working abroad when old;

2. *temporary emigration*   working and studying abroad when young, and working at home when old;

3. *brain drain*   working and studying at home when young, and working abroad when old; and

4. *no emigration*   working and studying at home when young, and working at home when old. A worker chooses the option that yields the highest utility.

14.10   Illegal Migration

Some countries impose restrictions on emigration of their residents, and nearly all countries have limitations on immigration of residents from other countries. Despite these restrictions, economic and other conditions have driven many people to make attempts to move from their home countries to other countries. Some of these attempts are not permitted by the source and host countries.

Illegal migration is caused by government restrictions and people's desire to move from one country to another. In a sense, it is similar to smuggling in the theory of international trade (Bhagwati and Hansen, 1973b; Pitt, 1981),[21] and thus can be analyzed along the same line. Illegal migration has some characteristics that distinguish it from smuggling, and careful analysis is needed.

Because most countries have heavier restrictions on inflow of foreign residents than on outflow of domestic residents, illegal migration is usually re-

---

21. See Bhagwati (1981) for a survey and references.

garded as a problem of the host country (Ethier, 1986b; Bond and Chen, 1987; Djajić, 1987). I now examine some of the issues raised in these papers.

The first issue to address before a rigorous model of illegal migration can be constructed is why a country would like to restrict inflow of foreign residents. Two economic reasons can be offered.

Monopsony Power

I explained in Chapter 11 that a country that has influence on the price of an incoming factor has monopsony power. The country can limit the inflow of the factor to increase its national welfare. Such a policy requires a simultaneous tax on the income earned by the migrants; the tax being either discriminatory so that only migrants are subject to the tax, or nondiscriminatory so that native and foreign workers are subject to the tax. In many countries, a discriminatory tax is unconstitutional, or is not feasible for ethical or other reasons. If the tax is nondiscriminatory, native workers could be hurt twice by immigration. First, immigration drives down the wage rate; second, the tax lowers the after-tax income. In this case, the government can use other means (through lump-sum transfers or welfare programs) to compensate the native workers.

If no taxes are imposed on foreign workers (legal or illegal), and if foreign workers receive the same wage rates as native workers do, quantitative restrictions on immigration is never optimal. The analysis in Chapter 11 shows that inflow of a foreign factor monotonically improves national welfare until the prices of the moving factor in both countries are equalized.

Ethier (1986b) and Bond and Chen (1987) examine a way in which the host country exploits its monopsony power. Instead of having the host government impose an income tax on the illegal workers, they consider a case in which domestic firms can identify legal and illegal workers. The firms then pay a lower wage rate to illegal workers. In equilibrium, this wage rate is equal to the prevailing wage rate in the source country (plus any moving costs). Hiring illegal workers is prohibited in the host country, however, and the government does check, assumed to be done randomly, the legality of the workers a firm hires. If it is found that a firm has hired an illegal worker, a fine has to be paid. This means that to a firm that hires illegal workers, the cost per illegal worker is not just the (lower) wage rate, but also a fine should employing the illegal worker be discovered. In equilibrium, a risk-neutral firm that hires both types of worker must pay the wage rate to a legal worker the same as the wage rate to an illegal worker plus the expected fine.

If firms cannot identify legal and illegal workers, all workers receive the same wage rate. In equilibrium, the wage rate is the foreign level plus the expected fine where the probability of hiring an illegal worker and the probability of being caught are taken into account. Bond and Chen (1987) show that enforcement is less likely a desirable policy.

Income Distribution

Another reason for restricting the inflow of foreign workers is due to the income distributional effect of immigration. When foreign workers move in, workers in the host country who are close substitutes of foreign workers are hurt in one way or the other. If wage rates are perfectly flexible and full employment is attained, immigration will drive down the wage rates. If wage rates are fixed and unemployment exists, as in the Harris-Todaro model, immigration will make it more difficult for the native workers to get a job.

Restricting immigration clearly helps native workers. Thus if a government has a social welfare function that has a strong weight on the welfare of the native workers, then restrictive immigration policies are likely to be imposed. Alternatively, as Djajić (1987) assumes, native workers lobby for restricting the inflow of foreign workers. Because the presence of illegal foreign workers is possible, he assumes that native workers lobby not for the official level of legal immigration, but for the government expenditure on enforcing the ban on immigration. Because of bureaucratic lags, however, government expenditure adjusts only slowly. Djajić (1987) then does some comparative statics experiments to show how the source and host countries are linked by illegal migrants.

Another issue about illegal immigration is how to limit the inflow of foreign workers. Ethier (1986b) distinguishes between two types of enforcement: border patrol and inspection of firms for possible employment of illegal workers. Border patrol is usually costly, and there is a need to look for less costly ways to stem the inflow of foreign illegal workers. Inspection of firms could be less expensive, and Bond and Chen (1987) focus on this means of enforcement. Ethier (1986b), however, shows that if the host government has as a policy parameter for a particular wage rate for the native workers, and if both border enforcement and internal enforcement are available, there may be a trade off between these two types of enforcement. Then the host government can choose a combination of them to minimize the fiscal cost of enforcement.

References

Alam, M. Shahid (1981). "Welfare Implications of Growth under Quotas." *Economics Letters* 25: 177–180.

Alam, M. Shahid (1988). "Domestic Monopoly, Quotas, Two-Way Trade and Tariff-Equivalence." *Southern Economic Journal* 55: 202–205.

Aliber, Robert Z. (1970). "A Theory of Direct Foreign Investment." In Charles P. Kindleberger (ed.), *The International Corporation*. Cambridge, MA: MIT Press, 17–34.

Amano, Akihiro (1968). "Stability Conditions in the Pure Theory of International Trade: A Rehabilitation of the Marshallian Approach." *Quarterly Journal of Economics* 82 (No. 2): 326–339.

Amano, Akihiro (1977). "Specific Factors, Comparative Advantage and International Investment." *Economica* 44: 131–144.

Anderson, James E. (1988). *The Relative Inefficiency of Quotas*. Cambridge, MA: MIT Press.

Arrow, Kenneth J. (1962). "The Economic Implications of Learning by Doing." *Review of Economic Studies* 29: 155–173.

Arrow, Kenneth J. (1964). "The Role of Securities in the Optimal Allocation of Risk-bearing." *Review of Economic Studies* 31: 91–96.

Arrow, Kenneth J., H. D. Block, and L. Hurwicz (1959). "On the Stability of the Competitive Equilibrium, II." *Econometrica* 27: 82–109.

Atkinson, Anthony B. (1973). "How Progressive Should Income Tax Be?" In Michael Parkin (ed.), *Essays in Modern Economics*. London: Longman, 90–109.

Axelord, Robert (1981). "The Emergence of Cooperation Among Egoists." *American Political Science Review* 75: 308–318.

Azariadis, Costas, and Allan Drazen (1990). "Threshold Externalities in Economic Development." *Quarterly Journal of Economics* 105 (No. 2): 501–526.

Baldwin, Robert E. (1948). "Equilibrium in International Trade: A Diagrammatic Analysis." *Quarterly Journal of Economics* 62: 748–762.

Baldwin, Robert E. (1952). "The New Welfare Economics and Gains in International Trade." *Quarterly Journal of Economics* 65: 91–101.

Baldwin, Robert E. (1971). "Determinants of the Commodity Structure of U. S. Trade." *American Economic Review* 61 (March): 126–146.

Baldwin, Robert E. (1984). "Trade Policies in Developed Countries." In Ronald W. Jones and Peter B. Kenen (eds.), *Handbook of International Economics*, Vol. I. Amsterdam: North-Holland, 571–619.

Batra, Raveendra N. (1971a). "Factor Market Imperfections and Gains from Trade." *Oxford Economic Papers* n.s. 2: 182–188.

Batra, Raveendra N. (1971b). "Factor Market Imperfections, The Terms of Trade and Welfare." *American Economic Review* 61: 946–955.

Batra, Raveendra N., and François R. Casas (1976). "A Synthesis of the Heckscher-Ohlin and the Neoclassical Models of International Trade." *Journal of International Economics* 6: 21–38.

Batra, Raveendra N., and P. Pattanaik (1970). "Domestic Distortions and the Gains from Trade." *Economic Journal* 80: 638–649.

Batra, Raveendra N., and Rama Ramachandran (1980). "Multinational Firms and the Theory of International Trade and Investment." *American Economic Review* 70: 278–290.

Batra, Raveendra N., and William R. Russell (1974). "Gains from Trade under Uncertainty." *American Economic Review* 64: 1040–1048.

Batra, Raveendra, and Gerald W. Scully (1971). "The Theory of Wage Differentials: Welfare and Immiserizing Growth." *Journal of International Economics* 1: 241–247.

Beladi, Hamid (1990). "Unemployment and Immiserizing Transfer." *Journal of Economics/Zeitschrift für Nationalökonomie* 52: 253–265.

Ben-Zvi, Shmuel, and Elhanan Helpman (1992). "Oligopoly in Segmented Markets." In Gene M. Grossman (ed.), *Imperfect Competition and International Trade*. Cambridge, MA: MIT Press, 31–53.

Berry, R. Albert, and Ronald Soligo (1969). "Some Welfare Aspects of International Migration." *Journal of Political Economy* 77 (No. 5): 778–794.

Bertrand, Trent J. (1972). "An Extension of the N-Factor Case of Factor Proportions Theory." *Kyklos* 25: 592–596.

Bertrand, Trent J., and F. Flatters (1971). "Tariffs, Capital Accumulation and Immiserizing Growth." *Journal of International Economics* 1: 453–460.

Bertrand, Trent J., and Jaroslav Vanek (1971). "The Theory of Tariffs, Taxes and Subsidies: Some Aspects of the Second Best." *American Economic Review* 61: 925–931.

Bhagwati, Jagdish N. (1958). "Immiserizing Growth: A Geometric Note." *Review of Economic Studies* 25: 201–205.

Bhagwati, Jagdish N. (1964). "The Pure Theory of International Trade: A Survey." *Economic Journal* 74: 1–78.

Bhagwati, Jagdish N. (1965). "On the Equivalence of Tariffs and Quotas." In Robert E. Baldwin et al. (eds.). *Trade, Growth and the Balance of Payments—Essays in Honor of Gottfried Haberler*. Chicago: Rand McNally, 53–67.

Bhagwati, Jagdish N. (1968a). "The Gains from Trade Once Again." *Oxford Economic Papers* 20: 137–148.

Bhagwati, Jagdish N. (1968b). "Theory and Practice of Commercial Policy: Departures from Unified Exchange Rates." Special Papers in International Economics, No. 8. Princeton: Princeton University Press.

Bhagwati, Jagdish N. (1968c). "Distortions and Immiserizing Growth: A Generalization." *Review of Economic Studies* 35: 481–485.

Bhagwati, Jagdish N. (1968d). "More on the Equivalence of Tariffs and Quotas." *American Economic Review* 58: 142–146.

Bhagwati, Jagdish N. (1971). "The Generalized Theory of Distortions and Welfare." In Jagdish N. Bhagwati, Ronald W. Jones, Robert A. Mundell, and Jaroslav Vanek (eds.). *Trade, Balance of Payments, and Growth: Papers in International Economics in Honor of Charles P. Kindleberger*. Amsterdam: North-Holland, 69–90.

Bhagwati, Jagdish N. (1972a). "The Heckscher-Ohlin Theorem in the Multi-Commodity Case." *Journal of Political Economy* 80 (No. 5): 1052–1055.

Bhagwati, Jagdish N. (1972b). "The United States in the Nixon Era: The End of Innocence." *Daedalus*.

Bhagwati, Jagdish N. (1973). "The Theory of Immiserizing Growth: Further Applications." In M. Connolly and A. Swoboda (eds.). *International Trade and Money*. Toronto: University of Toronto Press, 45–54.

Bhagwati, Jagdish N. (ed.) (1976a). *The Brain Drain and Taxation: Theory and Empirical Analysis*. Amsterdam: North-Holland.

Bhagwati, Jagdish N. (1976b). "The Brain Drain Tax Proposal and the Issues." In Jagdish N. Bhagwati and Martin Partington (eds.), *Taxing the Brain Drain: A Proposal*. Amsterdam: North-Holland, 3–29.

Bhagwati, Jagdish N. (1981). "Alternative Theories of Illegal Trade: Economic Consequences and Statistical Detection." *Weltwirtschaftliches Archiv* 117: 409–427.

Bhagwati, Jagdish N. (1982a). "Directly-Unproductive Profit-Seeking (DUP) Activities." *Journal of Political Economy* 90: 988–1002.

Bhagwati, Jagdish N. (1982b). "Shifting Comparative Advantage, Protectionist Demands, and Policy Response." In Jagdish N. Bhagwati (ed.). *Import Competition and Response*. Chicago: University of Chicago Press, 153–184.

Bhagwati, Jagdish N. (1985a). "Protectionism: Old Wine in New Bottles." *Journal of Policy Modelling* 7: 23–34.

Bhagwati, Jagdish N. (1985b). *Investing Abroad: Esmee Fairbairn Lecture*. Delivered at the University of Lancaster.

Bhagwati, Jagdish N. (1988). *Protectionism*. Cambridge, MA: MIT Press.

Bhagwati, Jagdish N. (1989). "Is Free Trade Passé After All?" *Weltwirtschaftliches Archiv* 125: 17–44.

Bhagwati, Jagdish N., and Richard A. Brecher (1980). "National Welfare in an Open Economy in the Presence of Foreign-Owned Factors of Production." *Journal of International Economics* 10: 103–115.

Bhagwati, Jagdish N., and Koichi Hamada (1974). "The Brain Drain, International Integration of Markets for Professionals and Unemployment: A Theoretical Analysis." *Journal of Development Economics* 1: 19–24.

Bhagwati, Jagdish N., and Koichi Hamada (1982). "Tax Policy in the Presence of Emigration." *Journal of Public Economics* 18: 291–317.

Bhagwati, Jagdish N., and Bent Hansen (1973a). "Should Growth Rates Be Evaluated at International Prices?" In J. Bhagwati and R. Eckaus (eds.), *Development and Planning: Essays in Honour of Paul Rosenstein-Rodan*. Cambridge, MA: MIT Press, 53–68.

Bhagwati, Jagdish N., and Bent Hansen (1973b). "A Theoretical Analysis of Smuggling." *Quarterly Journal of Economics* 87: 172–187.

Bhagwati, Jagdish N., and Murray C. Kemp (1969). "Ranking of Tariffs under Monopoly Power in Trade." *Quarterly Journal of Economics* 83: 330–335.

Bhagwati, Jagdish N., and M. Partington (eds.) (1976). *Taxing the Brain Drain: A Proposal*. Amsterdam: North-Holland.

Bhagwati, Jagdish N., and V. K. Ramaswami (1963). "Domestic Distortions, Tariffs and the Theory of Optimum Subsidy." *Journal of Political Economy* 71: 44–50.

Bhagwati, Jagdish N., and Carlos A. Rodriguez (1975). "Welfare-Theoretical Analyses of the Brain Drain." *Journal of Development Economics* 2: 195–221.

Bhagwati, Jagdish N., and T. N. Srinivasan (1969). "Optimal Intervention to Achieve Non-Economic Objectives." *Review of Economic Studies* 36: 27–38.

Bhagwati, Jagdish N., and T. N. Srinivasan (1971). "The Theory of Wage Differential: Production Response and Factor Price Equalisation." *Journal of International Economics* 1: 19–35.

Bhagwati, Jagdish N., and T. N. Srinivasan (1974). "On Reanalyzing the Harris-Todaro Model: Policy Rankings in the Case of Sector-Specific Sticky Wages." *American Economic Review* 64: 502–508.

Bhagwati, Jagdish N., and T. N. Srinivasan (1980). "Revenue Seeking: A Generalization of the Theory of Tariffs." *Journal of Political Economy* 88: 1069–1087.

Bhagwati, Jagdish N., and T. N. Srinivasan (1983a). *Lectures on International Trade*. Cambridge, MA: MIT Press.

Bhagwati, Jagdish N., and T. N. Srinivasan (1983b). "On the Choice Between Capital and Labor Mobility." *Journal of International Economics* 14: 209–221.

Bhagwati, Jagdish N., and Ernesto Tironi (1980). "Tariff Change, Foreign Capital and Immiserization." *Journal of Development Economics* 7: 71–83.

Bhagwati, Jagdish N., Richard A. Brecher, and Tatsuo Hatta (1983). "The Generalized Theory of Transfers and Welfare: Bilateral Transfers in a Multilateral World." *American Economic Review* 73: 57–76.

Bhagwati, Jagdish N., Richard A. Brecher, and Tatsuo Hatta (1985). "The Generalized Theory of Transfers and Welfare: Exogenous (Policy-Imposed) and Endogenous (Transfer-Induced) Distortions." *Quarterly Journal of Economics* 3: 697–714.

Bhagwati, Jagdish N., Richard A. Brecher, and Tatsuo Hatta (1987). "The Global Correspondence Principle: A Generalization." *American Economic Review* 77: 124–132.

Bhagwati, Jagdish N., Elias Dinopoulos, and Kar-yiu Wong (1992). "*Quid Pro Quo* Foreign Investment." *American Economic Review* 82 (May): 186–190.

Bhagwati, Jagdish N., V. K. Ramaswami, and T. N. Srinivasan (1969). "Domestic Distortions, Tariffs, and the Theory of Optimum Subsidy: Some Further Results." *Journal of Political Economy* 77: 1005–1010.

Bhagwati, Jagdish N., Klaus-Werner Schatz, and Kar-yiu Wong (1984). "The West German Gastarbeiter System of Immigration." *European Economic Review* 26: 277–294.

Bhagwati, Jagdish N., Richard A. Brecher, Elias Dinopoulos, and T. N. Srinivasan (1987). "*Quid Pro Quo* Foreign Investment and Welfare: A Political-Economy-Theoretic Model." *Journal of Development Economics* 27: 127–138.

Binh, T. N. (1985). "A Neo-Ricardian Model with Overlapping Generations." *Economic Record* 61: 707–718.

Blomström, M., and H. Persson (1983). "Foreign Investment and Spillover Efficiency in an Underdeveloped Economy: Evidence from the Mexican Manufacturing Industry." *World Development* 11: 493–501.

Boadway, Robin W. (1974). "The Welfare Foundations of Cost-Benefit Analysis." *Economic Journal* 84: 926–939.

Boadway, Robin N., and Neil Bruce (1984). *Welfare Economics*. New York: Basil Blackwell.

Bond, Eric W. (1990). "The Optimal Tariff Structure in Higher Dimensions." *International Economic Review* 31 (No. 1): 103–116.

Bond, Eric W., and Tain-Jy Chen (1987). "The Welfare Effects of Illegal Immigration." *Journal of International Economics* 23: 315–328.

Brander, James A. (1981). "Intra-industry Trade in Identical Commodities." *Journal of International Economics* 11: 1–14.

Brander, James A. (1986). "Rationales for Strategic and Industrial Policy." In Paul R. Krugman (ed.), *Strategic Trade Policy and the New International Economics*. Cambridge, MA: MIT Press, 23–46.

Brander, James A., and Paul R. Krugman (1983). "A 'Reciprocal Dumping' Model of International Trade." *Journal of International Economics* 15: 313–323.

Brander, James A., and Barbara J. Spencer (1981). "Tariff and the Extraction of Foreign Monopoly Rents under Potential Entry." *Canadian Journal of Economics* 14: 371–389.

Brander, James A., and Barbara J. Spencer (1984). "Tariff Protection and Imperfect Competition." In Henryk Kierzkowski (ed.), *Monopolistic Competition and International Trade*. Oxford: Clarendon Press, 194–206.

Brander, James A., and Barbara J. Spencer (1985). "Export Subsidies and International Market Share Rivalry." *Journal of International Economics* 18: 83–100.

Brecher, Richard A. (1974a). "Minimum Wage Rates and the Pure Theory of International Trade." *Quarterly Journal of Economics* 88: 98–116.

Brecher, Richard A. (1974b). "Optimal Commercial Policy for a Minimum-Wage Economy." *Journal of International Economics* 4: 139–149.

Brecher, Richard A. (1982). "Optimal Policy in the Presence of Licensed Technology from Abroad." *Journal of Political Economy* 90 (No. 2): 1070–1078.

Brecher, Richard A. (1983). "Second-Best Policy for International Trade and Investment." *Journal of International Economics* 14: 313–320.

Brecher, Richard A., and Jagdish N. Bhagwati (1981). "Foreign Ownership and the Theory of Trade and Welfare." *Journal of Political Economy* 89 (No. 3): 497–511.

Brecher, Richard A., and Jagdish Bhagwati (1982). "Immiserizing Transfer from Abroad." *Journal of International Economics* 13: 353–364.

Brecher, Richard A., and Ehsan U. Choudhri (1982a). "The Factor Content of International Trade without Factor-Price Equalization." *Journal of International Economics* 12: 277–283.

Brecher, Richard A., and Ehsan U. Choudhri (1982b). "The Leontief Paradox, Continued." *Journal of Political Economy* 90: 820–823.

Brecher, Richard A., and Ehsan U. Choudhri (1982c). "Immiserizing Investment from Abroad: The Singer-Prebisch Thesis Reconsidered." *Quarterly Journal of Economics* 47: 181–190.

Brecher, Richard A., and Ehsan U. Choudhri (1987). "International Migration versus Foreign Investment in the Presence of Unemployment." *Journal of International Economics* 23: 329–342.

Brecher, Richard A., and Ehsan U. Choudhri (1990). "Gains from International Factor Movements without Lump-sum Compensation: Taxation by Location versus Nationality." *Canadian Journal of Economics* 23 (No. 1): 44–59.

Brecher, Richard A., and Carlos F. Diaz Alejandro (1977). "Tariffs, Foreign Capital and Immiserizing Growth." *Journal of International Economics* 7: 317–322.

Brecher, Richard A., and Robert C. Feenstra (1983). "International Trade and Capital Mobility between Diversified Economies." *Journal of International Economics* 7: 317–322.

Brecher, Richard A., and Ronald Findlay (1983). "Tariffs, Foreign Capital and National Welfare with Sector-Specific Factors." *Journal of International Economics* 14: 277–288.

Bruce, Neil, and Richard G. Harris. "Cost-Benefit Criteria and the Compensation Principle in Evaluating Small Projects." *Journal of Political Economy* 90 (1982): 755–776.

Buckley, Peter J. (1985). "A Critical View of Theories of the Multinational Enterprise." In Peter J. Buckley and Mark Casson (eds.), *The Economic Theory of the Multinational Enterprise*. London: Macmillan, 1–19.

Buckley, Peter J., and Mark Casson (1976). *The Future of the Multinational Enterprise*. London: Macmillan.

Bulow, Jeremy I., Jonh D. Geanakoplos, and Paul D. Klemperer (1985). "Multimarket Oligopoly: Strategic Substitutes and Complements." *Journal of Political Economy* 93 (No. 3): 488–511.

Calvo, Guillermo, and Stanislaw Wellisz (1983). "International Factor Mobility and National Advantage." *Journal of International Economics* 14: 103–114.

Cantwell, John (1991). "A Survey of Theories of International Production." In Christos N. Pitelis and Roger Sugden (eds.), *The Nature of the Transnational Firm*. London: Routledge, 16–63.

Carmichael, Calum (1987). "The Control of Export Credit Subsidies and Its Welfare Consequences." *Journal of International Economics* 23: 1–19.

Casas, François R. (1991). "Lerner's Symmetry Theorem Revisited." *Keio Economic Studies* 28: 15–19.

Casas, François R., and E. Kwan Choi (1984). "Trade Imbalance and the Leontief Paradox." *Manchester School of Economics and Social Studies* 52: 391–401.

Casas, François R., and E. Kwan Choi (1985). "The Leontief Paradox: Continued or Resolved?" *Journal of Political Economy* 93 (No. 3): 610–615.

Caves, Richard E. (1971). "International Corporations: The Industrial Economics of Foreign Investment." *Economica* 38: 1–27.

Caves, Richard E. (1982). *Multinational Enterprises and Economic Analysis*. Cambridge: Cambridge University Press.

Caves, Richard E., Harold Crookell, and J. Peter Killing (1983). "The Imperfect Market for Technology Licensing." *Oxford Bulletin of Economics* 45 (No. 3): 249–267.

Chacholiades, Miltiades (1978). *International Trade Theory and Policy*. New York: McGraw-Hill.

Chamberlin, Edward H. (1933). *The Theory of Monopolistic Competition*. Cambridge, MA: Harvard University Press.

Chan, Kenneth S. (1988). "Trade Negotiation in a Nash Bargaining Model." *Journal of International Economics* 25: 353–363.

Chan, Hsiu-Yi, and Kar-yiu Wong (1994). "Intra-Industry Trade and Investment." Mimeo, University of Washington, Seattle.

Chang, Winston W. (1981). "Production Externalities, Variable Returns to Scale, and the Theory of Trade." *International Economic Review* 22 (No. 3): 511–525.

Chang, Winston W., and Seiichi Katayama (1992). "Recent Developments in the Theory of Trade with Imperfect Competition." *Kobe Economic & Business Review*, 37th Annual Report.

Chao, Chi-Chur, and Eden H. S. Yu (1991). "Immiserizing Growth for a Quota-Distorted Small Country under Variable Returns to Scale." *Canadian Journal of Economics* 24: 686–692.

Chen, Edward K. Y. (1983). *Multinational Corporations, Technology and Employment*. London: Macmillan.

Cheng, Leonard K. (1988). "Assisting Domestic Industries under International Oligopoly: The Relevance of the Nature of Competition to Optimal Policies." *American Economic Review* 78 (No. 4): 746–758.

Cheng, Leonard K., and Kar-yiu Wong (1990). "On the Strategic Choice between Labor and Capital Mobility." *Journal of International Economics* 28: 291–314.

Cheng, Leonard K., and Kar-yiu Wong (1993). "Strategic Policies toward International Factor Mobility." Mimeo, University of Washington, Seattle.

Chipman, John S. (1965). "A Survey of the Theory of International Trade: Part 2, The Neoclassical Theory." *Econometrica* 33: 685–760.

Chipman, John S. (1970). "External Economies of Scale and Competitive Equilibrium." *Quarterly Journal of Economics* 34: 347–385.

Chipman, John S. (1971). "International Trade with Capital Mobility: A Substitution Theorem." In Jagdish Bhagwati et al. (eds.), *Trade, Balance of Payments, and Growth: Papers in International Economics in Honor of Charles P. Kindleberger*. Amsterdam: North-Holland, 201–237.

Chipman, John S. (1974). "The Transfer Problem Once Again." In G. Horwich and P. A. Samuelson (eds.), *Trade, Stability and Macroeconomics: Essays in Honor of Lloyd A. Metzler*. New York: Academic Press, 19–78.

Chipman, John S. (1979). "The Theory and Application of Trade Utility Function." In Jerry R. Green and Josi Alexandre Scheinkman (eds.), *General Equilibrium, Growth, and Trade*. New York: Academic Press, 277–296.

Chipman, John S., and James C. Moore (1972). "Social Utility and the Gains from Trade." *Journal of International Economics* 2: 157–172.

Chipman, John S., and James C. Moore (1973). "Aggregate Demand, Real National Income, and the Compensation Principle." *International Economic Review* 14: 153–181.

Choi, Jay Pil (1995). "Optimal Tariff and the Choice of Technology: Discriminatory Tariff vs. 'Most Favored Nation' Clause," *Journal of International Economics* 38: 143–160.

Coase, R. H. (1937). "The Nature of the Firm." *Economica* n.s. 4, (No. 16): 386–405.

Collie, David (1991). "Export Subsidies and Countervailing Tariffs." *Journal of International Economics* 31: 309–324.

Contractor, Farok J. (1985). *Licensing in International Strategy: A Guide for Planning and Negotiation*. Westport, CT: Quorum Books.

Copeland, Brian R. (1989). "Tariffs and Quotas: Retaliation and Negotiation with Two Instruments of Protection." *Journal of International Economics* 26: 179–188.

Corden, W. M. (1984). "The Normative Theory of International Trade." In Ronald W. Jones and Peter B. Kenen (eds.), *Handbook of International Economics*, Vol. I. Amsterdam: North-Holland, 63–130.

Corden W. M., and Ronald Findlay (1975). "Urban Unemployment, Intersectoral Capital Mobility and Development Policy." *Economica* 62: 59–78.

Das, Sanghamitra (1987). "Externalities, and Technology Transfer through Multinational Corporations." *Journal of International Economics* 22: 171–182.

Das, Satya P., and Seung-Dong Lee (1979). "On the Theory of International Trade with Capital Mobility." *International Economic Review* 20: 119–132.

De Meza, David (1979). "Commercial Policy towards Multinational Monopolies —Reservations on Katrak." *Oxford Economic Papers* 31: 334–337.

Deardorff, Alan V. (1974). "Factor Proportions and Comparative Advantage in the Long Run: Comment." *Journal of Political Economy* 82 (No. 4): 829–833.

Deardorff, Alan V. (1979). "Weak Links in the Chain of Comparative Advantage." *Journal of International Economics* 9 (May): 197–209.

Deardorff, Alan V. (1980). "The General Validity of the Law of Comparative Advantage." *Journal of Political Economy* 88 (No. 5): 941–957.

Deardorff, Alan V. (1982). "The General Validity of the Heckscher-Ohlin Theorem." *American Economic Review* 72 (No. 4): 683–694.

Deardorff, Alan V. (1984). "Testing Trade Theories and Predicting Trade Flows." In Ronald W. Jones and Peter B. Kenen (eds.), *Handbook of International Economics*, Vol. I. Amsterdam: North-Holland, 467–517.

Deardorff, Alan V. (1986). "Firless Firwoes: How Preferences Can Interfere with the Theorems of International Trade." *Journal of International Economics* 20: 131–142.

Deardorff, Alan V., and Robert W. Staiger (1988). "An Interpretation of the Factor Content of Trade." *Journal of International Economics* 24: 93–107.

Dei, Fumio (1985). "Welfare Gains from Capital Inflows under Import Quotas." *Economics Letters* 18: 237–240.

Dei, Fumio (1990). "A Note on Multinational Corporations in A Model of Reciprocal Dumping." *Journal of International Economics* 29: 161–171.

Diewert, W. Erwin (1974). "Applications of Duality Theory." In M. D. Intilligator and D. A. Kendrick (eds.), *Frontiers of Quantitative Economics*, Vol. II. Amsterdam: North-Holland, 106–206.

Diewert, W. Erwin, A. H. Turunen, and Alan D. Woodland (1989). "Productivity- and Pareto-Improving Changes in Taxes and Tariffs." *Review of Economic Studies* 56: 199–215.

Dinopoulos, Elias (1983). "Import Competition, International Factor Mobility and Lobbying Responses: The Schumpeterian Industry Case." *Journal of International Economics* 14: 395–410.

Dinopoulos, Elias (1989). "*Quid Pro Quo* Foreign Investment." *Economics and Politics* I: 145–160.

Dinopoulos, Elias (1992). "*Quid Pro Quo* Foreign Investment and VERs: A Nash Bargaining Approach." *Economics and Politics* IV: 43–60.

Dinopolous, Elias, and Kar-yiu Wong (1991). "*Quid Pro Quo* Foreign Investment and Policy Intervention." In K. A. Koekkoek and C. B. M. Mennes (eds.), *International Trade and Global Development: Essays in Honour of Jagdish Bhagwati*. London: Routledge, 162–190.

Dixit, Avinash (1984). "International Trade Policy for Oligopolistic Industry." *Economic Journal* supplement: 1–16.

Dixit, Avinash (1986a). "Comparative Statics for Oligopoly." *International Economic Review* 27: 107–122.

Dixit, Avinash (1986b). "An Agenda for Research." In Paul R. Krugman (ed.), *Strategic Trade Policy and the New International Economics*. Cambridge, MA: MIT Press, 283–304.

Dixit, Avinash (1988). "Anti-Dumping and Countervailing Duties under Oligopoly." *European Economic Review* 32: 55–68.

Dixit, Avinash (1990). "Trade Policy with Imperfect Information." In Ronald W. Jones and Anne O. Krueger (eds.), *The Political Economy of International Trade*. Cambridge, MA: Basil Blackwell, 9–24.

Dixit, Avinash, and Gene M. Grossman (1986). "Targeted Export Promotion with Several Oligopolistic Industries." *Journal of International Economics* 21: 23–49.

Dixit, Avinash, and Victor Norman (1980). *Theory of International Trade: A Dual, General Equilibrium Approach*. Cambridge: Cambridge University Press.

Dixit, Avinash, and Victor Norman (1986). "Trade Gains without Lump-sum Compensation." *Journal of International Economics* 21: 111–122.

Dixit, Avinash, and Joseph E. Stiglitz (1977). "Monopolistic Competition and Optimum Product Diversity." *American Economic Review* 67: 297–308.

Dixit, Avinash, and Joseph E. Stiglitz (1993). "Monopolistic Competition and Optimum Product Diversity: Reply." *American Economic Review* 83: 302–304.

Dixit, Avinash, and Alan Woodland (1982). "The Relationship between Factor Endowments, and Commodity Trade." *Journal of International Economics* 13: 201–214.

Djajić, Slobodan (1986). "International Migration, Remittances and Welfare in a Dependent Economy." *Journal of Development Economics* 21: 229–234.

Djajić, Slobodan (1987). "Illegal Aliens, Unemployment and Immigration Policy." *Journal of Development Economics* 25: 235–249.

Djajić, Slobodan (1989a). "Migrants in A Guest-Worker System: A Utility Maximizing Approach." *Journal of Development Economics* 31: 327–339.

Djajić, Slobodan (1989b). "Skills and the Pattern of Migration: The Role of Qualitative and Quantitative Restrictions on International Labor Mobility." *International Economic Review* 30: 795–809.

Djajić, Slobodan, and Ross Milbourne (1988). "A General Equilibrium Model of Guest-Worker Migration." *Journal of International Economics* 25: 335–351.

Dollar, David (1986). "Technological Innovation, Capital Mobility, and the Product Cycle in North-South Trade." *American Economic Review* 76: 177–190.

Dornbusch, Rudiger, Stanley Fischer, and Paul A. Samuelson (1977). "Comparative Advantage, Trade and Payments in a Ricardian Model with a Continuum of Goods." *American Economic Review* 67: 823–839.

Drabicki, John Z., and Akira Takayama (1979). "An Antinomy in the Theory of Comparative Advantage." *Journal of International Economics* 9: 211–223.

Dunning, John H. (1977). "Trade, Location of Economic Activity and the MNE: A Search for an Eclectic Approach." In Bertil Ohlin, Per-Ove Hesselborn, and Per Magnus Wijkman (eds.), *The International Allocation of Economic Activity*. London: Macmillan, 395–418.

Dunning, John H. (1981). "Explaining the International Direct Investment Position of Countries: Towards a Dynamic or Developmental Approach." *Weltwirtschaftliches Archiv*, Band 117, Heft 1: 30–64.

Dunning, John H. (1983). "Market Power of the Firm and International Transfer of Technology: A Historical Excursion." *International Journal of Industrial Organization* 1: 333–351.

Eaton, Jonathan (1987). "A Dynamic Specific-Factors Model of International Trade." *Review of Economic Studies* 54: 325–338.

Eaton, Jonathan, and Gene M. Grossman (1986). "Optimal Trade and Industrial Policy under Oligopoly." *Quarterly Journal of Economics* 101: 383–406.

Eaton, Jonathan, and Arvind Panagariya (1979). "Gains from Trade under Variable Returns to Scale, Commodity Taxation, Tariffs and Factor Market Distortions." *Journal of International Economics* 9: 481–501.

Edgeworth, F. Y. (1894). "The Theory of International Value, I." *Economic Journal* 4: 35–50.

Ethier, Wilfred J. (1979). "Internationally Decreasing Costs and World Trade." *Journal of International Economics* 9: 1–24.

Ethier, Wilfred J. (1982a). "Decreasing Costs in International Trade and Frank Graham's Argument for Protection." *Econometrica* 50 (No. 5): 1243–1268.

Ethier, Wilfred (1982b). "National and International Returns to Scale in the Modern Theory of International Trade." *American Economic Review* 72: 389–405.

Ethier, Wilfred J. (1984). "Higher Dimensional Issues in Trade Theory." In Ronald W. Jones, and Peter B. Kenen (eds.), *Handbook of International Economics*, Vol. I. Amsterdam: North-Holland, 131–184.

Ethier, Wilfred J. (1985). "International Trade and Labor Migration." *American Economic Review* 75 (No. 4): 691–707.

Ethier, Wilfred J. (1986a). "The Multinational Firm." *Quarterly Journal of Economics* 101: 805–833.

Ethier, Wilfred J. (1986b). "Illegal Immigration: The Host-Country Problem." *American Economic Review* 76: 56–71.

Ethier, Wilfred J. (1988). *Modern International Economics*, second edition. New York: W. W. Norton & Company.

Ethier, Wilfred J., and Lars E. O. Svensson (1986). "The Theorems of International Trade with Factor Mobility." *Journal of International Economics* 20: 21–42.

Feenstra, Robert C. (1986). "Trade Policy with Several Goods and 'Market Linkages'." *Journal of International Economics* 20 (May): 249–267.

Feenstra, Robert C., and Kenneth L. Judd (1982). "Tariffs, Technology Transfer, and Welfare." *Journal of Political Economy* 90 (No. 6): 1142–1165.

Feenstra, Robert C., and Tracy R. Lewis (1991). "Distributing the Gains from Trade with Incomplete Information." *Economics and Politics* 3: 21–39.

Ferguson, Donald G. (1978). "International Capital Mobility and Comparative Advantage: The Two Country, Two Factor Case." *Journal of International Economics* 8: 373–396.

Findlay, Ronald (1970). "Factor Proportions and Comparative Advantage in the Long Run." *Journal of Political Economy* 78 (No. 1): 27–34.

Findlay, Ronald (1974). "Relative Prices, Growth and Trade in A Simple Ricardian System." *Economica* 41: 1–13.

Findlay, Ronald (1978). "Relative Backwardness, Direct Foreign Investment, and the Transfer of Technology: A Simple Dynamic Model." *Quarterly Journal of Economics* 62 (No. 1): 1–16.

Findlay, Ronald (1984). "Growth and Development in Trade Models." In Ronald W. Jones and Peter B. Kenen (eds.), *Handbook of International Economics*, Vol. I. Amsterdam: North-Holland, 185–236.

Findlay, Ronald, and Harry Grubert (1959). "Factor Intensities, Technological Progress and the Terms of Trade." *Oxford Economic Papers* 11: 111–121.

Findlay, Ronald, and Henryk Kierzkowski (1983). "International Trade and Human Capital: A Simple General Equilibrium Model." *Journal of Political Economy* 91: 957–978.

Findlay, Ronald, and Stanislaw Wellisz (1982). "Endogenous Tariffs, the Political Economy of Trade Restrictions, and Welfare." In Jagdish N. Bhagwati (ed.), *Import Competition and Response*. Chicago: University of Chicago Press, 238–243.

Fischer, Stanley, and Jacob A. Frenkel (1972). "Investment, the Two-Sector Model, and Trade in Debt and Capital Goods." *Journal of International Economics* 2: 211–233.

Flam, Harry, and Elhanan Helpman (1987a). "Industrial Policy under Monopolistic Competition." *Journal of International Economics* 22: 79–102.

Flam, Harry, and Elhanan Helpman (1987b). "Vertical Product Differentiation and North-South Trade." *American Economic Review* 77: 810–822.

Foster, E. (1976). "The Welfare Foundations of Cost-Benefit Analysis—A Comment." *Economic Journal* 86: 353–558.

Fukushima, T. (1979). "Tariff Structure, Nontraded Goods and Theory of Piecemeal Policy Recommendations." *International Economic Review* 20: 427–435.

Fung, K. C. (1991). "Collusive Intra-Industry Trade." *Canadian Journal of Economics* 24: 391–404.

Gale, D., and H. Nakaido (1965). "The Jacobian Matrix and Global Univalence of Mappings." *Mathematische Annalen* 159: 81–93.

Galor, Oded (1986). "Time Preference and International Labor Migration." *Journal of Economic Theory* 38 (No. 1): 1–20.

Galor, Oded, and Oded Stark (1990). "Migrants' Savings, The Probability of Return Migration and Migrants' Performance." *International Economic Review* 31 (No. 2): 463–467.

Geanakoplos, J. (1987). "Overlapping Generations Models of General Equilibrium." In J. Eatwell, M. Milgate, and P. Newman (eds.), *The New Palgrave: A Dictionary of Economics* Vol. 3. New York: W. W. Norton, 767–779. Also in J. Eatwell, M. Milgate, and P. Newman (eds.), *General Equilibrium*. New York: W. W. Norton, 1989, 205–233.

Geanakoplos, J. (1990). "An Introduction to General Equilibrium with Incomplete Asset Markets." *Journal of Mathematical Economics* 19: 1–38.

Geanakoplos, J., and H. Polemarchakis (1986). "Existence, Regularity, and Constrained Suboptimality of Competitive Allocations When Markets are Incomplete." In W. Heller, R. Starr, and D. Starrett (eds.), *Equilibrium Analysis: Essays in Honor of Kenneth Arrow*, Vol. 3. Cambridge: Cambridge University Press.

Gorman, William M. (1953). "Community Preference Fields." *Econometrica* 21: 63–80.

Graaf, J. (1949–50). "On Optimal Tariff Structures." *Review of Economic Studies* 17: 47–59.

Graham, Edward M., and Paul R. Krugman (1993). "The Surge in Foreign Direct Investment in the 1980s." In Kenneth A. Froot (ed.). *Foreign Direct Investment*. Chicago: University of Chicago Press, 13–33.

Graham, Frank (1923). "Some Aspects of Protection Further Considered." *Quarterly Journal of Economics* 37: 199–227.

Grandmont, J. M., and D. McFadden (1972). "A Technical Note on Classical Gains from Trade." *Journal of International Economics* 2: 109–126.

Grinols, Earl L. (1981). "An Extension of the Kemp-Wan Theorem on the Formation of Customs Unions." *Journal of International Economics* 11: 259–266.

Grinols, Earl L. (1984). "A Thorn in the Lion's Paw: Has Britain Paid Too Much for Common Market Memberships?" *Journal of International Economics* 16: 271–293.

Grinols, Earl L. (1987). *Uncertainty and the Theory of International Trade*. Chur, Switzerland: Harwood Academic Publishers.

Grinols, Earl L. (1991). "Increasing Returns and the Gains from Trade." *International Economic Review* 32 (No. 4): 973–984.

Grinols, Earl L. (1992). "Increasing Returns to Scale and Trade-Related Industry Enlargement: A Generalization and New Proof of Welfare Gains." *Economics Letters* 38: 61–66.

Grinols, Earl L. (1994). "Pure and Mixed Quality, Price and Income Compensation in International Trade: Breaking Political Roadblocks to Trade Reform," presented in a conference in honor of Jagdish N. Bhagwati.

Grinols, Earl L., and Kar-yiu Wong (1991). "An Exact Measure of Welfare Change." *Canadian Journal of Economics* 24 (No. 2): 428–449.

Gros, Daniel (1987). "A Note on the Optimal Tariff, Retaliation and the Welfare Loss from Tariff Wars in a Framework with Intra-Industry Trade." *Journal of International Economics* 23: 357–367.

Grossman, Gene M. (1983). "Partially Mobile Capital." *Journal of International Economics* 15: 1–17.

Grossman, Gene M. (1984). "The Gains from International Factor Movements." *Journal of International Economics* 17: 73–83.

Grossman, Gene M. (1986). "Strategic Export Promotion: A Critique." In Paul R. Krugman (ed.), *Strategic Trade Policy and the New International Economics*. Cambridge, MA: MIT Press, 47–68.

Grossman, Gene M., and Elhanan Helpman (1991a). *Innovation and Growth*. Cambridge, MA: MIT Press.

Grossman, Gene M., and Elhanan Helpman (1991b). "Endogenous Product Cycles." *Economic Journal* 101: 1214–1229.

Grossman, Gene M., and Elhanan Helpman (1991c). "Quality Ladder and Product Cycles." *Quarterly Journal of Economics* 106: 557–586.

Grossman, Gene M., and Elhanan Helpman (1994). "Foreign Investment with Endogenous Protection," presented in a conference in honor of Jagdish N. Bhagwati.

Grubel, Herbert G., and Peter J. Lloyd (1975). *Intra-industry Trade: The Theory and Measurement of International Trade in Differentiated Products*. New York: Wiley.

Grubel, Herbert G., and Anthony D. Scott (1966). "The International Flow of Human Capital." *American Economic Review* 56 (No. 2): 268–274.

Gruenspecht, Howard K. (1988). "Export Subsidies for Differentiated Products." *Journal of International Economics* 24: 331–344.

Haberler, Gottfried (1950). "Some Problems in the Pure Theory of International Trade." *Economic Journal* 60: 223-240.

Haberler, Gottfried (1990). "Strategic Trade Policy and the New International Economics: A Critical Analysis." In Ronald W. Jones and Anne O. Krueger (eds.), *The Political Economy of International Trade*. Cambridge, MA: Basil Blackwell, 25–30.

Hagen, E. (1958). "An Economic Justification of Protectionism." *Quarterly Journal of Economics* 62: 496–514.

Hahn, Frank H. (1962). "The Stability of the Cournot Oligopoly Solution." *Review of Economic Studies* 32: 329–331.

Hamada, Koichi (1966). "Economic Growth and Long-Term International Capital Movement." *Yale Economic Essays* 6 (No. 1): 48–96.

Hamada, Koichi (1974). "An Economic Analysis of the Duty-Free Zone." *Journal of International Economics* 4: 225–241.

Hamada, Koichi (1977). "Taxing the Brain Drain: A Global Point of View." In Jagdish Bhagwati (ed.), *The New International Economic Order: The North-South Debate*. Cambridge, MA: MIT Press, 125–155.

Hamada, Koichi, and Jagdish N. Bhagwati (1976). "Domestic Distortions, Imperfect Information and the Brain Drain." In J. Bhagwati (ed.), *The Brain Drain and Taxation: Theory and Empirical Analysis*. Amsterdam: North-Holland, 139–153.

Hamilton, C., and Lar E. O. Svensson (1982). "On the Welfare Effects of a 'Duty-Free Zone.' " *Journal of International Economics* 12: 45–64.

Hamilton, C., and Lar E. O. Svensson (1983). "On the Choice between Capital Import and Labor Export." *European Economic Review* 20: 167–192.

Harris, John R., and Michael Todaro (1970). "Migration, Unemployment and Development: A Two-Sector Analysis." *American Economic Review* 60: 126–142.

Harris, Richard (1985). "Why Voluntary Export Restraints Are 'Voluntary.' " *Canadian Journal of Economics* 17 (No. 4): 799–809.

Hart, Oliver D. (1975). "On the Optimality of Equilibrium When the Market Structure Is Incomplete." *Journal of Economic Theory* 11: 418–443.

Hatta, Tatsuo (1977a). "A Recommendation for a Better Tariff Structure." *Econometrica* 45: 1859–1869.

Hatta, Tatsuo (1977b). "A Theory of Piecemeal Policy Recommendations." *Review of Economic Studies* 44: 1–21.

Heckscher, E. (1919). "The Effect of Foreign Trade on Distribution of Income." *Ekonomisk Tidskrift*, 497–512; reprinted in H. S. Ellis and L. A. Metzler (eds.), *A. E. A. Readings in the Theory of International Trade*. Philadelphia: Blakiston, 1949, 272–300

Helpman, Elhanan (1981). "International Trade in the Presence of Product Differentiation, Economies of Scale and Monopolistic Competition." *Journal of International Economics* 11: 305–340.

Helpman, Elhanan (1984a). "The Factor Content of Foreign Trade." *Economic Journal* 94: 84–94.

Helpman, Elhanan (1984b). "Increasing Returns, Imperfect Markets, and Trade Theory." In Ronald W. Jones and Peter B. Kenen (eds.), *Handbook of International Economics*, Vol. I, Amsterdam: Elsevier, 325–365.

Helpman, Elhanan (1984c). "A Simple Theory of International Trade with Multinational Corporations." *Journal of Political Economy* 92 (No. 3): 451–471.

Helpman, Elhanan (1985). "Multinational Corporations and Trade Structure." *Review of Economic Studies* 52: 443–458.

Helpman, Elhanan, and Paul R. Krugman (1985). *Market Structure and Foreign Trade*. Cambridge, MA: MIT Press.

Helpman, Elhanan, and Paul R. Krugman (1989). *Trade Policy and Market Structure*. Cambridge, MA: MIT Press.

Helpman, Elhanan, and Assaf Razin (1983). "Increasing Returns, Monopolistic Competition, and Factor Movements: A Welfare Analysis." *Journal of International Economics* 14: 263–276.

Hennart, Jean-François (1991). "The Transaction Cost Theory of the Multinational Enterprise." In Christos N. Pitelis and Roger Sugden (eds.), *The Nature of the Transnational Firm*. London: Routledge, 81–116.

Herberg, Horst (1969). "On the Shape of the Transformation Curve in the Case of Homogeneous Production Function." *Zeitschrift für die gesamte Staatswissenschaft* 125: 202-210.

Herberg, Horst, and Murray C. Kemp (1969). "Some Implications of Variable Returns to Scale." *Canadian Journal of Economics* 2: 403–415.

Herberg, Horst, and Murray C. Kemp (1971). "Factor Market Distortions, the Shape of the Locus of Competitive Outputs, and the Relation between Product Prices and Equilibrium Outputs." In J. N. Bhagwati, R. A. Mundell, R. W. Jones, and J. Vanek (eds.), *Trade, Balance of Payments and Growth: Papers in International Economics in Honor of Charles P. Kindleberger*. Amsterdam: North-Holland, 22–48.

Herberg, Horst, and Murray C. Kemp (1975). "Homothetic Production Functions and the Shape of the Production Possibility Locus: Comment." *Journal of Economic Theory* 11: 287–288.

Herberg, Horst, and Murray C. Kemp (1991). "Some Implications of Variable Returns to Scale: the Case of Industry-Specific Factors." *Canadian Journal of Economics* 24: 703–704.

Herberg, Horst, Murray C. Kemp, and Makoto Tawada (1982). "Further Implications of Variable Returns to Scale." *Journal of International Economics* 13: 65–84.

Hicks, John R. (1940). "The Valuation of Social Income." *Economica* 26 (May): 105–124.

Hicks, John R. (1953). "An Inaugural Lecture." *Oxford Economic Papers* n.s. 2: 117–135.

Hirsch, Seev (1976). "An International Trade and Investment Theory of the Firm." *Oxford Economic Papers* n.s. 28 (2): 258–270.

Hood, Neil, and Stephen Young (1979). *The Economics of Multinational Enterprise*. London: Longman.

Horst, Thomas (1971). "The Theory of the Multinational Firm: Optimal Behavior under Different Tariff and Tax Rules." *Journal of Political Economy* 79: 1059–1072.

Horst, Thomas (1973). "The Simple Analytics of Multi-National Firm Behavior." In Michael B. Connolly and Alexander K. Swoboda (eds.), *International Trade and Money*. London: Allen & Unwin, 72–84.

Horstmann, Ignatius J., and James R. Markusen (1986). "Up the Average Cost Curve: Inefficient Entry and the New Protectionism." *Journal of International Economics* 20: 225–247.

Horstmann, Ignatius J., and James R. Markusen (1987a). "Licensing versus Direct Investment: A Model of Internalization by the Multinational Enterprise." *Canadian Journal of Economics* 20 (No. 3): 464–481.

Horstmann, Ignatius J., and James R. Markusen (1987b). "Strategic Investments and the Development of Multinationals." *International Economic Review* 28 (No. 1): 109–121.

Horstmann, Ignatius J., and James R. Markusen (1992). "Endogenous Market Structures in International Trade (Natura Facit Saltum)." *Journal of International Economics* 32: 109–129.

Hotaka, R. (1971). "Some Basic Problems on Excess Demand Functions." *Econometrica* 39 (2): 305–307.

Hufbauer, Gary C., and John G. Chilas (1974). "Specialization by Industrial Countries: Extent and Consequences." In Herbert Giersch (ed.), *The International Division of Labour: Problems and Perspective*. Tübingen: Mohr.

Husseini, S. Y., J.-M. Lasry, and M. J. P. Magill (1990). "Existence of Equilibrium with Incomplete Markets." *Journal of Mathematical Economics* 19: 39–67.

Hwang, Hong (1984). "Intra-industry Trade and Oligopoly: A Conjectural Variations Approach." *Canadian Journal of Economics* 17: 126–137.

Hwang, Hong, and Chao-cheng Mai (1988). "On the Equivalence of Tariffs and Quotas under Duopoly." *Journal of International Economics* 24: 373-380.

Hwang, Hong, Kaz Miyagiwa, and Kar-yiu Wong (1993). "Optimal Technology Choice and Immiserizing Export Subsidy." Mimeo, University of Washington, Seattle.

Hwang, Hong, Kaz Miyagiwa, and Kar-yiu Wong (1994). "Revenue Constraints and Choice of Export Subsidy Policy." Mimeo, University of Washington, Seattle.

Hymer, Stephen H. (1960). *The International Operations of National Firms: A Study of Direct Foreign Investment*. Ph. D. dissertation, MIT. Published by The MIT Press, 1976.

Hymer, Stephen H., and Robert Rowthorn (1970). "Multinational Corporations and International Oligopoly: The Non-American Challenge." In Charles P. Kindleberger (ed.), *The International Corporations*, Cambridge, MA: MIT Press, 57–91.

Ide, Toyonari, and Akira Takayama (1991). "Variable Returns to Scale, Paradoxes, and Global Correspondence in the Theory of International Trade." In Akira Takayama, Michihiro Ohyama, and Hiroshi Ohta (eds.), *Trade, Policy, and International Adjustments*. San Diego: Academic Press, 108–154.

Ide, Toyonari, and Akira Takayama (1993). "Variable Returns to Scale, Comparative Statics Paradoxes, and the Theory of Comparative Advantage." In Horst Herberg and Ngo Van Long (eds.), *Trade, Welfare, and Economic Policies: Essays in Honor of Murray C. Kemp*. Ann Arbor: University of Michigan Press, 67–119.

Inada, Ken-Ichi, and Murray C. Kemp (1969). "International Capital Movements and the Theory of Tariffs and Trade: Comment." *Quarterly Journal of Economics* 83 (No. 3): 524–528.

Inoue, Tadashi (1981). "A Generalization of the Samuelson Reciprocity Relations, the Stolper-Samuelson Theorem and the Rybczynski Theorem under Variable Returns to Scale." *Journal of International Economics* 11: 79–98.

Ishikawa, Jota (1992). "Learning by Doing, Changes in Industrial Structure and Trade Patterns, and Economic Growth in a Small Open Economy." *Journal of International Economics* 33: 221–244.

Ishikawa, Jota (1994). "Revisiting the Stolper-Samuelson and the Rybczynski Theorems with Production Externalities." *Canadian Journal of Economics* 27 (No. 1): 101–111.

Itoh, Motoshige, and Kazuharu Kiyono (1987). "Welfare-Enhancing Export Subsidies." *Journal of Political Economy* 95 (February): 115–137.

Jensen, Richard, and Marie Thursby (1986). "A Strategic Approach to the Product Life Cycle." *Journal of International Economics* 21: 269–284.

Johnson, Harry G. (1953–4). "Optimum Tariffs and Retaliation." *Review of Economic Studies* 21 (No. 55): 142–153.

Johnson, Harry G. (1954). "Increasing Productivity, Income-Price Trends and the Trade Balance." *Economic Journal* 64: 462–485.

Johnson, Harry G. (1955). "Economic Expansion and International Trade." *Manchester School of Economic and Social Studies* 23: 95–112.

Johnson, Harry G. (1957). "Factor Endowments, International Trade, and Factor Prices." *Manchester School of Economic and Social Studies* 25 (No. 3): 270–283.

Johnson, Harry G. (1965). "Optimal Trade Intervention in the Presence of Domestic Distortions." In Richard E. Caves, Harry G. Johnson, and Peter B. Kenen (eds.), *Trade, Growth and the Balance of Payments: Essays in Honor of Gottfried Haberler*. Amsterdam: North-Holland, 3–34.

Johnson, Harry G. (1966). "Factor Market Distortions and the Shape of the Transformation Curve." *Econometrica* 34: 686–698.

Johnson, Harry G. (1967a). "The Possibility of Income Losses from Increased Efficiency or Factor Accumulation in the Presence of Tariffs." *Economic Journal* 77: 151–154.

Johnson, Harry G. (1967b). "Some Economic Aspects of Brain Drain." *Pakistan Development Review* 7: 379–411.

Johnson, Harry G. (1970). "The Efficiency and Welfare Implications of the International Corporation." In Charles P. Kindleberger (ed.), *The International Corporation*. Cambridge, MA: MIT Press, 35–56.

Jones, Ronald W. (1956–57). "Factor Proportions and the Heckscher-Ohlin Theorem." *Review of Economic Studies* 24: 1–10. Reprinted in Jagdish N. Bhagwati (ed.), *International Trade: Selected Readings*. Middlesex, England: Penguin Books Ltd., 1969, 77–92.

Jones, Ronald W. (1965). "The Structure of Simple General Equilibrium Models." *Journal of Political Economy* 73: 557–572.

Jones, Ronald W. (1967). "International Capital Movements and the Theory of Tariffs and Trade." *Quarterly Journal of Economics* 81: 1–38.

Jones, Ronald W. (1968). "Variable Returns to Scale in General Equilibrium Theory." *International Economic Review* 9: 261–272.

Jones, Ronald W. (1971a). "A Three-Factor Model in Theory, Trade, and History." In J. N. Bhagwati, R. A. Mundell, R. W. Jones, and J. Vanek (eds.), *Trade, Balance of Payments and Growth: Papers in International Economics in Honor of Charles P. Kindleberger*. Amsterdam: North-Holland, 3–21.

Jones, Ronald W. (1971b). "Distortions in Factor Markets and the General Equilibrium Model of Production." *Journal of Political Economy* 74: 437–459.

Jones, Ronald W. (1980). "Comparative and Absolute Advantage." *Schweizerische Zeitschrift für Volkswirtschaft und Statistik* 3: 235–259.

Jones, Ronald W., and Stephen T. Easton (1989). "Perspectives on 'Buy-Outs' and the Ramaswami Effect." *Journal of International Economics* 27: 363-371.

Jones, Ronald W., and J. Peter Neary (1984). "The Positive Theory of International Trade." In Ronald W. Jones and Peter B. Kenen (eds.), *Handbook of International Economics*, Vol. I, Amsterdam: North-Holland, 1–62.

Jones, Ronald W., and Roy Ruffin (1975). "Trade Patterns with Capital Mobility." In M. Parkin and A. R. Nobay (eds.), *Current Economic Problems*, Cambridge: Cambridge University Press, 307–322.

Jones, Ronald W., and J. Scheinkman (1977). "The Relevance of the Two-Sector Production Model in Trade Theory." *Journal of Political Economy* 85: 909–935.

Jones, Ronald W., Isaias Coelho, and Stephen T. Easton (1986). "The Theory of International Factor Flows: The Basic Model." *Journal of International Economics* 20: 313–327.

Jones, Ronald W., J. Peter Neary, and Frances P. Ruane (1983). "Two-Way Capital Flows: Cross-Hauling in A Model of Foreign Investment." *Journal of International Economics* 14: 357–366.

Kaldor, Nicholas (1939). "Welfare Propositions of Economics and Interpersonal Compensations of Utility." *Economic Journal* 49: 549–552.

Katrak, Homi (1977). "Multinational Monopolies and Commercial Policy." *Oxford Economic Papers* 29: 283–291.

Katz, Eliakim, and Oded Stark (1984). "Migration and Asymmetric Information: Comment." *American Economic Review* 74 (No. 3): 533–534.

Katz, Michael L., and Carl Shapiro (1985). "Network Externalities, Competition, and Compatibility." *American Economic Review* 75: 424–440.

Kemp, Murray C. (1962a). "The Gains from International Trade." *Economic Journal* 72: 803–819.

Kemp, Murray C. (1962b). "Foreign Investment and the National Advantage." *Economic Record* 38: 56–62.

Kemp, Murray C. (1964). *The Pure Theory of International Trade*. Englewood Cliffs, N.J.: Prentice-Hall.

Kemp, Murray C. (1966). "The Gain from International Trade and Investment: A Neo-Heckscher-Ohlin Approach." *American Economic Review* 56: 788–809.

Kemp, Murray C. (1969). *The Pure Theory of International Trade and Investment*. Englewood Cliffs, N.J.: Prentice-Hall.

Kemp, Murray C. (1974). "Learning by Doing: Formal Tests for Intervention in an Open Economy." *Keio Economic Studies* 11: 1–7.

Kemp, Murray C. (1993). "The Welfare Gains from International Migration." *Keio Economic Studies* 33: 1–5.

Kemp, Murray C., and Ken-ichi Inada (1969). "International Capital Movements and the Theory of Tariffs and Trade: Comment." *Quarterly Journal of Economics* 83: 524–528.

Kemp, Murray C., and Ngo V. Long (1979). "The Under-Exploitation of Natural Resources: A Model with Overlapping Generations." *Economic Record* 55: 214–221.

Kemp, Murray C., and Takashi Negishi (1969). "Domestic Distortions, Tariffs and the Theory of Optimum Subsidy." *Journal of Political Economy* 77 (No. 6): 1011–1013.

Kemp, Murray C., and Takashi Negishi (1970). "Variable Returns to Scale, Commodity Taxes, Factor Market Distortions and Their Implications for Trade Gains." *Swedish Journal of Economics* 72 (No. 1): 1–11.

Kemp, Murray C., and Michihiro Ohyama (1978). "The Gain from Trade under Conditions of Uncertainty." *Journal of International Economics* 8: 139–141.

Kemp, Murray C., and Masayuki Okawa (1995a). "The Gains from Free Trade under the Condition of Imperfect Competition: A Conjectural Variations Approach." in Murray C. Kemp (ed.), *The Gains from Trade and the Gains from Aid.* London: Routledge (forthcoming).

Kemp, Murray C., and Masayuki Okawa (1995b). "The International Diffusion of the Fruits of Technical Progress under Imperfect Competition." in Murray C. Kemp (ed.), *The Gains from Trade and the Gains from Aid.* London: Routledge (forthcoming).

Kemp, Murray C., and Albert G. Schweinberger (1991). "Variable Returns to Scale, Non-Uniqueness of Equilibrium and the Gains from International Trade." *Review of Economic Studies* 58: 807–816.

Kemp, Murray C., and Henry Y. Wan, Jr. (1972). "The Gains from Free Trade." *International Economic Review* 13: 509–522.

Kemp, Murray C., and Henry Y. Wan, Jr. (1976). "An Elementary Proposition Concerning the Formation of Customs Unions." *Journal of International Economics* 6: 95–97.

Kemp, Murray C., and Henry Y. Wan, Jr. (1986a). "Trade Gains with and without Lump-sum Compensation." *Journal of International Economics* 21: 99–110.

Kemp, Murray C., and Henry Y. Wan, Jr. (1986b). "The Comparison of Second-Best Equilibria: The Case of Customs Unions." In D. Bös and C. Seidl (eds.), *Welfare Economics of the Second Best*, Supplementum 5 of *Zeitschrift für Nationalökonomie*. Vienna: Springer-Verlag, 161–167.

Kemp, Murray C., and Henry Y. Wan, Jr. (1989). "Distorting and Non-Distorting Compensation: The Case of Trade Gains." Mimeo, University of New South Wales, Sydney, Australia.

Kemp, Murray C., and Henry Y. Wan, Jr. (1993). *Welfare Economics of International Trade and Investment*. Chur, Switzerland: Harwood Academic Publishers.

Kemp, Murray C., and Kar-yiu Wong (1993). "Paradoxes Associated with the Administration of Foreign Aid." *Journal of Development Economics* 42: 197–204.

Kemp, Murray C., and Kar-yiu Wong (1995a). "Gains from Trade with Overlapping Generations." *Economic Theory* (forthcoming). Also in Murray C. Kemp (ed.), *The Gains from Trade and the Gains from Aid.* London: Routledge (forthcoming).

Kemp, Murray C., and Kar-yiu Wong (1995b). "Gains from Trade when Markets Are Possibly Incomplete." In Murray C. Kemp (ed.), *The Gains from Trade and the Gains from Aid.* London: Routledge (forthcoming).

Kemp, Murray C., and Kar-yiu Wong (1995c). "Gains from Trade for a Monetary Economy when Markets Are Possibly Incomplete." In Murray C. Kemp (ed.), *The Gains from Trade and the Gains from Aid.* London: Routledge (forthcoming).

Kemp, Murray C., Yoshio Kimura, and Makoto Tawada (1990). "The Global Correspondence Principle." *Economics Letters* 34: 1–4.

Kenen, Peter B. (1971). "Migration, The Terms of Trade, and Economic Welfare in the Source Country." In Jagdish Bhagwati et al. (eds.), *Trade, Balance of Payments, and Growth: Papers in International Economics in Honor of Charles P. Kindleberger*. Amsterdam: North-Holland, 238–260.

Kennan, John, and Raymond Riezman (1988). "Do Big Countries Win Trade Wars?" *International Economic Review* 29 (No. 1): 81–85.

Kindleberger, Charles P. (1969). *American Business Abroad*. New Haven: Yale University Press.

Kohli, Ulrich (1991). *Technology, Duality, and Foreign Trade*. Ann Arbor: University of Michigan Press.

Kojima, Kiyoshi (1978). *Direct Foreign Investment: A Japanese Model of Multinational*. London: Croom Helm.

Kreps, David, and José A. Scheinkman (1983). "Quantity Precommitment and Bertrand Competition Yield Cournot Outcomes." *Bell Journal of Economics* 14: 326–337.

Krishna, Kala (1989). "Trade Restrictions As Facilitating Practices." *Journal of International Economics* 26: 251–270.

Krishna, Kala, and Marie C. Thursby (1990). "Trade Policy with Imperfect Competition: A Selective Survey." In Colin A. Carter, Alex F. McCalla, and Jerry A. Sharples (eds.), *Imperfect Competition and Political Economy: The New Trade Theory in Agricultural Trade Research*. Boulder: Westview Press, 9–35.

Krishna, Kala, and Marie C. Thursby (1991). "Optimal Policies with Strategic Distortions." *Journal of International Economics* 31: 291–308.

Krueger, Anne O. (1974). "The Political Economy of the Rent-Seeking Society." *American Economic Review* 64: 291–303.

Krueger, Anne O. (1984). "Trade Policies in Developed Countries." In Ronald W. Jones and Peter B. Kenen (eds.), *Handbook of International Economics*. Vol. 1. Amsterdam: North-Holland, 519–569.

Krueger, Anne O., and Hugo Sonnenschein (1967). "The Terms of Trade, the Gains from Trade and Price Divergence." *International Economic Review* 8: 121–127.

Krugman, Paul R. (1979a). "Increasing Returns, Monopolistic Competition, and International Trade." *Journal of International Economics* 9 (November): 469–479.

Krugman, Paul R. (1979b). "A Model of Innovation, Technology Transfer, and the World Distribution of Income." *Journal of Political Economy* 87 (No. 2): 253–265.

Krugman, Paul R. (1980). "Scale Economies, Product Differentiation, and the Pattern of Trade." *American Economic Review* 70 (December): 950–959.

Krugman, Paul R. (1981). "Intraindustry Specialization and the Gains from Trade." *Journal of Political Economy* 89 (No. 5): 959–973.

Krugman, Paul R. (1983). "The 'New Theories' of International Trade and the Multinational Enterprise." In Charles P. Kindleberger and David B. Audretsch (eds.), *The Multinational Corporation in the 1980s*. Cambridge, MA: MIT Press, 1983, 57–73.

Krugman, Paul R. (1984). "Import Protection as Export Promotion: International Competition in the Presence of Oligopoly and Economies of Scale." In Henryk Kierzkowski (ed.), *Monopolistic Competition and International Trade*. Oxford: Clarendon Press, 180–193.

Krugman, Paul R. (1987a). "Increasing Returns and the Theory of International Trade." In Truman F. Bewley (ed.), *Advances in Economic Theory, Fifth World Congress*. Cambridge: Cambridge University Press, 301–328.

Krugman, Paul R. (1987b). "Is Free Trade Passé?" *Journal of Economic Perspectives* 1 (2): 131–144.

Krugman, Paul R. (1987c). "The Narrow Moving Band, the Dutch Disease, and the Competitive Consequences of Mrs. Thatcher: Notes on Trade in the Presence of Dynamic Economics." *Journal of Development Economics* 27: 41–55.

Krugman, Paul R. (1991). *Geography and Trade*. Cambridge, MA: MIT Press.

Kuhn, Peter, and Ian Wooton (1987). "International Factor Movements in the Presence of a Fixed Factor." *Journal of International Economics* 20: 123–140.

Kuhn, Peter, and Ian Wooton (1991). "Immigration, International Trade, and the Wages of Native Wages." In John M. Abowd and Richard B. Freeman (eds.), *Immigration, Trade, and the Labor Market*. Chicago: University of Chicago Press, 285–304.

Kwok, Viem, and Hayne Leland (1982). "An Economic Model of the Brain Drain." *American Economic Review* 72 (No. 1): 91–100.

Kwok, Viem (Peter), and Hayne Leland (1984). "Migration and Asymmetric Information: Reply." *American Economic Review* 74 (No. 3): 535.

Laffont, Jean-Jacques (1989). *The Economics of Uncertainty and Information*. Cambridge, MA: MIT Press.

Lai, Edwin L. C. (1994). "The Product Cycle and the World Distribution of Income: A Reformulation." Mimeo, Vanderbilt University, Nashville.

Laing, N. F. (1961). "Factor Price Equalisation in International Trade and Returns to Scale." *Economic Record* 37: 339–351.

Lancaster, Kelvin (1979). *Variety, Equity, and Efficiency*. New York: Columbia University Press.

Lancaster, Kelvin (1980). "Intra-industry Trade under Perfect Monopolistic Competition." *Journal of International Economics* 10: 151–175.

Lancaster, Kelvin (1984). "Protection and Product Differentiation." In Henryk Kierzkowski (ed.), *Monopolistic Competition and International Trade*. Oxford: Clarendon Press, 137–156.

Lawrence, Colin, and Pablo T. Spiller (1983). "Product Diversity, Economies of Scale, and International Trade." *Quarterly Journal of Economics* 98: 63–83.

Leamer, Edward E. (1980). "The Leontief Paradox, Reconsidered." *Journal of Political Economy* 88: 495–503.

Leamer, Edward E. (1984). *Sources of International Comparative Advantage*. Cambridge, MA: MIT Press.

Lefeber, Louis (1971). "Trade and Minimum Wage Rates." In J. N. Bhagwati, R. A. Mundell, R. W. Jones, and J. Vanek (eds.), *Trade, Balance of Payments and Growth: Papers in International Economics in Honor of Charles P. Kindleberger*. Amsterdam: North-Holland, 91–114.

Leontief, Wassily W. (1953). "Domestic Production and Foreign Trade: The American Capital Position Re-Examined." *Proceedings of the American Philosophical Society* 97: 329–349. Reprinted in Jagdish N. Bhagwati (ed.), *International Trade: Selected Readings*. Middlesex, England: Penguin, 1969, 93–139.

Lerner, Abba P. (1952). "Factor Prices and International Trade." *Economica* n.s. 19: 1–15.

Lerner, Abba P. (1936). "The Symmetry between Import and Export Taxes." *Economica* 3: 306–313.

Levinsohn, James A. (1989). "Strategic Trade Policy When Firms Can Invest Abroad: When Are Tariffs and Quotas Equivalent?" *Journal of International Economics* 27: 129–146.

Lien, Da-Hsiang Donald (1987). "Economic Analysis of Brain Drain." *Journal of Development Economics* 25: 33–43.

Lien, Da-Hsiang Donald (1993). "Asymmetric Information and the Brain Drain." *Journal of Population Economics* 6: 169–180.

Lipsey, R. G., and Kelvin Lancaster (1956–57). "The General Theory of Second Best." *Review of Economic Studies* 24: 11–32.

Lipsey, Robert E., and Merle Yahr Weiss (1981). "Foreign Production and Exports in Manufacturing Industries." *Review of Economics and Statistics* 63 (No. 4): 488–494.

Lipsey, Robert E., and Merle Yahr Weiss (1984). "Foreign Production and Exports of Individual Firms." *Review of Economics and Statistics* 66 (No. 2): 304–308.

Little, Ian M. D. (1949). "The Foundations of Welfare Economics." *Oxford Economic Papers* n.s. 1: 227–246.

Little, Ian M. D., and J. A. Mirrlees (1969). *Manual of Industrial Project Analysis in Developing Countries*, Vol. 2. Paris: Organisation of Economic Cooperation and Development.

Lloyd, Peter J. (1973). "Optimal Intervention in A Distortion-Ridden Open Economy." *Economic Record* 49: 377–393.

Lloyd, Peter J. (1974). "A More General Theory of Price Distortions in Open Economy." *Journal of International Economics* 4: 365–386.

Lucas, Robert E. Jr. (1988). "On the Mechanics of Economic Development." *Journal of Monetary Economics* 22: 3–42.

MacDougall, G. D. A. (1960). "The Benefits and Costs of Private Investment from Abroad: A Theoretical Approach." *Bulletin of the Oxford University Institute of Statistics* 22 (No. 3): 189–211.

Magee, Stephen P. (1973). "Factor Market Distortions, Production and Trade: A Survey." *Oxford Economic Papers* n. s. 25: 1–43.

Magee, Stephen P. (1976). *International Trade and Distortions in Factor Markets*. New York: Marcel Dekker.

Magee, Stephen P. (1977). "Information and the Multinational Corporation: An Appropriability Theory of Direct Foreign Investment." In Jagdish N. Bhagwati (ed.), *The New International Economic Order*. Cambridge, MA: MIT Press, 317–340.

Mai, Chao-cheng, and Hong Hwang (1988). "Why Voluntary Export Restraints Are Voluntary: An Extension." *Canadian Journal of Economics* 16 (No. 4): 877–882.

Markusen, James R. (1981). "Trade and the Gains from Trade with Imperfect Competition." *Journal of International Economics* 11: 531–551.

Markusen, James R. (1983). "Factor Movements and Commodity Trade As Complements." *Journal of International Economics* 14: 341–356.

Markusen, James R. (1984). "Multinationals, Multi-Plant Economies, and the Gains from Trade." *Journal of International Economics* 16: 205–224.

Markusen, James R. (1988). "Production, Trade, and Migration with Differentiated, Skilled Workers." *Canadian Journal of Economics* 21: 492–506.

Markusen, James R., and James R. Melvin (1979). "Tariffs, Capital Mobility, and Foreign Ownership." *Journal of International Economics* 9: 395–409.

Markusen, James R., and James R. Melvin (1981). "Trade, Factor Prices, and the Gains from Trade with Increasing Returns to Scale." *Canadian Journal of Economics* 14 (No. 3): 450–469.

Markusen, James R., and James R. Melvin (1984). "The Gains-from-Trade Theorem with Increasing Returns to Scale." In Henryk Kierzkowski (ed.), *Monopolistic Competition and International Trade*. Oxford: Clarendon Press, 10–33.

Markusen, James R., and Lar E. O. Svensson (1985). "Trade in Goods and Factors with International Differences in Technology." *International Economic Review* 9: 395–410.

Markusen, James R., and Albert G. Schweinberger (1990). "The Positive Theory of Production Externalities under Perfect Competition." *Journal of International Economics* 29: 69–91.

Markusen, James R., and Anthony J. Venables (1988). "Trade Policy with Increasing Returns and Imperfect Competition: Contradictory Results from Competing Assumptions." *Journal of International Economics* 24: 299–316.

Marshall, Alfred (1879). *Pure Theory of Foreign Trade*, originally printed for private circulation, reprinted by London School of Economics and Political Science, 1930.

Marshall, Alfred (1890). *Principles of Economics*, eighth edition. London: Macmillan, 1920.

Martin, Philip L. (1994). "Germany: Reluctant Land of Immigration." In Wayne A. Cornelius, James F. Hollifield, and Philip L. Martin, *Controlling Immigration: A Global Perspective*. Stanford: Stanford University Press.

Martin, Ricardo (1977). "Immiserizing Growth for a Tariff-Distorted, Small Economy: Further Analysis." *Journal of International Economics* 7: 323–328.

Maskus, Keith E. (1985). "A Test of the Heckscher-Ohlin-Vanek Theorem: The Leontief Commonplace." *Journal of International Economics* 19: 201–212.

Mayer, Wolfgang (1974a). "Short-run and Long-run Equilibrium for a Small Open Economy." *Journal of Political Economy* 82: 955–967.

Mayer, Wolfgang (1974b). "Homothetic Production Functions and the Shape of the Production Possibility Locus." *Journal of Economic Theory* 8: 101–110.

Mayer, Wolfgang (1974c). "Variable Returns to Scale in General Equilibrium Theory: A Comment." *International Economic Review* 15: 225–235.

Mayer, Wolfgang (1981). "Theoretical Considerations on Negotiated Tariff Adjustment." *Oxford Economic Papers* n.s. 33 (1): 135–153.

McCulloch, Rachel, and Janet L. Yellen (1975). "Consequences of a Tax on the Brain Drain for Unemployment and Income Inequality in the LDCs." *Journal of Development Economics*, 2. Reprinted in J. Bhagwati (ed.), *The Brain Drain and Taxation: Theory and Empirical Analysis*. Amsterdam: North-Holland, 155–170.

Meade, James E. (1952). *A Geometry of International Trade*. London: Allen and Unwin.

Meade, James E. (1955). *Trade and Welfare*. London: Oxford University Press.

Melvin, James R. (1968). "Production and Trade with Two Factors and Three Goods." *American Economic Review* 58: 1248–1268.

Melvin, James R. (1969). "Increasing Returns to Scale as a Determinant of Trade." *Canadian Journal of Economics* 2: 389–402.

Melvin, James R., and Robert D. Warne (1973). "Monopoly and the Theory of International Trade." *Journal of International Economics* 3: 117–134.

Metzler, Lloyd (1949). "Tariffs, the Terms of Trade and the Distributions of National Income." *Journal of Political Economy* 57 (No. 1): 1–29.

Mill, J. S. (1909). *Principles of Political Economy*, ed. Sir W. J. Ashley, Book III, Chapter 18. London: Longmans, Green & Company.

Minabe, Nobuo (1966). "The Stolper-Samuelson Theorem under Conditions of Variable Returns to Scale." *Oxford Economic Papers* 58: 204–212.

Minabe, Nobuo (1981). "Tariffs, Capital Export and Immiserizing Growth." *Journal of International Economics* 11: 117–121.

Minhas, B. S. (1962). "The Homohypallagic Production Function, Factor Intensity Reversals, and the Heckscher-Ohlin Theorem." *Journal of Political Economy* 70: 138–156.

Miyagiwa, Kaz (1991). "Scale Economies in Education and the Brain Drain Problem." *International Economic Review* 32 (No. 3): 743–759.

Miyagiwa, Kaz (1993). "On the Impossibility of Immiserizing Growth." *International Economic Journal* 7: 1–13.

Motta, Massimo (1992). "Multinational Firms and the Tariff-Jumping Argument." *European Economic Review* 36: 1557-1571.

Mundell, Robert (1957). "International Trade and Factor Mobility." *American Economic Review* 67: 321–335. Reprinted in Jagdish Bhagwati (ed.), *International Trade: Selected Readings*. Cambridge, MA: MIT Press, 1987, 21–36.

Mussa, Michael (1974). "Tariffs and the Distribution of Income: The Importance of Factor Specificity, Substitutability, and Intensity in the Short and Long Run." *Journal of Political Economy* 82: 1191–1204.

Neary, J. Peter (1978a). "Dynamic Stability and the Theory of Factor-Market Distortions." *American Economic Review* 68: 671–682.

Neary, J. Peter (1978b). "Short-run Capital Specificity and the Pure Theory of International Trade." *Economic Journal* 88: 488–510.

Neary, J. Peter (1993). "Welfare Effects of Tariffs and Investment Taxes," in Wilfred J. Ethier, Elhanan Helpman, and J. Peter Neary (eds.), *Theory, Policy and Dynamics* in *International Trade*. Cambridge: Cambridge University Press, 131–156.

Neary, J. Peter, and Frances Ruane (1988). "International Capital Mobility, Shadow Prices, and the Cost of Protection." *International Economic Review* 29 (No. 4): 571–585.

Neary, J. Peter, and Albert G. Schweinberger (1986). "Factor Content Functions and the Theory of International Trade." *Review of Economic Studies* 53: 421–432.

Negishi, Takashi (1965). "Foreign Investment and the Long-Run National Advantage." *Economic Record* 41: 628–633.

Negishi, Takashi (1972). *General Equilibrium Theory and International Trade*. Amsterdam: North-Holland.

Newbery, David M. G., and Joseph E. Stiglitz (1984). "Pareto Inferior Trade." *Review of Economic Studies* 51: 1–12.

Ng, Yew-Kwang (1983). *Welfare Economics: Introduction and Development of Basic Concepts*, revised edition. London: Macmillan.

Ohlin, Bertil (1933). *Interregional and International Trade*. Cambridge, MA: Harvard University Press.

Ohyama, Michihiro (1972). "Trade and Welfare in General Equilibrium." *Keio Economic Studies* 2: 37–73.

Oniki, H., and H. Uzawa (1965). "Patterns of Trade and Investment in A Dynamic Model of International Trade." *Review of Economic Studies* 32 (No. 1): 15–38.

Panagariya, Arvind (1980). "Variable Returns to Scale in General Equilibrium Theory Once Again." *Journal of International Economics* 10: 499–526.

Panagariya, Arvind (1981). "Variable Returns to Scale in Production and Patterns of Specialization." *American Economic Review* 71 (No. 1): 221–230.

Panagariya, Arvind (1983). "Variable Returns to Scale and the Heckscher-Ohlin and Factor-Price-Equalization Theorems." *Weltwirtschaftliches Archiv* 119: 259–280.

Panagariya, Arvind (1986). "Increasing Returns, Dynamic Stability, and International Trade." *Journal of International Economics* 20: 43–63.

Piore, Michael J. (1979). *Birds of Passage: Migrant Labor and Industrial Societies*. Cambridge: Cambridge University Press.

Pitt, Mark M. (1981). "Smuggling and Price Disparity." *Journal of International Economics* 11: 447–458.

Pomery, John (1984). "Uncertainty in Trade Models." In *Handbook in International Economics*, R. W. Jones and P. B. Kenen (eds.), Vol. I. Amsterdam: North-Holland, 419–465.

Prebisch, Raúl (1959). "Commercial Policy in the Underdeveloped Countries." *American Economic Review, Papers and Proceedings* 44: 251–273.

Quibria, M. G. (1988). "On Generalising the Economic Analysis of International Migration: A Note." *Canadian Journal of Economics* 21: 874–876.

Radner, Roy (1972). "Existence of Equilibrium of Plans, Prices, and Price Expectation in a Sequence of Markets." *Econometrica* 40 (No. 2): 289–303.

Ramaswami, V. K. (1968). "International Factor Movement and the National Advantage." *Economica* 35: 309–310.

Rauch, James E. (1989). "Increasing Returns to Scale and the Pattern of Trade." *Journal of International Economics* 26: 359–369.

Ray, Edward John (1989). "The Determinants of Foreign Direct Investment in the United States, 1979–85." In Robert C. Feenstra (ed.), *Trade Policies for International Competitiveness*. Chicago: University of Chicago Press, 53–77.

Razin, Assaf, and Efraim Sadka (1992). "International Migration and International Trade." Cambridge, MA: NBER working paper no. 4230.

Razin, Assaf, and Kar-yiu Wong (1993). "International Capital Movements under Uncertainty: An Extension." In Horst Herberg and Ngo Van Long (eds.), *Trade, Welfare and Economic Policies: Essays in Honor of Murray C. Kemp*. Ann Arbor: University of Michigan Press, 301–324.

Ricardo, David (1817). *The Principles of Political Economy and Taxation*, reprinted by London: J. M. Dent & Sons Ltd., 1977.

Riezman, Raymond (1982). "Tariff Retaliation from a Strategic Viewpoint." *Southern Economic Journal* 48 (No. 3): 583–593.

Riley, John (1970). "Ranking of Tariffs under Monopoly Power in Trade: An Extension." *Quarterly Journal of Economics* 84 (No. 4): 710–712.

Rivera-Batiz, Francisco L. (1982). "International Migration, Non-Traded Goods, and Economic Welfare in the Source Country." *Journal of Development Economics* 11: 81–90.

Rodriguez, Carlos A. (1974). "The Non-Equivalence of Tariffs and Quotas under Retaliation." *Journal of International Economics* 4: 295–298.

Rodriguez, Carlos A. (1975a). "Trade in Technological Knowledge and the National Advantage." *Journal of Political Economy* 83: 121–135.

Rodriguez, Carlos A. (1975b). "Brain Drain and Economic Growth: A Dynamic Model." *Journal of Development Economics* 2: 223–247.

Ruffin, Roy J. (1979). "Growth and the Long-Run Theory of International Capital Movement." *American Economic Review* 69 (No. 5): 832–842.

Ruffin, Roy J. (1981). "Trade and Factor Movements with Three Factors and Two Goods." *Economics Letters* 7: 177–182.

Ruffin, Roy J. (1984). "International Factor Movements." In Ronald W. Jones and Peter B. Kenen (eds.), *Handbook of International Economics*, Vol. I. Amsterdam: Elsevier, 237–288.

Rugman, Alan M. (1981). "Internalization as a General Theory of Foreign Direct Investment: A Re-Appraisal of the Literature." *Weltwirtschaftliches Archiv* 116: 365–379.

Rybczynski, T. (1955). "Factor Endowment and Relative Commodity Prices." *Economica* 22 (84): 336–341.

Salvatore, Dominick (1991). "Trade Protection and Foreign Direct Investment in the U. S." *Annals*, AAPSS, No. 516, 91–105.

Samuelson, Paul A. (1939). "The Gains from International Trade." *Canadian Journal of Economics and Political Science* 5: 195–205.

Samuelson, Paul A. (1947). *Foundations of Economic Analysis*. Cambridge, MA: Harvard University Press.

Samuelson, Paul A. (1948). "International Trade and the Equalization of Factor Prices." *Economic Journal* 58: 181–197.

Samuelson, Paul A. (1949). "International Factor-Price Equalization Once Again." *Economic Journal* 59: 181–197.

Samuelson, Paul A. (1950). "Evaluation of Real National Income." *Oxford Economic Papers* 2 (January): 1–29.

Samuelson, Paul A. (1951). "Abstract of a Theorem Concerning Substitutability in Open Leontief Models." In T. C. Koopmans, *Activity Analysis of Production and Allocation*. New York: Wiley, 142–146.

Samuelson, Paul A. (1952). "The Transfer Problem and Transport Cost: The Terms of Trade When Impediments Are Absent." *Economic Journal* 64: 278–304.

Samuelson, Paul A. (1953). "Prices of Factors and Goods in General Equilibrium." *Review of Economic Studies* 21: 1–20.

Samuelson, Paul A. (1956). "Social Indifference Curves." *Quarterly Journal of Economics* 70: 1–22.

Samuelson, Paul A. (1958). "An Exact Consumption Loan Model of Interest, with or without the Social Contrivance of Money." *Journal of Political Economy* 66: 467–482.

Samuelson, Paul A. (1962). "The Gains from International Trade Once Again." *Economic Journal* 72: 820–829.

Samuelson, Paul A. (1971). "On the Trail of Conventional Beliefs about the Transfer Problem." In in Jagdish N. Bhagwati, Ronald W. Jones, Robert A. Mundell, and Jaroslav Vanek (eds.), *Trade, Balance of Payments, and Growth: Papers in International Economics in Honor of Charles P. Kindleberger*. Amsterdam: North-Holland, 327–351.

Sapir, André (1983). "Foreign Competition, Immigration and Structural Adjustment." *Journal of International Economics* 14: 381–394.

Savosnick, K. M. (1958). "The Box Diagram and the Production Possibility Curve." *Ekonomisk Tidskrift* 60 (No. 3): 183–197.

Schweinberger, Albert G. (1979). "The Theory of Factor Price Equilisation, the Case of Constant Absolute Differentials." *Journal of International Economics* 9: 95–115.

Scitovsky, T. (1941). "A Note on Welfare Propositions in Economics." *Review of Economic Studies* 9: 77–88.

Segerstrom, Paul S., T. C. A. Anant, and Elias Dinopoulos (1990). "A Schumpeterian Model of the Product Life Cycle." *American Economic Review* 80: 1077–1092.

Serra, Pablo (1991). "Short-run and Long-run Welfare Implications of Free Trade." *Canadian Journal of Economics* 24: 21–33.

Shea, K-L., and A. E. Woodfield (1993). "Optimal Immigration, Education and Growth in the Long Run." Mimeo, University of Hong Kong.

Shephard, R. W. (1953). *Cost and Production Functions*. Princeton: Princeton University Press.

Sheshinski, Eytan (1967). "Optimal Accumulation with Learning by Doing." In Karl Shell (eds.), *Essays on the Theory of Optimal Economic Growth*. Cambridge, MA: MIT Press, 31–52.

Shy, Oz (1988). "A General Equilibrium Model of Pareto Inferior Trade." *Journal of International Economics* 25: 143–154.

Singer, H. W. (1950). "The Distribution of Gains between Investing and Borrowing Countries." *American Economic Review, Papers and Proceedings* 40: 473–485.

Smith, M. Alasdair M. (1977). "Capital Accumulation in the Open Two-Sector Economy." *Economic Journal* 87 (No. 346): 273–282.

Smith, M. Alasdair M. (1984). "Capital Theory and Trade Theory." In Ronald W. Jones, and Peter B. Kenen (eds.), *Handbook of International Economics*, Vol. I. Amsterdam: North-Holland, 289–324.

Smith, M. Alasdair M. (1987). "Strategic Investment, Multinational Corporations and Trade Policy." *European Economic Review* 31: 89–96.

Sohn, Kiyohn (1993). *International Market Share Competition with Export Subsidies and Retaliation*. Ph. D. dissertation, University of Washington.

Spence, Michael (1976). "Product Selection, Fixed Costs, and Monopolistic Competition." *Review of Economic Studies* 43: 217–236.

Spencer, Barbara J., and James A. Brander (1983). "International R & D Rivalry and Industrial Strategy." *Review of Economic Studies* 50: 707–722.

Srinivasan, T. N. (1983). "International Factor Movements, Commodity Trade and Commercial Policy in a Specific Factor Model." *Journal of International Economics* 14: 215–230.

Srinivasan, T. N., and Jagdish N. Bhagwati (1975). "Alternative Policy Rankings in a Large, Open Economy with Sector-Specific, Minimum Wages." *Journal of Economic Theory* 11: 356–371.

Staiger, Robert W. (1986). "Measurement of the Factor Content of Foreign Trade with Traded Intermediate Goods." *Journal of International Economics* 21: 361–368.

Staiger, Robert W. (1988). "A Specification Test of the Heckscher-Ohlin Theory." *Journal of International Economics* 25: 129–141.

Stern, Robert M., and Keith E. Maskus (1981). "Determinants of the Structure of U.S. Foreign Trade, 1958–76." *Journal of International Economics* 11: 207–224.

Stiglitz, Joseph E. (1970). "Factor Price Equalization in A Dynamic Economy," *Journal of Political Economy* 78:456–488.

Stolper, Wolfgang F., and Paul A. Samuelson (1941). "Protection and Real Wages." *Review of Economic Studies* 9: 58–73.

Suzuki, K. (1989). "Choice between International Capital and Labor Mobility for Diversified Economies." *Journal of International Economics* 27: 347–361.

Svensson, Lar E. O. (1984). "Factor Trade and Goods Trade." *Journal of International Economics* 16: 365–378.

Takayama, Akira (1972). *International Trade*. New York: Holt, Rinehart and Winston.

Takayama, Akira (1985). *Mathematical Economics*, second edition. Cambridge: Cambridge University Press.

Tawada, Makoto (1989). *Production Structure and International Trade*. Berlin: Springer-Verlag.

Thompson, Henry (1986). "Free Trade and Factor-Price Polarization." *European Economic Review* 30: 419–425.

Tinbergen, J. (1945). *International Economic Co-operation*. Amsterdam: Elsevier.

Tinbergen, J. (1954). *International Economic Integration*. Amsterdam: Elsevier.

Tirole, Jean (1988). *The Theory of Industrial Organization*. Cambridge, MA: MIT Press.

Tower, Edward (1975). "The Optimum Quota and Retaliation." *Review of Economic Studies* 42: 623–630.

Travis, W. P. (1964). *The Theory of Trade and Production*. Cambridge: MA: Harvard University Press.

Tu, Pierre N. V. (1991). "Migration: Gains or Losses?" *Economic Record* 67: 153–157.

Turnovsky, Stephen J. (1974). "Technological and Price Uncertainty in a Ricardian Model of International Trade." *Review of Economic Studies* 41: 201–217.

Uekawa, Yasuo (1972). "On the Existence of Incomplete Specialization in International Trade with Capital Mobility." *Journal of International Economics* 2: 1–23.

Uzawa, Hirofumi (1963). "On a Two-Sector Model of Economic Growth." *Review of Economic Studies* 30: 105–118.

Uzawa, Hirofumi (1969). "Shihon Jiyuka to Kokumin Keizai (liberalization of Foreign Investment and the National Economy)." *Ekonomisuto* (December 23): 106–122 (in Japanese).

Vanek, Jaroslav (1965). *General Equilibrium of International Discrimination: The Case of Customs Unions*. Cambridge, MA: Harvard University Press.

Vanek, Jaroslav (1968). "The Factor Proportions Theory: The N-Factor Case." *Kyklos* 21 (No. 4): 749–756.

Varian, Hal R. (1992). *Microeconomic Analysis*, third edition. New York: W. W. Norton & Company.

Venables, Anthony J. (1982). "Optimal Tariffs for Trade in Monopolistically Competitive Commodities." *Journal of International Economics* 12: 225–241.

Venables, Anthony J. (1985). "Trade and Trade Policy with Imperfect Competition: The Case of Identical Products and Free Entry." *Journal of International Economics* 19: 1–19.

Venables, Anthony J. (1990). "International Capacity Choice and National Market Games." *Journal of International Economics* 29: 23–42.

Vernon, Raymond (1966). "International Investment and International Trade in the Product Cycle." *Quarterly Journal of Economics* 83 (No. 1): 190–207.

Viner, Jacob (1931). "Cost Curves and Supply Curves." *Zeitschrift für Nationalökonomie* 3: 23–46.

Viner, Jacob (1950). "Supplementary Note to 'Cost Curves and Supply Curves'." In R. V. Clemence (ed.), *Readings in Economic Analysis*, Cambridge, MA: Addison-Wesley, Vol. II, 31–35.

Vousden, Neil (1990). *The Economics of Trade Protection*. Cambridge: Cambridge University Press.

Weymark, J. A. (1979). "A Reconciliation of Recent Results in Optimal Taxation Theory." *Journal of Public Economics* 12: 171–189.

Wong, Kar-yiu (1983). "On Choosing Among Trade in Goods and International Capital and Labor Mobility: A Theoretical Analysis." *Journal of International Economics* 14: 223–250.

Wong, Kar-yiu (1986a). "The Economic Analysis of International Migration: A Generalization." *Canadian Journal of Economics* 19: 357–362.

Wong, Kar-yiu (1986b). "Are International Trade and Factor Mobility Substitutes?" *Journal of International Economics* 21: 25–43. Reprinted in Jagdish N. Bhagwati (ed.), *International Trade: Selected Readings*, Cambridge, MA: MIT Press, 1987, 37–53.

Wong, Kar-yiu (1986c). "International Factor Movements, Repatriation and Welfare." *Journal of International Economics* 21: 327–335.

Wong, Kar-yiu (1988). "International Factor Mobility and the Volume of Trade: An Empirical Study," in Robert C. Feenstra (ed.), *Empirical Methods for International Trade*, Cambridge, MA: MIT Press, 231–250.

Wong, Kar-yiu (1989a). "The Japanese Challenge: Japanese Direct Investment in the United States." In Kozo Yamamura (ed.), *Japanese Investment in the United States: Should We Be Concerned?* Seattle: Society for Japanese Studies, 63–96.

Wong, Kar-yiu (1989b). "Optimal Threat of Trade Restriction and *Quid Pro Quo* Foreign Investment." *Economics & Politics* 1 (No. 3): 277–300.

Wong, Kar-yiu (1989c). "Validity of the Rybczynski and Stolper-Samuelson Theorems under Variable Returns to Scale," Mimeo, University of Washington, Seattle.

Wong, Kar-yiu (1990). "Factor Intensity Reversal in a Multi-Factor, Two-Good Economy." *Journal of Economic Theory* 51: 434–442.

Wong, Kar-yiu (1991a). "Welfare Comparison of Trade Situations." *Journal of International Economics* 30: 49–68.

Wong, Kar-yiu (1991b). "Incentive Incompatible, Immiserizing Export Subsidies." Mimeo, University of Washington, Seattle.

Wong, Kar-yiu (1993a). "International Trade in Goods and Factor Mobility with Oligopoly: A General Equilibrium Approach." Mimeo, University of Washington, Seattle.

Wong, Kar-yiu (1993b). "Gains from Trade with Lumpsum Compensation." Mimeo, University of Washington, Seattle.

Wong, Kar-yiu (1994a). "A Comment on 'Some Implications of Variable Returns to Scale: the Case of Industry-Specific Factors.'" *Canadian Journal of Economics* (forthcoming).

Wong, Kar-yiu (1994b). "Curvature of the Production Possibility Frontier under Variable Returns: Was J. Tinbergen Wrong?" Mimeo, University of Washington, Seattle.

Wong, Kar-yiu (1995a). "Fundamental Trade Theorems under External Economics of Scale," Mimeo, University of Washington, Seattle.

Wong, Kar-yiu (1995b). "International Trade and Factor Mobility under External Economies of Scale," Mimeo, University of Washington, Seattle.

Wong, Kar-yiu, and Xiaokai Yang (1994). "An Extended Dixit-Stiglitz Model with the Tradeoff between Economies of Scale and Transaction Costs." Mimeo, University of Washington, Seattle.

Wong, Kar-yiu, and Kozo Yamamura (1995). "Japanese Direct Investment in the United States." In Ramon H. Myer (ed.), *Integrating the World Economy: Japanese Foreign Direct Investment, 1972–1990*. Stanford: Hoover Institute Press (forthcoming).

Woodland, Alan D. (1980). "Direct and Indirect Trade Utility Functions." *Review of Economic Studies* 47: 907–926.

Woodland, Alan D. (1982). *International Trade and Resource Allocation*. Amsterdam: North-Holland.

Yang, Xiaokai, and Ben J. Heijdra (1993). "Monopolistic Competition and Optimum Product Diversity: Comment." *American Economic Review* 83: 295–301.

Young, Alwyn (1991). "Learning by Doing and the Dynamic Effects of International Trade." *Quarterly Journal of Economics* 106: 369–405.

Young, Leslie (1991). "Optimal Tariffs: A Generalization." *International Economic Review* 32 (No. 2): 341–372.

Index